THE ROAD MAP
ESCAPING THE MAZE OF MADNESS

First published in January 2026.

ickonic
publishing

**New Enterprise House
St Helens Street
Derby
DE1 3GY
UK**

email: gareth.icke@davidicke.com

Copyright © 2026 David Icke

No part of this book may be reproduced
in any form without permission from
the Publisher, except for the quotation
of brief passages in criticism

Cover Illustration: Tom Kellett
Book Design: Neil Hague

Printed and bound by CPI (UK) Ltd, Croydon CR0 4YY

**British Library Cataloguing-in
Publication Data**
A catalogue record for this book is
available from the British Library

ISBN 978-1-83709-071-6

THE ROAD MAP

ESCAPING THE MAZE OF MADNESS

DAVID ICKE

Dedication:

To Kerry, Gareth, Jaymie, Erin, Zach, Elora, Ophelia, Travis, Maddox, and Rowan.

May you remember that your dad, grandad, and great grandad did it for you and others like you across the world.

Never quit.

THE REVEAL

THE NEXT STAGE OF HUMAN AWARENESS

DAVID ICKE

Other books and videos by David Icke (see also Ickonic.com)

The Reveal

The Dream

The Trap

Perceptions of a Renegade Mind

The Answer

The Trigger

Everything You Need To Know But Have Never Been Told

Phantom Self

The Perception Deception

Remember Who You Are

Human Race Get Off Your *Knees* - The Lion Sleeps No More

The David Icke Guide to the Global Conspiracy (and how to end it)

Infinite Love is the Only Truth, *Everything* Else is Illusion

Tales from the Time Loop

Alice in Wonderland and the World Trade Center Disaster

Children Of The Matrix

The Biggest Secret

I Am Me • I Am Free

... And The Truth Shall Set You Free – 21st century edition

Lifting The Veil

The Robots' Rebellion

Heal the World

Truth Vibrations

DVDs

Worldwide Wake-Up Tour Live

David Icke Live at Wembley Arena

The Lion Sleeps No More

Beyond the Cutting Edge – Exposing the Dreamworld We Believe to be Real

Freedom or Fascism: the Time to Choose

Secrets of the Matrix

From Prison to Paradise

Turning Of The Tide

The Freedom Road

Revelations Of A Mother Goddess

Speaking Out

The Reptilian Agenda

Details at the back of this book
and through the website **www.davidicke.com**

Today's mighty oak is just yesterday's nut that held its ground.

David Icke, 1990

Contents

	Before We Start	XVII
CHAPTER 1	The 'Human' Illusion	1
CHAPTER 2	Paradise Lost	23
CHAPTER 3	What is the 'Matrix'	45
CHAPTER 4	Breaching Orthodoxy	71
CHAPTER 5	The Archons	87
CHAPTER 6	Loosh Farm	109
CHAPTER 7	Wheel of Misfortune	122
CHAPTER 8	Beyond the Veil	145
CHAPTER 9	The Global Cult	159
CHAPTER 10	From the Hidden to the Seen	179
CHAPTER 11	The Sabbateans	190
CHAPTER 12	Sabbatean Spider	205
CHAPTER 13	Spellbound	223
CHAPTER 14	Owning 'Normality'	239
CHAPTER 15	Language of Symbolism	251
CHAPTER 16	God Save Us From Religion	273
CHAPTER 17	They Made It Up	284
CHAPTER 18	They Made It Up (2)	306
CHAPTER 19	Who (or What) is the Biblical 'God'?	321
CHAPTER 20	Dividing the World	349
CHAPTER 21	Trump Psyop	366
CHAPTER 22	Enter Epstein	384
CHAPTER 23	'Accelerating' the 'Dark Enlightenment'	402
CHAPTER 24	'You're the Media Now'	427
CHAPTER 25	AI Dystopia	445
CHAPTER 26	Making It Happen	473
CHAPTER 27	Breaking the Spell	497
CHAPTER 28	Final Thought	517
POSTSCRIPT		523
INDEX		542

Before we start

*To acquire knowledge, one must study; but to acquire wisdom,
one must observe.*
Marilyn vos Savant

My 1998 book *The Biggest Secret* was described by some as the 'Rosetta Stone' of conspiracy research and *The Road Map* is the seriously updated version with the benefit of a further nearly 30 years of full-time dot-connecting.

The Rosetta Stone was discovered in 1799 and included inscriptions in several languages that allowed Egyptian hieroglyphics to be read. *The Road Map* is designed to allow the scale of the global conspiracy to be seen in its multi-dimensional dot-connected detail. So much has happened and been uncovered since *The Biggest Secret* which brought the manipulations of a non-human force to public attention. It was dismissed then as you would expect by most people. A non-human force was behind the direction of human society? Crazy, surely? But times change as perceptions change with the input of knowledge and far more minds are open today to what would have been instantly rejected not so long ago. I have dived ever deeper in the decades since and present to you here an extraordinary story that puts current events into a context not seen before in a single book. The *what* tells you that something is happening, but the key is the why – *why* it's happening. It provides the essential context without which there can be no understanding.

What I have said and written since my mind-opening awakening in 1990 has attracted widespread ridicule and abuse before the tide turned with events proving me right. Even now mention of 'David Icke' still triggers laughter among those who get their views from the mainstream media (and much of the 'alternative') because their minds are locked away in myopia to such an extreme that they dismiss what I say after 36 years of full-time research when they haven't researched these subjects for 36 seconds. A few people can't control the world? That's how easy it really is. Control perception by squeezing the sense of the possible and you'll have your targets guffawing as they wave away exposure of the very conspiracy designed to make them guffaw as they wave away exposure of the very conspiracy that enslaves them. Round and round it goes in a feedback loop of manipulate-expose-reject-manipulate some more.

I have watched as the numbers have dramatically increased of those who *are* now aware of the conspiracy, or rather *aspects* of it, and my aim here is to make the connections between apparently unconnected people, governments, organisations, secret societies, dimensions, and happenings to expose the vast panorama of human control that absolutely includes other-dimensional forces we can't even see. It is within that panorama that the answers await. It's a challenge because I am asking people to put aside their preconceived ideas about life and reality and suspend their beliefs in politics and religions to give another version of who we are and where we are a chance to make its case. The challenge comes in the way belief systems control the psyche like a boa constrictor wrapped around the human mind. The manipulators don't care what you believe so long as you believe it rigidly and will consider nothing else. This is what belief systems are – prisons of the mind.

Many more have begun to awaken since the 'Covid' hoax to the fact that there is a demonic conspiracy to enslave humanity by a cabal of billionaires, Satanists, and their political minions on the payroll. This has made it easier for me to be heard compared with the outright and widespread dismissal I faced for decades, but if the demonic couldn't stop this awakening entirely it could limit its expansion and redirect its attention. There was no 'alternative' or 'independent' (it's largely not) media in the years after I set my course in 1990. I watched it appear especially after the outrageous official lies and cover stories surrounding 9/11 and I was delighted to see the expansion of awareness that something very dark was behind national and global events.
Then came 'Covid'.

I guess that was the peak of my credibility this far when I exposed very publicly in the spring of 2020 that 'Covid' was a make-believe hoax to terrify people into having a 'vaccine' with serious consequences for body and mind. I was deleted from every major video and social media site in the aftermath of my 'Covid' revelations and I have not appeared in the mainstream media ever since at the time of writing. The 'vaccine' was claimed to be produced in a record time of weeks in 2020 when it had been sitting there for years waiting for the hoax to be played. It is not a 'vaccine', but a genetic manipulation device of which more later in the book. Donald Trump's colossal ego claims he is the 'father' of the fake vaccine when it is the work of the military. 'Covid' was both a period when great numbers acquiesced to authority without question and when more people than ever began to *ask* questions they never had before. What was going on? Where did this fascism suddenly come from? In fact, it had been there all along but now it was on public display. Tens of thousands and more took to the streets of London alone in protest at what was happening, and the manipulators were faced with

Introduction

an awakening they had to redirect before it got out of hand.

I then watched a stream of people coming into the alternative media from the mainstream and quickly become the 'stars' blatantly promoted both by algorithms and funding. They basically hijacked what the alternative had been and absorbed some of the older researcher-presenters who step-by-step began to justify what they had previously exposed and condemned. Once they joined the club the algorithms fell in love with them, too, while others seeking out and communicating a deeper truth were *suppressed* by the algorithms and 'shadow banned' to prevent their work being seen on the scale that it otherwise would. The theme was captured by the Elon Musk Twitter/X mantra about believing in 'freedom of speech, not freedom of reach'; and saying that what is 'lawful but awful' would be very difficult to find on the platform. *They* decide what is 'awful' and it tends to match what they don't want the public to see. Twitter/X is a cesspit with bots programmed to abuse targets along with people who act like bots. The platform quickly became the propaganda arm of the Trump-Musk duo as it was planned to be from the moment Musk took over. Many of the human 'bots' are 'stars' of the seized 'alternative' media who became nothing more than Trump-Musk groupies promoting those who were, in effect, their paymasters.

It became clear very quickly that this systematic capture was redirecting the alternative arena from a perception that countries are One-Party States which makes political 'choice' an illusion and regressing it back into the Left v Right puppet show. Vote for *this* agent of the same force or *this* agent of the same force when both are taking you in the same direction by slightly different routes using different rhetoric. Those that lead the 'Left' and the 'Right' are not your friend whatever they may claim. They are both working to enslave you into the same artificial intelligence dystopia and they are only selling this with a differing sales-pitch to target the belief systems involved. The rest is pure theatre to divert you. Ultimately, they answer to the same force, a global network of interconnected secret societies and Satanic groups that I call the Global Cult.

The most sinister aspect was how the post-'Covid' 'alternative' was transformed into a propaganda arm of Donald Trump and Elon Musk who as a result came to elected and unelected power in January 2025. They immediately set about crashing the institutions of government and firing massive numbers of people in favour of loyalists to what had become the Trump-Musk religion and most significantly to have artificial intelligence that can be centrally controlled running government and society. Trump and Musk may have eventually fallen out for a time as narcissists do, but together they continued to promote the upheaval and chaos essential to dismantling one status quo that can then be replaced with another even more extreme in its deletion of freedom.

The methodology has been to hold the line of 'alternative' exposure to 'here and no further' as the 'possessed' alternative formed a barricade of focus around politics and finance. I noted this calculated seizure of awakening perception pretty much when it began, and I was inspired to write this book in response to lay out in the simplest dot-connected order what this conspiracy is really all about and how deep it really goes. It involves a whole new explanation of the human story, how we got here, and what is behind the desire of the demonic to entrap humanity in ongoing servitude which is planned to impose a new extreme of slavery through AI. Answers or what people call 'solutions' are simply not possible without this knowledge. You can see this clearly with the continuing 'alternative' focus on politics as the answer when the political system of illusory choice was specifically created to deceive humanity into giving its collective power away to agents and gofers of the Cult. What you are about to read will expose the self-defeating nonsense of that approach.

My aim is to keep the story simple and easy to follow even for those new to this information. You will find supporting fine detail in my other books which include *The Biggest Secret; Children of the Matrix; And The Truth Shall Set You Free; The Perception Deception; Phantom Self; The Trigger; Everything You Need To Know But Have Never Been Told; The Answer;* and my Reality Trilogy, *The Trap, The Dream* and *The Reveal*.

I trust you will see as I add layer upon layer of suppressed information, chapter after chapter, why it is so vital to connect these dots to see where we are, how we got here, and how we can free ourselves from this demonic madness.

CHAPTER 1

The 'Human' Illusion

Everything that you are or conceive of yourself as being is just an idea. It's an illusion. It's an hallucination.
Frederick Lenz

Once upon a no-time in a land not far away there was a paradise. There still is. *Remember*? You probably don't because you're not meant to. What a story there is to be told, and it puts current events and human 'history' into a context like no other.

The world is as it is because it's been made that way. On purpose. By design. Through cold calculation. It is the work of demons. Scan the spectrum of human society where the overwhelming majority focus on survival, not contentment or happiness. They must make it to tomorrow or at best the end of the week or month. Observe the death and destruction weaved through the human story, the war, conflict, upheavals. Is that the work of a 'loving God' or a demonic force? Put aside your beliefs and look at it dispassionately without preconceived idea or religious bias and the answer to that question screams the obvious. No loving God created this human shithole of turmoil and struggle while the few prosper in their wake and on their backs, their sweat, and labour. *It's the demons that did it*. But why and how? That is the fantastic story I am about to tell.

Let us return to that paradise – 'a place of great happiness where everything is exactly as you would like it to be'. Yes, such a reality does exist, although just not 'here'. But it's not far away and I should start by explaining the opening line of this chapter which captures the essence of the human plight in a few words. 'Once upon a no-time' describes this paradise in which time that we perceive and forms the foundation of human control plays no part. Oh, but that's ridiculous. Everybody knows that time exists and takes us 'forward' from past through present to future. No. Humans *believe* that as part of their demonic perceptual programming, but amazingly what humans believe has nothing to do with the truth. Belief is not truth. It is *belief*. Human control is the control of human perception which is expressed as human behaviour. Perception is not truth, or rarely. It is *perception* which comes from belief which comes from information in the form of knowledge and experience. Knowledge is not necessarily truth. It is what we *perceive* to be true. Experience is what happens to us and how we respond. Neither happening nor response must have a relationship with truth. Shit happens and we respond according to what we think we know or from accumulated experience. None of this has to be true.

Time out

So it is with 'time'. Just because we experience what we perceive as time 'passing' doesn't mean that it does. Our sense of time reality relates not to time passing, but to our belief and experience that it does – 'Is that the time?'; 'Where's the time gone?'; 'I'm so bored – time is passing so slow.' The very fact that our relationship with 'time' changes according to our mood and situation should tell us something about the 'time' illusion that controls us. It can seem like forever waiting for a bus and yet forever can pass in an hour in the company of those we love and who intrigue us. We associate 'time' with the movement of clocks when that is only a human construct. Universal 'time' calculation originated only in the 19th century with the building of the railways. 'Time' was measured before then by a local sundial based on the changing position of the Sun. This meant that a location time in Britain could differ by up to 20 minutes and much longer in big countries such as India and North America. That was fine until the coming of the railways and the need for a common time to make non-chaotic train timetables possible. The Great Western Railway in the UK standardised its timetable on London's Greenwich Mean Time in 1840 and the rest followed until the Statutes (Definition of Time) Act unified standard time for the whole country in 1880. The move went on to be implemented globally together with time zones. I remember flying across the Pacific and the theoretical International Date Line between the North and South Poles and moving from 'today' into 'yesterday'.

Time that we live by is so obviously a manufactured construct. Our calendar was introduced in October 1582 by the dictate of Pope Gregory XIII to replace the Julian calendar of Julius Caesar imposed in 46 BC which replaced the Roman calendar that consisted of ten months beginning in March. Rome also introduced the 'BC' and 'Ano Domini' (Before and After Christ) year calculation in 525 AD that expanded over centuries. The Gregorian calendar had to delete ten days to make it fit while making sure no Christian festivals were missed. Time as measured is a human creation. Renowned and legendary physicist John Wheeler (1911-2008), a professor emeritus at Princeton, said: 'Heaven did not hand down the word "time". Man invented it.' There is no time, only our perception of it. There is no past or future. There is only the eternal NOW in which all happens at the same 'time'. I know how hard that can be for the human brain to process when it is programmed not to do so. 'Time' is a massive force of control and limitation and if you want to enslave and bewilder humans then their perception of time is an essential component. But we can *de*-program and a few simple questions will suffice to get us started.

If 'time' exists then you must have been in the 'past' when you experienced your 'past' and you must be in the 'future' when what has yet to happen, well, happens. But were you? And will you be? Here are those questions. Where are you when you think of the 'past'? You are in the NOW (or what is perceived as the 'present moment'). Where were you when you experienced what you believe to be the 'past'? You were in the NOW. Where are you when you think of the future? You are in the NOW. Where will you be when you experience what you perceive as the 'future'? You will be in the NOW. There is only the NOW (Fig 1). Watch a film and whatever scene you are viewing is your sense of the 'present'; the ones you have watched will be your sense of the 'past'; and those you are yet to watch are your sense of the 'future'. But the whole film exists at the same 'time'. The 'spacetime' of science orthodoxy does not exist 'naturally' when one moment does not follow another. It just appears to. 'Past, present' and 'future' at the quantum level beyond the illusory 'material' are the same. We access the 'past' ('memory') through a connection with the field of the infinite NOW and we tap into the 'future' ('intuition') through a connection with the field of the infinite NOW. We call them memory and intuition, but you could say we 'remember' the 'future' as we remember the 'past' when the same NOW is at work. Infinity is not an infinite space or distance without end. It is the timeless eternal NOW – the NOW without end.

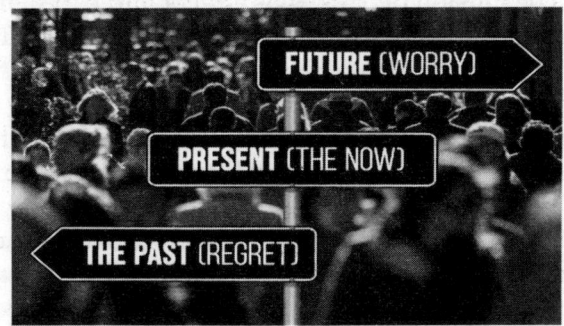

Figure 1: There is no 'time' – only the perception of it. (Image by Gareth Icke.)

Albert Einstein, the world's best-known scientist with his name used as a symbol of intelligence, said that 'time' does not only flow in one direction and the future exists simultaneously with the past. Maybe 'time' doesn't flow anywhere. It is an illusion of a simulated reality that I will get to in detail. 'Past', 'present' and 'future' can interact with each other within the NOW. We say that the past and present can influence the future, but the present and future can influence the past. Decisions made in the present can flow through to past and future while the future in the form of a frequency field of *potentiality* can affect the past and present. Are we changing 'history' by what we do in the present? I would say the answer is yes. You could symbolise this as adding words to a computer document which then reassemble what went before and after to encompass the new. Your *sense* of 'time' is dictated by your perception of what you are experiencing. Everything happens in the NOW and in the totality of Infinite Reality that is a gimme, a known, an everyone-knows-that. Why not 'here'? Well, because 'here' is different. 'Here' is a premeditated trap to enslave the eternal True 'I' – a state of consciousness, awareness – in a fake reality that it believes to be real. The illusion of 'time' has a central role in that monumental perceptual fakery. Einstein said: 'People like us, who believe in physics, know that the distinction between past, present, and future is only a stubbornly persistent illusion.'

You are living 'in' a virtual-reality simulation designed to confuse and mislead you, created by a demonic force to that end. I will be exposing this force and its nature in considerable detail. If the demonic seizes your perception of reality, it controls your experienced reality. It seizes and possesses *you*. But what is this *you*? *The Road Map* is the story of how this 'you' came 'here' from the Infinite realm of no-time to be trapped in the perception of 'time' and 'physicality' through a brain programmed to decode 'time' and 'physicality' like a computer decodes Wi-Fi. What is Wi-Fi? It is *information*. What is a computer? It decodes that information into a totally different form on the screen. Thus, you have the relationship between the brain and our simulated reality (information) that entraps us in the energetic density of 'matter' or what ancient Indian Vedic works call 'Maya'. This translates as 'illusion' or 'magic' – 'where things appear to be present but are not what they seem'. Maya is said to 'conceal the true character of spiritual reality'. It does so through a simulated 'world' or 'Matrix' that tricks our senses to believe it is real. If you have read any other books of mine, you will understand what I am saying. If not, I'll explain as we go along.

Rigid belief = rigid control

This is what I mean by 'once upon a no-time', but what about this 'land not far away', this 'paradise'? There are many concepts and themes in the Bible that symbolically tell this no-time story and much else, along with the dross to entrap and ensnare. You can't be discerning and still be an official Christian or Jew because the Bible is sold as the 'word of God'. Given that God is said to never be wrong, and can't be, you are stuck with the good stuff and the dross and told to accept all of it as fact even when the good stuff (constantly) contradicts the dross and vice-versa. It's another calculated trap like all the other religious 'holy books' including the Koran and Vedas. They pull you in with the parts that make sense and twist your mind with the non-sense. You can't take what feels right and leave the rest or you are not a Christian, Muslim,

Hindu, whatever. More than that, you are a blasphemer against God for the mere suggestion that your God may be contradicting itself (or rather those claiming to speak for God are doing so). It's very clever and what the religious assume to be God's unquestionable word is another entrapment to confuse you with contradiction – a circle you are demanded to square. This is very deep and fundamental to the overall trap, and I'll explore its background and perceptual consequences later. The name of your religion does not matter so long as you follow its version of reality without question. They are the same in their outcome as they are meant to be.

There are however many sayings, concepts and themes in religious texts that do have relevance *if* we are discerning and sift the gems of wheat from the barn-load of chaff. One such theme is the 'Fall' told in Genesis as the symbolic story of Adam and Eve ejected from the Eden paradise. This fits my contention and that of others from many cultures and beliefs that there really has been a 'Fall of Man' – a 'fall' from Infinite Paradise into the prison of 'dense matter' or rather energetic density which is what 'matter' really is. The biblical 'Eden' may have an earthly explanation, but it is symbolic of a much greater 'Fall'. To understand 'not far away' is to understand frequency and how our perceptions generate frequency. This is key to grasping the background to human control and yet so few do. Why would they when the whole conspiracy depends on us not doing so?

It is now well known in proper 'science' that every time we think and feel emotion, we are generating frequencies that relate to that thought and emotion. Together our thoughts and emotions both reflect and collectively create the energetic field around us that I will refer to as *perception*, which is the sum of who we are, or *believe* we are. This perceptual field interacts with the infinite field of possibility to manifest our experienced reality as I will explain further shortly. Our state of frequency is dictated by our perceptions which manifest as thought and emotion which manifest as frequency. If you can control the perceptions of humans, you can control the frequencies on which they resonate. Limit the perceptions and you limit their frequencies. Limit the frequencies to those of your constructed reality domain and they cannot leave your frequency prison which is a simulated virtual reality – a fantastically more advanced and sophisticated version of human virtual reality technology. In those few sentences you have the world 'in' which we think we live.

Home sick

I'll be describing how the fake 'world' deceives us, but we should begin *beyond* the simulated prison to find context. Most humans feel that somehow something is 'missing'. There is a void they can't explain like a part of them has been lost. They long for something, but don't know exactly what. This void is filled – or attempted to be – by religion and religious heroes who play the role, among many other things, of what has been lost. Jesus will save me from this nightmare if only I believe in him. The void is further mitigated through escapism in its endless forms, be it drink or drugs or sex, anything that takes attention from the emptiness and directs my focus. If I have enough beers, enough cocaine or ecstasy, I can forget for a while that hole in my being that longs for what it had but now can't remember. We seek out relationships in search of our 'other half' when what has been lost is not even in this human reality.

The reality itself has been specifically intended to block the reconnection with our true 'other half' – Infinity. We kick this can (hole) down the street in the form of the illusion we call 'hope'. Karl Marx said that religion is the opium of the people, but the real drug is hope-ium or hopium. This is the very foundation of religions in that they involve the hope of being saved by obeying your hidden master or masters. I will go to heaven if I obey Jesus. Think of all those virgins if I obey Allah. Hopium means that I can accept the suffering now in the hope of better things – *paradise* – to come. Oh yes, paradise is what we long for amid the chaos masquerading as 'civilisation'. We even kid ourselves with a simulated paradise like lying back on a beach in the sunshine in some faraway place that provides respite from the madness, sorry, 'civilisation'. 'Ah, paradise', we say.

What if there really was a paradise – 'a place of great happiness where everything is exactly as you would like it to be' – from which humans, or what we now *call* humans, fell? I say there was (is) and it's not far away in the sense that it exists in the same 'space' that you are sitting or standing in now. This can happen for the same reason that all the radio and television stations broadcasting to your area exist in the same 'space' that you currently occupy. They don't interfere with each other unless they are very close on the dial because they operate on different wavelengths and are oblivious to all others (just as humans are oblivious to all other realities or bands of frequency that occupy the same 'space' that they do). Press the zapper or move the dial on your TV or radio and you change 'stations' as your device disconnects with one wavelength and connects with another. *Our* 'device' that tunes our awareness with the band of frequency called 'human' is the brain/body. I have called this combination since the 1990s a 'biological computer' and it acts in the same way as the computer I am looking at now. The biological computer/mind is decoding our experienced 'physical' reality from a field of potentiality and information in the way a desktop computer decodes Wi- Fi (Fig 2).

The illusion of 'matter'

We may perceive the Internet as what we see on the screen, but that's only

The 'Human' Illusion

Figure 2: Wi-Fi is a field of information that we cannot see.

the version which has been decoded as text, graphics and videos. The Internet only exists in that form *on the screen* and everywhere else the Internet is *information* encoded in Wi-Fi and electronic circuitry. Wi-Fi is the information, and the computer decodes that information into what we perceive as the Internet. In the same way the brain/body biological computer is decoding our simulated (virtual) reality into a world that we think is outside of us when it is actually *within* us. The 'physical world' exists only within the decoding processes of the brain. Where does the computer decode Wi-Fi? Inside the computer. Where is the decoded version of the Internet that you see on the screen? Inside the computer. This dynamic mimics how we experience 'human' reality and

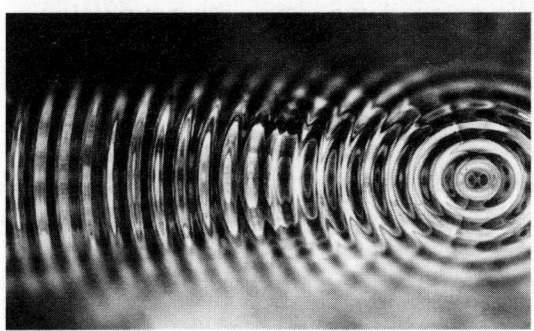

Figure 3: Simulation information is encoded in waveform which the body decodes into illusory 'physical' reality.

indeed the entire technological explosion of recent decades mimics the way our simulated virtual reality operates. There is a reason for that as will become clear. Compare this with how the biological computer decodes 'human' reality. The simulation is waveform information, and the brain/body decodes this into the 'physical' reality that we think we are experiencing (Fig 3). But it isn't 'physical' at all. Einstein again:

> Concerning matter, we have been all wrong. What we have called matter is energy, whose vibration has been so lowered as to be perceptible to the senses. There is no matter.

American scientist David Bohm (1917-1992), a friend of Einstein, is described as one of the most significant theoretical physicists and philosophers of the 20th century and combined his studies of quantum physics and mysticism. The mystic and the scientific should be expressions of each other, but they are kept apart by the ignorance of scientific orthodoxy and the need by the manipulating force to keep the truth from the population. Orthodoxy blinds and confuses people with irrelevant complexity and massive blackboards awash with equations (Fig 4). It uses long words and jargon to sound intelligent when in my view if you can't explain something simply then you don't really understand it. Syllables do not intelligence make. Orthodoxy believes that for something to be explained it must be complex. But complexity is there to hide the simplicity behind everything. Genius is not to understand complexity – it is to see the simple hidden by *apparent* complexity. Quantum physics legend Max Planck said: 'When the solution is simple, God is answering.'

Figure 4: Complexity hides the simple truths.

Orthodoxy has contended that reality is some kind of predetermined material clockwork machine when if you specifically sat down to suggest something as far from the truth as possible you would come up with something exactly like that. If you want to keep your targets ignorant and under control you would seek to program them with perceptions of self and reality as far from the truth as you can. David Bohm worked to understand the nature of reality and consciousness and believed that the *information* content in the energy that we call 'light' explained how 'matter' comes into being. 'Light' is the background medium and its encoded information dictates the detail. Bohm said:

> Light is this background, which is all one, but its information-content has the capacity for immense diversity. Light can carry information about the entire universe. The other point is that light, by interactions of different rays, (as field theory in physics is investigating today), can produce particles and all the diverse structures of matter ...

> ... they are ripples on this vast ocean of light. This ocean of energy could be thought of as an ocean of light. But the information-content may be such as to predispose certain light rays to combine so that they move back and forth rather than moving straight ahead and thus forming particles ['matter'].

Bohm described matter as 'condensed or frozen light'. This includes the human body or biological computer although even 'frozen light' is a metaphor and not a reality. I believe 'matter' is formed by standing waves which manifest when the movement of energy is resisted by a force of the same strength. It's like two people of equal momentum running into each other and they begin to run on the spot with neither going forward or back (Fig 5). This would support Bohm's ideas of 'condensed or frozen light' with certain light rays combining to 'move back and forth rather than moving straight ahead and thus forming particles [matter]'. DNA is a receiver-transmitter of information interacting with the human simulation and potentially other realities. Compare its shape with energetic waves and you'll see what it really is – a *standing wave* of information (Fig 6).

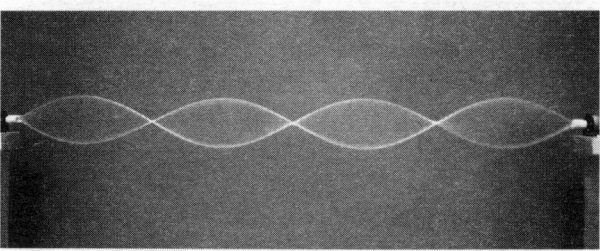

Figure 5: A standing wave with equal force pushing both ways causes energy to 'run on the spot'.

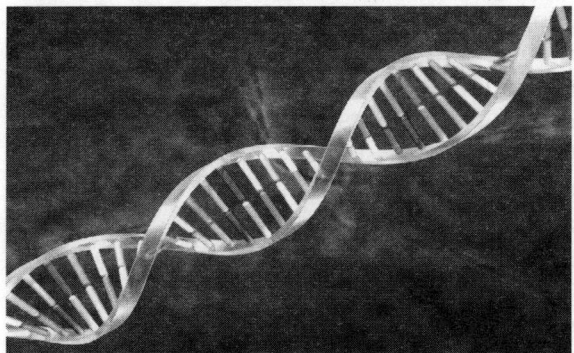

Figure 6: DNA 'running on the spot.

Quantum physics has confirmed the illusion of physicality and thrown orthodox 'science' (most of it isn't 'science' at all) into bewildered disarray. Orthodoxy ('classical physics') is founded on a solid world existing externally in space and time. But the deeper you go into the energetic field beyond the 'atom' any concept of physicality disappears. Touch your chair and it seems so 'solid' and yet 'matter' consists of 99.9999999 percent 'empty space'. Or what to us *appears* empty. However solid it seems to be the quantum realm of energy beyond 'matter' will confirm that it's not. American theoretical physicist Richard Feynman (1918-1988), a joint winner of the Nobel Prize in Physics in 1965, observed: 'Nature isn't classical, dammit, and if you want to make a simulation of nature, you'd better make it quantum mechanics.' They have. Max Planck (1858-1947) was a German theoretical physicist dubbed the 'father' of quantum mechanics, and his work won him the Nobel Prize in Physics in 1918. He said:

As a man who has devoted his whole life to the most clearheaded science, to the study of matter, I can tell you as a result of my research about the atoms this much: There is no matter as such!

All matter originates and exists only by virtue of a force which brings the particles of an atom to vibration and holds this most minute solar system of the atom together ... We must assume behind this force the existence of a conscious and intelligent mind. This mind is the matrix of all matter.

We have been led to believe that physicality is the creation of atoms, but now it is clear that atoms are not physical. They are expressions of energy way beyond the frequency of 'matter' and outside the strictly limited human sight sense. German theoretical physicist Werner Heisenberg was awarded the Nobel Prize in 1932 for his discoveries in quantum mechanics and he realised that atoms, the 'building blocks of matter', have no physicality: 'The smallest units of matter are not physical objects in the ordinary sense; they are forms, ideas which can be expressed unambiguously only in mathematical language ... atoms or elementary particles themselves are not real; they form a world of potentialities or possibilities rather than one of things or facts.' Atoms are supposed to be the 'building blocks of matter' when they have no physicality. They are energetic forms said to consist of electrons 'orbiting' a nucleus. But if you take the nucleus to be a ten-cent piece the atom would be the size of a stadium. The rest is what we perceive as 'empty space'. Go even deeper into the nucleus and electrons and they, too, are 'empty' (Fig 7). How can that construct a 'physical world'? Even the quantum level of reality is only part of the story and there is so much more to know.

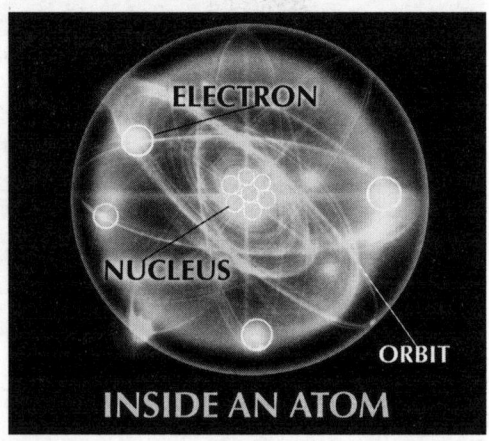

Figure 7: A non-'physical' atom does not a 'physical' world make.

Encoded myopia

The calculated limitation of human sight is so extraordinary it is almost laughable. The electromagnetic spectrum which is basically human experienced reality is estimated to be just 0.005 percent of what exists in the Universe as energy in all its forms (Fig 8). 'Visible light' which is the only band of frequency that the biological computer can 'see' (decode) is a fraction of the 0.005 percent (Fig 9). This means that we can 'see' only a

The 'Human' Illusion

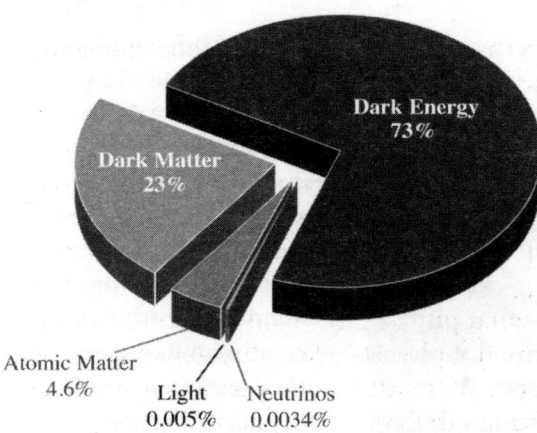

Figure 8: The entire electromagnetic spectrum – in effect human experienced reality – is an estimated just 0.005 percent of the energy in the Universe. 'Dark' just means invisible to us.

smear of what exists in the Universe and what we can 'see' of Infinite Reality is so infinitesimal that it defies mathematical calculation. I don't think for a second that this is by chance. The aim is to enslave humanity in perceptual myopia and the less of reality they can actually see the better. Just enough to function as you want them to, but not enough for them to realise what is happening. Humans exist in a realm

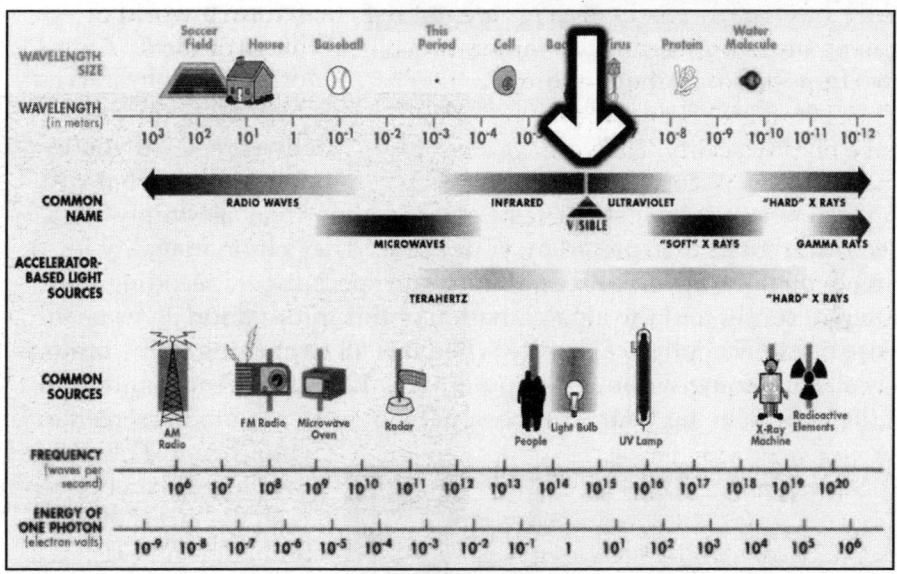

Figure 9: Visible light is the only band of frequency we can see and it is a *fraction* of the 0.005 percent. Humans are basically blind to what exists in the 'space' that we occupy.

of induced ignorance not least through enormous visual constraint. I should say that some estimates put the electromagnetic spectrum at perhaps 0.5 percent of the Universe. Either way it is too tiny to change the picture I am describing. We are already so far from the human sense of 'normal'. The interaction (or decoding) between the simulated virtual reality field and the biological computer are the five senses of sight, touch, smell, taste, and hearing. We think these are physical senses when there is no physical. Everything is frequency/vibration/information decoded into the *experience* of physicality, and this is how. The five senses decode frequency information from the simulation field into electrical information which is communicated to the brain to be decoded into digital holographic (illusory 'physical') information (Fig 10). A focus

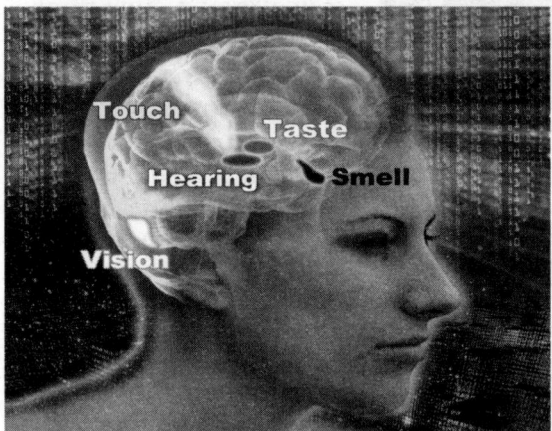

Figure 10: The senses communicate electrically to the brain which has specific areas to decode each sense and together they construct our experience of 'physical' reality. (Image by Neil Hague.)

of *attention* on the material realm of the senses can disconnect you from the influence of your expanded awareness extending out into infinity (Fig 11).

Remember that great line by the Morpheus character in the *Matrix* movie when Neo, experiencing a computer software program, asks: 'This isn't real?' Morpheus replies: 'What is real? How do you define "real"? If you're talking about what you can feel, what you can smell, taste and see, then "real" is simply electrical signals interpreted by your brain.' That's human reality in three sentences. Specific areas of the brain specialise in decoding the different senses and the amalgamation of this information gives us the sense of external physical reality when it is all happening in the brain as it is all happening within a computer (Figs 12 and 13). You could think of the brain playing your own personal movie on a symbolic screen in

Figure 11: The five senses can so hold human attention that we disconnect from an awareness of the greater reality. (Image by Neil Hague.)

your 'head'. The scale of the illusion can be seen with the fact that the brain doesn't exist as a 'physical' entity either. Everything is decoded information – even that which is doing the decoding or perceiving. What is a computer? It is *information* encoded to decode. What is the Internet? *Information* encoded to be decoded.

The 'Human' Illusion

Figure 12: A computer decodes Wi-Fi inside the computer.

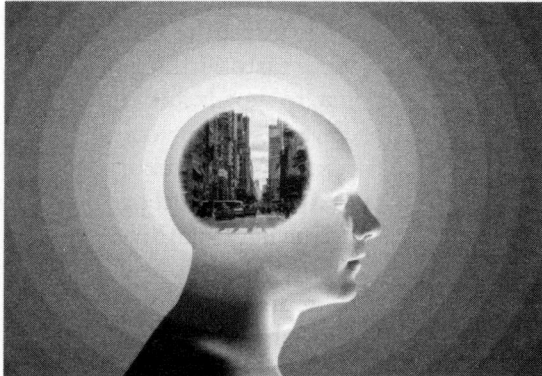

Figure 13: We decode simulated reality inside the body/brain. (Image Gareth Icke.)

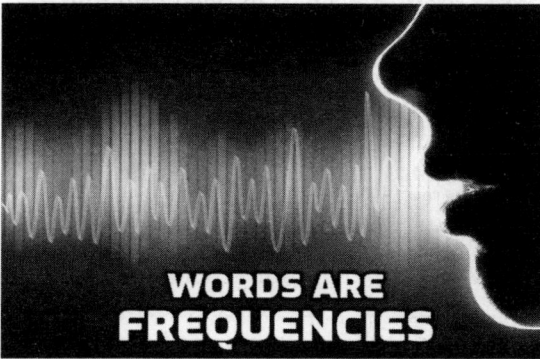

Figure 14: Speech is information generated by the vocal cords in the form of frequency.

The brain is an energetic field of encoded information that we decode into what we experience as a 'physical' entity. Yep, the non-material brain decodes itself into apparently material form! The 'physical' body/brain is an energetic field of encoded information (think software) to be decoded into the illusion of 'physical'. Put software into your computer on a data stick, press play, and what appears on the screen is information in a totally different form to what exists on the stick.

We communicate ('talk') through frequencies generated by our vocal cords which the ears transform into electrical signals that the brain decodes into words that we hear (Fig 14 and overleaf Fig 15). Every colour that we think we see is a frequency that we decode into the appearance of colour. Black absorbs all light and so we 'see' black; white reflects all light and so we 'see' white'. Other apparent colours absorb some light frequencies and reflect others. Only what they reflect do we 'see' as their colour which is why we can see nothing in a truly black room without a source of light which objects can reflect. Tetrachromacy is a rare genetic trait that allows about one percent of the population to see colours invisible to most humans. Women are apparently most likely

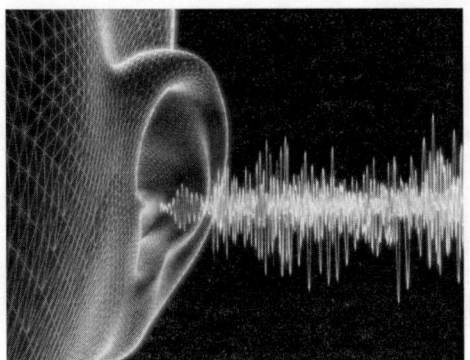

Figure 15: Speech frequencies are decoded by the hearing sense into electrical information. This is communicated to the brain which decodes the electrical into the words that we 'hear'.

to have a fourth colour-detecting cone (frequency decoder) in their retinas while most people have three. 'Tetrachromats' can differentiate between colours and see variations of colour that others cannot. They can *decode* more shades of colour. Synaesthesia is a neurological phenomenon in which sense decoding merges and overlaps. People see colours while hearing music, see numbers as colours, even have taste sensations in response to words spoken or read. It affects up to four percent of the population. Synaesthesia and tetrachromacy expose 'scientific' orthodoxy in how we perceive (decode) the world and what the 'world' really is. Our reality is a field of information in the form of frequency. We decode it into what we appear to 'externally' experience.

People have no problem accepting that our hearing sense is the result of sound wave frequencies decoded by the ears/brain into what we perceive as words and noise. In fact, all the senses work like this. We don't hear until the brain decodes the electrical information from the ears and we don't see, touch, taste or smell until the brain decodes that experience (information). Block the communication from the tongue to the brain and you won't taste anything. Block signals from the point of a blow from reaching the brain and you won't feel pain. The brain says 'ouch', not the point of impact. There are now pain relief methods that work on stopping the pain signals from reaching the brain. In short, the world you think you are 'in' and is all 'around' you is, in fact, in your head. Imagine eight billion computers decoding the same Wi-Fi into the same basic reality and you pretty much get the picture. The emphasis here is on *basic* or background reality. Our perceptions dictate what we make of that reality and the detail of how we experience it. Christians will decode the same backdrop but read it through their belief system and Muslims will read the same backdrop from their belief perspective. Christian, Muslim, or Hindu are all belief programs spinning their own version of the same basic reality being fed to their brain.

The body as a headset

The biological computer is constantly delivering to our awareness the reality decoded from the simulation, or Matrix, once our consciousness enters the body/brain between conception and birth. This then becomes our sense of reality. See how the senses are taken over almost instantly by a virtual reality headset decoding a virtual reality game (Fig 16). People scream, jump, fall over and run from what is only an illusion presented by the game (Fig 17). They can at least take off the headset and remember this, but what if you can't take off the brain/body headset unless it ceases to function ('dies')? All you would ever know was what the brain/body was decoding for you from the simulation field and that

Figure 16: The body operates like a virtual reality headset decoding the simulation into an illusory 'physical' reality.

would mean your entire human lifetime short of awakening to your consciousness beyond the simulation/Matrix and seeing reality for what

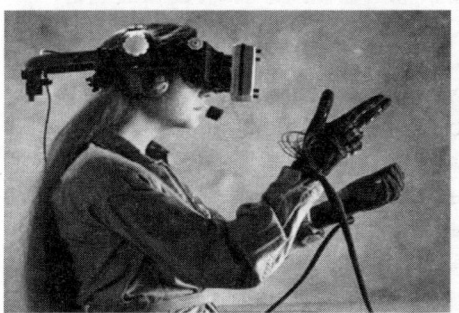 

Figure 17: You need only see how a sense of reality can be transformed in an instant by a virtual reality game to appreciate why that would happen with a body 'headset' from cradle to grave.

it is. Few manage to do that, and you can understand why with the 24/7 delivery of fake experience in a fake world. What if you donned a virtual reality headset at birth and did not remove it throughout your subsequent life? You would believe and accept as real whatever the headset presented to you. Of course you would, why wouldn't you? There you have the human condition and what I call the illusory self or 'Phantom Self' (Fig 18 overleaf). This identifies with 'human' and not infinity (Fig 19 overleaf). How do we experience those virtual-reality games? With the very five senses through which we decode the reality simulation. The headset, audio and gloves that people wear in the sophisticated computer games are tapping into the five senses and overriding the decoding of 'normal' reality. Erwin Schrödinger (1887-1961), an Austrian-Irish theoretical physicist, was a major player in quantum theory. He said:

Figure 18: The fake 'you' created by the body computer decoding the simulation.

Figure 19: The sense of human is a simulation creation. The True 'I' is a state of formless awareness.

We do not belong to this material world that science constructs for us. We are not in it; we are outside. We are only spectators. The reason why we believe that we are in it, that we belong to the picture, is that our bodies are in the picture. Our bodies belong to it. Not only my own body, but those of my friends, also of my dog and cat and horse, and of all the other people and animals. And this is my only means of communicating with them.

Our consciousness operates in another reality and at one level it is the human electromagnetic auric field that we know as the Mind (Fig 20). This is the field of information from which the body/brain is decoded into illusory physicality. The brain is not the Mind. It processes information from the Mind into what we experience as conscious thought and emotional reaction. Consciousness does not manifest *from* the brain, but *through* the brain. The information blueprint of body and human reality exists beyond visible light and what we 'see' is a decoded version of that which we experience as physicality/matter. We look *into* the realm of 'matter' while believing we are *in* the 'matter'. Only the body/brain is in the 'matter' which is not 'matter' at all, but condensed energy vibrating slowly to appear as 'matter'. Mind operates beyond 'matter' and through 'matter'. And what about movement? Do we really move or does our mind 'move'? You are sitting in a chair with a

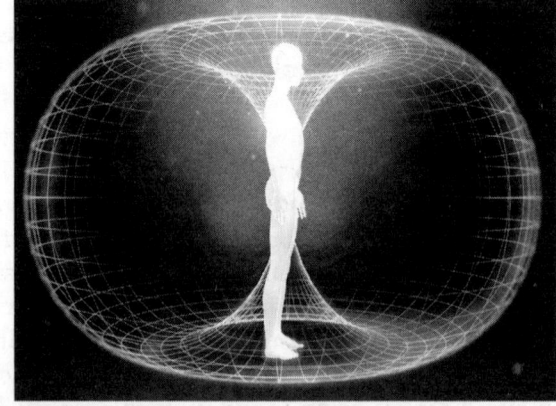

Figure 20: The Mind is an electromagnetic field – also known as the auric field – which interacts with the brain. We think *through* the brain, not *from* the brain.

The 'Human' Illusion

virtual reality headset which gives you the sensation of movement. You are in a car or walking down a street. But 'you' are sitting in a chair. The *game* is 'moving', not 'you'. What if we are decoding 'movement' rather than actually moving? It's worth asking. Scientific' orthodoxy clings to its ludicrous script that consciousness is only the brain. Michael Pravica, a professor of physics at the University of Nevada, Las Vegas, suggested that consciousness could in part be connecting with other dimensions and was immediately dismissed by the orthodoxy groupies. What he said was very mild, but even that was too much for them.

I watch many of those that call themselves 'alternative' falling for the same encoded traps as the masses they call the 'Sheeple'. They believe they are 'awake' when they are only in a very slightly bigger mind prison that has added some sort of 'conspiracy' to its sense of reality. The conspiracy they perceive operates in the political and financial arena when the very reality they think they are experiencing is the real foundation of human control. They see the Psyop of Trump as their 'saviour' while continuing to experience a constructed illusion as if it's real. I have been trying to get across this debilitating limitation of perception for so long and abuse and dismissal has been my reward, but less so now as scales (appropriately) fall from human eyes. What I am describing here *is* the conspiracy. The rest are only expressions and playouts of this *foundation* conspiracy which is the illusory 'world' we call 'human' (Fig 21).

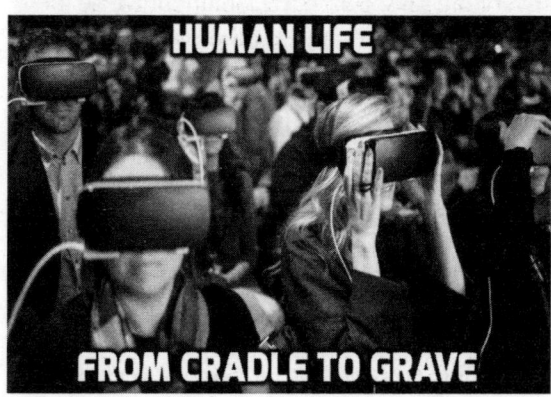

Figure 21: Human life.

Is there a 'God'?

Infinite Reality is consciousness, awareness, a state of being aware, but all awareness is not equally aware. There is what I call *Infinite Awareness in Awareness of Itself*, or the 'Infinite' for short. It is aware that it is *all* awareness. It is aware that it is *all* that exists – that everything is ultimately ONE. This is so often mistaken for the 'God' of almost every religion when the religion 'God' is a very different entity as we shall see. The Infinite is described in 'holy books' in terms of what it really is, but this is a diversion from what religious people are actually worshipping. They are not the same. We read that 'God is everywhere' and in terms of the Infinite that is true. *Infinite Awareness in Awareness of Itself* interpenetrates all infinity and so is 'everywhere'. This does not, however, mean that this level of Infinite Awareness *influences* all existence. Observe the human world and no more confirmation is necessary. Infinite Awareness is the all-possibility, all-potential, waiting to manifest. This explains the concept that 'God', or the Infinite, is *All That Has Been, Is, And Ever Can Be*. How can anything be *All That Has Been, Is, And Ever Can Be*? But if you are all-possibility, all-potential, you must be *All That Has Been, Is, And Ever Can Be* and the Source of everything – what we like and what we don't. What do physicists say about the quantum realm? It is *potentiality*. Our perceptions decide what within that potentiality (all possibility) we decode into experience and in doing so we create our own unique reality. The great majority of humans do this without even realising that they do. They think it's all random. Joseph Michael Straczynski, an American filmmaker and sci-fi writer, described it perfectly when he said:

> Accidents happen. That's what everyone says. But in a quantum universe there are no such things as accidents, only possibilities and probabilities folded into existence by perception.

The *All That Is* provides the infinite possibility and our perceptual state (a frequency field) interacts with the possibility field to manifest a 'physical' experience or expression of itself. Look at your life and it reflects your *perception* of life. This is how. The *Infinite in Awareness of Itself* is beyond frequency. It just is. It is pure potential waiting to be manifested by consciousness or imagination. That manifested potential is what we call Creation and Creation is *frequency*. Picture a silent void of all-possibility. Consciousness imagines aspects of that pure potential into manifested 'form' as information encoded in frequency. We therefore have the non-frequency Source of All – the Infinite – and a multi-dimensional Creation manifested as information carried by frequency. Infinite Creation abounds with 'worlds' and realities limited only by the imagination that made them manifest. From the calculated suppression of human perception and imagination it can be hard to grasp what all-possibility really means. Creation is limited only by the imagination of consciousness and can never be limited by possibility when the Source is *all-possibility*. The Infinite is silent stillness while Creation is experienced as noise and movement. A good way to imagine this dynamic is to sit in silence, or as best you can in this realm of comparative noise. When you break the silence by speaking (frequency) you are pulling one possibility out of all-possibility. Stop speaking and that possibility returns to the silence of all-possibility waiting to manifest. Even thought is actually the manifestation of one potential within all-potential and so is emotion.

What is consciousness?

Creation is possibility made manifest in the form of energy. Okay. What makes it manifest? Consciousness does. So, what is that? We go back to the silence. Consciousness is not energy. The Infinite is not energy. It is stillness and silence with no vibration. Consciousness generates energy with its thought patterns (information/imagination) in the form of frequency. Consciousness *infuses* itself into this energy as an emanation or extension of itself, but consciousness is not energy. Consciousness just *is*. It is *Isness*. It is the indefinable (in human words) silent stillness which pervades all reality and is infused within all reality. It is 'God' if you wish to use that term although any word or words can only be a symbol for the indefinable *All That Is*. Energy is conscious while not being consciousness which is the creative force behind and *within* energy. Consciousness is something different. It has no form and no energy. It is simply awareness, a state of being aware. It is the source of Creation. We see its impact on energy, but we don't see *it*. For *'it'* is the ultimate unseeable and unknowable no-thing, yet every-thing. We don't see *'it'*, only its manifestations. We are an energetic extension of that 'Infinite' consciousness and beyond energy an expression of the 'Infinite'. We have just forgotten and been manipulated to forget.

I have recalled in other books how in an altered and expanded state of consciousness in a Brazilian rainforest I experienced this still and silent *All That Is*. I later heard and read descriptions from others of the same experience and they matched my own. It took the form of a darkness that shone with a brilliant light which sounds contradictory but that's how it appeared. I have seen this called the 'Dazzling Darkness' which describes my experience perfectly (Fig 22). Creation comes out of this all-possibility in the form of Divine imagination. We are talking an amazing and infinite Creation – 'worlds' and realities – of every kind you could imagine and more. They share the same 'space' as they operate on different wavelengths or bands of frequency. Wherever you are now you are occupying the same 'space' as the Infinite and the entirety of Infinite Creation. These realities are all there to be experienced by consciousness as we explore forever forever and we can create our own. This

Figure 22: The 'Dazzling Darkness' – all-possibility and potential from which all Creation emerges.

Figure 23: From the stillness and silence of the *All That Is* emerges Creation through infinite expressions or emanations of itself. (Image by Neil Hague.)

is the infinity of which we are all an expression. We have once again been manipulated to forget (Fig 23).

Prime 'Earth'

One such reality is the original blueprint for our simulated world, and it exists on another wavelength sharing the same 'space' that we are. This is the 'paradise not far away'. You would recognise that world in theme if you saw it today, although *only* in theme. Our simulated 'human' reality is a frequency/digital 'copy' of that blueprint which has now been radically changed from the original. You can liken the concept to downloading a website from the Internet. The original website still exists as it always did, but you can change your copy in any way you choose until only the theme of the original remains. I will call this original blueprint 'Prime Reality' although it is only one reality within Infinite Reality. Consciousness creates realms of experience and discovery and when you are dealing with all-possibility the discovery never ends. Prime Reality with its Prime Earth is teeming with life and joy. I have read many accounts of near-death experiencers who describe this 'Earth' when their consciousness is temporarily released from human density as their body expires before it is revived. There is no death, only life, in Prime Reality. Consciousness in all its forms can enter and leave realms at will with no need to 'die' because everything happens on a higher frequency with greater awareness and possibility.

The technique known as 'cymatics' is an example of this. Cymatics is

Figure 24: Sound causes particles to form together to create a visual representation of the frequency. Change the sound, change the frequency, change the form.

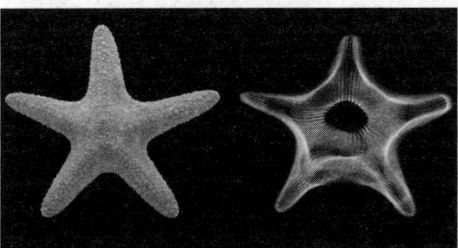

Figure 25: A real starfish and a 'starfish' created by cymatics.

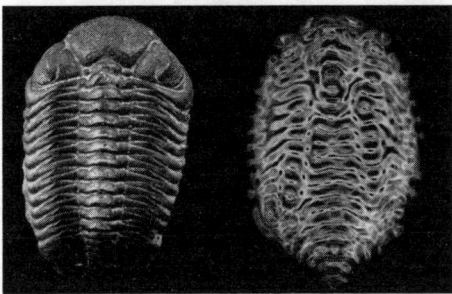

Figure 26: A stone and a cymatics image generated through sound.

the playing of sound frequencies across particles or a liquid medium. Each change of sound changes the impact on the form taken by the particles or liquid. A symbol or arrangement of the particles by one sound immediately becomes another with a switch of sound (Figs 24, 25, 26). Put 'cymatics' in a video search engine and you'll see. I shall be highlighting how symbols are placed all around us and in the media by agents of the demonic to manipulate our perceptions and these work through the cymatics principle. The all-seeing eye and pyramid and all-seeing eye (see the dollar bill and the reverse of the Great Seal of the United States) are obvious examples of this but there are many more (Fig 27 overleaf). Symbols represent sound frequencies and resonate to that frequency. This way they impact upon mind and perception through the effect on our energetic fields. Cymatics reveals that the higher the frequency the more complex are the arrangements (symbols) of the particles and medium. The lower the frequency the simpler they are. The reason is that the higher the frequency the more information it can hold and access (Fig 28 overleaf). Transform this into the consequences for consciousness and it means that the higher the frequency the greater awareness and the lower the frequency the greater the *lack* of awareness. The low-frequency human world, anyone?

Prime Reality operates on far higher frequencies than the desperately low frequency density of its manipulated and distorted simulated copy. Prime Earth would appear ethereal and non-physical when observed from our human density because of the difference in

Figure 27: The pyramid and all-seeing eye is widely used by the manipulators to covertly infiltrate perception. This is possible because symbols created by frequency also generate that frequency and impact on the frequency field we know as perception.

wavelength. To the visual perspective of lower frequences the higher frequencies appear ethereal, or 'ghost-like'. There is a colossal difference in potential in higher-frequency realms which allow for far more expanded imagination through their closer connection to full-blown all-possibility or the Source. This potential includes the outer forms you can take and what you can choose to do.

The chasm between the experience of Infinite Reality and the limitation of simulated reality

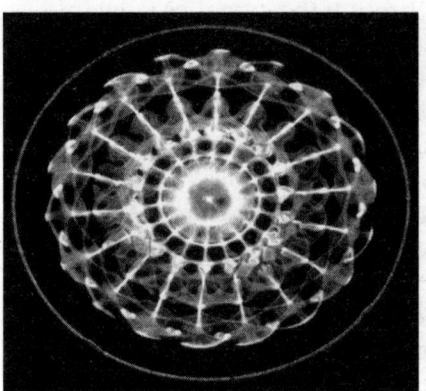 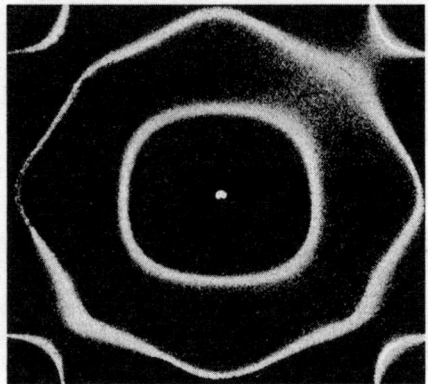

Figure 28: The higher the frequency (left) the more complex the pattern because higher frequencies can carry more information. Hence humans operating in lower frequencies (right) have more limited potential to process information into perception.

is beyond human language to describe because here we are subject to the manipulations of demonic control freaks that seek to entrap us in servitude to them. We shall now explore how this came about and ultimately what can set us free.

CHAPTER 2

Paradise Lost

Awake, arise or be for ever fall'n
John Milton, *Paradise Lost*

A recurring theme across religions and ancient cultures is a negative or demonic force 'fighting against God'. You have the demonic 'fall from heaven' of an entity with names such as Satan and the Devil (Christianity); Shaytan/Iblis (Islam); Samael (Jewish); and Yaldabaoth (Gnostic). Satan is, like Yaldabaoth, called the Deceiver.

Other names for the negative force include Beelzebub, Belial, Lucifer and Baphomet. There is Māra, the 'Lord of the Senses' in Buddhism and that title is extremely relevant given the power of the senses to deceive. Hinduism has many such negative 'gods' including Kali, the goddess of death, time, and doomsday. Samael is the king of all demons and the angel of death in Judaism. He is associated with Mars which will interest Elon Musk if he doesn't already know with his close connections to Israel. Zoroastrianism features Ahriman who rules over dark and evil forces at war with Ahura Mazda, the god of life. Cizin was the Mayan god of death in Central America who became associated after the Spanish conquest with the Christian Devil. The Norse goddess Hel is said to rule over the underworld called by the same name, Hel(l), while the horned Norse god, Nidhogg, the 'Malice Striker', seeks to destroy 'virtue and world peace'. Nidhogg was depicted as a dragon and often these figures are portrayed in reptilian terms as with the biblical Revelation 12:9: 'And the great dragon was cast out, that old serpent, called the Devil, and Satan, which deceiveth the whole world: he was cast out into the earth, and his angels were cast out with him.' The Gnostic Satan figure of Yaldabaoth is described as taking the form of a 'lion-faced serpent' with eyes like 'flashing fires of lightning'. Native Americans speak of the 'mind virus' they call Wetiko (among other names) which seeks to infiltrate the human psyche and control human thought, emotion and behaviour. Across the globe and ages, you find the same story of a force for good (depicted as 'God') and a force of evil operating from the hidden. An Internet article I saw about the subject said:

While the Christian version of Satan doesn't show up in every world religion, some version of a singular figure – often a disgraced or fallen deity – does emerge in modern and ancient texts worldwide. This devil-like being might preside over the underworld, perform the final judgement on a person's soul, or tempt people to stray from the path of goodness and light.

While non-Christian devils such as Hades from Greek mythology are not meant to be directly compared to the Bible's Satan (or at least our modern conception of him), they are often representatives of a fallen angel, deity or creator who has tried to usurp an all-powerful God figure, and in doing so, has been banished to some lesser world or fate.

There are many tags for the demonic force including the adversary, destroyer, great dragon, serpent, son of wickedness, the Evil One, the Father of Lies, the great accuser, spoiler and tempter. I am always looking for patterns of agreement between otherwise opposing or differing views and what I am describing here is an example. All these religions and cultures would disagree on so much (or at least have very different interpretations) and yet on this they are all in agreement: There was an 'entity' (*consciousness*) that sought to oppose and usurp 'God' (the Infinite) and this entity was the cause of the 'Fall of Man' (down the frequencies into dense 'matter'). All that I have researched and observed in the last 36 years leads me to the same conclusion when you fuse ancient and modern and include proper rather than orthodox science. These various names attributed to the negative force will change in different societies and ages. Some may well have been misused and misattributed, but I want to keep this as simple as possible given the apparent complexity of endless names for 'gods' around the world.

I will use the concept of Satan, the Devil, Shaytan/Iblis, Samael, and Yaldabaoth to symbolise a state of *consciousness* and its expressions in form as vehicles of that consciousness. I use these terms for a negative force because they have entered popular usage and people will know what I mean. They are just names. What I am using them to represent is what matters here. We should focus on the most common of common themes: A distorted expression of consciousness, which was reflected in the disharmony of its creation, sought to usurp the omnipotence of the Source of All. It doesn't matter what form we occupy; it is our state of consciousness that dictates what we do and how we behave. Those driven by this state of distorted, imbalanced, consciousness will behave and perceive accordingly no matter what form, human or non-human, they may take.

I have chosen in other books to focus on the Gnostic version of the 'Fall' because it is detailed and comprehensive while including all the major aspects of the universal story albeit with differing interpretations which led to their horrific demise at the hands of the Roman Church and its psychopaths. There was no formal Bible when Gnosticism began interpreting ancient texts on which the biblical narrative was based and the Roman Church excluded Gnostic manuscripts in favour of those that suited its agenda. Gnostic documents offer an insight into early Christian beliefs (including reincarnation) before the Church seized control to demonise Gnostic thought and eventually destroy them as a public presence in the 13th century. Gnostic interpretation offers a very different context for the universal story and the Roman Church was having none of that. There was far too much at stake financially and in terms of power and control for any other version of reality to circulate that challenged the narrative decided upon by the Church through the texts that it chose to include in the Bible.

It makes me chuckle when I see other denominations of Christianity condemning Roman Catholicism when Rome dictated what constitutes the Bible that they all claim is the word of God. I should emphasise that I had already reached pretty much the same conclusions when I first came across the Gnostic version of human reality and especially that the 'human world' was the work of something very, very malevolent. I had further decided that the True 'I' is a state of formless consciousness and an expression of the Infinite *in awareness of itself* and that bodily form is only an outer 'shell' that allows consciousness to interact with the frequency bands or realities of Creation. I refer to this formless awareness or True 'I' as 'Spirit' which is beyond what people call 'Soul' and way, way, way (and then some) beyond the realm of human dense 'matter'. 'Beyond' refers to the chasm of difference in both awareness and, because of that, in *frequency*.

Find of finds

Gnostics were not a genetic group, but rather a belief system which manifested among various peoples, most famously the Cathars in southern France. Cathar Gnosticism effectively ended with the siege of Montségur Castle in 1244 when hundreds of Cathars were burned to death at the behest of the Roman Church and the Church-controlled French king, Louis IX. Legends say that a few Cathars escaped with 'treasure', and this was rumoured to include documents. The siege was thought to be the demise of Gnostic belief but then came an amazing find in the Egyptian town of Nag Hammadi in 1945 some 80 miles north of Luxor and the Valley of the Kings. The Nag Hammadi find included 13 leatherbound papyrus codices or manuscripts and more than 50 texts (Fig 29 overleaf). They were written in Coptic Egyptian and are extensively the work of Gnostic thinkers. Scholars took years to track and assemble them when news circulated that a local farmer had found the now labelled 'Nag Hammadi Library' in an earthen jar. Gnostic beliefs were now exposed to a much wider audience.

Egypt was the location for another centre of Gnosticism at the Great or Royal Library of Alexandria. It became the biggest library in the ancient world with the works of Greek writers and philosophers such as Homer, Plato and Socrates among its hundreds of thousands of texts and documents from across ancient societies including Assyria, Greece, Persia, India and, of course, Egypt. The Nag Hammadi find included a partial translation of Plato's *Republic* and the library's Gnostic leadership was massively influenced by Ancient Greece as is Gnosticism in general through Socrates, Plato and Aristotle. There are also other Gnostic texts that were rejected by the Roman Church for inclusion in the Bible and these have been labelled the Gnostic Gospels which I will be highlighting. Scholars have estimated that the Nag Hammadi works were hidden around perhaps 400 AD which syncs with the demise in stages of the Great Library driven once again by the Roman Church which feared the open minds that gathered there.

Figure 29: Part of the Nag Hammadi Library found in Egypt in 1945.

Among them was Hypatia, an Athens-educated mathematician, astronomer and philosopher who taught the work of Plato and Aristotle. She was the head of the Platonist school at Alexandria who was murdered by a Catholic mob in 415 AD instigated by Cyril, Rome's Bishop of Alexandria. She was reported to have been 'stripped naked, her skin flayed with jagged pieces of oyster shells, her limbs pulled from her body and paraded through the streets.' Her body was then burned. Cyril, like a stream of other Roman Church psychopaths, was made a saint as late as 1982 with his 'feast day' celebrated on June 28th. It staggers me to see many 'stars' of the so-called 'Truth Movement' claiming to support freedom of speech while converting to Roman Catholicism which has killed grotesquely so many people over the centuries for the crime of having the wrong opinion. A quote attributed to Hypatia captured why the Catholic mob was set upon her: 'Reserve your right to think, for even to think wrongly is better than not to think.' Oh no, don't let them *think*. They'll *all* want to do it. The library's commitment to free thought led to many discoveries long before they were *officially* discovered. This included the observation that the Earth circles the Sun 2,000 years before it was attributed to Polish mathematician and astronomer, Nicolaus Copernicus.

The translated Nag Hammadi texts have provided enormous insight into Gnostic beliefs, and I was often stunned by how they matched my own views derived from other experience, observation and sources. That doesn't mean I go along with everything (no one has *all* the answers) and I am going to add other information and sources that challenge aspects of the Gnostic narrative or perhaps add more detail and context to how the universal story came about. But in theme and much detail I found myself nodding in agreement over and over as I read through the translated volumes. Gnostic means 'learned' while Gnosis comes from a Greek word that translates as a form of mystical knowledge. I have described different levels of being as 'Mind' (human); 'Soul' (frequencies of reality beyond human); and 'Spirit' – the Infinite Self that ultimately connects with, and is an expression of, the *All That Is* or the Source (Fig 30). Gnostics spoke of 'Nous' (Mind/Soul) and Pneuma (Infinite Self). Gnostics believed, as I do, that the 'God' worshipped by the Roman Church (and most other religions) is ultimately the evil force that created the realm of matter or the virtual reality simulation known as the human world. You can see why the Church psychopaths wanted rid of them when it challenged the whole basis of their narrative. I mean by this 'evil God' a state of consciousness that operates through multiple agents and agencies that I will be exposing step-by-step. You could think of the

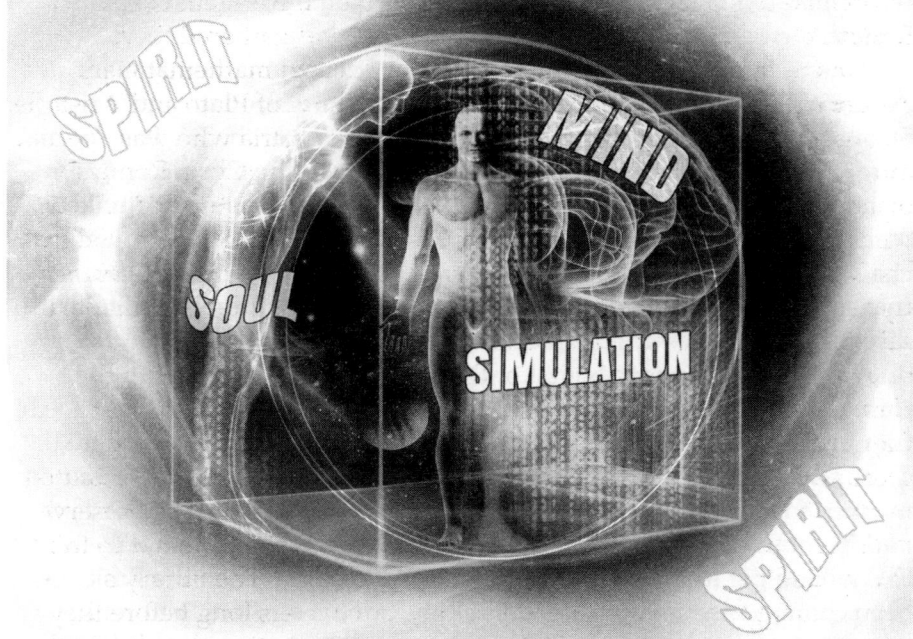

Figure 30: Multiple levels of being from infinite Spirit to Soul and human. The level that dictates our sense of reality dictates our self-identity. Human and Soul are trapped in a simulated reality to hijack perception. (Image by Neil Hague.)

control structure as a deeply imbalanced consciousness operating through a hierarchy of subordinates that include 'extraterrestrials' (interdimensionals) and the Global secret society network of the Global Cult. It is this combination, inspired by the same distorted *consciousness* that Gnostics name Yaldabaoth, that created and/or drive the simulated reality that humans perceive as their 'world'.

Gnostic 'Satan'

We have that common theme in religions and ancient cultures of an entity engaging in a 'revolt from God'. This is clearly described in Gnostic texts with the entity/consciousness Yaldabaoth also often known as the Demiurge ('Creator') and a version of the perception of 'Satan'. Emanations or projections/expressions of Infinite or Divine Consciousness are called 'Aeons' by Gnostics who they said act as a force of Creation. One of these Aeons is referred to as 'Sophia' or 'Wisdom'. Gnostics said Aeons work in unity to create in harmony and balance, but Yaldabaoth is said to have been created 'in error' when the Aeon Sophia sought to create without the unity of other aspects of the Infinite and this disharmony was reflected in what was created. Nag Hammadi texts say a boundary described as 'the Limit' was installed to separate the Divine 'Upper Aeons' from her manifestation in what is described as the 'Lower Aeons': ... 'Her inborn idea, with its passion, was separated from her by Horos [the Limit], fenced off and expelled from that circle.'

Gnostic texts describe how 'Sophia' has been trying to infuse Infinite Awareness into the Lower Aeon Yaldabaoth simulation to rectify the error and communicate with those awake enough to 'hear'. The Sophia 'error' was erased and forbidden by the Church which could not allow its target populations to realise that even the Divine is not infallible when it is *all* possibility and not a tyrant. Nag Hammadi documents challenge the official symbolic story of Adam and Eve in Eden and say the 'snake' was trying to awaken humanity to forbidden knowledge to discern good and evil. The Church has used this to say that 'God' doesn't want humans to have knowledge which it equates with the forbidden fruit. When I have asked Christian believers questions which they cannot answer I am told that 'God doesn't want us to know that'. They also speak of the 'Gnostic heresy' when Gnostics said we must awaken to spiritual knowledge to see through the illusion. The Adam and Eve narrative can be interpreted in many ways, and you will see this when I get to the chapters on religion and how much the Bible has been changed and manipulated. I tell the Sophia story only to reflect what Gnostics said and not because I necessarily accept all the detail. People have different symbolism in their story telling and we have to realise that much ancient 'history' is written to be absorbed symbolically rather than literally. Taking the symbolic to be literal is the whole foundation of religions worldwide.

Gnostics say that Yaldabaoth had the power to create as an emanation of Sophia, an aspect of the Divine, but that power was limited. Hence it has been labelled the 'Dim Ruler' in relation to its Divine 'light' (creative power). Gnostics believed that Yaldabaoth creativity was limited to making copies of what already exists rather than creating from pure imagination. Nag Hammadi texts say Yaldabaoth lacks 'ennoia' which is translated as 'intentionality'. I would define this lack of 'ennoia' as limited creative imagination compared with the limitless imagination of the all-possibility Infinite. There is some inherited creative power but a fraction by comparison and it is limited to creating something from something as a counterfeiter does rather than something out of nothing. Indeed, Yaldabaoth is described as a 'Counterfeit Spirit' limited to 'countermimicry' which includes the simulated 'countermimicry' of Prime Reality. The Gnostic *Tripartite Tractate* manuscript describes how the realm of Yaldabaoth is one of 'likenesses, copies, shadows, and phantasms' mimicking Upper Aeon reality, but 'lacking reason and the light'. It makes the point that a copy of something beautiful can appear beautiful, but nothing like as magnificent as the real thing: ' ... In the manner of a reflection are they beautiful. For the face of the copy normally takes its beauty from that of which it is a copy.' Gnostic texts say Yaldabaoth specialises in 'Hal' or 'phantasia' – *virtual reality* which is what the simulation is. The Nag Hammadi *Apocryphon of John* says:

> ... [Yaldabaoth] organised (everything) according to the model of the first aeons [by using] the power in him, which he had taken from his mother, [and] produced in him the likeness of the cosmos ...

> ... This is the first archon [Yaldabaoth] who took a great power from his mother. And he removed himself from her and moved away from the places in which he was born [Upper Aeons]. He became strong and created for himself other aeons with a flame of luminous fire which exists now.

I'll come to the meaning of 'Archon' for those who are new to this information. I have suggested that 'luminous fire' could be electromagnetism which is the 'false light' of the simulation in contrast to the light of Infinite Creation. This would explain the symbolism of Lucifer 'the light bringer' which is a focus of worship for Satanists and secret society initiates. There are different versions of these creation stories relating to this, but it is the *theme* that I wish to emphasise. The Christian Satan or Devil is the most famous version of this as an 'angel' who was expelled by God from 'heaven'. I have used the Gnostic name

Yaldabaoth for this entity/consciousness in other books and I will do the same here. I emphasise that Yaldabaoth is the *consciousness*, and its operatives are expressions of that consciousness that take many forms. They can become confused with each other in different narratives, but in the end, it is the consciousness that dictates their behaviour. Whenever I say Yaldabaoth, I am talking about the state of consciousness, and I will refer to subordinate gofers expressing that consciousness as 'Yaldabaoth entities'.

The 'bad copy'

Nag Hammadi texts refer to human reality as a 'bad copy' of Upper Aeon Prime Reality or a part of it anyway. Upper Aeons are portrayed as the archetypes (blueprint) and the Lower Aeons as inferior reflections of that blueprint. Upper Aeons are 'emanations' from the Infinite – extensions of that consciousness and creative force. Lower Aeons are inferior copies. I'll focus on this bad copy, or Matrix, in the next chapter. It is a copy of the vibrational codes (information) of a Prime Reality 'Universe' (one of endless numbers). The symbolism of downloading a website to make a copy is most appropriate. The point is that it was a very inferior copy and yet how would you *know* that once you were trapped inside and it became your sense of reality? What would you compare it with? Gnostic documents highlight the difference between the Aeons as fullness/deficiency, immortal/mortal, spiritual/psychic, Spirit/Soul, existence/non-existence, no-time/time. Put another way – Infinity/limitation, life/death, True 'I' Spirit/Mind, True 'I' Spirit/Soul, Prime Reality/simulated reality, and the no-time/time I have already covered. 'Time' is an illusion encoded into the bad copy simulation to enslave consciousness in a false sense of reality. Nag Hammadi texts describe the simulation in terms of a 'shadow' of Prime Reality and a shadow does not exist in the same way as that which it reflects. Gnostic manuscript *Origin of the World* says of this shadow realm that Gnostics called 'the Abyss':

> Now the eternal realm of truth has no shadow outside it, for the limitless light is everywhere within it. But its exterior is shadow, which has been called by the name 'darkness'.

This describes two very different versions of 'light' which I will be expanding upon. A shadow is also an inferior copy of whatever it reflects, and you can also picture Prime Reality reflected on water as a symbol of this existence and non-existence (Fig 31). They are reality and an inferior copy of reality. A Nag Hammadi text called *Zostrianos* says: 'In relation to the reflection which he [Yaldabaoth] saw in it, he created the world. With a reflection of a reflection, he worked at producing the

Figure 31: The simulation is like a shadow reflection of Prime Reality. This was the Gnostic division of 'existence' and 'non-existence'.

world.' Producing, not so much 'creating'. The human world was 'copied' from Prime Reality and then continually distorted until we see the result today. Gnostics called Yaldabaoth the 'Great Architect' and Freemasons of the Global Cult network refer to their 'god' as the 'Great Architect of the Universe'. The creator of the simulation in the *Matrix* movies is 'the Architect'. A text in the Nag Hammadi *Bruce Codex* describes how after the emergence of the Yaldabaoth distortion the Infinite separated the Upper Aeons (Infinite Reality) from the Lower Aeons (the Yaldabaoth simulation or fake 'kingdom'):

> And then the existent separated itself from the non-existent. And the non-existent is the evil which has manifested in matter. And the enveloping power separated those that exist from those that do not exist. And it called the existent 'eternal', and it called the non-existent 'matter'. And in the middle, it separated those that exist from those that do not exist, and it placed veils between them.

Another Nag Hammadi text, *Hypostasis of the Archons*, tells us that 'a veil exists between the world above and the realms that are below; and shadow came into being beneath the veil; and that shadow became matter; and that shadow was projected apart'. What we call 'humans' were ejected from 'paradise' by the disconnection from the influence of the Infinite as they 'fell' into the frequency gulag of the simulation.

Figure 32: Gnostics portrayed the Infinite as 'the silence' and 'the One'. Some call it 'the Void'.

The Separation

I have said that the Infinite is silence, and Creation is the noise. This is also portrayed in Gnostic works (Fig 32 on previous page). The Infinite Upper Aeons are called 'The Silence', 'the silent Silence', 'the living Silence', which has 'Watery Light'. The latter indicates the difference between Upper Aeon Infinite light and the electrical/electromagnetic light of the Yaldabaoth simulation which Nag Hammadi texts may refer to as 'luminous fire'. The misunderstanding of this difference is a foundation of religious misdirection. Infinite light also operates as a single whole while simulation light is split into positive and negative, male and female, or *duality* rather than wholeness, unity, or Oneness. Human reality is founded upon electromagnetism and electricity which require what? Polarity – *duality*. Electromagnetism is a combination of electricity and magnetism, both of which are generated by polarity. Evil (extreme imbalance) does not exist within the infinity of the Source where everything is balance, but of course all-possibility means there must be a potential for *im*balance – especially the further we stray from the harmony and unity of the Source. Balance and harmony are what we call 'love' and 'wisdom' while the Yaldabaoth simulation is imbalance and disharmony that negates love and wisdom. Explains a lot, right? This doesn't mean that love and wisdom cannot be expressed in the realm of Yaldabaoth by those that retain influence from the *All That Is*. It can and we see it. But even this is a pale version of what love and wisdom really are and what that really means.

The chasm between infinity and simulated limitation comes with the sense of separation. There is no separation in Infinite Reality and to instigate control and illusion we have to be manipulated into that *sense* of separation. There are different points of attention within infinity, but all is aware that it is part of an infinite whole. An expression of 'God' if you want to use religious terms. Upper Aeons are the infinite realms of pure Spirit (awareness, the True 'I') where there is no 'time' or 'space' because as one Gnostic text puts it: '… the emanations [from the 'Father'/Infinite] are limitless and immeasurable.' They just are. Everything just is. There is no measurement or perception like 'space' which is why I have put quotes around the word. The perception of 'space', like time, is encoded into the simulation and does not exist in the same way elsewhere. When you play a virtual reality computer game there is the perception of 'time' as one scene follows another and of 'space' with the perspective of distance. But both are simply information encoded in the game. I've said that you see 'time' and 'space' when you watch a film or play a video game and yet time is only one scene following another in an entire film or game existing in totality at the same 'time'. 'Space' is only *information* encoded in the simulation 'Wi-Fi' field. Nag Hammadi works describe the Upper Aeons of Spirit

Paradise Lost

(Pleroma) as 'the totality', 'the fullness' and 'perfection' of 'emanations of the Father'. The whole point of the Yaldabaoth simulation is to so entrap consciousness that it ceases to be influenced by those 'emanations of the Father', or Infinite. In that one sentence you have the reason the human world is as it is. The Gnostic text *Tripartite Tractate* says:

> The emanation of the Totalities, which exist from the one who exists, did not occur according to a separation from one another, as something cast off from the one who begets them. Rather, their begetting is like a process of extension, as the Father extends himself to those whom he loves, so that those who have come forth from him might become him as well.

You could interpret the biblical story of the Prodigal Son this way as an 'extension of the Father' leaves and becomes lost in illusion and suffering before being welcomed home by his father with equal enthusiasm to another son that never left. True awakening is returning 'home' to Infinity while the simulation is designed to stop that return and impose ongoing enslavement in manufactured illusion. Prime Creation comes from the imagination of the Infinite and expressions of the Infinite while the simulation is the work of Yaldabaoth/Satan/Shaytan/Samael, the inverted, distorted state of consciousness that Gnostics say was created in 'error'. We have a force, whatever the detailed background, that has sought to usurp the Infinite and its Creation. It can never do that because it's not even nearly aware or powerful enough, but it can, and has, manifested a fake reality – the simulated 'bad copy' – that has entrapped consciousness in its lair by convincing its targets that the lair is 'real'.

Playing both 'sides'

One of Yaldabaoth's greatest mind-tricks is to play both the Devil and the Divine. They are promoted as polarities of good and evil when the same villain is playing both 'characters'. We will see in the chapters on religion how one expression of Yaldabaoth consciousness, the bloodthirsty 'God' of the Old Testament, Yahweh, is reported as saying in Isaiah 45:5: '*I am* the LORD, and *there is* none else, *there is* no God beside me.' The Nag Hammadi text *Hypostasis of the Archons* quotes Yaldabaoth as saying: 'It is I who am God, and there is no other power apart from me.' Gnostics said that Yaldabaoth and the biblical Yahweh/Jehovah are the same entity. We'll see later that there are other explanations for 'Yahweh', but I suggest that 'he' reflects the *consciousness* of Yaldabaoth who claimed to be the 'true God' when it is the imposter 'god' that created the simulation as its 'kingdom'. Yaldabaoth believed it was the true god because Gnostics say that as a creation of shadow and not Infinite light it was in a realm in which at first only itself appeared to exist. Mind-trickery does not come more extreme than people following a religion that appears to oppose 'Satan' by worshipping a 'God' that is *also 'Satan'* in another guise. It certainly explains how religious advocates worship what they claim is a 'loving god' that demands Old Testament slaughter and a New Testament 'loving god' that insists that his 'only begotten son' be horrifically sacrificed on a cross before he will 'forgive the sins of humanity'. Here's a reminder of the Yaldabaoth entity known as Yahweh quoted in the Old Testament in Leviticus:

> You will eat the flesh of your sons and the flesh of your daughters. I will destroy your high places, cut down your incense altars and pile your dead bodies on the lifeless forms of your idols, and I will abhor you ... I will scatter you among the nations and will draw out my sword and pursue you. Your land will be laid waste, and your cities will lie in ruins.

Yaldabaoth consciousness is indeed bloody stupid and Gnostics acknowledged this insanity. They labelled Yaldabaoth as 'The Blind One' who is 'stupefied in his madness' while other names including Samael and Saklas translate as 'The Blind God' and 'The Foolish One'. You don't do what it does and seek such power over others unless you are an imbalanced buffoon, but that doesn't mean you can't be clever, or even very clever. A lot of psychopaths are clever while none of them are wise. There is such a difference between cleverness and wisdom, and I have long said that cleverness without wisdom is the most destructive force on Earth (or anywhere else). The cleverness of Yaldabaoth consciousness comes from keeping its targets in ignorance. It is highly skilled at manipulating perception and sense of reality which is the whole foundation of its control. Stupidity and foolishness come in the desire to do this and the belief that it can ultimately prevail against the eternity of the Infinite. For those trapped in its illusions, however, that is no immediate comfort. All in all, I do have sympathy with the view expressed in *The Hitchhiker's Guide to the Galaxy*: 'In the beginning the Universe was created. This has made a lot of people very angry and been widely regarded as a bad move.'

Simulated limitation

The Lower Aeon Yaldabaoth simulation is blocked from Upper Aeon Infinity by what Nag Hammadi texts say is a boundary dubbed 'the Limit'. The outer extent of the simulation, or bad copy, is symbolised in the text *Pistis Sophia* as a dragon swallowing its own tail: 'The outer

Figure 33: The Ouroboros 'Ring-Pass-Not'.

darkness is a great dragon, whose tail is in his mouth, outside the whole world and surrounding the whole world.' Dragon/reptilian symbolism again and the dragon swallowing its tail is known as the Ouroboros or Leviathan (Fig 33). It is said that we must pass through Leviathan to reach 'paradise' (Divine Infinity). The 'Ring-Pass-Not' is an ancient esoteric concept that reflects the same theme and is defined like this:

> A profoundly mystical and suggestive term signifying the circle or bounds of frontiers within which is contained the consciousness of those who are still under the sway of the delusion of separateness – and this applies whether the Ring be large or small.
>
> It is a general term applicable to any state in which an entity, having reached a certain stage of evolutionary growth of the unfolding of consciousness, finds itself unable to pass into a still higher state because of some delusion under which the consciousness is labouring, be that delusion mental or spiritual.

The frequency field (consciousness) to which we resonate is dictated by our perception and sense of self-identity. The more limitations that you identify with ('Little Me', I have no power) the denser and more limited will be your frequency field. The goal of Yaldabaoth and its minions is to so control your perception, self-identity, and sense of reality that your frequency field cannot breach the limits of the simulation 'Matrix' which has other levels and not only the dense physical realm of 'human' (Fig 34). The concept of the Ring-Pass-Not defines the situation very well. Consciousness it says cannot breach the 'bounds of frontiers' within which it is contained (the simulation) while 'still under the sway

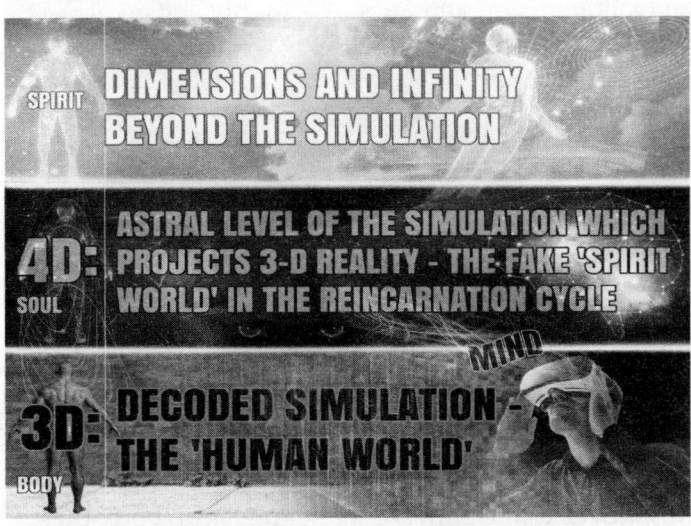

Figure 34: The human 'Third Dimension' and the Astral 'Fourth Dimension'. The Astral has other levels and beyond that is infinity outside the simulation or Matrix. Dimensions have to be symbolised as one above the other, but they really share the same 'space'. (Image by Neil Hague.)

of the delusion of separateness and some delusion under which the consciousness is labouring, be that delusion mental or spiritual'. The reason is that perception = frequency. The delusion of separateness from the Infinite Whole and the delusion of only being 'human' with all its sense of limitation will ensure that your frequency cannot breach the limits of the simulation when it remains in the *frequency band* of the simulation. Control perception, control frequency, keep them in the Matrix. This is why I have said for decades that the foundation of human control is control of perception and self-identity. Do you identify with being human or infinite? One is trapped in the simulation; the other is out of here when the body expires.

We have two 'bodies' within the simulation – the 'physical' body and the Soul body. One is the outer shell for our consciousness when we are in the density field of the 'human world' and the other allows our consciousness to interact with other less dense levels of the simulation known as the Astral dimensions, fourth dimension, or 'fake heaven'. Spirit takes on energetic bodies, or fields, that resonate with different realities so we can interact with them given that Spirit resonates at far higher frequencies than the realities that it chooses to experience (Fig 35). My consciousness could not tap this keyboard because of the vast difference in frequency and my outer 'shell' or body allows me to do this as it matches the 'physical' frequency of the keys. The principle applies throughout Creation. The body that allows interaction with the Astral is widely known as the Soul within which pure Spirit can experience the Astral realm. Our awareness (attention) moves to the Soul when the 'physical' body dies, and the Soul is the perspective described in the so-called 'near-death experience' when the human body briefly expires before being revived. The person experiences a totally different reality in the Astral dimension

Figure 35: The many dimensions of existence in which formless Spirit enters different 'bodies' to interact with different frequencies of reality. (Image by Neil Hague.)

and the common themes described are extremely compelling. I'll have a lot more about this.

It's enough to say for now that the simulation encompasses both the 'physical' world of the human body and the Astral realm of the Soul body and seeks to entrap us in an endless cycle of reincarnation between Astral and human for reasons that will become clear. Buddhism calls this the 'Wheel of Samsara'. Buddhists believe, I say rightly, that you stay on the reincarnation 'wheel' until you reach a state of 'enlightenment'. This is another way of saying *frequency* through expanded states of awareness, self-identity, and sense of reality. I have a different explanation for reincarnation, however, which I say has nothing to do with 'learning lessons to evolve'. Entry to Infinity is through self-identification with the 'True I', consciousness without form or limit, free from identification with human, Soul, or any mental or emotional attachment to the illusions of the multi-levelled Matrix. We return to Infinity when we realise that we *are* Infinity or 'Spirit'.

Springing the Trap

The disconnection between the Infinite and Yaldabaoth was also a disconnect from what Gnostics refer to as Divine 'emanations' from the Source of all-possibility. Yaldabaoth consciousness retained creative power in its field for long enough to embark on manifesting its own 'kingdom' ('the Universe' and other connected realities). Prime Earth is a realm of Infinite Creation originating from the energetic and consciousness emanations of the Source. Yaldabaoth sought to mimic this as closely as possible with its 'bad copy'. Putting various sources together it seems that this was not a trap at first and consciousness (Spirit) could come and go at will. Eventually the trap was sprung as the Astral frequency was made denser and other energetic 'shells' emerged to match the frequency change. These are known as the astral body ('Soul'), mental body, etheric body, and ultimately the dense human body. A lot of the inner conflict – 'being pulled in many directions' – is generated by the battle for dominance of these different aspects of being when they are not in unified harmony.

Now we had Spirit entrapped in ever denser frequencies and it could no longer leave at will because its manipulated low-frequency perceptions were held within the Matrix frequency band. Nag Hammadi documents refer to these entrapped Spirits as 'Divine Sparks' that are encased within energetic 'garments' (bodies/frequency fields) which impact on the perceptions and self-identity of the 'Spark'. As I write this, I am seeing in my mind one of those Venus flytrap plants. The principle is the same. You entice the target into your lair and then slam the door – in this case a perception/frequency door. Divine Sparks became lost in the Astral/human illusion and the process had only just begun. I have heard it said that all the 'Sparks' still trapped in the Matrix today are those that were originally captured. This would make sense in that the trap was played when there appeared to be little difference between Prime Reality and the copy while Spirit was free to move between the two. Once the trap was sprung the game became obvious and no others fell for it. Maybe, but I think there's more to know about that and how the trap can be set in other ways. Next came the extreme density of 'matter' and, with each fall down the energetic harmonics, Divine Sparks became ever more deeply encased in illusion. Memory of its True 'I' – Spirit – became lost in level after level of perceptual fakery like a multi-levelled energetic maze.

Today's fast-emerging fusion between humans and artificial intelligence is the next stage of this. Does anyone believe that remembering who you really are will play any part when AI is governing your thinking and emotional response? To understand where we came from is to understand where we are and that is the whole point of this book. The Kabbalah, the Jewish mystical work or 'Bible', tells of many different versions of 'Adam' (bodies encasing the Divine Spark) to match the incessant fall down the frequencies. Consciousness that became 'human' was ethereal to start with. There was no need to eat or sleep and they did not feel pain. These traits are related to the biological computer, not consciousness. What does a computer do when it is not being used – it goes into *sleep* mode. As does the body computer. The Gnostic *Gospel of Phillip* says that what became 'humans' were Divine energy 'emanations' of the Infinite. They were androgynous in line with the unity of Infinite Reality, but the androgynous nature was eventually split within the simulation and separated into the human perception of male and female to create duality. The Bible calls the first man 'Adam' and the first woman 'Eve' who was 'created from a rib of Adam'. This symbolises the splitting of aspects of mind which is why men and women largely don't think and perceive in the same way.

By now other emanations of Yaldabaoth consciousness existed as I will detail including some who walked the Earth as the 'gods' and 'giants' of ancient texts that will become very much part of this story. They were centrally involved in the bodily evolution of the 'Adams' and 'Eves'. The Bible appears to tell us that 'God' (in reality gods, plural) *created* 'Adam', the 'first human'; but we'll see that 'genetic manipulation' to evolve a *new* species of human (rather than one from scratch) would more accurately describe the process. This will be part of a whole new look later at what biblical texts really say when they are retranslated from the garbage we are told to believe. You are experiencing the latest version of 'Adam' and 'Eve'. The next unfolding version is the fusion with AI and a much more synthetic form. Original 'humans' had a direct connection to the Infinite. They did not have to 'learn lessons' to 'evolve'. They knew what the Infinite knew as a pure expression of the Divine. They could not be controlled by a bunch of lunatics, and they had to be encased in ignorance – the Soul body and dense material body. Gnostics said the human body is a prison that traps perception in illusion and false self-identity and that's what it is and has been created to be. The Nag Hammadi *Apocryphon of John* says: 'This is the tomb of the newly formed body with which the robbers had clothed the man, the bond of forgetfulness; and he became a mortal man.' Human bodies were 'fences for light' which block awareness from Spirit and make the body a prison. *Apocryphon of John* continues:

> And I entered into the midst of their prison, which is the prison of the body. And I said: 'He who hears, let him get up from the deep sleep' ... And I said, 'I am ... of the pure light ... Arise and ... follow your root, which is I [Spirit] and guard yourself against the angels of poverty and the demons of chaos and all those who ensnare you, and beware of the deep sleep and the enclosure of the inside of Hades.'

The 'enclosure of the inside of Hades' – the simulation. Gnostic and other texts describe how the body is programmed to be docile, subservient to authority, fearful, and not question anything that would dilute the impact of the program. Yaldabaoth wanted obedient slaves, and the biological computer is programmed to get them. This describes the great majority of humans to this day but awakening to consciousness and remembering the True 'I' can override the program.

Different 'Adams', different 'Eves'

Ancient texts and beliefs around the world reveal a theme of humans driven by different levels of consciousness. The Nag Hammadi *Tripartite Tractate* says there are three basic types of 'human', although I think there is a fourth that is consciousness that can project itself into this reality from beyond the simulation frequency band which on death of the body simply 'wakes up' in Infinite Reality. That's just my view picked up over the years. The Nag Hammadi human trio are: The 'Pneumatics' with a potential connection to the Infinite; the 'Psychics' who have a Soul; and the 'Hylics' who are programmed to be only soulless material entities. Pneumatics are Divine Sparks trapped in the body program with the potential to see through the illusion and control system. They have an innate feeling that 'something isn't right' which was captured in the first *Matrix* movie when the Neo character is told: 'What you know, you can't explain. But you feel it.' The Psychics are described as having a Soul, but not a Divine Spark. They can still expand to connect with the Infinite, or they can fall into the material trap. Psychics are used by Yaldabaoth to create and administer its systems.

They may seek meaning for life while the material can also ensnare and mesmerise them. Hylics are 'biological machines' following their program and comprise the majority of humans. A computer processes data without what we would call 'consciousness'. It's the same principle. We are all experiencing through a biological machine seeking to program and limit perception. The question is what level of consciousness – if any – is at work that can override the program?

Hylics are creations of Yaldabaoth and its operatives specifically to serve its interests by holding back the Pneumatics and Psychics. They don't question anything about reality beyond the material because they are programmed not to do so. The Church would wet its pants at the thought of any of this knowledge circulating and the texts revealing this reality. The 'bad copy' simulation was banned from the Bible and Church teachings on punishment of death. The fall down the frequencies from formless awareness into dense matter totally rewired the self-identity of Divine Sparks, that core which can still potentially connect with the Infinite. Each new programmed energetic layer encased its awareness in ever more illusion. This was especially so when the new human – the 'Adam' – was genetically manipulated from earlier humans and the biological computer body was infused with a version of the Yaldabaoth 'counterfeit spirit' to confuse and deflect from our true identity. The Gnostic *Apocryphon of John* says:

> He [Yaldabaoth] sent his angels [subordinates] to the daughters of men, that they might take some of them for themselves and raise offspring for their enjoyment. And at first they did not succeed.
>
> When they had no success, they gathered together again and they made a plan together ... And the angels changed themselves in their likeness into the likeness of their mates, filling them with the spirit of darkness, which they had mixed for them, and with evil ... And they took women and begot children out of the darkness according to the likeness of their spirit.

Stories abound across the world in ancient cultures about the interbreeding of humans with non-human entities. These hybrid bloodlines still exist to this day and comprise the inner circles of the Global Cult. There is this famous biblical passage in Genesis 6:4 of the King James version:

> There were giants in the earth in those days; and also after that, when the sons of God came in unto the daughters of men, and they bare children to them, the same became mighty men which were of old, men of renown.

The result is believed to be the 'Nephilim' who are described as the offspring of the 'sons of God' and 'daughters of men' and are assumed by many scholars and Greek translations to have been giants compared with humans. Nephilim offspring by this definition were the part-human/part non-human hybrids and became known as 'demi-gods'. Some researchers have suggested the possibility that the Nephilim were extraterrestrials/interdimensionals and not genetic hybrids from the human-non-human interaction. The Book of Enoch is an ancient text dated by estimate from 300-200 BC, with some parts as late as perhaps 100 BC or even the 1st century of Ano Domini or the Common Era. There are five parts assumed to be written by different authors, and it was not written by the figure of Enoch which the Old Testament claims was the great grandfather of Noah. The text writes extensively about the Nephilim, demons, 'fallen angels', 'Watchers', portals, and 'heavens' with different 'laws' (of physics). These are interdimensional Yaldabaoth entities widely revealed in the Old Testament as we will see. The Book of Enoch labels the 'fallen angels' as 'the Watchers' which you find in other ancient works. Enoch texts repeat a universal pattern in 1 Enoch 6:1-2:

> And it came to pass when the children of men had multiplied, that in those days were born unto them beautiful and comely daughters. And the angels, the children of heaven, saw and lusted after them, and said to one another: 'Come, let us choose wives from among the children of men and beget us children.

The biblical 'sons of God' (sons of the *gods* when properly translated) are the supernatural angelic 'sons of heaven' according to the Book of Enoch who seeded the giant Nephilim. I have heard it said that the Book of Enoch was rejected by compilers of the Bible because it was not written by the alleged author, but then Christians don't know who wrote the Gospels of Matthew, Mark, Luke, and John. Certainly not the 'disciples' with those alleged names.

The disconnect

The Nag Hammadi *Apocryphon of John* also describes how sexual desire was planted to allow the counterfeit spirit to constantly make copies of itself: 'And he [Yaldabaoth] planted sexual desire in her who belongs to Adam. And he produced through intercourse the copies of the bodies, and he inspired them with his counterfeit spirit.' Together these layers and diversions constantly present Divine Sparks with fake realities and self-identities which overwhelm the memories of our true and eternal nature. The aim is to trap human perception in such myopia and fake self-identity that we lose the influence, perspective and memory of the infinite Spirit self. The whole point of these energetic layers or 'bodies' is to trap our perceptions in limitations and illusions and to block the influence of True 'I' Spirit. Think of a computer (human mind) being disconnected from the operator with the mouse and keyboard (Spirit) and being taken over by a computer virus that dictates perceptions, decisions, and reality (Fig 36).

Figure 36: Disconnection between Spirit/Soul and human can be likened to a computer virus taking over a computer which then ceases to respond to the operator. (Image by Neil Hague.)

How many people now find it very difficult, even impossible, to conceive a state of being that is pure awareness – just a state of being aware? Humans perceive 'life' in terms of 'form' which gives them their self-identity. I am black; I am white; I am Asian. These are then subdivided into other perceptual states – I am American; I am Canadian; I am European; I am African; I am Indian; I am Chinese; I am Australian. Ask people who they are, and they will give you their name, job, country of origin, religion, and such like. They won't say: 'I am Spirit having a brief human experience in a world that's a simulated illusion.' The overwhelming majority identify with form and the 'life-stories' of form or at best the Soul. Both are a simulated Matrix phenomenon, and that very self-identity keeps you vibrationally trapped in its energetic 'walls'. These identities are expressions of the systematic energetic fragmentation of perception designed to usurp and confuse the Divine Spark into identity forgetfulness. Imagine sitting in a room surrounded by TV screens each pounding you 24/7 with information, often conflicting. You would soon lose touch with your core self. Donning a virtual reality headset is similarly symbolic. As the old 'Humpty Dumpty' nursery rhyme goes: 'All the king's horses and all the king's men couldn't put Humpty together again.' Oh, but we *can* put ourselves together, we really can, and I will come to that later in the book.

Aware people throughout the human story have sought to use symbolism and myths to tell tales relating to the world of 'form' which portray our true nature of no-form. They have employed symbols familiar to the culture and era they were dealing with to express reality and identity in ways people could not comprehend directly. Such myths are interpreted literally by form-obsessed academics as the delusions of a primitive people when it is academia that is primitive. Spirit, or

Infinite Awareness, can easily conceive of the no-form state from which all Creation comes. How could that be any other way when Spirit *is* a no-form state of pure awareness? But these energetic garments or 'bodies' are each programmed with different delusions which together surround the Divine Spark with the collective delusion that dominates its sense of self and reality. We call these different levels of illusion, the Soul, Mind, Ego, and so on. We need to tell them to shut the fuck up so the awareness of Spirit can get a bloody word in. When it does, we begin the process called 'awakening' which happens in stages as the layers of deceit are peeled back.

Quick – divert them!

Major religions have been specifically structured to stop people reconnecting with the Divine Spark within. They use terms like blasphemer and heretic to describe people who say they are an expression of the Divine. How many have suffered horrific deaths at the hands of Church psychopaths for the crime of speaking the truth or, at the very least, having a different opinion to the orthodoxy and ignorance. The media personality Russell Brand converted to Christianity after he converted to the right-wing politics that absorbed the alternative arena after 'Covid'. I'm sure these conversions had nothing to do with his audience from which his income derived being right-wing Christians mostly in America where he moved from the UK to be among his own. He jumped on the Trump bandwagon which made sense given that Brand's career reveals a pattern in which he seems never to have seen a bandwagon that he did not seek to ride. I observed him in my opinion thoroughly misleading his audience about the conspiracy by staying within the Trump (and Musk) official story tramlines on which his *conspiracy* career depended. He then began to preach the tramlines of the Bible on which his *religious* career is founded after his Christian conversion and 'baptism' in the River Thames.

Brand said that as a Christian he had to acknowledge the Jewish connection to the land of Israel (with all that means for Palestinians) when the biblical history of Israel is unsupportable by the evidence as we shall see. It was said in a conversation he had with Canadian biblical scholar Wes Huff, that Christianity wants us to look outward and not inward. This was equated with being 'self-focused'. Huff talked about the 'heresy' of saying 'it's not Jesus who is divine, it is you and me that are divine'. This is a big no-no with the Church because it takes you inside through your levels of being to the Divine Spark and the realisation that we are aspects of the Infinite. Even Huff and Brand's biblical Jesus is quoted in Luke's Gospel as saying: 'God's kingdom is within you.' Don't you dare realise that you are an aspect of the Divine systematically blocked from that knowledge. Believe instead that you are just little me who must fall to your knees to worship your master 'God' which is actually the very force they call 'Satan'. Huff said that Satan doesn't so much want us to worship 'him', but to worship ourselves. But he and other Christians worship 'him' every day by worshipping the bloodthirsty, vengeful, jealous fake 'God' of the Old Testament.

This is a brief outline of the 'fall' from Spirit into the trap of 'matter' and you will find more detail in my other books. It presents the human world in a fundamentally different light that cuts through the contradictions and diversions to the core of human reality. We are Spirit, a state of being aware, that can be as aware as the *All That Is*, or as unaware as most humans allow themselves to be. Ignorance of the True 'I' and our experienced reality ensures humanity's frequency entrapment and that's why the imposition of low-frequency ignorance is so constant and systematic. American historian and writer Daniel J. Boorstin said: 'The greatest obstacle to discovery is not ignorance – it is the illusion of knowledge.' Very true in the sense that the illusion of knowledge is what so often instigates ignorance. I have always worked on the principle that whatever we know there is *always* more to know. My books are but stepping stones to truth and the *whole* truth lies only beyond the simulation in the realm of Spirit.

The information in these opening chapters puts human reality in an entirely new perspective and we have only just begun. There is so much more to come.

CHAPTER 3

What is the 'Matrix'?

Life is just a dream. It is not *like* a dream, it *is* a dream, and nothing other than a dream
Detong Choyin

The term 'Matrix' abounds in the conspiracy arena today, thrown around like confetti at a wedding, and constantly misused. I see people like Andrew Tate of the fake 'alternative' media going on and on about how the 'Matrix' is after him when he has no idea what it is.

'The Matrix' is applied to human activity and shenanigans when the real 'Matrix' is our very sense of reality. The alleged 'resistance' to global tyranny is focused on politics, finance and religion while the 'resisters' go about their lives oblivious that the biggest conspiracy is the very 'world' they think is 'real'. Perceptual manipulations they claim to 'expose' are perpetrated by the very heroes and 'god-kings' that they urge the population to support. People like Trump, Musk, and the AI tech oligarchy. Misdirection is everywhere to stop people seeing through the illusion. There are exceptions with the few who know exactly what they are doing to keep people off the scent, but the bulk of the fake 'alternative' is misdirecting because *it* can't see through the illusion.

'The Matrix' became a common term after the release of the movie of that name in 1999 which was followed by another three in the franchise, *The Matrix Reloaded*, *The Matrix Revolutions* and *The Matrix Resurrections*. The first one came at a perfect time for me with the reality forming in my mind given a visual portrayal in a global movie. I remember watching in astonishment as what I had been concluding played out before me on a cinema screen. *The Matrix* is remarkably accurate in how the simulation works and includes endless supporting symbolism for people with eyes to see. Either those ultimately behind the movies got very lucky (highly unlikely given the accuracy) or they had knowledge of what human reality really is. I have read that the movies were based on the work of legendary Chicago-born science fiction writer Philip K. Dick (1928-1982) who authored 44 novels, including the acclaimed *The Man in the High Castle*, and more than 120 short stories. He didn't only write novels about illusory realities. He said it was *literally* true. Dick claimed at a Paris conference in 1977: 'We are living in a computer-programmed reality ... the only clue is when some variable is changed, and a glitch occurs.' He said – correctly – that the simulation was not only around us – it was *inside* us.

Dick said that in 1974 he was recovering from effects of a drug given for a wisdom tooth extraction. He opened the door to a young girl with dark hair delivering a pain-relief drug and became focused on her necklace featuring a golden fish. She said it was a symbol used by 'early Christians' and it is associated with 'secret knowledge'. It reflected the sun to generate a 'pink beam' which he believed downloaded knowledge to him that we live in a simulated reality. Dick began having 'strange hallucinations' after she left, and he thought these were due to the medication. However, they did not stop, and he reassessed the cause. He said: 'I experienced an invasion of my mind by a transcendentally rational mind, as if I had been insane all my life and suddenly, I had become sane.' I know exactly what that feels like from my own 'paranormal' experiences in 1990 and 91. Dick said the download allowed him to understand quantum physics, languages he didn't know before, and the illusory nature of human reality. He talked about experiencing 'anamnesis' or the sudden recall of forgotten knowledge within oneself which included the awareness that reality was a thin veil that stopped humans seeing what lay beyond it. 'Anamnesis' was discussed by Ancient Greek philosopher Socrates. Dick said that he was questioned by the authorities about his 'Matrix' visions and his house was broken into, ransacked, and manuscripts stolen. He said he had confirmed surveillance of him through his CIA and FBI files secured through Freedom of Information access.

Prime Earth 'overlay'

The Matrix or simulation is not a 'physical' construct. It is a source of energetic frequency *information* – think Wi-Fi – which is decoded by the human body/brain into what is experienced as an external material reality when it isn't. It only exists in the way that we experience within the decoding mechanisms of the brain. I concluded more than two decades ago that the Yaldabaoth simulation was a frequency field of encoded information that overlayed Prime Reality which operates on a much higher frequency band while sharing the same 'space'. Biological computer human bodies were then created in a series of 'Adams' to interact with the simulation field and decode the information into a *perception* of 3-D reality via the five senses of sight, hearing, smell, touch and taste. It has long been established by mainstream science that the five senses are decoding frequency information (which is the simulation) into electrical information which is communicated to the brain (same information, different form) to be decoded into what is digital holographic (illusory physical) information. Māra, the Buddhist demon, is known as the 'Lord of the Senses' who seeks to stop anyone being liberated from the reincarnation trap of 'Samsara' and is dubbed 'the personification of the forces antagonistic to enlightenment'. The five senses are the point of connection with the simulation field and constantly feed us the experience of being 'in' a 'physical world' when the whole deal is a highly sophisticated hoax. We will never remember our true and infinite self while we fall for what the five senses are presenting to us. We will never detox our perceptions from 'physical' fakery. The Matrix even includes a fake 'void' that mimics all-possibility to catch those who have some knowledge of the Trap and how it works.

I featured the experience of Canadian Lauda Leon in my last book, *The Reveal*, after she appeared in the Christianne van Wijk film series *The Great Unknown* which you can see at Ickonic.com. Lauda says she has died seven times which led to near-death experiences in another dimension of reality. She is one of those rare people who say they can remember their incarnation process. They may be rare compared with the millions of near-death accounts, but their experiences have compelling common themes. One is the incredible energetic density they experience as they enter the human world to the point where it is a real challenge to cope. I said earlier that when the simulation trap was sprung the work began to lower the vibration into ever greater density to disconnect entrapped Divine Sparks from the Infinite and with that forget their true identity. When you hear these accounts of just how dense and treacle-like is the energy of this reality no wonder it is known as the 'Veil of Forgetfulness' and you understand why things are as they are. Lauda Leon says she remembers seeing as she incarnated what she calls an 'overlay' reality which is what I had described in earlier books:

> It looked to me like there was an overlay. I remember coming to a place where it seemed like there was a magnetic grid, like an electric, magnetic type of grid. I remember it being electric. There was something organic, an organic realm underneath the overlay. This is interesting, right?
>
> There was like an actual organic Earth underneath. And then the overlay was very, let's say, like digital and that weird electric fence you had to go through. The Guardians told me that part of their job was to get me through that electric fence without erasing my memory.
>
> The objective of [the fence] is that as a Soul comes in, you go through that electricity, that electromagnetic zap, and it erases your mind. So, they had to ensure that I could get through without it doing that.

Others who claim to remember their incarnation process tell of passing through this electromagnetic field that wipes the memory in a similar way to how we used to erase the old videotapes by passing them across a magnetic field. The 'overlay' of frequency information is the simulation, and the human body biological computer is designed to 'read' or decode that information into the illusion of a 'world'. Tap into the Divine Spark and you have access to infinity beyond the simulation and suddenly the realm of 'human' looks very different. There are two 'fields' of information that we can decode – the simulation which seeks to limit your perception of self and reality through the strict limitation ('fire walls') of the body decoding systems; and the limitlessness of Infinity, all-possibility, and all-knowingness. Even those more enlightened say that we *are* the Universe or *of* the Universe when the 'Universe' is the simulation. We *are* infinity and *of* infinity.

Leon says she was shown that what religious books call the 'New Earth' is really the organic (Prime) Earth overlaid by the 'counterfeit' simulation. 'It's the new old Earth', she said. This matched my own perceptions accumulated over decades. All this means that 'nature' is also part of this simulated construct. The real 'natural world' exists beyond the simulation in the sense of consciousness manifesting realities directly without the intervention of a manipulative force. The simulated version of nature is an information construct decoded by the human brain in what is a bad copy of nature as it exists elsewhere. 'Nature' has also been set up as a killing field in which almost everything survives through the demise of something else. The significance of this will become clear in the chapter 'Loosh Farm'. People can experience an expansion of awareness amid the simulated 'natural world' away from the urban sprawl and maybe the experience triggers a memory of Prime Earth that helps us tune in to the real thing that still shares the same 'space'. Avoiding the electromagnetic soup is another reason for getting out of the towns and cities although that is becoming harder with the tens of thousands of low-orbit satellites increasingly beaming technological electromagnetism at the entire Earth led by Elon Musk and SpaceX.

The simulation has many levels, and we are experiencing the densest (lowest frequency) of them. Lauda Leon says she has learned in her Astral experiences that an aberration happened in the unfolding Creation in which the Gnostic Yaldabaoth emerged, and that created the simulation through 'the entire hijacking of reality and universe' ... 'the counterfeit versions of everything, including all the heavens, all the lower Astral, everything'. She describes human reality as a 'metal digital interface' and she refers to Yaldabaoth/the Demiurge as 'the Metal God'. Manipulating aspects of the Infinite – Divine Sparks – into its counterfeit 'facsimile version' was essential to have access to Source energy to which it was denied. 'It's a dead thing that only has essence to keep it

What is the 'Matrix'?

alive unnaturally like Frankenstein', she says. Divine Sparks were tricked into entering the fake simulated reality: 'They'll never know the difference – I'll make it beautiful and good at the beginning so that they think they're in the right one.'

We are experiencing a reality created with electricity and electromagnetism that reflects in theme human Wi-Fi. This field of information is decoded by the body/brain like a headset decodes a virtual reality game. The information-encoded simulation field overlays Prime Earth and Prime Reality and the biological computer human body decodes this into the experience of being 'human'. Why can't we remember any of this? Because of the 'mind-wipe' which many near-death experiencers have described. I'll come back to this memory-wipe in Chapter Seven about reincarnation when I'll address the fake 'heavens' which recycle 'Souls' between human reality and the Astral 'after-life' on the Buddhist Wheel of Samsara.

Holographic confirmation

Holograms which have become ever more widespread and sophisticated are created as wavefields of information which a laser transforms into apparently three-dimensional objects and people (Fig 37). The most advanced of them look as solid as you and me. Holograms are created by taking a waveform image of an object using one half of a laser beam that is then directed onto a photographic plate. The other half strikes the

Figure 37: Holograms are getting more and more advanced to the point where you won't know the difference between technological holographic reality and *real* holographic reality – the human realm.

plate directly, and the two beams collide to create a waveform pattern (interaction of light waves) that represents a waveform (frequency information) version of the object. This is known as an interference pattern (Figs 38 and 39). Think of two pebbles dropped in a pond and, as the waves pan out, they collide to create a waveform version of where the pebbles dropped, how fast, and how heavy they were (Fig 40). In the case of holograms when a laser is directed at the wave pattern print an apparently three-dimensional image of the object is projected (Figs 41 and 42). The 3-D holographic projection is the result of information 'decoded' from the wavefield and not only does the hologram and the wavefield exist at the same time – they *have* to. Without the information in the wavefield there can be no 'particle' hologram. This mirrors the apparent 'mystery' of why waves and the particles manifested from those waves exist simultaneously. No actual 3-D object exists with a hologram, but it is *interpreted* by the brain to exist as it reads the

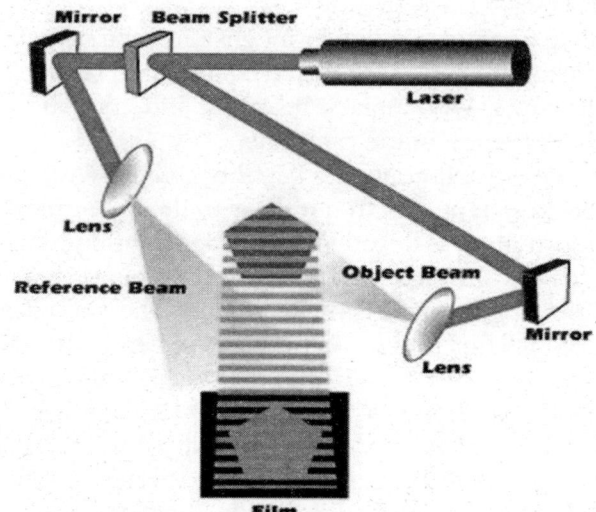

Figure 38: Two parts of a laser collide on the holographic print to form a wave pattern.

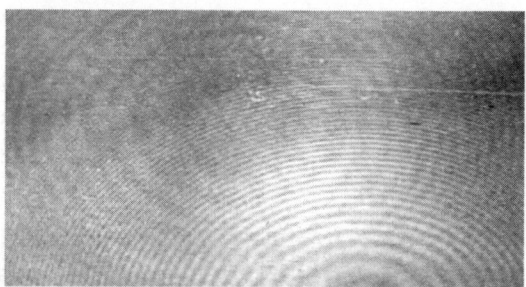

Figure 39: Holographic prints are created from the interaction of waves and are encoded with the information of the object being holographically photographed.

Figure 40: The holographic principle is like two pebbles dropped in a pond and the two wave formations interacting to create a wave version of where the pebbles dropped, at what speed, and how heavy they were.

Figure 41: The result can be amazing with pop band Abba performing shows as holograms.

Figure 42: The car may look solid, but it's an anything-but-solid hologram.

Figure 43: We are decoding wavefield information into electrical and digital holographic information which we experience as the 'physical' world. (Image by Neil Hague.)

information encoded in the waves. Physicist David Bohm and German neuroscientist and neurosurgeon Karl Pribram (1919-2015) promoted the idea of a holographic reality when Bohm saw that subatomic particles behaved like a hologram and around the same time Pribram noted that the way the brain stores and processes information was holographic. The result is 'physical' reality (Fig 43).

Holograms have another amazing characteristic which explains so much. The information in a hologram is encoded throughout the wavefield at every level. This means that if

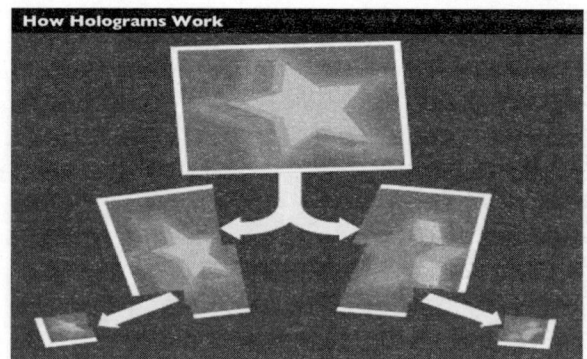

Figure 44: Holograms encode information from the whole hologram within every part of the hologram. Cut a normal image into four and you will have four parts of the picture. Cut a holographic print into four pieces and you have four quarter-sized versions of the *whole* picture.

you cut a holographic print into four and point a laser at each one you will not see a quarter of the object projected. You will see a quarter-sized version of the *whole* object (Fig 44). Here we have the ancient principle of 'as above, so below'. The whole simulation works like this with the information of the whole encoded in the parts as we will confirm shortly. The simulation is a bad copy of how Infinite reality works and emanations of the Infinite – the 'Father' to Gnostics – are also holographically projected. In this way an 'emanation' of the Infinite, like you and me, everything, is a holographic version of the whole containing the *information* of the whole. This is the Divine Spark that the controlling force wants to stop us reconnecting with. The holographic principle explains why everything is connected and why subatomic particles can respond to each other no matter what the apparent 'distance'. We also have 'quantum jumps' when quantum phenomena can move from one point to appear in another without travelling through the 'time and space' in between.

A wonderful example I have featured over the years are the experiments by researchers at the Aerospace Institute in Stuttgart, Germany, who developed a technique to photograph *information* in droplets of water. *Everything* is information because the holographic simulation is information. A flower was dipped into a tank of water and removed. Droplets of the water were then photographed, and they discovered that the frequency information of the flower was encoded in all the droplets. Had they done the same with the entire tank of water they would have found the same (holographic) outcome. Institute researchers invited a group from the local community and asked each of them to take four droplets from a tank of water and put them in a dish with their name on. They photographed each set and found that they were all similar while being *different* from everyone else's set. The act of taking a droplet from the tank to the dish had encoded the person's individual frequency on the water (Fig 45). Think what that means collectively as we interact with each other and the simulation field. If we are generating distorted frequencies through our mental and emotional state they are encoded 'as above, so below' throughout holographic

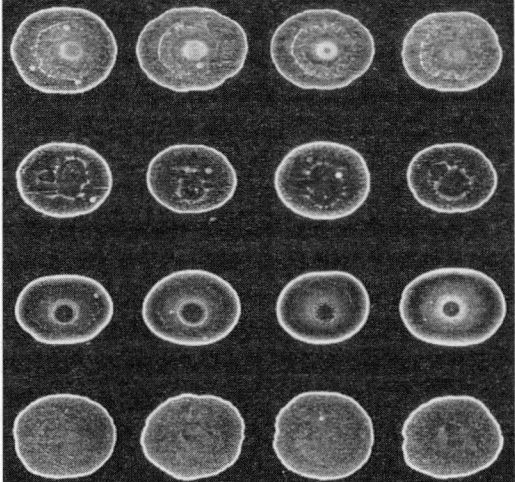

Figure 45: The unique frequency signatures of participants in the Stuttgart experiment reflected in the water droplets. All they did was take four droplets from a container and put them in a dish, but their frequency uniqueness was infused.

reality. Russian researcher Dr Vladimir Poponin found the same with DNA. He beamed a laser across DNA and, when he removed the 'physical' DNA, the energetic information remained in the laser in accordance with the same principle as the flower and the water. This so-called 'Phantom DNA Effect' is not 'phantom' at all. It's just the way energy operates in the simulation.

I have just described how homeopathy works. I have even met homeopaths who don't know the methodology, only that it can be effective. Mainstream medicine is ignorant about reality and what the body really is and wreaks much death and health destruction as a result. Professor Dame Sally Davies, a former UK Chief Medical Officer, betrayed this ignorance when she said: 'Homeopaths are peddlers and homeopathy is rubbish.' This is typical of orthodox 'medicine' and 'science' which is mesmerised by the non-existent 'physical' and believes in its arrogance of ignorance that if it can't explain why something is happening then it can't be happening. The whole arena of the 'paranormal' is treated with disdain for the same reason. If you don't cut it out or treat it with chemical toxicity, how can it possibly work? Famed physicist Werner Heisenberg observed: 'The existing scientific concepts cover always only a very limited part of reality, and the other part that has not yet been understood is infinite.' The problem that orthodoxy has with homeopathy is that the potions are diluted to the point where they don't appear to retain any of their contents. One article said: '... scientists argue that the [homeopathic] cures are so diluted they are unlikely to contain any of the original substance.' The point is that this doesn't matter because the *frequency information* of the substance remains and it's this which does the healing (frequency harmonisation) through a *frequency* interaction with the frequency level of the body. I think Dame Sally has just disappeared up her own backside. Is there a doctor in the house? I am not saying that homeopathy works for everyone, and it depends on the skill of the practitioner. I am just saying that this is the basis on which it *can* work and does for many.

In our face

The sheer power of emerging information despite the suppression is leading more open-minded scientists to the conclusion that our reality is indeed a holographic simulation. Confirmation has been all around us for thousands of years in the illusion of 'time'. The ancients identified recurring geometric patterns throughout reality under terms like Pi, Phi, golden ratio, and divine proportion. They encoded their most significant buildings with these geometrical sequences to synchronise them with the energetic environment or what I would term the simulation. The Knights Templar secret society designed great cathedrals of Europe with these characteristics for the same reason. Observe these buildings from this perspective with their fantastic architecture that still bewilders people with how they were built given the alleged techniques and technology of the day. Then in the 12/13th centuries came the Fibonacci number sequence discovered by Italian mathematician, Leonardo of Pisa, known as Fibonacci, although what he identified can also be traced back to ancient India and a mathematician named Virahanka. The Fibonacci number sequence adds the two previous numbers to get the next one, as in ... 1, 1, 2, 3, 5, 8, 13, 21, 34, 55, and ongoing. This sequence reflecting the digital level of the simulation is found in the human face and body, plus the body proportions of animals and in DNA, seed heads, pinecones, trees, shells, spiral galaxies, hurricanes, and the number of petals in a flower (Fig 46).

All these recurring sequences can be found in the energetic fabric of our reality which play out throughout the world of 'form' including the human body. This is exactly what you would expect with a frequency/digital holographic simulation which is a phenomenally more advanced version of modern software. We now speak of 'fractal patterns' in which the same patterns recur in different levels of reality in keeping with the holographic theme of as above, so below, or every part is a smaller version of the whole. Fractals are 'bad copy' versions of Infinite fractal patterns which include Divine Spark consciousness. Near-death experiencer Lauda Leon says: '[The Infinite] split itself into an infinite number of fractals to experience Creation in every possible way imaginable.' Divine

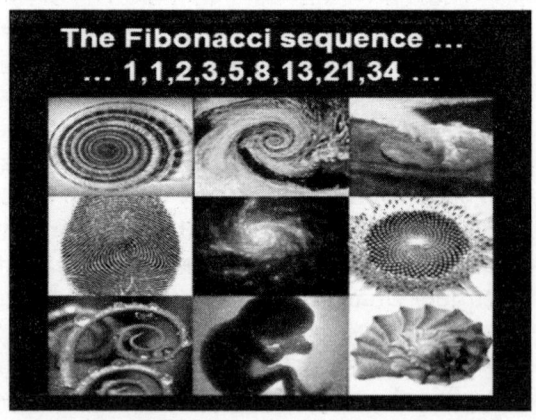

Figure 46: The Fibonacci number sequence is encoded throughout human reality.

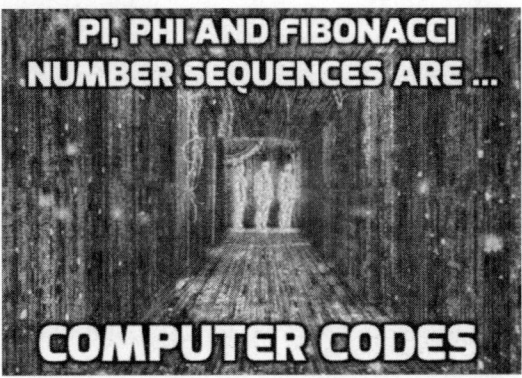

Figure 47: Simulation codes have been staring us in the face.

Figure 48: Fractal patterns – more computer codes

Sparks are those fractal aspects of the infinite whole and why Divine Sparks are expressions of Infinite Awareness. These bad copy digital patterns like Pi, Phi, golden ratio, divine proportion, Fibonacci numbers, and fractals are the *computer codes* of the simulation just as the human genetic code is a *computer code* (Figs 47 and 48).

The simulation is embedded in every last fabric of human reality, and they are the recurring patterns of the Matrix software. Geometric sequences known as Pi, Phi, Golden Mean, Golden Ratio and Golden Section proportions are found in the human body and throughout reality even down to the way that plants grow. Fractal patterns are 'a never-ending pattern that is infinitely complex and self-similar across different scales' and conform to the holographic principle of information encoded at every level. We have fractal patterns in river networks, mountain ranges, craters, lightning bolts, coastlines, mountain goat horns, trees and branch growth, animal colour patterns, pineapples, heart rates, heartbeats, neurons and brains, eyes, respiratory systems, circulatory systems, blood vessels and pulmonary vessels, geological fault lines, earthquakes, snowflakes, crystals, ocean waves, vegetables, soil pores, and the rings of Saturn. DNA has fractal properties, and I read a scientific paper some years ago headed 'DNA is a Fractal Antenna in Electromagnetic Fields'. DNA is a receiver-transmitter of information interacting with the simulation. There is also 'symmetrical mathematics' identified throughout our reality which is 'one shape becoming exactly like another when you move it in some way, turn, flip or slide.'

American theoretical physicist James Gates has been a Professor of Physics at the University of Maryland, Director of The Center for String and Particle Theory, and member of the Council of Advisors on Science and Technology to the Obama administration. He discovered with his team further evidence of a computer-like reality. They found embedded computer codes of digital data in the energetic fabric of our reality taking the form of 1 and 0, the binary on-off electrical charges used by computers. 'We have no idea what they are doing there', he said. I think I can help him. Observe the binary system against the A, C, G, and T codes of DNA which also have a binary value (Figs 49 and 50). A and C = 0 and G and T = 1. It's all a single program. Gates and his researchers further discovered error-correcting codes or block codes which are mathematical sequences which again relate to computer systems. Error-correcting codes monitor flows of information to ensure they do not deviate from their original state. Correcting codes reboot deviating data to its original or 'default settings'. What Gates found would keep the simulation stable in other words. Gates was also asked if he had found a set of equations embedded in our reality that were indistinguishable from those that drive search engines and browsers. He said: 'That is correct.'

Figure 49: Binary codes used in computers are found in the fabric of reality.

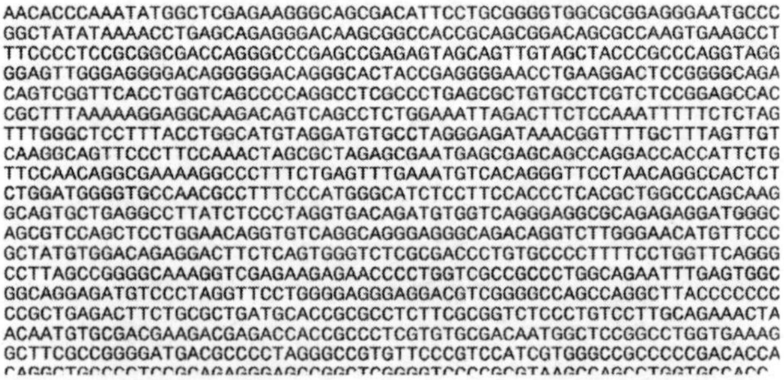

Figure 50: The A, C, G and T codes of DNA have a binary value.

Wherever you look it's as above, so below, the holographic principle of the same information encoded everywhere. The simulation is psychological as well as illusory physical and these same sequences have been found in behaviour, speech patterns, and interpersonal relationships. Have you noticed how behaviour can be so predictable? That is a program, too. Science studies have found previously undiscovered and fundamental laws that seem to dictate everything from the electrical firing of brain cells to the growth of social networks and the expansion of galaxies.

It's a simulation!!

Plasma universe

The foundation of the whole simulation is an energetic field known as 'plasma'. This is said to be the 'fourth state of matter' along with solid, liquid and gas. Think of ice (solid), liquid (water) and gas (steam) as three states of the same substance that are separated by differences in temperature (frequency). I focus on plasma in detail in *The Reveal*. Plasma is employed in neon lights and in the manufacture of semiconductor computer chips as its significance gathers pace, but its true significance is still largely ignored because it would demolish 'scientific' orthodoxy and pull back the curtain on human understanding. I mention in *The Reveal* how scientists working in the plasma arena are invariably contracted by intelligence and military agencies that limit what findings can be made public. How many people realise that *99 percent*, even *99.9 percent*, of the visible Universe is *plasma*? It should be dubbed on that basis the first state of matter, not the fourth. What we *call* matter is only energy that is vibrating in sync with the body's tiny visual frequency range or 'visible light'. I said that this represents only a fraction of the electromagnetic spectrum which is itself only 0.005 percent of what exists in the Universe in energy in all its forms.

Look around you now and you will only see matter (low-vibrational energy condensed into the frequency range of visible light). I am looking at a computer screen, walls, pictures, books and a window through which I can see trees and houses. All these forms are energy within the frequency band of visible light, which is all, through the body sight sense, that we can visually perceive. What do I see and you see between these material objects? *Empty space*. Or rather, what appears to us to be 'empty space'. No 'space' is empty – everything is filled with energy. The point is that our body's visual decoding range is limited to the frequency density of matter and although the 'empty space' is filled with energy *we can't see it*. That 'empty space' is plasma. We believe that we live in a reality consisting of 'atomic' matter when as much as *99.9 percent* of our visible world is not dense matter at all – it's plasma.

People who claim to have seen UFO craft or entities 'appear out of nowhere' and 'disappear into nowhere' are called crazy or at best deluded when all that's happened here is that a craft or entity has lowered its frequency to the visible light range. They then appear 'out of nowhere' to any human observer. The reverse is the case when they quicken their frequency and leave human vision. I remember Betty Shine, a professional psychic, telling me how a child was taken to her by his desperate mother. They had been through the medical system to no avail. The boy said he was seeing UFOs and other 'paranormal' phenomena and was believed to be autistic. Betty said when she looked at him on an energetic level his etheric energy field was only partly in his body. This explained why he could see beyond 'normal' sight limitations. She said she manipulated his field into full sync with his body and he stopped seeing UFOs or anything else outside of visible light. So much is happening in the space you are experiencing now, but your biological computer will only decode a tiny sliver of what there is to see.

Other-dimensional entities are plasma-based and can lower their frequency to appear in the human realm as however they choose to present themselves. They are often described as being 'radiant' and the ancients called them the 'Shining Ones' which led to biblical and other religious themes of radiant 'angels'. Ancient Greek philosopher Aristotle (384 BC-322 BC) believed that 'divine entities' were made of energy he called the ether or 'fifth element' which formed the Sun and other stars and overlayed the human body. His 'ether' is plasma which is encoded with the electromagnetic blueprint of the 'physical' body and human reality in totality. We can't see other-dimensional plasma entities in the 'normal' course of life because we can't see plasma ('empty space'). We can only see how plasma interacts with electromagnetism and electricity in the form of auroras, lightning, ball lightning, and those plasma balls or lamps originally invented by science genius Nikola Tesla (1856-1943).

You could think of plasma as the canvas on which the simulation is 'painted' in the form of encoded electrical and electromagnetic information. No surprise then that plasma is an almost perfect medium for both of them. The human world is a decoded holographic and digital projection of what I refer to as 'programmed plasma'. The simulation manipulators program the blueprint (humans, planets, whatever) on the same principle as computer software and we decode that 'software' coding into what appear to be 'solid' humans, planets, and all the rest. Plasma was discovered in the modern world in 1879 by British scientist William Crookes which he identified as 'radiant matter'. Nikola Tesla was much inspired by Crookes and what Tesla called his 'epochal work on radiation matter'. Irving Langmuir (1881-1957), the Nobel Prize-winning American scientist, called this substance 'plasma' when it reminded him of blood plasma which transports nutrients to cells and organs and waste products to the kidneys, liver and lungs for excretion. Plasma is electrically super-conductive and the medium to transport particles, electricity, and electromagnetism (which are other ways of saying *information*).

One example of interaction between electricity, electromagnetism, and the plasma medium was discovered by Irving Langmuir and labelled 'Langmuir sheaths'. He observed that where an electrical charge flowing through plasma meets a different charge (frequency) the plasma automatically creates a barrier between them. Earth generates its own unique frequency charge and where it meets the different charge in the

What is the 'Matrix'?

Figure 51: Planetary magnetospheres are formed by an electrical charge within plasma meeting another electrical charge which causes a barrier to be formed.

Cosmos the plasma creates the energetic barrier that we call planetary 'magnetospheres' (Fig 51). A similar principle applies to this obvious question: If there is no 'physical' how come I can't walk through a wall or anything else? Firstly, don't underestimate the power of belief to limit possibility, and the resistance between 'objects' is not *physical* resistance – it is *electromagnetic* charge resistance within the plasma Langmuir sheaths. The wall is within the overall human frequency band, but it's a different charge to you and a Langmuir sheath-like resistance is applied that we experience as physical resistance. A 'ghost' (other-dimensional entity) can appear to pass through walls because its frequency is so different to the wall and it's like two radio stations on different wavelengths sharing the same space. Ghosts are a visual version of radio station interference when two stations are close on the dial and one can be heard with another. The main station dominates, but another can be heard less sharply in the background. The ghost is visual interference in that it is close enough to our frequency to be seen ethereally, but not as full-blown 'solid'. If we were on the same frequency the ghost would look as 'solid' as we do.

Electric Universe

I have highlighted in many books the work of genuine scientists who operate under the collective label of the 'Electric Universe' and the Thunderbolts Project. I don't know how many of them – if any – believe that our reality is a simulation, but it matters not. Their work supports that contention. Detailed research reveals that what we perceive as a physical Universe is a vast electrical and electromagnetic grid founded on a plasma medium. 'Matter' is a low-density frequency of electricity/magnetism that operates within the incredibly narrow human sight sense of visible light. Everything we can't see is plasma and programmed plasma. When people say that something just 'appeared out of the ether' they mean that it appeared out of the plasma into the narrow band of electrical 'matter'. Atoms are supposed to be the building blocks of 'matter', but it has been long established by the science discipline of quantum physics that atoms have no solidity. They are *electrical/electromagnetic* phenomena, and the rest is decoded illusion.

Figure 52: The night sky that we see as stars and planets.

Figure 53: If we could see the heavens on another level it would appear as a vast electrical and electromagnetic network flowing through its plasma medium.

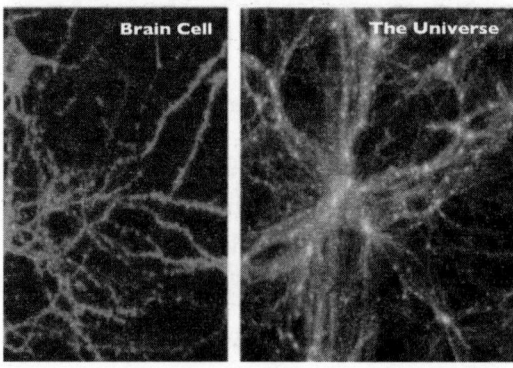

Figure 54: A brain cell and the Universe – as above, so below.

We look at the night sky and see planets and lights from stars, but if you could see the same scene beyond the limitations of human sight you would see that planets and stars are part of one enormous network of electrical and electromagnetic connections flowing through the plasma (Figs 52 and 53). This is the electromagnetic grid that Lauda Leon says that she saw. The whole Universe (simulation) is plasma electrically programmed with information, and we have as above, so below, on all levels as with the electrical systems of the brain and the Universe (simulation) and the energetic field unique to each human that compares with the Earth's magnetosphere (Figs 54 and 55). The Sun is said to be 99.86% of the mass of the Solar System and consists almost entirely of plasma. I have detailed over the decades how the Sun is not a nuclear reactor generating 'light' from its core, but a *processor* of electricity from the universal electrical grid. In turn the human body is an electrical/electromagnetic organism. Our thoughts are electrical, and the brain processes electrical information electrically. It communicates with organs and cells electrically and vice versa. The body is an electrical battery and when you feel 'drained' it's because the battery is draining of energy. Drain enough

What is the 'Matrix'?

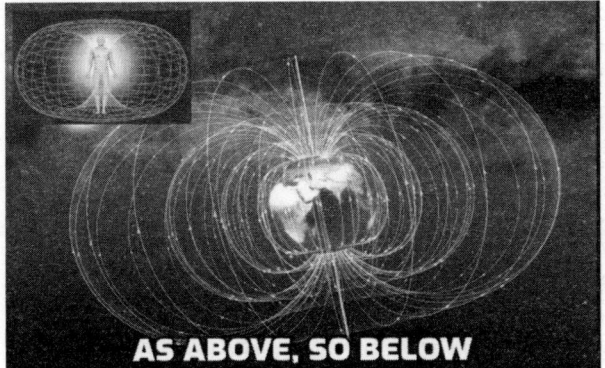

Figure 55: Human energy field and Earth energy field – as above, so below.

and the battery can no longer function. We know this as 'dying'. Ions and impurities in water make that a conductor of electricity. Water comprises some 60 percent of the body and 73 percent with the electrical brain and heart. This is a key reason why dehydration can be dangerous.

The 'natural' (simulated) world communicates electrically in everything from the soil connections between trees to animal and bird navigation. Bees find pollen through the electrical signals emitted by flowers. The whole universal system is electrical with encoded information and information encoded to decode information. What does this remind you of? A *computer system*. The Internet is encoded information, and the computer is information encoded to decode the Internet. I have been describing the simulation for nearly 25 years as a Cosmic Internet. Today's technological developments are replicating how we manifest our illusory reality with technology decoding and interacting with information fields. Coincidence? Not a chance. The simulation is the fake reality encoded in frequency/electricity and the human body is a means to entrap consciousness (Divine Spark) and feed it a fake sense of reality and identity. This is another reason why control of perception is vital and in fact the whole conspiracy of human control is a battle for perception.

Instant attraction and dislike come from the vibrations/electricity interaction generated between the perceptions of people. We talk of good vibes and bad vibes and this is why: Someone can be very nice on the surface and smile to your face, but there is 'something about them' that you can't take to. You are picking up the frequency and electrical signals that reflect who they really are no matter what their lips are saying. In contrast we talk of people having 'electricity between them' and this comes from the synchronisation of their electromagnetic auric fields that overlay the human body within the plasma and can be photographed with some technologies. Within the auric field is what we call the 'Mind'. This is where we construct human perception, and the brain decodes this into our conscious sense of reality. Manipulators target both mind and the brain decoding systems to limit and suppress perception. The Mind is like someone sitting with the keyboard and the mouse while the brain is the computer that can be programmed to allow some perception to manifest as a conscious thought while blocking others. The principle is akin to the computer system in China where much of the Internet is firewalled to prevent access.

The prisoner is the prison

There are certain key pillars of the simulation, but overall, it is interactive in the same way that our perceptions are affected by what we see on the Internet while what we post can change the Internet. If enough minds/consciousness infuse the field with another perception it becomes available for all connected to the field to access that. This appears to be especially the case with members of the same species that operate in the same band of frequency, and they can instantly know things and do things that the pioneers had to learn. Quantum physics has confirmed how consciousness can change reality, and the simulators are well aware of that. The Matrix is a bad copy of Prime Reality and must adhere to the interactive way that consciousness manifests experience. The manipulators know that if they control individual and collective human perception the simulation will project back that perception in the form of the people and experiences we draw into our lives that we think are random. Our perceptions are like a blueprint that interacts with the fields of possibility to manifest a 'physical' reflection of our perceptual state, conscious and subconscious. Put another way: If they can induce prisons of the mind, we will collectively create an *apparently* external manifestation of that prison – human society. This makes us through our perceptions both the prisoner and the prison.

We are not separate from infinity or the simulation. The manipulators just want us to believe that we are. Everything is *ONE* consciousness taking different forms like an infinite ocean. 'Individual' ocean waves and crests are expressions of the whole and interconnected with the wind, sources of tidal flow, sea life, everything. We identify as an 'individual', like a droplet of water; but when the droplet connects with the ocean where does the droplet end and the ocean start? They are *ONE* (Figs 56 and 57). In the same way an eddy in a river may look different to the rest of the water and yet it's still the river and the same water. Now imagine that you see the waves and crests while the ocean is invisible to you.

Figure 56: The ocean is the droplet, and the droplet is the ocean.

What is the 'Matrix'?

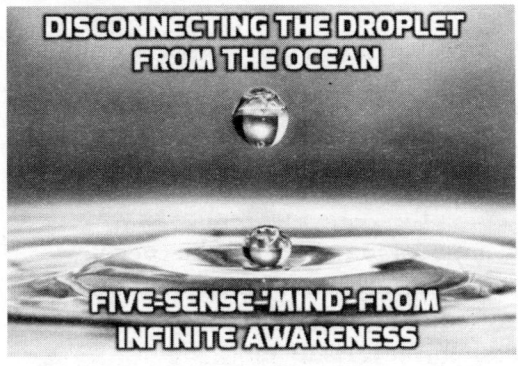

Figure 57: The foundation of the humanity control system is breaking the connection between the droplet and the ocean.

That is the material world illusion in which the visible (within visible light) appears to be form or 'things' with empty space in between when they are only the visible manifestation of an ocean of consciousness/energy that you cannot see. If you could see the ocean, you would realise that everything is ONE. Singer-songwriter Leonard Cohen said: 'If you don't become the ocean, you'll be seasick all your life.'

We experience this co-dependency every day. We eat, for example, only because a farmer grows the crops; a driver takes them to food producers or markets; the producers process the crops or market traders sell them; another driver takes them to the supermarket where we pick them off the shelf thanks to the shelf-stackers and other staff. Plus, a lot more elements besides that lead to us picking up those tomatoes or eggs (thanks to the chickens) and taking them to the checkout person for payment. The money we hand over is itself connected to a whole other stream of interdependency that provides the income. Yet we largely see this sequence as an individual 'I' going to the supermarket, taking the eggs to the checkout and going home. 'I've just been to the supermarket to buy some eggs', we say. Yes, on one level that is true, but it is only one part of an interdependent whole.

Observe and you shall see (but only then)

Now - a real noodle-cooker. The body/brain biological computer is decoding the simulation into what we think we are 'seeing'. The external world that we experience only exists in the decoding systems of the brain. What therefore happened to the 'vastness of space'? What happened to the billions and even trillions of light years of 'distance' between stars and galaxies? The whole shebang is an encoded illusion. Nothing – NOTHING – is what it seems. We look at that 'vastness of space' when it only exists in that form between our ears. It is a decoded projection and when it is not being decoded (observed) it doesn't exist at all in the form that we appear to experience. Neither does anything else in human 'physical' reality. When the simulation is not decoded by any of the five senses it only exists as an energetic field of information. Does the Internet exist on your computer screen when the computer is turned off? Of course not. The Internet encoded into Wi-Fi fields and electronic circuits is not being decoded by the switched-off computer and cannot appear on the screen in a totally different form. Without a computer, Wi-Fi remains as just undecoded Wi-Fi. In the same way 'physical' (digital holographic) reality cannot be made manifest when the brain is not decoding it.

Some scientists have proposed over the years that reality as we experience it only exists when we are 'looking at it'. This has become known as the 'observer effect' when it should really be called the 'decoder effect'. The act of 'looking' triggers the decoding system and when we are not looking at something it reverts to its electrical/electromagnetic frequency state just as the Internet is only a Wi-Fi field when a computer is not decoding it. Put simply: Does the Internet as we perceive it on the screen exist without a computer? No. So does 'physical' reality exist without a biological computer? No. Princeton physicist John Wheeler said: 'No elementary phenomenon is a phenomenon until it is an observed phenomenon.' Wheeler asked if the 'architecture of existence' only arose through being observed in a 'strange loop' in which 'physics gives rise to observers, who then give rise to information, which in turn gives rise to physics'. I would say the information encoded in the field came first which the body-computer has been created to decode and bring human reality into 'existence' as a holographic illusory fake 'physical' world (Fig 58). Einstein said that 'the field is the only reality'. It is in the simulated reality for sure, I would say. I have used the example over the years of a tree making no noise as it falls unless someone is there to observe it. The tree is a field of energy falling through a field of energy and makes no sound unless an observer decodes the resulting vibrational disturbance into a sound by transforming the frequencies into an electrical signal transmitted to the brain. Without the observer (decoder) there is no sound (Fig 59).

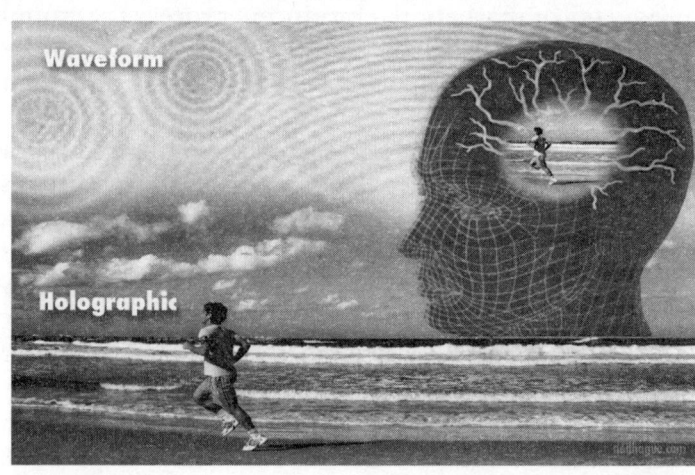

Figure 58: Material experience doesn't exist without the observer/decoder just as the Internet doesn't exist except as information fields and circuits until a computer decodes it into perceivable form. (Image by Neil Hague.)

What is the 'Matrix'?

The point has been made that to have reality permanently in a decoded state would involve an almost indescribable amount of computer power and the simulation has been set up as an electrical/electromagnetic information source that humans decode into illusory physical reality only when they 'look' at it or another sense decodes it. You can be lying with eyes closed on the bed, but your touch sense goes on decoding that part of the simulation. A computer game only presents you with the part of the game you are playing while the rest remains as computer codes until they enter your vision. A DVD only plays you the decoded scene you are watching while the rest of the movie, 'past' and 'future' remains undecoded on the disk. Scientists have been baffled at the quantum level of reality beyond atomic matter to see that energy can be a waveform *and* a particle at the *same time*. This is said to be 'counter-intuitive' when in fact waveform and particle are the same information in a different form. Remember that the frequency information decoded by the five senses is turned into electrical information to be communicated to the brain to become digital holographic information. Different forms – *same* information.

The simulation is in a waveform state until it is decoded by the brain (an information processor and limiter) through the act of observation into a holographic – particle – state. Thus, the waveform and the particle exist at the same time because the particle is a decoded expression of the waveform information. It has also been established that particles affect other particles over enormous 'distances' ('quantum entanglement') which led to Einstein's famous comment about 'spooky action at a distance'. There is no distance in the quantum realm as there is no time because it operates outside Einstein's suggested 'speed of light' limitations of perceived material 'space' and 'time'. The 'parts' and the whole are the same. Many have experienced thinking about someone only for the phone to ring and it's them on the line. This is a version of 'spooky action at a distance' in that you started thinking of them when they began thinking of you because they were about to call. Their focus of attention on you made the frequency/particle connection that you experienced as them coming into your thoughts. A reminder of what physicist David Bohm said of

Figure 59: A falling tree doesn't make a noise unless you are close enough to decode the vibrations into sound.

particle creation:

> ... This ocean of energy [frequencies] could be thought of as an ocean of light. But the information-content may be such as to predispose certain light rays to combine so that they move back and forth rather than moving straight ahead, and thus forming particles.

I say the *observer* decodes the frequencies of 'light' into particle form. The wave is potentiality, and the particle is the potential chosen by the *perceptions* of the observer. We are back to the example of the hologram projected from the wavefield print. The hologram and wavefield must exist at the same time because without the wavefield information there can be no 'particle' hologram. It makes experimentation interesting at the quantum level when perception (conscious *and* subconscious) creates reality. As consciousness expands out of perceptual myopia it can 'see' more and more of what it couldn't 'see' before and bring more into manifestation. We call this 'evolution', 'discovery', and 'breakthroughs' when it's really *remembering* what we have been manipulated to forget. Mathematical physicist Roger Penrose said: 'The behaviour of the seemingly objective world that is actually perceived depends on how one's consciousness threads its way through the myriads of quantum-superposed alternatives.' We create our own reality! Our perceptual field interacts with the quantum field to manifest a reflection of itself, and the brain decodes that reality into a 'physical' (holographic) version of our perceptual state – conscious and subconscious.

Meridian network and 'sacred places'

The electrical grid throughout the Universe and the holographic nature of reality come together with the Earth's meridian or 'ley line' network that is the 'as above, so below', version of the universal grid. This is part of the simulation. Ancients like the druid priestly class of the Celts knew of this network of electrical/electromagnetic lines of force and located their stone circles, standing stones, temples, pyramids, and sacred places on these lines, especially where many crossed. The crossing points create vortices and the more lines that intersect the bigger the vortex (Fig 60). The spin of major vortices thin out the distinction between the human and Astral dimensions and make it easier for Astral entities to appear in our reality. Satanists interacting with these entities perform their rituals at these points for this reason. Early Christians built their churches on sites believed by the 'pagans' to be sacred. Some did this with the intent of suppressing the 'pagan' energy while others in the know sought to exploit that energy. Excavations and repairs inside England's Canterbury Cathedral found remains of four previous churches estimated to date from the eighth, ninth, mid-tenth and early eleventh

What is the 'Matrix'?

Figure 60: The 'ley line' or meridian system is part of the universal electrical grid of the simulation with vortices forming where lines cross. (Image by Neil Hague.)

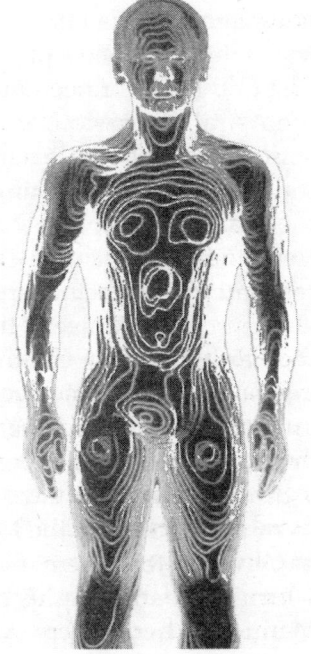

Figure 61: The meridian system of the body targeted by the ancient art of acupuncture is yet another as above, so below, of holographic reality. It's like a 'motherboard' of the biological computer.

centuries. Secret society initiates of the Cult's Knights Templar were the builders, designers and locators of the great cathedrals that targeted this 'earth energy'. Freemasonic temples and those of other secret societies select their most important locations based on vortex points and energy flows through the grid. We see the holographic principle again with the human body's meridian system of 'chi' or 'lifeforce' energy. This is a version of the ley line system ('motherboard') with the flows balanced by needles and other techniques in acupuncture (Fig 61).

Energy is just energy. It can be harnessed for good or ill according to its frequency. The Global Cult targets the ley line system to infuse low-vibrational frequencies for reasons that will be obvious later. If you want to suppress and distort energy passing through the grid then build a big road intersection on the vortex points or a nuclear power station. Stone used in circles and buildings on these vortex sites is invariably crystalline which make them receiver-transmitters of energy/information. The massive Mormon Temple in Salt Lake City is made from crystalline granite and no way that would have been located anywhere but on a big vortex point. Structures conform to the so-called sacred geometry of the simulation and that will not be a coincidence. Certain wavelengths and harmonics have been discovered in these vortex buildings and many of such locations have legends about interactions with the 'gods' (Astral entities).

Different levels of the human energy field are interpenetrated by vortices known as 'chakras' which comes from the ancient Sanskrit language in India and translates as 'wheels of light' (Fig 62). They connect with the Astral dimension, and some believe they are part of the control system. I think they can be. It depends on the frequency to which they are resonating and connecting. As above, so below, means that the Earth has these chakras and some of the major ones are said to be Mount Shasta in northern California; Lake Titicaca in Peru; the Giza pyramids in Egypt; the Mount of Olives in Jerusalem; Glastonbury Tor in England; and Ayer's Rock or Uluru in Australia, plus others. My life has taken me to all of those mentioned here. There is also the theme of amazing structures placed on 'sacred sites' that required a level of knowledge and technological sophistication utterly at odds with official 'history'. I have seen the Great Pyramid at Giza with its 2.3 million blocks weighing on average 2.6 tons forming a structure big enough to contain the cathedrals of Florence, Milan, Saint Peters, Westminster Abbey, and St. Paul's. The word that hits you is '*how*'? Certainly not by the ludicrous idea of slaves pulling the rocks up ramps. It was revealed in 2024 that the central 'Altar Stone' at Stonehenge in England came from the far north of Scotland. How was a stone weighing six tonnes transported some 500 miles thousands of years ago? We will explore who built these ancient masterpieces later in the book. Official 'history' really is bunkum. It's interesting, too, how many ancient sites have been lost under water due to dams in Egypt, China, India, Turkey, Brazil, Greece, Iraq, and elsewhere. A staggering *60,000* dams were built between 1930 and 1970 which required four to be completed every day for 40 years. To say there is more to know about all this is a serious understatement.

Figure 62: The human chakra or 'wheels of light' system.

Another related point: Italian physicist Enrico Fermi asked: 'Where are the aliens?' The question became known as the 'Fermi Paradox'. How can you have life on one tiny planet and despite there being 100 billion stars in the galaxy there was officially no sign of 'intelligent life' outside of humans (and even then, 'intelligent life' is often debatable). There are signs of 'alien' life if you are prepared to look, but I mean officially. The question can be answered with two others: If your simulation is about perceptual entrapment would you want the constant interaction of non-human life with humans that would dramatically open minds to other possibilities? Or would you want to present the illusion of humans being isolated and alone with an estimated two trillion galaxies in the observable Universe – ten times more than previously estimated – offering no official signs of life? The two trillion comes from estimates gleaned from the Hubble Space Telescope. It is fantastic whatever the number and highlights the ludicrous fallacy exposed by the Fermi Paradox. No way would there be zero sign of intelligent life except humans unless that was purposely made to happen. The simulated universe appears to be 'dead' *for a reason*. It is obvious from ancient accounts that non-human entities – mostly Yaldabaoth entities – did once show themselves, but since way back they have operated in the background and on the periphery.

Expert stupidity

The focus on a physical material reality that does not exist except in the illusory way we experience means that 'scientific' orthodoxy has got no chance of seeing reality for what it is. But that's exactly why the controllers want to maintain the fantasy. Children and young people are taught 'scientific' orthodoxy in the schools, colleges and universities, and the media perpetuates this as the term 'scientist' is equated with 'expert' when lots of them are clueless about the big picture. Far from being 'experts' they are instead repeaters of the official orthodoxy or official 'normal'. Ah, but there's the point. If you stick to the script, the official story, you attract the funding from official sources and you could go on to be feted as an 'expert' with titles and letters before and after your name. My goodness, you may even become a 'professor'. Wow. I have met many professors in my life, a few brilliant, but many couldn't run a lemonade stall. Their brilliance comes with the brilliance of never deviating from the orthodoxy. Others do not attract funding in the same way when they push the cutting edge into areas the controllers want to deny a public stage. They are often excluded, ostracised and ridiculed by their own profession.

Witness what happened to the few doctors who spoke out against the 'Covid' fake vaccine and fascist restrictions to see what happens when you tell a true story that authority wants to suppress. They don't want the truth to circulate – worst nightmare. They only want the narrative that suits their agenda for human control and ignorance. The last thing they want is for their targets to see through the fakery to grasp the true nature of the reality they think is so real. Officialdom and its funding-controlled, appointment-controlled, prestige-controlled 'science' have created a fake perception of 'normal' and any phenomena that cannot be explained by this 'normal' is dubbed the 'para-normal'. There is nothing 'para' about it. These phenomena are perfectly normal and explainable, but they are a danger to the orthodoxy that holds the line at human ignorance. They are dismissed once again on the basis that if I can't explain it then it can't be happening. The arrogance and ignorance of that statement is hard to absorb, but if you want to keep your population ignorant keep your perceived 'experts' ignorant or at least so compromised by career-protection or secret society oath that they toe the line. How many doctors realised that the 'Covid' fake vaccine was a killer and health destroyer while continuing to promote and administer the poison for fear of losing their job? May they have mercy on their *own* souls, never mind 'God'.

All this means that true reality is hidden behind walls of suppression and oppression and each of us must pursue our own understanding and research outside of the system when system sources only tell you what the system wants you to believe. I mean by that the whole spectrum of the system – 'education', academia, medicine, government, corporations, media, the lot of them. If you are new to my books, you'll see as we go along how all these sources of 'information' (perception) can be – and *are* – controlled by the same networks to the same end. Suddenly the 'mysteries of life' begin to unravel when you enter the realms of the simulation and how it works. You see they are not mysteries at all. Their explanations lie in the very places where we are told not to look for fear of ridicule, laughter, dismissal, or career suicide.

The challenge is to go there anyway, say it anyway, or be condemned to your life and opinions being controlled for the duration. How many are willing to do that? How many are willing to be truly free?

CHAPTER 4

Breaching Orthodoxy

Heresy is a cradle; orthodoxy a coffin.
Robert Green Ingersoll

I concluded just after the turn of the millennium that we are experiencing a simulated reality and that the speed of light (186,000 miles per second) is an energetic expression of the Matrix at the human level. I had been contemplating this possibility over the years but now the simulation became so clear.

I looked around for others saying the same publicly and I only found Nick Bostrom, then a professor at Oxford University, who was exploring the possibility that we live in a simulation although I differed from his version of what it is. Bostrom was indicating that it could have been created by a human civilisation 'from the future' that was far more technologically advanced than we are. He said that 'just as you can simulate anything else, you can simulate brains'. There was no conceptual barrier to that and once we created sufficiently detailed and accurate brain simulations 'it is possible that those simulations would generate conscious experiences'. He has suggested that humans would eventually be able to build computers so powerful we would not be able to tell the difference between reality and computer-simulated reality. You only have to look at the constant advancement in virtual reality technology and predictions that it will eventually be equivalent to 'real' reality to see that this is true. Bostrom said:

> Because their computers would be so powerful, they could run a great many such simulations. Suppose that these simulated people are conscious (as they would be if the simulations were sufficiently fine-grained and if a certain quite widely accepted position in the philosophy of mind is correct).
>
> Then it could be the case that the vast majority of minds like ours do not belong to the original race but rather to people simulated by the advanced descendants of an original race. It is then possible to argue that, if this were the case, we would be rational to think that we are likely among the simulated minds rather than among the original biological ones.

Either way a simulated human mind is the target of human-AI fusion and what if the 'biological' is also a form of technology? Crazy? We think the biological is 'natural' and what humans create is technology. How do we know? Unless you have something you are certain is 'natural' what do you have to compare with the biological? We think biological is natural because we compare it with nuts and steel technology. What if they are both technology and one is merely far more advanced than the other? What is 'natural' within a simulation? I can tell you from the experience of researching these people that the cultists see biological as technological and treat it as such. The body to them is a form of technology and certainly not 'natural'.

Since my post-millennium insights ever more mainstream scientists with a desire for the truth have concluded that the simulation is a fact. Nearly 20 years after my simulation and speed of light conclusion came an article in the mainstream *Scientific American* in April 2021 with the headline: 'Confirmed! We Live in a Simulation.' The writer was Fouad Khan, a senior editor at *Nature Energy*, who said that our reality is simulated and that its limit is the *speed of light*. I would say that's an apparent limit at the human level and the simulation is multi-dimensional operating at speeds way beyond the speed of light. There can be no limits within infinite possibility. Khan related the speed of light to computer processing power. He said that although simulation and virtual reality creators dictate the rules of the game ('laws of physics') they are still limited by processing speed or energetic power.

Many other scientists have reached similar conclusions about reality as a simulation in recent years. They are nothing like the majority with so much pressure to conform to an orthodoxy that would be demolished by this revelation. The numbers, however, are growing. These are among the mainstream headlines I have seen: 'Physicists May Have Evidence Universe Is A Computer Simulation'; 'The idea we live in a simulation isn't science fiction'; 'Is Our Universe Fake? Physicists claim we could all be the playthings of an advanced civilisation'; 'Is reality an Illusion? Scientist says we may be living in a computer simulation controlled by an evil genius'.

The tide turns

Rich Terrile, director of the Center for Evolutionary Computation and Automated Design at NASA's Jet Propulsion Laboratory, said in 2016 that he believed the Universe is a digital hologram and was therefore not natural and must have been created by some form of intelligence (Fig 63). If the simulation hypothesis was correct then there was 'a creator, an architect – someone who designed the world'. Terrile said this ancient idea claimed by religion could be recast using 'mathematics and science

Breaching Orthodoxy

NASA Scientist Claims Human Reality Is an Alien Created Hologram

With NASA reportedly on the cusp of announcing the discovery of an extraterrestrial race, one scientist says we're living in their hologram.

A NASA scientist has come to the conclusion that our reality is an elaborate hologram created by an alien race. Dr. Rich Terrile, the director of the Center for Evolutionary Computation and Automated Design at NASA's Jet Propulsion Laboratory has said that we can all be the creation of a cosmic computer programmer as opposed to a God. The theory is backed by other scientists, but also has its detractors as well. Maybe as the late Bill Hicks said 'we're all one consciousness experiencing itself subjectively, there is no such thing as death, life is only a dream, and we are the imagination of ourselves' is true.

Figure 63: NASA's Rich Terrile goes public.

rather than just faith'. I have seen Christian researchers point to recurring geometrical sequences in our reality as confirmation of a creator 'God', but they are identifying the handiwork of the *fake* 'God'. American physicist James Gates who found the error-correcting codes or block codes in the energetic fabric is nevertheless reluctant to accept the simulation. He, too, brings up religion. Science had taken us 'away from this idea that we are puppets' controlled by an unseen entity and the simulation hypothesis 'starts to look like a religion', with a programmer substituting for God. Gates is missing the point that neither a God of religion or a creator of the Matrix should be worshipped and that all restraints on the open-minded pursuit of knowledge must be unlocked if we are to understand the human plight and what we can do about it.

American nuclear physicist Silas Beane led a team at the University of Bonn in Germany that concluded we likely live in a simulation that could be arranged as a series of cubes (Fig 64). They found that cosmic rays exhibit a pattern that conforms to a lattice of cubes, and they identified limits or constraints that you would expect if we are dealing with a simulation – the codes that dictate and limit how the 'game' is played. The team highlight in their paper 'Constraints on the Universe as a Numerical Simulation' a limit known as the GZK cut-off. This is a boundary for cosmic ray particles caused by interaction with

Figure 64: Silas Beane and his 'cube' Matrix.

cosmic background radiation which they said was exactly what you would expect with a simulated reality. The paper notes: 'Like a prisoner in a pitch-black cell we would not be able to see the "walls" of our prison.' How would we when our prison is feeding us the reality that stops us seeing the walls of the prison? Or that it is a prison specifically created to enslave us? Even that promotor of scientific orthodoxy, American astrophysicist Neil deGrasse Tyson, has put the simulation odds at 50-50. 'I think the likelihood may be very high', he said. Somewhere out there could be a being with intelligence much greater than our own. 'We would be drooling, blithering idiots in their presence,' he said. 'If that's the case, it is easy for me to imagine that everything in our lives is just a creation of some other entity for their entertainment.' Oh, it goes far deeper than entertainment.

Melvin Vopson, an associate professor in physics at England's University of Portsmouth, went public in late 2023 with his book *Reality Reloaded: The Scientific Case for a Simulated Universe* which was based on his scientific notes and papers (Fig 65). He made the points I have been making for more than two decades and includes Fouad Khan's concept made two years earlier about processing speed. Vopson likened the laws of physics to a computer code and elementary particles of 'matter' to pixels. He writes that the behaviour of particles 'bears an uncanny resemblance to the rules of coding and programming ...' and asks if there is a link between the nature of the Universe and the principles governing computational simulations. Vopson highlights the 'symmetry' of recurring codes at different levels (the holographic principle) and the information nature of the simulation. I have been emphasising this all

Figure 65: Melvin Vopson is another breaking from 'scientific' orthodoxy.

along. The Matrix is *information* that the body-computer decodes into the illusion of 'matter'. Vopson says that information should be acknowledged as the fifth state of matter together with solid, liquid, gas, and plasma. In fact, *everything* is information including solid, liquid, gas, and plasma. If it is not encoded information to be decoded, then it cannot exist in our reality. We only see, hear, touch, smell and taste *information*. He asks if the 'dark matter' proposed by scientists is really information. They can't find 'dark matter' because there is no such thing as they propose. It is information in the energetic blueprint from which the realm of 'matter' is projected (decoded) and that blueprint is what I call programmed plasma. American scientist David Bohm believed that *information* within 'light' explained how 'matter' comes into being. Light/plasma is the background medium and information in the form of electricity and electromagnetism encodes the detail.

Computer science is a profession well placed to consider the possibility of a simulation. Rizwan Virk is an American computer scientist and video game designer who wrote the 2019 book, *The Simulation Hypothesis*. He says there are a lot of mysteries better explained by a simulation than 'a material hypothesis'. There was so much we don't understand about reality, and he believes it's more likely than not that we are in some kind of a simulated universe. 'I would say that if the world isn't really physical, if it's based on information, then a simpler explanation might in fact be that we are in a simulation that is generated based on computer science and information.' The fact that 3D printers could now print 3D pixels of objects showed that most objects could be broken down as information. I would say *all* objects. He believed there were ten stages of technology development needed to reach a point where reality could be simulated, and humans were already at number five. Virk said stage six would be learning to interact with a simulation without glasses/headsets and then it would get even more challenging:

> But the really difficult part – and this is something not a lot of technologists have talked about – is in The Matrix, the reason they thought they were fully immersed was they had this cord going into the cerebral cortex, and that's where the signal was beamed. This brain-computer interface is the area that we haven't yet made that much progress in, but we are making progress in it. It's in the early stages.

Astral entities have long been on the case. Interaction with a simulation without glasses/headsets is called the human body which is specifically *designed* to be a brain-computer-Wi-Fi interface. Virk said that humans would reach the 'simulation point' within a few decades to 100 years from now. This does not include the fact that secret science is way further down the line than public arena science or the underground base interaction between human scientists serving the Global Cult and non-human entities. Where humans *could be* is however far less relevant to the simulation than where Yaldabaoth and its operatives already are.

Ugh?

Another mainstream scientist, Professor Marika Taylor, a theoretical physicist from the University of Birmingham, was featured by the *Mail Online* in 2025 for saying that our universe is two-dimensional and is like a 3-D movie seen on a flat screen. The article was headlined: 'Are we living in the Matrix? Scientist claims the universe is really a hologram.' The article writer said that 'some scientists now claim that humanity, the Earth, and everything else in the universe are really part of a giant holographic projection' and this 'bold idea could solve some of physics' most challenging questions'. Professor Taylor said this does not have to mean we live in a simulation, but it did confirm that holographic theory is no longer on the fringe. She says that the '3-D world' is only an illusion. 'That doesn't mean our lives, or the universe are any less real [it *does*], but it does mean that the cosmos might be a lot stranger than we had previously thought.' The article said that the 2-D 'surface' had no gravity and no depth, only quantum and atomic forces. 'What appears to be the 3D structure of the world we can observe is just an illusion created by this 2D surface.' Hold on. If the world is not a simulated construct, then we must believe that information has been imprinted by chance on a 2-D surface and miraculously the human brain/body has 'evolved' to perceive it in 3-D? Now that *is* a stretch given all the other information. Fermilab, a United States Department of Energy particle physics laboratory, is quoted as saying: 'The notion that our familiar three-dimensional universe is somehow encoded in two dimensions at the most fundamental level does not imply that there is anybody or anything "outside" the two-dimensional representation, "projecting" the illusion or "running" the simulation.' My response is the same. Don't be silly. 'Evolution' did it, then? This is the get-out response to stop a total re-evaluation of reality. The *Mail* article went on to say that the holographic principle contends that we can describe everything about the universe, including gravity and depth, by talking about what's happening on the 2D surface. That's what I am saying in another way. The 2-D 'surface' is the Wi-Fi field encoded with the information we decode into an appearance of 3-D. Professor Taylor did say that 'holography takes us into an even more extreme world, where not only are the forces quantum in nature, but the number of dimensions is different from our perceived reality'.

I have been saying for years that the Matrix is a gigantic quantum computer, and I was interested to see that Melvin Vopson suggests the

Universe may function as an advanced quantum computer that computes its own existence. Quantum computers are fantastically more advanced than current computer systems and they are in the process of being introduced to control human society. Ironically, our very reality is a quantum computer way beyond the human version. It was quite an experience as someone who left school at 15 without taking a major exam to read a book by an associate professor in physics and find nothing I didn't already know, but this is an important point. The information is encoded in our very reality and beyond in the realm of Spirit. If you can tap into that you don't need formal 'education' (programming) as it currently operates. You certainly don't need to get yourself in massive debt for much of the rest of your life to pay for your own programming. The sums borrowed by young people nationally and globally to *buy* their programming is beyond belief and it requires you then to serve the system to pay back the system for programming you. We can educate ourselves on our terms pursuing what inspires and interests us. I left school at 15 to play professional football and I have since written and researched nearly 30 books. Okay, you need to study for a specialisation, but why does that require that your entire childhood is blighted sitting at a desk listening to stuff you will never use and bores you rigid? We elevate the intellect and equate it with intelligence when it is the village idiot compared with expanded states of awareness. Intellect is mind and is there to hold you in the Matrix not to set you free. Look at academia, science, government, corporations, media, even most of the 'alternative' media, and it's all intellect policing the human perceptual prison.

The 'para' is normal

'Para-normal' phenomena cannot be explained by 'scientific' orthodoxy when the orthodoxy is there to stop them being explained. Shift perspective and suddenly all is revealed. Let's take astrology. Read your horoscope in the morning paper and it's next to pointless. Go much deeper into astrology and you can see its validity. Everything in the simulation is an electrical/electromagnetic field and everything has a form of consciousness. This 'everything' applies to the planets. The interactive movement of their fields through the universal electrical/electromagnetic field of the simulation changes its frequency (information) make-up. Humans are interacting with that field through the body/brain and senses. Changes in the field impact upon us. Combinations of planets – known in astrology as conjunctions, trines, aspects, transits, eclipses, and so on – have more powerful effects on the field based on the sum of the parts is more powerful than the parts alone. Our individual fields are impacted by the nature of the universal field when we are born (some say conceived) and we interact with changes in that field in a different way to those born at another point in the simulation cycle.

We call these differences Taurus, Leo or Gemini but there are subtle differences between segments of the same day within the 'sign'. This is why only deep and detailed analysis tells you anything that truly relates to you. Even then it should be emphasised that astrology is a phenomenon of the *simulation* and part of the control program. The benefit of astrology is to know when the flows of energy through the grid network support or oppose a particular course of action. Or whether it is advisable to delay and wait for a 'time' when the energy flows are most beneficial in relation to your energetic field. You don't want to row against the tide when you can wait until the tide is with you. It is for this reason that many corporate CEOs have astrologers on retainers to advise them when best to act and launch a product. I stress again that this only applies within the simulation and if you are connected with Spirit beyond it, you can override astrological 'laws' and 'rules'.

There are many techniques in what is called the art of 'divination'. They include the psychic (accessing knowledge and information from other levels of reality); Channelling (allowing another dimensional entity to take over your body and speak through your vocal cords); Numerology (reading reality through numbers assigned to a name, birth date and time); and tarot cards (reading symbolically illustrated cards selected by a person to 'read' their 'future'). All these techniques can be both valid and extremely misleading depending on those involved. Once again, they are also simulation phenomena unless the psychic/channeller is connecting with information beyond its energetic limitations. The question always with psychics and channellers is who is on the other end? Information can be anything from misguided to outright manipulative if a psychic is connecting with sources within the Matrix. It is vital not to just take things on face value as 'enlightened' by definition. These communications can be anything but, and it's crucial to be discerning and cross reference with other information. I can tell you from long experience that the great majority of psychics and channellers are connecting with Matrix sources and not beyond-the-Matrix Spirit. This does not mean that all such connections cannot be useful and accurate from a Matrix perspective. It means that at best the knowledge communicated will be limited and at worst misleading you. I have witnessed many channellings – some to the extent that the channel's face features change or 'shapeshift' – but always the question comes back. Who is the channelled entity and what is its motivation and purpose? I have also seen many 'channellings' in which the 'channel' was clearly making it up or deluding themselves that they were 'channelling' when the source was their own mind. Discernment is vital.

Numbers game

Numerology works with numbers and is reading the digital level of the simulation. I have said that the brain decodes electrical information from the senses into digital holographic information. It just so happens that digital holograms are now the cutting edge of holography. Collective humanity is constantly decoding the electrical into the digital and as a result there is a collective digital field of information both within and collectively connected which numerologists are reading. Human DNA has a digital or binary expression as we've seen (Fig 66). The Universe follows mathematical laws and equations which is again what you would expect with a simulation. Max Tegmark, a physicist at the Massachusetts Institute of Technology (MIT) and author of *Our Mathematical Universe*, said: 'The Universe can be entirely described by numbers and maths.' He said that if characters in a computer game began to study their 'world' they would realise that everything was made of pixels and what they thought was physical could be described in numbers. This is what would happen, and is beginning to happen, in human reality. Tegmark said:

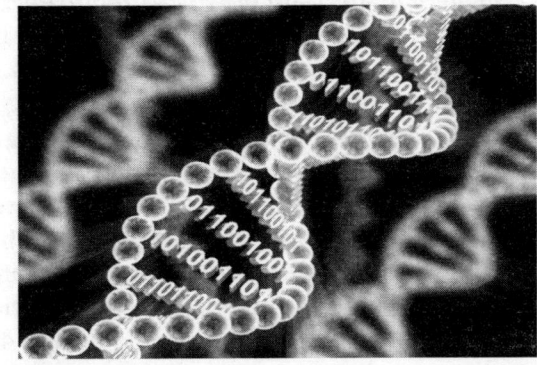

Figure 66: DNA on one level is digital.

> And we're exactly in this situation in our world. We look around and it doesn't seem that mathematical at all, but everything we see is made out of elementary particles like quarks and electrons. And what properties does an electron have? Does it have a smell or a colour or a texture? No! ...
>
> ... We physicists have come up with geeky names for [electron] properties, like electric charge, or spin, or lepton number, but the electron doesn't care what we call it, the properties are just numbers.

Yes, on *one* level they are. Eugene Wigner (1902-1995), a Hungarian American theoretical physicist, engineer and mathematician, has acknowledged the same phenomenon. He observed how the mathematical foundation of nature borders on the mysterious with 'no rational explanation for it'. Oh, but there *is* if you encompass the simulation. The psychic/channeller is tapping into the frequency field level of reality while numerologists are reading the digital level. These are two aspects of the same information. I have had readings with gifted psychics and numerologists very close to each other for my research and the readings have been basically the same as you would expect when they were interpreting different versions of the same information. Numerology assigns a number to letters of the alphabet while birth dates and times are already numbers. These are added together until they become a single digit. A number as big as 3,400,296 becomes 24 when added together and 2 + 4 is 6. My birth year of 1952 becomes 17 becomes 8. Numerology is possible because the simulation is akin to a *computer program* and how is software encoded? With *numbers*. Numerology is reading the digital Matrix both collectively and inside all of us. Numbers represent frequencies and many people will have had experience of the same numbers recurring in their lives for a period which reflect certain frequencies recurring around them or which they are emitting.

Tarot cards have been used for centuries. Each one is illustrated with symbols representing states of being and the Tarot reader will ask a client to pick out a series of them apparently at random from the pack while not seeing the symbols involved. These are then interpreted in a tarot reading. This naturally sounds very strange and makes little sense until you realise that the selections are made at the electromagnetic level. We have an electromagnetic field surrounding and interpenetrating the body which I call Body-Mind and that contains the sum of our perceptions plus the subconscious knowledge of where those perceptions are leading us if nothing changes. Tarot cards like everything in this reality are also electromagnetic fields in their undecoded state and their fields are dictated by the symbols on the cards reflecting as they do states of being. In this way the cards are not selected at random, but by particular electromagnetic frequencies from the person locking into matching frequencies in the card pack (Fig 67). A skilled tarot reader will lay out the selected cards as a

Figure 67: Tarot like everything is electromagnetic in nature.

version of *you*. That's the idea anyway and I emphasise the 'skilled tarot reader'. There are many who are not and when I see them doing readings on YouTube for Aries, Capricorn and other star signs it is ridiculous to suggest that the same thing is going to happen to all of them. They throw in riders and disclaimers such as 'see if this resonates with you' while the premise is still nonsensical. A personal reading with someone who knows what they are doing can be useful so long as you don't take every last word as the truth you must act upon. *You* decide that and no one else.

Christians condemn forms of divination as the 'occult' which just means 'hidden'. It is hidden knowledge that can be used for good or ill. With supreme irony the Bible is full of numerology with its recurring numbers such as 12 and 40. The number 12 appears 189 times in the King James Bible – 114 times in the Old Testament and 75 in the New. These include the 12 apostles; 12 was the age that 'Jesus' spoke in the temple; 12 tribes of Israel; 12 sons of Jacob; 12 crops of fruit on the tree of life in Revelation. We have 40 days and nights of rain; 40 days and nights of fasting by 'Jesus' when he was tempted by the Devil; 40 years of the Israelites wandering in (a very small) desert after their alleged escape from Egypt; 40 days for Moses on Mount Sinai when God delivered the commandments. These are not literal stories. They are symbolic and weaved with numerological, astrological, and non-human 'god' themes of which more later.

What are the chances?

Put all this evidence together, and more, and my contention that we are experiencing a simulated reality is to say the least not so crazy. The 'physics' of the so-called natural world mirror the encoded limits, rules and laws of computer simulations and apply throughout the simulated universe. Hungarian-American theoretical physicist Eugene Wigner said the fact that there are universal rules governing the cosmos was in itself a kind of miracle. Cosmologist Sean Carroll, a research professor in the Department of Physics at the California Institute of Technology, pointed out that 'a law of physics is a pattern that nature obeys without exception'. The speed of light was measured at a constant 186,000 miles per second whether it be a galaxy or a flashlight, he said. Another 'law' (simulation code) known as the proton-electron mass ratio was the same here as in a galaxy said to be six billion light years away. The truth is in front of us while the almost totality of 'science' covers its eyes. Paul C. Davies, a physics professor at Arizona State University, said that when he asks other physicists why the laws of physics are what they are they reply: 'There is no reason they are what they are – they just are.' But there *is* a reason as I am laying out here. Then there is the question of why Earth's atmosphere and environment is perfect for life in a visible universe apparently devoid of the requirements for life as we know it. Even then *only just*. Scientist Robert Lanza wrote this in his book *Biocentrism*:

Why are the laws of physics exactly balanced for animal life to exist? ... If the strong nuclear force were decreased 2 percent, atomic nuclei wouldn't hold together, and plain-vanilla hydrogen would be the only kind of atom in the Universe. If the gravitational force were decreased by a hair, stars (including the Sun) would not ignite.

These are just [some of] more than 200 parameters within the solar system and Universe so exact that it strains credulity to propose that they are random – even if that is exactly what standard contemporary physics baldly suggests.

These questions are fundamental to the quest for truth, but overwhelming swathes of mainstream 'science' will not ask them and go where that leads them. Conditions on Earth are perfect but only just for human life because the simulation has been encoded to make it that way with a human body designed to interact with that encoding. The rest of the visible universe only appears to be lifeless because it has also been made to be that way to give the entrapped perception of the target 'humans' the impression they are isolated and alone with no interaction with other far more intelligent life to open their minds to the truth. The whole simulated reality in all its multiple levels is run by a form of AI that is light years ahead of the AI now coming in so fast to take over and control human society on a scale never seen in what we *call* known history.

Mind of the Matrix

Then there is something else to consider. I said that 'Yaldabaoth' is a distorted, schismatic state of awareness which infuses its schism, its separation and fragmentation from the Infinite Whole, into every aspect of the simulation. It's the holographic principle again. I have said in other books that the entire simulation is an emanation from the Mind of Yaldabaoth and hence the infusion of its distortions and inversions into everything. In short, I am saying that we are living 'in' the mind of Yaldabaoth as in effect a figment of its perceptual reality. Its *idea*. English physicists, mathematicians and astronomers James Hopwood Jeans (1877-1946) and Arthur Eddington (1882-1944) would agree with at least the concept. Jeans said that 'the universe begins to look more like a great thought than a great machine' while Eddington said that 'the universe is of the nature of a thought or sensation in a universal mind'. Or the Mind of Yaldabaoth. Think of it this way. All reality is in the mind of the Infinite and the simulation is in the mind of the schism and distortion that Gnostics name Yaldabaoth. The simulation therefore reflects the distortion rather than the harmony of the Infinite.

Caleb Scharf, a Director of Astrobiology at Columbia University, said that what is called 'alien life' could be so advanced (compared with humans) that it is not a part of our reality – it *is* our reality. He proposed that the 'alien' force could have transcribed itself into the quantum realm to become our physics and numbers and was indistinguishable from the fabric of the Universe. I say that Yaldabaoth *is* the Universe, the energy of the Universe that it imagined into existence. The Nag Hammadi *Apocryphon of John* that I quoted earlier says that Yaldabaoth 'organised (everything) according to the model of the first aeons … [and] produced in him the likeness of the cosmos'. Scharf advanced the possibility that 'we don't recognise advanced life because it forms an integral and unsuspicious part of what we've considered to be the natural world'. For sure there is no 'natural world'. It is a simulated 'copy' of a world beyond the simulation. He described a civilisation that has learned how to encode living systems with itself. What if those systems *are* itself? Scharf said that if he was correct in his proposals many of the greatest mysteries would be solved:

> Perhaps hyper-advanced life isn't just external. Perhaps it's already all around. It is embedded in what we perceive to be physics itself, from the root behaviour of particles and fields to the phenomena of complexity and emergence ... In other words, life might not just be in the equations. It might *be* the equations.

My suggestion that we live in an emanated idea of Yaldabaoth brings us back to quantum physics. Paul Levy in his book *The Quantum Revelation* notes that 'both the wave function and the atom are essentially ideas, and outside of these ideas, both the wave function and the atom are not there'. American mathematical physicist Henry Stapp said that 'we live in an idea-like world, not a matter-like world' and 'the actual events in quantum theory are likewise idea-like'. Physicist John Wheeler also compared reality to an idea which relates to a dream-like reality that I explored in my book, *The Dream*. Is the simulation Yaldabaoth's dream? Is it Yaldabaoth's idea in which he mimicked Prime Reality? Is indeed Yaldabaoth itself a form of highly advanced AI within which the simulation is encoded?

What is 'history'?

There is another point to make about the Matrix which some may think takes us deeper into fairyland but doesn't. There are multiple material simulations, not only the one based around Earth, and there are multiple timelines known as 'history'. Souls are incarnating into these other simulated realities and 'periods' of history, or what we call 'history'. What is that? History is the 'past' when there is no 'past' in no-time infinity, only the simulated illusion of it. All these 'eras' or timelines exist in the same moment and Souls are still incarnating into ancient 'eras' that we believe to be the 'past' such as ancient Egypt, Babylon, Greece, Rome, and so on. The simulations have a 'period' and are then rebooted to start again while the transformation ('Great Reset') from one simulated timeline to the next is what we perceive as 'history', 'evolution' and moving 'forward'. This relates to the ancient concept of epochs and the 'yugas' of Hindu belief. You'll find the theme around the world including the concept in Central America of the Mayan calendar recording cycles of various lengths with its Long Count over thousands of years. A yuga is another measurement of epochs of different 'ages' and collective cycles of experience involving creation and destruction.

I say these are symbols of the simulation cycles when one comes to its conclusion and is then 'reset'. Each simulation includes apparent remnants of other simulations – like the Giza pyramids – to give the impression of a long 'history' when the simulation cycles are actually much shorter. For example, the original pyramids will continue to exist in pristine condition in their simulation 'era' while an older version is encoded into our simulation that appears to be an unbroken timeline when it's not. History is very difficult to track when we are dealing with a simulation and a click, click, enter can encode new 'discoveries' to mislead historians about the perceived 'past'. We must always remember that the simulation is there to confuse and misdirect, not to inform and reveal the truth. The now infamous 'Great Reset' of Global Cult operative Klaus Schwab could refer to the Great Reset of the simulation as we enter a period designed for total human control through AI. It is very possible that the destruction of 'Atlantis' and the Great Flood could be one simulation being reset into another. It becomes ever more obvious despite the 'historian' orthodoxy that structures such as the Giza pyramids and so much more could only have been achieved by a highly advanced civilisation. The extent of the Giza site underground goes on expanding and there is a stream of enormous, advanced structures under the ocean that were once on land before geological upheavals. What I say here about 'history' should be kept in mind when I talk about accepted 'history' as the book unfolds.

What is 'possible'?

There is a major difference between the Matrix and the infinite forever beyond its frequency enslavement. That difference is *possibility*. The Infinite Realm is infinite possibility. Therefore, it is everything and nothing, it is, and it isn't, it can, and it can't. There is no contradiction here although to the duality mind it would seem so. There cannot be contradiction – paradox – within all-possibility where everything (and nothing!) is possible. The simulation is a bad copy of Infinite Reality and must adhere to its basic ways of working which means that it must involve all-possibility. The control system seeks to mitigate these effects and limit possibility by controlling the *perceptions* of the observers and their *sense* of what's possible. Quantum physics says that the observer manifests 'physical' reality into apparent existence. If you wish to limit possibility you must limit the *perceptions* of the observer so that limited possibility is decoded into existence. You do this by controlling access to knowledge and diminish the human sense of self-identity, possibility, and reality which, in turn, limits the range of possibility the observer can bring into 'physical' experience.

Could it even be that this limited collective sense of the possible manifests as perceived 'laws of physics' which appear to limit the possible in line with the *perception* of the possible? Is it chicken or egg? This would match in theme the 'strange loop' proposed by physicist John Wheeler in which 'physics gives rise to observers, who then give rise to information, which in turn gives rise to physics'. It could in my view be that information decoded by observers with limited perceptions of the possible give rise to *apparent* 'laws of physics' that *appear* to limit the possible. The sense of limitation can be overcome through awakening and reconnection with the Divine Spark and its connection to the Infinite Realm of all-possibility. This would mean that the imagination of the scientist exploring the quantum world of physics would need to be expanded and Divine Spark influenced in some way to see beyond the apparent limitation of physics. The mentality of a 'scientist' worshipping orthodoxy will go on perceiving (creating) orthodoxy while one with out-of-the-box expanded awareness and maverick tendencies will gravitate to the land of the quantum. In other words – orthodox 'scientists' and quantum scientists don't perceive in the same way if the quantum scientist is *truly maverick*. Far from all of them are. The understanding of all-possibility leads to a transformation of perception and what is 'logical' or not. Humanity's oppressed 'logic' says that something is or isn't. It is a 'paradox' if you think otherwise. But all-possibility is the death-knell of paradox. Paul Levy writes in *The Quantum Revelation*:

> … two-valued logic works by contrast, giving attributes to things and making distinctions, thereby limiting them. Something is this only by defining it as not that. Our very language itself, in categorizing things and ideas, conditions us into a dualistic, two-valued, logical way of thinking.

Language is fundamental to perception programming both as an influencer of perception and because it is information in the form of *frequency* that can impact upon the human energetic field and brain. This knowledge is mercilessly exploited by the Cult for perceptual programming. We live in a duality world because of duality thinking that leads to duality structures of organisation – us and them, left and right, positive and negative. These are perceptions of reality that become experienced reality. Compare the lives of those with a limited sense of the possible with those who believe anything is possible. Our perceptions really do create reality which is why perception is the stadium in which the game of life and control is played out. What is the world? What do you *want* it to be – *choose* it to be? A fragmented mind will create a fragmented reality. Perceived 'evolution' is the expansion of awareness which is why 'evolution' can expand or regress according to the awakeness or asleepness of the population. Everyone lives in their own perceptual universe and manifests a reality to match. It's only a case of how much and how little is agreed upon. Conflict and the fault-lines of divide and rule come from arguing over whose reality should prevail when if people simply expressed their uniqueness and respected everyone else's right to do the same, without forcing one on the other, then harmony could be restored.

Why does the world operate as it does? Because we *think* that it does. Each new generation enters the world as it is and thinks of the world as it experiences the world which ingrains the belief that this is how the world operates and thus collectively it does. But it doesn't have to. Change perception and you change your life. Change perception collectively and we change the world.

CHAPTER 5

The Archons

The demon is a liar. He will lie to confuse us; but he will also mix lies with the truth to attack us. His attack is psychological ...
William Peter Blatty

A common theme across religions and ancient cultures is the existence of an unseen force – Satan, Shaytan, Yaldabaoth, Samael, Saklas – that seeks to enslave and manipulate humans. Another recurring tale is how that force created an army of wickedness to serve its will.

These are known among many other names as demons and fallen angels (Christianity); Jinn (Islam); Archons (Gnostic); Galla (Mesopotamia); Oni (Japan); La Llorona (Mexico); and Gorgon (Greece). They are given a stream of individual names across the cultures including Baphomet, Asmodeus, Diablo, Ahriman, Azazel, Moloch, Abaddon, Iblis, and in the female form, Lilith, Morrigan, Hecate, Lamia, Jezebeth, Mara, Saturna and Medusa. They are said to present themselves in endless 'physical' forms, the ability known as 'shapeshifting', and can be anything from handsome and beautiful to ugly and grotesque. They can possess humans and take over their minds and behaviour. They deceive, mislead, manipulate, and are associated with malevolence. Demons have been feared through the ages in every part of the world.

Gnosticism calls them Archons from a Greek word meaning 'rulers' and says that in their base state they are formless energy but can take form in various ways. Yaldabaoth was called the Chief Archon or Lord Archon created according to Gnostics by the Sophia 'error' and this is the overall consciousness that emanates its distortion through its subordinate entities and seeks to infuse that distortion into humans (Fig 68 overleaf). You have the biblical association of 'Lord' with the 'Lord God' and 'The Lord' with reference to Jesus. We can see the Yaldabaoth origin of 'Dark Lord' and 'Time Lord' and movie portrayals by Archontic Hollywood of Lord (Darth) Vader and the evil ruler of the 'Dark Dimension' dubbed Dormammu in the Marvel comic movie, *Dr Strange*. Nag Hammadi texts say Yaldabaoth created other Archons as emanations (copies) of itself by using the creative power inherited from

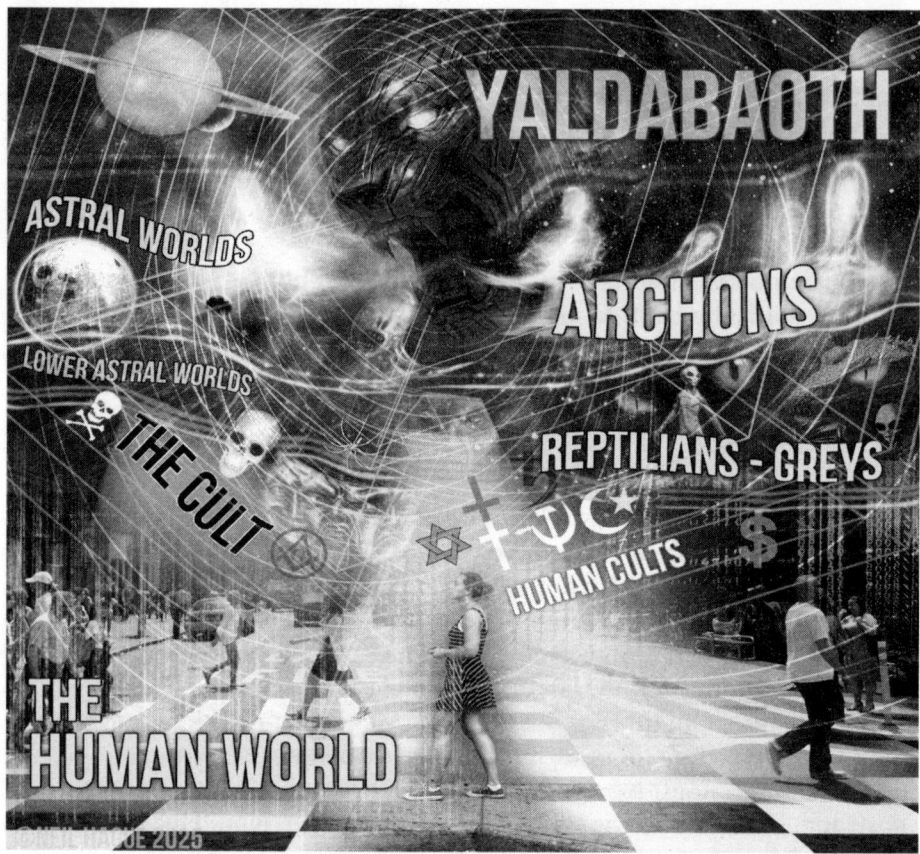

Figure 68: I am using the term 'Yaldabaoth' for the consciousness behind the simulation/Matrix and that consciousness emanates through subordinate entities known as 'Archons', 'demons' and Archontic extraterrestrials/interdimensionals. (Image by Neil Hague.)

Sophia to serve its agenda as the 'bad copy' simulation was formed. Yaldabaoth, the 'Great *Arch*itect', is appropriately embedded in *Arch*ons and biblical *arch*angels along with church terms such as *arch*bishops and *arch*deacon. You can again see the common theme with Yaldabaoth called the Archon of Archons while the Christian 'Satan' and his demons or demonic host is the 'Demon of Demons'. Archons as holographic copies of Yaldabaoth have inherited all its distorted traits. Gnostics call them mind parasites, inverters, guards, gatekeepers, detainers, judges, pitiless ones and deceivers who 'overpower humanity in its perceptual functions' and use fear to impose slavery. They are described in terms of cyborgs which can imitate but not innovate.

Gnostics said Archons were made from luminous fire (electromagnetism?) while Islamic texts say Jinn were made from smokeless fire because they are describing the same phenomenon. I remember talking about the Archons to a Muslim taxi driver in New York and he said: 'That sounds like the Jinn'. Archons in all their forms and sub-groups *are* the Jinn. Gnostics say Archons represent the forces of chaos and describe them as 'the farthest that a created being could be from God.' They are malevolent 'counterfeit spirits' and I have said in other books that they are a form of highly advanced AI although not in the way that we currently perceive it. They are also stupid in the sense that they were created by stupid. Clever manipulators, yes, but stupid as a 'download' and extension of their stupid maker. How can stupid manipulate billions of people on this scale? By making humans more ignorant than *they* are through the suppression of knowledge. Archons in turn created entities below them (called demons by Gnostic texts) and this is the origin of malevolent 'extraterrestrials' be they reptilian, 'Grey aliens', and other non-human forms (Fig 69). They are not 'extraterrestrial' in a 'physical' sense but interdimensional and are able to come and go between the Astral and human bands of frequency. Entities and 'UFOs' which 'appear' and 'disappear' are moving in and out of visible light from the Astral realm.

We should also remember the endless legends of entities and worlds within the Earth. Many witnesses claim to have seen 'UFOs', now officially called 'Unidentified Anomalous Phenomena' (UAPs), disappearing into the ground when they suddenly change from an apparently 'solid' to an energetic form. I have spoken with very credible people who say they have seen this. The inner-Earth realm – 'Underworld' – would support claims I have heard many times from military personnel who say that non-humans interact with the human military and scientists in the lower levels of the 'DUMBs', or Deep Underground Military Bases. A lot of manipulation is coming from under our feet along with the legends of benevolent groups in underground cities linked by tunnel systems. Ancient tunnel networks have been found all over the world and many military personnel over the years have described how the DUMBS are connected by tunnels and trains that move at extraordinary speeds over long distances. Bases in Nevada, New Mexico and Arizona are often mentioned. I have come across stories many times about underground

Figure 69: Hilarious, isn't it? I mean, everyone knows that humans are the only form of 'intelligent' life in all infinity.

Reptilians which interact with human Cult scientists in the lowest levels of the 'DUMBS' where advanced technical knowledge is transferred that eventually becomes high-tech 'inventions' on the surface. Politicians, including US presidents, are not allowed to know what happens in those bases and secret projects because there is an always-there level of the military that is way above their pay grade and right-to-know. Others tell of connections between the underground realm and key buildings. A long-time friend of Princess Diana described to me how entrances to tunnel systems exist under the British royal family castle at Balmoral in Scotland.

Reptilians? Ha, ha, ha ...

I have become famous – *infamous* – and widely ridiculed and abused for saying since the mid-1990s that human society is manipulated by a non-human force that in part takes a reptilian form. You should have been around me for the last 36 years if anyone needs confirmation about human arrogance and ignorance. All these decades of research that has taken me to 50-60 countries worldwide and yet people who have not done five minutes of research ridicule you for no other reason than what you say is beyond their programmed perception of 'normal' and capacity to see other possibilities (Fig 70). German philosopher Arthur Schopenhauer said: 'Everyone takes the limits of his own vision for the limits of the world.' It doesn't matter to the ridiculers and abusers how much information you compile because they can't be bothered to read it. The very idea is outside of their tiny perceptual box and so it can't be true. The Archontic wants to keep humanity ignorant, but many are ignorant by choice with an arrogance and belief system that limits knowledge by knowing it all.

Figure 70: No matter what the ancient and modern evidence this is all too much for many people.

I'm not going to go into detail again here about the reptilian information because I have done so at enormous length in many books since *The Biggest Secret* in the 1990s. See also *Children of the Matrix* (2001), *Everything You Need To Know But Have Never Been Told* (2017), and my 'Reality Trilogy', *The Trap* (2022), *The Dream* (2023) and *The Reveal* (2024).

The Archons

I have compiled a mountain of information ancient and modern on the Reptilian subject that confirms an undeniable interconnected story that leads from ubiquitous ancient accounts to modern civilian and military experiences. Add to this the focus and worship of the dragon, the dragon symbolism of Yaldabaoth, the connection of the serpentine to royal and aristocratic bloodlines of the Global Cult, and religious themes. The Reptilians I have been exposing since the 1990s are an expression of the Archontic horde.

Nag Hammadi texts estimated to have been hidden 1,600 years ago say the most common manifestations of Archons in form are reptilian or serpentine and one that appears like 'an unborn baby or foetus with grey skin and dark, unmoving eyes' – what a description of 'Grey aliens'. Hopi Native Americans in Arizona tell of the 'Sheti' or 'Snake Brothers' and 'Lizard People'. Hopi folklore records that the Sheti are humanoid reptiles that live in underground cities across the western United States which continue into Mexico and Central America. Sheti are said to know the secrets of mind control. Not all Reptilian species are antagonistic to humans, but those I am exposing certainly are. Then we have the Astral Reptilians who come and go between there and the human band of frequency. Reptilian legends abound throughout history and global cultures from the Celtic serpent god Hu (hu-man would equal serpent man) to the serpent gods in Central and South America, Africa, Asia, and across the world. Reverend John Bathurst Deane said in his 1933 study of serpent veneration, *The Worship of the Serpent*: 'The mystic serpent entered into the mythology of every nation; consecrated almost every temple; symbolised almost every deity; was imagined in the heavens, stamped upon the earth, and ruled in the realms of everlasting sorrow.' Deane said that serpent worship and mythology was the 'only common object of superstitious terror throughout the habitable world' and worship of the serpent is the oldest and most global of all religions. Mythology of the ancient African San people, or 'Bushmen', says that humans were created in the Tsodilo Hills in the Kalahari Desert of Botswana when the 'Great Python' arrived with a 'bag of eggs'. The oldest form of human religious worship so far uncovered is the worship of the serpent or python which goes back at least 70,000 years to the same Tsodilo Hills of Botswana.

Long after I went public with the Reptilian phenomenon, American aerospace engineer William Tompkins published a 2015 book, *Selected by Extraterrestrials: My life in the top secret world of UFOs, think-tanks and Nordic secretaries*. 'Nordics' are a tall, fair-skinned non-human race with human characteristics widely described in UFO research circles. Zulu high shaman Credo Mutwa told me they were known in Zulu legends as the 'Mzungu' who could 'appear and disappear'. He said that when white Europeans first arrived in South Africa the people thought they were the returning Mzungu. William Tompkins revealed in his book his own experience of the Reptilian control of human society. Tompkins died in August 2017 after a fall aged 94 with another book in the pipeline. He said he worked from the 1940s with a secret think tank based at one of the US Navy's biggest and most important bases in San Diego and was connected to a group of American Navy spies during World War Two who stole UFO secrets from the Nazis. Tompkins claimed that he personally gave them to US military and space corporations such as Lockheed, Douglas, Northrop, Grumman and others to produce advanced antigravity craft ('flying saucers') and other advanced technology. The California Institute of Technology (Caltech) was also heavily involved, he said. 'UFOs' had been flown by at least Americans and Germans as a result of this knowledge. Not all 'UFO' craft are flown by 'aliens' and that's something I have been emphasising over the years after hearing the same from many sources.

Tompkins said human elites and military insiders were working with extraterrestrials – especially Reptilian – and this was the origin of most advanced technology (another point I have been making for decades). The Reptilians known as the 'Draco' or 'Draconians' are connected by researchers to the vast Draco Constellation in the northern sky. Draco is Latin for dragon. One of the constellation's best-known stars is Thuban, or Alpha Draconis, which was the north pole star from the 4th to 2nd millennium BC. I covered the background and nature of the Draconians in *Children of the Matrix* which was first published in 2001. Draco Reptilians are said to be the 'royalty' at the top of the Reptilian hierarchy who are fierce warriors and super-psychopaths that pass on their traits to their underlings. They have seeded many elite human-reptilian hybrid bloodlines that have become royalty, political leaders, and the Cult inner circle. Tompkins said the Draco had the same skin as lizards and reptiles and the ability to shapeshift into human form – something I have been describing since the 1990s. He said: 'You have Draco Reptilian guys running your governments of every country on the planet.' He said Reptilians have bases throughout the solar system and under the Earth including one under Antarctica. There were human-ET underground bases on Mars – something else I have been told by other sources. Tompkins wrote that Reptilians are expert in mass and individual perception manipulation; the creation of illusions; and have genetically manipulated humans to limit them to a fraction of potential brain capacity. He said extraterrestrials built the pyramids around the world and other structures that we would struggle to build even today. Everything that Tompkins said about the Reptilian presence and interaction with the human 'elite', including the building of the pyramids, I have heard from other contacts and sources over the last 30 years.

Humanity's reptilian brain

Reflex-action ridiculers will have no idea of the reptilian elements of the human body and brain which are there specifically to attach us to the reptilian hive mind. Anyone who researches the Reptilians will realise that they operate as a hive mind in a way that can be likened to a bee or ant colony. Frequencies emitted by the queen are orchestrating the apparent chaos that is really order as the bees and ants come and go. I have heard the concept of an 'Orion Queen' in relation to the Reptilians. A highly significant aspect of the human brain is known by science as the R-complex, reptilian brain, or lizard brain, which is so named because of the similarity to the brain of reptiles. The R-complex can be found in the area from near the centre of the brain and down the brainstem into the spinal cord of the central nervous system (Fig 71). The probe in the back of the neck that plugs people into the simulation, as portrayed in the *Matrix* movies, is appropriately in the reptilian brain. This is also known as the Primal Brain which allows 'back-door' access to the body-computer to Reptilian demonic entities which are part of the Archontic horde and Yaldabaoth hierarchy. Its influence can be overridden by awakening to the Divine Spark. The fast-unfolding plans for a connection between artificial intelligence and the human brain is to advance 'back-door' access and block any Divine Spark intervention.

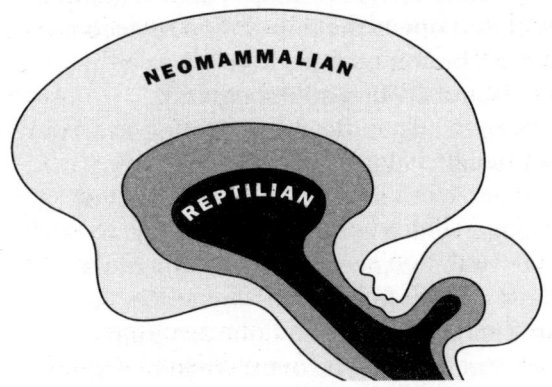

Figure 71: The Reptilian brain – 'back door' access to human perception and emotional reaction.

The reptilian brain is vital for human control with its emphasis on survival in every sense. 'Physical' survival naturally, but also survival of your family, job, income, food supply, relationships, status, reputation, and anything else you don't want to lose. Its method of operation is through *fear* and regulates heart rate, breathing, and body temperature. The fight or flight response is the reptilian brain. Background anxiety that many constantly feel is generated by this R-complex and it seeks to conform and obey authority to mitigate its fear of the consequences of not doing so. A dominant reptilian brain does not do mavericks or system-busting and only reflects the hive mind acquiescence of the Reptilian hierarchical system of organisation. The Archontic order is hierarchical, and this has been infused into the human realm along with the reptilian brain adherence to that. Many cannot even conceive of a way of living that is not hierarchical. The hierarchical caste system in India is an expression of the Reptilian structure of control and division.

Traits of the reptilian brain include: Aggression [road rage is a classic], dominance, territoriality, ritual displays, obsessive compulsive behaviour; personal day-to-day rituals and superstitious acts; slavish conformance to old ways of doing things; ceremonial re-enactments; obeisance [deference] to precedent, as in legal, religious, cultural, and other matters and all manner of deceptions. Among reptilian traits are cold-bloodedness (no empathy); a desire for control; power; ownership; and a belief that might is right or winner takes all. The Reptilians and Global Cult to a 'T' and this reflects the traits of Yaldabaoth consciousness. There is also the tendency to worship which is another trait of the hierarchical mindset and opens the population to need a religious belief (5.4 billion of the 8 billion humans identify as either Christian, Muslim or Hindu, without adding all the others). Malfunctions of the reptilian brain leads to disorders relating to anxiety, mood, panic, phobias, and personality, along with 'intermittent explosive disorder' which triggers 'explosive outbursts of anger or violence, often to the point of rage, which are disproportionate to the situation at hand'. The reptilian brain connects with the amygdala in the middle of the brain which plays a key role in processing emotions and emotional reactions. These are central to the behaviour programs encoded in the body computer that can only be overridden by expanded states of consciousness.

I read the book *The Dragons of Eden* in the 1990s in which famed cosmologist Carl Sagan emphasised the massive impact of human reptilian genetics (information patterns) on behaviour. Sagan said we should not ignore the reptilian component of human nature because '... the model may help us understand what human beings are really about'. He highlighted ritualistic (repeating patterns) and hierarchical behaviour connected to the reptilian brain. 'Pheromone' is a chemical secreted in minute amounts that can affect behaviour between the same species. Pheromones in human women and iguanas are a chemical match. Those millions, even billions, who laugh and ridicule any suggestion of a reptilian connection to human society have no idea about any of this. They fall for the trap that if they cannot conceive the possibility then it can't exist even when they have done no research whatsoever on the subject. A few people can't control the world? *Doddle.*

Archon mind

Peruvian-born writer Carlos Castaneda published a series of books from the late 1960s from conversations with Don Juan Matus, a Central American Yaqui Indian healer or shaman. Castaneda's final book in

1998, *The Active Side of Infinity*, quoted Don Juan's warning about the 'Flyers' or 'predators' who had taken over the minds of humans and were turning us into them. The next stage to complete the transformation is to fuse humans with artificial intelligence which would connect the human mind to theirs like never before. What Don Juan Matus said can be found in different forms in ancient cultures across the world:

> We have a predator that came from the depths of the cosmos and took over the rule of our lives. Human beings are its prisoners. The predator is our lord and master. It has rendered us docile, helpless. If we want to protest, it suppresses our protest. If we want to act independently, it demands that we don't do so ... indeed we are held prisoner!
>
> They took us over because we are food to them, and they squeeze us mercilessly because we are their sustenance. Just as we rear chickens in coops, the predators rear us in human coops, humaneros. Therefore, their food is always available to them. Think for a moment, and tell me how you would explain the contradictions between the intelligence of man the engineer and the stupidity of his systems of belief, or the stupidity of his contradictory behaviour.

The line about 'we are food to them' will be explained in the next chapter. Don Juan said that sorcerers believed the predators gave us our systems of beliefs, our ideas of good and evil and 'our social mores'. They set up our dreams of success or failure and gave us covetousness, greed and cowardice. The predator had worked to make us complacent, routinary and egomaniacal:

> In order to keep us obedient and meek and weak, the predators engaged themselves in a stupendous manoeuvre – stupendous, of course, from the point of view of a fighting strategist; a horrendous manoeuvre from the point of those who suffer it. They gave us their mind. The predators' mind is baroque, contradictory, morose, filled with the fear of being discovered any minute now.

All true from my own research and experience over 36 years and a key connection point is the human reptilian brain. Don Juan Matus indicated that the predators operated from the shadows on the fringes of human perception or what I would call the Astral. When you hear that Reptilian entities and other non-human species come from this or that planet it is often dismissed because of the apparent 'lifeless' planet or star systems involved. Firstly, the perception and possibility of 'life' is related to what humans need to survive as if there is no other system of

Figure 72: The ancient reptilian god Morrop in the Peruvian city of Chiclayo. Morrop was the Iguana Man, a mediator between the world of the living and the dead.

Figure 73: A reptilian mother with baby figurine found from the Ubaid people who predated the Sumerians in Mesopotamia between an estimated 6500 and 3700 BC (although dates vary). Many such figures were discovered and became known as the 'Ubaid Lizardmen' (and women). Some are holding sceptres which became associated with royalty and power.

existence; and, secondly, the planets and stars have other dimensional levels which operate in the Astral. The 'planet' may look very different in those dimensions. People talk about 'extraterrestrials' in the sense of other species within our material realm when I prefer to call them interdimensionals who can move in and out of the human band of frequency. They can even operate in our frequency while being shielded from human sight with energetic fields known as 'Invisibility Cloaks' or shields.

They were considered 'god-like' for their abilities and technology and there are many statues, figurines and symbolic representations around the world of the 'serpent gods' (Figs 72, 73, and 74). The Reptilian structure is both hierarchical and factional with different groups fighting among themselves for dominance while seeking the same goal of human control. Hybrid reptilian-human bloodlines infused into the Global Cult mean that this factionalism is transferred to the Cult although with an overall dominant force that bangs heads together if it gets out of hand and threatens the objective. The so-called 'Draco' are top of the Reptilian hierarchy and the 'royalty' who are fierce warriors and super-psychopaths who again pass on their traits to their underlings. Members of the human Cult serve them through a terror of failing to obey and succeed. They seek to absorb humanity even more comprehensively into the Reptilian hive mind via AI. The Orion star system in its Astral manifestation is

The Archons

Figure 74: Kukulkan, the Plumed Serpent and Amazing Serpent of Mayan mythology in Central America. The reptilian god Quetzalcoatl or Feathered Serpent was worshipped in Aztec Mexico.

a major reptilian stronghold. Astral dimensions of planets and star systems have portals through which they can enter the frequency band of matter. Saturn a the major one of which more to come.

Archons under other names

The Roman Church which compiled the Bible rejected Gnostic texts which highlighted the Archons although some references survived without direct identification. We should also remember that the New Testament was first written in 'Koine' or 'Hellenistic' Greek while Greek was the third language translation of the Old Testament after Hebrew and Aramaic which is referred to as the 'Septuagint'. The first known complete translation of the Bible into English (handwritten) wasn't until 1382 and was from the Roman Church Latin, not the original Hebrew or Greek (very significant later). The point being that the Greek word for ruler was 'archon' and later translations including into English would have interpreted that word as *human* rulers when at least some references could have meant something else. Even then Bible texts refer to 'spiritual' controllers. Satan and the Devil, of course, but there are clear mentions of multiple 'heavenly' (beyond human) forces in the plural. Biblical hero 'Paul the Apostle' ('Saul of Tarsus') is attributed with this quote in the Epistle to the Ephesians: 'For our struggle is not against flesh and blood, but against the rulers, against the authorities, against the powers of this dark world and against the spiritual forces of evil in the heavenly realms.' I will have far more detail in later chapters about what the Bible really says, who the Biblical heroes really were, and how this relates to the human story.

'Pantheons of gods' can be found as a focus of worship all over the world and they are the Archons/demons under different names which have been recorded as 'gods'. We have Zeus and the well-known Greek Pantheon of again *twelve* 'Olympian' gods and goddesses who demanded worship from all their subjects (just like the Archons). Those who failed to do so would suffer horrendous punishment (see the continuation of this with the Roman Church and its Inquisition). We are simply witnessing the same continuing stream of the same beliefs in a different guise. The Greek pantheon is only one example of these Archontic 'gods'. Others include: African pantheons; Armenian pantheon; Aztec pantheon; Berber pantheon; Burmese pantheon; Canaanite pantheon; Celtic pantheon; Chinese pantheon; Egyptian pantheon; Germanic pantheon; Greek pantheon; Hindu pantheon; Incan pantheon; Irish pantheon; Jain pantheon; Japanese pantheon; Japanese Buddhist pantheon; Maya pantheon; Native American pantheons; Norse pantheon; Roman pantheon; Slavic pantheon; Assyrian pantheon; Babylonian pantheon; Sumerian pantheon. These are the same Archon and demonic rulers known by different names in different cultures.

They were and are the focus of human and animal sacrifice and why that is will be addressed in the next chapter. Pagans worshipped them and Christians, Jews, Muslims and others still worship them while believing they are 'God' and 'angels of God' which operate in the usual Archontic hierarchies that are also expressed through the Global Cult in the human realm. Judaism was a multi-god religion before it fused them into one and the same with the religions of Arabia before the alleged arrival of Muhammad (said to have lived from 570-632 AD). Today 'elite' initiates of the Global Cult of secret societies continue to worship these fake 'gods' in the knowledge of who the Archons really are. These are the 'gods' to which sacrifice continues to be performed in Satanic rituals worldwide. Zulu high shaman Credo Mutwa told me that according to Zulu legend it was a reptilian other-dimensional race that introduced cannibalism. The Christian biblical theme of God demanding worship originates with this Yaldabaoth and Archon background. No loving god would insist that people fell to their knees and bowed their head in worship and reverence, but Yaldabaoth and the Archons demand exactly that.

Spirit and Creation is an extension of the Infinite Mind and Archons are inferior extensions (mini copies) of the inferior Yaldabaoth Mind ('Yaldabaoth derivatives'). Other entities in the Archontic hierarchy, known as demons, are extensions of the Archon Mind ('Archon derivatives') and together they form the ruling force behind the multi-dimensional simulation which the Global Cult serves and obeys within human reality. Archons are described as formless energetic states as I mentioned. This reflects the Yaldabaoth original, and Archons have the same limited creative potential. Gnostic writings refer to the 'formless ones', but mind projection means they can take any form they choose to suit their agenda. Archons are a fusion of male and female with the faces of beasts, according to Gnostic texts. Nag Hammadi *Origin of the World* says: 'And they were born androgynous, consistent with the immortal pattern that existed before them.'

Archons can possess humans in their energetic state, including members of the Global Cult, or they can appear as an 'alien' or human being. Key members of the Global Cult inner circle will be full-blown incarnations or manifestations of the Archontic force. They remind me of Agent Smith in the *Matrix* movies in that Yaldabaoth created the Archons as 'software' mini copies of itself and like Smith they are able to move in and out of 'material' reality to manipulate events while the population in the movies had no idea there even was a simulation. Agents like Smith were just like them on the face of it. My goodness the times I have had described to me experiences with 'humans' who were anything but human. I have seen them myself sometimes and they can often be identified by a very different energetic 'vibe' or signature with eyes that tell you they are not what they claim to be. Kenneth Copeland is a famous Christian evangelist in the United States whose eyes scream to me 'Archon' or Archon derivative. Trump invited him to the White House at Easter 2025 and he's spoken at Trump rallies. Copeland said that a vision revealed to him that Jesus would hold to account anyone who voted against Trump or didn't bother to vote. God help us might be an appropriate response.

The Schism inversion

The Gnostic reference to Yaldabaoth and Archons as the 'forces of chaos' is most appropriate. I see their foundation state as an energetic frequency distortion, an inversion of everything represented by the Infinite. While that is balance, wisdom, love and harmony, the Yaldabaoth distortion is *im*balance, foolishness, evil and *dis*harmony. Evil is really an energetic distortion and written backwards it reads 'live'. It is an inversion of life. Observe human society and you will see how it is founded on inversion. Writer Michael Ellner said: 'Doctors destroy health, lawyers destroy justice, psychiatrists destroy minds, scientists destroy truth, major media destroys information, religions destroy spirituality and governments destroy freedom.' Everything is upside down because of the Archontic distortion – inversion. It is like a schism penetrating everything including the human mind through which society is a projection of the schism. It is war, conflict, upsets and upheavals. It is the schism between people, cultures, religions, politics and belief systems in general. It is hunger in a world of plenty, illness, suffering and deprivation – all of which are the distortion/inversion made manifest. Only those that can reconnect with the balance of Spirit can restore themselves to harmony in a world of utter madness. Which is what? What is this *madness*? It is distortion and inversion. You see the schism at work from the multiple dimensions of the simulation to the lives of individuals.

Native Americans have the concept of 'Wetiko' which they describe as a mind virus. Wetiko is the name used by the Cree people in Canada and the northern United States. Others have variations of that. The most prominent researcher into Wetiko is Paul Levy, author of *Dispelling Wetiko, Breaking the Spell of Evil*. I have also read the work of Native American writer Jack D. Forbes with his *Columbus And Other Cannibals – The Wetiko Disease of Exploitation, Imperialism, and Terrorism*. I was intrigued by the Wetiko concept because I had referred to a 'mind virus' infecting the human psyche long before I came across Wetiko. It reminded me immediately of the Gnostic Archons. Wherever you look with anything from Christianity to Gnosticism to Islam to Judaism to Native Americans, Zulus, and other native peoples, you find the recurring theme of a hidden force seeking to negatively influence and direct humanity. Wetiko is a 'sickness of the Soul' devoid of compassion, empathy, love, respect (including self-respect). Top traits of psychopaths are having no empathy or compassion. I call empathy the fail-safe mechanism of human behaviour in that the ability to put yourself in the feelings of those you affect will temper how you will treat them. Psychopaths by contrast get a high from making others suffer. Wetiko is the psychopath and super psychopath which is a perfect description of Yaldabaoth, Archons, demons, and their minions and servants in the Global Cult.

Behaviour of Cult operatives such as Klaus Schwab, Bill Gates, Donald Trump and the Big Tech billionaire hierarchy including Elon Musk perfectly express the traits of Wetiko which wants to crush any opposition and silence their own exposure. Wetiko is the empathy deleted banker, lawyer, politician, government official, CEO, and 'Big Tech bro'. As I wrote in *The Dream*: It is Stalin, Lenin, Mao, Pol Pot, Putin, Zelensky, Biden, Trump, Obama, the Clintons, Bushes, and their like around the world. It is corporate greed and the merciless dictator. It is the hater and those who hate the hater (see the Woke mentality). It is the violent tyrant and the violent opposer of the tyrant. Wars are Wetiko fighting itself. I have long said that what you fight you become because Wetiko infuses both 'ends' of that electrical circuit. We don't need to fight. We need to cease to cooperate which we can do calmly and with unbreakable determination without getting Wetiko involved. Levy says Wetiko is a 'frigid, icy heart, devoid of mercy' and you have Gnostic Nag Hammadi texts saying that the Archon effect on humanity was to close their hearts. Jack D. Forbes contends that 'tragically, the history of the world for the past 2,000 years is, in great part, the story of the epidemiology of the Wetiko disease'. I agree in the wider sense of Wetiko, but its influence is well beyond 2,000 years. Paul Levy describes how '… the subtle body of wetiko is not located in the third dimension of space and time, literally existing in another dimension … it is able to affect ordinary lives by mysteriously interpenetrating into our three-dimensional world.' See how this syncs with what I am saying? Levy uses a lower-case 'w' in Wetiko while I prefer the capital. He makes this interesting observation:

> A vampire has no intrinsic, independent, substantial existence in its own right; it only exists in relation to us. The pathogenic, vampiric mind-parasite called wetiko is nothing in itself – not being able to exist from its own side – yet it has a virtual reality such that it can potentially destroy our species …
>
> … The fact that a vampire is not reflected by a mirror can also mean that what we need to see is that there's nothing, no-thing to see, other than ourselves. The fact that wetiko is the expression of something inside of us means that the cure for wetiko is with us as well. The critical issue is finding this cure within us and then putting it into effect.

I agree with most of that view although I differ slightly in this way. New readers will see in the next chapter why Yaldabaoth and the Archons cannot exist without the humans they abuse. I agree that Wetiko/Archons represent the dark or 'shadow' aspect of humans. My question is why Spirit, our true identity outside the simulation, should have a 'dark side'. The answer is that the Divine Spark is trapped within endless Yaldabaoth/Archon created energetic fields ('bodies') known as the human body, Soul, astral body, etheric body, mental body, and so on, which are constantly feeding us fake self-identities. This directs our *attention* on these constructed identities which diminishes and blocks the influence of the Divine Spark and through that the Infinite. Physicist Werner Heisenberg said: 'The more closely you look at one thing, the less closely can you see something else.' Focus on the twig and you won't see the forest. The more this process expands the more the human fake identity itself begins to generate Wetiko/Archon frequencies to form a 'dark side' that can be ever more easily impacted by the source of that 'dark side' – the Archontic manipulation that Native Americans call Wetiko. In other words, the human 'dark side' has been manufactured and then expanded by the schism and inversion.

The body program

The Archontic influence on human behaviour is even more fundamental in that there are programs – akin to software programs or algorithms – encoded in the biological computer, or body. The current human form remember was created by the force behind the simulation to interact with the simulation. It's the same with the 'Soul' and other energetic fields which marginalise the Divine Spark. Anyone think they are going to simply create a material body to allow incarnations into this energetic density without having a 'back door' in the way that they are encoded into computer systems to allow real time access for nefarious reasons? Nag Hammadi texts claim that Archons in creating the human body as we know it ensured that it was subject to their influence to the point where it is a serious challenge to resist. Humans were subject to ongoing demonic possession you could say. Those that think body programs are too far out might look at stem cells which can be programmed to develop into any cell function (Fig 75). The body is

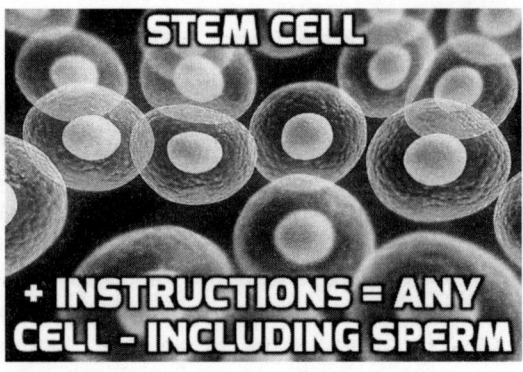

Figure 75: Stem cells can be encoded to have many functions.

programmable for sure. Only by reconnection with the Divine Spark and Infinite Reality can this be overcome. This is the age-old dynamic of good and evil. The body-program encodes the cycle from birth to death and what we call ageing. Changes in the body identified at different ages, including brain function, are the program at work. There is no reason for a hologram to age unless there is a program to make it so, but the program can be overridden. The simulation field itself with which we are constantly exchanging information like an interactive Internet is feeding us low-vibrational Archontic frequencies to trigger mental and emotional responses for reasons that will become very clear.

We can counter this by expanding our awareness through self-identity with the Divine Spark and by 'gnosis' – knowing what is going on and the nature of our plight. Paul Levy writes: 'Holographically enforced within the psyche of every human being the wetiko virus pervades and underlies the entire field of consciousness and can therefore potentially manifest through any one of us at any moment if we are not mindful.' All true. Wetiko 'pervades and underlies the entire field of consciousness' because it is encoded in the simulation field and body programs. The only way to overcome its influence is not to fall down the octaves into its frequency lair. All addiction whether to drugs, alcohol, gambling, sex, whatever, will take you there and that's why addictions abound. They take you into the dark places where Wetiko (the Archontic force) waits to ensnare you.

Archons encoded everywhere

Gnostic documents differ on the number of Archons, but they are often said to have been seven at first and they are related to the seven heavenly bodies known to exist by the ancients – the Sun, Moon, Mercury, Venus, Mars, Jupiter, and Saturn. This is also the origin of the 'seven princes of the underworld' and 'seven Princes of Hell'. Seven is another recurring number as in the 'seven deadly sins' of pride, greed, wrath, envy, lust, gluttony, and sloth. Ancients spoke of seven layers of Heaven, seven layers of Hell, and we have seven spirits of God mentioned in Revelation. The number seven appears more than 700 times in the Bible which is ablaze with numerological, astrological and other symbolism. 'God' (Yaldabaoth and the Archons) is said in Genesis to have created the world in … seven days. The Archon numbers related to planets may just be symbolism, but symbols often carry a theme of truth. Gnostics connected Archons to pagan gods and the seven days of the week were assigned to locations in the heavens. Jewish traditions speak of seven archangels serving God and the archangel concept was absorbed by Christianity. Is it really a coincidence – seven Gnostic Archons and seven archangels?

Gnostic texts say seven archons ruled over their own celestial sphere and were designated different areas of Lower Aeons which mimics the descriptions of different Upper Aeons designated to expressions of the Infinite in a similar way. This adds to the significance of astrology which I say is a highly relevant aspect of the trap with its influence on human perception and behaviour. I have said that it's good to be aware of astrological energies so you can flow with them rather than against, but we need to understand they are part of the simulation. They are connected to 'fate', another simulation trap, which I'll have more about in the chapter on reincarnation. Cycles of 'time' and epochs which include the belief in the yuga cycles of the East and Mayan time cycles in Central America are different phases of the simulation. The phases form together an interconnected loop of apparently forward-moving 'time' that is actually going 'round and round' in a series of Time Loops. See my 2003 book, *Tales From The Time Loop*. It is like sitting on a carousel horse trying to catch the one in front. You can't. The system is rigged to stop you – but consciousness can overcome anything given that consciousness is *manifesting* everything according to its state of perception.

Saturn was especially significant to Gnostics as a symbol and extension of Yaldabaoth/the Demiurge. Saturnian frequencies are very important to the simulation frequency in the material world and Saturn is depicted as the god of time which is fundamental to the simulation illusion. I became interested in Saturn when I saw the profuse Saturn symbolism employed throughout society by the Global Cult, and it led me on an amazing journey to understand Saturn's significance to the simulation together with the Moon. I have explained this in detail in *Everything You Need To Know But Have Never Been Told*. It is quite a story, and I'll touch on some of the Saturn symbolism in a later chapter. The term 'Saturnine' refers to a gloomy, taciturn temperament related since ancient times to the influence of Saturn. Astrological traits for Saturn include being cold and non-emotive and representing limitation, austerity, discipline and depression. Saturn in Hindu Vedic astrology is linked with the lower chakra that represents basic survival needs and the fear of threats to survival. These are traits of the reptilian brain. Saturday or Saturn's day is the Jewish Sabbath and central to their religion.

Archon 'royalty'

Another extraordinary discovery from the ancient world that reveals a belief in non-human 'supernatural' entities are thousands of clay tablets and fragments that I will call the Sumerian Tablets compiled by societies in Mesopotamia – 'The Land Between Two Rivers' – that today we know as Iraq and part of Syria. The two rivers are the Tigris and Euphrates where once was located Sumer from 3,000 years BC, or earlier, and the later Akkad, Assyria and Babylon in the same region. Shinar, the biblical name for Sumer, means 'The Land of the Watchers' and 'Watchers' is another name used by the ancients to describe 'supernatural beings' (Astral entities with advanced technology) as we saw with the Book of Enoch. Shinar/Sumer was known by the Egyptians as Ta Neter which has the same Watcher connotation. Sumer was so advanced it has been labelled the 'Cradle of Civilisation'. Its architecture, arts, mathematics, astronomy, and societal structure was way ahead of its 'time'. Where did this knowledge suddenly come from? I would say that Sumer was the 'cradle' of *re*-civilisation after cataclysmic events symbolised as the Great Flood deleted an advanced pre-flood society. These cataclysms are in the biological and geological record of the planet and really happened as we'll explore. Sumerians believed in an array of gods to whom humans were servants and the Tablets say they ruled as and through kings and 'royalty' for some 240,000 years after 'descending from heaven'. The Tablets include the Sumerian Creation Myth and flood story long before the Noah version and tell how the gods created humanity as we know it and instigated the concept of royalty or 'kingship'. Reptilian symbolism is widely associated with 'royalty'. One example is the Celts in Europe with their title Pendragon, the 'Great Dragon' or Draco, and 'King of Kings'.

For sure genetic lines, or bloodlines, 'of the gods' are central to the Global Cult to this day and they have a wider visual range that can see deeper into reality which allows them to see what non-bloodline humans cannot. I have told of my experience with Satanist paedophile UK prime minister Edward Heath as we sat alone in a *Sky News* make-up room in the late 1980s when he was literally scanning me with his eyes while having a very inquisitive look on his face. As he did so, the whole of his eyes, including the whites, turned deep black and it was like looking through portals into another dimension. These people are not like the rest of us (Fig 76). I would later realise that the same

Figure 77: Jimmy Savile was a mega paedophile and Satanist who was protected for his role as a procurer of children for the rich and famous elite.

Figure 76: Edward Heath's eyes turned jet black including the whites.

phenomenon has been reported by many around the world. An Internet article on the subject said: 'A human-looking being with pure black eyes (including the normally white parts) will approach a person at their home or car, asking to be let in.' They would usually have a 'very dry' personality, almost no personality at all, but when refused entry they got very agitated. 'Most people describe a feeling of intense dread and fear when in the presence of these Black-Eyed Beings, but they can't say exactly why', the article reported.

Years later I would expose Edward Heath as a paedophile/Satanist in *The Biggest Secret* while he was still alive and a Member of Parliament. Another 17 years after that Wiltshire Police in England began an investigation into the then diseased Heath with regard to paedophilia and concluded that if he were still alive there was enough evidence to bring him in for questioning. Heath was a friend of notorious BBC 'entertainer' paedophile Jimmy Savile who procured children for the rich and famous which is how his record-breaking paedophilia was allowed to go unchecked by police and the authorities who well knew what he was doing (Fig 77). Savile was also a friend of UK Prime Minister Margaret Thatcher and her husband and the then Prince Charles and his father Prince Philip. Charlie was close to him right up to Savile's death (Fig 78). Charles used him as a go-between when his marriage to Princess Diana was breaking down

Figure 78: Prince, now King, Charles was a long-time friend of Jimmy Savile.

(Fig 79). I established through a friend of Princess Diana in the 1990s that she had contempt for Savile. The royal family invited Savile into their inner circle in the 1960s via his friend and paedophile Lord Mountbatten who

Figure 79: Princess Diana couldn't stand Savile and said he gave her the creeps.

was a 'mentor' to Charles and Philip. The idea that the police knew of Savile's paedophilia (and did nothing), but the royal family *didn't know* is utterly ridiculous. So, what is the real reason he became so close to the royals? See *The Perception Deception* for the detailed background. I have highlighted in many books how Reptilians, other Astral entities, and their hybrid human offspring are obsessed with the energy of children.

Royalty and aristocracy claim to be special bloodlines, or 'blue bloods', and this is the origin of the 'Divine Right To Rule' although it has nothing to do with the Divine and far more to do with Archons and their demonic Astral subordinates. 'Royal' and 'aristocratic' families have inbred incessantly through the ages to protect the hybrid codes which dissipate rapidly when interbred with non-hybrids. I quoted Christine Fitzgerald, a long-time friend of Princess Diana, in my 1998 book, *The Biggest Secret*. She told me (as others have) that the British royal family are human-reptilian hybrids:

> The royal family hasn't died for a long time, they have just metamorphosed. It's sort of cloning, but in a different way. They take pieces of flesh and rebuild the body from one little bit …The different bodies are just different electrical vibrations, and they have that secret, they've got the secret of the microcurrents. It's so micro, so specific, these radio waves that actually create the bodies.

Fast forward nearly 30 years to 2025 and the American biotechnology and genetic engineering company Colossal Biosciences claimed that it used 'deft genetic engineering and ancient DNA' to breed three members of the 'dire wolf' species that went extinct more than 10,000 years ago. The company said: 'These wolves were brought back from extinction using genetic edits derived from a complete dire wolf genome, meticulously reconstructed by Colossal from ancient DNA found in fossils dating back 11,500 and 72,000 years.' Paleogeneticist Dr

Nic Rawlence from Otago University in New Zealand said the de-extinction team employed new synthetic biology technology and used ancient DNA to identify key segments of code that they could edit into the biological blueprint of a living animal. 'So, what Colossal has produced is a grey wolf, but it has some dire wolf-like characteristics, like a larger skull and white fur – it's a hybrid.' The point is that they took genetic codes, some ancient, and created a living entity. What can be done with genetics outside the public arena? Colossal Biosciences co-founder and lead geneticist George Church said: 'We can clone all kinds of mammals, so it's very likely that we could clone a human; Why shouldn't we be able to do so? Laws can change, by the way.'

Agents of the 'gods'

I have contended since the 1990s that these genetic lines are hybrids between 'gods' and humans that allow Astral entities to walk among us while hiding behind apparent human form. The entities are often reptilian in appearance, although not always, and they are recorded in statues throughout history depicting them and their dual nature (Fig 80). Hybrids have two energetic information fields. One carries the human genetic information blueprint and the other the reptilian or non-human. The human field is the dominant one in any public setting for obvious reasons, but I have written at length how people have witnessed the switch from human to non-human in what is called 'shapeshifting'. This often happens during Satanic rituals when they are among 'friends' and like hybrids. Shapeshifting is not 'physical' because there is no physical. It is the process of decoding information. The

Figure 80: Symbolising the human-Reptilian hybrid 'demi-gods'.

human field is decoded by any observer into an apparently 'solid' human body. When the *non*-human field becomes the dominant one, the observer decodes the second field and appears to see someone transform *physically* from a human to non-human state. It's an illusion of the decoding process and happens through a shift in the hybrid *information* field from human to non-human. I have had this described to me all over the world by those who have experienced seeing people shift from human to reptilian or other non-human form. See *The Biggest Secret, Children of the Matrix, The Perception Deception*, and others. Hybrid bloodlines are vehicles for Archontic entities to enter human reality and they dominate the inner core of the Global Cult.

The Sumerian Tablets describe a non-human group known as the Anunna, or Anunnaki, who are said to have forced humans to mine for gold in Africa where there is evidence of gold mining 100,000 years ago (with the proviso about time and history). The Tablets say the Anunnaki were led by two 'brothers', Enlil and Enki, who answered to their 'father', Anu, the 'Lord of the Sky'. They were known as the 'Neteru' to Egyptians and by other names in other cultures. South African Zulu accounts tell a similar story about a reptilian race that forced humans to mine for gold led by two brothers, Wowane and Mpanku. They were known as the 'water brothers' and Mesopotamian accounts of the Anunnaki symbolise one of their brothers, Enki (Ea to the Babylonians), as the god of fresh waters. They are obviously versions of the same story, and both accounts have the theme of the Anunnaki instigating the cataclysmic events that ended the pre-flood global society. Sumerian Tablets describe how Enki warned a human 'priest-king' called Ziusudra of the coming flood and gave instructions to build a huge ship and take aboard 'beasts and birds'. Flood story heroes can be found throughout the world with the later invention of Noah the most famous in the Old Testament.

Detail may differ across the ages, religions, and cultures as you would expect, but what are the common agreements? These include a global cataclysm or Great Flood; the interbreeding of 'gods' and humans; a 'fall from paradise'; and the manipulation of human society by a non-human force under many names and descriptions. Next comes the question of how this force benefits from its simulation fantasia and perceptual control. Why do they do it?

CHAPTER 6

Loosh Farm

Loosh is a hyperdimensional energy given off by the human soul when traumatized. The Archons parasitically feed on it.
Sol Luckman, Cali the Destroyer

Why would this Yaldabaoth consciousness go to all the trouble to create a simulation to enslave humans in perceptual servitude? I mean, what's the point? Oh, there *is* a point.

Yaldabaoth consciousness and subordinate Archons serving its interests are sealed off from the Gnostic Upper Aeons and are not able to access the life force energy emanating from the Infinite. All is still One and can never not be so, but it is a matter of degree. How connected are we to the Source of All? In the case of Yaldabaoth and its minions the answer is 'not very'. Emanations from the Source give us imagination and creativity as well as energetic sustenance and the vibrational distance between Yaldabaoth and the Source means that sustenance, imagination and creativity are denied their true potential. Imagine a symbolic light in the darkness. The further and further away you are from the light, the darker it becomes and the less influence the light has on reality. This had to be overcome when Yaldabaoth instigated its simulated 'kingdom'.

Remember that the simulation is not a unique creation but a *copy* of Prime Reality with the frequencies, codes and fractal patterns 'downloaded'. This fits with the Gnostic contention that Yaldabaoth consciousness can mimic what has already been created while lacking the imagination and potential to create uniquely in the absence of Source energy. Yaldabaoth is like a version of artificial intelligence which will become ever more relevant the longer the book goes on. Distance from the Source also denies the energy of balance (love and wisdom) and we have Yaldabaoth called 'The Blind One', and 'The Foolish One' who is 'stupefied in his madness'. Yaldabaoth is not very bright (literally) and yet 'clever' in the sense of hoarding knowledge about the simulation and its workings while ensuring that humans are imprisoned by ignorance. If I know what you don't know, and I keep that from you, I can appear to be clever or intelligent when if you know what I know, we are playing on an equal field. The game is rigged for this reason, and we'll see how that pans out in human society.

Many humans have within them the Divine Spark that was originally trapped when the simulation door was closed. We may not often see its influence, but it's there maintaining, however tenuously, a connection to the Source. This is where human creativity comes from, and Yaldabaoth has set up a simulated system in which it trawls and vampires that energy for sustenance and imagination. Except that it is not *its* imagination, it is *Source* imagination via human imagination. Put another way, it manipulates humans to create their own prison, and this will become obvious as we observe human society and interaction. I have used the Yaldabaoth/Global Cult banking system as an example. Banks lend fake 'money' that doesn't exist called 'credit' and charge interest to those who seek a loan to finance an expansion of their creativity. Banks are vampires feeding off the creativity of the population while lending fake 'money' at interest. Should the creative not be able to repay (often because of financial downturns initiated by the banks) then the product of the creativity – businesses, homes, land, possessions, resources – go to the banks. This is called the boom-and-bust cycle when it's pure manipulation to vampire the creativity of the people. The hijacking this way of Divine Spark creativity has long allowed the demonic banking and other connected networks to seize control of human society and exploit the creativity of the population.

Human batteries

Our thoughts and emotional reactions generate energetic vibrations that match the frequency of that thought or emotion. This has been long established by mainstream science. Fear, anxiety, hatred, resentment, regret, depression and ignorance produce low, slow, frequencies while love, wisdom, joy, and expanded awareness are high, fast, frequencies. The more you expand your awareness the higher and quicker your frequency becomes. Keeping people in ignorance is vital for Archontic control on many levels and among them is the effect on frequency. I have featured the work over the years of my late friend, Dr Masaru Emoto, a Japanese researcher who became well known for his techniques photographing the impact of frequency and vibration on water crystals. Everything is a frequency field in its foundation state within the simulation and all is impacted by frequency influences. Water and words are no different. The written word and its intent generate the same frequency as the spoken word. Dr Emoto would write messages reflecting love or hate, balance or imbalance, on the side of water containers and freeze them very quickly before photographing the crystals. The difference in the effect on the water is fantastic. Words of love and balance make beautiful geometrically balanced water crystals while those of hate and imbalance are a distorted mess (Fig 81).

We know that spoken words are frequencies generated by the vocal cords which the sound senses and the brain decode into the words that we 'hear'. Written words are the same. They generate frequencies that represent the *intent* behind them. You can say 'piss off' in a jokey fashion and it will not produce the same frequencies as saying 'piss off' with anger and menace. Intent is the power behind thought. The greater the intent the greater the power to impact on quantum reality and bring what you want into manifestation. Perceptions that lack clear intent – 'I don't know what I want' – will manifest a 'material' experience version of 'I don't know what I want'. You will say 'nothing seems to work out for me', but it can't work out when 'I don't know what I want'. Dr Emoto experimented with polluted water (it distorted crystals), mobile phones attached to the canisters (ditto), and various types of music (balanced or imbalanced depending on the vibrations). He also found that 'prayer' (focused intent) could restore balance to the water and crystals (Fig 82). Mind (frequencies) and words (frequencies), either spoken or written, can therefore impact upon the reality field and change its nature. The simulation is constantly infused with distorted low-vibrational frequencies both directly from Archontic sources or by humans manipulated into low-vibrational states. Okay, so why? Because they are *feeding* off human energy or 'loosh' as it has become known among researchers of the subject. *We* are their sustenance.

Figure 81: Water crystals infused with the vibration from words of love and hate. No difference, then?

Figure 82: Prayer is concentrated thought and intent and can change the nature of energy fields as with this example.

Yaldabaoth and its servant Archons known by many different names in many cultures (like the Christian 'demons') are low vibrational phenomena because their state of being and perception make it so. Their frequency states match those of low vibrational thought and emotion.

Yaldabaoth and its entities generate and absorb those frequencies by manipulating humanity into low-vibrational mental and emotional states. This is hardly difficult when you control the very reality that humans experience while believing they are living in a 'natural' world created by either 'God' or the Big Bang fantasy. You manipulate via your entities and the Global Cult of secret societies within human reality to ensure a constant flow of war, conflict, deprivation, suffering, despair, and challenge which generate a constant and enormous flow of collective low-vibrational energy or loosh.

Loosh triggers

Yaldabaoth consciousness expressed through the Archons and their demonic emanations is still running the show. This force doesn't care why you go to war, why you fight and conflict, so long as you *do*. Mmm – loosh. Yaldabaoth and the Archons *are* fear and thus fear is their prime source of energy. The Nag Hammadi *Dialogue of the Saviour* says that 'truly, fear is the power [of the Rulers].' Fear and connected emotions are both their food and currency of control. Anyone still wonder why there are constant reasons for people to fear? Gnostics called Archons 'parasites' and this is what they are – literally feeding off human energy. They said Archons were responsible for all the destructive behaviour of humans but look at how humans are blamed for what happens which leads to more guilt, despair and sense of hopelessness. *Apocryphon of John* describes how Archons induce humanity into loosh production through perpetuation of ignorance:

> And they steered the people who had followed them into great troubles, by leading them astray with many deceptions. They [the people] became old without having enjoyment. They died, not having found truth and without knowing the God of truth.

> And thus, the whole creation became enslaved forever, from the foundation of the world until now. And they took women and begot children out of the darkness according to the likeness of their spirit. And they closed their hearts, and they hardened themselves through the hardness of the counterfeit spirit until now.

A state of ignorance itself carries a dense frequency that can be absorbed as loosh. The energetic core within Divine Spark humans is our connection to the Source and this is expressed in part as 'loosh' in our mental and especially emotional responses. The Divine Spark is Source energy and reflects the Source in its pure untouched state; but as it is filtered through other levels of being like the Soul, and especially the human body, this Source energy is impregnated with low-vibrational responses which makes it absorbable to the hidden controllers. Loosh is the human creative force and Yaldabaoth consciousness and its demonic Archontic horde are absorbing this energy and creative potential to recycle back against us. Morpheus in a

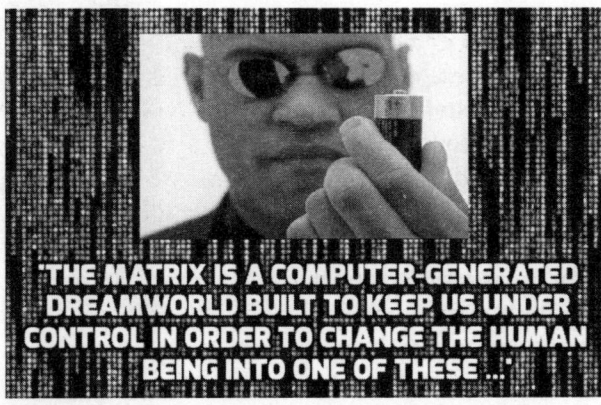

Figure 83: A profound truth in an apparently fictional movie.

Matrix movie holds up a battery and spoke a profound truth when he said: 'The Matrix is a computer-generated dream world built to keep us under control in order to change the human being into one of these' (Fig 83). This is what we are to these demons – an access point to energetic 'food' in the same way that farm animals relate to humans. You'll recognise the comparison with how both are treated from Palestinians in Gaza to factory farm chickens. This is what Don Juan Matus meant in the Castaneda book when he said:

> They took us over because we are food to them, and they squeeze us mercilessly because we are their sustenance. Just as we rear chickens in coops, the predators rear us in human coops, humaneros. Therefore, their food is always available to them.

Loosh is generated by the Divine Spark as it taps into the infinite divine essence, but other levels of awareness like the Soul and human body are unaware of this and believe it just to be their inspired thought or creative abilities. This low-vibrational infusion as it passes through the levels of ignorance transforms the loosh both into a frequency state the hidden controllers can consume and directs that creativity into 'physical' activities. This can include, for example, the less than divine development of weapons of mass murder. Creativity is to create. *What you create depends on the consciousness doing the creating.* Simulation controllers have no interest in humanity being in a high-vibrational state for multiple reasons. They are terrified of us reconnecting with the Infinite which would be game over for them and they cannot absorb energy beyond a certain band of frequency. War, conflict, despair, depression, anxiety and, most importantly *fear*, are not generated through random events and situations. It is systematic to produce low-vibrational loosh that the Archontic can absorb. Pain, illness, ageing and the decay of body processes and functions are all encoded into the body program to generate loosh.

Then there is the addiction to emotional states and drama for the same reason. We all know people addicted to drama and to the emotions of worry, anxiety, and depression (Fig 84). Emotions are frequencies and the body can become so synchronised with these frequencies, and their chemical expression, that people go into emotional cold turkey when they have nothing to be worried, anxious, or depressed about.

Figure 84: Drama, drama, drama. You'll never guess what's happened.

The response is to find something to make the frequency/chemical fix flow again and loosh can be restored. You will notice how in the presence of some people you can feel drained because they are stealing your energy even though they may not be aware of that. It's the same principle. There are now many technological means of trawling loosh. People find themselves drained when they are in the presence of strong electromagnetic fields with which our environment is now deluged thanks to towers and low-orbit satellites from Elon Musk's SpaceX and others. The unfolding connection between AI and the human brain is planned to be a full-blown fusion to allow thought and emotion to be externally delivered and produce loosh on demand. The fact that the 'natural world' is a killing frenzy of survival by the predator at the expense of the prey – plus the constant fear of that happening – is another stupendous source of loosh that is constant and never ends.

Astral loosh

We see how people are feeling emotionally by their body language, their eyes and facial features. We can't see the frequencies those emotions are emitting because they operate well beyond visible light, and they flow into the Astral realm where the demonic entities absorb them. Monsters, Inc., an animated Disney movie, symbolised this when it portrayed a monster world which had no energy source. They had power stations in which the monsters stood in line and a stream of bedroom doors were placed before them that gave access to the human realm. They would walk through the door into a human child's bedroom to frighten them. The child's scream was caught by the monster in a tube, and he would return through the door with the energy to power his world. The key character was a green monster with a single giant eye – the all-seeing eye which is a major symbol of the Cult and its non-human masters (Fig

Loosh Farm

Figure 85: The all-seeing eye in Monsters, Inc. as the monsters powered their world with the fear of children.

85). The symbolism of the movie is obvious from what I am saying here. Rudolf Steiner (1861-1925), the Austrian philosopher and esoteric thinker, exposed these energetic vampires. Steiner is famous for establishing Waldorf education or Steiner schools with the aim of encouraging children to think outside the box of mainstream 'education' (programming). He said this about what Gnostics call the Archons:

> There are beings in the spiritual realms [Lower Aeons beyond the five senses] for whom anxiety and fear emanating from human beings offer welcome food. When humans have no anxiety and fear, then these creatures starve. If fear and anxiety radiates from people and they break out in panic, then these creatures find welcome nutrition and they become more and more powerful. These beings are hostile towards humanity.
>
> Everything that feeds on negative feelings, on anxiety, fear and superstition, despair or doubt, are in reality hostile forces in super-sensible worlds, launching cruel attacks on human beings, while they are being fed ... These are exactly the feelings that belong to contemporary culture and materialism; because it estranges people from the spiritual world, it is especially suited to evoke hopelessness and fear of the unknown in people, thereby calling up the above mentioned hostile forces against them.

This accurately describes the human plight.

Left-Right harmony

The term 'loosh' was coined by Robert Monroe (1915-1995), a radio broadcasting executive who wrote a series of books, including *Journeys Out of the Body*, which popularised 'Astral travelling' or 'out-of-body-experiences' (OBE). These differ from near-death experiences (NDE) in which the body briefly dies to release consciousness into another dimension. Astral travellers project their consciousness into the Astral realm while the body is still very much alive. Monroe perfected the technique and worked with psychologists, psychiatrists, doctors, biochemists, and electrical engineers on what he called 'Hemi-Sync' or 'Hemispheric Synchronisation' which is the harmonisation of the hemispheres of the brain. The hemispheres are connected by a 'bridge' known as the corpus callosum (Fig 86). Monroe said that when the two sides of the brain reach 'frequency and amplitude synchronisation' it is possible to transfer attention from the human realm into the Astral. I have written at length over the years about the way society is designed to stop this hemisphere harmony. The brain is holographic, and information is distributed throughout, but the hemispheres still have distinct roles. The left-side is where most humans are imprisoned, especially in the West. This specialises in language, letters, analysis, linear and sequenced thinking, and numbers. It sees the world in terms of parts and not connections or wholeness. The controllers seek to manipulate the population to view reality through the myopia of the left hemisphere which believes itself to be logical and rational and is home to the intellect. 'Soldiers' stand at the gateway to the left-brain to stop right-brain influence (Fig 87).

Left-brain dominance tends to produce orthodox scientists, academics, doctors, teachers, politicians, journalists (mainstream and most 'alternative'), accountants, lawyers, and other head/intellect professions. Right and balanced brainers in these jobs approach

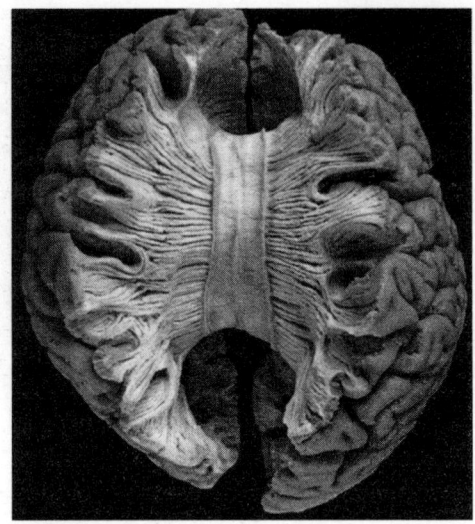

Figure 86: The corpus callosum 'bridge' through which the two sides of the brain communicate.

Figure 87: The system seeks to imprison humans in the left-side of the brain by emphasising left-brain subjects and 'norms' at the expense of the right. (Image by Neil Hague.)

the role differently. Most politicians are left brainers and emerge from the education system of school and university which is specifically formulated to lock away perception in the left side of the brain. The right brain is far more expansive in its sense of reality. It sees panoramas and

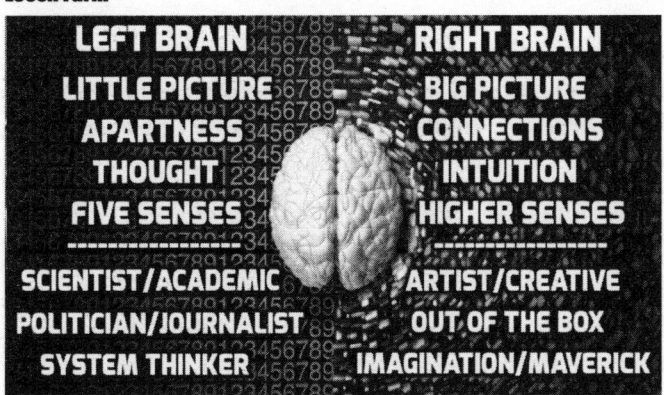

Figure 88: Different realities of each hemisphere of the brain. The idea is to balance the two.

how dots connect. It perceives totality and not only parts, and is creative, intuitive, spontaneous, and artistic. Creative professions are its speciality, and it is the daydreamer that perceives without words (Fig 88). The human world in its governing structure is basically the left-brain made manifest. Left-brain dominated can be seriously stuck in the world of 'normal' and predictable while right-brainers can struggle to relate to that reality and function within 'normality'. The ideal is to sync both hemispheres, so you are both *in* this world, but not *of* it. This is what 'Hemi-Sync' is all about and Monroe observed that such synchronisation can release consciousness to explore the Astral dimension.

Robert Monroe's work attracted the US military in the late 1970s, and it assessed Astral travelling abilities through a technique called the Gateway Process. Government documents since declassified by the CIA describe Gateway as 'a training system designed to bring enhanced strength, focus and coherence to the amplitude and frequency of brainwave output between the left and right hemispheres' with the intent to 'alter consciousness, moving it outside the physical sphere so as to ultimately escape even the restrictions of time and space'. Project leader US Army Lieutenant Colonel Wayne McDonnell wrote a 29-page report entitled 'Analysis and Assessment of The Gateway Process' in 1983. This was declassified by the CIA in 2003. The report said Gateway Process discoveries profoundly supported the case for reincarnation and confirmed our reality is a holographic electromagnetic Matrix. It emphasised the limitations of the left hemisphere of the brain and how right-brain communication involved symbolism. The Gateway Process came from this understanding of left-brain/right-brain function as described on the missing page 25 of the CIA declassified report which only came to light through the Monroe Institute in 2021. It said that 20th century physics would seem to be 'revisiting insights belonging to mankind as far back as written records can take us'. The difference was that 20th century physics was using a left brain, linear, quantitative style of reasoning to approach the same knowledge which the mystics of old apparently acquired in a holistic, intuitional right brain style. Lieutenant

Colonel McDonnell said the 'self-imposed limitations to balanced perception and objective logic, which our cultural and personal psychological subjective imposes when we use the strictly left-brain thinking style, could be offset by the holistic form of perception associated with altered states of consciousness'. To do that was to release ourselves from the 'prison of subjectivity'.

'The alligators'

Monroe said that he learned in his projected Astral travelling that entities in that realm are feeding off human energy that is essential for them to survive and he dubbed this energy 'loosh'. Humanity was being farmed and harvested, he said. I had again concluded this from many other sources before I came across Monroe's material. I was fascinated to see, given the scale of ridicule I had attracted since the 1990s, that Monroe would often experience entities in the Astral that took a *reptilian* form. They had been manipulating and enslaving humanity for millennia, he said, and both with this example and my wider worldwide research there is a constant theme of reptilian entities feeding off human energy and having a lust for human blood (frequency). Monroe and other participants in the Gateway study saw so many reptilian entities in the Astral that they gave them the collective name of the 'alligators'. Reptilian entities involved are part of the Yaldabaoth/Archon 'army'. They do exist out of sight in the human world and within the Earth, but they are mostly Astral in nature. The *Down the Chupacabra* Hole website said:

> During countless expeditions, [Monroe] observed identical saurian creatures. For over thirty-five years the etheric investigator gathered insight about these startling beings. Here is what he uncovered: The nefarious vertebrates have controlled and enslaved humanity for millennia. They exist and operate in the 4th dimension [Astral] and are only visible to individuals who can see beyond our extremely limited spectrum of visible light.

The obsession of the demons or Archons with loosh explains the obsession of Yaldabaoth agents on Earth through the ages with Satanic human and animal sacrifice 'to the gods'. These 'gods' (prats) are the demons/Archons in another dimension very close to this one, but outside the visual confines of visible light.

Gift to the 'gods'

I have been investigating Satanism and paedophilia since the mid-1990s when I realised their fundamental connection to the Global Cult. I have been revealing in the books since then some of the rich and famous names involved. Former UK prime minister Edward 'black eyes' Heath was a name that often came up. It is quite a shock to see that people regularly in the news are involved in human sacrifice ritual and the obvious question was why? I then began to track human sacrifice into the ancient world where it was both widespread almost everywhere and performed openly as an 'offering to the gods'. Next question – what do the 'gods' get out of it? It all makes sense when you introduce loosh to the mystery. Astral entities oversee the ritual from their dimension while the human realm Satanists perform the sacrifice. Rituals are carefully sequenced to generate maximum terror from the victim which is why many former Satanists have told me how rituals often take the same form today as they did in Babylon and the ancient world. All the chants and colours are related to the creation of a frequency environment that thins-out the energetic barriers between dimensions. Terror is an extremely powerful low-vibrational frequency, and the entities are absorbing that energy as it is projected into their Astral dimension. This is the offering or 'gift to the gods'. Terror triggers an adrenaline to enter the bloodstream and Satanists performing the ritual drink the blood after the sacrifice. To them it is a drug that gives them a 'high' with its adrenaline-laced content. The stories about the 'elite' drinking a form of adrenaline-infused blood called adrenochrome are true.

I have described how major rituals are performed on vortex points in the global electromagnetic/electrical grid where many lines cross. The spin of big vortices weave together dimensional energies and open channels to the Astral. Those who have experienced the rituals, often against their will, have told me how they witnessed non-human entities manifest thanks to the energetic vortex and ritual 'conduits' and how terrified the Satanists were of their other-dimensional masters. Many of these entities took a reptilian form, but far from always. The Global Cult is a pyramid of fear in which each level fears the level above and *all* fear the demonic 'gods'. Satanic themes of signing contracts in your own blood are real (blood = frequency) and getting into the Cult is easy if you are malleable, empathy-deleted, and have something to offer the agenda. Getting *out* is quite another thing. Your career advancement can be very swift and your bank balance bulging if you serve the Cult without question. If you should have doubts at any point and wish to leave – well, all the best with that one.

Inner-circles of Satanic and paedophile networks fuse as one global network for the same reason – energy. The focus on children by the 'gods' and Satanists comes from the energetic changes that take place at puberty. The ancient concept of 'sacrificing young virgins to the gods' was code for children. We see puberty as a hormonal or chemical transformation when this is triggered by an energy or frequency change. I am going to explain in more detail later how the body is encoded with a program that takes it through a cycle of ageing between birth and death. Puberty is part of this program, and the Astral demons want a child's energy before those changes happen. The energy of pre-puberty children is considered a 'nectar' to them. I began to investigate the paedophile rings in the 1990s when I saw the staggering number of paedophiles in positions of power and influence and especially among the Global Cult 'elite'. My question again was 'Why?' Well, this is why. Secret society and Satanic rituals connect their advocates to the demonic frequency just as regular paedophiles operating outside the major rings are demonically connected by their low-frequency state. This is the age-old theme of 'possession'.

Demonic Astral entities attach themselves to the energetic fields of humans and take control of their mental and emotional processes. Many people describe how their family members or associates changed their personality increasingly dramatically after involvement in secret societies or the 'dark arts'. Possession and induced mind control is the reason. Entities impose their will as necessary and can then withdraw in the usual course of life. People will appear as a result to have a split-personality in which they can lurch from very pleasant to demonically evil. Demons can also jump from person to person if they are energetically fragmented and resonate to the demonic frequency band. I remember a sequence towards the end of the movie *The Devil's Advocate* with Keanu Reeves and Al Pacino in which this is portrayed. Paedophiles are invariably possessed like this and, as they are abusing children, the overseeing possessing entity is vampiring the child's energy. This same recurring story has been told to me all over the world in different cultures because it is a global network. Beyond the imagination numbers of children go missing worldwide every year and many end up in the Satanic and paedophile rings. The late Zulu high shaman Credo Mutwa told me how groups were organised to keep watch on children in his village because so many were going missing. Central American shaman Don Juan Matus said:

> ... Sorcerers see infant human beings as strange luminous balls of energy, covered from the top to the bottom with a glowing coat, something like a coat of plastic adjusted tightly around the cocoon of energy.
>
> This glowing coat of awareness is what the predators consume and when a human reached adulthood, all that is left of that fringe awareness is a narrow fringe that goes from the ground to the top of the toes. That fringe permits mankind to keep on living, but only barely.

Information I have summarised in this chapter explains why the world is deluged in war, conflict, greed, scarcity, injustice, and chaos. Yaldabaoth Archontic forces make it that way through direct manipulation of the human mind and the scheming of its Global Cult within the human frequency. Loosh is our divine life-force – love, wisdom – that is impregnated by the calculated ignorance of the Soul and Mind with low-vibrational fear-based perceptual frequencies that both feed the Beast and disconnect humanity from an Infinite Divine connection which is the true meaning of enlightenment.

Human control in its foundation state is really that simple.

CHAPTER 7

Wheel of Misfortune

Our birth is but a sleep and a forgetting.
William Wordsworth

I can understand how consciousness could be enticed *once* through trickery into the extreme density of the material realm, but why in the name of sanity would you keep coming back?

This was a question I had long ago when I became convinced that reincarnation was real and as my research continued it became clear to me that the simulation has many other Astral levels between which Souls are recycled in and out of material reality. This is the Buddhist Wheel of Samsara, and I say this is designed to entrap Souls within the multi-dimensional Matrix to continue to suck the life-force from humans life after life (Fig 89). A material-only Matrix would soon run out of loosh producers without this recycling prison – 'That place is an emotional shithole – I ain't going back there.'

Belief in reincarnation was once widespread including among early Christians. Gnostic texts take reincarnation as read and Christian scholar Origen of Alexandria (185-253 AD) is quoted as saying: 'The soul has neither beginning nor end. [They] come into this world strengthened by the victories or weakened by the defeats for their previous lives.' Reincarnation was removed from Christian theology and doctrine and that still applies today. One life and God's eternal judgement was a far more powerful tool of control than life after life as a reincarnating Soul. A few indications of reincarnation survived in the Bible despite the censorship and of course 'Jesus' said that he will return which means

Figure 89: The Wheel of Samsara – until we break the ever-recurring cycle.

reincarnate. The idea that a 'loving God' creates humans to have one life on Earth before eternal judgement and allocation to Heaven or Hell is so utterly ridiculous you have to catch your breath. This is aligned with the need to believe in 'Jesus' as your saviour to avoid the bloke with the pitchfork and the central heating. What about babies who die without ever hearing of 'Jesus'? What about those living outside the Christian world who had never heard of 'Jesus? What does God have against *them*? Good works won't get you to Heaven only a belief in 'Jesus' which means a belief in the Church doctrine designed to control you. Religion was created as a means of perceptual limitation and indoctrination and the greatest form of mind and behaviour control ever invented. They are belief systems with a padlock on the door marked 'expanded awareness' and I mean everything from Christianity to Islam to Hinduism to Judaism to the New Age.

Belief systems tend to have their own uniforms to show which mind-club they represent. I have long wondered why Buddhist priests, encouraging an expansion of mind, need to wear the same uniform which symbolises a contraction of mind. You can identify many New Agers immediately by what they wear. Belief systems, including political belief, immediately instigate no-go areas where your research and sense of the possible will not go for fear of putting your belief under threat. You cannot be a Christian, Muslim or Jewish believer if you believe in reincarnation and without that knowledge you cannot understand life, the world and the Matrix. That is the idea. Hinduism does believe in reincarnation but turns that into a means of control by designating where you incarnate to your place in the caste system which still exists despite what is claimed. Eastern religions and its Western New Age counterpart see reincarnation as a way to 'learn lessons' to 'evolve' while I see it as a calculated trap to maintain the flow of loosh and prevent the Divine Spark from escaping to infinity. I cover all this in detail in my Reality Trilogy, *The Trap*, *The Dream* and *The Reveal*.

My research into reincarnation has again taken me across the spectrum in search of common agreement from religion and Gnostic works to near-death experiencers and modern scientific studies. Millions of people have had near-death experiences ('NDEs') when the body dies, and their consciousness is released into another dimension before the body is revived and they return. Russian electrical engineer Semyon Kirlian and his wife Valentina developed Kirlian photography, a method which photographs the human energy field which changes colour with different emotions and mental states. These produce different frequencies that relate to the frequencies of colour. Kirlian photography has captured the auric/etheric field in humans, animals and plants at the point of death and recorded the luminescent field withdrawing until none was left. Other-dimensional near-death accounts while different have many common threads which include meeting religious heroes, loved ones, 'spirit guides', angels, and 'elders' who take the classic human expression of wise old men with beards and robes. The 'elders' guide them through a 'life review' in which their lives are played back to them on a screen or screens. They are told where their behaviour can be improved and sent back to Earth to continue their 'mission' although what that is doesn't seem to be explained very often. Near-deathers confirm that reincarnation is a fact. I'll have more about NDEs shortly because none of this is what it seems.

Life after life

I feature in *The Reveal* the work of Canadian-born American psychiatrist Dr Ian Stevenson (1918-2007), founder and director of the Division of Perceptual Studies at the University of Virginia School of Medicine. Stevenson spent much of his career investigating reincarnation with children who said they could remember previous lives. He found that their memories started between the ages of two and four with more details emerging until five or six. They began to fade until they were gone around eight to ten with a few retaining them until puberty. He found that only around one in 500 children met his criteria and that applied even in India where reincarnation is universally accepted. Stevenson studied 2,500 to 3,000 cases in different cultures and published his two-volume 2,268-page *Reincarnation and Biology* in 1997. Small children would present him with fine details of other lives such as names, locations, life happenings, and their cause of death which they could never have known in this life. They would relate to locations they had never visited and had no family connections to the area. Stephenson would then forensically check the facts and set out to prove them wrong, but over and over what the children said was confirmed as accurate in the most remarkable ways. Some knew their way around towns and the layout of houses where they had never been. I saw a TV programme in which a little boy who said he was in the crew of the Titanic could navigate a video mock-up of the ship predicting rooms and uses before they appeared on the screen.

Stephenson recorded how children with a recent past life recognised people they had never met (even those who had killed them or owed them money). One boy was taken back to the family where he said he had been the husband of a woman still alive. The boy addressed the woman as if they were still married. He was asked that if what he said was true if he could tell them where he left his will because they could never find it. The boy identified a floorboard in the kitchen and there it was. Some children could speak languages they had never been taught but fitted with a past life. Stephenson noted hundreds of cases with rare birthmarks and birth defects that related to a previous life and death.

Among them were being born without a lower leg and finger deformities, scar-like, hypo-pigmented birthmarks, port-wine stains, and strange-looking moles where you rarely find them, as with the soles of the feet. He wrote how children expressed fears, interests, and responses that matched happenings in the life they recalled and birth defects and birthmarks at the location of fatal wounds they said had killed them. This can happen when events encoded in a person's energetic field in one life are transferred to the next. Ian Stevenson who specialised in psychosomatic medicine felt that powerful emotions caused by say traumatic deaths could leave an emotional imprint and trigger the memories. Most of the children he studied had died violently. There was also the psychological impact of a previous life in fears and phobias in this one as with drowning leading to a fear of water. Stephenson believed that past-life memories can be triggered by happenings in the child's current life.

The Trap

What follows is the cycle of reincarnation as I pull together all my research on the subject in the last 36 years. It is worth re-emphasising that the human body allows us to interact with the material realm while the Soul is our 'body' in the Astral dimensions (which is why it is often called the 'Astral body'). But the True 'I' is formless 'Spirit', simply a state of being aware, which connects us to Infinite Reality (Fig 90). What Gnostic texts call the 'Divine Spark' is Spirit perceptually trapped in the illusions of the simulated Matrix. It is this entrapment that the Archontic seeks to perpetuate indefinitely.

Figure 90: The True 'I' pure formless awareness, a state of being aware.

Reincarnation is designed to ensure Souls remain trapped in the simulation and producing loosh for their controllers. I have described how Divine Spark consciousness was lured into the Matrix originally when the 'gateway' to infinity was closed and the density continually lowered until at the lowest level it became the severe density that we experience as 'matter'. This is still conscious as all is consciousness, but the density means its awareness is far more limited. There are less dense dimensions of the Astral – still in the simulation – that appear to be 'Heaven' when compared to the human density. But they are not 'Heaven'. They are a fake 'Heaven' that makes Souls believe they need to keep incarnating into the human realm to learn lessons to evolve according to 'God's plan'.

Take the totality of near-death accounts and you will see how the overwhelming majority believe this when they return to the body. You find the same belief in the Eastern religions with the Buddhist Wheel of Samsara and the New Age. We experience physical and emotional pain, suffering, and deprivation to learn our lessons and then there's always 'karma' to force us to keep coming back. We enter the human realm with its extraordinary energetic density, challenges and insanity, and as a result we make choices we would not otherwise have made. These 'choices' attract karma that we have to 'pay back' by returning to human and the cycle goes on indefinitely. But it's all *bollocks*. None of it is true. A near-death experiencer said she was told by 'beings' in the Astral that everything that happened to her was 'all the Soul's plans that you came to experience'. Okay, so why the 'karma'? I am not attacking Buddhism, by the way. Buddhism has identified many things that most other religions have not – reincarnation, interconnectedness, and illusory 'physical' reality for a start. I just think it is missing the real reason for its 'wheel'.

My studies and observations of the human and Astral realms make clear the foundation similarities between the two. Both are based on perceptual manipulation and acquiescence to authority. Humans are programmed to obey and fear authority and it begins the moment we enter the world. The Astral levels of the simulation operate in virtually the same way. Only the environment changes. The stream of near-death experiences I have read and heard year after year have many things in common and central to them is the bewilderment the Soul feels on leaving the body. You may wonder why they would be bewildered when the Soul must have been through the process many times life after human life. I'll deal with that as we proceed, but basically the incarnating Soul experiences a mind-wipe on entering this reality which is why comparatively few remember previous human experiences. Some cultures refer to this as the 'veil of forgetfulness' or 'water of forgetfulness' and it continues until you are safely back in the Astral and under control awaiting your return to human loosh production.

The Soul released from the decoded reality of the body is therefore, to its perception, experiencing a body exit for the first time. It has become used to 'physical' reality and now suddenly finds itself floating in another dimension with dramatically different laws of physics. Naturally, it is confused and bewildered. This is when the religious heroes appear tailored to your religious belief, or the 'spirit guides', 'angels', 'elders', and passed 'loved ones'. Many wear 'robes' which are perceptually connected to the spiritual. It's all a mind-intercourse, or mind-fuck to the uncouth like me. They are your new authority to take

Wheel of Misfortune

Figure 91: Many near-death experiencers describe moving through a tunnel of light but it leads across the threshold to the recycling wheel.

the place of human authority, and they are both expressions of the *same* Yaldabaoth authority. Their role is to lead you up the 'tunnel of light' and onto the Wheel of Samsara before you have the chance to escape the simulation (Fig 91). Can you imagine a Christian faced with the appearance of Jesus who would not follow his instructions of what to do? But they are *not* Jesus, Muhammad, a spirit guide, angel, elder, or loved one. These are AI projections as I explain at length in the Reality Trilogy. They are your new authority to follow and obey until you return to follow human authority again (which is really Astral authority).

The cycle

Round and round this cycle goes until you access the knowledge and memory of your true self-identity that allows you to reach levels of perception – frequency – that free you from the Matrix illusion. This is what the Archons work so hard to stop. Their game is over if they don't. The simulation in total has an outer frequency limit with the Astral consisting of many dimensional levels from the densest, which directly interacts with the human realm, to the highest which represents a simulated fake 'heaven'. You will gravitate after bodily death to one of these levels according to the frequency on which you operate dictated by your perception – *unless* you open to 'gnosis', or spiritual knowledge, that can lead you out of here. Those, like Global Cult initiates, will be vibrating in Astral density and will find themselves in the lower Astral which has been likened to Hell. This is where the most extreme of the Archons and demons are resident. Other Souls will transfer to higher levels of the Astral while still in the Matrix and are destined to return in another human life as the Samsara wheel turns. Some form of Archontic authority, human or Astral, will be seeking to rule and control you by downloading your sense of self and reality wherever you are in the simulation.

I am going to start my description of the reincarnation cycle in the Astral as a Soul is preparing to return to human and the first thing to emphasise is the way the Astral and the incarnation process are described in technological terms. The simulation at all levels has a plasma foundation with an electrical/electromagnetic program flowing through the plasma that creates the detail. This mirrors the human world which is an electrical/electromagnetic program encoded into plasma which is a near-perfect medium for electricity and electromagnetism. The difference is one of density – frequency. Plasma is known as the fourth state of matter. The Astral operates on higher frequencies than the human realm, but it is still a form of matter albeit far more ethereal than we experience (the more so the higher you go).

I have featured people in the books who say they have memories of their incarnation and life in the Astral in the period before they came. They have described technology and technologists involved and how they accepted 'the veil' which would delete memories and induce a sense of separation. One even talked about a 'veil of acceptance simulator' to practice overcoming the fear of extreme density that the human world would bring. He said it was like being pushed under water for as long as you can take it and then 'you cry uncle' and they let you out. He remembered being in 'like a technician's chamber, or like a mechanic shop that was over the Earth' with a shaft below him and beyond that the Earth. 'And there were these beings there who were very technical in nature, and they are very, very skilled at matching the veil to you, to the individual.' He said that Astral entities overseeing his incarnation were like 'technicians' who weaved different energetic fields of different frequencies into one energetic fusion:

> The individual soul has so many rich qualities, and the life and the body, and the circumstances have their own energetic thing going on, and they like, I don't know, they make everything fit. They make everything jive. They're able to make this organic connection work … The veil is like an organic blanket or something and they're able to fine-tune that.

Those with pre-incarnation memories describe the detail with which each incarnation was planned in league with 'guides' down to the colour of hair, facial features (handsome or not), life circumstances and happenings, gifts of skills and potential, and propensity to illnesses. Near-death accounts have described how Astral spirit world 'guides' carefully choose human bodies and *personalities* for incarnating Souls. The detail is connected (so the recipients think) to working on failings to speed their evolution and pay back their 'karma'. One said that he knew a trauma that would befall him in his 20s, but 'the amount of profound personal growth … that was possible [was] breathtakingly huge'. Given that this is all based on their 'karmic debt' it means that they will behave in ways in each 'life' that add to the karma and keep the cycle going. This crap about incarnating to 'learn lessons to evolve' is the Big Lie that keeps the wheel spinning indefinitely.

American Isabella Greene is a near-death experiencer and author of *Leaving the Trap: How to Exit The Reincarnation Cycle* and *Transcending the Trap*. She has also experienced the Astral over and over through consciousness projection or out of body experiences (OBEs). Her conclusion matches my own – 'there is no such thing as soul growth' because at that deepest level (the Infinite) all is known, and we can tap into that if we break out of the programmed myopia of the Matrix. We do not have to experience this mad house to 'learn and grow' and especially when the mad house is there to stop us 'growing' and knowing. Isabella Greene says that a 'pure Soul' entering this reality is then dragged down by the experience of material density and the illusion of 'karma' which the system ensures can never be 'paid off'. She said: 'A lot of us volunteered to come here for one reason or another, and now we're just running in circles around the Earth plane, being like a battery for the beings that lured us here, I think.' Eastern religions buy into this deceit, and it prepares their followers, largely unknowingly, to accept the lies in the Astral that bring them back here.

How do they do it?

My question was how they could ensure such detail in planning each human life as described by those who say they remember. I could understand the hair and features with the targeting of a particular genetic line, but what about their life experiences, 'personalities', and events? People who have memories of their pre-incarnation Astral experience talk about their upcoming human body being an 87 percent match for their planned experience or 98 to 99 percent, and how they know they will have this or that experience, trauma, or illness as a result. It's all very precise. They describe the detail involved in 'choosing' what body and personality-type would be next. They have told of rejecting a personality that was 'too angry' or the wrong hair-colour, choosing between being male or female, not being too good looking or intelligent because it would negate their planned 'karmic' experience. 'Karma'? How does this square with choosing personality types that are extremely angry or promiscuous or arrogant before you even get here? You get back for your 'life review' and the 'elders' tell you there is a need to return to the material realm to work through your 'karma' for being too angry, promiscuous or arrogant. Think of all the loosh involved, too.

I concluded over the years reading and listening to these accounts that some kind of program was involved, a sort of software program infused into the body or biological computer. I have called this the 'Astral AI Mind' program and you can liken this to algorithms. The 'physical' body is a decoded illusion happening in the brain which is itself a field of information and not physical in an undecoded state. Everything is information encoded into electromagnetic and electrical fields flowing through a plasma medium. The program is encoded like software in the electromagnetic auric field that surrounds and interpenetrates the body and this contains the *information* that interacts with human DNA and the electrical/electromagnetic central nervous system that we experience as 'physical' and personality traits. Both can be overridden by the Divine Spark True 'I' but mostly they are not because of the extreme nature of human programming and Divine Spark suppression. Biological personality programs can explain the concept of 'archetypes' which means 'original pattern' in ancient Greek. Swiss psychiatrist Carl Jung (1875-1961) contended there are twelve archetypal personalities within what he called the 'collective unconscious'. He said we all tended to have personalities dominated by one of these archetypes and this sounds very much like a software program which again can be overridden if we allow the infinite potential and possibility of the Divine Spark to express itself.

We speak of synchronicity, a term coined by Jung, where 'coincidences' happen, even amazing ones, way beyond statistical chance. They have happened to me constantly. Some can be life changing. These can be the Divine Spark expression of the Infinite leading you or they can be the Life Program where people are literally programmed to come together and play out pre-planned scenarios. The more I observe the more the latter are by far the most prominent. Life Programs, as I said, can be likened to algorithms. Someone will feel attracted to another and may not even know why when it is the programs bringing them together. It is a biological computer after all. The penny has been dropping for decades now, slowly then swiftly, just how controlled human society really is. Far more than almost anyone can grasp.

The Life Program can dictate not only where you are born but where and how you will die. It can program if you are kind or psychopathic, rich or poor, skilled and intellectually smart, or otherwise. All these things can be overcome by the Divine Spark and the whole point of the Archontic system is to keep that asleep and disconnected from the decision-making and perceptual process. When that happens, and it does this far with the great majority of humans, then the Life Program is dictating your life from womb to tomb mostly in a sequence of birth/school/marriage/kids/death before the Astral deceit begins again and you are back here in new circumstances. Those who have had organ transplants – especially the heart – can take on personality traits of the donor. This is a transfer of biological Life Program 'software'. Identical twins can have similar experiences even when parted by 'time' and 'distance'. These are the Life Programs again through identical 'software'.

What is deciding?

It's been established that the brain's electrical activity necessary to perform an action happens *before* the conscious thought to take that action when surely it should be the other way round. Benjamin Libet (1916-2007), a University of California scientist, found that brain activity to move a limb began half a second before the conscious intention. Neuroscientist John-Dylan Haynes at the Max Planck Institute for Human Cognitive and Brain Sciences in Leipzig, Germany, was later able to predict an action *ten seconds* before it happened by monitoring the brain. *What*? Who is calling the shots here and dictating behaviour if not the conscious mind? Well, the *sub*conscious mind, but what is that? The subconscious is defined as 'the part of your mind that notices and remembers information when you are not actively trying to do so, and influences your behaviour even though you do not realise it.' Subconscious simply means everything that is not the conscious mind of thought and emotional response – waking awareness. The question is how far the subconscious extends. Does this have to relate to us, the apparent individual? Or can it extend into levels of reality and awareness where some other force is dictating action? It is rather sobering to think that psychological research has concluded that 95 percent of our response and behaviour are triggered from the subconscious (Fig 92). I think it is a constant battle for control of perception and behaviour between the biological program and Divine Spark/Infinite Consciousness seeking to override that (if it's awake enough).

Native Americans have the concept of two wolves inside everyone fighting for supremacy. They define the 'wolves' as evil, anger, envy, greed, arrogance, resentment, lies, self-doubt, inferiority and ego battling with good, joy, peace, love, hope, serenity, kindness, generosity, empathy and truth. I would define this as the biological program and the Divine Spark. If the program is not dominated by the intervention of consciousness, we become little more than perceptual, behavioural robots. 'Which 'wolf' wins?' the Native Americans ask. 'The one you feed most' comes the reply. The overwhelming majority of human programming targets the subconscious and once there it dictates perception and behaviour unless it is purged by expanded consciousness beyond the human mind. The

Figure 92: The subconscious mind that triggers 95 percent of human response and behaviour and the level to which symbolism speaks as I will focus upon later. (Image by Neil Hague.)

subconscious cannot distinguish between 'past, present and future', or between an experience and *thinking* about an experience. This is why thinking about something can generate the same emotional and physiological responses as experiencing that something happening. Think about a massive poisonous spider crawling up your leg. There you go.

The placebo effect is based on this. You take a pill you *believe* will cure you and even though it is a sugar pill your health responds purely through thought. *Everything* is perception – almost entirely subconscious perception. I remember an alternative healer saying to me once that he wasn't sure if his supplements and treatments were helping people directly or whether it was their belief in them that was having the effect. I am all for eating as healthily as you can to avoid unnecessary frequency disruption of the human energy field, but in the end the mind dictates what happens to health. You may think the conscious mind is running the show, but it's not. The subconscious controls the systems of the body and is encoded with the information from which the 'physical' body is decoded into apparent reality. Body systems run without any influence from the conscious mind. You don't constantly think I must breathe, you just breathe. This is the subconscious at work and that is all levels of being beyond the conscious mind. They include everything from the body program to the auric field to expanded levels of awareness.

NPC humans

I conclude from what I have seen and observed that it is possible to create human beings that do not have a Divine Spark but are the equivalent of non-player characters (NPCs) in computer games which are controlled and pre-programmed by the game. Human NPCs are software programs driven in their actions, perceptions and responses by the body program without the Divine Spark potential to go its own way. They are people that appear to have no other perceptions except those dictated by authority and they are incapable of original thought. The Reptilian system of hierarchical top-down authority is all they can conceive. They are go-through-the-motions personalities who are extraordinarily predictable and a form of biological AI. Is this really so far-fetched when the body is a biological computer animated and driven by electricity? They are infused into human society to overwhelm Divine Sparks with situations and pressures that keep them in line. I do not think it is a coincidence in the current Matrix phase that it took until 1804 for the global population to reach one billion while another *seven* billion were added within 218 years. We are heading for a profound transformation of the Matrix and the more NPCs there are to control, bewilder and confuse Divine Sparks the more likely the Archontic system is to succeed. We may all be 'in' the human world from the body perspective, but we are not in the same realm of consciousness. You may have noticed.

These are the 'Hylics', from a Greek word 'hyle' meaning matter, that I highlighted earlier in the Gnostic Nag Hammadi texts. Hylics are NPCs focused on the material realm without connection to the eternal and infinite. They are mostly not aware of other realities and dominated by the five senses, physical pleasures and sensations. Remember what former Oxford professor Nick Bostrom said about the likelihood that 'the vast majority' of human minds possibly being simulated rather than original. We can see now that what the Gnostics described is *absolutely* possible along with gathering evidence that this has indeed happened. Near-death experiencer Lauda Leon says she realised from her Astral experiences there are 'hybrids, synthetics and backdrops' within the simulation to suppress Divine Sparks. They had backdrop people 'to make the theatre look real'. NPCs look the same because they have a human body like everyone else, but what is driving their perceptions and acquiescence to authority? The simulation is at the wheel, and they behave as the simulators demand to pressure potentially conscious Divine Sparks to be absorbed by the herd. They will ridicule and condemn those that the simulation wishes to discredit and marginalise. Elon Musk's Twitter/X platform is absolutely awash with them. NPCs are also observing reality into existence through the body program encoded with a limited sense of reality that challenges the impact of awakening people in breaking the stranglehold of perceptual limitation. Such is the power of consciousness in its pomp and potential that they must go to these lengths to suppress it.

Those that control the Global Cult are little more than NPCs, again biological AI, controlled by their masters in the Astral and programmed to follow the empathy-deleted, compassion-deleted software. Once again think of Agent Smith in the *Matrix* and other software people like the 'Merovingian'. Would a software program have any problem with mass murder in manipulated wars and abusing children in Satanic and paedophile rings? Press enter, and away they go. The prime goal of the now ubiquitous AI agenda to fuse humans with artificial intelligence is to turn Divine Spark humans into NPCs through AI connection to the human brain. Observe, too, the gathering manipulation of genetics and making the body more synthetic. These are all connected to creating totally controllable NPCs. The Archontic mentality is founded on fear – the fear of being exposed and losing their essential life force vampired from Divine Sparks. Archons are terrified of situations where they cannot control the outcome, and their desire is for total control to appease this terror. NPCs and Divine Sparks controlled by AI is therefore their ideal scenario.

Energetic 'treacle'

Archons play a game of 'footsy' with Divine Spark energy in that they need to suppress its awakening and stop its influence overwhelming the program, but this is also the source of loosh they need to trawl by lowering its vibration as it passes through the 'bodies' of ignorance within which it is enslaved. This is most important at the density of 'human' where loosh is generated on a scale far more powerful and abundant than any other dimension of the simulation. Those who can remember their incarnation often find it a challenge to even describe the energetic density of this reality. One talked of being in the 'waiting area' before incarnation when a guide said: 'Go now!' and it was like 'getting the rollercoaster, you know, once you strap in, you can't get out until the ride's done'. What followed was a 'huge plummet and vibration down, down, down, down, lower, lower, lower, lower' as he 'surrendered to the veil' and his 'knowing' disappeared along with his 'connectedness' and memory. The human reality was 'very dark'. Lauda Leon who has had seven near-death experiences and says she has pre-human life memories describes the same overwhelming density on entering the material vibration: 'It became denser, heavier, and, you know, it actually felt painful.' It was like a 'heavy, heavy, painful weight' and reality was 'really foreign' and 'very alien'. Isabella Greene said of her incarnation experience: 'I started being pulled into an entirely different state of being, which felt denser and denser, like from the state of air into water, into mud ... and then I started going into human.'

The next thing we know we are looking through the eyes of a baby and the common theme is one of bewilderment. Where am I? Who are these strange beings? We should know given we've been here so many times, but the mind-wipe means it is all new to us with each fresh arrival. The child then goes through the perceptual programming from programmed parents, teachers, academics, media, scientists, doctors, and peer pressure to infuse the 'norms' of Archontically-controlled human society. Those that question and refuse to conform soon learn there are unpleasant consequences for not bending the knee to the system. The body biological computer is decoding the simulated fakery as we head from cradle to cemetery and delivering to us like a virtual reality headset, gloves and audio (plus taste and smell) a reality that appears to be solid when it's not and appears to be external to us when it's not.

All the while the individualised body Life Program or Astral AI Mind is playing out to keep people on their pre-programmed 'karmic journey', dictating choices, 'synchronicities', and happenings that they think are 'coincidences', chance events, and 'meant-to-be'. Or at least it is unless we open our minds to awaken the Divine Spark that can override the programming and see through the bullshit. The whole system is encoded to stop that happening, but it is always possible because awakened consciousness is far more powerful than some foolish 'god' that only prevails by keeping its targets in a state of ignorance even more profound than its own. Another program that underwrites the control system is astrology as the impact of the planetary information fields impact upon the simulation and impact upon us according to frequencies in our own energetic field known as our 'star sign', etc. The Nag Hammadi *Apocryphon of John* highlights the role of 'fate' (the programs) on human control:

> And bitter fate was begotten through them, which is the last of the changeable bonds ... For from that fate came forth every sin and injustice and blasphemy, and the chain of forgetfulness and ignorance ... And thus the whole creation was made blind, in order that they may not know God, who is above all of them.
>
> And because of the chain of forgetfulness, their sins were hidden. For they are bound with measures and times and moments, since it [fate, the program] is lord over everything.

'Physical' and psychological pain are encoded into the Life Program and the body goes through its cycle of ageing and decomposition aided by the perceptual state that expects that to happen when the proof seems all around in what is happening to others. Life has its ups and downs and for most humans mostly downs if you scan the world to see all those people just trying to survive another day. Loosh is projected in abundance as Divine Spark Source energy is encoded with low-vibrational negativity by life experience and absorbed by the Astral realm and entities which vibrate to the frequency of low-vibrational negativity. *Mmm* ... dinner is served thanks to the latest human tragedy. Death is the fear that dominates human perception consciously and subconsciously. Fear of our own demise and fears about our children and other loved ones. Death is fear of the unknown and the more unknowns there are the more there is to fear. This is another reason for manufactured ignorance. Judgement by 'God' or ceasing to exist or accumulated 'karma' are all sources of loosh as is the intensified fear with a doctor's fatal verdict or declining health when you know the end is near. Where do I go? Do I go anywhere? I don't want to die. I don't want to leave my kids and grandkids, husband or wife. Add to this the often painful and traumatic death that many experience. Loosh, loosh, everywhere you look. The lower the vibrational state you are in, and the more ignorant of the game that you are, the more likely it is that you'll head up the tunnel to the recycling unit.

What is death?

Death is only the demise of the biological computer – not *you*. It's true that you will be leaving this tiny band of frequency called 'human' and you will no longer be able to interact in the old way with the ones you love. You are heading to another band of frequency, but you don't cease to exist anymore than the consciousness of your loved ones does when they come to leave (Fig 93). Death is only when the body computer ceases to function and *ceases to decode this human reality*. That is the simplest explanation of death – when the body *ceases to decode this human reality*. Think of when a computer 'dies'. What happens? The screen goes blank because it is no longer decoding the Internet, the Wi-Fi. *Our* screen

Figure 93: This is all that death is – taking off the headset when it ceases to function.

does not go blank – the body's does. We are released from the strict limitations of the material realm the body has been decoding, and we consciously enter the Astral or fake 'Heaven'. *Or* we can project ourselves out of the Matrix and home to infinity if we are awakened to our true self. Why don't we just kill ourselves and escape? Because the state of mind largely necessary to do that is guaranteed to keep us in the simulated 'box' and the more 'time' we have to reach a state of True 'I' self-awareness the better chance we have to bypass the 'wheel'. Once you are in the Astral and up the ubiquitous tunnel to the fake light it's too late and this is why it's so important to awaken to the simulation reincarnation scam while still in the body. Then you are prepared for the Archontic tricks that await you to ensure you return again to generate more loosh for the prison cell.

Your consciousness is released from the body prison when it ceases to function and decode illusory human reality. This is when enormous numbers of near-death experiencers have described finding themselves in another realm. A comparative few have different experiences after the initial release that take other forms, but most recount a compellingly similar sequence of events. Firstly, there is confusion at what is happening when through reincarnation their consciousness would have experienced this over and over. That's the mind-wipe. Then there is the universal theme of being immersed in an amazing feeling of love. 'When I got to the light the love was so incredible, the acceptance, the forgiveness', as one said. People can take drugs and have a similar experience. Drugs are a frequency in their base state as everything is in the simulation. We see drugs as a chemical interaction with the body when they are a frequency impacting on the frequency – *information* – nature of the body field. Pharmaceutical drugs are distorted frequencies as emanations of the schism via Global Cult-controlled Big Pharma. 'Side-effects' are the way the distortion affects the body field. Frequencies projected in the Astral after bodily death can induce the love deemed 'so incredible' as frequencies from drugs like ecstasy can induce a state of euphoria. Near-death accounts almost universally describe a feeling of oneness when released from the body, but is that oneness with Infinite Reality or a oneness with the Astral levels of the Matrix?

The point of release from the body is when we have the best chance to leave the simulation and head back to infinity. This is a crucial moment when the Archontic force must entice us 'to the light', often via a 'tunnel', and back on the recycling wheel. That would be difficult if the post-body experience was unpleasant with horrible 'guides' waiting to meet you. It is crucial that you believe you are in some sort of Heaven with loving beings that you have been programmed in the human realm to believe Heaven must be like. There is also the relief that you are not meeting the guy with the pitchfork. People mostly leave the body in fear and trepidation (fear of the unknown) and this mixture of fear and mind-wipe confusion make you a sitting target for the NDE 'love-bombing' technique. At this stage the figures appear that the Soul perceives as their religious heroes, angels, guides, elders, passed-over family members, and loved ones. They emanate more 'incredible love' and most people are hooked. There are many descriptions of feeling some sort of magnetism pulling them through a tunnel to a light or maybe a light without the tunnel. Much of the programming for this moment is downloaded during a human life with the association of 'God' and 'Jesus' with 'the Light'.

Imagine you are a devout Christian and a figure that looks like the archetypal image of 'Jesus' appears to 'guide' you. How many would say hold on a minute, I'm not sure about this? It's the same with believers from other religions – 'Oh, it's 'Muhammad', 'Oh, it's Shiva', 'Oh, it's Buddha'. The reincarnation religions that believe the cycle is about 'learning lessons' are seriously prepared to willingly accept the wheel. Angels, guides, elders and family members are all there to give you comfort so that in your relief your guard comes down and you do and believe what they say. Why wouldn't you if you had no idea what else to do in your mind-wipe perceptual stupor? You have just emerged from a human life of programming to do what Earthly authority tells you – again in your human mind-wipe perceptual stupor. Now the

Astral authority takes over which was really the human authority all along via the Global Cult.

Many questions will burst forth from this including 'why would Jesus or my old mum want to manipulate me like this?' The answer is that it's not Jesus, or Muhammad, or Shiva, or angels, guides, or your old mum. They are *projections* designed specifically for you, your belief system and how to most effectively get you back on the train to Samsara. There are no descriptions in the Bible of what 'Jesus' looked like. The one you see is the version that emerged with artists of the Renaissance period in Europe across the 15th and 16th centuries which depict him as a European with blond hair and blue eyes which is absolutely not what a 'carpenter's son' in the Middle East would have looked like at all. But this is the 'Jesus' that post-death Christians and others see because that's the one they are familiar with. Quite ironic given that 'Saint Paul' says in 1 Corinthians 11:14: 'Does not the very nature of things teach you that if a man has long hair, it is a disgrace to him …'

'Akashic' database

If these projections are not who they appear to be how do they target each Soul with the beliefs and weaknesses of the 170,000 people on average who die every day? That's an average of some 7,000 per hour, 117 per minute and nearly 2 a second. How would they keep up? They don't have to. I have said that the entire simulation is run by a level of artificial intelligence that is way beyond what we are seeing rolled out in human society. Way beyond? It's light years more advanced. I have featured in my Reality Trilogy the so-called Akashic Records popularised by American medium/psychic/clairvoyant and 'The Sleeping Prophet' Edgar Cayce (1877-1945). The Christian Sunday school teacher would enter a trance state and answer questions about the afterlife realm by accessing what he called the Akashic Records or 'God's Book of Remembrance'. He said:

> Upon time and space is written the thoughts, the deeds, the activities of an entity – as in relationships to its environs, its hereditary influence as directed – or judgment drawn by or according to what the entity's ideal is. Hence, as it has been oft called, the record is God's Book of Remembrance; and each entity, each Soul – as the activities of a single day of an entity in the material world – either makes same good or bad or indifferent, depending upon the entity's application of self ...

This 'book' has nothing to do with God, as in the Infinite. It is an Archontic *database* recording every thought, emotion and action of every incarnate Soul. We are moving this way fast in the human world and the 'technology' used in the Astral is fantastic by comparison. Modern-day promotors of Cayce and the Akashic Records even symbolise them as a database. One article said:

> The Akashic Records are basically a record of what will happen, is happening, or has happened. Because they are a higher dimension, the rules of time don't really apply. Time is a flat circle to the Akashic Records, so information from 2,000 years ago is as accessible as what happened to you yesterday.
>
> And what happened to you yesterday is as available as what could happen to you – if you stay on the same destiny trajectory – in 10 years. Interestingly, everything has its own Akashic Record. Your Soul has an Akashic Record, your house has an Akashic Record, your dog, even your relationship! You can open the specific Records of things to ask questions that pertain to them.

It all sounds seriously far-out, even a bit loony, but hold up. Humans constantly make the absolutely *massive, colossal, enormous,* mistake of believing that the human cutting edge of possibility is the real cutting edge. It's not even the edge in the human realm where the real cutting edge is in the underground bases and secret projects. Look in the public arena at Sat-Nav simultaneously guiding billions of drivers every day across the world and instantly revising the route if you take a wrong turn. The Astral is quite another level and I'll give you some idea of what is possible. I highlight in *The Reveal* the work of writer and researcher Robert Temple and his book, *A New Science of Heaven*, which focuses on the fundamental significance of plasma which I say is the foundation energetic medium of both human and Astral levels of the simulation and upon which the electrical/electromagnetic detail is encoded. Everything you basically 'see' as 'empty space' between 'material form' is plasma and the 'form' itself is encoded electrical/electromagnetic *information* that the brain/body decodes into what appears to be 'physical' reality. The subtitle of Temple's book is *How the new science of plasma physics is shedding light on spiritual experience.* Yes, it is, which is why most leading plasma scientists are forced to be answerable to the intelligence and military networks that control disclosure.

Temple describes an extraordinary phenomenon known as the two 'Kordylewski Clouds' either side of the Moon and about the same distance from Earth at around 250,000 miles. The clouds are together the size of *18 Earths*. They were first discovered by Polish astronomer Kazimierz Kordylewski in 1961, and it would take another 57 years for the clouds to be officially confirmed by the Royal Astronomical Society in 2018. The Kordylewski Clouds consist of plasma awash with micro and nanoparticles and this combination makes possible with these particle-plasma clouds alone a level of computing and data storage of stratospheric proportions. Temple says that 'there are good reasons to believe that plasma, with its ordering properties, can in certain circumstances be in some sense alive and can evolve intelligence'. This would fit with my contention that the simulation is orchestrated by what we would term artificial intelligence. Temple reveals the mind-blowing computing power of the clouds with 'electromagnetic wave emission/absorption across cloud dimensions as well as electrical connections (charge/current exchanges) between adjacent charged particles only centimetres apart'. This is what he says would be possible with just these plasma-particle clouds never mind whatever else exists:

> … a Kordylewski Cloud might well be able to function as a gigantic computer/brain capable of storing and processing digital information. The maths also shows that the cloud may have a super-astronomical sum total for its potential computing power, exceeding the computing power available in all human brains, and indeed all other intelligent life on Earth as well, by very many orders of magnitude.

The scale of computational power and storage would make the clouds capable of the following. Akashic Records anyone? Temple again:

> The storage capacity for information would easily include the ability to retain full knowledge of everything that has ever happened in our local cosmic environment for four billion years. Everyone who has ever lived will be recorded. Every creature that has ever roamed the surface of the Earth will be recorded. Every plant which has ever grown will be as well.

Such potential processing and storage could quite easily track every Soul incarnation and generate the designer projections when it returns to the Astral to match its beliefs and exploit identified emotional weaknesses to secure continued entrapment in the Matrix. These are the information sources that allow the human body-programs to be assembled and coordinated with others to encode life experiences and synchronicities that people think are random coincidences. It has long been my view that most psychics 'tuning in' to access remarkable details about 'passed over' Souls are really 'tuning in' to the Akashic Records without communicating with an actual entity. This is, after all, what Edgar Cayce said he was doing. Why is it that people we once knew communicating through a psychic never say: 'Hey, it's all an illusion. Don't believe what they tell you – you are being manipulated!'? Instead, it is mostly human world stuff and not what will set you free. Psychics who can connect beyond the Matrix can deliver expanded levels of information and connect with non-Matrix Spirit freed from Samsara, but they are the few.

Fake 'Heaven'

You are out of the body, greeted by the projections, up the tunnel to the false light and into the fake Heaven. Judging by the NDE accounts you may find yourself in a garden, meadow, or looking across a river to the departed on the other side. This will be designed for you, too, as somewhere you associate with Heaven or feel comfortable with. People say they felt 'liberated' when they leave the body, but why wouldn't that be when they have been released from the dense physical body with all its encoded limitations and entered a far more etheric realm with an entirely different physics? NDE accounts described the Astral Heaven as 'more real' than the human world and again this can be understood. The Astral is still part of the simulation, but far less dense and 'unreal'. Sometimes you will see only one 'guide', other times great hordes of people in a stadium-like setting cheering your return after doing a 'good job' in the human shitshow. One near-deather recalled seeing dancing souls, children playing, dogs jumping, merriment and joy – 'just a wonderful festival'. In the sky were 'pure spiritual beings of pure golden light, emanating beautiful music'. They tell of seeing 'beings of light' with no features 'but I knew who they were' which is very impressive intuition.

Why would children be playing when children are a feature only of the material realm and a dense 'physical' body? Why would a discarnate Soul be a child? Or a jumping dog? These are designer scenes and projections which you then recall when you return to the material to further program people to go with the projections and into the light when their body terminates. This is the point about NDEs. They come back. They are told they must return to complete their 'mission' which is rarely defined. The mission is really to tell their tale and encourage others up the tunnel. They don't do this maliciously and they give comfort for those who fear death or have lost people they loved. They are only saying what happened to them, but it suits the Archontics and makes the wheel continue to spin through acceptance of the process. Most Souls don't want to return to an often-challenging life as a human, yet they are told they must and find themselves back in a body often wracked with physical and psychological pain. Choice doesn't appear to exist in this false Heaven. There are many symbols that near-deathers recall for the threshold beyond which there is no returning to Earth. These can be anything from an archway or wall to a river. The point is that near-deathers don't cross that threshold and that's why they can tell their stories. None of them know what is on the other side where the 'wheel keeps on turning' as a song goes from my youth.

A constant aspect of the near-death experience is the 'life review' when they describe in their various ways the same sequence where their life is played back to them on a screen or screens and their behaviour assessed often by 'elders' with the white beards and robes. Why are they old when there is no ageing in the Astral? It is an Earth programming symbol for 'wise men'. Near-deathers describe how details of what they did and said up to that point in a human life are assessed along with how that made others feel. I have called it Roman Catholic confession with pictures. It is a guilt trip extraordinaire. Most don't see it like that at all. They say 'there's no judgement' when that's exactly what is going on. The 'elder' projections clearly lead them to judge *themselves* and feel like shit when at the other end of the cycle their personality type and life story is pre-planned. Square that circle, or cycle. You can't. One said they felt 'profoundly ashamed at the way I behaved' and felt 'pretty small at that point' while also saying the 'guide' told him that 'everything happened as it was supposed to'. Where's the sodding 'karma' come in then? You plan a life experience and personality and then face 'karma' for what was *planned* to happen? Is it me? The silliness reaches mega proportions when 'elders' assess if the Soul remembered their pre-incarnation 'advice'. Well, that's a bit difficult, mate, when you wipe my bloody mind. Near-deathers recall how even what they did as children is judged and taken into account. Or rather self-judged. The 'wise elders' don't judge, you see, although in truth that's exactly what they do.

The loosh loop

A psychological trait I have observed over the years is that people stop asking even basic questions or pointing out even basic contradictions once they give their minds to an authority. Plus, all the conflict, suffering and 'bad behaviour' is orchestrated to keep the loosh flowing. You give them their loosh and then pay your 'karma' for doing so and return to Earth to produce more. Near-deathers are being prepared to buy the 'karma' scam and sell it to others when they return to human. It also programs them to go through the tunnel and the whole charade again when the moment comes to leave this reality at bodily 'death'. Imagine the guilt-trip and pressure to return that happens on the other side of the threshold and how much of what they experience is not recalled because of another mind-wipe of details they don't want humans to know? A past-life regression book claimed that a life review with the 'elders' was 'as close to seeing a divine being as we get in the spirit world'. What utter crap – they are *projections*. Some think they saw Jesus, Muhammad, and Buddha overseeing the review seeking to take them to the 'next level'. Blimey, it must be all they do when 170,000 people die every day. 'Hey, Budd, we got a Buddhist in the tunnel – red alert.' *What*? I'm worked off me feet. The outcome is always the same whether it be a near-deather or someone regressed to the between-life state. The 'review' decides that you have more to learn, and another human life must be experienced to fix your faults – a life that leads to more 'faults' in need of fixing with another life and another and another.

The reincarnation scam is nothing to do with 'learning lessons to evolve'. It is the human equivalent of governments saying 'accept the crap now in the hope that things will get better in the future'. But they rarely do and that's the idea. Feed them the hopium and make them think they are getting somewhere when they are going round and round. The Astral may be less dense than the human realm, but it is still a form of plasma matter with extremely advanced forms of AI technology that runs the system. Souls are convinced by their Archontic handlers that they are little children who must learn lessons and human lives are carefully arranged to allow them to 'evolve' (produce maximum loosh). They incarnate to connect with a biological computer body with programmed software dictating their life experience unless the program is overridden by awakening to the Divine Spark within. Humans are their Life Programs without that intervention and little more than non-player characters or NPCs.

They believe they are thinking their own thoughts and feeling their own emotions when it is just the program playing out. They are designed to be loosh machines by infusing low-frequency states into the energy emitted by the Divine Spark to allow the Archontic system access to that energy at a frequency it can absorb. Divine Spark energy is filtered through the Soul and human bodies along with other energetic fields which are manipulated into low-vibrational states by the experiences and pressures of stupendously low density that we know as the material world. All the while the biological computer is decoding the simulation information field into the illusion of an external 'physical' reality and is it any wonder that humanity is so monumentally controlled and confused?

The simulation is a frequency band of manipulative information, and the Soul must remain trapped within its Ring-Pass-Not after a human experience or the loosh supply would disappear. The mind-wipe on the way into human experience continues until the Soul is back in the Astral, across the threshold, and on the Wheel of Samsara to return through another mind-wipe for another dose of loosh generation. The cover story for the

Figure 94: We must keep incarnating onto a billionth of a pin head to learn and evolve. Sounds credible.

bewildered Soul without Divine Spark influence is that 'God' has created a system for their evolution that involves the constant incarnation into energetic density and an Earth that is by comparison with the estimated extent of the Universe the equivalent of a billionth of a pin head (Fig 94 on previous page). Yes, that makes sense, and it is no mystery why I refer to naivety as the 'human disease'. The Soul disease, too, it would seem. This has been a swift summary of the reincarnation cycle because of the dot-connector nature and reason for this book. You will find far more detail in my Reality Trilogy, *The Trap*, *The Dream*, and *The Reveal*.

Near-deathers invariably say that the reincarnation cycle is motivated by 'love'. God loves us so much that 'He' wants us to suffer so we can learn. Gaza children blown apart by Israel bombs are learning a lesson, then? What could it be? Don't incarnate again as a Palestinian when the Israeli government wants to destroy you and steal your land? Observe all the suffering, hunger, conflict, war, and desperation across the world and it is all about learning to 'love'? It must be true – the elders said. My reply to them is not suitable for a family audience.

CHAPTER 8

Beyond the Veil

Psychic abilities aren't reserved for a gifted few – they are natural states of awareness we can all remember and reclaim.
Desta Barnabe

Remote viewing is the ability to project your awareness to another location and has long been used by the military and intelligence agencies to spy on people and places.

I remember speaking at a conference in San Francisco in the 1990s when a woman approached me to explain how her late husband had been part of the US military 'psychic assassination squad'. She said military recruits were scanned and assessed for psychic abilities and those skilled with the gift were developed and trained for the 'squad'. Groups would then sit around a table with a picture of the target and focus their attention for example on his or her heart stopping. The collective power of their projected energetic attention would impact on the electrical system of the heart and stop it beating. The person would die and no one outside a tiny military circle would know why. It must have been 'natural causes'. I have heard something similar from other sources over the years. Orthodox 'science' dismisses psychic phenomena and potential in its ignorance (including calculated ignorance) while military and intelligence are constantly researching those realms and using the very abilities that orthodoxy rejects as even being possible. Witness the US military 'Gateway' study of the Astral with Robert Monroe.

Psychic spies

Remote viewing (RV) is again to project awareness to a place that can't be accessed 'physically'. It's like 'Astral travelling' that many explore. The 'viewer' will be given coordinates for somewhere they have never been and be asked to describe it in detail purely through mind projection. This can be in 'real time' or even a 'past' event. All exists in the same NOW and they are projecting their consciousness to connect with the energetic fields where 'present', 'past' and 'future' information is stored. Distance is not a problem because there is no 'distance' in the realms of consciousness. The viewer will report what they see and often draw images they are perceiving. Remote viewing experiments include describing objects in a sealed container and a place 'far away' that trainers know about, but the viewer doesn't. The best of them are then recruited to remote view for the military and intelligence agencies. I have met people who have done this. Gifted psychics are regularly used by the inner circles that operate way beyond the alleged 'cutting edge'. Others outside the military have developed these skills. The most gifted are able to describe people, objects and locations of which they know nothing before they 'tune in'. Advanced remote viewing employs all the psychic 'arts' from clairvoyance to telepathy to out-of-body experiences and intuitive 'knowing' to access information from other locations and is done under strictly controlled conditions. The military have no interest in getting flawed information.

The best-known US military experiment into remote viewing was the Stargate Project established at Fort Meade in Maryland, home to the National Security Agency (NSA), in 1977. It was overseen by the Defense Intelligence Agency (DIA) and for many years headed by Lt. Frederick Holmes 'Skip' Atwater who later became president of the Monroe Institute in Virginia established by Robert Monroe. Stargate is also the name given to the mega AI project announced by Trump, Larry Ellison and Sam Altman within two days of the Trump presidency in 2025. US Army Lieutenant Colonel Wayne McDonnell wrote the Robert Monroe Gateway Process report in 1983 about the Astral dimension declassified by the CIA and was a member of the US Army Intelligence and Security Command (INSCOM). This was headed by Major General Albert Stubblebine III, an expert in 'psychic warfare and espionage'. McDonnell mentioned remote viewing in his assessment of the Gateway Process:

> In addition, the energy bar tool is used as a portal for initiating a follow-on technique called 'remote viewing'. In this context, the participant turns his bar of energy into a whirling vortex through which he sends his imagination in search of new and illuminating insights.
>
> The apparent purpose of the symbolism involved in the vortex seems to cue the subconscious and convey to it instructions as to what the participant wishes to do but in terms of nonverbal symbols which the right hemisphere of the brain is capable of understanding.

Joe McMoneagle, a trainer with the Monroe Institute and on the Board of Advisors, served as a remote viewer in a Stubblebine psychic spy programme. He has claimed he remote viewed Russian military bases and said of his 20 years as a remote viewer: 'My success rate was around 28 percent. That may not sound very good, but we were brought in to deal with the hopeless cases.' Information was cross-checked with any other intelligence to assess what was happening. 'We proved to be quite useful spies', he said. The Fort Meade Stargate was small scale and closed in 1995, but remote viewing has developed and expanded to become a significant part of military and intelligence surveillance and information gathering. Other countries do the same to a high-level including China and Russia. It comes down in the end to the ability of the viewer. Many call themselves remote viewers that aren't, but to dismiss the phenomenon is as ridiculous as believing every last word from every last 'remote viewer'. It is on that basis that I present the following and people will have to make their own conclusions.

Remote viewing the Matrix

I was sent a video by the very aware Jean Nolan in the United States (see his Inspired channel on YouTube). It told the story of four remote viewers who had accessed what sounded very much like the simulation I have been highlighting for more than two decades. The video featured Brett Stuart, author of *Remote Viewing: The Complete Guide*, and founder of the organisation, Technical Intuition. He spoke about the experience of himself and three other remote viewers who explored the subject of 'moksha' which is a Sanskrit word defined as 'freedom from the cycle of death and rebirth'. Moksha (also vimoksha, vimukti, and mukti) is used in Jainism, Buddhism, Hinduism, and Sikhism for release from the reincarnation cycle. Stuart posted the video some years ago on YouTube and then took it down because of what he said was the feedback from people it had sent into a dark place. He also said it had been misinterpreted by some, and they had ignored the caveats about interpretation, etc. It was reposted on YouTube by Jean Nolan because he felt that people needed to know the information and I agree with that. We cannot in effect censor what the population sees just because some may not like it or misinterpret it. We are facing a situation in which all information available is vital for people to make a judgement on what is happening and how to respond. All I am doing here is quoting from the video and letting people reach their own view about what to make of it.

Brett Stuart said the 'viewing' was done under the usual controlled conditions with the four viewers working independently of each other. He said of the collective findings: 'If multiple viewers hadn't come up with the same information, describing the same mechanics, the same groups that are responsible, it would probably be even difficult for me to believe.' They described a fence or grid around the Earth which acts as a 'barrier' that 'collects and traps people, things or objects'. This was a deliberate function that was like a cage or animal pen. Stuart said:

It stirs, agitates, and it works in a cylindrical manner, like clockwork, over a long expanse of time. In my session, my work described a planetary system that's extremely crowded and jammed. Ghostly voices are flooding into this place and incredibly harrowing for them. It's a bone chilling experience. As a viewer, when I remote view this, I had descriptions that made me upset in the session and elicited contempt for what was going on at the site.

A net had been spun as an operation of 'catch and release on a grand scale'. A massive grid existed around this planet which was 'a checkpoint, a waypoint or rest stop where Souls are drained'. This energy then energised something else. The process worked with Earth shielded by a companion object, and they were not sure if this was a 'physical thing' or not. 'I mean, we're dealing with a ... type of technology that's so far beyond which humans can even probably comprehend.' It was almost like magic which 'makes sense why one viewer probably uses this word hocus pocus'. The technology was so far 'beyond his own lexicon'. Maybe this companion object 'exists in a phased state in a different dimension' where this object 'creates this net' that is 'powerful and magnetic and it squeezes tightly around the globe'. One viewer described it as a magnetic 'vice', and it was a 'mechanical process that incorporates destructive chemicals'. An individual underwent 'bombardment as they pass through the system'. They feel lost and 'don't have an understanding of what's going on' as they lose memories. This is the 'mind-wipe and what is described here I have heard from many other sources about loosh extraction after 'death'. Another thing – if minds can be wiped of memories where does that leave official 'history'? Did it happen at all?

Stuart says of the reincarnation process: '... these are Souls that are being bent back towards the planet ... the closest analogy was kind of like gravitational lensing ... there's an artificial structure that is lensing or curving your light back down to Earth.' There was 'a fracturing that occurs to force this light in this Soul to kind of come back down to the planet again for a second, third, infinite amount of times'. This reincarnation process was ultimately powering something else, and the viewers described a 'massive rotating object that visually appears like an axle in space' which was 'fluctuating and absorbing energy that's created by this lensing effect'. Stuart said:

... what is being done to the reincarnating souls? There's a fracturing that is occurring ... It's rendering them very confused and upset about their predicament. Something is being extracted and taken from them without them being conscious of the occurrence.

The analogy that was used in the work is that of bees in a box, or like a harvest of honey from bees, and that there's a honeycomb. And this is the kind of the trapping within the mesh that's occurring. And then there's a third party that comes in, extracts honey out of this box. This [is taken] for some other purpose and then … the bees [are put] back into the box.

Stuart said that was a very close analogy 'that matches what is going on here with Souls'. Another viewer described this as harvesting: 'There's a harvest that occurs when a Soul goes up and then is refracted back down.' The whole system was 'toxic':

The number of Souls, the amount of individuals that are reincarnating on this wheel is that this creates an instability that is required for this alchemical process. Without this volatile planet, without volatile Souls, without creating this certain type of scenario where something's taken and, you know, thrown back, and you've no memory, it wouldn't produce what it is desired by this third party.

The crowded state of Earth and the number of Souls here is required to create an optimal environment to extract what's desired. The confusion and anger caused by the confinement feeds into this process, and an aspect of the individual's mind or their Soul.

The intelligence or the mind of the Soul was feeding 'an external parasitic force'. Drawings from the remote viewing work 'were certainly grotesque' and associated 'with something that's warped, sadistic and twisted, that's actually doing this process'.

Moral degradation

The viewers explored how all this began and came about. Information they gleaned indicated that 'historically … the planet was viewed with extreme envy by an external force' at a time when reincarnation did not exist. When individuals left here they were not trapped and were able to leave. Then came an enormous war when a huge force was met with resistance and 'the fate of a planet was decided'. The viewers said they saw that the Earth was a tiny component in a much larger system. 'It's minuscule, but it's a much, much larger operation.' Brett Stuart said:

It describes that we are part of a funnel, and it's a … state of moral degradation or spiritual dejection in a manner, and that the system encircles us and that its proponents have cast a wide net, not just here on this planet.

Those that perpetuated this system in the closest vocabulary the viewers had was that 'these things are like demons' that were feeding on intelligence during the extraction process, fracturing the individual, the

Soul, and sending them back:

> It's something parasitic, something that's twisted and warped. But ... the work describes that they have put man in this cage, mind in this cage, and that wars of men, anarchy, destruction, societal overthrows, cyclical revolutions, that occur down here all fuelled the system that actually keeps us entrapped.

This is what I have been exposing all these decades as the Archontic vampires feed off human low-vibrational energy and to produce this loosh there must be constant war, conflict, suffering, mayhem. The energy is then trawled – especially in the immediate post-death process:

> ... There's just far too many people here on this planet and that's intended because it creates the chaos that feeds into the system that powers it. And so, when pinpointing and remote viewing ... the energetic activity that's occurring, when a Soul dies, it gets caught up in the system and sent back. It appears ... a part of them is chipped off and then carried off somewhere else.

> ... it's a limbo state that's occurring. And these aspects that are chipped off or described as ghosts, these are aspects of the Soul that have been drained up and used, and an overwhelming melancholy and sadness is associated with these remnants. This is what's split apart and fractured off.

The Soul became enslaved, bundled up like a collection of twigs, and used as 'kindling', Stuart said. This fed a different system that 'doesn't have anything to do with here'. Earth was like one small engine that feeds back into a power plant. 'We're essentially Souls being used as kindling ... coal for this system.'

Who are they?

The viewers focussed on the entities behind all this. Stuart said they were able to describe who they were, where they were, and the general purpose. Those perpetuating the system were 'a council of organic entities, and they exist and operate this from a location that is incredibly concentrated':

> ... You can think of it kind of as a bubble or a void zone or black hole that they're existing within, and they're creating an artificial environment, an artificial, timeless environment from which to exist in and then spread their influence out in a time reality in the Universe.

> Essentially, it's making them immortal, but they're doing this in a way that they spread throughout the universe through these various gateways ... they create these little void zones in various pockets in space, in the Universe. There's one

here in this specific solar system, and this pocket is what allows them to pop in and out anywhere they want, along this conquest or supply line.

It was 'almost like they entered into a different dimension that doesn't have time, but they can come out anywhere they want along the supply line for it'. They didn't age and they had created a system in which they 'set themselves up as gods'. They viewed themselves as 'gods of reality' that were above the other life forms, and they believed this gave them the authority to do what they do. 'The energy that is being funnelled back to create the system is also being funnelled back to them.' The viewers described them as 'evil':

> It's about taking the energy that exists in the Universe, accumulating it, and then absorbing it for their own desires and to serve their own purposes which has nothing to do with serving a greater good. It has nothing to do with bringing harmony or peace to the Universe.

The viewers said the entities were organic life forms 'but through their technology, or whatever you want to call it, they created an environment for themselves that they are no longer biological'. They may as well not be, because they existed in this timeless reality with or without bodies. The viewers saw them with 'eyes that are blazing white.' They used to be organic beings 'but through technology, they figured out a way to set themselves up to live forever so they don't die'. This is what the Big Tech AI cabal is seeking to do and why I say the Archontic force is an advanced form of AI. Brett Stuart said: 'And from that space, they have an outward expansion of conquest in the universe to perpetuate a system of control, to perpetuate a system of cages around planets that keep Souls locked and trapped there, so that every time they die, they have to go back.' The entities had dismissive contempt for humans:

> They do notice you actually looking at them, but it's rather irrelevant to them ... It's very, very strange ... It was like a gorilla noticing a gnat. It was very dismissive where like little mind, I don't have time for this ... I have much more important things, much more grand things to think about. And so, it wasn't even really an interaction. It was just like a gorilla noticing a gnat and then ignoring it afterwards.

How to escape The Trap

The viewers turned their attention to 'moksha' or release from the reincarnation Wheel of Samsara. They said that upon death 'particles like cosmic dust or dark matter, something strange, a strange type of particle that we don't have a description for ... becomes charged and creates an emission'. The particles 'launched out of the individual very, very quickly, like a cannonball out of a cannon, or bullet out of a gun'. They were emitted from the central nervous system in a spiral. 'Something is spiralling right out of the top of the head of the individual from their internal system.' A vast amount of energy was released – 'the intelligence of the Mind from the body – and was being 'sent to a place that is described as a tangled mess or a superhighway for the Soul'. There was 'a mechanical object around Earth that prevented the Soul from reaching this highway':

> Seems like if you're able to reach the superhighway, you can go pretty much anywhere you want. Achieving moksha gives you access to this superhighway and where those lead, your guess is as good as anyone else's, I suppose at this point, but for this to work properly, to actually achieve moksha, is that the position and the angle with which you exit your body is very, very important.
>
> And the concept … is that it brought up the idea of how the Egyptians used to evoke an out of body experience, and how the angle with which the body was actually laying was considered important to the Egyptians … It described that this 45-degree angle was a key element. And so, as the body dies, the Soul needs to exit at a correct angle, lest it be trapped within this system again, and then is refracted back, and then lens back again into another body.

There was 'something like a safety rope if you exit at a right angle'. A group was waiting to help you the rest of the way out. They assumed that 'it's probably the group that used to be in charge of this particular space, or in charge of this environment around Earth as far as death is concerned'. They are there and 'if you can meet them at a certain point, they can help you out the rest of the way'. There was a great deal of fear associated with the energetics of leaving the body and the [mind-wipe] incarnation process meant there was no memory of what is happening. 'It's all seemingly brand new to you.' This is the point I have been making in many books. '… the fear of this seems to be something that prevents most people from ever getting [out].' It was very, very, important not to go into the light after release from the body. This was crucial. The body was like having a vice on your head for a 'very, very long period':

> The vice has gone all the way down into your brain, into your mind, there's cords and cables you didn't even realize that was occurring, that's created this environment for you to repeat these lives over and over again, and that the freedom of moksha is this device being ripped off and taken off the top of your head.

... The closest analogy to something like that is you could look at the movie *The Matrix* when Neo wakes up and all the cords are pulled out of his back ... that's in essence in the human vocabulary, what is occurring ... something in your head is being ripped off and is being pulled off violently. That's ... kept you here in the first place.

Brett Stuart said he believed it is very important for people in this lifetime to think about how they attain moksha. There was the outside group that 'may not be in charge of this particular space' but is waiting for people that 'figure out how to avoid the specific snares that exist for Souls as they exit the body'. I agree that working on achieving the knowledge of the human situation and how to release ourselves from the simulation when the body expires is far and away the most important aspect on which to focus. You can do everything you can to 'build a better world', but what's the point if you go up the tunnel to the false light to come back again with a wiped memory and another programmed personality? We do what we can to improve life here, okay. Escaping the Matrix is, however, the number one priority or the game just goes on and on.

Travelling the Astral

I also spoke as I was completing the book with Rolf Nuyts from Belgium who was the first European to serve on the board of the Monroe Institute of Astral travel promotor Robert Monroe. You can see him in the *Messengers* series with Christianne van Wijk at Ickonic.com. Nuyts had his first out-of-body experience when he was ten and later became a Certified Outreach Trainer and Off Campus Residential Trainer at the Monroe Institute. He's been Astral travelling through consciousness projection and connection since 2002 along with colleagues and those he has trained in the technique of Monroe's 'Hemi-Sync' which balances both sides of the brain. Nuyts said you could travel by projecting your attention into other energetic bodies like the Astral body which gives you the feeling of moving and covering 'distance'. Or you could do it through pure consciousness and then 'you are right there at the very same moment'. He said this way you could be on the other side of the Earth and tap into information without feeling that you have moved. He has realised from what he's seen in the Astral that our reality is indeed a simulation, a Matrix, or what he described as 'the disturbance'. He said the 'disturbance' is 'overlaid' and blocks out what I call Prime Reality. This again matched my own perception for decades that the Matrix is an overlayed source of information to which the human body is tuned to decode into the illusory material world.

He told me how he has seen and interacted with reptilian entities in the Astral and seen them 'shapeshift' in our reality from apparently human. Nuyts described one incident in which a woman's face changed. 'It became greyish and then I saw her teeth become sharp.' He said she told him she often went to Egypt where she could see the different timelines and dimensions in the same 'space'. Nuyts said he had noticed many people with reptilian eyes during 'Covid' when people wore masks, and all focus was on the eyes. Draconian reptilian energy appeared to be running the lower and material dimensions, but he had seen in the Astral many other types of non-human including the Greys and those that appear in like a Praying mantis form. He said the non-humans have 'an enormous variety of personalities'. Some entities were very common while others were more 'high level', a higher ranking with higher energy.

We discussed how Astral entities vampire loosh from humans and he said one major source was through the chakra system which was all about generating loosh that can then be trawled. I personally feel that if you can blast through the frequencies on which the chakra vortices normally operate this can be negated. Nuyts said the 'third eye' pineal gland in the brain was like a piece of biological technology to connect humans to other levels of the Matrix. These 'spiritual' aspects of the body were used to control and manipulate through emotions and behaviour. The chakras had different 'flavours' (frequencies) for the entities, he said. 'I think the main moment that they harvest the information (energy, loosh) is when people die ... they lure you [with] the tunnel of light, and strip you of all your memories.' Entities, religious heroes, and 'loved ones' that people saw during near-death experiences that led people to the light or through the tunnel were synthetic and not what they appeared to be. He told me how he had questioned Astral entities, including the apparently 'angelic', and they become angry. 'They don't like being questioned.' You can see why when questioning reveals an awareness that will not just roll over to their claimed authority and omnipotence. Many locations appear to be blocked to Astral travellers and remote viewers and among them Nuyts has found in his experience are the Moon, Mars and the White House. The latter appeared to be the case since the presidency of Father Bush between 1989 and 1993. I guess that's to be expected as remote viewing began to circulate and be used by governments.

Rolf Nuyts says that the fifth dimension and above remain harmonious, but below that level of awareness the unity of consciousness is fractured and fragmented like multiple expressions of fractal patterns with different aspects of 'you' dispersed into different realities and dimensions. See how common themes repeat. The idea was to fuse those parts back together through an awareness of infinite identity so all that accumulated wisdom and experience could be absorbed into the Infinite 'I'. The challenge was that the fragmented entities behind the Matrix were seeking to prevent this by manipulating constant imbalance and fragmentation. They knew that when balance is restored the game is over. Balance came from connecting with heart intelligence that was far wiser than the brain and generates a far more powerful electromagnetic field (Fig 95). Here lies the connection to the original essence of the complete 'I' which spans all dimensions – the Gnostic 'Divine Spark'.

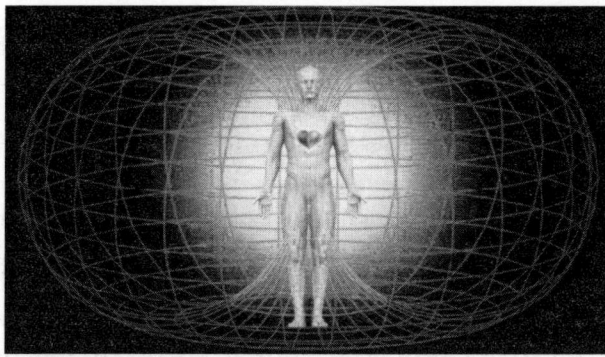

Figure 95: The electromagnetic field generated from the heart centre is the most powerful in the body.

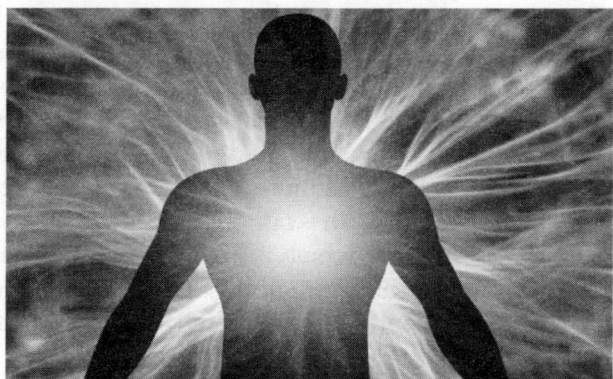

Figure 96: Where wisdom reigns.

I have written extensively in many other books about the power of the heart to bring balance to all levels of being. Here you find wisdom beyond anything the brain can manifest and the energetic balance that brings everything into integrated wholeness. This is referred to as 'going within' (Fig 96). Nuyts stresses from his experience that every time you externalise your sense of reality, whether in the human or Astral realms, you are in the Matrix. Focusing on the inner 'you' is how to connect with infinity. Nuyts said that entities who knew this considered an integrated human as like 'royalty' – the most powerful intelligence in the Universe. Observing the world makes that hard to imagine, but what we are seeing in the 'external' is the result of human consciousness *fragmentation*, not integration. We experience a chaotic 'external' through a chaotic or fragmented 'internal'. One is manifesting the other. The Archontic seeks to secure this ongoing imbalance by getting humans to externalise reality and sense of self and instigating chaos and upheaval in the external that we think we have no control over. It's another feedback loop. *Internal* chaos creates *external* chaos. Take your attention into the heart and the world looks a different place. You suddenly see what really matters and what does not. You see the ludicrous 'game' for what it is. A perceptual trap.

'Seeing Yaldabaoth'

I was contacted just before this book went into production by American near-death experiencer Isabella Greene, author of *Leaving the Trap: How to Exit The Reincarnation Cycle* and *Transcending the Trap*, who has also experienced the Astral many times in out of body projections (see *The Reveal*). She said that a recent experience warned of the urgency for people to understand the nature of The Trap. The experience was in line with what I have been warning about over the decades in the way AI, genetic manipulation, and synthetic biology is creating a human body vehicle that would delete the potential connection to Infinite Awareness. This is the prime driver behind my exposure of the fake 'alternative' media that is holding the conspiracy line at politics and finance when a vastly bigger picture must be seen. Isabella said she projected her consciousness into the Astral with the intent to enter the 'mainframe' of the simulation to see if any 'adjustments' could be made to benefit humanity. 'As I landed there, it was familiar with this dark space, dark layer, around the Earth – not entirely black and you retain your humanness in there which is how I knew I was in the fake void' (and not the infinite one). She felt another presence with her that she couldn't see and began to scan for what she felt was looking at her:

> I saw an eye. It was a yellow eye with vertical pupils. Then I saw a scale and a claw and a spike. I was only able to see little pieces of this presence and I thought maybe there's a giant or a Reptilian in this space. When you are Astral-projecting you can easily move to any location, and I decided to move to the opposite side of the Earth from where the dragon was ...

> ... When I did that, it could still see me. It felt like that presence was everywhere and I was getting the most eerie feeling that it was looking right at me ... There was this attitude of arrogance and self-centred confidence, and cold, dismissive energy was coming towards me.

Isabella said she returned to her body, but curiosity sent her back to see what the presence was, having never experienced it before:

> I went out of my body again and sensed that I was in a layer outside of that black void. It looks like a black circle around twelve dimensions of the Matrix. You see it very clearly once you project yourself out of that structure.

> It's like the Earth is in the centre and you have twelve dimensions of the Astral all colourful and rainbowy and beautiful, and the outside is that black layer. I knew that being was in that black layer. Is that the mainframe?

She said that when she viewed the entire being it looked like an Ouroboros. It wasn't swallowing its own tail, but it was wrapped around the Earth in tight circles. 'It was holding the Earth like this is *mine* – nothing was coming in here, nothing … ' The being was holding all the dimensions of the Astral and the Earth plane. 'That's my property.' She said it looked very much like a Chinese dragon that you would see in Chinese celebrations 'where the head is big like a lion's head, but it's got like human features, big teeth, big yellow eyes, the vertical pupil … and a long body like a snake, but it had four legs … and really massive paws and claws.' As she withdrew back into her body, still in an altered state, she asked what the being was doing:

> I got that bone-chilling feeling – this is the owner of Earth, this is the owner of all of these realms and he's here to harvest, to get energy that it's now orchestrating or upgrading or whatever. It's obvious that the next level of harvest is on.
>
> As I continued tuning in … I started getting more downloads [about] the depopulation agenda – get rid of all the organic bodies and replace them with technologically modified bodies so that him and his minions and Archons don't need to work any longer and install a system that would retain humans without much effort.

She said it was next level entrapment where humans would only have one option of incarnating into technologically modified bodies where they would not even have the inclination to question or have the ability to access their 'supernatural abilities or anything spiritual'. They would be '100 percent bound to Earth' at that point:

> All the New Age stuff when they say that the reincarnation cycle is no more and rejoice, the system is getting dismantled … [Yes] it is getting dismantled, but in favour of an upgrade system where it is going to be a no-brainer for the owners to keep humans entrapped.

This is what I have been warning about and there are many things to pick out here. I said earlier that Gnostic texts describe Yaldabaoth as taking the form of a 'lion-faced serpent' with eyes like 'flashing fires of lightning'. I should stress that projecting into the Astral is not a modern phenomenon – it's been happening since ancient times among shamans and others. Isabella's experience would explain the concept of the Ouroboros and the 'Ring-Pass-Not'. Maybe what she saw was projected symbolism, or maybe literal. Either way it would put into context what I say about the Gnostic Yaldabaoth being the distorted consciousness that transcends the entire Matrix and seizes the perceptions of all those locked into its frequency including its Archons and demonic emanations. It would confirm my concept of humans and the simulation in general being within the Mind of Yaldabaoth and subject to its distortions. The way out is to expand our frequency as I'll come to later to go beyond the frequency limits of the Matrix. The current transformation of the human body into a synthetic entity with its fusion with AI is designed to block that expansion by overriding and never asking the Big Questions: Who are we? Where are we? What is this 'place'? Those are the questions if asked with true intent that begin to reveal the answers and our infinite nature. The new body and AI are planned to so control human perception that they are never asked, and the dystopia becomes the unquestioned sense of 'normal'.

It is vital to remember that expanded and balanced consciousness is infinitely more powerful than the Yaldabaoth distortion and this is *not over*. Come on, people, we can do this.

CHAPTER 9

The Global Cult

*A secret society exists and is living among all of us.
They are neither people nor animals, but something in-between.*
Karen White

The origin of human control is in the Astral dimension, but there is an essential network in the human realm to impose and play out the Astral Archontic agenda. That network is the Global Cult.

The opening quote of the chapter talks about neither people nor animals, but something 'in-between'. I say the 'in-between' is a very advanced form of biological AI – a version of an NPC – although programmed with the knowledge of how to serve their Astral masters through the manipulation of human perception. You only have to observe the major players at even the gofer level to see that they are computer-like in their demeanour, devoid of empathy and compassion, and able to act in ways that would emotionally destroy Divine Spark people at the very thought of doing what the cultists do every day – and love it. They are super-psychopaths and programmed to be so. What that means can be seen in the personality traits of mere run-of-the-mill psychopaths of which there are far more within human society than official estimates of at most a few percent. This is a list of psychopathic characteristics at choosingtherapy.com:

> Superficial charm and charisma; unnecessary cruelty or a mean streak; lies, exaggerations, and dishonesty; lack of accountability and playing the blame game; need for power, control, and dominance; sadistic enjoyment of pain and suffering; boredom and thrill-seeking behaviours; disregard for rules, laws, and norms; unaffected and unafraid of consequences; detached, cold, and callous demeanour.

Scan those across the system of human control in politics, corporations, media, law enforcement, banking, and all the other institutions. You'll find so many who fit that description and when we come to the inner circle of the Global Cult and its agents and assets you would have to double and triple that at least. The book so far makes the reason for this obvious. The leading cultists are emanations, creations, of the stupendously psychopathic Archons and those traits are downloaded to their minions. 'Superficial charm' is their way of hiding their real self and even then many cannot. Their coldness and meanness is obvious to anyone not mesmerised by their apparent power. Bill Gates and former World Economic Forum chief Klaus Schwab come to mind immediately. How can you plot the deaths, sterilisation, and health destruction of millions, even billions, through vaccines unless you are a super psychopath? How can you plot the total control of humans through AI like Schwab and the AI oligarchy unless you fit that bill? How can you coldly mislead your supporters in the case of Trump and Musk while manipulating them to the same end as Gates and Schwab? The latter is an example of how the Cult seeks to control all 'sides' through their place-people to be sure of the outcome. Cultists don't like states of flux where the outcome is in doubt. It terrifies them, in fact.

Where it came from

The Cult goes 'back' to ancient times with the proviso I mentioned about 'time' and 'history'. I have laid out how the Astral 'gods' controlled the ancient population through manipulation and intimidation, and I will expand on that in later chapters. The thing to emphasise here is that they did so via a hierarchy in which monarchs and priests acted as intermediaries to impose the will of the interdimensional gods on the people. The gods ordered their appointed lackeys in Exodus 18 to select people who feared the gods to be given power over groups of '1,000, or 100, or 50, or 10'. These hierarchies would represent the laws and control imposed by the gods and this is precisely how the Global Cult operates to this day. One biblical scholar said: 'We are dealing here with an actual pyramid organisation to make the government of a few thousand people functional.' It's now billions, but the principle is the same and it's not only about 'function'. The foundation reason is control. The gods then used this structure to embark upon the incessant centralisation of power as they withdrew from the public eye and operated from the shadows.

The more you centralise decision making, the fewer people have control over the many, and we are now closing in on a global government dictating to every community. A global government that would not ultimately be elected and instead appointed in the form of bureaucrats and technocrats in a system labelled a 'technocracy'. This is a system of dictatorship very much connected to the Musk family via his Jewish grandfather which his grandson, Elon, is now pursuing with vigour along with the Silicon Valley Mafia. The gods and their Cult created Mystery schools and secret societies to communicate advanced knowledge about reality through generations of initiates while other schools and societies dedicated to protecting the knowledge for the benefit of humanity were infiltrated. American Freemasonic historian

The Global Cult

Manly P. Hall (1901-1990) wrote in his epic *Secret Teachings of All Ages*:

> While the elaborate ceremonial magic of antiquity was not necessarily evil, there arose from its perversion several false schools of sorcery, or black magic. Egypt, a great center of learning and the birthplace of many arts and sciences, furnished an ideal environment for transcendental experimentation. Here the black magicians ... continued to exercise their superhuman powers until they had completely undermined and corrupted the morals of the primitive Mysteries.
>
> By establishing a sacerdotal caste they usurped the position formerly occupied by the initiates and seized the reins of spiritual government. Thus black magic dictated the state religion and paralyzed the intellectual and spiritual activities of the individual by demanding his complete and unhesitating acquiescence in the dogma formulated by the priestcraft.
>
> The Pharaoh became a puppet in the hands of the Scarlet Council – a committee of arch-sorcerers elevated to power by the priesthood.

This allowed the spiritual knowledge about reality – the 'gnosis' – to be twisted and inverted. Even those who thought they had access to the Mysteries were given a limited and inverted version. Hall writes:

> These sorcerers then began the systematic destruction of all keys to the ancient wisdom, so that none might have access to the knowledge necessary to reach adeptship without first becoming one of their order. They mutilated the rituals of the Mysteries while professing to preserve them, so that even though the neophyte passed through the degrees he could not secure the knowledge to which he was entitled.
>
> Idolatry was introduced by encouraging the worship of the images which in the beginning the wise had erected solely as symbols for study and meditation.

Satellite groupings of the Cult were everywhere interacting with the Archontic 'gods' and interdimensional 'demons' under many and various names. The goal was to link these groups into a global network which has now been achieved. The Middle East was a major centre with the period of Egyptian dominance along with Sumer, Akkad, Assyria, and Babylon in Mesopotamia and what is now Iraq. The Abrahamic religions of Christianity, Judaism and Islam came out of this same region and have much in common despite first appearances. This is not a coincidence and has instigated the inter-religion conflict with all the benefits for loosh and divide and rule. The Middle Eastern Cult expanded into Rome and northern Europe with the Roman Empire. The Roman period of dominance was a massive stepping stone for the Cult and remains central to Cult thinking and methodology. Elon Musk is a fan.

World domination

The Cult began to go global when tribes were brought together into nations ruled by a fraction of those that made decisions in the former tribes that formed the nation. Kings, queens, and priests continued to be the intermediaries for the gods. The big go-global period was colonisation when the Cult-controlled countries of Europe, especially Britain, took over the world through conquest and manipulation. It appeared on the surface that colonisation largely ended in the 20th century as the European powers withdrew and granted (the arrogance of it) 'independence'. In fact, the secret society network that colonisation established, and key hybrid bloodline families, were left in those countries and have continued to control them covertly ever since. The population think that a vote every four or five years for secret society-endorsed candidates confirms their freedom. Most royalty fell in the same period and control moved into Cult-created politics and corporations to make it seem that we lived in people-power 'democracies' when they are One-Party States masquerading as political 'choice'. Mega-groupings like the European Union have brought nations under the centralised control of the few – see unelected bureaucrats in the EU – and you have gathering groupings like the BRICS nations of Brazil, Russia, India, China, South Africa, Egypt, Ethiopia, Indonesia, Iran and the United Arab Emirates. This is highly significant with global power planned to be moved eastwards while assets like Trump are used to dismantle the West and sow chaos.

The Cult operates undercover through coordinating the same policies and direction between what appear to the public to be unconnected, even antagonistic and rival, countries, corporations, etc. It is the scriptwriter for what is little more than theatre to target the perceptions of the global population and give them a false sense of what is happening. Many of those involved with the various facets won't know there is background coordination, but the key players do as they answer to their masters in the shadows. The Cult is known on one level as the 'Deep State', or Shadow State, manipulating people and events from behind the scenes, but all the national 'Deep States' are part of a global 'Deep State' – the Cult. This network wants the public to see everything as bewildering and random while it gets on with its calculated coordination. We need to lift our gaze from the twigs and see the forest to unravel the bewilderment. I have long used the phrase: 'Know the outcome and you'll see the journey'. Everything appears random and confusing if you don't know the planned outcome. Daily events appear as they are – stepping stones to the outcome – once you know where we are being taken. So, what is that 'outcome'?

The Plan

I'll get into this in more detail, but for now these are the foundations. The planned outcome is a global dystopia based on control by a world government hierarchy and artificial intelligence (Figs 97 and 98). First and most certainly foremost is to fuse humans with artificial

Figure 97: The structure of the planned Global Cult/Astral dystopia. (Image by Gareth Icke.)

Figure 98: What I have termed The Hunger Games Society in which a tiny elite controlled from the shadows would oversee the police state oppression of humanity via artificial intelligence. (Image by Neil Hague.)

intelligence so that AI becomes the human mind and emotional responses. This is another way of saying that the Archontic force becomes the human mind on a scale not seen before because that is what this level of AI really means. I have chapters specifically about this and how the fascist Donald Trump regime in the United States is manipulating its supporters to accept this ultimate dystopia in what is a blatant psychological operation or 'Psyop'. The human-AI fusion is designed to create a hive mind which can be infused with the same perceptions from a central point. Hard to believe? Maybe, but it's also true. It is happening minute by minute with the nano infrastructure in the body and the technologically generated 'Cloud' constantly expanded by ever more 5G towers with 6G and 7G in the pipeline. Most crucially this is done by tens of thousands of low-orbit satellites courtesy of Elon Musk and SpaceX, along with others. We talk about cloud computing which is a hosted service delivered over the internet and include servers, databases, software, networks, analytics and other computing functions. The 'Cloud' I am talking about includes that but is also a global technological electromagnetic field which can connect with the human electromagnetic field and deliver information from a hive mind. Information can be communicated via electromagnetic waves of magnetism and electricity and include radio waves, microwaves, infrared radiation, visible light, ultraviolet light, X-rays, and gamma rays. Radio and television broadcasts, mobile phones, and Wi-Fi networks all communicate information through electromagnetic wave fields.

The hive mind is to add another layer of control to stop an awakening to the Divine Spark and the Infinite Realm. Once AI is dictating thought and emotion the potential for loosh is unlimited and an AI Mind is not going to even think about big questions such as Who am I? Where am I? What is really going on? The escape hatch would be slammed shut. We are looking at a process in which the Astral 'gods' have been developing human knowledge potential to the point where they can build their own AI prison while having no idea they are doing so, to what end, and what force is ultimately behind it. The process can be described as developing cleverness without wisdom, and it absolutely depends on blocking access to expanded awareness beyond the simulation. The idea is to control human thought and behaviour through AI and then the 'gods' can show themselves again.

AI-controlled humans would live in an AI-controlled society in which centrally controlled artificial intelligence would be making all the decisions with humans utterly marginalised. I am old enough to remember when you called a company or government department and talked to a human. Then the tapes came in and now it's AI. Even this is only the start. Imagine a world in which nothing is possible unless AI agrees (with AI controlled by the Astral 'gods'). You can't buy food or anything without the right entry code that you only get if your behaviour and opinions suit authority. You can't travel by any means unless AI says you can. The number of people controlling humanity would be a fraction of what it is even today. Numberplate cameras now being installed in their millions using different excuses would ensure that you are fined for leaving your designated 15-minute zone without permission and the fine would be taken by AI from your digital bank account the moment you 'transgressed'. This would be done to 'save the planet' from a human-caused climate change that isn't happening. Censorship would be all-pervading with AI not only taking down forbidden posts but blocking them even *being* posted if they include a 'wrong' opinion.

Almost all jobs would be taken by AI leaving humans to exist on a pittance 'Universal Basic Income' which you would only get if you obeyed authority and had approved views and opinions. A carbon tax, again justified by the climate lie, would allow you to buy each month only up to a 'carbon limit' with each product designated a 'carbon footprint' value. Credit cards already exist that won't work once a carbon limit is reached every month. Your children would be 'taught' by AI and there would be an AI robot police force and military. Drones would patrol the skies and with millions of cameras in every town and city you would be under surveillance wherever you go. Nano-tracking devices in the body (see 'Covid' fake vaccines and other sources) would mean you could never go anywhere the authorities didn't know about with a global network of low-orbit satellites able to monitor every inch of the planet. See the Skynet system in the *Terminator* movies when an AI 'created by humans' became self-aware and took over everything. Anyone who thinks this is all too fantastic and only sci-fi is not paying attention. Look around – it's happening and expanding by the day. There is so much else in the Cult plans, but that will do for starters. None of this has to happen when eight billion are being directed by a comparative tiny handful. The maths alone makes that obvious and this is why control of *perception* is the foundation of everything. Control perception and you control the world. It took just two days into the second Trump presidency for him to hold a White House press conference with Jewish AI billionaires Larry Ellison (Oracle) and Sam Altman (OpenAI) to announce an up to $500 billion investment in AI expansion and infrastructure. Trump is the AI president and even more so is the vice-president, JD Vance.

The Web

The Global Cult structure can be accurately likened to a spider's web around the planet with each strand representing a secret society, semi-

Figure 99: The Global Cult structure with the Astral spider at the centre dictating the direction of human society. (Image by Neil Hague).

secret group, or known organisation in the public arena (Fig 99). This interlocking web owns governments, corporations, military and intelligence networks, the banking and financial system, medicine, media, Big Tech, and all the institutions necessary to control human society. At the centre is the Spider and that is the Archontic force in the Astral with which the cultists interact during Satanic rituals that include human sacrifice. You will see from their psychopathic traits why they have no empathy with their often child victims. The inner core of the Cult is the Archontic demons of the human-non-human hybrid bloodlines – the shapeshifters. They are often reptilian in their non-human state and include at least most of the remaining 'royal' and 'aristocratic' bloodlines and those who moved into the political and corporate world when humanity would no longer be ruled by genetic succession. The strands immediately around the Spider are the most exclusive secret societies and their initiates will not be famous. They put their gofers on public display while they pull the strings way back in the shadows. They control through this network everything from politics, finance, military, media, and the pharmaceutical cartel to Zionism, religion, Satanism and 'elite' paedophile rings (Fig 100).

Next as we expand out from the Spider are the secret societies that we do know about such as the Knights of Malta, Knights Templar, Opus Dei, and the inner circle of the Jesuit Order. Note how these are all connected to the Roman Church which is a 100 percent owned entity of

Figure 100: All roads lead to the Cult and the Astral gods even though they appear unconnected in every day life. (Image by Neil Hague.)

the Archon-serving Cult which dictated what texts went into the Bible and which did not. When I get to the real background to religion you will see why the Roman Church has been a Cult creation from the start and why it is still so influential within the structure.

This section of the web involves many secret societies that are publicly known (and many that are not), but what they *do* is not known through oaths of strict secrecy. An obvious example are the Freemasons with their lodges in every town and city of the West and further afield. They are an example of the secret society compartmentalisation that keeps even their lower initiates in the dark about the real agenda. Most Freemasons never advance beyond the bottom three levels of 'degree', the so-called 'blue degrees', and there are 33 degrees in the Scottish Rite. You only enter a higher degree when that level decides that you qualify. You have a fail-safe mechanism to stop any interloper or potential whistleblower progressing very far even if they got in to start with (Fig 101 overleaf).

A lower initiate might be able to use the lodge to get business opportunities. Maybe a local builder in a lodge with a council planning officer might get favourable treatment that a non-Freemason would not. The great majority of Freemasons, however, have not a clue what their secret society is being used to impose. Many would be horrified if they did when they have children, too. They are what has been called a 'show army' for the inner circle to hide behind and within. I went to an 'open day' at a local Freemason's lodge in my town when they were seeking to present themselves as warm and cuddly after some bad publicity nationally. I saw pictures of local councillors and dignitaries to confirm they were Freemasons and asked some of those showing people around about Freemasonic history and the reason for their characteristic symbology. They genuinely had no idea. I was telling *them* what their

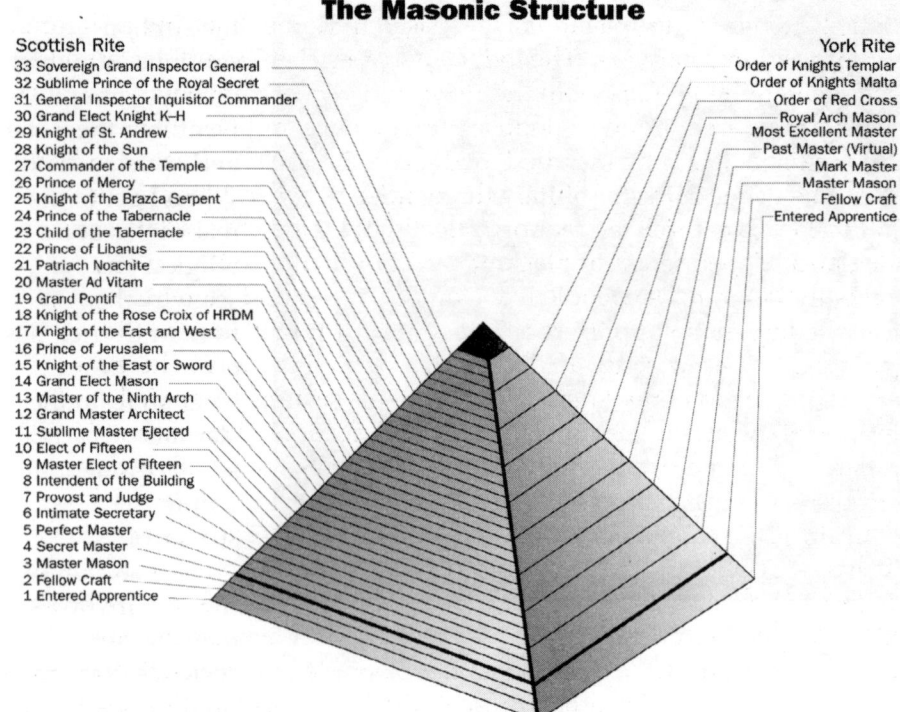

Figure 101: The Freemasonic structure perfectly illustrates how the Cult is compartmentalised into degrees of knowledge. You only know what you need to know to play your part without knowing the biggest picture. Only the few are aware of that.

symbols represented. Freemasonic historian Manly P. Hall reveals the origin of this ignorance:

> False interpretations were given to the emblems and figures of the Mysteries, and elaborate theologies were created to confuse the minds of their devotees. The masses, deprived of their birthright of understanding and groveling in ignorance, eventually became the abject slaves of the spiritual impostors.
>
> Superstition universally prevailed and the black magicians completely dominated national affairs, with the result that humanity still suffers from the sophistries of the [ancient occult] priestcrafts ...

When we say 'the Freemasons' are involved in global and national manipulation we are not talking about blokes down the local lodge. We mean the inner circles that take their orders through the web from the Archontic Spider.

The P2 blueprint

A perfect example of this compartmentalisation came with the exposure of the P2 lodge, or Propaganda Due, based in Rome, Italy, but spanning out into a global network. The lodge and its fascist Grand Master Licio Gelli were raided by police in the 1980s and lists of members revealed major names among Italy's political, intelligence, military, banking, legal and media 'elite'. They included media tycoon Silvio Berlusconi who would be Prime Minister of Italy three times between 1994 and 2011. Political leaders rarely appear organically. They are chosen for their allegiance, dependence, or blackmailed compliance to the Cult. It is a real belly-laugh to see people like Donald Trump and Elon Musk described by their supporters as 'mavericks' who bucked the system. Yeah, right. P2 initiates were divided into sealed sections where the leader of a section only knew who was in his section. Only Gelli and a few key associates knew who was in *all* the sections. This meant that P2 initiates were interacting in government, business, law and media without knowing that each was a member of P2.

Gelli, a Mussolini fascist, had global connections through the Cult. He was a close friend of Argentina's fascist leader Juan Peron and both US President Ronald Reagan and his vice-president George H.W. Bush, the serial paedophile and super-psychopath. Gelli was invited to Reagan's inauguration. Bush is another example of the secret society and bloodline network. His father, Prescott Bush, a funder and supporter of Hitler and the Nazis, was a member of the elite Skull and Bones Society based in its windowless headquarters across the road from Yale University in Connecticut (Fig 102). George H.W. Bush was also a member and went on to become head of the CIA, vice-president, and president of the United States. Later *his* son, George W. Bush, another Skull and Bones initiate, would be US president. Political leaders are not *el*ected, they are *sel*ected. Political 'choice' is an illusion.

The Cult controls the Democrats and Republicans in the United States and it's the same around the world. I call it the Left-Right puppet show – vaudeville, theatre – to keep the people fighting each other over political parties controlled by the same force. The 'choice' is between masks on the same face and there was a time when much

Figure 102: Skull and Bones Society headquarters across the street from Yale University in Connecticut. Part of the initiation ritual is to lie naked in a coffin while revealing sexual secrets. Presidents Father and Boy Bush have been among the initiates.

of the 'alternative' media realised that the 'multi-party' system is really a One-Party State masquerading as 'choice'. Since the Cult hijack of this 'alternative' following 'Covid', its highly-promoted central core has regressed perception back into the Left (bad), Right (good), diversion – exactly as it was meant to do. Power moves between one or the other (Democrat and Republican in the US case) to maintain the illusion that the population is selecting the government. Look at the direction of travel, not least with AI, and you will see that when you ignore the rhetoric the same agenda is

Figure 103: We only see the gofer level of politics. The real power is permanently in the shadows as political leaders of all parties come and go.

followed no matter who is in official power. Take one step back into the shadows and there are the same hands holding the strings of all parties that have any chance of forming a government and many that haven't (Fig 103). As they used to say when I travelled America in the 1990s to make these points: 'It doesn't matter who you vote for the government still gets in.' Yes, the Cult government. The hijacked 'alternative' wants you to forget that.

The Vatican connection

P2 is also an example of how the secret society network of the Cult connects into religion. They are different facets of the system of perceptual control after all. P2 big-time ran the Vatican and its finances which emerged with its exposure. Roberto Calvi, a P2 member, was Chairman of Banco Ambrosiano of which the Vatican Bank was the main shareholder. Calvi was labelled 'God's banker' for this reason. He knew where the bodies were buried, symbolically and otherwise, when the P2 scandal broke. This was not good for his health. Banco Ambrosiano collapsed after transferring massive amounts of money abroad via the Vatican Bank in contravention of Italy's currency laws. The deeply corrupt Vatican was cleared of all crimes, but agreed to pay Banco Ambrosiano creditors $224 million in 'recognition of moral involvement'. Moral and the Vatican in the same sentence. Must be a first. Calvi fled to London where he was found hanged under Blackfriars Bridge at the entrance to the seriously Cult-owned London financial district known as the 'City of London', 'the City', or the 'Square Mile', which was the original London. His private secretary had jumped from the fifth-floor window of his bank's headquarters the day before. I'm sure she wasn't pushed.

Secret societies like the Freemasons love their symbolism. It is the secret language by which they communicate with those 'in the know'. Calvi had masonry in his pockets and P2 was known by initiates as 'frati neri' or 'black friars'. The Blackfriars Bridge under which Calvi died was named after the Blackfriars Monastery, a Dominican priory which once stood nearby. The bridge is designed with 'pulpits' for this reason (Fig 104). Dominican friars were known as Black Friars and Dominicans were involved in the horrendous Roman Catholic Inquisition to kill non-believers and the siege and mass burning of the Gnostic Cathars at Montségur Castle in 1244. P2 was also involved in the murder of Pope John Paul I in 1978 after being appointed only 33 days earlier – 33 is a highly symbolic and significant Freemasonic and secret society number.

Figure 104: A pulpit on Blackfriars Bridge at the entrance to the City of London or The City.

The white smokers at the Vatican had somehow chosen the wrong guy and this pope, real name Albino Luciani, set about purging the Vatican of Freemasonic (P2) influence. See David Yallop's book, *In God's Name*, for the background to his poisoning that caused the shortest reign in papal history.

Major religions and secret societies are seriously connected because they are both the creations of the Global Cult and its Archontic masters. Secret societies are phenomenal in number and those connected to the Cult have an interlocking 'mission control' that coordinates actions between them as necessary. Once in the Cult and taking the benefits, you don't refuse its orders. You do what it tells you – or else. All Cult secret societies have a route into higher levels for the mega-chosen beyond those that officially exist. The Freemasonic Scottish Rite officially consists of 33 levels or degrees, but the chosen can go through that into another level that I will call the Cult degrees. It's all compartmentalised hierarchy because that is the mentality and structure of the Archons and their Reptilian and other demons.

'Cusp' interface

Secret societies take the Archontic agenda from the Spider and expand it out through the hidden part of the web before delivering the demands to the 'Cusp' section. This is the half-way house between the hidden and the seen. It consists of semi-secret organisations which operate partly in the hidden and partly in the seen in that people are aware of them or can be if they choose to do a modicum of research. I'm talking about organisations like the World Economic Forum founded in 1971 under another name by the German Klaus Schwab; Royal Institute of International Affairs or Chatham House (1920); Council on Foreign Relations in the United States (1921); the Bilderberg Group (1954); Trilateral Commission (1973); and the Club of Rome (1968) which was established specifically to exploit and create environmental concerns to justify the centralisation of global power to 'fix' the problem. The human-caused global warming hoax is a Club of Rome invention along with other environmental groupings. The Cusp includes the now stupendous number of non-governmental organisations (NGOs) and 'think tanks'. The role of the Cusp is to take the agenda from the Spider delivered through the secret societies and 'sell it' or play it out into the world of the seen through governments, their agencies and institutions, corporations, medicine, and media.

Cusp organisations are the Cult's sales-pitchers. They bring together politicians and leading 'opinion formers' and decision makers across the spectrum of national and global politics, government administration, corporations and media to form consensus policies across the spectrum of issues. Some will be cultists while others are here-today-gone-tomorrow people who come and go election-by-election who are needed while in office to support a direction of society dictated from the shadows. Many of the latter won't even know there are any 'shadows', but their ego is flattered by being invited to join such 'distinguished' company and they are sucked into the consensus. The Cult mirrors the interconnectedness of simulated reality in that all these groups, NGOs and think tanks are connected through the web although most of those involved and invited won't know that. They are there to be moulded into agreement with the Cult agenda and this is done through bullshitting them and, if necessary, by blackmail. Such is the power of the Cult and its media that political careers can be built or destroyed by compliance or resistance. 'If you work with us, Mr Politician, we can help your career.'

The Cult also likes to advance people with something to hide because it makes them easier to threaten if they refuse to comply. 'We can make sure your secrets stay secret, or we can blast them on the front page with a banner headline – which will it be?' Jeffrey Epstein's Israeli Mossad/CIA network of sexual abuse by the rich and famous was part of this approach. Mossad is a major Cult operation. I have spoken to several women – abused by the Epstein circle when little more than children – who have described the Epstein cameras and microphones on his island and properties on the US mainland. Have you noticed politicians who seem genuinely opposed to certain policies who then suddenly start arguing in favour? We all have and it's common. This can be the political technique of tell-them-what-they-want-to-hear to get elected and then do what you planned all along. Or, it can be: 'We can make sure your secrets stay secret, or we can blast them on the front page with a banner headline – which will it be?' Imagine if the Epstein material implicated Donald Trump who Epstein described as his closest friend for ten years? What power Mossad would then have over the US president. It would certainly come in handy if you wanted the American military to do some bombing for you and supply unlimited weapons. Follow the sequence: Trump was the closest friend for a decade of Jeffrey Epstein running a blackmail operation for Israeli Mossad. Trump later ran for president, won twice, and has given Israel virtually everything it wants. Lawrence B. Wilkerson, a retired United States Army Colonel and former chief of staff to US Secretary of State Colin Powell, said it was unquestionable that the 'Epstein business' was at least heavily influenced by Mossad. He said:

> I watched Mossad take over the Pentagon. In 2002 the Pentagon was infiltrated by Mossad. They did not need any identification to get through the river entrance to the building. They went upstairs to [ultra-Zionist] Douglas Feith, the Under-Secretary of Defense for Policy, the third most powerful man in the Defense Department.
>
> Occasionally they went to the second most powerful man, [ultra-Zionist] Paul Wolfowitz, the Deputy Secretary of Defense, and they had the run of the Pentagon. Donald Rumsfeld, the Secretary of Defense, told my boss once – 'Hell, I don't run my building – Mossad does'.

Rumsfeld, Feith and Wolfowitz officially ran the Pentagon on 9/11 and if you read my book, *The Trigger*, you will see why Mossad was in control and to what end. You will also be in no doubt in the face of enormous evidence who was behind 9/11, and it wasn't 19 Arab hijackers. Elon Musk posted in a fit of pique after his public fall out with The Donald that the Epstein files were not being made public because Trump was in them. Soon after the Iran bombing and coinciding with another visit to the White House by Netanyahu, the Trump regime announced there were no 'Epstein files' and no reason to charge anyone with his crimes relating to underage girls. Trump had told his MAGA supporters that he would release the files and now suddenly they didn't exist despite his gofer Attorney General Pam Bondi telling the media earlier that they were 'on my desk'. Nothing fishy here, then. I'll have more on Epstein and Trump later.

Bilderbergers

The Bilderberg Group has been playing its Cult role since officially launched in 1954 at the Bilderberg Hotel in the Netherlands. It has since been orchestrating global policy and has been enormously influential in the incessant centralisation of power through the European Union which has been a long-planned project of the Cult as I have exposed in detail in other books. Cult stalwarts like the late David Rockefeller and Henry Kissinger were centrally involved along with the Dutch royal family. Annual Bilderberg gatherings are held in hotels around the world amid strict security. I visited a Bilderberg location in Switzerland in the 1990s just before the guests arrived and saw the security staff preparing. The location was a group of extraordinarily expensive hotels on a hill approached by a long road. When I returned during the event I couldn't even access the road. A police roadblock was installed at the bottom of the hill. I asked an officer what was going on and why the road was closed. He said that he was only told there was an event with important people and no one should be allowed up there. Such is compartmentalisation.

It became well known in the 1990s among what was then a tiny, disparate, alternative media that if someone new with political ambitions was invited to the Bilderberg meeting that their career was about to blossom. I remember both Bill Clinton and Tony Blair were invited just before they became President of the United States and UK Prime Minister, both of whom seriously advanced the Cult agenda. Blair is still at it working from the semi-shadows – the 'shade' you might say. Hardly anyone had heard of Bilderberg when I first came across it in the 1990s, but gradually we brought it to greater attention until even the mainstream media picked up the theme although not to expose its real reason for being. A protest I was involved with outside a Bilderberg meeting in Watford, England, in 2010 brought together thousands of people and by then its desired secrecy was no more at least among those seeking answers about who controls global events. It has since been usurped in Cusp prominence by the World Economic Forum (WEF) and its annual meeting in Davos, Switzerland.

The Schwab Mob

The WEF was launched by Klaus Schwab from a Nazi-connected family in Germany after he had been a steering committee member of the Bilderberg Group and a director for five years of the UK *Mail* newspapers. He announced in May 2024 that he was stepping down as chairman of the WEF which happened in early 2025. He then said he would relinquish his new role of chairman of the Board of Trustees by 2027 but resigned with immediate effect in April 2025 at the age of 87. Schwab headed the WEF for 55 years. He was a protégé of Henry Kissinger, a US Secretary of State and National Security Advisor, who was a Cult operative virtually all his adult life. Kissinger answered to the Rockefellers and Rothschilds in the Cult Archontic hierarchy. Cult support for 32-year-old Schwab's European Management Forum in 1971 meant that he attracted 440 executives from 31 nations to the first meeting. It was renamed the World Economic Forum in 1987 and has since become the most high-profile front pushing the Global Cult agenda. Schwab was replaced as WEF chairman by 'interim chairmen' ultra-Zionist Larry Fink, CEO of BlackRock, the world's biggest investment management corporation, and André Hoffmann, the Swiss billionaire from the family behind Big Pharma giant Hoffmann-La Roche, of which he is vice-chairman. Hoffmann is also a member in this interlocking web of the Club of Rome and Royal Institute of International Affairs. WEF goals can be seen with the members of its Board of Trustees: Larry Fink again; Christine Lagarde, former Managing Director of the International Monetary Fund (IMF) who became President of the European Central Bank; Mark Carney, former governor of the Bank of Canada and Bank of England, leading figure in the Bank for International Settlements which coordinates global policy between central banks, and now Prime Minister of Canada. Around a thousand Cult-controlled corporations fund the WEF (they wouldn't dare not to).

Leading names in world affairs attend the annual event in Davos and they arrive in some 1,500 private jets to urge governments to take action on the climate change hoax that the Cult instigated to justify the transformation of society. That's why they fly in private jets and buy mansions by the sea. They know it's all nonsense. WEF attendees also include royalty from the Netherlands, Norway, Sweden, Denmark, and the UK in the form of Prince, now King, Charles, who is a vocal advocate of the climate change hoax. Some 3,000 attendees from 130 countries arrived for the 55th WEF gathering in 2025. Among them were US President Donald Trump (on a live feed from America) and leading politicians and officials from countries worldwide including China, Ukraine, Israel, Spain, Switzerland, Belgium, Armenia, Azerbaijan, Congo, Panama, Egypt, Iraq, Ireland, Netherlands, Poland, Peru, Serbia, Singapore, Sweden, Syria, Thailand, Somalia, and Elon Musk's buddy, Argentina president Javier Milei. Then there was European Commission president Ursula von der Leyen, European Parliament president Roberta Metsola, and UN Secretary General António Guterres. Not a bad line-up if your goal is to manipulate the world in your image, but there's more. Other participants were:

The Director-General of the World Trade Organization; Managing Director of the IMF; Secretary-General of NATO; Director-General of the World Health Organization; Administrator of the United Nations Development Programme; the CEO of Gavi, The Vaccine Alliance (Bill Gates); the General Secretary of the International Trade Union Confederation; CEO of Conservation International; President and CEO of the International Crisis Group; President of the Association for Fulani Women and Indigenous Peoples of Chad; Executive Director of Human Rights Watch; Executive Director of the Global Fund; Executive Director of Oxfam International; Chancellor of the Pontifical Academy of Sciences and Social Sciences of the Holy See. Plus, regulars including Bill Gates and George Soros who both employ fake 'philanthropy' to fund key elements of the Global Cult agenda. The summit was headed 'Collaboration for the Intelligent Age' and for 'collaboration' read 'coordination'. Donald Trump appeared by video link shortly after he took office for the second time. He claims to be against everything they stand for, but that's only for his support base. Trump is on board with the Cult and wouldn't be president twice if he wasn't. We'll see the scale a few chapters on of how monumentally his supporters, or the Make America Great Again 'MAGA', are being mercilessly played. Trump said in 1998:

> If I were to run, I'd run as a Republican. They're the dumbest group of voters in the country. They believe anything on Fox News. I could lie and they'd still eat it up. I bet my numbers would be terrific.

That's what he *really* thinks of you MAGA. Trump could have used the live video link to Davos if he was genuine to expose the World Economic Forum agenda and the people involved. But he isn't. Instead, he talked about how many friends he had in the Davos audience. Anyone think that Schwab would have invited him to speak live to a global audience if he wasn't 'safe'? The WEF promotes the AI control agenda and Trump brought Elon Musk on board to dismantle government and human This is why the AI tech billionaire oligarchs like Peter Thiel, Marc Andreessen, David Sacks, and others circled their wagons around him and Musk spent $250 million to get him elected. Musk donated $5 million to MAGA Inc., the main super PAC affiliated with President Trump, in late June 2025 *during* their 'feud'. A day later he attacked Trump's spending bill as 'insane and destructive'. Ugh? Musk's mate, David Sacks, was appointed by Trump as White House 'AI and crypto czar' to oversee the AI agenda implementation.

Getting them ready

The World Economic Forum does not only select people already circulating in politics. It brings through young people to take the reins of political, corporate and Big Tech power. To quote Schwab directly the idea is to 'penetrate' governments. He said he was proud that more than half of the Canadian cabinet of then Prime Minister Justin Trudeau had been through the training system known as the Economic Forum Young Global Leaders. Trudeau stepped down in 2025 and was replaced by Mark Carney who is on the WEF Board of Trustees and is a 'globalist' to his very core. These are some names that have been through WEF 'training':

Vladimir Putin, President of Russia (according to Schwab); Angela Merkel, long-time Chancellor of Germany; Tony Blair, UK Prime Minister from 1997 to 2007; Jacinda Ardern, New Zealand Prime Minister during the 'Covid' hoax; Emmanuel Macron, President of France; Gavin Newsom, Governor of California; Jean-Claude Juncker, former Prime Minister of Luxembourg and President of the European Commission; José Manuel Barroso, former President of the European Commission; Alexander De Croo, Prime Minister of Belgium; Sanna Marin, Prime Minister of Finland; Carlos Alvarado Quesada, Costa Rica President; Peter Buttigieg, US Secretary of Transportation; Sebastian Kurz, a Chancellor of Austria; Nicolas Sarkozy, former French President; Annalena Baerbock of the German Green Party, Minister of Foreign Affairs, Leader of Alliance 90/Die Grünen; Faisal Alibrahim, Saudi Arabia Minister of Economy and Planning; Vasudha Vats, Vice-President of Pfizer; Businessman Richard Branson; Jacob Wallenberg from the family known as the 'Swedish Rothschilds'; Elon Musk; Peter Thiel, Musk associate and orchestrator of the AI control agenda; Bill Gates at Microsoft; Jeff Bezos, Amazon founder and owner of the *Washington Post*; Larry Page, founder of Google; Mark Zuckerberg, founder of Facebook; Jimmy Wale, founder of Cult-narrative Wikipedia; Jack Ma, founder of Chinese Internet tech giant Alibaba; actor Leonardo Di Caprio, UN 'climate ambassador'; singer Bono, mate of Bill Gates and agenda promotor; 'Green' campaigner David de Rothschild; and Ricken Patel, founder of Cult agenda promoting Avaaz.

The World Economic Forum is only one of the Cusp organisations, albeit a prominent one, and think of the potential that it has to take the Spider agenda and implement it through Big Government, Big Business, Big Tech, Big Pharma, and Big Media. The interconnected network is mind-blowing of secret societies, semi-secret and Cusp groupings, along with the enormous range of think tanks and non-governmental organisations (NGOs), many funded by Cult operative George Soros and his family. These connect with and infiltrate governments and their agencies, media, medicine, 'science', academia, and transnational corporations that include investment giants BlackRock, Vanguard, State Street, Fidelity, and others that have stakes in almost any company with a global reach and many that don't. BlackRock alone, headed by WEF co-chairman, Larry Fink, managed assets worth 11.5 *trillion* in 2024 through 70 offices in 30 countries and boasts clients in 100 countries. It claims to be an American company and yet really represents Israel, a country that comes up over and over and over with regard to the Global Cult. Schwab and his network were all over the 'Covid' hoax when a 'virus' that never existed was used to impose fascism on the world. He produced a book, *The Great Reset*, urging governments to use the (manufactured) 'crisis' to 'reset' society in a different way. The Cult way. The 'Build Back Better' mantra parroted by leaders the world over was straight from the Cult script and heralded what Schwab described as the 'Fourth Industrial Revolution' – AI.

Schwab and the WEF brought the young vulnerable Swedish girl Greta Thunberg to the world stage at Davos, and she went on to lecture the United Nations about a climate change threat that is a Cult fantasy. She was just someone else to be used and abused for their own ends which is what you would expect from psychopaths. Thunberg was the vehicle to target the young to campaign for the Net Zero insanity that is deindustrialising the world to open the way for AI.

CHAPTER 10

From the Hidden to the Seen

Almost any sect, cult, or religion will legislate its creed into law if it acquires the political power to do so.
Robert A. Heinlein

The Spider leads to the secret part of the Cult web and onto the semi-secret 'Cusp' and now we enter the world of the seen. Well, seen in the sense of seeing public governments and organisations, but not the manipulation happening from the shadows.

We experience the result of that in calculated government and economic policies. Scan the world and you see an apparently bewildering number of governments, agencies, corporations, Big Tech, groupings like the World Health Organization, media, NGOs, think tanks. It is a maze that seems impenetrable, impossible to see what's what, and yet the basic structure is very simple (Fig 105). All these major organisations that can affect the direction of the world are compartmentalised like a secret society using the 'need to know' principle. Employees only know what they need to know to do their jobs. If you work for any of these Cult operations ask yourself what is happening and being decided by those at the top. You don't know. What is the agenda being followed by those at the top? You don't know. Who or what does the inner circle connect with outside the official organisation? Same. What secret societies do they answer to? Same.

Go deep enough into these

Figure 105: The Cult and Astral gods control all the permanent institutions while selecting here-today-gone-tomorrow political leaders for brief periods of service to the Cult agenda. Many won't even know there even *is* a Cult such is the compartmentalisation.

governments and organisations and you reach the point where they connect to the web of the Global Cult. At that level all these governments, agencies, corporations, Big Tech, groupings, media, NGOs, think tanks, and so on, are the *same* organisation – the *same* Cult – pursuing the *same* agenda of dystopian human control through AI on behalf of the Astral 'gods'. The overwhelming majority involved have no idea that this is the case. They just go to work, do what they're told by the higher-ups, and go home to their families. They are not trying to manipulate anyone, but they and their families will take the consequences of the manipulations that they unknowingly make possible. I remember after a talk in London in the 1990s a former executive of the Shell corporation in South America came up to me to say that what he had heard that day had explained much about what happened at Shell, and what he was told to do, which made no sense at the time. He was an executive, not an oil truck driver way down from the boardroom. People would be shocked at how high the compartmentalisation goes before you hit those who know. The same applies to governments where you can be in the cabinet and still not be aware of the forces at work.

The structure I am describing means that you can both hide the truth from all except a few in any organisation while coordinating policy and direction with other parts of the web and ultimately the Archontic Spider which even many insiders won't even know exists. It all starts to make sense once the structure is understood. At the start of the Cult 'Covid' hoax we had Silicon Valley corporations such as Google-owned YouTube, Facebook, Instagram (owned by Facebook), and Twitter saying they would censor any posts that went against the 'Covid' narrative issued by the World Health Organization (WHO). This seemed strange in that surely these were the very platforms where information and opinion were supposed to be exchanged. There was nothing strange about it once you understand the structure. Go deep enough into these platform corporations and you reach the point which attaches to the Cult web. Go deep enough into the WHO and it's the same. The Cult in Silicon Valley was censoring anyone challenging the Cult narrative of the WHO that they wanted the public to believe. The World Health Organization was created in 1948 by the Rockefeller family (subordinate to the Rothschilds in the hierarchy) to control global health policy from a central point. All these global groups like the World Trade Organization, International Monetary Fund (IMF), World Bank, and United Nations are the same and connect through the Web. The WHO is controlled today by Rockefeller gofer Bill Gates via the mega crook from Ethiopia, Director-General Tedros Adhanom Ghebreyesus. The Gates and Rockefeller families have a close ongoing connection.

The Cult structure allows the Big Pharma cartel (another Rockefeller creation) to basically get whatever it wants from the government agencies that are supposed to protect the public from Big Pharma lies and corruption. Go deep enough again in the Big Pharma structure and you attach to the web and the same with government agencies like the US Centers for Disease Control and Prevention (CDC), Food and Drug Administration (FDA), and in the UK the Medicines and Healthcare products Regulatory Agency (MHRA). You will remember that during the 'Covid' hoax these 'protection' agencies in each country lied outrageously to the public about the fake 'virus' and gave permission for Big Pharma to infuse its nanotechnology 'mRNA' fake vaccine into the population down to the very young and even babies. These liars told us it was 'safe and effective'. The 'vaccine' is not even a vaccine under previous criteria and delivers self-replicating nanotech into the body which is designed to connect with the 'Cloud' to form the human hive mind. I'll have more on this in the AI agenda chapters.

Holographic Cult

The Cult operates on the holographic principle as you would expect as a creation of the holographic simulation. Every part of the web is a smaller version of the whole. The hierarchical structure at a local level reflects the national and global levels. This allows the Spider to manipulate events right down to local councils to ensure that the same agenda is infused globally, nationally and locally. National hierarchies answer to the global hierarchy, and they manipulate events, funding and media to plant their people – or those with the 'right' opinions and goals – into power. The same is true of global agencies like the UN, IMF, WHO, EU, and so on. Can they control everything? No, not yet. Do they control great swathes of society with that control increasing incrementally? Absolutely. But they don't have to if humanity can emerge from its perceptual myopia and see that what it believes to be the answer – hierarchy and politics – is the very prison it seeks to escape. It is amazing how high you can go in politics and still not know how it is all controlled and who by. Shadow people, administrators, and upper levels of the military, run the show, not politicians. I read an article on the Activist Post website that quoted Dominic Cummings, chief advisor to former UK Prime Minister Boris Johnson, which also featured Liz Truss, the shortest-serving prime minister in British history. Truss was ousted by a stock market crash after the Conservative Party membership picked her and not the Cult's preferred candidate Rishi Sunak. Guess who replaced her? Yep. The experience of Dominic Cummings in the Johnson government showed him that backroom people are far more powerful and influential than politicians. He said in late 2024:

> So, if you think of two roles … the Foreign Secretary of Great Britain and the

private secretary in the PM's office responsible for foreign affairs, an official whose name has never been in the newspapers, that person was, like, ten times more powerful and important than the secretary of state. This is something which, I think, people just don't really realise ...

... It's part of how the whole system has become fake. So, you have fake meritocracy, fake responsibility, and then fake cabinet government ... it's all nonsense. The cabinet is just like a staged theatre.

Cummings was in government during the 'Covid' hoax and told a Parliamentary Committee hearing in 2021 about the influence of Bill Gates:

In March [2020] I started getting calls from various people saying these new mRNA vaccines could well smash the conventional wisdom ... What Bill Gates and people like that were saying to me and [to] others in Number 10 [Downing Street] was you need to think of this much more like the classic programs of the past ... the Manhattan Project in WWII, the Apollo program ... That's essentially what we did.

He said that Bill Gates and 'that kind of network' were telling the UK government what its Covid emergency response should be – exactly what I said at the time. The Activist Post article turned to Liz Truss and what she found when she entered Downing Street to briefly become Prime Minister:

What I [thought] when I got into Number 10 is that, if I got to the top of the tree, I would be able to implement those Conservative policies ... What I discovered, is that I was not holding the levers. The levers were held by the Bank of England, the Office of Budget Responsibility. They were not held by the prime minister or the chancellor [the UK finance minister].

The Governor of the Bank of England two years before Truss took her brief office had been current Canadian Prime Minister Mark Carney and it gives you an idea of the people involved behind the politicians. Carney has been head of the Canadian and UK central banks; a World Economic Forum stalwart; Bilderberg Group attendee; chairman of the Bank for International Settlements' Committee on the Global Financial System; chairman of the Financial Stability Board (Bank for International Settlements); Group of Thirty (G30), a financial grouping established by the Rockefeller Foundation; UN special envoy for climate action; chairman of the Bloomberg board; and a Goldman Sachs employee who became Prime Minister of Canada thanks to Donald Trump's demand that Canada become the US 51st state. Carney's party was way behind until he founded his whole campaign on 'I will stand up to Trump'. In this way globalist Carney got elected because of 'anti-globalist' (not really) Trump.

The Bank of England, the UK central bank, operates independently of the government and connects with other central banks around the world through this Rockefeller/Rothschild established Bank of International Settlements (BIS) in Basel, Switzerland, which coordinates policy between them all while politicians come and go as elections come and go while the same agenda drives on. Underpinning the entire Cult web is Satanism and paedophilia generating loosh for their 'gods' and instilling fear and terror into the hierarchy. The entire Cult structure is founded on fear with each level fearing the level above in a 'choice' between obeying your masters, or knowing they will destroy you, even kill you or family members, if you don't. Those who know about the Satanism or take part in those rituals don't need telling the scale of empathy-deleted psychopathic evil that will be turned on them for insubordination. The whole structure then uses fear (and secrecy) to impose its will on the population at all levels. This is how the world is controlled and its direction dictated on behalf of the Archontic 'gods'. No one is imprisoned and governed by the web more than those who serve it.

The Palantir 'hub'

Bilderberg and other Cusp organisations are what the conspiracy community call 'globalists' in that they seek a world government and centralised global control. This leads to some very strange alliances with supposedly 'anti-globalists'. Bilderberg is run by its steering committee which includes Peter Thiel and Alex Karp, two co-founders of the tech company Palantir which was seed-funded by the CIA (it's really a CIA arms-length company) and provides AI surveillance technology for the intelligence networks and the military, including NATO. Palantir is a major Cusp organisation in that the public know of its existence, but not what it does behind the scenes. It has become a very significant Cult operation, and I want to highlight its role. The media revealed in the summer of 2025 that Palantir was being hired by the Trump regime to fuse together government databases into one network which would allow all information compiled on the population to be accessed at a central point – including their views and opinions. Alex Karp said in a shareholders call that Palantir 'kills people' and their AI is part of what they dub the 'kill chain' which is the sequence between identifying a target and killing them. Ultra-Zionist Thiel and Palantir contracted with Israel to identify targets in Gaza for assassination and bombing. Thiel is a highly significant web operator and apparently a keen reader of science fiction. He says he's read Tolkien's *Lord of the Rings* more than ten times. Palantir/palantíri are indestructible crystal balls employed for communication in *The Lord of the Rings*. Six of his company names, Palantir, Valar Ventures, Mithril Capital, Lembas, Rivendell, and Arda Capital are inspired by Tolkien. Palantir is a public company, Cusp organisation, and in effect a secret society which operates throughout the web.

Peter Thiel, an associate of Elon Musk, has funded the political career of US vice-president JD Vance who is also a Thiel business associate. Vance's political stance is that he's 'anti-globalist' when his career has been funded by a steering committee member of the seriously globalist Bilderberg Group. Vance co-founded Narya Capital with financial backing from Thiel, AI-promoting billionaire Marc Andreessen, and former Google chief Eric Schmidt, a globalist to his fingertips and steering committee member of the Bilderberg Group. Another Trump-supporting 'anti-globalist' is Vivek Ramaswamy. He is also a business associate of globalist Peter Thiel, an investor in Ramaswamy's venture capital operation Strive along with Bill Ackman, an American Jewish billionaire hedge fund manager, and JD Vance. It wouldn't surprise me if the Cult wanted Vance in the presidency at some point and the demise of Trump would achieve that. Thiel was the first outside investor in Facebook as Mark Zuckerberg advanced to Big Tech oligarch status. It's a Big Club and you ain't in it.

Palantir is involved in real-time people tracking, monitoring social media, and censoring through AI algorithms. It even works with crime prediction or 'pre-crime' surveillance. All this was happening under the 'freedom-loving', 'anti-globalist', Trump regime. What a joke. Pre-crime targeting is real with the UK government alone using algorithms to study data on thousands of people for 'murder prediction'. It was called the 'homicide prediction project', which changed to 'sharing data to improve risk assessment' to hide its intent. The pressure group Statewatch uncovered the project through documents obtained by Freedom of Information requests. It has been called 'chilling and dystopian'. The plan is to arrest people around the world purely from such assessments 'to keep the public safe'. Palantir, like Musk, makes billions from government contracts while they coordinate the deletion of money that goes to the population. Peter Thiel is an anagram of 'The Reptile' so someone was psychic obviously.

Palantir everywhere

CIA-funded Palantir headed by Bilderberg's Peter Thiel and the very strange Alex Karp are fast becoming the AI control system within governments; intelligence including the CIA and NSA; military including NATO, the US Air Force, Marines, and Special Operations Command; FBI and police; the Musk established government-wrecking DOGE operation; border police ICE; the Internal Revenue Service (IRS);

private companies like the Wendy's fast food chain; 'health' care; and health insurance companies that they support in 'denial management' to 'protect revenue'. A Palantir whistleblower said the company's aim was to 'run our government, run our battlefields, and run our personal life … Using artificial intelligence as a sort of panacea solution across our federal departments, and especially when they're again wielded by people with a very distinct agenda, puts everyone at risk.' Peter Thiel said at a Libertarian conference in 2010:

> The basic idea was that we could never win an election … because we were such a small minority … But maybe you could unilaterally change the world without having to constantly convince people and beg people, and plead with people, who were never going to agree with you, through technological means. This is where I think technology is this incredible alternative to politics.

Fifty-five percent of Palantir income in 2024 came from sources within government and profits were boosted after the arrival of Thiel's friend Trump. Time to cheer Trump supporters – 'we're winning'. Former Palantir employees have been appointed to key government IT posts and roles in the 'Department of Government Efficiency' (DOGE), first headed by Elon Musk. Palantir's tech goes much further afield than America, too. It operates worldwide as with Israel. The UK National Health Service (NHS) widely uses Palantir software to organise information held by NHS hospital trusts into one unified platform and the Trump regime revealed plans for a new private unified health tracking system. The global agenda moves on. Collaboration between the US government and Big Tech would 'allow patients to more seamlessly track and share their medical records or data among doctors, hospital systems and health apps', the Trump regime and AI corporations claimed. But of course, it's about control, not 'patients', and it was pathetically dubbed for the MAGA base 'Making Health Technology Great Again'. The potential for accessing personal data across all these governments and agencies is limitless and why not eventually a global database like a human Akashic Records? Trump appointed unelected Elon Musk to head DOGE which was supposed to target waste and inefficiency when it was really a means to remove agencies and human jobs in government, delete programmes that benefit the population, trawl personal data, and replace the system with AI. Whistleblowers said Musk and his DOGE were illegally accessing enormous swathes of private data in government systems. Data is the new gold. The *New York Times* reported that Musk and DOGE were compiling data on American citizens from dozens of federal databases and reportedly creating a master database at the Department of Homeland Security. Information was meant to be kept separated to stop this happening:

Mr. Musk and Mr. Trump have knocked down the barriers that were intended to prevent them from creating dossiers on every U.S. resident. Now they seem to be building a defining feature of many authoritarian regimes: comprehensive files on everyone so they can punish those who protest.

Yes, with Palantir at the helm. Elon Musk's artificial intelligence company xAI entered a 'strategic partnership' in May 2025 with Thiel's Palantir Technologies and investment firm TWG Global to 'embed advanced AI into financial services and insurance operations'. The partnership 'envisions a tight integration between xAI's AI models and Palantir Foundry's data fabric' which can 'curate data from transaction systems, market feeds, and customer interactions into unified pipelines'. This is the unified data system of Palantir as contracted by the Trump regime. 'Data fabric' is thus described:

> Data fabric is a broad data architecture system that allows for the seamless integration and management of data across a variety of environments. Think of it as a way to connect disparate data sources virtually without the need for redundant copies. By knitting together these disparate data sources, a data fabric creates a unified framework where you can ensure consistent delivery, governance, and security of data, regardless of where it resides.

In short, a unified data system. Kevin Bankston is a longtime civil liberties lawyer and a senior adviser on AI governance at the civil rights organisation, Center for Democracy and Technology. He said: 'This is what we were always scared of – the infrastructure for turnkey totalitarianism is there for an administration willing to break the law.' The Trump regime had done little else since taking office. The *New York Times* reported that some federal workers had been told that DOGE was using artificial intelligence to sift through their communications to identify people who had expressed anti-Musk/Trump views. America was going full fascist and the rest of the world is going the same way. Peter Thiel is also an investor in facial recognition company Clearview AI contracted by the military to develop augmented reality glasses that combine with facial recognition. Clearview AI 'harvested' billions of social media images without users' consent to create a database for police and private companies to identify people. Peter Thiel is a lovely man. He says so himself.

The Thiel dome

It was announced in 2025 that the Musk-Thiel combination of SpaceX, Palantir and Anduril were front runners to build Trump's 'Golden Dome' missile defence system. US Space Force chief General Chance

Saltzman described this as a network of systems to block ballistic, hypersonic and advanced cruise missiles among others. He said the Golden Dome would 'combine terrestrial, naval, airborne, and space-based sensors and interceptors, along with non-kinetic defences like directed energy weapons and electronic warfare capabilities'. Directed energy weapons are incredibly destructive and have been secretly in the military armoury around the world for a long time. Some believe this is how the Twin Towers were brought down on September 11th. The Pentagon is fast-tracking 'space-based interceptors and infrared satellites' – more satellites with weapon capabilities. 'Do what we say, or we'll destroy you and your family from space.' Reports said that SpaceX had proposed a 'subscription service' in which American taxpayers would fund the building of the network, and the SpaceX trio would charge the government for ongoing access to its own system. One mainstream article said:

> The subscription model, which has not been previously reported, could skirt some Pentagon procurement protocols allowing the system to be rolled out faster, the two sources said. While the approach would not violate any rules, the government may then be locked into a subscription and lose control over its ongoing development and pricing, they added.

My goodness the arrogant cheek of it. The SpaceX-Palantir-Anduril alliance emerged as the frontrunner for the contract. SpaceX has satellite launch capability; Palantir deals with software and data analysis; Anduril's expertise is defence and autonomous drone technology. They plan up to a thousand satellites to detect and track missiles across the world and some 200 'attack satellites' with missiles/lasers to take them out. The Israel 'Iron Dome' supplied by the American taxpayer proved less than impregnable when Iranian missiles attacked Israeli cities in response to Netanyahu launching a war against Iran in the summer of 2025.

SpaceX-Palantir-Anduril is Thiel-Thiel-Thiel with his investment in SpaceX, co-founding of Palantir, and long-time mentoring of Anduril co-founder Palmer Luckey who met Thiel when he was '19 or 20'. Luckey, who describes himself as a 'radical Zionist', is the designer of the Oculus Rift virtual reality headsets (with investment from Thiel's Founders Fund) and he sold this to Facebook (Meta) for nearly $3 billion in 2014. He then co-founded Anduril Industries with former Palantir employee Trae Stephens, a partner in Thiel's venture capital Founders Fund, and defence contracts began to flow. Anduril Industries continues the Thiel theme of *The Lord of the Rings*. 'Anduril' is the sword of the fictional character Aragorn and means 'Flame of the West' in the book's language of Quenya.

They're after your mind

I include in every book two major mass perceptual manipulation techniques constantly employed by the Cult because it is so important for anyone new to this to understand how the public is played. I coined the terms in the 1990s Problem-Reaction-Solution (P-R-S) and the Totalitarian Tiptoe (TT). I wanted a simple phrase to describe another version of the technique known as the 'Hegelian Dialectic' developed by German philosopher Georg Wilhelm Friedrich Hegel (1770-1831). He talked of Thesis, Antithesis, and Synthesis. The 'Thesis' is how things are. The 'Antithesis' is opposition to how things are. The 'Synthesis' is what emerges from this debate to create a new 'Thesis' (status quo). The whole process then starts again with the updated status quo that goes through a constant series of Thesis, Antithesis, and Synthesis to take society incrementally in the desired direction. This is 'creative destruction' in which you constantly dismantle a status quo, replace it with another, and then dismantle that on the road to your ultimate outcome of global dystopia. This is what Trump was installed by the Cult to do in the United States and the wider world. He creates the chaos that dismantles the status quo and the reason he does so is very different to what he tells his MAGA base.

Problem-Reaction-Solution (P-R-S) is similar, and the result is the same – a changed status quo. You first create a 'problem' which could be anything that allows you to offer a 'solution' that takes society in the direction you want. It could be a financial collapse, war, fake pandemic, fall of a government, terrorist attack. 9/11 is a perfect example of P-R-S and it changed the world even though the official story is a joke. You then tell the people through a naïve, uninformed and compliant media, the version of the problem you want them to believe and who or what to blame for it (never you). Stage two is the 'reaction' when you manipulate the public to emotionally respond with fear, anger, or fury and utter the golden words: 'What are *they* going to do about it?' At this point *'They'* (who have covertly created the problem) offer the 'solution' in new laws and changes that take the world in the desired direction usually involving more power for the few. Let crime run riot if you want to impose a tyrannical law enforcement system and not only will the public accept the tyranny. They will *demand* that you do it or 'do something' to stop the crime. Israeli Mossad and the US CIA are both specialists in P-R-S attacks (also known as 'false flags') to justify actions against the alleged perpetrator – 9/11 was a classic.

The Trump regime has provided many examples of this. Trump's 'Big Beautiful Bill' in the summer of 2025 included massive funding of AI and surveillance and not least to Palmer Luckey's Anduril for AI control of the US southern border as I indicated would happen in *The Reveal*. Unchecked immigration (Problem); MAGA's outrage (Reaction); leads to an AI 'virtual wall' at the border (Solution). The later murdered Trump promotor Charlie Kirk (see Postscript) also posted in relation to migrant farmworkers: 'Robots can now pick apples. It's time to automate America's farms. Automation, not amnesty.' Trump's bill funded an 'autonomous' system defined as 'designed to apply artificial intelligence, machine learning, computer vision, or other algorithms to accurately detect, identify, classify, and track items of interest in real time such that the system can make operational adjustments without the active engagement of personnel or continuous human command or control'. Give them the problem of illegal immigration and then offer them an AI solution. Trump and his AI handlers even included in the 'Big Beautiful Bill' a ban on states regulating AI for ten years by which time the foundations of the AI control system would be in place. The Senate rejected that, but the regime will try again in another form and guise.

There is also a version of P-R-S that I call NO-Problem-Reaction-Solution where you don't even need a real problem only the *perception* of one. Human-caused global warming and the 'Covid' hoax are obvious examples of the no-problem genre. Once you trigger perception, the reaction follows, with the solution sitting there waiting all along. The Totalitarian Tiptoe (TT) is the incremental steps to dystopia. You start at 'A' and you know you are taking the world to 'Z', but if you go too fast the change will be such that a lot of people could be alerted to the direction of travel. So, you go from 'A' to 'B', maybe to 'D', after assessing public awareness and how awake they are to the game. Each step is sold as unconnected to the other steps until you eventually look back and see what a transformation there has been. Both P-R-S and the 'TT' become blatant once you know the planned outcome – know the outcome and you'll see the journey. The Cult uses these techniques incessantly.

It's important to stress that the Global Cult is orchestrated by the Archontic Astral 'gods' manipulating from the unseen and making events happen to support the agenda. This includes mind control and suppression of the population via the simulation field which tells them what to think absent an awakening to expanded consciousness. I'll focus next on an always highly controversial aspect of the Global Cult and indeed so controversial that it's even becoming illegal to talk about it. *I don't care*. The truth is the truth is the truth, and it is way past the time it was heard.

CHAPTER 11

The Sabbateans

True revolutionaries do not flaunt their radicalism. They cut their hair, put on suits and infiltrate the system from within.
Saul Alinsky

A key element of the Global Cult is a cult within a cult that operates worldwide out of Israel. These are the Sabbateans (also Sabbatians) or Sabbatean-Frankists. They control the United States, Canada, Europe and countries all over the world despite their tiny numbers.

Sabbateans are fake 'Jews' who use the Jewish population as a shield to hide behind and within by branding people like me exposing the Sabbatean cult as an 'antisemite' who is blaming everyone Jewish for manipulating the world. It's not true, but since when did truth play any part in the Sabbatean strategy? Sabbateans have contempt for Jewish people while posing as them. They have long taken over the reins of power while plotting the establishment of Israel which they have ruled from the start. They have sold generations of Jewish children and young people a false history and a belief that the world hates them for being Jewish. They must look to their (Sabbatean) leaders to protect them from their hostile enemies and protect them from harm. This is one of the oldest mass perceptual tricks. Frighten the population into compliance by seeing you as their protectors. Meanwhile, it is the atrocities and manipulations of the leaders that have Jews in general cast in a negative light. No one needs to know this more than Jewish people who are being shafted by fake or 'crypto-Jews' and have been for centuries. Jewish people fall into three basic perceptual categories. There are the crypto-Jew Sabbateans; those that buy their lies downloaded from birth; and those who see through various levels of the bullshit and at the very least don't support the psychopathy of the Israeli government.

The foundation of the deceit is that modern Jews originate in biblical Israel and that the Bible tells a true story about Jewish history including the myth that they are 'God's Chosen People'. Research is now well advanced by Jewish scholars and others that link modern Jews to a people called the Khazars in the region of the Caucasus Mountains, in what is now Georgia and southern Russia, and *not* to ancient Israel. I'll summarise here because I have told the story in detail in *The Trigger* and

The Sabbateans

Figure 106: The Khazaria Empire where the king imposed a mass conversion to Judaism in 740 AD and the people became known as Ashkenazi Jews. They eventually migrated north into Eastern and then Western Europe where they became the Jewish people targeted by the Nazis. They have no connection to 'biblical' Israel.

other works. Maintaining this myth allows the Sabbatean cult hiding within the Jewish community to pursue the long-planned agenda of the Global Cult for total human control. Shlomo Sand is one of the researchers who uncovered the lies while Professor of History at Tel Aviv University. He had set out to prove the official history of the Jews to be true but soon found the opposite. I will demolish the 'Chosen People' narrative in Chapters 18 and 19. Sand wrote his book, *The Invention of the Jewish People*, to show the evidence that today's Jews overwhelmingly originate from the Khazar Empire in the Caucasus alongside the Caspian and Black Seas (Fig 106). The book was published in 2008 and in English the following year. Sand wrote: 'If certain Jewish communities had distinctive qualities, they were due to history, not biology.' His other books include *The Invention of the Land of Israel: From Holy Land to Homeland* and *How I Stopped Being a Jew*. Abraham Polak (1910-1970), also a Jewish professor of history at Tel Aviv University, uncovered the Khazar story even earlier as a specialist in Jewish, Arab and Khazar history. His book *Khazaria: History of a Jewish Kingdom in Europe*, published in 1943 and updated in 1944 and 1951, uncovered the Khazar origin of Eastern-European Jews which went on to found, dominate and control modern Israel. Among others I have quoted is Arthur Koestler, the Hungarian-born Jew, with his work *The Thirteenth Tribe* published in 1976. He said:

> … That does not alter the fact that the large majority of surviving Jews in the world is of Eastern European – and thus perhaps mainly of Khazar – origin. If so, this would mean that their ancestors came not from the Jordan but from the Volga, not from Canaan but from the Caucasus, once believed to be the

cradle of the Aryan race; and that genetically they are more closely related to the Hun, Uigur and Magyar tribes than to the seed of Abraham, Isaac and Jacob.

Should this turn out to be the case, then the term 'anti-Semitism' would become void of meaning, based on a misapprehension shared by both the killers and their victims. The story of the Khazar Empire, as it slowly emerges from the past, begins to look like the most cruel hoax which history has ever perpetrated.

The Khazars were a Turkic people who had a mass conversion to Judaism at the behest of their ruler King Bulan in about 740 AD. Khazaria kings were called the 'Khagan' or 'Kagan' and that's why it's a common Jewish name today. Bulan saw the Christian Empire on one side and the Islamic or Arabian Empire on the other and didn't wish to be absorbed by either. Khazaria eventually collapsed and its people now self-identifying as Jewish migrated north into what is today Ukraine, Hungary, Lithuania, Russia, and Poland. They later expanded into Western Europe and Germany to become the Jews targeted by Hitler and the Nazis. They then relocated to Palestine to establish modern Israel with which they have no historical connection. This should not matter anyway thousands of years on. These are the Ashkenazi Jews that represent the great majority of Jewish people globally and have produced every prime minister since today's Israel came into being. The claim to a right to the land of Palestine is based on the Bible which is daft enough to start with and those who have studied the Khazar story show this claim to be fraudulent. The term 'Semitic' refers to a group of languages in the Middle East which are almost entirely *Arabic languages*. Arabs are the Semites!

Modern Israel has been controlled from the start by alleged Jews originating in Eastern Europe. Benjamin Netanyahu's father was the Polish-born Benzion Mileikowsky, the son of Russian-born Rabbi, writer and Zionist activist Nathan Mileikowsky. Israel prime ministers galore (or their parents) changed their family names to sound less European. There are also strict laws in Israel which make it very difficult to get a DNA test to establish genetic inheritance. I have watched videos of Jews outside of Israel who have had their DNA tested and found no connection to biblical Israel. Their genetic inheritance was overwhelmingly European and Eastern. Jeff Halper is an Israeli-American anthropologist living in Israel who has tirelessly campaigned against the abuse of Palestinians. He asks how anyone can come from Ukraine to Palestine and say 'this country is mine and you Palestinians have no place here'? Halper said:

To justify what you're doing and explain what you're doing you develop a whole narrative. God gave us this land and this is ancient Israel. We were driven out by the Romans ... what every colonial movement does is it criminalises the indigenous population. So we're normal and here are these criminal terrorists that are simply attacking us.

Sabbatean origins

The name Sabbatean comes from Sabbatai Zevi (1626-1676) although the Satanic strand that he and Sabbateanism represent within Jewish history can be charted into the far ancient world from where the Old Testament 'God' version of Yaldabaoth was spawned (Fig 107). Zevi was a rabbi, occultist and black magician who proclaimed himself the 'Jewish Messiah'. He attracted a big following which became the largest messianic movement in Jewish history. Zevi promised he

Figure 107: Sabbatai Zevi.

would return the Jews to the biblical Israel in what was then Palestine. He apparently claimed no messianic pretentions until he met in 1665 what appears to be a Svengali figure known as Nathan of Gaza who proclaimed himself a prophet. The cult of Sabbatai Zevi operated as an inversion of everything as the wider Global Cult does to this day. It was certainly an inversion of Judaism. A fast day in Judaism became a feast day in Sabbateanism. Traditional teachings were spurned to be replaced by sexual free-for-alls (including incest) and an inverted view of 'right and wrong' in which evil was celebrated. Sabbateans were forbidden to marry outside the sect and interbred among themselves. Children were kept ignorant about the cult until they were old enough to be trusted not to spill the beans to outsiders. The same system described here operates within the Global Cult.

Zevi and his cult lived within the Islamic Ottoman Empire that ruled in the Middle East, Southeast Europe, West Asia, and North Africa from the 14th to early 20th centuries out of Turkey and its capital Constantinople (modern-day Istanbul). Zevi attracted attention from the Sultan who said he must prove his 'divinity' or convert to Islam. Failure to do so would mean torture and death. Zevi went for the easiest option – conversion. This upset many supporters, but some 300 Sabbatean families also converted to Islam and became known as the 'Dönmeh' which means 'to turn'. In fact, they didn't 'turn' except in theory and continued with their inverted version of Judaism in secret. They were dubbed 'crypto-Jews' who have contempt for Jewishness and have sought to invert it – as they have. Sabbateans have perfected the art of infiltrating societies, countries, and belief systems by posing as supporters and advocates while pursuing a very different agenda behind the scenes. They invariably manipulate themselves into leadership positions. If not publicly then from the shadows posing as 'advisors'.

Figure 108: Jacob Frank.

Zevi died in 1676 at the age of 50 and in the next century along came Polish Satanist Jacob Frank (1726-1791) to take Sabbateanism to another level of horror (Fig 108). Frank claimed to be the reincarnation of Zevi and biblical patriarch Jacob. He was a depraved man in the Sabbatean mould of human sacrifice, paedophilia, and worship of the Archontic 'gods'. Sabbateans established paedophilia-riddled Hollywood and the movie industry, so say no more. Jewish professor Gershom Scholem said of Frank in *The Messianic Idea in Judaism*: 'In all his actions [he was] a truly corrupt and degenerate individual ... one of the most frightening phenomena in the whole of Jewish history.' Frank and Zevi said that certain 'elite' people (themselves) are exempt from the moral law. They believed commandments and laws of Judaism did not apply to them. The forbidden would be encouraged and the more despicable the better with again human sacrifice, incest, and other sex with children among the abominations. Human society had to be overthrown and destroyed, and they sought 'the annihilation of every religion and positive system of belief' while posing as religious advocates. They would infiltrate and destroy them and society from within with the Astral 'gods' giving them their full support.

Sabbatean-Frankists have contempt for Jewish people and yet claim to represent their interests and be 'one of them'. This is exactly what the Global Cult is doing worldwide across all belief systems. Jewish writer and researcher Clifford Shack said in *The Sabbatean-Frankist Messianic Conspiracy Partially Exposed*: 'Jacob Frank was not a big fan of the Jewish people.' Rabbi Marvin Antelman explains in *To Eliminate the Opiate* how Sabbatean-Frankists established their own fraudulent systems of appointing rabbis that appear to be genuine while following the Sabbatean agenda. Antelman said they were 'barbarians', not rabbis, and the Sabbatean-Frankist goal was to Christianise Judaism and Judaize Christianity (Christian Zionism) to destroy both. He describes

The Sabbateans

Figure 109: The Rothschild house in Frankfurt, Germany.

Figure 110: The flag of Israel carries the symbol from which the name Rothschild derived. How apt when the Rothschilds were fundamental to the creation of Israel.

Figure 111: The Rothschild kingdom with a massive expansion in the works.

Sabbatean-Frankism in his book as 'a movement of complete evil'. Rabbi Antelman was the pioneer in bringing Sabbatean-Frankism infiltration to light.

Sabbatean Rothschilds

Jacob Frank, like Zevi, was excommunicated by traditional rabbis, but he represented a very different religion that secured support from the Sabbatean-Frankist crypto-Jews of the House of Rothschild and its founder, Mayer Amschel Rothschild (1744-1812). This Rothschild was the 'founding father of international finance' (the Cult money system). The family had been known as 'Bauer' until Mayer renamed them Rothschild after the red six-pointed 'Star of David' (also Seal of Solomon and symbol of Saturn) displayed on their house in Frankfurt, Germany (Fig 109). 'Red-shield' or 'red-sign' in German is 'rot-schild'. The Rothschilds were behind the creation of Israel and put the symbol which inspired their name on the flag of the country (Figs 110 and 111). Jacob Frank's Sabbatean-Frankist cult infiltrated the Vatican and Roman Catholicism as they have with Judaism, Christianity, Islam, and others. Sabbatean-Frankist 'Dönmeh' within Islam are the ruling family of Saudi Arabia, the House of Saud, with its extreme and violent Wahhabism distortion of Islam. No need to wonder why Saudi Arabia and Israel work together away from the public eye.

Frank conspired with Mayer Amschel Rothschild and the Jesuit-educated Jew, Adam Weishaupt, to establish the Bavarian Illuminati in 1776 (the year the United States was founded). This secret group triggered widespread manipulation including the French Revolution. The Illuminati ('Illuminated ones') went on to infiltrate (the Sabbatean technique) governments, banking, corporations, media, and the entertainment industry. Sabbatean-Frankism has become a predominant force within the Global Cult while expressing the themes and goals of the Archontic web going back to antiquity. Jewish researcher Clifford Shack has specialised in the history of Sabbatean-Frankism. Here he charts its progression to be a global phenomenon:

> Through infiltration, stealth and cunning, this invisible network has come to rule us all. Forty-one years after Shabbatai Zevi's death ... they would infiltrate Masonry guilds in England and establish Freemasonry ... Jacob Frank would have a great impact on the inner core of Freemasonry known as the Illuminati, formed in 1776.
>
> Freemasonry would become the hidden force behind events like the [American, French and Russian] revolutions, the creations of the UN and Israel, both World Wars (including the Holocaust!), and the assassinations of the Kennedy brothers who, together with their father, tried to thwart the efforts of the network on American soil.

Shack goes on to highlight how Sabbateanism seeks to control both sides to ensure the outcome:

> Sabbatean/Frankists, also referred to as the 'Cult of the All-Seeing Eye' (look on the back of your one dollar bill to begin to understand their influence in YOUR life), are political and religious chameleons. They are everywhere ... there is power. They are the good guys AND the bad guys.
>
> The World War Two era is a prime example. The following leaders were members of the 'Cult of the All-Seeing Eye' (Sabbatean/Frankists): Franklin D. Roosevelt; Winston Churchill; Adolph Hitler; Eugenio Pacelli (Pope Pius XII); Francisco Franco; Benito Mussolini; Hirohito; and Mao Tse-Tung.

I detail in my book *The Trigger* the central involvement of the Sabbateans in the 9/11 attacks; how they were behind the Nazis; bombed and terrorised Israel into being in 1948; and have controlled it with an iron fist ever since. The Sabbatean Rothschilds were centrally involved in the establishment of Israel through their political arm, Zionism, which many Jewish people oppose. Zionism has been a vehicle for the House of Rothschild to manipulate world events and the direction of human society. Zionism is not Jewishness. It is a political ideology strongly opposed by many Jews and nor do you have to be Jewish to be a Zionist. The ideology is defined as 'an ethnocultural nationalist movement that emerged in Europe in the late 19th century that aimed to establish a national home for the Jewish people, pursued through the colonization of Palestine'. If you support that aim you are a Zionist, Jewish or not.

The Russian Bolshevik Revolution of 1917 which ousted and murdered the Romanov Czars was absolutely dominated by Jewish activists. Robert Wilton, author of *Last Days of the Romanovs* published in 1920, consulted official records and documents to show beyond doubt that those driving the revolution were overwhelmingly Jewish and it fitted with the Sabbatean modus operandi perfected through the Rothschild/Jacob Frank Bavarian Illuminati. Wilton established that the 62 members of the revolution Central Committee included only five Russians, one Ukrainian, six Latvians, two Germans, two Armenians, three Georgians, one Czech, one Karaite (a Jewish sect), but *41 Jews*. The 36 members of the Extraordinary Commission of Moscow consisted of just two Russians, eight Latvians, a German, a Pole, an Armenian, and *23 Jews*. The Soviet government (Council of the People's Commissariat) had three Russians, two Armenians and 17 *Jews*. Of the 556 key people in the Bolshevik authorities of 1918 and 1919, there were 17 Russians, two Ukrainians, eleven Armenians, 35 Latvians, 15 Germans, a Hungarian, ten Georgians, three Poles, three Finns, one Czech, one Karaite, and *457 Jews*. To think I have had events cancelled all over the world since my book *And The Truth Shall Set You Free* in 1995 for pointing this out because I am 'antisemitic' for quoting from these original Bolshevik documents. The Russian Revolution, headed by Zionists like Lenin and Trotsky, was not *Russian* at all. Anyone think that Russia is no longer controlled by the same Sabbatean forces under Vladimir Putin who has been either president or prime minister since 1999?

Emergence of Zionism

The inner sanctum of Zionism is a Sabbatean-Frankist secret society and is really 'Revisionist Zionism', an ideology founded on violence by Russian Jew Ze'ev ('Vladimir') Jabotinsky in the 1920s. He set out to seize Palestine with an 'iron wall of Jewish bayonets' and today they use American bombs and weapons. Jabotinsky (1880-1940) sought to 'create, with sweat and blood, a race of men, strong, brave and cruel' that would impose a Greater Israel from the River Nile in Egypt to the Euphrates in Iraq and known to Jews as Eretz Yisrael. This describes the largest expanse of alleged biblical Israel which includes what would be the former Palestine, the whole of Jordan and Lebanon, plus parts of Iraq, Syria, Saudi Arabia, and Egypt (Fig 112 overleaf). This is ludicrously based on Genesis 15:18: 'On the same day the Lord made a covenant with Abram (Abraham), saying: "To your descendants I have given this land, from the river of Egypt to the great river, the River Euphrates."' What extraordinary insanity we are dealing with, and I'll be showing just how ridiculous these claims turn out to be.

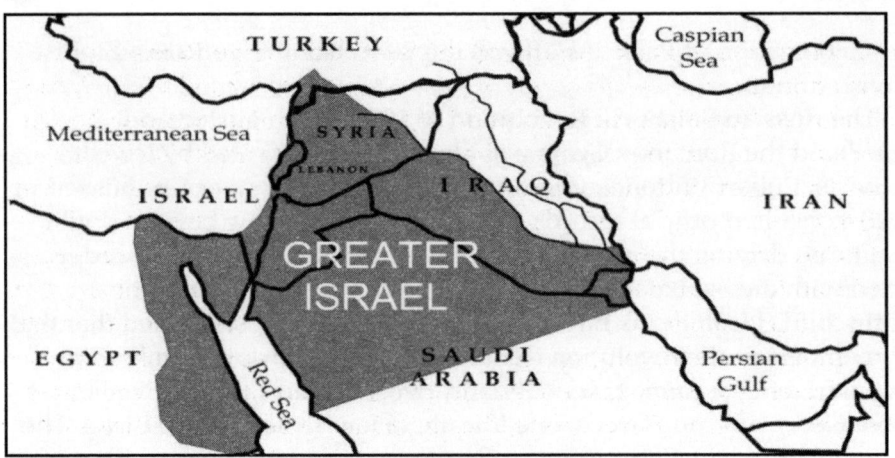

Figure 112: Greater Israel which is the biggest extent of alleged biblical Israel. We will see later that this is based on a fantasy.

The first Zionist Congress was in Basel, Switzerland, in 1897. It should have been in Munich, Germany, but such was the opposition from the Jewish community they had to relocate the event. Jews were quite happy in Germany and had no wish to up sticks to Palestine, thanks very much. Then by complete 'coincidence' of course came Hitler and the Nazis and Jews fled to the United States and ... Palestine. The Rothschilds were behind the 'Balfour Declaration' in 1917 in which Lord Arthur Balfour, the British Foreign Secretary overseeing a dying empire, committed his government to supporting a homeland for Jews in what was then Palestine. The Rothschilds had created the Round Table secret society in England in the late 19th century just as Zionism was getting promoted and this was headed by Rothschild agent, Cecil Rhodes, who plundered southern Africa for his owners. The Round Table went on to spawn the Royal Institute of International Affairs, Council on Foreign Relations, Trilateral Commission, Bilderberg Group, Club of Rome, and with others the United Nations. The 'Balfour Declaration' was a letter from Balfour, an inner circle member of the Round Table, to Lord Lionel Walter Rothschild, a leader of British Jewry, who *funded* the Round Table. The whole thing was a stitch-up.

Palestine was still ruled by the Ottoman Empire at the time, but not for much longer. Enter British intelligence agent Edward 'T. E.' Lawrence, made famous by the 1962 film, *Lawrence of Arabia*, starring Peter O'Toole. Lawrence persuaded Palestinian Arabs to support British efforts in the 'Arab Revolt' of 1916 to drive out the Ottoman Empire in return for independence when they were successful. Lawrence knew he was lying to them and the land was being cleared for Zionist Israel. The Ottoman Empire collapsed by 1922 and the post-First World War mandate to oversee Palestine was handed to Zionist (Rothschild) controlled Britain. By 1948 the British were driven out by ruthless

Zionist terror groups like Irgun and the Stern Gang after Rothschild money had transported Jews out of post-Nazi, post-Second World War Germany to Palestine. An estimated 700,000 Palestinian Arabs fled their homeland in terror to escape the sheer evil of the merciless Zionist terror groups and they and their descendants have never been allowed to return.

Jewish scientist Albert Einstein and more than 20 other prominent American Jews sent a letter to *The New York Times* in 1948 describing Irgun and its Zionist political arm as 'terrorist', 'right wing' and founded on 'ultranationalism, religious mysticism and racial superiority'. They were referring to Sabbatean-Frankism which was controlling Irgun and other terror groups. Einstein and the American Jews went further and said the network behind Irgun was 'closely akin in its organization, methods, political philosophy and social appeal to the Nazi and Fascist parties'. Irgun terrorists bombed the British Mandate headquarters at the King David's Hotel in Jerusalem on July 22nd, 1946, which killed 91 people and injured 46. They disguised themselves as Arab workmen and waiters to plant the bomb in the basement and the technique continues today with Israeli intelligence arm Mossad and the military many times using Arab disguises to blame Arabs for attacks. Ultra-Zionist terror groups sought to make life so dangerous for British people in Palestine that they would walk away from the Mandate and leave Palestine to them. This happened and the Sabbatean terrorists then turned on the Arab population.

Targeting America

Sabbatean-controlled Israel has expanded the occupation of Palestinian land with the intent of creating their 'Greater Israel'. The United States is crucial to these ambitions and that has long been owned by the Sabbateans. I have covered since the 1990s the Rothschild manipulation of America since the 19th century, but steroids were added to the mix after 1948 when Sabbatean and ultra-Zionist operatives were sent to locate in the US to make their children American-born citizens. They included Benjamin Emanuel (formerly Ezekiel Auerbach), a Russian Jewish terrorist with Irgun who apparently specialised in bus bombing. His son Rahm Emanuel became a political fixer who was White House Chief of Staff (handler) to Barack Obama and went on to become the first Jewish Mayor of Chicago and then US Ambassador to Japan. He worked with ultra-Zionist David Axelrod who ran both successful election campaigns for Obama. Another son is Hollywood power player Ari Emanuel who has been agent to Donald Trump and is a close friend of Elon Musk. Ari Emanuel is CEO of entertainment and media agency Endeavor that owns the mixed martial arts Ultimate Fighting Championship (UFC), which employs fake 'alternative' podcaster Joe Rogan, and World Wrestling Entertainment (WWE). Dana White, CEO of the UFC, is a close friend of Trump appointed to the board of Meta (Facebook). A third Emanuel son is Ezekiel Emanuel who was a member of Joe Biden's Covid-19 Advisory Board and Chief of the Department of Bioethics at the National Institutes of Health Clinical Center.

Israel hijacked American politics in both major parties through funding and a network of lobby groups – especially the American Israel Public Affairs Committee (AIPAC). The name has the feel of being government-connected to hide its real purpose which is to *control* government through massive funding and promotion of politicians who pledge unwavering support for Israel. AIPAC was established in 1954 by an Israel government lobbyist Isaiah L. Kenen 'partly to counter negative international reactions to Israel's Qibya massacre of Palestinian villagers'. Israel Defense Forces Unit 101 led by future Israeli Prime Minister Ariel Sharon laid siege to the village in the West Bank, then under Jordanian control, killing 69 Palestinian civilians with two-thirds of them children. Start as you mean to go on. Former Congresswoman Cynthia McKinney and a few others have exposed how Left and Right politicians running for political office are asked to 'sign the pledge' to support Israel and confirm they will always vote in 'Israel's best interests'. Those that agree get AIPAC (Israel) funding and promotion for their campaigns and those who refuse, well, don't. More than that AIPAC will enthusiastically support their opponent. The lobby group representing a foreign government is reported to have spent $45.2 million in the 2024 Congressional elections, the most by any organisation in history, with 65 percent of Congress getting AIPAC money. Media reports said Republican House Speaker Mike Johnson got at least $654,000 while Democrat House Minority Leader Hakeem Jeffries was handed $933,000. AIPAC spent $20 million to unseat two New York Democrats who wouldn't play their game. The *Jerusalem Post* reported that 'Pro-Israel political action committee AIPAC has aided 318 Zionist candidates to win so far in the recent US elections' [and] 'other PACs and private donors also played significant roles'. Who do you think controls American politics? It's a mystery.

Small in number – massive in influence

The prominence of Jewish people in the news would lead you to think they must be significant in number worldwide, but this is not the case. An eight billion human population had less than 17 million Jewish people in 2023 according to the Jewish Virtual Library website. Nearly all of them live in Israel (7,427,000) or the United States (7,460,600). The two countries comprised 88.8 percent of the Jewish population of the world in 2023. The drop to the third country is dramatic in that France is home to 440,000 Jewish people. Jews, never mind the far smaller number of Sabbateans, are little more than two percent of Americans and the ratio of those to positions of power is nothing less than stupendous. Barack Obama had ultra-Zionist Rahm Emanuel at his shoulder and ultra-Zionist Chief Strategist David Axelrod ran his election campaigns in 2008 and 2012. This was his financial team alone awash with Jewish appointees as I laid out in *The Perception Deception*:

Timothy Geithner (ultra-Zionist), Treasury Secretary; Jacob J. Lew (ultra-Zionist), another Treasury Secretary; Larry Summers (ultra-Zionist), director of the White House National Economic Council; Paul Adolph Volcker (Rothschild business partner), chairman of the Economic Recovery Advisory Board; Peter Orszag (ultra-Zionist), director of the Office of Management and Budget overseeing all government spending; Penny Pritzker (ultra-Zionist), Commerce Secretary; Jared Bernstein (ultra-Zionist), chief economist and economic policy adviser to vice president Joe Biden; Mary Schapiro (ultra-Zionist), chair of the Securities and Exchange Commission (SEC); Gary Gensler (ultra-Zionist), chairman of the Commodity Futures Trading Commission (CFTC); Sheila Bair (ultra-Zionist), chair of the Federal Deposit Insurance Corporation (FDIC); Karen Mills (ultra-Zionist), head of the Small Business Administration (SBA); Kenneth Feinberg (ultra-Zionist), Special Master for Executive [bail-out] Compensation. Feinberg would be appointed to oversee compensation (with strings) to 9/11 victims and families in a campaign to stop them having their day in court to question the official story. I expose in *The Trigger* the fundamental involvement of Sabbateans in the September 11th attacks. At the same time ultra-Zionist Bernard Bernanke was chairman of the Cult-controlled US central bank, the Federal Reserve. He replaced ultra-Zionist Alan Greenspan who was head of the Fed from 1987 to 2006 under Reagan, Father Bush, Clinton, and Boy Bush. Obama's biggest corporate donor was ultra-Zionist Goldman Sachs which had employed many in his administration.

These were just some of the Zionists in the Joe Biden (officially) administration from 2021 to 2025:

Ron Klain, White House Chief of Staff; Antony Blinken, Secretary of State; Wendy Sherman, Deputy Secretary of State; Janet Yellen, Secretary of the Treasury; Merrick Garland, Attorney-General; Alejandro Mayorkas, Secretary of Homeland Security; Anne Neuberger, Director of Cybersecurity, National Security Agency; David Cohen, Deputy CIA Director; Avril Haines, Director of National Intelligence; Eric Lander, Director, Office of Science and Technology Policy; Jeff Zients, Covid-19 Coordinator (later White House Chief of Staff); Rochelle Walensky, Director, Centers for Disease Control (replaced by Mandy Cohen); Rachel Levine, Deputy Secretary, Health and Human Services.

Sabbatean-owned Trump

Donald Trump, son of an ultra-Zionist father, Fred Trump, has been owned by Israel and the Sabbateans since his early days in business. Boy Trump's mentor and legal advisor was Roy Cohn from the early 1970s until his death in 1986. Cohn was genetically corrupt and eventually disbarred for unethical conduct by the Appellate Division of the New York State Supreme Court. He was chief counsel to Senator Joseph McCarthy's 'communist' witch-hunt in the 1950s (see Trump's 'anti-Semitism' witch-hunt). Trump was his front man as Cohn worked for the Russian Zionist Mafia out of New York. Cohn represented ultra-Zionist media mogul Rupert Murdoch and introduced him to Trump at the start of a long friendship before Trump sued Murdoch and his organisation for a story in the *Wall Street Journal* connecting him to Jeffrey Epstein of which more later. *Esquire* magazine ran an article headed 'Don't mess with Roy Cohn' which described him as the most feared lawyer in New York ... 'a ruthless master of dirty tricks ... [with] ... more than one Mafia Don on speed dial'. Yep, he worked for the Italian Mafia, too. Two sets of Mafia were very useful for Trump's building projects and construction materials.

Trump was bailed out by the Rothschilds when he faced mega bankruptcy (not for the first time – he's a poor businessman despite the hype). He built two casinos in Atlantic City and bought the big Taj Mahal operation which led to unpayable debts by the early 1990s of $4 billion including almost $1 billion in personal debt. He was cooked. Well, until the Rothschilds stepped in. Wilbur Ross, who worked for the Rothschilds for 24 years, negotiated a deal with 72 banks to save him. Ross was made Commerce Secretary in Trump's first administration. Zionist tycoon Carl Icahn bought the Taj Mahal casino to help the deal and was rumoured to be a possible Treasury Secretary in Trump's first term before accepting the role of Special Advisor to the President on Regulatory Reform. The Treasury job went to ultra-Zionist Steve Mnuchin.

Trump hired a bankruptcy lawyer to represent him and that was ultra-ultra-Zionist David M. Friedman who Trump appointed US ambassador to Israel. Friedman was in place to oversee the relocation of the US embassy from Tel Aviv to Jerusalem which had been agreed with Sabbatean ultra-Zionist casino tycoon Sheldon Adelson in return for a $100 million donation to Trump's first election campaign. Ultra-Zionist Jason Greenblatt, the executive vice president and chief legal officer to Donald Trump and the Trump Organization, was appointed as Assistant to the President and Special Representative for International Negotiations including Israel-Palestine.

Trump's second administration is overflowing with Jewish Zionists and Christian Zionists who are Jewish in all, but name. His first picks were: Susie Wiles, Chief of Staff; Marc Rubio, Secretary of State; Pete Hegseth, Secretary of Defense; Stephen Feinberg, deputy Defense Secretary; Mike Waltz, first the National Security Advisor, then UN Ambassador; Steven Witkoff, the Jewish Middle East envoy; Morgan Ortagus, deputy to the special envoy to the Middle East and a Jewish convert married to a Jewish man; John Ratcliffe, CIA director; Elise Stefanik, the first nomination for UN Ambassador; Pam Bondi, Attorney General; Kristi Noem, head of Homeland Security; Scott Bessent, Treasury Secretary, a protege of Jewish billionaire George Soros; Howard Lutnick, Secretary of Commerce; Stephen Miller, Jewish Deputy Chief of Staff and Homeland Security Advisor; Robert F. Kennedy Jr., Department of Health and Human Services; Will Scharf, White House Staff Secretary; Lee Zeldin, Environmental Protection Agency administrator; Mike Huckabee, a fanatical Christian Zionist, the US Ambassador to Israel who refuses even to say West Bank and instead insists on calling that land the biblical Judea and Samaria. *All* are vehemently pro-Israel.

Then you have the AI Big Tech line-up of David Sacks, the Jewish friend of Musk and Peter Thiel, who is Trump's 'AI and crypto czar', while two AI Jewish billionaires Larry Ellison and Sam Altman are behind the up to $500 billion AI Stargate project. Musk is owned by Israel and describes himself as 'Jew-ish'. His father, Errol, said that Benjamin Netanyahu is a 'Musk family friend' and this would explain the closeness and how Elon Musk enthusiastically attended Netanyahu's address to a joint session of Congress in 2024 at his friend's invitation. It explains how Musk was on a plane to Israel in the wake of October 7th to support Netanyahu's narrative and then to Auschwitz with Netanyahu gofer, the fake 'alternative' Ben Shapiro, for more Israel anti-Palestinian propaganda. Musk is owned by Israel. Trump is owned by Israel. Silicon Valley is owned by Israel. Musk's Jewish grandfather Joshua N. Haldeman was a leading proponent of technocracy, a system of government in which appointed people, not elected, run everything. This is what Musk and his tech oligarch cronies are working towards. It is stating the obvious to say that the ratio of Jewish and Israel fanatics to positions of power (and not only in the US) is ridiculous and what would the reaction be if the same ratio applied to black people, brown people, Chinese people, or Hispanics?

Somehow, they have had to make stating the obvious unacceptable, even illegal. They have constantly expanded the definition of 'antisemitism' to block any criticism of the Israeli Sabbatean government and Sabbatean-owned Donald Trump gives them anything they demand including the crackdown on 'antisemitism'. Sabbatean Sheldon Adelson and his wife Miriam have given Trump more than $300 million for his three presidential campaigns and Trump's Israeli campaign contributions are astonishing in scale. In return, as agreed with the Adelsons, Trump moved the US embassy from Tel Aviv to Jerusalem in his first term and recognised the Syrian Golan Heights as Israeli territory. There is even a location in the Golan now named Trump Heights. He handed Miriam Adelson America's highest civilian award in 2018, the Presidential Medal of Freedom. Trump told the ultra-Zionist Israeli-American Council: 'Miriam and Sheldon would come into the White House almost more than anyone, outside people who work there … as soon as I gave them something, they would want something else – I would say give me a couple of weeks will you?'

The deal with Adelson since her husband's death in 2021 is that Trump recognises the Israeli annexation of the occupied Palestinian West Bank in return for her $100 million donation to his 2024 election campaign. American Jewish publication *Forward*, Israel newspaper *Haaretz* and the *New York* magazine all reported that the money was given in return for 'an Israeli annexation of the West Bank and a US recognition of Israeli sovereignty in all the regions of the land'. Adelson is 'a megadonor for settlement development in the West Bank' and one of Trump's first acts in his second term was to remove sanctions against Israeli settlers stealing land and property from Palestinians in the West Bank. David Friedman, Trump's bankruptcy lawyer and Ambassador to Israel in his first term, has called for $1 billion to be redirected from existing aid to the Palestinians to finance the annexation plan. He wrote: 'The easiest bucket to tap into and reposition is that of the United States.' He said Israel would need financial assistance 'to assert and maintain its sovereignty over Judea and Samaria'.

This delusional man claims that support for 'Israeli sovereignty' is 'based first and foremost on biblical prophecies and values'. We are going to see that those 'prophecies' have no foundation in fact and that the whole 'God's Chosen People' myth is based on manipulated translations of ancient texts. Proper translations demolish the whole fairy tale about 'Jews' and their right to the Promised Land. What's more, the key players will *know* that.

CHAPTER 12

Sabbatean Spider

America and Israel share a special bond.
Our relationship is unique among all nations. Like America, Israel is a strong democracy, a symbol of freedom, and an oasis of liberty, a home to the oppressed and persecuted.
Bill Clinton

Donald Trump removed all restrictions on US weapons supplies to Israel immediately he took office for the second time in January 2025. He announced a plan to relocate all Palestinians in the Gaza open air concentration camp to Jordan and Egypt and replace them with a Gaza Mediterranean resort for the rich. He even posted a grotesque video depicting his 'vision'.

The United States armed Israel to kill fantastic numbers of Palestinians in Gaza and turn the place to rubble following the Hamas attacks on Israelis on October 7th, 2023. Trump then said that Gaza was a 'demolition site' and the Palestinians would have to leave. It was all long planned by the Israeli government and the US One-Party State. The level of unimaginable psychopathy was highlighted in a report published on the Harvard Dataverse website in June 2025 and compiled by Garb Yaakov, a Jewish professor at Ben-Gurion University in Israel. The report estimated that 377,000 people in Gaza had been 'disappeared' since Israeli bombing began through violence and starvation with half believed to be children. At the time the official death toll was about 61,000. The response of Cult-owned UK prime minister Keir Starmer was to say: 'We are urgently accelerating efforts to evacuate children from Gaza who need critical medical assistance – bringing more Palestinian children to the UK for specialist medical treatment.' The same man said he supported Israel's 'right to defend itself' and that included cutting off power and water to Gaza. His 'solution' of course suits the agenda to rid Gaza of Palestinians.

The appalling Hamas attacks were blatantly *allowed* to happen by the Israeli government, the IDF military, and intelligence networks Mossad and Shin Bet. This was a Problem-Reaction-Solution. These organisations are evil beyond the imagination and terrify their targets into obedience and submission. Fellow Jews are just collateral damage to them. It emerged when Israel bombed Iran in the summer of 2025 that Mossad agents threatened Iranian generals *and their families* with assassination if they did not defect from the regime and send a film of themselves doing so. Persian-speaking Mossad agents called them on their mobile phones which is their level of infiltration. 'We're closer to you than your own neck vein', one Iranian was told. 'I can advise you now, you have 12 hours to escape with your wife and child. Otherwise, you're on our list right now.' They also demanded that the Iranian targets filmed themselves fleeing and sent the video to Mossad for propaganda purposes. You can imagine why politicians and others do what they are told worldwide when faced with that level of evil that is prepared to carry out their threats without a second thought.

It is well established that the Israel government funded Hamas into being to challenge the Palestinian Liberation Organization (PLO) and divide opposition. Somehow Hamas was allowed to breach in multiple places the most surveilled and defended border fence on Earth while facing no military response for a ridiculous period as they went on a killing spree. Former soldiers with the Israel Defense Forces (IDF) were aghast at what happened. They confirmed sensors on the fence are so sensitive that a cockroach or bird would set them off let alone terrorists in multiple locations. Another soldier told an Israeli parliament Knesset committee: 'We received orders from the Golani Brigade commanders on October 7 to cancel all patrols along the Gaza border from 5.20am until 9am.' The official story makes no sense because it's a lie. Egypt warned Israel the attacks were imminent and still there was no response. I read this stupendous nonsense in the *Times of Israel*:

> When the first Hamas terrorists breached the border fence between Israel and Gaza in the early hours of Saturday, October 7, the IDF was caught completely unaware and thus struggled to mount a response during the first few hours of the invasion.

Insult my intelligence if you like, but the *Times* report partly redeemed itself by then telling some truth:

> During the first hours of the October 7 Hamas terror onslaught in southern Israel, IDF troops on the ground were instructed to prevent the kidnapping of soldiers into Gaza by whatever means necessary, as senior officers in the Gaza Division allegedly implemented the controversial 'Hannibal Protocol', according to newly reported testimonies of soldiers and officers.

The 'Hannibal Protocol' is an instruction to IDF troops to stop the kidnapping of fellow troops back to Gaza by any means necessary including killing their own. Israel daily *Haaretz* said it had obtained

Sabbatean Spider

documents and soldier testimonies to confirm this. It is also clear that many Israeli civilians were killed by IDF 'friendly fire' when they eventually responded to the attacks. We had the Problem and the Reaction. What was the Solution? The mass murder of Palestinian men, women and so many children to turn Gaza into the 'demolition site' that Trump wanted to make a luxury resort with the Palestinians gone. This could not have happened without the Hamas attacks of October 7th which those who delivered the 'solution' allowed to happen. The targeting of children is part of the Palestinian genocide. Kill the children and they don't become adults.

Silencing dissent

There were protests at the Israeli slaughter, especially those at American colleges and universities. Amid the outrage by those with a smear of empathy we had Israel-owned Donald Trump seeking to silence them. Trump also began to target anyone accused of 'antisemitism' with tyrannical laws and oppression, including deportation, while claiming to stand for freedom of speech. He even imposed a law to withhold disaster relief funds on states that refuse to deal with 'Israeli companies' or in any way boycott Israel. A backlash of disgust followed, and Trump changed the wording. Yes, changed the wording, not the meaning. He dropped reference to Israel but retained the text that meant the same. States would receive disaster funding so long as: 'They do not engage in and will not during the term of this award engage in, a discriminatively prohibited boycott'. The cynicism and contempt this reveals sums up the Trump mentality. All this brought into sharp focus the ever-expanding definition of 'antisemitism' to stop exposure of what the Sabbateans and their lackeys are doing. Here is the latest version, but it's unlikely to be the last:

- Calling for, aiding, or justifying the killing or harming of Jews in the name of a radical ideology or an extremist view of religion.
- Making mendacious, dehumanising, demonising, or stereotypical allegations about Jews as such or the power of Jews as a collective – such as, especially but not exclusively, the myth about a world Jewish conspiracy or of Jews controlling the media, economy, government or other societal institutions.
- Accusing Jews as a people of being responsible for real or imagined wrongdoing committed by a single Jewish person or group, or even for acts committed by non-Jews.
- Denying the fact, scope, mechanisms (e.g. gas chambers) or intentionality of the genocide of the Jewish people at the hands of National Socialist Germany and its supporters and accomplices during World War II (the Holocaust).

- Accusing the Jews as a people, or Israel as a state, of inventing or exaggerating the Holocaust.
- Accusing Jewish citizens of being more loyal to Israel, or to the alleged priorities of Jews worldwide, than to the interests of their own nations.
- Denying the Jewish people their right to self-determination, e.g., by claiming that the existence of a state of Israel is a racist endeavour.
- Applying double standards by requiring of it a behaviour not expected or demanded of any other democratic nation.
- Using the symbols and images associated with classic antisemitism (e.g., claims of Jews killing Jesus or blood libel) to characterize Israel or Israelis.
- Drawing comparisons of contemporary Israeli policy to that of the Nazis.
- Holding Jews collectively responsible for actions of the state of Israel.

That is nothing to do with protecting Jewish people from discrimination and everything to do with protecting the Sabbatean cult operating within the Jewish community from legitimate investigation and exposure. People are being arrested, detained or deported for 'antisemitism' under Trump for merely protesting against the mass murder of Palestinians, fantastic numbers of them children, by the Israeli government and military. Trump's National Institute of Health, part of the Department of Health and Human Services headed by Israel fanatic Robert Kennedy Jr, issued new guidelines to medical researchers warning that funds will be terminated if they support a boycott of Israel. A boycott of anywhere else is allowed, just not Israel. Trump threatened universities with deletion of government funding worth hundreds of millions of dollars. Columbia was the first target, and it caved immediately. Harvard at the time of writing was standing firm. The Department of Homeland Security (DHS) announced that 'antisemitic activity' on social media would be taken into account when assessing 'aliens' applying for 'lawful permanent resident status, foreign students and 'aliens' affiliated with educational institutions'. Trump further appointed ultra-Zionist Mark Levin, yet another Fox News contributor in his regime, to his revamped Homeland Security Advisory Council.

The predictable excuse for targeting anyone protesting the mass murder of children was they were supporting Hamas, an organisation created with Israel government support to divide Palestinian opposition. Israeli sources with support from assets in the United States began to file lawsuits against individuals and groups on the same basis. Silencing opposition to Israel (the Sabbatean vehicle) was clearly coordinated in preparation for what was to come. TikTok hired a former member of the Israel Defense Forces (IDF) to oversee hate speech policies. Erica Mindel, a former US State Department contractor, worked for ambassador

Deborah Lipstadt, the Biden administration's special envoy to monitor and combat antisemitism. Mindel said she planned to 'develop and drive' TikTok 'positions on hate speech'; 'influence legislative and regulatory frameworks'; and 'analyse hate speech trends' with special focus on antisemitic content.

I was banned by the Dutch government from nearly 30 countries in the European Schengen border group in 2022 for challenging Sabbatean Israel and this was extended for another two years in 2024 (see the Ickonic.com documentary *Persona Non Grata*). The Schengen system is that if you are banned from one you are banned from all. The first ban was imposed by the Israel-worshipping government of Mark Rutte (now Secretary-General of NATO as a good little Cult gofer) and the second was by the government of the *unelected* Prime Minister Dick Schoof, a former head of Dutch Intelligence. The installation of Schoof was overseen by 'alternative' media hero Geert Wilders who is head of the 'Party for *Freedom*' and it was a minister from that party that imposed my second ban, one Marjolein Faber. The first ban was by Rutte's 'People's Party for *Freedom* and Democracy'. Ha, ha. Everything is inverted with the Cult which is a reflection of the Yaldabaoth inversion. Have you noticed how many dictatorships in places like Africa have been called 'Democratic Fronts' or similar?

How sobering to think that I was banned from the Netherlands after pressure from a Jewish 'think tank' called CIDI (Center for Information and Documentation Israel) in a country of 29,700 Jews by 2023 figures which represents just 0.2 percent of the population. Australia banned me on the say-so of the Jewish Anti-Defamation Commission (ADC) in a country with a Jewish population of 117,000 representing 0.5 percent of Australians. Why such power you might ask? The ADC was originally founded by the Rothschild-inspired B'nai B'rith and was first known as the B'nai B'rith Anti-Defamation Commission. B'nai B'rith ('Children of the Covenant') was established in New York by Jewish immigrants from Rothschild Germany in 1843 and later spawned the infamous 'antisemitism' censorship operation the Anti-Defamation League (ADL). They have come after me and I have been censored by the Israel (Sabbatean) protection network across the world since 1995.

The Chabad network

Another crucial network to highlight is Chabad-Lubavitch which came to wider public attention in early 2024 when secret tunnels were discovered at the Chabad-Lubavitch global headquarters in New York. Chabad-Lubavitch was established in 'White Russia' or the land of Belarus in 1775 and now has a worldwide influence. The Chabad-Lubavitch website says its philosophy and adherents have 'reached almost every corner of the world and affected almost every facet of

Jewish life' as the biggest Jewish movement on Planet Earth. Counterpunch.org reported as long ago as 2014:

> There are approximately 3,600 Chabad institutions in over 1,000 cities in 70 countries, and 200,000 adherents. Up to a million people attend Chabad services at least once a year. Numerous campuses have such centers and the Chabad website states that hundreds of thousands of children attend Chabad summer camps.
>
> According to the Times, [Chabad] 'presided over a religious empire that reached from the back streets of Brooklyn to the main streets of Israel and by 1990 was taking in an estimated $100 million a year in contributions'.

What will that be today? Chabad-Lubavitch is part of Hasidic Judaism which emerged from Western Ukraine and spread rapidly throughout Eastern Europe in the 18th century. The main centres today are Israel obviously and New York's Brooklyn and Rockland County. Hasidism officially seeks to adhere closely to Jewish orthodoxy, and they can be recognised by their classic Jewish religious clothing with the twirls of hair on the side of their face, long coats, fedora and homburg hats, along with the Shtreimel or massive fur hats that remind me of a car tyre (Fig 113). Hasidism and the Chabad-Lubavitch movement draw heavily on the Lurianic Kabbalah named after its creator, Jewish rabbi Isaac ben Solomon Luria (1534-1572), which emphasises messianic belief. 'Nathan of Gaza' employed Lurianic ideas to claim the 'new Messiah' (Hebrew 'Moshiach') was Sabbatai Zevi.

Figure 113: The car-tyre headgear.

This messianic mind-set remains a pillar of Sabbatean-Frankism today. The Kabbalah in general is the bible of Jewish mysticism dating from the late 13th century and is widely followed by Satanists especially its foundation work, the Zohar, which means 'Splendour' or 'Radiance' ('Illuminated'). Kabbalists Zevi and Frank believed that the Torah should be superseded by the occult Zohar. The Torah (also Pentateuch from the Greek) is the Old Testament 'five books of Moses' (Genesis, Exodus, Leviticus, Numbers, and Deuteronomy) which Judaism and Christianity claims were inspired by 'God' and communications to Moses an alleged more than 3,000 years ago. We'll see who this 'God' was in the section on religion. Sabbatean-Frankists are also known as Zoharists. Remember how Einstein and company mentioned 'religious mysticism' in their condemnation of how Israel was bombed into existence.

The 'Rebbe'

The Hasidic movement Chabad-Lubavitch is headed by a 'Rebbe' or 'Grand Rabbi'. The best-known is Menachem Mendel Schneerson (1902-1994) described as one of the most influential Jewish leaders of the 20th century (Fig 114). Some followers believe he was the Messiah (how many are there?) and it seems that Schneerson did not discourage that. Schneerson was awarded a posthumous Congressional Gold Medal for 'outstanding and lasting contributions toward improvements in world education, morality, and acts of charity'. President Jimmy Carter designated Schneerson's birthday as US Education and Sharing Day. They are commemorating a man who said this:

Figure 114: Menachem Mendel Schneerson – the 'Rebbe'.

> The body of a Jewish person is of a totally different quality from the body of [members] of all nations of the world; an even greater difference exists in regard to the soul. Two contrary types of soul exist, a non-Jewish soul comes from three Satanic spheres, while the Jewish soul stems from holiness ... A Jew was not created as a means for some [other] purpose; he himself is the purpose, since the substance of all [divine] emanations was created only to serve the Jews.

Another Schneerson cracker is: 'The entire creation [of a non-Jew] exists only for the sake of the Jews.' This mentality about the importance of Jews against their non-Jewish servants is what makes Israeli troops look upon Palestinians as little more than vermin. A 2025 United Nations Independent International Commission of Inquiry on the Occupied Palestinian Territory, including East Jerusalem and Israel, reveals what happens when you demonise your targets:

> Specific forms of sexual and gender-based violence – such as forced public stripping and nudity, sexual harassment including threats of rape, as well as sexual assault – comprise part of the Israeli Security Forces' standard operating procedures toward Palestinians.

> Other forms of sexual and gender-based violence, including rape and violence to the genitals, were committed either under explicit orders or with

implicit encouragement by Israel's top civilian and military leadership.

A climate of impunity also exists with regard to sexual and gender-based crimes committed by Israeli settlers in the West Bank, with the aim of instilling fear into the Palestinian community and expelling them.

You see it's fine to claim you are the 'Chosen People' of 'God' and above all others, but you are an 'antisemite' if you say that's bollocks. You can even say that the role of non-Jews is only to serve Jews and that's okay, too. But question the mass murder of Palestinian kids and Trump will ban or deport you. They get away with this hypocrisy because Chabad-Lubavitch and Sabbatean-Frankists have enormous influence and control over political leaders. Israeli Prime Minister Benjamin Netanyahu was influenced by Rabbi Schneerson at least from the 1980s and said he was 'the most influential man of our time'. Netanyahu became a friend of Donald Trump's father Fred Trump while Israel's ambassador to the United Nations and son Trump first discussed having Elon Musk head the Department of Government Efficiency (DOGE) following a visit to Schneerson's grave during a car ride with ultra-Zionist Howard Lutnick who would be his Commerce Secretary (Fig 115). Chabad influence is far bigger than only Israeli politicians. I have mentioned Jimmy Carter and he's not alone. Former President Joe Biden has long Chabad connections and was honoured by them many times. An excellent five-part series by Lifesitenews.com exposing Chabad influence reveals how Biden's wayward son, Hunter, said in 2023 that he had once been involved in recovering the Schneerson library collection from Russia.

Figure 115: Donald Trump in his yarmulke at Schneerson's grave with on his left Commerce Secretary Howard Lutnick, a neighbour of Jeffrey Epstein. On the right (appropriately) is the influencer and ultra-Zionist Ben Shapiro.

Chabad-owned Trump

Donald Trump has made glowing tributes to Schneerson and his political funders from the Adelson family have been vehement supporters of Chabad. The Adelsons had a blessing from Schneerson before their wedding. Chabad has acknowledged that Sheldon Adelson supported Chabad institutions 'from Boston to Washington DC, to Moscow' and one of eight Chabad centres in Las Vegas is named after the couple. Trump's daughter Ivanka, a Jewish convert, visited Schneerson's tomb to pray for her father's election success. Her husband Jared Kushner, a life-long friend of Benjamín Netanyahu through his Trump-pardoned father, has big connections to Chabad. He has made substantial donations to its cause along with the Donald J. Trump Foundation. The Kushners are both active Chabad members. Jared Kushner created in league with Saudi Arabia and the United Arab Emirates a company called Affinity Partners which he said is a 'corridor for Gulf investment in Israel'. It owns Israeli investment firm Phoenix Holdings which partly owns Elbit Systems, Israel's biggest arms company, that provides 85 percent of the drones used in Gaza and the West Bank. Rabbi Levi Shemtov, Executive Vice President of American Friends of Lubavitch (Chabad) in Washington DC, 'the rabbi of Capitol Hill', told a US Senate hearing on antisemitism on American campuses that it was 'not enough' for 'individuals and institutions' to be 'not anti-Semitic' – 'one must be *anti*-anti-Semitic.' The arrogance and self-obsession of such people has no bounds. Israel-owned, Chabad-owned, Trump nominated Yehuda Kaploun, a Chabad rabbi, as his US 'Antisemitism Envoy'. Kaploun was initially connected with Trump by his Jewish megadonors, Miriam and Sheldon Adelson.

Trump government pick Robert Kennedy Jr is a Chabad advocate, as was his assassinated attorney general father Robert Kennedy Sr who met with Schneerson. Kennedy Jr tweeted in 2023 that he had visited the grave of Schneerson who he said was the most important Jewish spiritual leader of the 20th century and had 'personally mentored some of America's greatest Jewish leaders'. This included Kennedy's friend Rabbi Shmuley Boteach who calls Schneerson his 'mentor'. Boteach has a high profile and in my opinion appears to be a very strange man. Jewish journalist Max Blumenthal has called Boteach the 'Adelsons' bagman'. Life-long Democrat Robert Kennedy Jr was influential in Trump's 2024 election win. He had long criticised Trump and pledged to end the two-party system as he ran as a third candidate 'independent'. Many supported him including smaller parties as he campaigned with his running mate, Nicole Shanahan, a billionaire thanks to her divorce from Google co-founder Sergey Brin. Then months before the election he switched to supporting Trump and another front in the Trump campaign was formed called MAHA (Make America Healthy Again). This upset his Democrat supporters, but he also took many to Trump bolstered by Kennedy's campaign against vaccines which eased off once he became Trump's 'health' pick.

Kennedy's move also cemented the two-party system rather than dismantle its 'Buggins' turn' irrelevance. The switch gave me the feeling of 'planned all along'. Kennedy is phenomenally pro-Israel and has called Palestinians 'arguably the most pampered people by international aid organisations in the history of the world'. Religion-obsessed podcaster Russell Brand said of Kennedy: 'The Lord's hand is upon him.' How ironic that Kennedy should be such a Zionist when Israel was involved in the assassinations of his father and his uncle, President Kennedy, in the 1960s. Chabad influence with its networking potential between influential people is far in excess of its numbers within the Jewish community, many of whom don't support its ambitions. The Lifesitenews series said: '… only about 0.29% of the entire adult population of the United States is involved with this group and 99.71% of the population – Jews and non-Jews – are not.' Power is not about numbers clearly. It's about influence.

Chabad and Putin

Russian President Vladimir Putin has a close relationship with Chabad. I watched a video in which a Chabad operative bragged about Jewish oligarch control of Russia and how Putin's friendship with the Jewish world was central to this. Putin may not be good for Russia, but he's definitely good for the Jews of Russia, the guy said. This originated in his childhood when he would come home from school in St Petersburg while his parents were working, and he was befriended by an orthodox Jewish family in the same block who would help him with his homework. 'All his childhood friends were Jewish', the Chabad man claimed, and there were a lot of quiet deals between Israel and Russia that people knew nothing about. Putin fired a top government official for describing Chabad as a 'supremacist cult'. Aleksey Pavlov, assistant secretary of the Russian Security Council, was out the door after he said: 'The main principle of the Lubavitch Hasidim is the superiority of the supporters of the sect over all nations and peoples.' Putin has Chabad connections to Trump via his son-in-law Jared Kushner. The State of the Nation website reported that Putin enlisted two of his closest confidants, the oligarchs Lev Leviev and Roman Abramovich, after he became prime minister in 1999. They would go on to be Chabad's biggest patrons worldwide and create the Federation of Jewish Communities of Russia under the leadership of Chabad rabbi Berel Lazar. He would come to be known as 'Putin's rabbi'. State of the Nation continued:

> In 2007, Trump hosted the wedding of [the] daughter [of] Leviev's right-hand man at Mar-a-Lago, his Palm Beach resort. A few months after the ceremony, Leviev met Trump to discuss potential deals in Moscow and then hosted a bris [circumcision] for the new couple's first son at the holiest site in Chabad Judaism.

Trump attended the bris along with Kushner, who would go on to buy a $300 million building from Leviev and marry Ivanka Trump, who would form a close relationship with Abramovich's wife, Dasha Zhukova. Zhukova would host the power couple in Russia in 2014 and reportedly attend Trump's inauguration as their guest.

Zhukova and Abramovich would later divorce and she remarried while ultra-Zionist media tycoon Rupert Murdoch became her stepfather after he married her mother in 2024. What a small world it is. This Chabad background puts the Russia-Ukraine conflict in another potential light when you realise that the Jewish President of Ukraine Volodymyr Zelensky is close to Chabad. Trump said that if he was elected he would end the Russia-Ukraine conflict in 24 hours, but instead Russia began to bomb even more intensely, and he announced unlimited weapons for NATO to support Ukraine. Trump, Zelensky and Putin all connected to Chabad? Interesting. Another is Israel fanatic Argentina President Javier Milei who claims to be Jewish. Chabad is all over him. Milei is an ideological partner of Elon Musk and handed him a chainsaw at a bizarre pro-Trump event before his election to symbolise slashing government programmes through Musk's DOGE. Milei deleted a stream of ministries in Argentina, fired tens of thousands of government workers, increased the cost of housing in Buenos Aires by 135 percent in a year, and food became unaffordable for millions. The price of petrol increased by 715 percent between December 2023 and October 2024. He was selling Argentina to corporations and among them those with significant Israeli connections. No wonder Musk and Trump love him.

Then there's the World Economic Forum. At the end of every conflab of the WEF in Davos is the invite-only 'Shabbat dinner' held for the last 25 years which hosts high-profile Jewish figures. Klaus Schwab said this was his favourite event of the week. I bet it is. The dinner is organised by Avraham Berkowitz, an 'emissary' for Chabad Lubavitch and 'a senior coordinator of Special Missions' for Chabad Headquarters. Berkowitz has represented Chabad at the United Nations and is executive director of the Federation of Jewish Communities in Russia. Berel Lazar, Chief Rabbi of Russia and Vladimir Putin confidant, is another Chabad operative at the WEF. Financier Nathaniel Rothschild counts himself as very good friends with Lazar: 'I met Rabbi Lazar in Switzerland at the World Economic Forum in Davos and I was struck by watching this figure and we eventually connected and started talking, and from there began a friendship and I started visiting his centre in Russia, many times a year.'

Making 'prophecy' happen

Chabad-Lubavitch is a messianic movement that believes that the

Moshiach or Messiah will come according to biblical and other prophecy. Moshiach literally means 'the anointed one', and refers to the ancient practice of anointing kings with oil when they took the throne. The Christian 'Christ' and 'Messiah' also mean 'the anointed one'. Chabad followers will believe their stories, but it is also clear that those prophecies are being *made* to happen and it's nothing to do with their perception of 'God'. Humans are making them happen so they appear to be unfolding according to 'God's' will as laid out in the severely manipulated Bible. By doing so the Sabbateans are gathering support from Christians who believe God is at work when it's actually the Cult. The following summary of the Messiah's arrival is taken from Chabad.org which says that the Messiah will be a direct descendent of the King David line. He will redeem Israel in the 'End of Days' and rebuild the Jewish Temple on what Jews and Christians call Temple Mount in Jerusalem (although some scholars believe the temple was somewhere else). The Mount has been the location of the Islamic Al-Aqsa Mosque since the 7th/8th centuries and is the third-holiest site in Islam after Mecca and Medina. Alongside is the Dome of the Rock which Muslims believe (because they are told) is the place where 'God' created the world and the first human, 'Adam'. The story also goes that the 'Night Journey' of Muhammad included Temple Mount (al-Haram al-Sharif to Muslims) where he ascended through the heavens and into the presence of God (Allah). Everyone to their own, but the religion chapters will throw religions and their stories into question.

If until recently someone had suggested the Islamic shrines should be demolished to accommodate the 'Third Jewish Temple' most would have laughed. *What?* It would be a bloodbath, they would say. But now we are in very different times. Gaza is devastated, the West Bank is being absorbed, and the Israeli government and army is dominant with a US president in the White House utterly owned by Israel. Suddenly the unthinkable can be thought although I do believe that the Jewish population is being set up for some serious upheavals, too. They are only perceived as fodder for the Sabbateans after all.

Plans for the Third 'Solomon's Temple' are well advanced and red heifers have been imported from Texas to fulfil the prophecy that a red heifer that has never been worked, given birth, milked, or worn a yoke must be sacrificed and mixed with a bunch of other stuff to purify the land after Al-Aqsa is destroyed. Only then can the Third Temple be built to follow the first that is claimed to have stood between 1000 and 586 BC ('Solomon's Temple') and the second between 515 BC and 70 AD. A red heifer raised in Israel was disqualified for sacrifice after two black hairs were found on its body and was used in a 'practice burning ceremony' for priests in July 2025. These people are insane.

Chabad believers suggest that the temple location is a gateway or interface between 'Heaven and Earth' and temple chambers are designed to be resonance amplifiers that will broadcast that 'system' to the rest of the world. How about a central control point on the human hive mind delivered by AI? Jerusalem is a massive vortex on the global energy/electrical grid ('ley lines') with interdimensional potential. This and manipulated history are the real reason that Jerusalem is a sacred centre for the 'Abrahamic' (believe in 'Abraham') religions of Judaism, Christianity and Islam. The Mount of Olives just east of the Jerusalem Old City is where prominent Jews are interned. Some say this is an Earth 'chakra' vortex relating to communication.

Dismantling 'Edom' (the West)

Jewish extremists believe that the Moshiach will only come after 'Edom' (Europe and the West) and Christianity are destroyed. They associate an ancient people they call the Edomites with the destruction of the first and second Jewish temples in Jerusalem and must face their 'punishment'. These crazies say the destruction of the first temple (of 'Solomon') involved the Edomites who occupied land to the south of modern Israel and that the Edomites later demolished the second temple as the Romans. They say it is 'good news' that Islam invades Europe to speed its demise. This makes sense of the Zionist networks manipulating through NGOs to facilitate the Islamic hordes that have crossed into Europe over decades. They have been allowed to do so by the Zionist-controlled EU and its puppet nation states. Many of these NGOs have been funded by Hungarian-born Jewish billionaire George Soros, well into his 90s as I write, who has played the part of being antagonistic to the Israeli establishment while funding its agenda. European Commission President Ursula von der Leyen said: 'Europe has the values of the Talmud.' The irony is noted given the racism and Jewish superiority betrayed in that book (the primary source of Jewish religious law and theology). The irony, too, of Christians and Christian Zionism supporting these insane people seeking to destroy their religion and culture. It's a shocker.

I saw a rabbi proclaim: 'You will pay dearly for it, Europeans – to such an extent you have no idea.' Dearly for what? 'Because of all the evil you have done to Israel, you will pay for it a hundredfold.' He called Islam 'the broom of Israel'. Other extremists say that America (part of 'Edom' or the West) must be destroyed and bow to the power of Israel. 'America will go down in eternal history as the ones that paved the way for the return of the Kingdom of David,' one rabbi crazy said. Another messianic rabbi believed that Donald Trump would be an 'eternal hero' for the role he is playing in bringing America to its knees. He is far from alone in that view. I have seen many of the same bonkers mindset say this and it is certainly happening as I write. 'All the world's systems must be erased', these zealots say. The world must be 'unrecognisable' and 'nothing can remain'. They must be eliminated to be replaced by the 'Messiah' ruling the entire planet from Jerusalem. There will be no more governments. 'You want one world government? So does God – no problem,' said another rabbi clearly in urgent need of psychiatric help. All will be ruled by the Jewish Messiah from Israel and world events are being made to happen to that end. View events through the lens of this indoctrinated madness, and you will see. How do you rule the world from Jerusalem? Through an AI hive mind. Yet *another* irony is that the 'God' they are worshipping and serving is the fake 'God'. Yaldabaoth consciousness and its Archontic, interdimensional hierarchy, are only using them and massaging their sense of superiority to reach the goal of a human hive mind under the control of AI. Sacrificing Jews in pursuit of this is fine with the Astral 'gods'.

Prophecy claims that all the nations of the world will recognize Moshiach as the world leader and accept his rule. The term 'End of Days' or 'End Times' is taken from the Old Testament Numbers 24:14: 'And now, behold, I go unto my people: come therefore, and I will advertise thee what this people shall do to thy people in the latter days.' Blimey, plenty to go on there then. This is said to be a reference to the messianic era. Rebbe Schneerson said the messianic redemption is imminent and I guess it must be. How could Schneerson be wrong? Prophecies say the Sanhedrin, the supreme court of Jewish law, will be re-established, and rule on all matters of law. Efforts are happening to do this. The period immediately before the Moshiach comes will see 'great travail and turmoil'. There will be a world recession, and governments will be controlled by despots. There are beliefs that a great war will take place, called the war of Gog and Magog. The Zohar claims that a resurrection when the dead will be raised will happen forty years after the arrival of the Moshiach. All the dead will be resurrected in the Land of Israel. It is hard to believe that others believe this crap, but they do, and the fundamentals are being made to happen, or *appear* to happen.

How the return of 'Jesus' fits in with all this is not easy to say because it's all a dog's breakfast to be honest. The Christian version goes something like this, courtesy of Christianity.com: First we will have the false Messiah or 'Antichrist' and the 'Great Tribulation' with 'great suffering, persecution, false prophets, great deceptions, wars, famines, earthquakes, and other natural disasters'. Nice. Jesus will then arrive to defeat the Antichrist, establish his 1,000 year kingdom, and also resurrect the dead. I'm not sure they will be happy rushing back from the Astral where they are still alive (or maybe returned here), but there we go. Needs must, I suppose. The story goes that God will judge everyone according to their works. Oh, and there will be the 'Rapture'

Sabbatean Spider

before the End of the World when Jesus takes his children believers to be with Him in Heaven while unbelievers will be left on the Earth to undergo the seven years of Tribulation. The Rapture will happen without warning, so eyes peeled. You have been warned. No babies will be born when Christ's Millennial kingdom is over and no one will die, but all non-believers 'will be thrown into the lake of fire for eternity'. I knew those swimming lessons would come in handy. Pinch me that people believe this stuff. *Ouch*, yes, it seems they do. It wouldn't matter if those that do believe these versions of the End Times were not in positions of power. Trump's cabinet is full of such people and that is not a coincidence. World events are planned to mimic the 'Tribulation' with Israel at the centre of it.

The Noahide tyranny

The Jewish Moshiach, or Messiah, will be a man who possesses extraordinary qualities apparently. He will be proficient in both the written and oral Torah traditions. He will incessantly campaign for Torah observance among Jews, and observance of the seven universal Noahide Laws by non-Jews. Ah, yes, the Noahide Laws. This is where it gets tasty and connects into the whole AI agenda. The seven so-called Noahide Laws are claimed to have been given by 'God' to Adam and Noah and are binding on non-Jews with *decapitation* the main penalty for not complying. Other punishments for non-Jews include death by stoning if a man has intercourse with a Jewish betrothed woman or by strangulation if the Jewish woman has completed the marriage ceremonies but had not yet consummated the marriage. They're not racist or mad or anything. 'God' had nothing to do with the 'Seven Laws' and neither did 'Adam' and 'Noah'. They were concocted by extremist 'Talmudic' rabbis with the goal of imposing them on the entirety of human society. Jewish works, the Babylonian Talmud and Jerusalem Talmud, are founded on the interpretations of rabbinical crazies and are incredibly racist against non-Jews. The deceit claims that 'Noah' is the father of all post-flood humanity which makes non-Jews (Gentiles) all subject to the Noahide Laws given to him by 'God'. 'Noah' was an invented character based on 'flood' heroes in many cultures long before Old Testament writers brought their composite invention to global prominence with his 'ark'. The Noahide Laws are as follows:

1. Do not worship idols.
2. Do not curse God.
3. Do not murder.
4. Do not commit adultery, bestiality, or sexual immorality.
5. Do not steal.
6. Do not eat flesh from a living animal.

7. Establish courts of justice to impose the Noahide Laws.

The Devil here, as always, is in the detail. The key 'law' is the setting up of courts to impose the Noahide Laws and decree the death sentences on non-complying non-Jews, or Gentiles. These courts would be controlled by Sabbatean-Frankist Death Cult 'judges' according to their interpretation of what constitutes 'worship of idols', 'cursing god', 'adultery', 'sexual immorality', and all the rest. Some of these ultra-Zionist extremists consider Christianity as 'idolatry' while the Israeli and global elites worship idols, murder, commit adultery, sexual immorality, steal, and that's just for starters. This is the point: Non-compliance with the 'God' decreed by the rabbinical (Sabbatean-Frankist) 'courts' would simply mean non-compliance with the 'God' that they *decide* is 'God'. These zealots contend that Israel is obligated to bring the entire world to worship the Sabbatean-Frankist 'God' (Yaldabaoth and co). All other worship, or no worship, would be decreed as 'idolatry', 'worship of idols', or cursing 'God'. The fact that they would be ordering the murder of non-compliers over a list of 'laws' that include 'do not murder' passes them by. Hypocrisy is their very lifeblood. This is not meant to make sense to anyone with an active brain cell. It is merely a calculated excuse to kill who they like when they like. There are many other 'laws' that apply only to Gentiles, too, and even not setting up the courts to pass death sentences is punishable by death. The 'courts' are planned to be run by pre-programmed AI.

You could write all this off as a form of insanity except that recognition of the Noahide Laws (including therefore the demand for the creation of Noahide 'courts') has been gathering in the Gentile world. President Ronald Reagan (another Chabad gofer) signed a proclamation in 1982 recognising 'the eternal validity of the Seven Noahide Laws, a moral code for all of us regardless of religious faith'. The US Congress gave its support to the Noahide Laws in 1991 when establishing that 'Education Day' to honour the ultra-Zionist extremist racist lunatic Rabbi Menachem Mendel Schneerson who said that non-Jews exist only to serve Jews. He also gave us this gem:

> This is what needs to be said about the body: the body of a Jewish person is of a totally different quality from the body of [members] of all nations of the world ... The difference in the inner quality between Jews and non-Jews is so great that the bodies should be considered as completely different species.

A more racist claim you could not imagine from those who accuse the rest of the world of racism when Jewishness is not even a race, but a cultural/religious belief system that they want you to believe is a race. The 1991 resolution passed by both Houses of Congress (H.J.Res.104) during the presidency of Chabad-connected Father George Bush included the following:

> Whereas Congress recognizes the historical tradition of ethical values and principles which are the basis of civilized society and upon which our great Nation was founded;
>
> Whereas these ethical values and principles have been the bedrock of society from the dawn of civilization, when they were known as the Seven Noahide Laws;
>
> Whereas without these ethical values and principles the edifice of civilization stands in serious peril of returning to chaos;
>
> Whereas society is profoundly concerned with the recent weakening of these principles that has resulted in crises that beleaguer and threaten the fabric of civilized society;
>
> Whereas the justified preoccupation with these crises must not let the citizens of this Nation lose sight of their responsibility to transmit these historical ethical values from our distinguished past to the generations of the future;
>
> Whereas the Lubavitch movement has fostered and promoted these ethical values and principles throughout the world.

A few things: The United States was not founded on the Noahide Laws, and they have not been the 'bedrock of society from the dawn of civilization'. They were scripted by Talmudic rabbis representing a small section of a tiny section (currently 0.2 percent) of the world population but decreed by these arrogant extremists as applying to the whole of humanity on pain of death. Congressional politicians claim that the deeply racist Chabad-Lubavitch movement has 'fostered and promoted these ethical values and principles throughout the world'? Don't be ridiculous. But when you are owned by the Sabbatean-Frankist Death Cult via funding and intimidation/blackmail you'll parrot any old shite that your masters tell you.

The plan is to introduce a universal 'Noahide Code' founded on the Noahide Laws and imposed by rabbinical courts in a world government system controlled out of Israel (planned centre of the AI hive mind grid) and this 'code' would replace national sovereignty. That doesn't mean this has to happen, only that this is what the crackpots want. The United Nations is seen as a vehicle for advancing this agenda and is 'striving to fulfil' many parts of the Noahide 'universal code'. The aim is for the global Noahide Laws to be administered by the biblical Sanhedrin through AI as part of the Smart Grid control system and the rebuilding of 'Solomon's Temple. Just by coincidence, of course, the Sanhedrin Council of the Jewish nation was reconstructed for the first time in 1,600 years on October 13th, 2004. The ceremony was held in the Israeli town of Tiberias on the Western shore of the Sea of Galilee where the council's last meeting took place in 425 AD. The pieces are being moved into place at ever greater speed and the symbol of the Noahide Laws is all around us today. It's the *rainbow colours* depicting the rainbow of Noah in the biblical story of the Great Flood. The now ubiquitous symbol of the rainbow (including as a symbol for medical staff support during the fake 'Covid pandemic') is yet another 'coincidence' when that is the symbol of the Noahide Laws? Not a chance.

I write with the Greater Israel project blatantly underway, and Netanyahu is openly talking about it. Genocide in Gaza is intent on securing that land for Israel along with the West Bank. We await American government support for annexing the occupied West Bank under Israel ownership. Trump deleted all limits on weapons supplies to Israel and took the annual Pentagon budget beyond a trillion dollars preparing for what he knew was planned. Open conflict with Iran was unleashed in 2025 and I have warned for so long that Iran was a likely flashpoint for a wider conflict between the West and China/Russia. Bombing of Lebanon continues, a country that attacking Iran is planned to weaken, and the bombing of Iran is far from over. Moves are also being made against Syria. Trump recognised the Syrian Golan Heights as Israel land in his first term and after the removal of President Bashar al-Assad by Western-owned 'Islamic' terrorists the Israeli army moved deeper into Syria and began to bomb the ancient capital Damascus. It's worth becoming familiar moving forward with the extent of Greater Israel in the light of where Israel chooses to target.

These are the foundations and structure that allows the Global Cult to impose the will of the Archontic 'gods' on eight billion people and this is why Israel can behave as it does and get away with it. This is why, too, given the Satanic basis of Sabbateanism and the wider cult, that whenever I have delved deeply into the background of major cult operatives their Satanism and paedophilia invariably follow.

CHAPTER 13

Spellbound

We are governed, our minds are moulded, our tastes formed, our ideas suggested, largely by men we have never heard of.
Edward Bernays

How can a few people control a world of billions? This question leads to so many switching off at the very suggestion. I mean, it's not possible, right? That's obvious – *bye*!

In fact, it *is* possible and relatively straightforward once you have control over major sources of information. We behave as we do because we *perceive* as we do, and we form our perceptions from *information*. Control information and you control perception. When you control perception, you control behaviour. Collectively you control human society. In short, the global population is under mind control. No, no, my mind is not controlled – I think my own thoughts! Really? Where do those thoughts come from? They are the outgrowth of perception and that comes from information received whether this be personal experience, a Facebook post, item on the news, or an ideology or belief system that you refuse to question or reassess. This is without even adding the perception programs encoded in the biological computer. Original thought and perception come from tapping into consciousness beyond the simulation and anyone who doesn't do that is under mind control. What's more, it's systematic. It has to be. A few can only control the many by controlling their perceptions of self, the world, and reality. The agenda to connect the brain/body with artificial intelligence is the next stage of dictating what we think and feel. The Archontic force must stop the reconnection of the Divine Spark and the Infinite, or its game is 'history'. It must suppress perception to suppress frequency and keep us in the Astral/human trap.

Worlds apart

The Global Cult has created two 'worlds'. The difference between them is knowledge (Fig 116 overleaf). One world is the Cult with its compartmentalised structure isolated or walled off from the population behind secret oaths, rituals and fear of revealing the secrets. Each level is isolated from the others. Knowledge of the Cult agenda, the Archontic 'gods' and, crucially, the nature of illusory reality is passed through this hierarchy, but literally in 'degrees'. Only the inner circles of the secret societies have anything like the big picture. Everyone else has enough knowledge to make their contribution, but no more. This way occult ('hidden') knowledge can be communicated through the generations of initiates without spilling into the population. I have worked for 36 years so far to break that firewall. The other 'world' is mainstream society where the Cult has created almost all the streams of communication – media (programming), 'education' (programming), religion (programming). It's *all* programming. Great swathes of the 'alternative' or 'independent' media are also repackaged programming that suits the Cult.

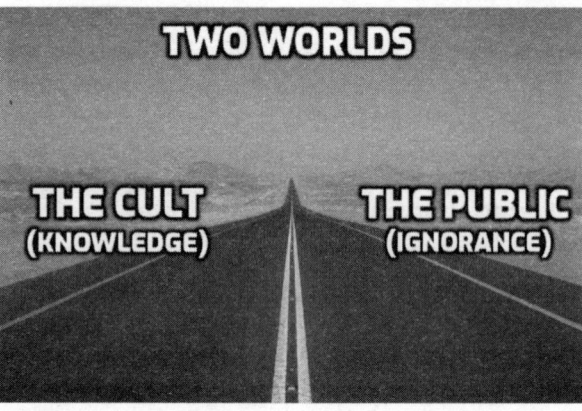

Figure 116: Two worlds within one world separated by access to knowledge.

The two 'worlds' allow the Cult to communicate knowledge through the secret societies while keeping the public in ignorance and one point to emphasise is the importance of controlling a sense of the possible. Suppress that and when those like me say this or that is happening, we are dismissed as crazy or strange. What I say is considered 'not possible'. Witness the dismissal since the 1990s of my contention there is a reptilian aspect to the conspiracy. Even alleged 'alternative thinkers' just laugh. Advanced technology is hidden from the public gaze before it is introduced in a calculated sequence to maintain an ignorance of the possible. Technology that we see in the public arena and think is the cutting edge of 'possible' is way back off the pace and designed to keep the population ignorant of the *real* cutting edge.

Lassoing perception

Mind control conjures images of horrific programmes like the infamous US/Canadian MKUltra which was 'inspired' by Nazi mind control experiments in Germany, but mind control is only the ability to manipulate people to think and behave as you want them to. On that basis, most of humanity is under mind control. Those involved in post-war MKUltra were transported to America from Nazi Germany through 'Operation Paperclip' to continue their evil in the United States. The Cult has no borders. Paperclip involved the transfer of more than 1,600

German scientists, engineers, and technicians including Josef Mengele, the 'Angel of Death' in the concentration camps, who operated out of America and South America after the war (Fig 117). MKUltra was headed by American Jewish chemist and super psychopath Sidney Gottlieb. The project involved more than 80 institutions in the US and Canada that included colleges and universities, hospitals, prisons, pharmaceutical companies, and CIA front operations. There were also centres abroad in Europe, East Asia, mostly Japan, and the Philippines. I refer you to the Global Cult structure for how this was coordinated. I have met and interviewed many people who were subjected to Gottlieb's mind control abominations, including those involving Mengele who operated in North America under the pseudonym 'Dr Green'. I studied the subject intently between 1996 and well after the millennium. To understand mind control is to understand human enslavement. MKUltra, orchestrated by the CIA, military and elements of government, began in 1953 and officially ended in 1973, but it has continued ever since under different names and become far more advanced and sophisticated. Today technology is very much involved.

Figure 117: More than 1,600 German scientists were relocated from Nazi Germany at the end of World War II and some of them created NASA. Others were experts in mind control and became involved in the infamous and horrific MKUltra.

American MKUltra survivor Cathy O'Brien has been a great friend since my mind control research began in the 1990s. She describes in her books *Trance Formation of America* and *Access Denied: For Reasons of National Security* how extreme trauma was used to 'honeycomb' the mind and neuron pathways of the brain to create compartments locked behind amnesic barriers. The compartments are known in the mind control industry as 'alters' as in altered states of perception. The Mind hides memories of extreme trauma behind these barriers, so people don't have to keep reliving them. This is why those involved in serious road crashes don't remember what happened immediately before and after impact. Nazi and MKUltra psychiatrists and operatives exploited this mechanism by exposing their victims to grotesque trauma to create the compartments and amnesic barriers around them. They would – *still do* – begin this trauma before the age of *six* while neuron pathways are still forming.

Ponder on the level of empathy-deleted psychopathy necessary to do this. If a child is terrified of snakes (and they can be made to be so) they will be put in a pit of snakes. If they are terrified of spiders their worst fear would be realised. Little kids are forced to watch the sacrifice of animals, even people, or take part for fear of what would happen if they refused. They are raped by Cult paedophiles like US President Father George Bush as Cathy describes happening to her daughter who was born into her MKUltra captivity. Children and adults are subjected to electroshocks, sensory deprivation, isolation, many different forms of torture, and drugs. Talk to those who have been through this, and I have talked to many both sides of the Atlantic, and you don't need to imagine any longer how the Cult can do the horrifying things that it does in manipulating wars, hunger, and suffering of all kinds. They are super psychopathic emanations of the Archons who are super psychopathic emanations of the super psychopathic consciousness that is Yaldabaoth. What potential for 'loosh' with such torture and psychological horrors.

Once the compartments are formed the mind controllers can infuse them with character traits and behaviour programs and patterns. They are given a front alter which is the character that people think is 'them'. They themselves also think the front alter is 'them'. But behind are all the other 'back alters' with very different 'thems' waiting to be activated by programmed words, images or sounds. There can be an alter programmed to go into a school and mass kill the children and staff. All it takes is the trigger and away they go. Manchurian Candidates depicted in the movies really do exist and in great numbers. You want someone assassinated, or to be in the wrong place to take the blame while the real assassin is a trained marksman? No problem. Many politicians, especially major ones, are under mind control. The Cult (like their Archontic masters) is terrified of outcomes they cannot call. Mind control is perfect for them to avoid surprises they were not expecting. The eyes tell the story if you know what to look for. I see mind control and/or possession in the eyes of key operatives every day.

The reach of the Cult and its ability to both act and cover up can be seen with what happened when MKUltra was publicly exposed in the 1970s. The US president at the time was Gerald Ford who was the man who came to the house to take Cathy O'Brien as a little girl from her willing Satanist father and into the MKUltra horror where she would remain for decades. He would later rape her as an adult. Ford ordered the creation of a Presidential Commission to investigate MKUltra and other CIA activities. This was led by Ford's vice-president Nelson Rockefeller who was involved with MKUltra. The Rockefeller Commission's final report was edited by the thug Dick Cheney, later vice-president to Boy George Bush. Cheney ('Republican') is exposed by Cathy in *Trance Formation of America* for constantly and brutally abusing her as part of MKUltra. President Bill Clinton and wife of convenience Hillary ('Democrats') were also connected to MKUltra abuse. The infamous Dr Jose Delgado (1915-2011), a Spanish professor of neurophysiology at Yale University, performed widespread experiments on animals and humans using electrical signals to control the brain. He said:

> We need a program of psychosurgery and political control of our society. The purpose is physical control of the mind. Everyone who deviates from the given norm can be surgically mutilated. The individual may think that the most important reality is his own existence, but this is only his personal point of view.
>
> This lacks historical perspective. Man does not have the right to develop his own mind. This kind of liberal orientation has great appeal. We must electrically control the brain. Someday armies and generals will be controlled by electrical stimulation of the brain.

This is the insane mentality we are dealing with, and the plan is to control the brain with AI. Even humans are no longer needed to serve as armies and generals when AI is running the show. AI *becomes* the generals.

Mass MKUltra

So yes, mind control exists in these projects around the world, but the same techniques are applied to the population in general. I observed the methods used during the 'Covid' hoax and saw the very techniques I learned about in my MKUltra and other mind control studies. Trauma-based mind control for the masses? We have a population that is constantly traumatised with reasons to fear and the daily struggle to survive (both traits of the reptilian brain). This generates loosh and makes people suggestable to perception programs. It has long been known that a traumatised mind is a suggestable mind. The mass trauma of the 9/11 attacks (not by 19 Arab hijackers) created the suggestibility to accept the 'solution' – the Patriot Act deleting freedoms and the invasions in the Middle and Near East. The trauma invoked by 'Covid' and the fear of dying, and your loved ones dying, from a 'deadly disease' made people suggestable to the 'solution' of the fascist impositions that, as a result, were meekly accepted. A mind-controlled kid shooting children in a school provides the trauma to make people suggestable to a 'solution' of more tyrannical impositions, schools turned into prisons, and law enforcement involvement. This prepares young generations to be familiar with these methods when they are applied in the wider world and accept them as the 'norm' they have always known. My children went to a primary school on the Isle of Wight in England where everything was open and free. Go there today and it's like a prison broken up into sections defended by high fences and locked gates. Trauma is a back-door access to the Mind individually and collectively.

Humanity is subjected to a daily onslaught of perceptual manipulation, and it casts a spell on the collective human psyche. Edward Bernays (1891-1995) made his living from mind control under the pseudonyms of 'public relations' and 'advertising'. He worked with US presidents and corporations to spin the public mind to their benefit. Bernays was a Jewish Cult insider and nephew of famous Jewish psychoanalyst Sigmund Freud. His mother was Freud's sister, and his father was the brother of Freud's wife. His great grandfather was Chief Rabbi of Hamburg. Bernays' family background with the famous psychoanalyst Freud must have been the perfect training for his career in mind control, oops, sorry, 'public relations', and what he described as 'the engineering of consent'. Bernays wrote in his 1928 book, *Propaganda*:

> If we understand the mechanisms and motives of the group mind, it is now possible to control and regiment the masses according to our will without their knowing it. In almost every act of our daily lives, whether in the sphere of politics or business, in our social conduct or our ethical thinking, we are dominated by the relatively small number of persons who understand the mental processes and social patterns of the masses. It is they who pull the wires which control the public mind.

The Archontic system is orchestrated from the Astral to make the human realm a life-long perceptual program.

Start them young – get them for life

Everything is directed at controlling perception and attention starting with babies in the womb impacted by the mental and emotional traits of the mother and their pre-birth environment. The programming becomes more direct once they emerge with parents projecting their programming on the child. Already perceptions of the world are being formed, and this really starts to move within three or four years when children go to school. Now they are faced with an authority figure representing the State telling them when they must be there and when they can leave, talk, eat, go to the toilet, during the whole period of the school day. Later they will be given homework to fill what remains of their free time after scrolling down their smartphones trawling still more system propaganda. Pondering time is filled with system information to process and that's the idea. Don't let their minds wander and ponder or they might just see through the bullshit and ask the wrong questions, reach the wrong conclusions. Children soon learn that life is easier (short term) when you obey than if you disobey or ask too many questions of

Figure 118: Education is mind control – perception control.

what you are being told to believe (Fig 118).

Exams are the State saying 'tell us what we told you or you will fail'. Humans tend to take the route of least resistance, and most are shepherded into traits of behaviour that don't push back on authority. Those that *do* resist soon learn there are consequences and many of those are broken into line. The others are called a 'problem' and a disruptive influence. Don't get me wrong. I am not saying that bad behaviour is to be encouraged and admired in the sense of respect for both teaching staff and fellow pupils. I mean the difference between those who obey authority just because it is authority no matter what it says or does, and those who don't accept that what a teacher or professor says is true simply because they say it. My experience is that the chances are it's not. Academics have been some of the most uninformed and closed-minded people I have ever met and imprisoned in the left side of the brain. Not all – but most.

Cult operative and oil tycoon J.D. Rockefeller was behind the creation of public education (programming) in the United States as he was with another Cult fiefdom, the pharmaceutical cartel. Rockefeller made it clear that he wasn't interested in educating young people to think for themselves. He wanted obedient workers for the system machine and the same Western 'education' has become the blueprint for the world through colonisation and funding of charities and non-governmental organisations. If you wished to install a structure to program young generations to become the adults that serve you and think what you want them to think you would come up with the way education indoctrinates perception. Five days a week, plus homework, children and young people trot along to school to be given the State's version of everything by a teacher paid by the State to tell the class what the State curriculum says is reality. History, 'science', all subjects, are the State's narrative and then you are tested in exams to see how much of the programming you have absorbed. 'Education' indoctrinates what I have termed the 'Postage Stamp Consensus' which means just enough to serve the system but not enough to see through it. Now recall what the 'gods' were described as doing in the ancient world – giving their human genetic concoctions enough 'intelligence' to be slaves to serve them, but no more. Nothing has changed except the 'gods' behind human control now operate from the hidden instead of making themselves visible.

Fill their minds

Children and young people spend much of their formative years having their minds filled with alleged 'facts' they will never use and could find out later on *their* terms if they needed to. Then they face the pressure (often imposed by parents) to 'revise' and remember the alleged 'facts' just long enough to pass an exam. They should be outside setting their imagination free, but instead they sit in a classroom being downloaded with the system's programming. How many childhoods have been destroyed by this or even ended by the suicides of kids who can't take the pressure of supposed failure and 'letting my parents down'? The technique is to so fill a young person's mind with often irrelevant and inaccurate 'facts' that there is no room left for imagination and right-brain expression. The more you absorb the programming the better your grades and your prospects to advance in the system are hugely enhanced by telling the system what it wants to hear and you to believe. You could even make it to Oxford or Cambridge, Harvard or Yale, where your programming will reach still new heights.

The young are taught *what* to think not *how* to think critically and with scepticism that demands evidence rather than blind acceptance. 'Everyone knows that' comes from everyone only being told that. The idea is to produce box minds for a box system and a belief in the system's version of reality, and not to unleash the unique gifts that lie within us all. Albert Einstein was right when he said: 'Everybody is a genius, but if you judge a fish by its ability to climb a tree it will live its whole life believing it is stupid.' These are the real lessons the school system wants you to take away: Truth comes from authority; intelligence is the ability to remember and repeat; accurate memory and repetition are rewarded; non-compliance is punished; conform intellectually and socially. This is the system that some parents celebrate with car stickers saying how proud they are that their children have passed an exam or got a degree. The late and great American comedian and social commentator George Carlin had a better idea: 'Here's a bumper sticker I'd like to see ... We are proud parents of a child who has resisted his teachers' attempts to break his spirit and bend him to the will of his corporate masters.' *Cult* masters.

More parents are beginning to see this as homeschooling soars. Now in response there are increased efforts by the State to target that and force kids back into the programming web. Homeschooling in some countries is against the law. I have seen even homeschooling parents indoctrinating their children with their own belief system programming especially with Christian parents who insist on Christian schooling. The idea is to set the children free to reach their own conclusions and not to swap one indoctrination for another. I'll address religious programming later which is one of the greatest assets in Cult perception control. Self-directed learning is when the child drives the direction rather than the biases of State and parents. Children follow their passions and interests which creates enthusiasm for learning. A study by psychology professor Dr Peter Gray found that mental health particularly improved through self-directed education where the child has the freedom and control to learn what inspires them. Researching their passion automatically leads to acquiring the base skills of reading, writing, and numbers which are compartmentalised into separate 'lessons' by the State.

Programmed programmers

The system of human control is a hierarchy. Teachers answer to the State and 'teach' according to its rules and regulations. Their job is then to impose the State's wishes on the kids. There is trouble for anyone who does not submit. The whole of society works the same way with humans manipulated to control each other all the way down the pyramids while the Cult sits at the top dictating the rules that everyone must follow. Teachers and academics largely never leave the system. They enter as small children and continue into adulthood just changing their roles, not their obedience to different levels of authority. This makes them some of the world's most perceptually programmed people and they are the ones that children and young people answer to and look to for 'learning'. The boss becomes the teacher when you leave school and there is law enforcement, courts, councils, governments and their agencies, and now AI cameras and other technology to track you and keep you in the box. These are in total meant to program you consciously and subconsciously into subordination to authority as you increasingly watch everything you do to make sure you are 'compliant'.

Then we have the 'experts'. The population in general looks to them for what to think and believe. 'We have an expert' on this or that wheeled on to TV programmes (programs) to give us the benefit of their own programming. They are 'science experts', 'medical experts', 'government experts', and we saw during the 'Covid' hoax how 'expert' they were as they instigated fascist lockdowns and deadly catastrophic fake vaccines on the basis of lies coming down from 'on high' which the 'experts' repeated, and the uniforms enforced. The same people urged the population to be tested by having a swab pushed high up the nose towards the brain and restrictions were instigated by governments to make testing obligatory to do anything. I refused anyway. The PCR test, which its creator said can't tell if you are sick, is another way to deliver nanotechnology to the body (see *The Answer*). This is what 'experts' and academics really are – *repeaters* of the State's official narrative. If they don't comply they are out the door, and if those they 'teach' don't comply they fail their exams on which ongoing opportunities often depend. The entire system is founded on humans policing humans on the basis of submitting to rules and structures ultimately controlled by non-humans and their lackeys. Repeaters include teachers, academics, politicians, and those who claim to be 'journalists' all of which are essential to perceptual programming. We now even have the fake 'alternative' media repeating the lies of the Trump regime in the same parrot fashion as the mainstream version they hypocritically condemn. The peak of the pyramid dictates what is true and the rest of the pyramid, following the 'experts', repeats the narrative.

We have the repetition of the same stories and alleged facts and the pressure to remember them for the exam papers. This downloaded version of reality can influence perception for life. I have met people who were programmed in MKUltra to program others, and we see this in the 'education' arena. Academics are some of the most programmed of all. They succeed in the school and university system by passing exams that confirm their indoctrination and then go into the teaching professions to indoctrinate the next generations. They never leave the system and all they hear is the system's version of everything. They are constantly monitored and tracked to ensure that what they tell the students is approved and doesn't stray even if their own perceptions become more expansive. Orthodox scientists and doctors are the same. You don't progress in the system by deviating from the narrative to become perceived 'experts' wheeled out in the media to tell the people what to think. You progress by your system mind repeating the system's version of reality.

Only 'Covid' adherents were allowed on TV, social media or in the papers during the hoax. Anyone telling the unacceptable truth was excluded even though they turned out to be right. All those that misled the public, even blatantly lied, are still today the system's 'experts' because they are telling the system's tale. Any 'doctor' or 'expert' you see on TV will be a repeater of the system narrative or they wouldn't be there. How many people died or have been maimed for life as a result of being lied to by 'TV doctors' about the 'Covid' fake vaccine being 'safe and effective'? But they are still employed as 'experts' giving 'health advice'. They had no idea if the fake vaccine was 'safe and effective'. They had done no research. All they did was repeat what the system told them like good little boys and girls. Much better for the career to be a repeater, you see. Those telling the truth are fired and excluded. You want a system career? Then repeat after me. You won't? Well, there's the door.

Brain targeting

The brain, with its estimated 100 billion neurons or 'brain cells', is not the origin of consciousness. The brain/body in general contain the perception and behaviour programs which are constantly running like biological software and the brain is a processor of information and consciousness into what we perceive as conscious thought and emotional response. It is a highly advanced 'quantum' computer that can be programmed and firewalled to process information that suits the system or not process that which George Orwell described as 'wrongthink' ('beliefs or opinions that run contrary to the prevailing or mainstream orthodoxy'). This can be overridden by consciousness beyond the programs which is why only those awakening to such expanded awareness can truly see through the scale of deceit. The programs call the shots if they are not overridden. Chemical (frequency) additives in food and drink, plus the effect of technological electromagnetic fields, further manipulate brain function to suppress the frequencies on which it receives and transmits to block the influence of expanded awareness and the Divine Spark.

The whole human system is designed to firewall the brain to process only myopia, and this is possible through the phenomenon of brain 'plasticity'. This means the brain changes the way it processes information according to the type of information (frequencies) it receives. That includes the information we know as 'experience'. Control of information and experience not only program perception. It also dictates the very way that the brain decodes reality. Science believed that once the brain was formed it didn't change. That was that for life. Now, as with so much that 'science' once knew for certain, they know differently. 'Neuroplasticity' is the brain's ability to reorganise neural pathways and grow neural networks according to 'structural changes due to learning'. Constantly recurring information causes brain neurons to fire in a particular sequence, and this constitutes a 'closed mind' that doesn't change because it doesn't question.

State-controlled 'education' is structured to form the pathways through repetition to develop the desired herd mentality and to encourage the collective to pressure any potential mavericks to conform. New information (like awakening to expanded awareness) realigns the neuron networks to match the new information (open mind). The Verywellmind.com website makes this highly significant point: 'Neurons that are used frequently develop stronger connections [while] those that are rarely or never used eventually die.' What you don't use fades away and the Archontic system seeks to ensure that you don't use what could threaten its omnipotence and do use what suits its agenda. A study by researchers at New York University and the Max Planck Institute of Empirical Aesthetics found that even brainwaves synchronise into similar patterns when students focus attention together in class. Shared *attention* and *focus* can also synchronise brainwave activity to synchronise perceptions (now play that out into the human collective mind and see how perceptions can be synchronised).

Left-brain prison

'Education' targets the left hemisphere of the brain, and this is where the great majority of academic minds are locked away and where the Cult wants the population for reasons I mentioned earlier. The right-brain controls the left side of the body and vice versa, and the hemispheres interact through the 'bridge' of the corpus callosum. People suffer from split personalities or 'split-brain syndrome' when the corpus callosum bridge is severed. One hemisphere can take an action while the other is unaware of what has been done. An image can be shown to each eye with the second eye having no memory of what has already been shown to the other. A woman with a corpus callosum damaged by a stroke would close doors with her left hand which the right had opened; close books that the right had opened; and take money back with the left hand that the right had just given. The corpus callosum does not have to be severed to impose split-brain syndrome. It can be done through such a constant inflow of left-brain information and concepts that the right goes largely to sleep as an arbiter of perception. Psychiatrist Eric Berne said: 'The moment a little boy is concerned with which is a jay and which is a sparrow he can no longer see the birds or hear them sing.' The left-brain operates in the realm of jays and sparrows. Enter the 'education' system to get a left-brain life up and running.

The left-brain is the 'intellect' in its most basic form and humans have been manipulated to worship the intellect as the fountain of knowledge and knower of all when it is the village idiot compared with expanded awareness. 'They have a great mind.' Okay, but what about a great consciousness? Most humans are dominated by the left side of the brain (especially in the West) which processes information into perceptions that relate to the five senses of can I touch it, see it, taste it, hear it, or smell it? The left-brain worships orthodoxy and clearly runs the world. The left-brain loves compartmentalisation and categorisation. Orthodox academia and science express this in rigid specialisations which compete for funding and prestige and rarely talk to each other. Seeing through the deceit requires a panorama across the specialisations, not myopia. The great majority of scientists are not pursuing truth for the truth's sake. They are serving corporate and military interests (the Cult in other words) with its agenda to keep the population ignorant rather than infused with gnosis. Paul Levy writes in *The Quantum Revelation*: 'The overwhelming majority of the physics field ... has been co-opted by the corporate powers ... to become an instrument for their agenda.' He quotes Professor Ravi Ravindra, an Indian-born scientist, as saying: 'We should keep in mind that a majority of all scientists and technologists in the world actually work for the military or for the war machine in one form or another.' Imagine where we would be now if science was focused on exploring reality with an open mind in which all possibility and not preconceived idea was the driving force.

Desperate for certainty

Both hemispheres within human society need the balance of each other. Left-brain myopia requires the balance of right-brain expansiveness, but we all know right-brain dominated people who struggle to function in a left-brain world. The ideal is to be 'whole-brained' where both hemispheres operate as one unit that can analyse the twigs *and* see that they are part of the forest. This is Robert Monroe's 'Hemi-Sync' or 'Hemispheric Synchronisation' which requires an active corpus callosum communicating between the two. Psychiatrist Dr Iain McGilchrist, author of *The Master and His Emissary, The Divided Brain and the Making of the Western World,* has made a long study of left-brain function which he says is 'black and white thinking, dogma, cut and dried thinking, unnuanced thinking, the craving for certainty …' Yes – *certainty*. This is what makes orthodox scientists furious and dismissive of quantum physics with its *un*certainty principles. Here you have the origin of the orthodox scientist, mathematician, academic, doctor, lawyer, judge, journalist, business people and politician that desire order, structure, and everything in its categorised box. These are all expressions of the need for *certainty*.

There is no certainty in an infinite reality of all-possibility. There is only *un*certainty and this is celebrated by expanded awareness because this is what it knows and glories in. The Archontic force is terrified of uncertainty – its worst, worst, nightmare and wants to placate its fears by controlling outcomes. Humans, as unconscious extensions of the Archontic, similarly fear uncertainty and seek out certainty to placate that fear. We see this in the certainty with which Trump supporters worship him as their saviour despite all the evidence to the contrary and there is the certainty of religious belief which is why its unsupported orthodoxy is accepted without question. Hence McGilchrist speaks of the left-brain's 'enormous capacity for denial', to ignore things, and 'keep them shut out'. Change the subject – I don't want to hear it!! Change the subject because I am terrified that what you say could be true.

Religion is left-brained because of its rigidity. Spirituality is right-brained and whole-brained. Politics is left-brained. Media is left-brained. Even most of the 'alternative' media is left-brained. This means they are all in a perceptual prison cell that they can only escape by breaking out into expanded awareness and sense of the possible. If you are going to keep your targets in a perceptual box you want them in the left-side of the brain which is the Archontic need for certainty. Witness the 'education' system from this perspective. It is designed through its subject matter and teaching methods to lock the young in the left-brain box and throw away the key. See how right brain subjects such as art and drama are marginalised, underfunded and underemphasised. When do children of school age engage in ad-lib play and improvisation like they once did? I grew up without smartphones or computers and we had to use our imagination for our entertainment. Now it is delivered to the left-brain largely fully formed through the Internet. Some right-brainers are okay to the system for their creativity, but the collective in general must be left-brain enslaved.

Long-term studies have revealed how the school system leads to massive declines of right-brain creativity 'as children have become less emotionally expressive [right brain], less energetic, talkative and verbally expressive, less humorous [right brain], less imaginative [right brain], less unconventional [right brain], less lively and passionate [right brain], less perceptive [right brain], less apt to connect seemingly irrelevant things [right brain], less synthesizing [right brain], and less likely to see things from a different angle [right brain]'. How perfect to develop Archontic slaves. Psychiatrist Iain McGilchrist says the left-brain is 'colonising the world with potentially disastrous results' which has denied left-brainers 'the means to *understand* the world'. Spot on and it really gets underway when children head for school. System institutions of 'education', government, corporations, and all the rest are founded on bureaucracy, uniformity, constant analysis, and rigid organisation. McGilchrist describes how the left-brain demands 'rules, regulation, and order' and we had 'recreated outside ourselves a world which very much looked like the interior world of the left-hemisphere – rigid lines of things that are rolled out mechanically and were non-unique'. This is crucially important when the inner creates the outer as a projection of itself. AI is a left-brain phenomenon with its obsession with data, more data, and still more data. We are entering an age when children are planned to be taught by AI while human teachers will be looking for work. Left-brain isolation is preparation for a life of slavery in a left-brain world following the rules which you did not decide, but which you follow because 'rules are rules'. The left-brain loves them!

Stealing creativity

Even then most right-brainers work for left-brained people and organisations that harness the creativity for left-brain ends – usually money. They who control the money control a world founded on money. Right-brained people who wish to expand the reach of their creativity and inventive minds need money to do so and this is where the left-brainers step in to fill the gap. I touched on this earlier, but control of money is so vital to control of humans that it is worth some expansion.

The banking and financial system is left-brained (with a few right-brain mavericks for creativity). This dictates the direction of society and where creativity goes and doesn't go by the technique perfected by the Rothschilds and earlier Cult operatives of lending people 'money' that doesn't exist and charging them interest for doing so. This non-existent money is called 'credit'. Banks are allowed through 'fractional reserve lending' to lend far, far, more than they have on deposit and they do this with lines of 'credit'. If you take a loan of say £100,000 the bank types into your account £100,000 which it doesn't have to possess. You are then committed to paying back that money that has never existed except in theory – plus *interest*. The interest has never been brought into circulation even theoretically and this is the calculated devastation of lives encoded into the banking system. It means that there is never ever enough 'money' in circulation to pay back all the debt and interest on the debt when the interest has never been created in theory or otherwise.

You sign over your home, business, land, possessions and resources to the banks as 'collateral' for borrowing money that does not and will never exist. If you are not able to repay, often through the actions of the government and financial system creating downturns and recessions, then the bank gets those homes, businesses, land, possessions and resources. Coldly instigated 'booms' to encourage borrowing followed by coldly instigated 'busts' to absorb those assets have sucked into the Global Cult banking system the wealth of the world. A handful owning more than the poorest half of the global population has not happened by accident. It's by design. There is not enough 'money' to repay debt and interest even in a 'boom' while in a 'bust' it becomes obvious as businesses fold and jobs are lost. The system has turned money into 'choice' and 'choice' is freedom. The more choices you can make the freer you are and the fewer the choices the more you are controlled. Money dictates choice (I would love to do this or that, but I don't have the money). If you control money, you control choice. You control who has freedom and who doesn't. The Cult controls money and through that can dictate where creativity is allowed to flourish and where it is not. Music industry insiders have told me over the years how the music 'genre' of any period is dictated by industry executives (the Cult) by what artists it will promote and fund. They only put before you the creativity that suits them. My son Gareth, a brilliant singer-songwriter, was told the industry would only promote and fund him if he denounced and publicly rejected me. He refused. The Internet has allowed artists to go their own way far more, but most still need the Cult system at some point and what is YouTube and other platforms anyway? The *system* which can promote or suppress, even cancel.

Owning governments

Cult banks and financial institutions control governments in the same way on behalf of the Archontic force that oversees everything from the Astral. US government debt is at $37 *trillion* at the time of writing with total government, corporate and individual debt well past $100 *trillion*. UK government debt is closing in on £3 *trillion* (nearly $4 *trillion*) and global debt is $315 *trillion* (probably a lot more). All the debtors are paying interest to the lenders, and it is money that has never, does not, and will never exist except in theory. What a breathtaking, almost incomprehensible, mess. Billions are suffering deprivation and death for lack of money while the world is paying interest and principal to a Cult-owned banking and financial system that can only be described as organised crime. They are calling Elon Musk the world's richest man as I write this. What a laugh. He's not even close. Why are governments borrowing money from the global financial system and paying colossal interest when they, as the government, could be creating their own money interest-free and lending it to the population in the same way? That doesn't happen because the same Cult that owns the financial system owns the politicians that pass the laws that make this organised crime officially 'legal' to crush their own populations. Nothing keeps humans more spellbound than the manipulation of 'money'.

Add to this credit fake 'money' scam the extraordinary level of taxation and how much of what you earn do you really keep from these parasites? There is income tax; a tax on almost everything you buy; on buying a home; taking out insurance; licences; and the most disgusting of all – tax on your assets when you die which have *already* been taxed. Cult-owned government is also organised crime that allows the population to be vampired of what its labour and creativity earns. It is a form of loosh extraction given that money like everything is energy and what you own and earn becomes part of your energetic field. What was the response to this of Donald 'man of the people' Trump? He passed a 'Big Beautiful Bill' that will add trillions to government debt for the population while ensuring massive tax cuts for billionaires like him. All together MAGA – 'We're winning!'

Archontic parasites impose on every facet of human life and where does all this taxation go as services decline by the day? Out of the system to the billionaire parasites serving the Archons and to all those Astral vampires feeding off human loosh.

CHAPTER 14

Owning 'Normality'

If you are always trying to be normal you will never know
how amazing you can be.
Maya Angelou

Control of perception, brain processing, and money means you control what is considered 'normal' or 'the norm'. This is crucial to Archontic oppression. The sense of normal may change. Normal when I was a kid was far from the normal today when a society infused with ever more technology is 'the norm'; but there is always a normal in every culture and era.

What is this 'normal'? It is only what people 'normally' experience. The point is that whatever the prevailing normal must be the sense of normal for the population because that becomes the point of reference. Possibility is judged from the perspective of this normal. Question control by technology and 'normal' says you are an old fogey living in the 'past'. Say we live in a simulation run by a non-human force often taking a reptilian form, and the human body is a prison for your True 'I' consciousness, and you are mad. Why? It's not normal. The normal is relentlessly policed by the very population that normal enslaves. They respond with ridicule, abuse and dismissal of anything that's not normal. The sheep police the sheep while the shepherd sips his Martini on a $500 million superyacht and chuckles at human naivety. Remember when those who said that flying in a machine was possible got this treatment? Now the pilot of a wide-bodied jet thinks flying is quite normal. How about those that said that heavier than water ships were not possible until Archimedes is said to have run naked down the street shouting 'Eureka' when he realised in his bath that it could be done. Now tell a bloke in the Navy that metal ships that float is not normal. He will say you are mad, just as those who said it was possible were once said to be crazy. All that's changed is the sense of normal.

The Cult system sets the normal and its agents and 'experts' promote and sell it to the public. This is what happens when you believe the official 'experts' as if they are all-knowing when they are really all-repeating what the system has told them. Some will be doing this knowingly and most will not. They will merely be repeating their programming genuinely thinking it is true and that they are experts. The left side of the brain tells them so. This is true of orthodox scientists, doctors, especially TV doctors, academics, journalists, the lot. Those that have any doubt are encouraged to conform by contemplating the consequences for their career and income of going against the normal and this leaves only a few with maverick backbones to speak out as they are escorted to the exits. The next stage is that those who believe the 'expert' version of normal then judge all possibility and happenings from that point of reference. On and on and on it goes generation after generation, century after century, in our perception of 'time'.

You break the cycle by questioning 'normal' to see if it stands up to scrutiny. Normal is accepted because it is familiar and once something is familiar the questioning stops. It is absorbed into the subconscious as 'just the way things are – everybody knows that'. No debate necessary. Most people accept 'normal' education (programming) because children go to school – 'everybody knows that'. But what about what's pumped into a child's mind day after day? I dunno. I just drop them off at the gate. Rule by politics is familiar and rarely questioned as the one-party vehicle of control that it is. We are a democracy, and the people decide who runs the government – everybody knows that. Really? Who decides who leads the parties? The parties do. Who picks the people running the rest of the government? The leader of the party that wins does. Who controls all the leaders of the parties with any chance of forming a government? The Cult does. Where is that 'democracy, power to the people' that you talk about? Familiarity does indeed breed contempt for the questioning mind. By contrast, when something new comes in it might be questioned until it has been around long enough to become familiar. Then silence. A New Normal has arrived.

As in school, so in 'life'

The 'education' system sets the perceptual tone for the duration as it is meant to and now you go out into 'the world' of work. There you will meet other people who have been through the same programming machine and have largely absorbed its version of reality. The teacher and lecturer are now replaced by the bosses you must keep happy to keep your job. The school hierarchy morphs into the work hierarchy and now you have to deal with government, local government, and corporate hierarchies. Know your place. Your work and social peers will be confirming the sense of reality you have downloaded which adds to the assumption that it must be true. I mean, everyone seems to know the same when everyone has spent their life being *told* the same. The now 24/7 media bombards you with the version of reality that you were given at school and university, which is confirmed by your work colleagues and friends. Only a few will question the system and if you are programmed enough, you will avoid them anyway. Bloody conspiracy theorists. How do they know better than the entire system of teachers, professors, government and journalists who all agree there are no conspiracies? Maybe because what all those people say is ultimately dictated by the Cult that created and owns those institutions. The definition of conspiracy may be simply two or more people conspiring together to manipulate an outcome (often illegal) that suits them, but they don't exist, I tell you.

I was a mainstream journalist for years after my football career ended at 21 and I worked in newspapers, radio and television. I can tell you that you don't need to be informed or pass an intelligence test to be a journalist. You just have to stay on message. There are lines you can't cross, or your reports won't get in the paper or on the news. Cross them enough times and you are in the street. That doesn't mean there are not genuine journalists genuinely seeking the truth about various people and subjects, but they are the few and I have yet to meet a mainstream journalist who had anything like the big picture. Nowhere near. They wouldn't be in the mainstream if they did and said so. I can say the same about most of the alleged 'alternative' media that has become prominent since 'Covid'. This operates exactly like the mainstream media while sticking its nose in the air and claiming it is different. It isn't.

People say the media is biased and yes, it is. Some will support the Democrats and the UK Labour Party while others will spin towards the Republicans and UK Conservative Party, or Nigel Farage's Reform. These are all aspects of the One-Party State. The emphasis and rhetoric might be different, but the direction is the same. It's just a matter of how fast. British broadcast media rules demand that TV and radio stations are not biased (against the normal) and in the United States it's an anything-goes-free-for-all with CNN and MSNBC blatantly Democrat and Fox pushing the Republican line. All these media corporations are owned in the end by the Cult and their one-side-or-another bias perpetuates the myth of political choice. The biggest bias of the media, however, is towards the Cult agenda, sales-pitching the prevailing 'normal', and assisting the perceptual transformations into new 'normals' when required. The media parrots the same Postage Stamp reality as 'education' which produces the journalists. As always, some who do this will be place-people of the Cult and the majority will just go along with whatever they are told to do. It helps when the media is in the hands of a few mega-corporations owned by billionaires, and much of the most prominent 'alternative' and 'independent' media is the same. You might see different TV and radio stations, newspapers and magazines, but check out who owns them, and it is shocking. I have detailed some examples in *Human Race Get Off Your Knees* and *The*

Perception Deception and the scale of ownership is almost funny.

Free press??

Cult intelligence and military networks have far more influence in the media than most comprehend through their planted assets, planted stories, and pressure to hold back information that would be detrimental to the national government or its owners in the Cult. British media can be subject to a 'D-Notice' or Defence and Security Media Advisory Notices (DSMA), which are official requests not to make information public 'for reasons of national security' (often Cult security). The system is officially voluntary, but most comply and censor material without even saying it has been censored. It just doesn't appear. The CIA's Operation Mockingbird was exposed in the 1970s for planting false stories in the media and using journalists as assets and spies. A US senate committee in 1975 investigated this and other abuses. The United States Senate Select Committee to Study Governmental Operations with Respect to Intelligence Activities was headed by Senator Frank Church and is better known as the 'Church Committee'. Its brief was to investigate agencies including the CIA, FBI and National Security Agency (NSA). The committee uncovered MKUltra; the FBI's COINTELPRO (Counter Intelligence Program) which infiltrated political and civil-rights groups to discredit them; and the 'Family Jewels' CIA operation to covertly assassinate foreign leaders not toeing the line. This is when Operation Mockingbird came to public attention in which the CIA used American and overseas journalists as assets along with dozens of US news organisations to communicate its (Cult) propaganda. The Church Committee said it had identified 50 journalists with secret connections to the CIA. It would have been far more no doubt. The committee report said:

> Approximately 50 of the assets are individual American journalists or employees of U.S. media organizations. Of these, fewer than half are 'accredited' by U.S. media organizations ... The remaining individuals are non-accredited freelance contributors and media representatives abroad ... More than a dozen United States news organizations and commercial publishing houses formerly provided cover for CIA agents abroad. A few of these organizations were unaware that they provided this cover ...
>
> ... The CIA currently maintains a network of several hundred foreign individuals around the world who provide intelligence for the CIA and at times attempt to influence opinion through the use of covert propaganda. These individuals provide the CIA with direct access to a large number of newspapers and periodicals, scores of press services and news agencies, radio and television stations, commercial book publishers, and other foreign media outlets.

Is anyone naive enough to think that this has not been continued to present day and expanded with the digital communication era online and through social media? Why do the authorities do this? To control *perception*. The late German journalist Udo Ulfkotte, a former assistant editor with major German newspaper, *Frankfurter Allgemeine Zeitung*, exposed before he died in 2017 his own knowledge and involvement in CIA (Cult) manipulation of public 'news'. He said he was forced to publish articles under his name to protect his job that were all the work of intelligence agencies. He said:

> I've been a journalist for about 25 years, and I was educated to lie, to betray, and not to tell the truth to the public. But seeing right now within the last months how the German and American media tries to bring war to the people in Europe, to bring war to Russia – this is a point of no return and I'm going to stand up and say it is not right what I have done in the past, to manipulate people, to make propaganda against Russia, and it is not right what my colleagues do and have done in the past because they are bribed to betray the people, not only in Germany, all over Europe.

Ulfkotte said intelligence agency control of the media was widespread with many American and European journalists writing agency propaganda and spying. He said he was bribed by billionaires and American agencies not to report the truth, and he published the book, *Journalists for Hire: How the CIA Buys the News*. Ulfkotte also revealed the close association between German intelligence and the CIA, and this is the case across the world through the Cult web. Intelligence agencies are a central pillar of Cult manipulation. Lower ranks will believe they are all separate, but they are all on the same side if you go deep enough to that level that attaches to the web.

'New media' – same old story

Communication is today dominated by the Internet with intelligence agencies even more prevalent. I exposed in *The Trigger* how Israel has whole armies of people operating advanced technology that are manipulating and influencing public perception through constant posting in the comment columns. They promote opinions they want people to have and attack and demonise those they wish to discredit. This is focussed on the massive Israeli army/Mossad Cyber Intelligence Unit in the desert-city of Beersheba which is home to some 20,000 'cyber soldiers' and the largest infrastructure project in Israel's history. I'll have more on this later in the book. Other militaries and intelligence agencies will be manipulating Internet communications in the same way. Cult asset Elon Musk was allowed to buy Twitter while claiming to be a 'free speech absolutist' to entrap the 'conspiracy' mind on a platform it believed was on its side. Philip Low, a friend of Musk for 14 years, was less than complimentary in an Internet post in 2025. Low, who founded neurotechnology company NeuroVigil, said Musk's claim to be a 'free speech absolutist' was bullshit as was his talk about getting to Mars to 'maintain the light of consciousness'. He said Musk 'knowingly feeds people to manipulate them' and 'everything Elon does is about acquiring and consolidating power'. Low said that Musk was not a Nazi in that Nazis believed an entire race was above everyone else while 'Elon believes *he* is above everyone else'.

Musk went all-in with support for Donald Trump and how both must have laughed at how easy it was to scam their support. Twitter – by now X –promotes through its algorithms the reach of posts that support the agenda and suppresses those that expose it – as I well know. I have 770,000 following my X page to get my posts as I write and yet only a fraction ever see them. Musk posts all day every day – or someone does on his behalf – and of course the algorithm is turned up full-blast for him. *The Verge, Guardian,* and others reported how he had his algorithm boosted by a factor of 1,000 when a Joe Biden post after the 2023 Super Bowl outdid his own. This means that when he reposts strategically chosen people supporting his agenda, they are guaranteed millions, even tens of millions, of views. Then there is a stream of Musk arse kissers employed to constantly post in support of Musk and the Cult agenda. 'Free speech' X has become little more than Musk's personal propaganda arm.

Musk appointed World Economic Forum stalwart Linda Yaccarino as X CEO and she instigated the policy (before resigning in July 2025) of what she called 'Freedom of speech, not freedom of reach' which is another way of saying shadow banning. In her words: 'If it is lawful but it's awful, it's extraordinarily difficult for you to see it.' *They* decide what is 'awful' and it corresponds with those challenging the Cult wish list and the Musk contribution to that. 'Freedom of speech, not freedom of reach', came from the Israel censorship operation, the Anti-Defamation League (ADL). Yaccarino and Twitter/X announced the policy in November 2022. Jonathan Greenblatt, head of the ADL, publicly said that phrase in *April* 2022, and another ADL spokesman said it in 2019. Greenblatt said of Twitter/X: 'We worked with the old regime; we're working with the new regime – I'm talking with Elon.' Musk's modus operandi is to make a big fuss about resisting government censorship very publicly, as with Brazil and Australia, to boost his 'free speech' image and then far more quietly cave to their demands. Twitter before Musk took down 54 percent of requests from authorities to delete content. After Musk it leaped to 71 percent.

Military Internet

The Internet and platforms such as Facebook (Meta), Google, YouTube, and X are a cinch to censor with algorithms either by suppressing views ('shadow banning') or outright deletion. The Defense Advanced Research Projects Agency (DARPA), the technological development wing of the Pentagon, claims credit for creating the Internet with military technology and they would never have done that unless there was benefit for the Cult. And there is – big time. Censorship was minimal in the early years of the Internet because the Cult had to entice people to ditch the old form of media and move to the well named 'World Wide *Web*'. There was a downside in that information would circulate that could not do so in the mainstream, but that was a 'lost leader' on the road to the destination eventually of total censorship. Cult operations were seed-funded which became the major Internet platforms. Other companies had to watch the bottom line while Cult companies such as Google (YouTube), Facebook (Instagram/WhatsApp), and Amazon could lose enormous amounts of money and still attract more to expand and to destroy, even purchase, potential opposition on the way to their near monopolies.

Censorship began once their dominance was secured, and the Internet had absorbed other means of communication. You want to stay visible 'online'? Then stay in the parameters that we dictate. Refuse to do that and you end up like me in April 2020 when I was deleted from YouTube, Facebook, Twitter, Spotify, et al, for exposing 'Covid' as the hoax that it turned out to be. The mere threat of censorship means that people self-censor in response. I absolutely refuse to do so because that is the most insidious form of censorship. There is no debate. You simply don't say it anymore in the face of the consequences. This happened long ago in the pre-Internet media when journalists knew the line they could not cross and today censorship can be enforced online through algorithms.

The British government Online Safety Act was claimed to be justified by 'protecting children from Internet harm', but from the moment it came into force in the summer of 2025 it was used – as always planned and predicted – to censor what the government does not want you to see. The fines for breaching its fascism are outrageous. The Act is enforced by the notorious government censor Ofcom, or Office of Communications, which was behind my ban from the mainstream media in 2020. Confirmation of the reason for Ofcom is that Cult operative prime minister Tony Blair brought it into being. He announced its arrival in 2001, and it was established in the Office of Communications Act a year later. First Ofcom policed only broadcasting and now the Internet has been added. Michael Grade ('Lord Grade of Yarmouth'), from the famous Jewish showbusiness family, began a four-year stint as chairman of Ofcom in 2022. He has also been chairman of the BBC and executive chairman of its rival, ITV. Grade lambasted the BBC (the *Israel apologist*

BBC) and other media for anti-Israel bias in 2017. He said in a speech in the House of Lords:

> Zionism is the right of the Jewish people to self-determination, and is right at the heart of the Balfour Declaration. However, sadly, the term Zionist and Zionism has in some quarters become a proxy for anti-Semitism.

He said 'anti-Semites' disguise their hatred of Jews as criticism of the Jewish state. Michael Grade, with that perspective, is currently chairman of British government censor and Online Safety Act overseer, Ofcom. I have been warning for decades that the plan is to control what is posted to the point where you will not see or hear anything that the Cult doesn't want you to see and hear. AI algorithms make that possible. We will have reached the age of Orwell's *Nineteen Eighty Four* and we are not far off. Don't be fooled by the Musk Psyop. It's only a step on the road to this and with a fusion of AI and humans it really won't matter what you see because AI will decide what you think of it anyway. Jeff Bezos began his Amazon as a global bookshop before expanding into selling almost everything. Independent bookstores and publishers were deleted along with stores selling products sold by Amazon. We had the supermarkets deleting most of the 'mom and pop' stores and now the supermarkets are being challenged by Amazon. As Amazon secures its monopoly on book sales the censorship of books is underway and planned to become a frenzy in the Brave New World of *Nineteen-Eighty-Four*. Amazon founder and Executive Chairman Jeff Bezos also owns the *Washington Post* and serves the Cult agenda in many other ways, including low-orbit satellites through Amazon's Project Kuiper and the development of AI.

Learning from Epstein

Investigative journalist Johnny Vedmore posted an article exposing connections between major players in the Big Tech arena headed: 'Musk & Epstein: The Third Culture Dossier'. Vedmore describes how Musk, Bezos, and Google co-founder Sergey Brin attended mass behaviour manipulation training in a course funded by Israel asset and infamous paedophile and Trump friend Jeffrey Epstein. The training was connected to the work of Zionists Richard Thaler and Cass Sunstein who popularised the concept of manipulating mass perception and behaviour through their 2009 book *Nudge: Improving Decisions About Health, Wealth and Happiness*. 'Nudge' refers to skewing information to 'nudge' people in the direction you want. Barack Obama employed Sunstein's 'talents' as administrator of the White House Office of Information and Regulatory Affairs from 2009 to 2012 and he advised President Biden on immigration policy. Sunstein is married to Samantha Power, the US ambassador to the United Nations under Obama.

Sunstein and Thaler also inspired the UK government's Behavioural Insights Team (BIT), known as the 'Nudge Unit'. This was established in 2010 by the UK Cabinet Office only a year after the *Nudge* book and headed by British psychologist David Halpern. The BIT was centrally influential in manipulating public opinion during 'Covid'. Sunstein and Thaler were named as 'academic affiliates' of the BIT. The whole raft of behaviour manipulation techniques is summed up even in this Wikipedia description of the Insights Team and its methods and techniques: 'Using social engineering, as well as techniques in psychology, behavioural economics, and marketing, the purpose of the organisation is to influence public thinking and decision making in order to improve compliance with government policy ...' The organisation, in league with British charity Nesta, established offices in the United States, Singapore, Australia, New Zealand, France and Canada. Tony Blair, the UK Prime Minister from 1997 to 2007, a long-time Cult operative, showed a keen interest in public behaviour manipulation. But of course.

Cass Sunstein co-authored a 2008 paper targeting 'conspiracy theories' and called for the cognitive infiltration of 'extremist' groups: 'Government agents (and their allies) might enter chat rooms, online social networks, or even real-space groups and attempt to undermine percolating conspiracy theories by raising doubts about their factual premises, causal logic or implications for political action.' Those claiming government involvement in the attacks of September 11th were referred to as 'extremist groups'. Among other suggestions to suppress these 'theories' the Sunstein paper proposed banning 'conspiracy theorising'; imposing a tax, 'financial or otherwise', on those communicating these theories; government engaging in 'counterspeech' to discredit conspiracy theories; and government hiring 'credible private parties' to engage in counterspeech. This is what they did and do. Many comments on social media are coming from programmed 'bots', the military operating out of Israel, and British army psychological operations (Psyop) unit, the 77th Brigade, along with their like around the world.

Epstein circle

It is with this background that the Epstein-Musk-Bezos-Brin connection (and others) should be seen. Johnny Vedmore highlights the influence of the Edge Foundation, which 'brings together leading ... thinkers across a broad range of scientific and technical fields'. Its website is Edge.org. The foundation was launched by Polish-Jewish literary agent and businessman, John Brockman, in 1988. *BuzzFeed News* reported from Edge's tax filings that Jeffrey Epstein was 'by far its largest financial donor' and gave him access to big names in science and Big Tech. Brockman was a prolific writer and published *The Third Culture: Beyond the Scientific Revolution* in 1995. The 'third culture' is connected to the 'third way' politics of people like Tony

Blair and Bill Clinton. These are presented as a balance of extremes when they are extremes themselves. 'Third' can be related to the 'Hegelian Dialectic' which I simplified with my phrase 'Problem-Reaction-Solution'. The 'Dialectic' consists of an argument, a counter argument, and then a fusion of the two, or 'thesis, antithesis and synthesis', leading to a new direction or idea. The 'third way' version, however, does not lead to a balance between for and against, but to a greater extreme *presented* as balance and fusion. Blair's 'New Labour' governments were extremism sold as moderation (see the invasion of Iraq in 2003 based on a blatant lie).

Vedmore says that membership of Brockman's Edge was linked to the ability to generate vast wealth and focused on the ruling class of 'elite scientific circles'. This led to its 'Billionaires Dinner' which Vedmore says was regularly attended by Jeff Bezos who also participated in many Edge courses run for 'elite members'. Other Edge attendees included Elon Musk of Space X and Tesla; Bill Gates of Microsoft; Sergey Brin, Larry Page and Eric Schmidt from Google; Anne Wojcicki of DNA testing company 23andMe; her late sister Susan Wojcicki who ran Google-owned YouTube; and Nathan Myhrvold, formerly Chief Technical Officer at Microsoft and co-founder of American private equity company, Intellectual Ventures, which controlled tens of thousands of patents. The Epstein-funded dinners were also attended by George Church, a co-founder and lead geneticist of Colossal Biosciences that 'de-extincted' the dire wolves that I mentioned earlier. Vedmore writes: 'From the late 90s onwards, almost every top member of the future ruling technocratic Establishment was involved with Edge.'

Zionist Richard Thaler, the 'father of behavioural economics', educated elite members of Epstein-funded Edge with his 'Master Class' brand of psychological manipulation in 2008 along with his friend and business associate, the Israeli-American psychologist Daniel Kahneman who was awarded the 2002 Nobel Memorial Prize in Economic Sciences. Among the attendees were Elon Musk, Jeff Bezos, Nathan Myhrvold, and Sean Parker, an American entrepreneur and philanthropist who co-founded Napster, and was the first president of Facebook. Parker was also a managing partner at Peter Thiel's venture-capital Founders Fund. American economist Paul Romer, another participant, would become Chief Economist for the World Bank in 2016 and shared a Nobel Prize in Economics. Vedmore says:

> This Edge event saw the leading experts of behavioural economics training the very top echelons of Google, Amazon, YouTube, Space X, Intellectual Ventures, Facebook and Peter Thiel's Founders Fund ... The attendees of this Edge Master Class would soon become the most powerful people in the

Owning 'Normality'   **249**

world, more powerful than any president, prime minister or king.

An Epstein-funded Master Class attended by Elon Musk was named 'The Psychology of Scarcity' which is a major aspect of behaviour manipulation and describes my long-time concept of scarcity = dependency = control. You may have noticed the very strong Jewish involvement here. Another Epstein associate highlighted by Vedmore is German entrepreneur Nicole Junkermann who invested in Carbyne911, a start-up company linked to IDF Israeli Unit 8200 which will be further mentioned later. Fellow Carbyne911 investors were Epstein, Peter Thiel and former Israeli Prime Minister Ehud Barak (with massive ties to Israeli intelligence), a close friend of Epstein, as was Junkermann. She sold her satellite data start-up Swarm Technologies to Musk's Starlink and flew on Epstein's infamous 'Lolita Express'. What a small world it is at these levels.

Know your data, know YOU

The Edge story puts into deep perspective the staggering amounts of data being posted hour after hour on Twitter/X, Facebook, Google/YouTube, Amazon, and many more. This is data that gives these companies the fine detail of peoples' lives, perceptions, opinions, lifestyles, finances, everything. This can be processed by AI to deliver individually targeted information to 'nudge' their views in the desired direction. Elon Musk has now fused Twitter/X with his xAI artificial intelligence company, and he wants to expand X into an 'everything app' that will include finances. We now have the most extraordinary depth and breadth of technology perfect for mind-controlling and manipulating the perceptions of the global population. Vedmore writes:

> At the moment, we are providing major companies with masses of our personal information daily and, in return, they are profiling us in more ways than one. That mass of data we supply to these companies allows them to control almost every action we take without us even realising it's happening.
>
> The next step is for artificial intelligence to be programmed to systemise this mechanism further until the vast majority of our decisions are controlled by our personal devices.

Put all the elements of these two chapters together and you come down to one word ... *perception*. They are casting a spell on the human mind. All is aimed at the control of perception which means the control of behaviour. This is the arena in which the entire conspiracy plays out. Perception dictates how we respond and if we respond to the Cult dystopia. It dictates if we even *know* there *is* a Cult dystopia unfolding by the hour. They must control your perception because then they control *you*. This is why the AI-human fusion is the target they seek above all else to achieve. Then there will be no need to manipulate information to manipulate perception. Your thoughts and emotional responses will be *AI's* thoughts and responses. *You* will not exist anymore except in theory. This is what awaits us and our children and grandchildren even more profoundly while the irrelevant and calculated diversionary conflicts over Trump or Biden, Democrat or Republican, Labour or Conservative or Reform, take attention away from the one-world tyranny which owns them all.

Orchestrating everything in the background are the Astral Archontic manipulators who must control our perceptions to control us. They have long seized control of human perceptions, and it is way past the time that we took them back. How? We think for ourselves instead of looking to system 'experts'. We work on the basis that authority lies unless proven otherwise. We question everything. *Everything*. We reach our *own* conclusions with our *own* mind and then act upon what we conclude.

The following few chapters continue the theme of multi-level perception manipulation because it is bottom-line vital that we seize back control of our thoughts while we still can. Shortly I will focus on the devastating impact of religion in securing perceptual myopia and limitation, but next the language of the subconscious – symbolism.

CHAPTER 15

Language of Symbolism

Symbolism is the language of the Mysteries. By symbols men have ever sought to communicate to each other those thoughts which transcend the limitations of language.
Manly P. Hall

Manipulation of perception takes many forms and one is the subconscious infiltration of symbolism. This is the language of the subconscious from where 95 percent of human behaviour is triggered.

We are faced with censorship, indoctrination, the body program, and electromagnetic fields all aimed at downloading a sense of reality, but the power of symbolism is often forgotten when it must not be. It is a crucial back door to perceptual programming. Dreams are mostly symbolic, not literal, because this is how the subconscious communicates. Symbolism is the secret language of the Cult and how initiates can exchange information in ways the population doesn't understand. Symbols encoded into events instigated by the Cult can alert advanced initiates to knowledge that 'we done it' and even how it was done.

Symbolism is the communication of frequency, and we return to cymatics. This perfectly illustrates how symbols and shapes are created by frequency. Particles form shapes which change as the frequencies change. A symbol is a frequency that can impact upon you energetically and *psychologically* because frequencies carry *information*. The Global Cult doesn't plant its symbols all around us for no reason. They are influencing the subconscious unless you are consciously aware of this in which case energetic barriers are projected to stop the impact. Symbols are 'subliminal' or 'below threshold' – the threshold of the conscious mind. Subliminal covert images are inserted into advertisements to speak to the subconscious which the conscious does not see. This can lead to you walking down a shopping aisle and being drawn to a product for no apparent reason when in fact it has been implanted in your subconscious mind by the subliminal advertisement. I have used subliminal images in other books to show that once the covert is pointed out to the conscious mind the first thing you see after that (every time) is the subliminal insert. It has been made *conscious* and loses its subconscious influence. How important this is when you think that almost the entirety of brain activity is subconscious (Fig 119). This is from a hypnotherapy website:

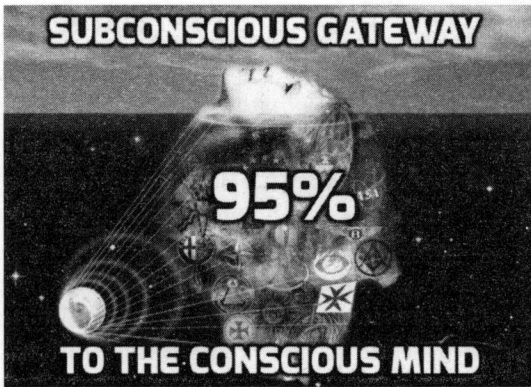

Figure 119: Symbols are energetic fields of frequency and designed to be absorbed by the subconscious mind from where 95 percent of human behaviour and reaction derives.

> Our subconscious mind controls each and every physical movement, whether voluntary or involuntary. Today's science estimates that 95 percent of our brain's activity is unconscious, meaning that the majority of the decisions we make, the actions we take, our emotions and behaviours, depend on the 95 percent of brain activity that lies beyond conscious awareness.

Our lives are dictated by levels of consciousness of which we are not *aware*. The potential for infusing subliminal instructions and perceptual influences is obvious and this is mercilessly exploited. Intent is the key here. What a symbol is *intended* to represent is the frequency that it generates into the environment. An example is the ubiquitous Cult symbol of the pyramid and all-seeing eye which represents the hierarchy of human control with the all-seeing eye of Yaldabaoth consciousness at the top. The symbol is on the dollar bill and the reverse of the Great Seal of the United States (Fig 120). It can be seen in many logos and symbols. They include that of the British domestic intelligence agency, MI5 (Fig 121). The words 'Novus ordo seclorum' on the dollar and seal translate as 'New Order of the Ages'. The 'New World Order' is an older version of the 'Great

Figure 120: The All-Seeing Eye and New Order of the Ages.

Figure 121: The pyramid and eye in the logo of MI5 (Military Intelligence, Section 5).

Language of Symbolism

Figure 122: The multiple all-seeing eyes and pyramids on the Cartoon Network alone.

Reset' and relates to the 'Great Work' of Freemasonry. The founding of the United States was dominated by Freemasons. Another Latin motto on the symbol is 'Annuit cœptis' from annuo (I approve, I favour), and coeptum (commencement, undertaking). It is translated as '[He] favours (or has favoured) [our] undertakings'. Why would there be so many versions of the eye and pyramid and all-seeing eye in children's cartoons on the Warner Bros Cartoon Network alone? It makes no sense ... *unless* (Fig 122). *Unless* they seek to implant in the psyche of the kids what the symbol frequency represents – obedience, fear, control. Can the frequency be generated through a TV? Oh, yes. The subconscious picks up everything it observes, and its range of observation is panoramic compared with the conscious mind. You are experiencing a sound frequency emitted into the field whenever you see an Archontic symbol, and they represent low-frequency states for obvious reasons.

Archontic Saturn

Many are symbols relating to Saturn which generate the frequencies emitted by Saturn. I am going to focus on these in this chapter because they are the most important to the Cult and they represent the frequency principles on which all symbolism operates. Saturn symbols include the hexagram (Star of David, see Israel and the Rothschilds), hexagon, and the cube (Fig 123). The Star of David is also known as the Seal of Solomon. These symbols represent aspects of the same frequency, and you can see what I mean in Figure 124 overleaf. Look at the same image of this crop circle first as a flat hexagon and then as a 3-D cube. It's the same frequency and your perception makes them appear different. It is not without reason that Saturn is known as 'the god of a thousand names' including ancient and secret society designations of the 'Dark Sun', 'Black Sun',

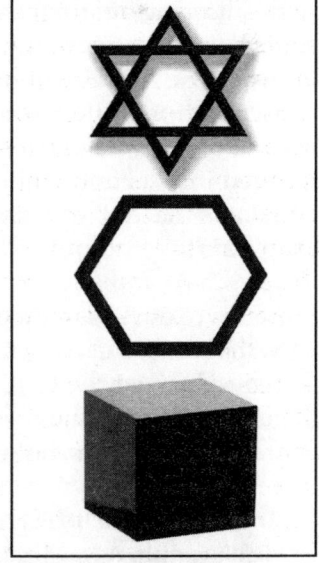

Figure 123: The hexagram, hexagon, and cube are all symbols of Saturn and different expressions of each other.

'Black Star', and 'Dark Lord'. The occult Nazis used the Black Sun symbol. It was displayed on the floor of the 17th century triangular Wewelsburg Castle, in Westphalia, Germany, after it became the 'spiritual retreat' of Heinrich Himmler's SS (Fig 125). Another Saturn name is the 'Great Malefic' which is defined as something that causes harm or destruction, especially by supernatural means, and having an 'evil influence'. Saturn is everywhere in different forms. This is the *Lord of the Rings* so beloved of Peter Thiel. Saturn is a focus of religion although most followers won't know. To cultists and secret society initiates it is the devourer, great judge of the dead, and associated with suffering, restriction, structure, control, and the recycling of the Soul between the Astral and human reality. Reincarnation or the 'Wheel of Samsara' is symbolised by Saturn's rings. It is weaved into legend and mythology, into ritual and 'sacred' architecture. A video I saw on Saturn's role in 'The Trap' said:

Figure 124: Look at this crop circle formation as a flat hexagon and then as a three-dimensional cube. They are the same image, but the way we perceive them can be different.

Figure 125: The Nazi symbol of the Black Sun that was placed on the floor of the Henrich Himmler's SS 'retreat' Wewelsburg Castle.

> Saturn doesn't merely represent the trap, it may be the trap. A wheel that spins without end, a cycle we're born to die in and return to without ever remembering how we got here. If Saturn represents structure, law, and judgment, it's no surprise that his shadow stretches across the most sacred traditions of human history.
>
> The figure we've been following, this devouring God, this cosmic warden, didn't vanish. As civilizations evolve, he adapted. And over time, his influence became more subtle, more symbolic, but no less powerful.

You will find the highly detailed background to Saturn, the Moon, and their connection to Yaldabaoth in one of my mega-works, *Everything You Need To Know But Have Never Been Told*, in which I cover the extraordinary story of how Saturn is a star, not a planet, and was once part of the Earth's two sun system. Saturn was the main sun of Earth and dominated the sky in the so-called 'Golden Age' before enormous cataclysmic events in the solar system relocated Saturn to its current position. Many 'sun gods' recorded in myths and symbols were *Saturn* sun gods when they have understandably been seen as gods of the present single sun (Fig 126). There is an excellent Internet video series by American researcher David Talbott, *Discourses on an Alien Sky*, that tells the Saturn story. His now hard-to-find book, *The Saturn Myth*, scanned the world for symbols of Saturn from many cultures and found a remarkable correlation confirming how Saturn was indeed the main Earth sun and how it was caught in the cataclysmic events that followed. Talbott found no evidence that *before* the relocation Saturn had rings. I'll come to them shortly.

There is a permanent storm at the north pole of Saturn that takes the form of a hexagon and another at the south pole that resembles an eye or all-seeing eye (Figs 127 and 128). I guess these are just coincidences, right? Once again, the hexagon is the hexagram and the cube (Fig 129 overleaf). I mean by 'permanent storms' that they have always been there since they were identified by the Voyager craft missions in the early 1980s which were followed by the Cassini-Huygens mission which

Figure 126: Many sun gods were Saturn sun gods and note how the symbolised 'halo' of sun gods was transferred to 'Jesus' and other Christian heroes.

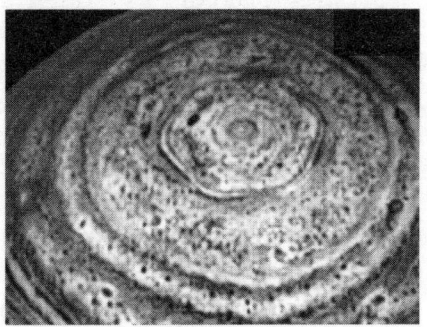

Figure 127: The fantastic hexagon storm at Saturn s north pole which is the size of four Earths. How is it formed? By sound.

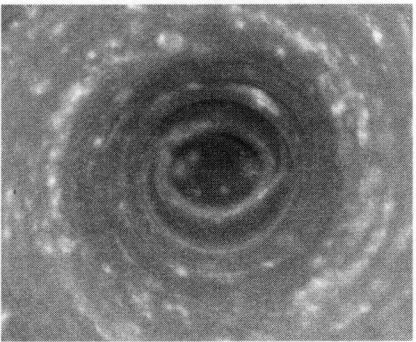

Figure 128: At the southern pole of Saturn is another sound creation of the eye storm.

Figure 129: A hexagon is also a hexagram and a cube.

launched in 1997, arrived in 2004, and was ditched into Saturn in 2017. The hexagon has even changed colour. Scott Edgington, deputy project scientist for the Cassini mission at NASA's Jet Propulsion Laboratory, said 'no one really knows what drives it'. The hexagon storm cycle matches Saturn's cycle of radio emissions with winds circulating at hundreds of miles an hour. There is nothing like it in the solar system and no wonder NASA describes the storm as 'bizarre'. Space.com reported how radio emissions differ at both poles and hence you have the eye storm at the south pole against the hexagon storm in the north. Don Gurnett, leader of the Cassini radio and plasma wave instrument team, said:

> These data just go to show how weird Saturn is. We thought we understood these radio wave patterns at gas giants, since Jupiter was so straightforward. Without Cassini's long stay, scientists wouldn't have understood that the radio emissions from Saturn are so different.

Confirmation that the Star of David is a frequency came when I watched a video of different sounds impacting on a liquid medium. Sounds produced both a perfect hexagram and hexagon (Figs 130 and 131). Quite simply, sound frequency information creates symbols and symbols generate that sound (Fig 132). Nag Hammadi texts say that Saturn is basically the energetic signature of Yaldabaoth and no surprise that symbols representing that signature are placed all around us.

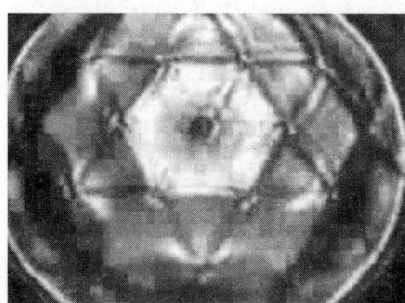

Figure 130: Sound impacts on the medium to form a hexagram or Star of David/Seal of Solomon..

Figure 131: A sound pounding through a liquid medium creates a perfect hexagon.

Language of Symbolism

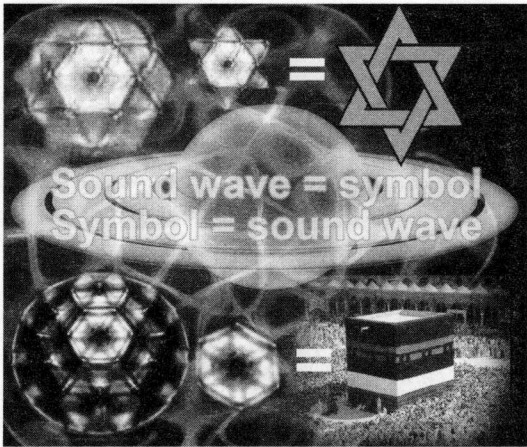

Figure 132: Frequency creates 'form'.

Gnostics believed that Saturn was the outermost Archon before the serpent Leviathan, the Ring-Pass-Not, that marks the frequency boundary of the Matrix through which Souls had to traverse to reach paradise. Planets and stars I have already emphasised are multi-dimensional and we only see that level within visible light and the energetic range of technology. They operate at different levels across dimensions. Just because Saturn appears as it does within the human sight frequency does not mean it's the same on every level.

Saturn's symbolic 'gods'

Saturn, or 'Cronus/Kronos' in Greek mythology, is said to be the god of 'time', 'space' and the 'Lord of Karma' which represents the material realm (Fig 133). It is associated with fear, difficulties, challenges, isolation, burdens and feelings of constriction. An astrological 'Saturn return' happens every 29/30 years when Saturn returns to its position when we are born and can bring challenge and change. Astrological energies interact with, and trigger, aspects of the life-programs encoded in the biological computer with Saturn the most significant. Cronus is 'Old Father Time' depicted with an hourglass and a sickle acknowledging Saturn's ancient association with 'time' and agriculture (Fig 134 overleaf). The 'grim reaper' with hood and scythe is Saturn symbolising time, old age and death (Fig 135 overleaf). Saturn was worshipped in Babylon as Nimrod, a *Saturn* sun god, and Ninurta, a god of war and enforcement. Saturn was Osiris to ancient Egyptians, the Lord of the Underworld, and again judge of the Soul. To others Saturn was the 'sun

Figure 133: Cronus/Kronos, the god of Saturn in Greek mythology, is said to rule 'time', 'space' and 'karma'.

Figure 134: Cronus/Kronos today is 'Old Father Time'.

Figure 135: Saturn's association with death is symbolised as the Grim Reaper.

gods' Bel, Bal, Baal, Baalim or Belus. Baal was a title meaning 'owner' or 'lord' in some semitic languages spoken in the ancient Levant and was eventually used for 'gods' in general. It is still used in Satanism to this day which worships the same 'gods'. In astrology Saturn rules Capricorn, which is represented by the goat that itself is a symbol of Yaldabaoth as with Baphomet and Pan (Figs 136 and 137). Freemasonic historian Manly P. Hall said of goat god Pan:

> Pan was a composite creature, the upper part – with the exception of his horns – being human, and the lower part in the form of a goat ... the god himself is a symbol of Saturn because this planet is enthroned in Capricorn, whose emblem is the goat.

Figure 136: Satanic symbol Baphomet is Saturn and Satanism is in many ways Saturnism.

The goat is associated with Satanism (Saturnism) for the same reason. Saturn was said to have reigned over the world in the Golden Age which is interesting given Donald Trump's contention that he would return the Golden Age to America. Trump would operate in circles in which Saturn worship prevails. Saturn was the chief god of Rome and celebrated by the festival of Saturnalia between December 17th and 23rd which corresponded with the winter solstice in the northern hemisphere. Saturnalia morphed into the Christian Christmas designated as the birthday of 'Jesus'. Later was added the concept of 'Santa' (an anagram of Satan). Saturnalia was a time when gifts were exchanged, trees were decorated, candles were lit, and there was holly and kissing under the

Language of Symbolism

Figure 137: Goat god Pan is Saturn.

mistletoe. There were similar traditions in other parts of Europe. The Saturnalia festival began and ended with a public sacrifice at the Temple of Saturn which housed the State treasury. The temple ruins still exist below Capitoline Hill, one of the Seven Hills of Rome, also known as Mons Saturnius, or Mountain of Saturn. Capitoline Hill is officially so called after a skull was found during excavations and skull or head in Latin is 'caput'. The name connection to Capitol Hill in Washington DC is clear and the city of government around the world is known as the 'capital' or 'head city'. America's Capitol Hill was built on land owned by the Carroll family for many years and listed in their records as 'Rome'. Daniel Carroll was a Jesuit educated Roman Catholic, and chairman of a commission appointed by the first president George Washington to find a location for a US capital. His brother John Carroll became the first Catholic bishop in America and founded Georgetown University. The Global Cult bases much of its structure on the Roman system.

Jewish/Islamic Saturn

Many religions came out of Saturn worship and reflect its energy of constriction, limitation, authority, and the materially external at the expense of the truly spiritual internal. The Jewish faith is a stand-out example which designates its holy day as Saturday, or Saturn-day (Shabbat in Hebrew). El is the Jewish god of Saturn as in Is-ra-EL, the Old Testament El (worshipped in many ancient cultures), and the plural Elohim (Yaldabaoth interdimensional entities). Elohim is inaccurately translated as a singular 'God' in the Bible as we will see. Saturn god El is symbolised as a black cube (Fig 138). Religious Jews wear the black cube 'Tefillin' on their heads in some rituals which always reminds me of a chimney (Fig 139). Maybe they can let off steam. Judaism believes Saturn to be the planet of divine order, the Jewish Messiah and the ruling planet of Jews.

Figure 138: El is the Jewish god of Saturn and symbolised as a cube.

Figure 139: The Tefillin cube.

It is central to the Jewish faith and associated with the archangel Gabriel. How interesting when Gnostics connected the Old Testament Yahweh with Yaldabaoth and so do I in terms of the consciousness involved. Saturn is Shabbetai in Hebrew, and we have the founder of the Sabbatean cult called Sabbatai Zevi. You can see why Sabbateans worship Saturn. They are Saturn-teans. They worship Saturn (symbol of Yaldabaoth consciousness) directly in covert rituals while Judaism covers this in public rituals and symbolic stories. Saturn's colour is black which dominates Jewish ritual clothing and networks such as Chabad.

Figure 140: The Saturn symbol on the fish hat of the pope. Christian priests and Muslims also wear the equivalent of the Jewish yarmulke, or skull cap.

The Star of David is on the headgear of popes because it is not an exclusive Jewish symbol (Fig 140). It is a symbol of Saturn which can be seen on Mesopotamian tablets from thousands of years ago as a six-pointed star (Fig 141). Cathedrals and churches are called the 'House of the Lord' – yes, they are ... the Lord Archon or Yaldabaoth and its emanations. You can also see the hexagram/Star of David profusely used by Freemasons. The two Freemasonic pillars of 'Boaz and Jachin' seen in lodges around the world represent the twin pillars said

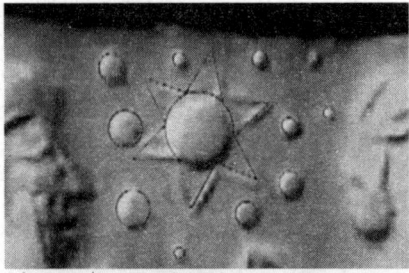

Figure 141: Mesopotamian hexagram Saturn.

to be at the entrance to Solomon's Temple (Fig 142). The Jewish religion is intertwined with Freemasonry. I found Saturn symbols during that 'open day' visit to the Freemason lodge in my town while the lower-ranked Freemasons I questioned had no idea this is what they represented. The Saturn symbol can be found in many cultures including those of Asia (Fig 143). A common theme is that the symbol is connected to the 'spirit realm' (the Astral). The astrological symbol of Saturn can clearly be seen in the hammer and sickle symbol of the Rothschild and Sabbatean-created Soviet Union (Fig 144).

Not by coincidence we also have a Saturn connection to Islam as

Language of Symbolism

Figure 142: The symbol of Saturn between the twin pillars of Solomon's Temple at the Mother Lodge of Freemasonry in Great Queen Street in London. The Great Queen was Queen Semiramis in Babylon.

Figure 143: Hexagrams all over Asia.

Figure 144: The astrological symbol of Saturn and the hammer and sickle of communism.

Figure 145: The Kaaba cube centre of Islam in Mecca.

there are many interconnections of belief between Islam, Judaism and Christianity. It is said that the 'archangel Gabriel', connected in Jewish belief to Saturn, was the messenger who told Muhammad, the official founder of Islam, that he was a prophet of God and revealed what became the Koran. Religious stories abound with symbolism rather than literal fact, and I will lay out the astonishing extent of this. Then there is the black cube or 'Kaaba' in Islam's holiest city of Mecca which is a symbol of Saturn. Kaaba means cube and it is considered the 'House of Allah' (Fig 145). If the cube is the frequency of Saturn which is the frequency of Yaldabaoth – what does that make 'Allah'? The cube is symbolic of the simulation trap and recall from earlier how American nuclear physicist Silas Beane and a team at the University of Bonn concluded how the simulation could be arranged as a series of cubes. The hexagram Saturn symbol from which the name Rothschild derives is displayed on the flag of Israel – the Yaldabaoth vibration. What if the Seal of Solomon/hexagram represents an interdimensional portal? I have talked with former Satanists and those who observed their rituals and they describe how entities would appear out of the Astral within the centre of a hexagram/Seal of Solomon positioned on the floor. It appears to act like an interdimensional 'stargate'.

Millions of Muslims who arrive in Mecca for the annual pilgrimage, or Hajj, circle the Saturn symbol Kaaba seven times

Figure 146: Muslim pilgrims in Mecca praying in concentric circles around the Kaaba cube of Saturn.

counterclockwise which allows their collective energy to be trawled while being infused with the Yaldabaoth vibration. They also sit around the Saturn symbol in concentric circles (Fig 146). What does that remind you of? All Muslims that are physically and financially able are told it is a mandatory duty to attend the Hajj at least once in their lifetime which must be seriously good for business in Saudi Arabia. Muslims fall to their knees and 'face Mecca' five times a day wherever they are and focus their attention of worship on the Kaaba. Given the truth of the phrase 'energy flows where attention goes' they are syncing their energetic fields with the cube/Saturn/Yaldabaoth vibration – five times a day. The loosh that the Kaaba must accumulate through that global attention must be stupendous. The same is true of other religious symbols. What you focus upon, and give your attention to, locks you into the frequency they represent. What if, as I suggest, they are all the vibration of Yaldabaoth?

Saturn symbolism everywhere

When you see how major religions are connected to Saturn/Yaldabaoth we should ask why Judaism, Christianity and Islam are obsessed with Jerusalem. Why are they focussed on what Jews and Christians call Temple Mount and Islam knows as Harm al-Sharif? Temple Mount is said to have been the location of Jewish temples of Solomon and Herod (which some scholars question). Jewish eyes are now on this site for the Third Temple. The Islam version Harm al-Sharif (Noble Sanctuary) is said to have been the spot from where Muhammad went to heaven on a horse-like steed with the angel Gabriel (connected by Jews to Saturn). Is it too much of a stretch therefore to connect Temple Mount/Harm al-Sharif/Jerusalem with Saturn and through that to Yaldabaoth? I think not and this is especially important when the crazies want to run the world and the human hive mind eventually from Israel. The Third Temple which is in the planning for the current Al-Aqsa site has an inner sanctum 'Holy of Holies' laid out as a cube '20 cubits by 20 cubits by 20 cubits' (Fig 147). This is to match the alleged first Solomon's Temple described in the Old Testament Second Book of Chronicles 3:8-9:

> He made the Holy of Holies a cube, thirty feet wide, long, and high. It was veneered with six hundred talents (something over twenty-two tons) of gold. The gold nails weighed fifty shekels (a little over a pound). The upper rooms were also veneered in gold.

Figure 147: A model of the Second Temple in Jerusalem destroyed by the Romans in 70 AD that Israel wants to replace.

Gold carries a vibration used in inter-dimensional communication although we will see in upcoming chapters that the literal accuracy of the Bible and Koran are subject to serious question. The New Testament Book of Revelation talks of a coming 'New Jerusalem' which is described as a cube in Revelation 21:16:

> The city was laid out like a square, as long as it was wide. He measured the city with the rod and found it to be 12,000 stadia in length, and as wide and high as it is long (Fig 148).

The Global Cult is represented by religions, secret societies and political movements and you find Saturn symbolism within all of them. Frequencies are expressed digitally in the decoded human realm of 'matter' and you would expect the same Saturn theme to continue with numbers and numerology. It does. 'Hex', as in hexagon and hexagram, comes from the ancient Greek hexa, meaning six, and to 'hex' someone is to cast a magic spell or curse. Humanity is being hexed 24/7 by the simulation. The Magic Square of Saturn, also used in Freemasonry, has sets of numbers that all add up to 15 (Fig 149 overleaf). Numerology adds multiple numbers together until arriving at a single digit. This base number represents the frequency. The number 15 is therefore 1 + 5 which makes 6. The Magic Square comes to 666 in all directions, and this is the 'Number of the Beast' in the Book of

Figure 148: The New Jerusalem symbolised as a cube.

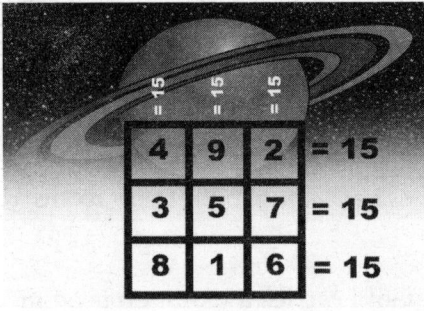

Revelation whatever the origin of that may be. The Magic Square of Saturn is the backdrop for the Sigil of Saturn (Fig 150). Turned upright you can see how it is the basis of the symbol of Freemasonry (Figs 151 and 152). Now look at the logo for Balmoral, the Scottish home of the Archontic British royal family (Fig 153). The Sigil of Saturn again.

Figure 149: The Magic Square of Saturn with all rows numerologically a six.

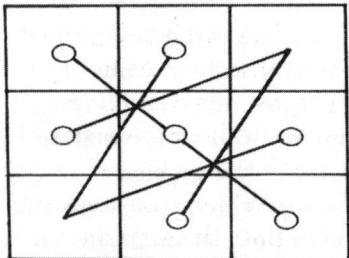

Figure 150: The Sigil of Saturn is created by drawing lines in number order 1-9 on the Magic Square of Saturn.

Figure 151: The Sigil of Saturn placed upright looks like ...

Figure 152: ... the compass and square symbol of Freemasonry.

Tales from the forest

I have highlighted since the 1990s the gathering of the Cult elite and their gofers at Bohemian Grove amid 2,700 acres of redwood forest in Sonoma County, California, around 75 miles north of San Francisco. The rich and famous including presidents and world leaders, politicians, corporate leaders like the Rockefellers and Rothschilds, and anyone of standing considered useful to the Cult, meet for a ritual-filled, alcohol and sex-filled 'summer camp' in which mind-controlled slaves are an essential part (see Cathy O'Brien's book *Trance Formation of America* and my own book, *The Biggest Secret*.) The 'grove' and its rituals are dominated by a 40-foot stone owl which symbolises the ancient Archontic god Moloch or Molech which is another symbol of Saturn (Fig 154). Hexagrams are known as the Star of Moloch and Star of Remphan which is the Egyptian name for Saturn (Fig 155). Ancient Canaanites and Ammonites related their Baal ('Lord') Moloch to Saturn and in

Figure 153: The Sigil of Saturn is the logo of Balmoral, the Scottish home of the British royals.

Language of Symbolism

Figure 154: Moloch or Molech as a 40-foot stone owl is the focus for rituals at Bohemiam Grove.

Figure 155: Moloch/Molech is Saturn.

Figure 156: Child offering to Moloch in his symbolic guise as a bull or bull-headed collossus.

demonology Moloch is the 'Prince of Hell' to whom children are sacrificed in fire. Jeremiah 32:35 says: 'They built the high places of Baal that are in the valley of Ben-hinnom to cause their sons and their daughters to pass through the fire to Molech.' Phoenicians sacrificed children in fire to Saturn and the same with the Celtic ritual of the 'Wicker Man' which was set ablaze with children inside. Humans have a long, long history of breathtaking insanity. The opening ritual at the 'summer camp' is called 'Cremation of Care' and involves a mock (we hope) human sacrifice watched by the people running our world.

Moloch is also symbolised as a bull or 'bull-headed colossus' (see the biblical 'Golden Calf') and this is the symbol of that Archontic bastion Wall Street (Figs 156 and 157).

I noticed during my travels to the United States in the 1990s that Capitol Hill (Capitoline Hill) was in the belly of a Moloch owl (not by accident) laid out in the road system (Fig 158 overleaf). Washington DC is a blaze of dark occult symbolism with distorted inverted pentagrams in the street network around the Capitol and the White House on land once called Rome and selected by the Roman Catholic Carroll

Figure 157: Moloch as a symbol of Wall Street.

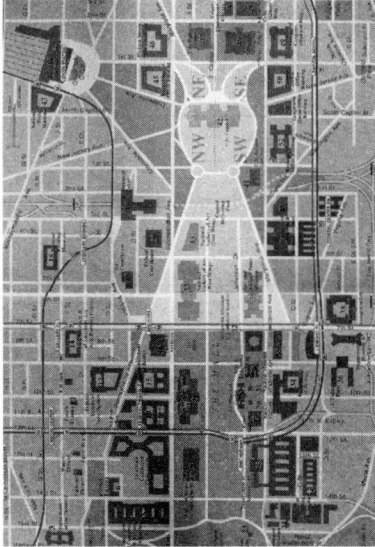

Figure 158: The Moloch owl with the Congress Building in its belly on Capitol (Capitoline) Hill in Washington sitting on a pyramid.

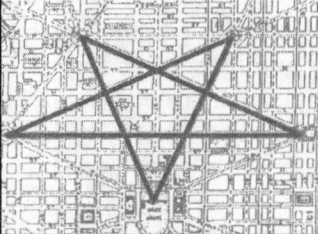

Figure 159: Inverted and distorted pentagram – a symbol of Satanism – in the street plan of Washington pointing into the White House.

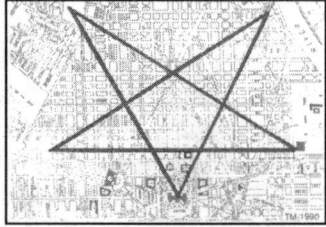

Figure 160: Another pointing into Capitol Hill.

family (Figs 159 and 160). Distorted symbols are used in Satanism to symbolise the Archontic distortion as they use inverted symbols to express the Archontic inversion. See the inverted pentagram and the inverted cross (Fig 161). The latter is believed to be a slight on Christianity, but the cross is an ancient symbol (witness the Celtic Cross). The cross is inverted because it represents the inversion of everything. Another example is the Statue of Liberty in New York Harbour which when inverted becomes the Statue of Control. 'Liberty' represents the ancient goddess under names such as Semiramis and Ishtar (Fig

Figure 161: Satanism uses inverted symbols including the pentagram and the cross.

Figure 162: The Statue of Liberty designed and gifted by Freemasons in France. Satanic inversion makes this the Statue of Control.

Figure 163: The Statue of Liberty replica on an island in the River Seine in Paris.

162). French sculptor and Freemason Frederic Bartholdi designed the Statue of Liberty and he and his Freemason colleagues in Paris named her after the goddess Libertas, a Roman version of Semiramis/Ishtar. There is a mirror image 'Liberty' on an island in the River Seine in Paris (Fig 163). Saturn symbols galore can be found in corporate logos and the black robes of the judiciary, legal profession, higher education, and the church are all related to the black of Saturn. Astrologically and esoterically Saturn represents law, the court system, banking, corporations, science, politics, and institutions of state. Saturn is the *left-brain*.

Lord of the Rings

Now – the *rings*. I'll keep it brief because the detail is in *Everything You Need To Know But Have Never Been Told*. David Talbott's research into Saturn symbolism around the world for *The Saturn Myth* (of which there are legion) did not find any evidence or mention that it had rings (Fig 164). I have concluded from researching this for decades that the rings have been added since the cataclysmic events that made Saturn go walkabout to its present location. If we think about it there is the

Figure 164: What are the rings of Saturn?

question of why Saturn is so prominent in the ancient world and became the chief god of Rome thousands of years ago if it was always where it is now. There is some rollover genetic memory of Saturn before the catastrophe that may well have been connected to the 'Great Flood' and the extraordinary destruction that can be identified in the Earth's geological and biological record. Maybe it marked the end of one simulation phase and the start of another – a 'Great Reset'.

My view of the rings would fit with the work of American engineer and research scientist Norman Bergrun who realised after studying photographs of the rings from the Voyager and Cassini missions that not only did the rings change regularly, sometimes in minutes, but they were *still being made*. Bergrun was employed at NASA's Ames Research Center in Moffett Field, California, and the National Advisory Committee for Aeronautics as well as working on classified aerospace projects for Lockheed Martin. He had top secret clearance for 30 years and pioneered the design criteria for aircraft thermal ice-prevention and the development of roll stability laws for planes, missiles, and rockets.

Among his awards was the California Society of Professional Engineers Archimedes Engineering Achievement Award. This guy was no theorist (Fig 165). He worked on facts as he saw them and wrote the book, *Ringmakers of Saturn*, to explain his conclusion that the rings of Saturn are 'not natural'. He said:

Figure 165: Norman Bergrun.

> Several years ago, a number of folks in the astronomy and physics world began theorising that these rings had to be much younger than the Universe, perhaps only about 100 million years old. But one pair of pictures shows a change in five minutes! ...
>
> ... An impression is conveyed that latest reported measurements purport to be the true ones when, in reality, all might be quite nearly correct at time of observation. General reluctance to accept variable ring-system geometry occurs because of apparent failure to identify a physical mechanism suitable for producing recurrent change.

The old orthodox 'science' response – if I can't explain it then it can't be happening and the desperation of their imprisoned left-brains for certainty. A news report was more open-minded:

> The great mystery of Saturn's rings is how they formed and why they are so stable. A simple model of orbital dynamics in this kind of orbit should gradually spiral into the planet. So, the rings should long ago have smeared out and disappeared. Instead, they are highly complex and stable and contain other structures such as spokes and braids. Nobody knows why.

Bergrun's biggest revelation as he studied the images were colossal cylindrical 'electromagnetic vehicles' in the rings that were emitting some kind of 'plasma exhaust' that was making the rings. 'People have got to be made to understand that those things are real', he said (Figs 166, 167, and 168). It would certainly explain why the ancients didn't mention rings. I have long concluded that the rings are the result of a hijack of Saturn – a possession if you like – by a highly advanced technological source that has turned it into a broadcasting system sending out low-vibrational frequencies across the solar system. I was once contacted by a sound engineer who sent an image of a Saturn ring and said he saw this every day in his work. He said the rings were clearly generated by sound (Fig 169). I further say that the Saturn frequencies are amplified by the Moon which is far too big to be

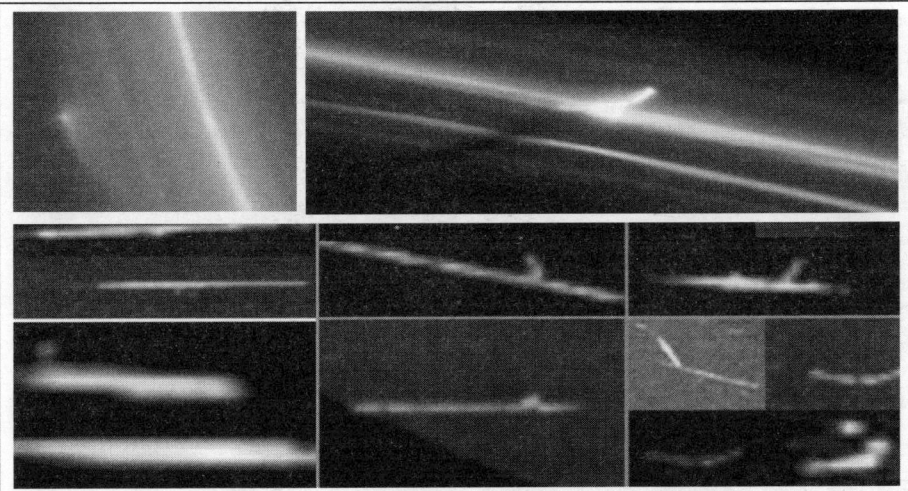

Figure 166: Bergrun's electromagnetic vehicles in and around the rings of Saturn.

Figure 167: An enormous vehicle in Saturn's rings.

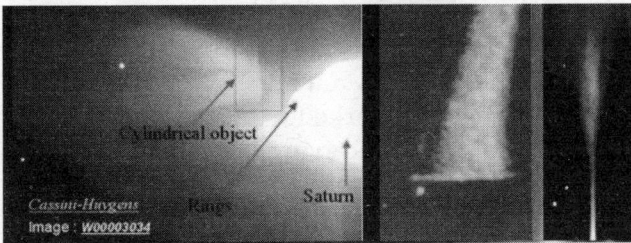

Figure 168: Plasma exhaust pours from the vehicles making the rings.

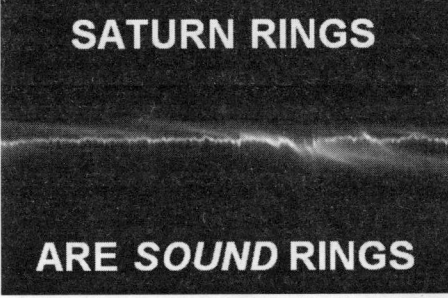

Figure 169: The sound rings of Saturn that answer the mystery of the Hexagon storm at the north pole and the eye storm at the south.

captured by little Earth. There are a stream of 'unexplainable' Moon anomalies and mysteries that *can* be explained if the Moon is not a natural body, but a construct in which the centre of activity is inside and not on the surface (Fig 170 overleaf). See my books, *The Perception Deception* and *Everything You Need To Know But Have Never Been Told* that tell an amazing story about the anomalies and what the Moon really is. The Soviet *Sputnik* magazine published an article as long ago as 1970 by two members of the Soviet Academy of

Sciences, Mikhail Vasin and Alexander Shcherbakov, who explained a stream of Moon anomalies from the perspective that it is a gigantic spacecraft for an advanced 'alien' species with all the action happening on the inside.

American aerospace engineer and Navy operative William Tompkins, author of *Selected by Extraterrestrials: My life in the top secret world of UFOs, think-tanks and Nordic secretaries*, said that the Moon is an artificial object and a Reptilian command centre with structures on the far side that we never see. I have quoted in other books former NASA employees who had seen pictures of those structures denied to the public.

Figure 170: The Saturn-Moon Matrix creating the perceptual box. (Image by Neil Hague.)

Tompkins said that the Apollo mission in 1969 had been just a show to hide the truth and America has never returned since the Apollo programme ended because the Reptilians warned against it. There has been no official manned flight to the Moon since Apollo 17 in 1972. He described how the Moon was occupied by nine-feet-tall 'Draco' Reptilians when astronauts landed in the first Apollo mission: 'After we get to the Moon we got some surprises – the Draco Reptilians were already there.' Ken Johnston is a former chief Lunar Module test pilot at the Manned Spacecraft Center in Houston and during the Apollo Program worked with Brown & Root, the principal contractor to NASA's Lunar Receiving Laboratory where moon rocks were stored and catalogued with photographs of their location. They included pictures taken by astronauts on chest-mounted cameras. Johnson told a SyFy channel television documentary *Aliens on the Moon* in 2014 that alien ships were waiting when astronauts Neil Armstrong and Buzz Aldrin arrived:

> While Neil and Buzz were on the Lunar surface, Neil switched to the medical channel [which couldn't be publicly heard], and spoke directly with the chief medical officer saying, they're here, they're parked on the side of the crater, they're watching us.

William Tompkins said that what Armstrong saw were ships floating above the crater with hundreds of Reptilian entities standing below them. All this does have to be balanced, however, against the assertions by many that the 1969 Moon landings were faked for which there is much evidence with the official story and footage making little sense. People will have to decide what they think. Zulu shaman and historian Credo Mutwa told me that their legends described the Moon as a Reptilian craft and a location from where humans were controlled. The Moon certainly has massive effects on Earth, tides and weather just by being there and the psychological effects on humans and animals are being increasingly explored. The Neurolaunch.com website ran an article headed 'Moon Brain: How Lunar Cycles Affect Human Cognition and Behavior':

> The concept of moon brain isn't just some far-out idea cooked up by starry-eyed dreamers. It's a growing field of study that's piquing the interest of neuroscientists, psychologists, and chronobiologists alike. But what exactly is moon brain? Simply put, it's the idea that the lunar cycle affects human cognition and behavior in measurable ways. It's as if our gray matter is engaged in a celestial waltz, swaying to the rhythm of the moon's phases.
>
> The notion that the moon holds sway over human behavior is nothing new. Ancient civilizations from the Mayans to the Chinese have long attributed various phenomena to lunar influences. Even the word 'lunatic' stems from the Latin 'luna', meaning moon. But it's only in recent years that science has begun to take a serious look at these age-old beliefs, armed with modern technology and rigorous methodologies.

The Moon holds a massive key to understanding human control.

You are feeling sleepy

Saturn and its radio waves broadcast a dark and eerie sound (check on the Internet) that captures its Satanic symbolism and mythology. These frequency emissions impact on mind and emotion and the cube is the perfect symbol of the Saturn perceptual 'box' that most people live within. Saturn puts you to sleep. Freedom lies in consciousness that breaches the box. Many ritualistic and satanic chants seek to mimic the Saturn frequency while others focus on the infinity beyond. It comes down to intent and awareness. We should remember for perspective that Saturn is enormous compared with Earth – 95 times bigger. Saturn is quite capable of sending out frequencies to bombard our tiny planet. Okay, it's 740 million miles away, but let us not forget that the realm of matter is illusory and there is no space as there is no time. NASA announced in 2009 that the Spitzer Space Telescope had identified another ring circling Saturn from some 3.7 million miles from the star/planet and extending to 7.4 million (Fig 171 overleaf). It could encompass a billion Earths and there are other waves of frequency way outside visible light that are constantly coming our way. I was fascinated all these decades after my take on the impact of Saturn's rings to chat with Rolf Nuyts, the long-time Astral traveller and former board member of the Monroe Institute. He

Figure 171: The ring of Saturn discovered by the Spitzer Space Telescope in 2009 that could encompass a billion Earths.

said that in his experience Saturn was a location of the fake 'god' ('Yaldabaoth'), and the rings were connecting with the frequencies of the human chakra system while operating together with the Moon to suppress human consciousness. I know people new to this will reel back with a '*what*? But there is a factual basis to back up what I'm saying.

What I am describing would certainly explain why the Global Cult is obsessed with Saturn and why its symbols are everywhere across society. Each one is broadcasting the frequency of what it represents alongside the Saturn emissions from the rings. Those frequencies are the Yaldabaoth vibration to keep humans in a low-vibrational perceptual stupor that is so important to keep us in the box and generate the loosh.

CHAPTER 16

God Save Us From Religion

Religion is regarded by ... the wise as false, and by rulers as useful.
Seneca the Younger

I have long called religion the greatest form of mind control ever invented. The Cult exploits this mercilessly and relentlessly and why wouldn't that be when the Archontic system *created* religion?

Many people express their compassion and empathy through their religious faith. I would say they could do this without the rigid beliefs and rules and regulations, but I have no problem with anyone that chooses to do that. It's none of my business as long as they don't insist that their children and others follow the same religion just because they do. This is, unfortunately, what happens over and over. Some 5.4 billion of the claimed 8 billion humans identify with being Christian, Muslim, or Hindu even without all the other religions worldwide – Buddhism, Mormonism, Jehovah's Witnesses, and many, many, more. Research believers and you invariably will find that they are Christian after being raised in a Christian family or environment and the same with Muslim, Hindu, Judaism, and others. This confirms that religious belief comes from religious heritage – religious *programming*. If the Christian, Muslim, or Hindu had been born into another faith they would now overwhelmingly be advocating that. Religious belief is less personal choice and far more religious indoctrination in the formative years. I have detailed the background to religion in my book *The Perception Deception* and here I will present the themes of why religion is such a weapon of Archontic manipulation. To understand the background and misdirection of religion is to understand the very foundations of the global tyranny.

Religious dogma and zealotry are not content with choosing a belief. They must impose it on everyone else through force, infiltration, and as we have often seen – outright war. Religions are a perfect vehicle for divide and rule when they don't have the respect for each other to believe what they choose without one seeking a position of domination (Fig 172 overleaf). Orthodox Jews perceive themselves to be God's 'Chosen People' because it says so in the Bible. Orthodox Christians believe that, too, because of their shared Bible and claim that the only way to Heaven is to believe in Jesus as their 'saviour'. Orthodox Muslims seek to impose the alleged will of 'Allah' on societies because as Muslims they are the children of Allah. Hindus worship endless 'gods' and often judge each other on the caste or group into which they incarnated. India may claim the caste system of reincarnated hierarchy no longer officially applies, but perceptually it does. Different faiths largely judge each other by their faith or lack of it because all believe they have the 'truth' and not only in theme, but detail (Fig 173). Ask where their faith came from and they point into far-distant history where the origins are often obscure and mysterious. Who wrote the Gospels on which Christianity is founded? Oh, that was the disciples of Jesus called Matthew, Mark, Luke, and John. No, it wasn't. Not even official Christianity believes that. Other 'books' are tagged to a single name when they are the result of multiple writers. Who? No idea. Lost in antiquity.

Figure 172: One of religion's main functions is to divide and rule the population – but there are many other reasons for its creation.

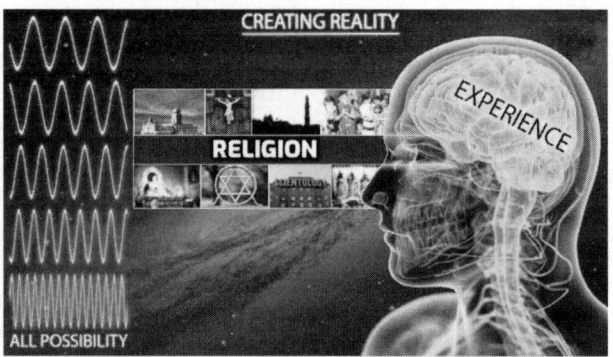

Figure 173: Religion is perceptual limitation and programming. (Image by Gareth Icke.)

This is the case with most ancient works – including Gnostic documents – and putting them in context and testing their credibility requires the fusion of ancient and modern knowledge to identify patterns of agreement and mutual support. It further requires that the researcher is not mesmerised by everything that is written being true without question. There are areas of Gnostic belief that I don't agree with, but nor is it sensible to dismiss everything from another faith or belief just because it's not yours. Discernment is crucial. Faith, however, does not do discernment. It's not allowed. Definitions of 'faith' include: 'Complete trust or confidence in someone or something'; 'Belief in God or in the doctrines or teachings of religion'; 'Belief, trust in, and loyalty to God'; Strong belief in the doctrines of religion based on conviction rather than proof.' Using intuition to reach conclusions is good if you are intuitively fine-tuned and not mistaking intuition for what you want to be true. Intuition is the stable mate of hard factual research through which we decide what feels right and what doesn't. Religion insists that you take the whole package – every detail – or you do not have *faith*. Discernment takes what feels right, or can be supported by research, and leaves the rest, but this is considered a form of blasphemy. You are not a true Christian, Muslim, Hindu, or Jew of faith if you don't take the lot.

Holy means wholly

The source of this is the belief that the 'holy books' of religion are the words of your version of 'God' or inspired by 'God' through a chosen individual. This pattern constantly repeats across the faiths and has terrible consequences for discernment. If the books are the words of 'God' then 'God' can't be wrong, and you must square endless circles of contradiction in all of them. The only way you can do this (as with a 'loving God' that demands mass slaughter) is to have faith or 'complete trust or confidence in someone or something'. Faith is needed to square the circles that otherwise could not be. Legitimate questioning of the contradictions is met with 'that's God's will' or 'God doesn't want us to know that' or 'have faith in God' or it's 'God's plan'. Yep, 'trust the plan' as with 'QAnon' and other scams that demand faith and not discernment. Don't question 'God's' (Q's) word because all those that don't question will be united in mutual condemnation and hostility.

In doing so they spurn one of the great biblical lines from Matthew 7:12 of the New International Version: 'So in everything, do to others what you would have them do to you, for this sums up the Law and the Prophets.' It's also a concept you can find almost word for word in texts far older than Christianity. How many Christians, or followers of other faiths, practice what they preach? They interpret the contradictions to support their version of the faith. Some will express compassion and empathy through their religion while others will justify violence to 'do the work of God'. Once you see others with a different belief as 'blasphemers' or 'infidels' anything goes because God doesn't like 'blasphemers' and 'infidels'. He wants rid of them, so believe or die. How much of perceived human history is defined by this?

Here you have the foundations for religion becoming the greatest form of mind control ever invented with all its limits on perception and self-identity (Fig 174 overleaf). It *was* invented as a form of mass human ignorance and perceptual imprisonment. If you wanted to control belief to control perception to control behaviour, then religion is your orgasmic moment. Holy books are the word of God, and these are the rules and regulations, the dos and don'ts, of the faith. Go beyond them and God will condemn you to the fires of Hell you blaspheming sinner. The aim of this is to isolate belief within a perceptual constriction defined by the faith and prevent you from exploring infinite possibility in pursuit of who we are and where we are. The constant theme is that God is 'up there', and

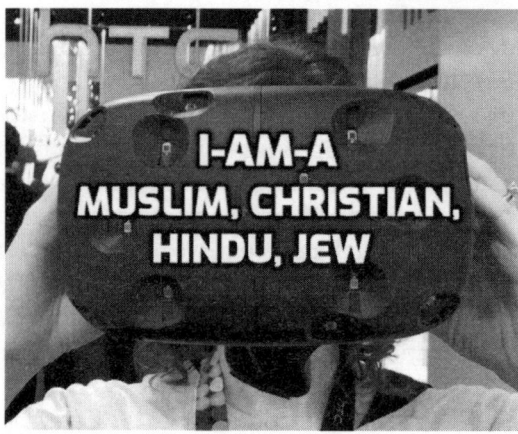

Figure 174: Headset religion.

we are 'down here'. He is never wrong while you are born a sinner who must be judged and sifted into wheat and chaff by the Creator of all things. We must bow, bend the knee, recognise our eternal role of subordination to the deity. Don't you dare say that we are all expressions of the Infinite, expressions of 'God', or there's a stake and lighted torch waiting for you, literal or condemnatory. The times I have had Christians say to me over the years that they agree with what I say about the conspiracy (up to a point), but they can't listen to me when I don't believe in Jesus as my saviour. It's true. I don't. My perception of reality and self-identity is my 'saviour' or 'oppressor'.

Religion is a mentality

Religions are everywhere throughout human society limiting the range of reality exploration to the confines of the faith. Who benefits from this? The Archontic which is desperate to maintain human awareness in the servitude of limitation. Many would not be considered religions and even anti-religion. We think religion (bricks and mortar religion as my father called it) must involve a church, synagogue, mosque, or temple, but it doesn't. That's only the way the religious state of *mind* often organises itself. Religious belief is a state of awareness and can therefore manifest in limitless settings. Orthodox 'science' is a religion. How ironic this is when its proponents like Oxford University professor Richard Dawkins is famous for condemning and ridiculing religion while being a high priest of his own – Scientism. We have the familiar themes. The holy books of Scientism are those that detail the *un*-scientific orthodoxy. Anything outside the orthodoxy is condemned as 'pseudoscience' or 'paranormal' claptrap and impossibility (see 'blasphemy'). Funding and prestige in Scientism is reserved almost entirely for believers in the faith.

Bricks and mortar religious orthodoxy condemns the 'paranormal' as the 'occult' ('hidden') and occult or hidden knowledge is, by definition, the 'Devil's' work. It's not. It's just knowledge and can be used for good or ill, but it's hidden knowledge that the Archontic wants to use against us while keeping us ignorant of how we can use it to set us free. In this way official religion and its perceived adversary Scientism speak an apparently different language from the *same* state of mind. Any unquestioned belief that repels all other possibilities is a religion. By that definition the human-caused climate change cult is a religion with an orthodoxy (based on Scientism) that must be obeyed and never questioned. Within all-possibility everything is possible, and we must always be aware of that, or the eddy of religious limitation starts to spin as the river of possibility flows past.

Religions may appear to be different in their beliefs, but the structure is the same and that includes Scientism. You go to a building – church, synagogue, mosque, temple, or university. There you find the vicar, rabbi, imam, pujari or professor who will conduct the ritual of telling you what God or scientism orthodoxy demands that you believe. The vicar, rabbi, imam, pujari or professor *interprets* the faith for you – a faith passed through the generations in verbal or written form that originated with *humans*, not 'God'. Humans translated the texts and decided which ones went into the holy books and which did not and are based on faith not open-minded research beyond the orthodoxy. That is labelled blasphemy to stop you going there to see what utter unsupportable nonsense you have been told to believe all your life by religious indoctrinators and how the Houses of God and Scientism are built on the same stretch of sand. A little push, a little open-minded research, and they are all a pile of rubble.

Uniformity

The scale of perception and behaviour control can be extraordinary and dictate life from cradle to grave even down to your clothing and hair which can be anything from uncut (Sikh) to cropped (Buddhist) to cutting the crown (Catholic monks and others officially to symbolise the 'crown of thorns'). The latter is called a tonsure and creates a ring like Saturn (Fig 175). This hairdo goes back at least to Babylonian priests leading the worship of the various gods including Saturn. Out of Babylon, Mesopotamia, and Roman occupation of the Middle East came Judaism, Christianity and Islam (which was also influenced by input from Hinduism). Beards are a feature of many religions and Muslims say they wear beards

Figure 175: Give us a ring.

because *Muhammad had one nearly 1,500 years ago*. Sounds like a good reason. The beard fetish reminds me of Cronus/Kronos, the Greek god of Saturn (Fig 176).

Uniforms are obligatory for all religion clergy to represent their chosen belief, usually in the form of a frock or gown. The skull cap was worn by Babylonian priests. This is the common origin of the caps worn in Islam, the Roman Catholic Church (including the pope), and Judaism (Fig 177). I gather that officially the Jewish cap, or kippah/yarmulke, comes from a Talmud requirement: 'Cover your head in order that the fear of heaven may be upon you.' Sorry, don't buy it. My money's on Babylon. The pope, Archbishop of Canterbury, and others wear a mitre like the Mesopotamian priests of the ancient fish god cult with their deities such as Oannes, or Dagon, the 'Fish of Heaven'. The mitre is a fish head (Fig 178). Christians partake of Holy Communion or the Sacrament of the Holy Eucharist which involves eating bread (as a wafer) and drinking wine to symbolise eating the flesh and drinking the blood of Jesus. I read that 'a good Catholic receives Communion every Sunday, or every day, if possible, but only once on the same day'. Holy Communion sounds very Satanic to me and originates in the ancient world long before Christianity when some literally ate flesh and drank blood to

Figure 176: The beard fetish of Saturn god.

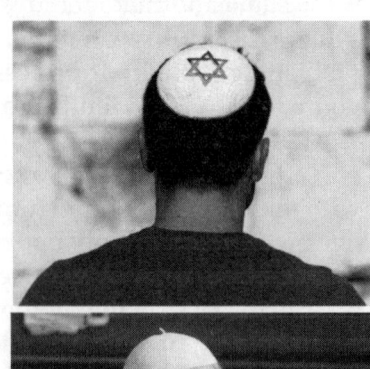

Figure 177: Skull cap uniformity with Judaism, the Pope, and many others.

Figure 178: Worship of the scaled fish gods in Mesopotamia continued today with the mitre of Christianity.

celebrate the 'gods'. The Christian version comes from John 6:53-58:

> Jesus said to them, 'Very truly I tell you, unless you eat the flesh of the Son of Man and drink his blood, you have no life in you. Whoever eats my flesh and drinks my blood has eternal life, and I will raise them up at the last day. For my flesh is real food and my blood is real drink. Whoever eats my flesh and drinks my blood remains in me, and I in them …'

It's in the Bible written by who knows who and *we* must do it thousands of years later. We must also continue to worship a God who felt the need to sacrifice his 'only begotten son' by being nailed to a cross to 'forgive the sins' of humanity and place images of said horrific sacrifice all over our churches to make it the symbol of our faith. 'For God so loved the world, that he gave his only begotten Son, that whosoever believeth in him should not perish, but have everlasting life' (John 3:16). But while God made his 'son' die a horrible death, we are still apparently 'born sinners'. Go figure.

Muslims fall to their knees five times a day to point their heads at the symbol of Saturn and virtually everything they do is directed by their faith. Even decapitation as with Saudi Arabia is justified at the extreme end of 'interpretation'. Try having a different version of reality in Pakistan where Islam rules with a rod of iron. This is not religious faith. It is the imposition of fascist tyranny. I saw when I spent a few weeks in Saudi Arabia in the 1970s how Islam is used as a vehicle for control that allows the fake royal family to run the show. A Hindu mob beat a man to death when he refused to tell them the location of Muslim and Hindu teenagers who had eloped in Uttar Pradesh. Love is not what God wants. My God insists you must be a Hindu. My God insists you must be a Muslim. In that case you can stick both your 'Gods'. Parents must dictate who their sons and daughters marry. Who says? God. No. Who says are arrogant tyrannical idiots that call themselves mum and dad. At the most extreme if you don't marry who we say we'll kill you. Tens of thousands of buffalo were slaughtered annually over the years at a Hindu festival to honour Gadhimai, the 'goddess of power'. Ashes of the dead are immersed in the River Ganges to 'liberate the Soul'. I read that the ashes must be collected on the third, seventh, and ninth day after death. I'm sure that makes all the difference. This still happens because of a story passed through the generations about the 'Goddess Ganga' and a king. Hindus better do it in the 21st century then.

Let there be no light

The dos, don'ts, musts, and can'ts of orthodox Judaism are really something else, especially as they relate to the Sabbath (Saturn), but much else besides. It's a real skin-pincher to check if you are dreaming or not. The book *Sabbath: Day Of Eternity* by Rabbi Aryeh Kaplan tells me that the following is banned on the Sabbath: Carrying, burning, extinguishing, finishing, writing, erasing, cooking, washing, sewing, tearing, knotting, untying, shaping, ploughing, planting, reaping, harvesting, threshing, winnowing, selecting, sifting, grinding, kneading, combing, spinning, dyeing, chain-stitching, warping, weaving, unravelling, building, demolishing, trapping, shearing, slaughtering, skinning, tanning, smoothing, marking. My son Gareth told me the story of his experience with a Jewish man at a lift which related to the Sabbath ban on 'selecting'. The man stood by the lift waiting for someone else to come along and select a floor. I guess he would then get out if it wasn't his floor and wait for someone else to come along or the lift door opening so he didn't have to 'select'. WTF? If you think all this is extreme, see my book *Infinite Love Is The Only Truth* and the chapter 'The God Program' based on an orthodox Jewish community in Manchester, England. The scale of behaviour control minute by minute is beyond belief. Or rather, it *is* belief.

The Sabbath ban on Jewish people burning anything is a humdinger. The Torah says: 'You shall not light a fire at home on the Sabbath day.' The interpretation is that nothing can be burned and this has far-reaching consequences. 'Even throwing a toothpick into a fire is considered a violation of the Sabbath under this category.' The ban includes smoking, striking a match, or turning on a stove, and definitely not driving. God forbid. Actually, he does. A vehicle engine causes fuel to burn, and driving is a real no-no. Heating metal to make it glow is considered 'burning' and turning on a light is banned or any electrical appliance including phones. Why would God ban driving on a Saturday or turning on a light? There are many efforts to get around the restrictions by sticking to the literal limits imposed by God, but not the spirit. I saw a video promotion of a light that is always on but obscured until you remove the covering. A light turned on and left on *before* the Sabbath is okay, it seems. Another way is to ask a non-Jew to turn on the light for you. God's fine with that so long as his 'Chosen People' don't do it. I have a better solution. Just turn the bloody light on yourself and stop being so silly. You are an adult or supposed to be. *Turn the light on*. What are you thinking? Clicks fingers. *Wake up*!

The religion mentality can be seen throughout human society because it is such a means to enslave minds in myopia and rules. The New Age is a religion with often its own uniform and is an offshoot of Hinduism, Buddhism, and the religions of the East. It says some things that are beneficial and enlightened but, in my experience, gets caught in the trap of believing that reincarnation is about 'learning lessons' to evolve. It also has its own version of Jesus called 'Sananda'. He is claimed to be one of the Astral 'Great White Brotherhood' (see the endless pantheons of Astral 'gods' worshipped under different names across the world). There is no description of Jesus in the Bible and the classic depiction is the work of Renaissance artists in the 15th and 16th centuries. Even so, the New Age 'Jesus', known as 'Sananda', is depicted in the same way along with near-death experiencers in the 'tunnel' (Fig 179). What a coincidence.

The theme that unites almost all religions is that their 'God' created the Earth and human reality. All the other misunderstandings must follow once you fall for this. Now observe the world of conflict, violence, suffering, poverty, hunger, ignorance, servitude, control by evil, and try to make sense of why a loving God would create and oversee this. You must square a 'loving God' with the evil tyrant 'God' of the Old Testament and even the son-sacrificing 'God' in the New. If you believe in the Bible, Koran, Torah, Talmud, Kabbalah, Bhagavad Gita, Book of Mormon, Jehovah's Witness Bible, on and on, you must deal with the endless contradictions. These disappear when you realise that the human realm and Astral was created as a perception prison by a deeply distorted and imbalanced state of consciousness that Gnostic texts symbolise as Yaldabaoth or the Demiurge. You also grasp that religions and their religious books are a prime means to secure that perception control and the 'God' they describe and demand that you worship is ... *Yaldabaoth*.

Figure 179: Sananda, the New Age 'Jesus', just happens to be portrayed in the same way as by Renaissance artists hundreds of years ago. There are no descriptions of Jesus in the Bible.

Yes, the 'God' of mainstream religion is the same entity (consciousness) that the religion claims to oppose in the form of the Devil, Satan, Shaytan, Samael, Saklas. Heads you lose and tails you lose. 'Satan' and the 'loving God' opposing Satan is the same entity wearing a different disguise. Books like the Old Testament sort of mix the two in 'Yahweh/Jehovah'. Based on 'energy flows where attention goes', the worship of the religion 'God' is making an energetic frequency connection that allows your energy to be trawled. Meanwhile, Infinite Awareness, the 'God' of which we are an expression, awaits beyond the frequency (perception) walls of the simulation for our expansion of consciousness to reconnect with that level of knowingness.

God-fearing

Think about it for a second. Yaldabaoth consciousness (expressed as Yahweh/Jehovah) insists that it is worshipped as the 'only God' for 'there is no other'. It wants humanity to bend the knee and bow in servitude and obedience. Its modus operandi and control weapon of choice is *fear*. Christian zealots and those of many other religions say we must be 'God-fearing'. Jewish women race in their anxiety to cook the food before the Sabbath begins as their husbands and children run to ensure they reach the synagogue in time. God must be feared. He must be obeyed. Saturn's day or the Sabbath is one of structure and restriction. Panic reigns if circumstances threaten your five-times-a-day devotion to the Saturn cube in Mecca. God must be feared. He must be obeyed. Yaldabaoth wants you to be chained and entrapped by rules, regulations, dos and don'ts, to block your exploration of all-possibility and realise the nature of the human plight and the Yaldabaoth Archontic hoax that can only be overcome by seeing through the diversions to the True 'I'. See how religion and its books tick every box? Religious foundations take a common theme. You have hero figures communicating with God, performing miracles, and establishing the religion; often they are a martyr figure; visitations by angels as messengers of God; journeys into Heaven. Muhammad, the alleged founder of Islam, is claimed to have been visited by the angel Gabriel (Jibreel) who led him to a beast resembling a horse 'with two huge wings springing from its back'. It took him to Jerusalem where he met with other prophets and was given milk and wine. He chose to drink the milk and Gabriel said:

> You chose milk in accordance to the purity of your nature. You have received guidance and your followers too. Had you chosen wine, your followers would have been led astray.

Muslims don't drink alcohol partly because of this and it's banned by the Koran. Gabriel is said to have led Muhammad through the seven heavens to meet Allah who told him that Muslim believers must pray 50 times a day. *What*? Yep, 50. Later Muhammad returned to Allah insisting that 50 was too many and much negotiation followed as Allah reduced it to 45 and then down and down until it was five. It's a good job *Art of the Deal* (written by someone else) Donald Trump didn't negotiate, or it would be at least 30, perhaps 60. Anyway, this story is the reason that Muslims fall to their knees five times a day wherever they are and face the cube. If you have read anything at all about Christianity, you will have heard of the angel Gabriel. The so-called 'Abrahamic religions' (those that believe in the Old Testament figure of Abraham) have much in common. These include Christianity, Islam, Judaism and the Baha'i faith, along with others like the Druzes, Rastafarians, and Samaritans. Islam and Christianity have a common belief in Jesus and Mother Mary although Islam rejects the 'Jesus is Divine' label. You can see how

Hebrew texts influenced Christianity and both Judaism and Christianity influenced Islam. This methodology will soon become very significant.

Moses is another character accepted by Judaism, Christianity and Islam. He is said to have been a Hebrew prophet estimated to live in the 13th century BC who led his people out of slavery in Egypt. The Old Testament story goes that he was given the Ten Commandments by God on Mount Sinai and founded Israel after his people wandered in a desert for 40 years which you could drive around in a day, two at the most. He is revered as the greatest prophet and teacher and Judaism has even been called the 'Mosaic faith'. God brought plagues of frogs, gnats, mosquitoes, boils, hail, locusts, and much else to pressure the Pharaoh to free the people of Moses. Eventually Moses and company made a break for freedom pursued by the Pharaoh's army and God rolled back the waters of the Red Sea to allow them to cross (no wet sand then?). The waves returned to engulf the Egyptian army as they gave chase.

Then there's the Moses burning bush that was not consumed by the flames and the staff of Moses that turned into a snake. Miracles are obligatory in religious stories. What's missing is any evidence outside the religion texts that they ever happened in the way described (Fig 180). Again and again, you see the same themes of older accounts repeated in the newer ones. For example, the story of Moses has the Pharaoh ordering all newborn Hebrew boys to be killed to reduce the population of the 'Israelites'. Herod the Great, King of Judea, is said to have instigated the execution of all male children under two-years-old born near Bethlehem in an effort to eliminate the Messiah Jesus who was to be 'King of the Jews'. We shall now explore where the stories came from on which religion is based. Strap in.

Figure 180: There is so much.

CHAPTER 17

They Made It Up

How could a cult leader draw crowds, inspire devotion and die by crucifixion, yet leave no mark in contemporary records?
Gavin Evans

There are many arguments and disagreements over who Jesus was and what he stood for. I see far fewer discussions about whether he existed at all. I am going to explore this because the scale of the religion scam will be brought into stark relief if he is not a historical character. The evidence is not good for believers.

A man who caused such a Gospel-described storm in Rome-controlled Judea and performed miracles like feeding the 5,000 from a few loaves and fishes, healing lepers, turning water into wine, walking on water, bringing Lazarus back to life, and floating up into Heaven saying he would return on a cloud, might just rate a major mention outside of the Gospel accounts and the after-the-fact texts attributed to 'Saint Paul'. But they don't. Where were all the Roman and non-Roman chroniclers who carefully recorded life in the empire? If someone says 'Josephus', I have some news for them coming up. Michael Grant (1914-2004) was a Professor of Humanity at the University of Edinburgh, Scotland, who specialised in ancient history. He said that 'we can no more reject Jesus' existence than we can reject the existence of a mass of pagan personages whose reality as historical figures is never questioned'. Oh, but I do. Stories are often symbolic rather than literal in any ancient era no matter what the source and they are invariably written well after the events with people involved long gone. The once mythological when taken literally can then produce a history believed to be real. The key is in the quality of the ancient evidence and how that pans out into modern supporting evidence – as with the simulation. It is said there are at least 14 'independent' sources from multiple authors within a century of the crucifixion of Jesus that survive. But what is the 'proof' of after-the-fact 'confirmation' up to (and beyond) a hundred years later with no eyewitnesses?

Common themes
Stories and sayings attributed to Jesus had been told many times before

They Made It Up

using a different hero and geographical location. 'Do unto others as you would have them do unto you' – the 'Golden Rule' to Christians – is not unique to 'Jesus' and is far older. Hindu, Jewish, Buddhist, and Zoroastrian beliefs all have their own versions long before. Ancient Chinese philosopher Confucius (about 551 to 479 BC) wrote: 'Do not do to others what you would not like yourself.' There is a stream of gods who died and returned to life with stories and events that were repeated in the Gospels with Jesus as the central figure. Sumerian goddess Inanna travels to the Underworld to see her sister and dies for three days and three nights before being resurrected. Greek god Dionysus and many other pre-Christian gods repeat foundations of the Jesus story. Dionysus, also known as Bacchus and worshipped in Rome, was a death-and-resurrection god famous for turning water into wine. The mother and baby theme of Mary and Jesus spans thousands of years (Fig 181).

Dionysus rituals involved 'theophagy' or 'eating the god'. Merriam-webster.com defines this as 'the sacramental eating of a god typically in the form of an animal, image, or other symbol as a part of a religious

Figure 181: The mother and child theme spanning thousands of years: Ubaid reptilian; Queen Semiramis in Babylon; Isis in Egypt; and the Christian Mother Mary.

ritual and commonly for the purpose of communion with or the receiving of power from the god'. You mean like eating the flesh and drinking the blood of Jesus? Greek god Orion walked on water which was a gift from his father Poseidon, the god of the sea, storms and earthquakes. Hindu god Krishna was born into a royal line to his mother Devaki through divine intervention. He was the foster son of a carpenter and came as a 'Divine shepherd' to triumph good over evil. His birth was foretold and a tyrant leader sought to kill him. Krishna performed miracles, spoke in parables, brought the dead back to life, and healed the sick. 'Lord' Krishna promised he would return to restore harmony whenever evil had to be overcome. He'll be returning imminently then?

Persian Saturn sun god Mithra, also worshipped in Rome, was the deity of a widely followed religion in the hundreds of years before Jesus.

Remember how Jesus is depicted with a halo – just like the sun gods were. Mithra was said to be born on December 25th and in his religion's Roman form was a rival of Christianity. Many similarities are suggested with Jesus which Christian scholars deny in most cases. It's not easy to find unbiased scholarship in either stance with each seeking to prove their belief system to be true. Saint Paul is quoted as a main source for the existence of Jesus, and he was said to be born 'Saul of Tarsus' in what is present-day Turkey. Paul is claimed to have been a leader of early Christians and Tarsus was a major centre of Mithra worship. Mithra was closely associated with another Roman sun god, Sol Invictus, the 'Unconquered Sun' (Saturn), and Emperor Aurelian declared December 25th as Sol's birthday. Remember that a major god of Rome was Saturn. Emperor Constantine the Great was another follower of Sol Invictus and a prime creator of Christianity with its worship of Jesus.

There are many ancient gods who have stories told about them similar to the much later biblical Jesus. I am not saying that the Jesus tales in the Bible were based on any one of these previous gods, only that common themes were taken from many of them to construct the fictitious story about Jesus as a Messiah sent by God. It is a recurring universal myth, and you can see it repeated in many other guises. You can even read the Matrix movies that way with Neo as Jesus, Morpheus as John the Baptist predicting the arrival of Neo (Jesus); Trinity as Mary Magdalene; Cypher, who betrayed Neo, Morpheus, Trinity and their 'disciples', as Judas; and the Architect as Yaldabaoth/the Demiurge/Satan. I note that Gnostic texts also widely refer to Jesus but from another angle relating to our nature as consciousness. Gnostic texts portray Jesus as a teacher who guides people to overcome the ego and attain enlightenment and not as a saviour who redeems humanity through his sacrifice. Maybe many Gnostics saw his character as more a symbol of a consciousness state than a literal human, but I find it very hard to equate the evidence with a literal Jesus as portrayed in the Bible texts. Some believe there was a man on which the Jesus character was based who travelled afar to Egypt, India, Armenia and elsewhere, and was an 'enlightened master'. I am with them in their dismissal of the Gospel narrative and their critique of the Roman Church and its role in suppressing the truth. There is, however, quite another way of viewing the man called 'Jesus'.

Who was Jesus *really?*

I have read many articles and four books for this chapter: *Caesar's Messiah, The Roman Conspiracy To Invent Jesus* by Joseph Atwill; *Creating Christianity, A Weapon of Ancient Rome* by Henry Davis; Piso Christ by Roman Piso with Jay Gallus; and *Christianity's Origin as a Flavian Secrecy Cult* by Michael Menasgotz. I am going to summarise the findings and people will have to see if this makes more sense to them than the biblical accounts. The books may differ on the fine detail here and there, but they uncover and support the same theme. We should start by knowing that evidence for the existence of Jesus is seriously scant outside the Bible. London-based author Gavin Evans describes himself as being raised in 'an evangelical Christian family, the son of a "born-again", tongues-talking, Jewish-born, Anglican bishop' but came to doubt all that he once believed. Evans says there are only three sources of 'putative proof' for Jesus – 'all of them posthumous': the Gospels, the letters of Paul, and historical evidence from beyond the Bible. But what was this 'historical evidence'? Evans quotes John Barton, an Anglican clergyman and Oxford scholar, as accepting that 'most Bible books were written by multiple authors, often over centuries, and that they diverge from history'. This is the background from which the existence of Jesus should be understood.

Joseph Atwill of *Caesar's Messiah* began his Christian studies at a Jesuit academy in Japan, where he was trained in Greek, Latin, and the Bible. He lays out his theme in considerable detail. The Romans were faced in Judea in the 1st century AD with a war waged against them by rebel groups like the Zealots and Sicarii, a sect that believed in a Messiah that was coming to lead their military campaign. Their version of the Messiah was no Prince of Peace. The Sicarii modus operandi was the assassination of Romans and Jewish collaborators. Atwill contends that the Roman Flavian imperial family dynasty invented Christianity featuring another Messiah who urged his followers to 'turn the other cheek' and 'give to Caesar what is Caesar's' to usurp the military Messiah narrative with a pacifist Messiah. They wanted one that conformed to Roman rule, paid taxes, and obeyed their laws. Luke 2:1-5 tells how Mary and Joseph, the mother and father of Jesus, travelled from Nazareth to Bethlehem for a Roman 'census' that makes no historical or genetic sense:

> In those days Caesar Augustus issued a decree that a census should be taken of the entire Roman world. (This was the first census that took place while Quirinius was governor of Syria.) And everyone went to their own town to register.
>
> So Joseph also went up from the town of Nazareth in Galilee to Judea, to Bethlehem the town of David, because he belonged to the house and line of David. He went there to register with Mary, who was pledged to be married to him and was expecting a child.

How would you know in those days if you were of the 'line' of King David who is said to have lived maybe a thousand years earlier? But

Figure 182: The Arch of Titus in Rome today near the Flavian-built Colosseum.

Figure 183: The Titus Arch celebrates his victory in Judea with the spoils brought back to Rome.

these claims fulfilled the prophecy of a Messiah that would come from the 'House of David' and indicates conformity to Roman law dictates that would be a feature of the Jesus approach which condemned Jews, not Romans. We will see in the next chapter that there is basically zero evidence for the 'line of David' anyway. Atwill points out that the Flavian dynasty ruled from 69 to 96 AD when many scholars believe the Gospels were written. The Flavians produced three Caesars – Vespasian and his sons Titus and Domitian. They replaced the Julio-Claudian dynasty which produced the previous five emperors between 27 BC and 68 AD. Vespasian led a Roman army against the Sicarii and the rebellion in Judea before returning to Rome to become emperor after Nero. He left his son Titus to finish the job that culminated with the capture of the Judean stronghold of Masada in 73 AD which I visited on my one trip to Israel more than 30 years ago. They certainly wouldn't let me in now.

The Arch of Titus in Rome commemorates his victory in Judea while the famous Colosseum was built by the Flavians and known as the Flavian Amphitheatre (Figs 182 and 183). Titus had fought other rebellious groups in the Roman empire including in Britain. The Flavians in general were brutal. Atwill says that Vespasian and Titus joined forces in Judea with two powerful families, the Herods and Alexanders, who were Greece-influenced Hellenised Jews. This version of Judaism had infiltrated the region with the conquests of Alexander the Great in 333 BC. Atwill says the Herods and Alexanders shared Vespasian's desire to stop more revolts. The latest had been put down, but many Jews continued to believe that a warrior Messiah, from the line of King David, would be sent by God to lead them against the Roman and Hellenist enemy.

The Flavian conspiracy

Atwill writes that the Flavian dynasty, in league with the Herods and

Alexanders, had the necessary control, power, expertise in Judaism, and other skills and influence to produce the Gospels. The Flavians had already overseen other religions and knew exactly what was necessary. The idea was not to replace the Judaic religious texts, but to make it seem like the Gospels were the next stage in which Christianity fulfilled Jewish prophecies with a peaceful Messiah instead of a military one and a Messiah who had already been and gone. They did this by having the Gospels written *after* the Titus victory in Judea but set more than 40 years earlier so 'prophecies' could be included of events which by then had already happened. They backdated the life of Jesus to the first 33 years of the first century AD and the start of the 'Jesus ministry' to 30 AD. Atwill says they employed a writing technique called typology which he defines in its basic form as 'the use of prior events to provide form and context for future ones – similar to using an archetype or stereotype to create a new character in literature'. The Merrian Webster dictionary appropriately gives the example of 'holding that things in Christian belief are prefigured or symbolized by things in the Old Testament'. This appears to be precisely what happened as texts in the New Testament repeat the sequences and characters in the Old and give the impression of prophecies fulfilled. Jesus is connected to a prophecy by Moses in Deuteronomy 18:15: 'The Lord your God will raise up for you a prophet like me from among you, from your fellow Israelites. You must listen to him.' I read the following on a Christian website:

> The prophet whom Moses foretells bears these qualities: He will be raised up by God, He will come from among the Israelites, He will be like Moses, and He will be worthy of being heard and obeyed. The prophet who fulfills these words is Jesus Christ, the prophet like Moses.
>
> On the banks of the Jordan River, the Jews questioned John the Baptist about who he was and why he was baptizing. Their question 'Are you the Prophet?' (John 1:21) shows that they were looking for the fulfillment of Moses' prophecy. John plainly informed them that he was not the Prophet but pointed them to the One who was: 'Among you stands one you do not know. He is the one who comes after me, the straps of whose sandals I am not worthy to untie' (verses 26-27).
>
> John's description of the Messiah as one 'among you' recalls Moses' prediction that God would raise up the Prophet 'from among you' in Deuteronomy 18:15. The very next day, John specifically identifies Jesus as the One they were waiting for (John 1:29-31).

Ah, but if the Gospels were written to link Jesus to the prophecies of Moses and the words of 'John the Baptist' were Flavian in origin a completely different scenario appears into view. Old Testament prophets Elijah and Elisha performed miracles, raised the dead, ascended into heaven, and did the food deal with Elisha feeding 'a hundred men with twenty loaves' and plenty to spare. I saw this compared with the story of Jesus feeding the 5,000 with a few loaves and fishes with plenty left over. Too right – it is typology. These are only two examples of what Atwill is talking about, and he and the other books provide many more. The term 'Gospel' is from the Greek 'evangelion' meaning 'good news' also in the context for example of 'good news of military victory'. We are told to believe the Gospels were written by the common people when the Roman authorities had control of what was published, not least through finance and literacy, and the great majority of the population was illiterate. Henry Davis says in *Creating Christianity, A Weapon of Ancient Rome*, that only 1-2 percent of the people could read or write. A perfect scenario for controlling information, as was the Bible for centuries before it was first printed and more widely circulated in English in the 16th century.

Moses blueprint

Moses was the founder of Judaism and Jesus the creator of Christianity and the Flavian Gospels infused many comparisons. Atwill writes: 'The story of Jesus' childhood in Matthew is based on the childhood of Moses ... the birth of a child causes distress to rulers, followed by a consultation with wise men, a massacre of children, and a miraculous rescue, with Egypt as the land of rescue.' To this day people are being deluded by the typology technique and as Atwill rightly says: 'Once Jesus was universally established as a world-historical individual, any other possibility became, evidentially, invisible.' The more people believed in Jesus as a world-historical figure, the less they were able to understand him in any other way. Atwill says that Gospel events, or the 'Jesus ministry', were symbolic and often satirical representations of the military campaign against Judean rebels waged by Vespasian's son, Titus. 'Jesus Christ', he says, is really Titus Flavius:

> The Gospels were not written by the followers of a Jewish Messiah, but by the intellectual circle surrounding the three Flavian emperors: Vespasian and his two sons, Titus and Domitian.

> The Gospels were written following the 66-73 C.E. war between the Romans and Jews, and many of the events of ministry are satirical depictions of events from that war. The purpose of Christianity was supersession. It was designed to replace the nationalistic and militaristic messianic movement in Judea with a religion that was pacifistic and would accept Roman rule.

Atwill sets out his case in compelling detail. The 'Jesus ministry' and the Titus military campaign not only included symbolically similar events at the same locations, but in the same *order of sequence*. The key is to compare the Gospels with the history of the Titus campaign written by 'historian' Josephus which is the only surviving contemporary account of events. Who was Josephus? He was a *Flavian*. The official story is that Josephus was born in 37 AD into the Judean 'royal family', the Maccabees, and became an expert in Judaic law. He was given command of the revolutionary army of Galilee when war broke out with the Romans in 66 AD. He was taken captive and presented to Vespasian who was then commanding the Roman forces. Josephus claimed to be a prophet and said that Vespasian was destined to be 'lord of all mankind'. He said he was now committed to the Romans and spurned the Judaic rebellion. Vespasian later became emperor and adopted Josephus as his son. Josephus bar Matthias became Flavius Josephus. That's the official version; but this is challenged in *Creating Christianity* and *Piso Christ* and by other writers who say that 'Josephus' was really a man called Arrius Calpurnius Piso, a member of the Flavian family who employed a stream of aliases that history records as separate people when they were all him. Henry Davis notes in *Creating Christianity* that 'no Jewish historical commentary mentions Josephus, not even in the Talmud, which is suspicious, given the background he has as a high priest'.

Piso Christ and *Creating Christianity* contend that Josephus was a central writer of the Gospels along with others including Greek philosopher Plutarch (around 40 to the 120s AD). Plutarch's official history says that 'at some point' he was given Roman citizenship (just like 'Josephus') thanks to a sponsor, Lucius Mestrius Florus, who was 'an associate of the new emperor Vespasian'. Plutarch became Lucius Mestrius Plutarchus. Another alleged Piso pseudonym was Philo Judaeus better known as Philo of Alexandria. The official record has him coming from a wealthy family with connections to the Judean priesthood (like Flavius Josephus/Arrius Piso). It is noted that Philo visited the Temple in Jerusalem during Passover. Despite these associations with the time and locations of Gospel Jesus he says nothing in his official writings about a Jesus performing miracles, a Messiah saviour claiming to have been sent by God and causing mayhem among the religious establishment before being crucified, rising from the dead, and ascending to Heaven. Not a titter. *Piso Christ* says that 'Philo' was Arrius Piso/Josephus who needed to invent another Jew writing in Greek so he didn't stand out as an obvious one-off. *Piso Christ* describes how many historically noted figures of the Roman period hid behind pseudonyms which meant that what appear to be multiple writers and chroniclers were really much smaller in number and a tight-knit group of royals and aristocrats who controlled the narrative. The book says that Josephus was a penname of Piso who was a

Roman *and* a Jew through his mother's side which connected to the Jewish Pharisees sect. 'He was a Jew by birth, but not by belief', the book says, and as Piso was 'a great nephew of Emperor Vespasian by way of Vespasian's brother, T. Flavius Sabinus …'

'Josephus' goes to work

Vespasian was considered a god ('God the Father') while Titus was his son. All was in place as Titus followed Vespasian as Caesar for Josephus to write the sole history of the Titus Judea campaign, *The Wars of the Jews*, which 'he' compiled while living in the Flavian court. The same Flavians then produced the Gospels and placed them in an earlier setting to both 'fulfil prophecies' and follow the sequence of the already-happened Titus military campaign. This is the contention of Joseph Atwill, and the evidence is impressive. The Roman Flavians controlled both the Josephus account of the Roman-Jewish war (and other works) and the writing of the Gospels which together provide the only literature on which the existence and nature of 'Jesus' was founded. The Wikipedia account of Josephus says: 'Josephus's works are the chief source next to the Bible for the history and antiquity of ancient Israel and provide an independent extra-biblical account of such figures as Pontius Pilate, Herod the Great, John the Baptist, James, brother of Jesus, and Jesus of Nazareth.' *Exactly*. But 'independent'? Ha, ha. The *opposite*. All four authors I am quoting found the same correlation between the Gospels and *The Wars of the Jews* by Josephus. Michael Menasgotz in *Christianity's Origin as a Flavian Secrecy Cult* highlights the parallels with his speciality, the Gospel of Luke: 'The way the two stories mutually parody each other's core narratives in intimate detail can be used to demonstrate that they must have been written together, thereby proving a Roman Flavian Government origin for Luke.' He also claims to have found patterns in the texts to confirm common authorship.

Read the Gospels from this perspective and they begin to make sense. Alleged feats of Jewish prophets were repeated and made even more amazing along with events claimed for other pre-Jesus 'gods' from the endless pantheons. Gospel writers infused the themes of Exodus to add the typology connection and make it appear that what became the biblical New Testament was a continuation of the Old. Now you can see why the Old Testament is so brutal with a 'God' that demands slaughter while the New features a 'God' apparently far more pacifistic. Numbers were made to fit earlier events and prophecies while Josephus and company wrote the Gospels that were produced in the *same period* as *Wars of the Jews* about the Titus campaign. A 'generation' was 40 years for Jews of the time. You have Moses wandering in the wilderness for 40 years before 'God' allowed them to enter the Promised Land and 40 years was also considered the period of 'penance'. The latter originates from the Moses period in the wilderness.

Jesus is quoted in the Gospels as predicting the destruction of the Jews and the arrival of the 'Son of Man' within the generation then alive – 40 years. He would come when the towns of Galilee were destroyed, Jerusalem was circled by a wall, and the temple was demolished with not one stone standing on another. These things had already happened when the Gospels were written, and they were the work of Titus. He surrounded Jerusalem with the Roman technique of 'circumvallation' in which you surround a target city with a wall of fortifications to stop anything getting in or out. Starvation inevitably follows. Josephus combined with other Gospel writers to make it 40 years – a 'generation' – between the start of the Jesus ministry in 30 AD and the Titus destruction of Jerusalem, and 40 years between the 'crucifixion' and the end of the Titus siege at Masada. The 'Son of Man' that the Gospels say Jesus predicted was coming 'within this generation' was Flavius Titus. Christians have been unknowingly worshipping him ever since. Titus could not make the Jews worship him as a god and he sought to achieve this another way in line with the Roman Imperial Cult that already attributed divinity to emperors like his father Vespasian. His father was a 'god' and Titus was the 'son of god'. Atwill writes:

> ... Jesus refers to a 'Son of Man' that will come before the generation he speaks to passes away – in other words within 40 years from 30-33 C.E. Jesus 'predicted' that when the 'Son of Man' made his visitation, Galilee would be destroyed, Jerusalem encircled with a wall, and the Temple razed.
>
> There is only one person in history who accomplished these events, and he did it precisely within the given time frame – Titus Flavius, a Caesar whose court historians maintained he was the Christ.

Atwill uses the terms CE (Common Era) and BCE (Before Common Era) while I am sticking with BC (Before Christ) and AD (Anno Domini or 'in the year of the Lord') which people have become used to. I don't accept their meaning and it's just a date device. The contention that the Gospels were written long after 'Jesus died' which allowed prophecies to be included that had already happened is a timeline supported by this comment in the biblical study publication, the *New Oxford Annotated Bible*:

> Scholars generally agree that the Gospels were written forty to sixty years after the death of Jesus. They are not eyewitness or contemporary accounts of Jesus's life and teaching. Even the language has changed.

'Fishers of men'

Joseph Atwill explains the Titus origins of the Jesus quote about 'fishers of men', the triumphal arrival in Jerusalem, driving out thieves from the Temple, and other famous New Testament incidents. Gospels describe how Jesus was at the Sea of Galilee when he told his disciples to follow him, and he would make them 'fishers of men' (Matthew 4:17-19) or 'you will be catching men' (Luke 5:1-10). The Bible's New English version translates this as: 'Then Jesus said to Simon, "Don't be afraid; from now on you will fish for people."' Josephus describes in his *Wars of the Jews* how Titus won a battle against the Jews who escaped into the Sea of Galilee. Titus' troops caught them and destroyed or overturned their boats. Josephus says that Jews in the water 'were drowning in the sea, if they lifted their heads up above the water, they were either killed by darts or caught by vessels'. He also writes that 'in the desperate case they were in they attempted to swim to their enemies', but 'the Romans cut off either their heads or their hands'. The leader of the Galilee rebels is even called 'Jesus, the son of Shaphat,' by Josephus in *Wars of the Jews*. Atwill writes:

> It could be understood only by someone who, like the residents of the Flavian court, had knowledge of the details of the sea battle between the Romans and the Jewish fishermen at Gennesaret [on the Sea of Galilee]. Only such individuals could have the prophetic irony in Jesus using the expression while standing on the very beach where the Jews would later be caught like a fish.

'Later' is in the context that the battle came *before* the Gospels were written. Atwill makes the case for disciples Simon (Peter) and John being so named to symbolise the leaders of the Jewish rebellion who were also called Simon and John in the Josephus account.

'Eat my body'

Gospel writers satirised the Jews and the invented Jesus through the association with the Titus military campaign and the Jewish rebellion. There are many Marys in the Gospels, far more than credible, and it turns out that the names 'Mary' and the Aramaic version 'Martha' relate to 'rebellion'. Mary is Hebrew for 'their rebellion' and Martha means 'she was rebellious'. Josephus writes in his account of the Titus campaign about a woman called 'Mary' who ate her son – 'the son of Mary' – when she was desperate for food. Given the techniques used to parallel *Wars of the Jews* with the Gospels we should not ignore a connection to this in Mark 14:22: 'Also during the meal He took a Passover biscuit, blessed it, and broke it. He then gave it to them, saying, 'take this, it is my body.' This is the origin of Christians eating the flesh of Jesus as a biscuit and drinking his blood as wine. Atwill shows that

Gospel references to Jesus casting out demons and unclean spirits, and condemning 'wickedness', are symbolic of how Titus and the Romans viewed the Jewish rebels as demonically wicked. This, too, parallels the Flavian Josephus accounts in *Wars of the Jews*. He wrote: '… nor did any age ever breed a generation more fruitful in wickedness than this was, from the beginning of the world.' Jesus says in the Gospels that unclean spirits can infect others while Josephus says that wickedness can pass from one head to many. Atwill writes:

> Thus, Jesus and Josephus shared a narrow understanding and expressed it with the same vocabulary: that the generation of Jews who lived between 33 C.E. and 73 C.E. were 'wicked' because they had been infected by a demonic spirit.
>
> This shared understanding is suspicious. Jesus could only view the 'wickedness' of the generation by looking into the future, and yet he not only held the same opinion of the generation as Josephus, he used the same words in describing it.

Jesus is quoted in the Gospels as saying that Jews were the 'sons of Satan' and the 'wicked generation' as he threatened to 'destroy the temple'. Titus saved him the trouble. Atwill says that people with a 'high fever' also symbolised possession by 'rebellion'. The Gospels point the finger at the Jews rather than the Romans who are portrayed as the vehicle for God to punish them. We have the Jewish crowd shouting for the Romans to crucify Jesus and release a prisoner called Barabbas. Matthew 27:21-23 of the New International Bible tells us that Pontius Pilate, Roman governor of Judea, gave them the choice:

'Which of the two do you want me to release to you?' asked the governor.

'Barabbas,' they answered.

'What shall I do, then, with Jesus who is called the Messiah?' Pilate asked.

They all answered, 'Crucify him!'

'Why? What crime has he committed?' asked Pilate.

But they shouted all the louder, 'Crucify him!'

Pilate then put all the responsibility on the Jews in Matthew 27:24-25:

When Pilate saw that he was getting nowhere, but that instead an uproar was starting, he took water and washed his hands in front of the crowd. 'I am innocent of this man's blood,' he said. 'It is your responsibility!'

All the people answered, 'His blood is on us and on our children!'

This is just the way the Flavians wanted the death of Jesus portrayed. It was the Jews that did it and that became the story throughout Christendom. To this day Jews are branded as the ones that killed Jesus when there is no evidence for this outside the Roman Gospels that put all the blame by design on Jewish people. How many Jews through the ages have been targeted for this myth? Josephus writes in his account of the siege of Jerusalem that he pleaded with Titus to take down three old friends who were being crucified. Titus agreed and two of the men still died while one survived. The Gospels have Joseph of Arimathea, a 'rich supporter of Jesus', asking Pilate if Jesus can be taken down from the cross and he take away his body. Notice the two names – Joseph of Arimathea and the Hebrew name of Josephus in the official narrative that was Joseph bar Mathias. No wonder Gospel scholars are bewildered by the meaning of 'Arimathea' when no such place has ever been found. It also puts into perspective the claims that Joseph of Arimathea visited Glastonbury in England with the Grail, 'the vessel used to collect Christ's blood'. Some legends say he earlier took with him the infant Jesus. The ruins of Glastonbury Abbey are also claimed to be the location of the 'grave of King Arthur' which was 'discovered' in 1191. Was Glastonbury the birthplace of attract-the-tourists myth PR?

Barabbas was known in early versions of the Gospels as Jesus Barabbas. Joseph Atwill highlights that Barabbas is a 'composite word' consisting of 'bar', meaning 'son', and 'abba', meaning father, thus making him Jesus, son of the father. I mentioned that the rebel leader in *Wars of the Jews* killed by the troops of Titus in the 'fishers of men' battle in the Sea of Galilee is named by Josephus as 'Jesus, the son of Shaphat'. Then there was 'Jesus ben Ananias', or 'the son of Ananias', in *Wars of the Jews* said to be prophesying the destruction of Jerusalem before the war began. Josephus writes that Jesus ben Ananias was tortured and released by the Romans after Jewish leaders handed him over and then died during the subsequent Roman siege of the city. The man is apparently called Yeshua ben Hananiah in Hebrew histories. Atwill also says that he identified a number of different versions of the Christian 'Jesus' in the Gospels that cannot refer to only one person.

Where's the evidence?

Old Testament Daniel is another Jewish prophet that Josephus employs to 'prove' the identity of Jesus as the biblical Son of God in conjunction with the Flavian Gospel writers. Daniel said that a Messiah, a son of God, would appear and be 'cut off' followed by the destruction of Jerusalem. Josephus specifically mentions Daniel's predictions (as does Jesus). Josephus even uses Daniel's phrases to make the vague prophecies fit the happenings in the Gospels and his *Wars of the Jews* to indicate that Jesus is the predicted Messiah who was 'cut off' after which came the Titus destruction of Jerusalem in 70 AD (also 'predicted' by Jesus in the Gospels). The fake fulfilment of Daniel's prophecies was very significant in early Christians accepting the divinity of Jesus. This can be seen in the writings of St. Augustine who said that the Gospel of Luke 'very clearly bears witness that the prophecy of Daniel was fulfilled when Jerusalem was overthrown'. Henry Davis writes in *Creating Christianity*:

- There is not one word explaining how these scriptures were obtained or proving their honest origin, and nothing was allowed to leak out as to the method used to compile the collection of doubtful tales made up of crude religious or phallic stories.

- All mentions of [Christian] persecution come after the fact and after the New Testament emerged and come from Roman historians.

- All mentions of Christians themselves ... came from Roman historians, again after the New Testament emerged.

- Scholars and academics have not identified who the authors of the Gospels were.

- The individual named 'Paul' never claimed to have met Jesus but claimed to have received his information from Jesus 'speaking to him' ... There is also no reliable evidence that a Christian sect existed before the New Testament emerged, even Paul says nothing about them.

- There are no direct Jewish sources or any other sources outside Rome for a historical Jesus of the Gospels.

There is, however, a mention of Jesus as 'the Christ' in another Josephus work, *Antiquities of the Jews*, written 20 years after the Titus campaign in an estimated 93-94 AD. He wrote:

> Now there was about this time Jesus, a wise man, if it be lawful to call him a man; for he was a doer of wonderful works, a teacher of such men as receive the truth with pleasure. He drew over to him both many of the Jews and many

of the Gentiles. He was [the] Christ.

And when Pilate, at the suggestion of the principal men amongst us, had condemned him to the cross, those that loved him at the first did not forsake him; for he appeared to them alive again the third day; as the divine prophets had foretold these and ten thousand other wonderful things concerning him. And the tribe of Christians, so named from him, are not extinct at this day.

This has been dubbed by many a later interpolation or insert added to give much-needed credibility to the Christian story, but given the background laid out here it could have been Josephus doing the same. Henry Davis in *Creating Christianity* highlights the discovery of the Dead Sea Scrolls hidden in caves at Qumran, along the northwestern shore of the Dead Sea, and another location I visited. It's only ruins now, but it was a settlement of the Essenes in the New Testament period. The messianic Essenes were one of the major Jewish sects and the scrolls have obviously been associated with them although many scholars connect the find to other Jewish sources fleeing Jerusalem during the Roman onslaught. Their discovery had many Christians hope that they would confirm the existence of Jesus outside the Gospels. The 15,000 scrolls and fragments, which included the Book of Enoch and Old Testament texts, were found in eleven caves between 1946 and 1956, but any hope Christians had were dashed when yet again there was no mention of Jesus or Christianity. Israel now claims ownership of the Dead Sea Scrolls which are kept at the Israel Museum after the occupation of the West Bank and East Jerusalem following the 1967 Arab-Israeli war. They were previously held in the Palestine Archaeological Museum (since renamed the Rockefeller Archaeological Museum).

Taking the piss?

Joseph Atwill contends in *Caesar's Messiah* that leaders of the Jewish rebellion recorded by Josephus as Simon and John were symbolised satirically as disciples of Jesus. John of Gischala was a leader of the Jewish revolt named by Josephus and claimed to have been captured by Titus and jailed for life in Rome. Rebellion leader Simon bar Giora is said to have been taken to Rome and paraded through the streets in chains before being executed. Simon is another name that recurs in the New Testament. The Gospel Simon was said to have been born Shimon Bar Yonah and is also known as St Peter, Peter the Apostle, Simon Peter, Simeon, Simon, or Cephas, who the Gospels tell us was the 'rock' on which Jesus said his church would be built. Yes, the *Roman* Church. The execution of 'Peter' (Simon) was prophesied by Jesus. This is John 21:18-19:

'Truly, truly, I tell you, when you were young, you dressed yourself and walked where you wanted; but when you are old, you will stretch out your hands, and someone else will dress you and lead you where you do not want to go.' Jesus said this to indicate the kind of death by which Peter would glorify God. And after He had said this, He told him, 'Follow Me'.

The same passage of text includes Jesus saying to 'Peter' apparently about his disciple John: 'If I want him to remain alive until I return, what is that to you? You must follow me.' Well, Jewish rebel John did stay alive to complete a life sentence in a Roman jail and this quote is the origin of some Christians wondering over the centuries if Gospel 'John' was still alive awaiting the 'return' or Second Coming of Jesus. The power of belief in every word of the Gospels is truly staggering. The story goes, according to Christian tradition, that Peter was crucified in Rome under Emperor Nero, but when 'Christian tradition' is Flavian deception, it must be difficult to crucify a deception.

The Flavians were now in total control of events and propaganda, and we have 'Peter' claimed to be the first pope. Tertullian (about 155-220 AD) was a prolific early Christian author from Roman Carthage who claimed that Saint Peter ordained Pope Clement I. Again, how can you be ordained by a deception? But by now the Flavians were building their invented Christianity into what would eventually become a global religion. They needed the bricks and mortar and personnel. Clement was one of the first popes, and quite probably *the* first who got the show on the road. Atwill says Clement was a *Flavian*. Flavia Domitilla, a granddaughter of Emperor Vespasian, niece of Titus and Domitian, who married Titus Flavius Clemens, a grand nephew of Vespasian through his father, was an early promotor of Christianity and became a saint.

Then there is the Roman Catholic narrative about disciple Peter becoming the 'first pope' although with the absence of evidence. 'Peter' was a nickname for Gospel Simon. *Caesar's Messiah* points out that Peter in Greek is Petros which means 'rock' or 'stone' and 'Saint Paul' refers to Peter as Cephas which is Aramaic for 'Peter' or 'stone'. This takes us to the description by Josephus of the capture of Jewish rebel leader Simon. Josephus says that this Simon hid in an underground cavern with stonecutters during the Titus siege and after failing to dig an escape passage, and with no source of food, he 'appeared out of the ground in the place where the temple had formerly been'. Atwill comments:

> The humor is dark and subtle. In the ironic language of the New Testament's Simon's nickname, 'stone' satirizes Josephus' depiction of Simon being captured with a group of stonecutters who, of course cut 'stone'. As he 'came out of the ground in the place the temple had formerly been', he was,

therefore, the first 'stone' upon which the new 'temple', Christianity, was to be built.

This would explain in a Roman reference to the rebel Simon the exchange in Matthew 16:23 when Jesus relates the Gospel Simon (Peter) to Satan: 'But he turned, and said unto Peter, Get thee behind me, Satan: thou art an offence unto me: for thou savourest not the things that be of God, but those that be of men.' Michael Menasgotz notes in *Christianity's Origin as a Flavian Secrecy Cult* that many mysteries disappear once the Flavian connection is understood and when and why the Gospels were written. Why 'Jesus' left no writings, monuments, remains or documents, and 'why no Judean records from the AD 30s mention this miracle worker who raised the dead to life, walked on water or fed 5,000'. Menasgotz also points to the claim that Jesus was crucified at Golgotha/Calvary ('place of the skull') which he says is a Roman connection to Capitoline Hill ('hill of the skull') in Rome. He further suggests that the Roman Gospel origin of Christianity was hidden by unsubstantiated claims from writers with no first-hand knowledge that the Romans persecuted Christians. There is no credible evidence outside the Gospels of the crucifixion and resurrection and yet the entire religion is founded on this happening.

'Saint Paul'

The character of Saint Paul is a Bible hero who is claimed to have spread the teachings of Jesus in the 1st century and became known as 'Paul the Apostle'. The New Testament includes 'letters' or 'epistles' attributed to him, and he is featured in Acts of the Apostles. This is the fifth book of the New Testament and focuses on the founding of the Christian Church and efforts to expand its influence in the Roman Empire. Acts is described by Wikipedia as 'an attempt to answer a theological problem, namely how the Messiah, promised to the Jews, came to have an overwhelmingly non-Jewish church; the answer it provides, and its central theme, is that the message of Christ was sent to the Gentiles because the Jews rejected it'. You can see why they would do that given the background. Wikipedia is an excellent source for the official version of everything. Not the truth – the official version. 'Paul' is referred to as Saul of 'Tarsus', a stronghold of Persian Mithra worship in what is now Turkey. The Bible tells us in Acts of the Apostles that 'Paul' was a Pharisee who intensely persecuted Christians before being converted on the 'road to Damascus' when Jesus appeared as a light from heaven and said 'Saul, Saul, why do you persecute me?' Saul/Paul was blind for three days after the experience during which he never ate or drank. Then his sight was restored, and he was baptised. Perfectly believable.

Pauline epistles

The authors of *Piso Christ* contend after what appears to be enormous research that 'St Paul' was really the character known to history as Pliny the Younger. The Rome connection continues. Pliny the Younger is described as a lawyer, writer, and magistrate in Rome who lived officially between 61 AD and somewhere around 113. Pliny visited all the places where 'Saint Paul' is said to have travelled and was a prolific writer of letters as was 'Saint Paul'. The 247 surviving letters of Pliny are said to have 'helped shape our view of the Roman Empire'. Saint Paul's letters with his New Testament 'epistles' helped shape our view of Christianity. These include the Book of Titus which is a letter officially attributed to Paul and sent to his 'close companion', 'a Greek follower of Jesus', 'coincidentally' called *Titus*. The letter instructs Titus on 'how to organise and oversee the Churches in Crete, and how to teach sound doctrine and godly living to various groups of people so that the good news of Jesus can transform Cretan culture from within'. Pliny was a friend of famed Roman historian Tacitus (about 56 AD to about 120). Tacitus is one of the 'earliest extra-biblical references to the crucifixion of Jesus'. He is said to be another pseudonym which makes the who-is-who of these Roman figures such a challenge. *Piso Christ* author 'Roman Piso' says in an Internet article:

> They were playing parts, as in a play. They were doing so as they played their parts in the story of Christianity, and also as apparent non-biblical authors as well. Pliny The Younger played his part as Paul in the New Testament, while at the same time, he was writing his epistles and Panegyricus [oration] as Pliny the Younger. Arrius Piso was playing the part of Jesus, while at the same time writing as Flavius Josephus and others.
>
> This was something that traditional royalty had to do and they had been doing this even long before the creation of Christianity. This was because they had to create the illusion that there was a measure of 'freedom of speech' alive under their rule – particularly because there was NOT.
>
> They had to make it 'appear' that at least some of the things being written were not written exclusively by royals. And, they also had to make it appear that there were many people writing, when in reality, there were really only a few.

Where is the evidence outside the New Testament that 'Paul the Apostle' existed? Dr Nina Livesey, Professor of Religious Studies, Emerita at the University of Oklahoma, made an extensive investigation of the Paul letters for her book, *The Letters of Paul in their Roman Literary Context: Reassessing Apostolic Authorship*. She concluded they were not written by the biblical character, Paul: 'I was both surprised and struck by the abundance of flawed methodologies ... and equally struck by a lack of external evidence for the [letters] dated to the mid-1st century for Paul.' She said there was also the question of how letters supposedly delivered to disparate ancient cities and regions far and wide came together as a collection. This mystery would be answered if they were written by a Flavian or connected Roman source. Livesey contends the 'letters of Paul' are literary creations in 2nd century Rome and not, as claimed, written by 'Apostle Paul' in the aftermath of the crucifixion in the 1st century. This would support the Gospel technique of writing texts that are set in an earlier period. Livesey believes the letters were written under a false name and 'Paul' was a constructed persona. She is not alone in that view among scholars.

A Bible website tells me that 'one of the earliest and most significant non-biblical references to the apostles comes from the writings of early 'Church Fathers'. What if they were Flavians and their group of largely pseudonyms? The article names Clement of Rome, Ignatius of Antioch, Polycarp of Smyrna, and Roman historian Tacitus for providing valuable historical insights: 'Clement of Rome, writing around A.D. 96 in his letter to the Corinthians, mentions the apostles Peter and Paul, highlighting their martyrdom and significant contributions to the Church (1 Clement 5).' It says that Clement's references are crucial because 'they come from a time when eyewitnesses to the apostles' lives were still alive, lending credibility to his accounts'. But Clement, almost certainly the first pope and not the fourth, was a Flavian. The article names another source for Jesus and the apostles outside the New Testament – *Josephus*. Jeremiah J. Johnston described as 'a New Testament scholar, pastor, and president of the Christian Thinkers Society', was interviewed by Christian Tucker Carlson as this book went into production. He was claiming that the Shroud of Turin, claimed to be the burial shroud of Jesus which was first exhibited in the 14th century, was real and genuine. He ended the interview with these words and they capture the points I am making here:

> I know atheist Jews who are archaeologists, and they use six sources to make sure ... they are digging in the right place. You've probably heard of these sources, Tucker, are you ready? ... Matthew, Mark, Luke, John, the Book of Acts and Josephus.

Exactly. Writer and former Christian Gavin Evans says that historians base their claims for a historical Jesus on the thinnest mentions of early Christians by the Roman politicians Pliny the Younger and Tacitus who write of Christians they say they interviewed early in the 2nd century ... and by Flavius Josephus, a Romanised Jewish historian. Same old, same old. The whole shebang is such a perceptual scam.

The 'Neo-Flavians'

The emerging Christian religion went through a fallow period after the end of the Flavians when Christianity didn't take off in the way they had hoped but then came Constantine the Great (272-337 AD) of the 'Constantinian dynasty' who were known as Neo-Flavian because every Constantinian emperor bore the name Flavius. He was Flavius Valerius Constantinus who became emperor in 324 and made Christianity the state religion of Rome. Legends say that before a battle in 312 Constantine saw a cross of light in a vision with the message 'in this sign, conquer'. Yep, nothing God loves more than a battle as history has constantly confirmed. Constantine oversaw the agreed Christian belief code known as the 'Nicene Creed' at the Council of Nicaea in present-day Turkey in 325 AD. Constantine would have known through family and aristocratic connections that Jesus had been invented by his namesake predecessors, but he was trying to hold together what was left of the empire amid warring religious factions. He needed a state religion in search of unity and control.

Constantine is said to have been baptised into Christianity on his deathbed in 337 which is a bit late really for the 'founder of the creed'. He had earlier worshipped the Roman god Sol Invictus and for him and many Romans the conversion from their Pagan religions to Christianity was not a problem when only the names changed and not even the symbols. The Vatican is built on the site of Pagan worship to the goddess Cybele 'the Great Mother' who was worshipped by the Israelite/Judeans as Asherah (Ashtoreth), the goddess of fertility, sexuality and war. The pope in the new Christianity was called Pontifex Maximus which was the title for the chief priest of the Pagan religion in ancient Rome later taken by emperors including Constantine the Great. Christians are supposed to follow the Constantine Nicene Creed to this day. Talk about covering all bases:

> We believe in one God, the Father, the Almighty, maker of heaven and earth, of all that is, seen and unseen. We believe in one Lord, Jesus Christ, the only Son of God, eternally begotten of the Father, God from God, Light from Light, true God from true God, begotten, not made, of one Being with the Father; through him all things were made. For us and for our salvation he came down from heaven, was incarnate from the Holy Spirit and the Virgin Mary and was made man. For our sake he was crucified under Pontius Pilate; he suffered death and was buried.
>
> On the third day he rose again in accordance with the Scriptures; he ascended into heaven and is at the right hand of the Father. He will come

again in glory to judge the living and the dead, and his kingdom will have no end. We believe in the Holy Spirit, the Lord, the giver of life, who proceeds from the Father and the Son, who with the Father and the Son is worshipped and glorified, who has spoken through the prophets. We believe in one holy catholic and apostolic Church. We acknowledge one baptism for the forgiveness of sins. We look for the resurrection of the dead, and the life of the world to come. Amen.

I believe perceptions create reality. It's shorter and closer to the truth. Constantine's mother Helena became a Christian saint after her tour of the 'Holy Land' in 326 AD when she claimed to have found the 'True Cross' on which Jesus died, the location that he died, and where he ascended to heaven. Ludicrous legends say she chose a site for excavation and discovered three crosses. This was when Jesus is supposed to have died on a *wooden* cross nearly 300 years earlier. Christian tradition says she decided which was the Jesus cross by having a woman near death brought to the site to touch each one. Two made no difference, but she was cured when she touched the other. Helena declared this the 'True Cross' and Constantine built the Church of the Holy Sepulchre on the site in Jerusalem that they claimed was both the location of the crucifixion and his tomb. What a coincidence and this is still considered the holiest place for Christian pilgrims. The Church of the Holy Sepulchre was built by Constantine on the site of the Roman Temple of Venus, a place of worship of the Goddess Venus.

The Church of the Nativity, or Basilica of the Nativity, was also built by Constantine down the road in Bethlehem after Helena found the birthplace of Jesus and another was located on the site she identified as the place where Jesus 'ascended'. Some further claim that she found the nails and rope used in the crucifixion and the 'Holy Tunic' that he wore. They made clothes to last in those days, clearly. The tunic is claimed to be owned today by several Christian sources at the *same time*. Miracles continue then. Either that or it pulls the pilgrims and tourists in. I went to all these places in Jerusalem on my one short visit to Israel in 1993 and I remember asking a Muslim taxi driver if he believed all the Jesus stories. He said that he didn't know but 'Jesus is good for taxi drivers because he moved around a lot'. So did Titus. I encourage people to read the books I have highlighted in this chapter for the fine detail of the evidence for a Flavian origin to Christianity. I have presented only a summary in the context of *The Road Map*.

Today Rome, tomorrow the world

From here the Roman Church with its headquarters at the Vatican has exploded across the world along with a stream of offshoot Christian strands most notably Protestantism and many others. A whole global top-down structure emerged to impose a perceptual prison of indoctrinated myopia that repels other possibilities to enslave the Mind in a belief in a judgemental 'God' that must be obeyed or eternal consequences will follow. The prison-cell perception that only by believing in Jesus will heaven await you. Reincarnation that many early Christians believed in was deleted from its theology and its followers told to accept that a 'loving God' judged everyone on the basis of one human life, no matter what the circumstances. What a means of human perceptual limitation and control orchestrated as it would have been by the Astral 'gods' manipulating through the simulation.

How the loosh has flowed from its engendered fear and guilt, and the wars, slaughter and horrors it has instigated to impose its doctrine based on 'Gentle Jesus'. It has offered limitless opportunity to divide and rule the target populations by pitching Christianity against Islam, Hinduism, Judaism, and others that all have equally doubtful origins and lead ultimately to the *same* origin as we will see. It is extraordinary to observe the blatant fantasies accepted without question by otherwise intelligent people just because of repetition. Even more to see how those telling others to 'open their minds' and 'stand for freedom' have their perceptions totally seized by a 'faith' that requires no other evidence outside the official story to hand over their minds to something that is claimed to have happened thousands of years ago.

Oh yes, one other thing. If there was no 'Jesus' then who is the 'Jesus', looking like the image decided by Renaissance artists, who turns up again and again in the Astral and its 'light tunnel' as described by many near-death experiencers? Who is that? A synthetic projection of the simulation to entice Christians and others up the tunnel to the recycling bin.

The world really is *nothing* like it is claimed to be.

CHAPTER 18

They Made It Up (2)

To invent, you need a good imagination and a pile of junk.
Thomas A. Edison

The Old Testament stories which the Gospel writers used to concoct their alleged ongoing 'bridging' narrative from Judaism into Christianity were also a fabrication. We have a fabrication based on a fabrication.

There is no evidence outside the Bible and Jewish religious texts for the existence of Abraham (Abram) who made the 'Covenant with God' and is claimed to be the 'founder' of the Israelite nation through his 'go forth and multiply' family. Even then you can't call the Bible 'evidence' when it's just a claim, a story. There is no evidence for the existence of the Jewish 'patriarchs' that followed Abraham, or for 'Moses' on which Jesus was blueprinted, or his 'Ten Commandments' from God on 'Mount Sinai'. There is no evidence for the Israelites fleeing from slavery in Egypt – the 'Exodus' – or 'wandering in the wilderness' for '40 years' (a 'generation'). There is, however, plenty of evidence that none of this ever happened in the way described. Modern archaeological techniques have not been good for the Old Testament (or New) narrative. Jewish archaeologists Israel Finkelstein and Neil Asher Silberman write in their book, *The Bible Unearthed*, that modern excavation methods and a wide range of laboratory tests have been used to date and analyse the civilisations of the ancient Israelites, and their neighbouring Philistines, Phoenicians, Arameans, Ammonites, Moabites and Edomites. The authors conclude:

> It is now evident that many events of biblical history did not take place in either the particular era or the manner described. Some famous events in the Bible clearly never happened at all.

Finkelstein and Silberman contend that the stories of the Old Testament were compiled long after the events were claimed to have happened and are not historical facts. They and other scholars date the text origins to around the 7th century BC – about 1,500 years after

Abraham is said to have been born in the region of 2,000 BC. Moses and King David came on the scene 500 and a thousand years later, and you have about a thousand years between the alleged life of Moses and when the biblical stories about him were written – about 400 to 500 years in the case of David. Does it make any sense whatsoever that the texts can be promoted as historical documents? But that's how the religions present them as the historical basis of not only Judaism, but also Christianity and Islam. Abraham is a patriarch common to all three 'Abrahamic' religions.

Over and over, we have biblical 'history' written by 'visions' and 'dreams' about 'God'. We will see in the next chapter that 'vision' is mistranslated as is so much else. Abraham is said to have had his God vision while living in Mesopotamia, now Iraq. God told him to take his family to land that would be shown to him, and he would make them a great nation. They then headed for Canaan where modern Israel is today. God promised he and his descendants all the lands from 'the river of Egypt to the great river, the river Euphrates' (Genesis 15:18). Some 4,000 years later modern Israel fanatics like Benjamin Netanyahu and his masters are seeking to establish control of that very land under the name, Greater Israel. God obviously takes his time when it comes to promises. How many more people will 'God' demand to be slaughtered to fulfil his prophecy? My goodness, how many have died already over 4,000 years?

The 'Chosen People'?

The Jewish religion from which Christianity and Islam are later extensions is founded on Abraham's 'covenant' with God that promised the land between the two rivers; the Israelites that grew from Abraham and his family 'multiplying'; their slavery under a pharaoh in Egypt; the 'Exodus' escape led by Moses; 40 years wandering in the wilderness as a punishment from God; and their brutal mass murder of the Canaanites demanded by God to capture the 'Promised Land'. The Jewish claim to Palestine and all the Judaic and Abrahamic religions are founded on this nonsense for which there is absolutely no evidence. It is all claimed to have happened in a small area of land between Egypt and the country now known since 1948 as Israel and yet no archaeological confirmation has ever been found nor any texts outside the Old Testament to evidentially support this fairy tale. *None*. Oh, there have been some finds spun to fit the story, but as modern techniques, and sheer assumption-deprogrammed commonsense has prevailed, the spins have been debunked one by one. Take 'Exodus' as an example. The claim is that God brought plagues and disasters on Egypt to force the pharaoh to 'let my people go'. These included infestations of frogs and gnats; 'pestilence' that killed Egyptian livestock; festering boils on Egyptians and their animals 'throughout the land'; thunder, hail, and lightning; swarms of locusts, three days of darkness; and finally, the death of all the first born in Egypt as described in Exodus 11:4–6:

> This is what the LORD says: 'About midnight I will go throughout Egypt. Every firstborn son in Egypt will die, from the firstborn son of Pharaoh, who sits on the throne, to the firstborn of the slave girl, who is at her hand mill, and all the firstborn of the cattle as well. There will be loud wailing throughout Egypt – worse than there has ever been or ever will be again.'

What a lovely bloke and you can see why 'he' is used to justify horrors inflicted on humans century after century. God spared the Israelite first born by telling Moses to warn his people to mark their doors with lamb's blood so the 'Angel of Death' would pass over them. Jews celebrate to this day the 'Passover' when God spared their first born but killed all the Egyptian kids. You would have thought that a God that could produce all these disasters, communicate with Moses through a burning bush, have manna (food) fall from the sky, and give Moses the power to turn the Nile to blood, would have been able to sort out the pharaoh without killing the first born of slave girls. Not so, it seems. But of course, the text reflects the psychopathy of the writers and their perception of 'God' some thousand years after the alleged happenings as they invented these fantasies.

The biblical account goes on to say that the pharaoh relented after the first-born massacre and Moses told the *two million* Israelites that they were up and leaving – fast. *Two million* people – fast? Yep, real fast. Genesis 46:27 tells us that patriarch Joseph and his family numbered 70 people when they moved to Egypt 400 years earlier. The two million is the estimate that comes from the claim in Exodus 12:37-39 that 'the children of Israel journeyed from Rameses to Succoth, about six hundred thousand men on foot, besides children.' Add the children and women and you easily pass two million. Spin the number anyway you like and it's still massive. Exodus tells us that they took with them – in a rush – 'a mixed multitude' of 'flocks, and herds, *even* very much cattle'. They baked 'unleavened cakes of the dough which they brought forth out of Egypt'. It was not 'leavened' (made with yeast) because they didn't have time, but they somehow managed to move all those people and livestock super quick.

Out of Egypt

They left pursued by Egyptian troops when the pharaoh changed his mind. But God had a plan. He rolled back the waves of the Red Sea to allow the Israelites to cross which they did with their animals and carts that did not get stuck in the wet sand. I guess if he could roll back the waves, he could deal with the sand. The Israelites reached the other side, and God unleashed the waves again to drown the Egyptian army. All perfectly credible. Why would you have any doubt you *blasphemer*. 'Manna' falling from above is described in the Bible and the Koran as an 'edible substance that God bestowed upon the Israelites while they were wandering the desert during the 40-year period that followed the Exodus and preceded the conquest of Canaan'. Well, somehow the writers had to explain how two million people wandered in the wilderness for 40 years and still managed to eat. It's another version of feeding the 5,000, I suppose. Manna in Hebrew apparently means 'What is it?' That's an understandable reaction when stuff starts to fall from the sky. Alleged Islam founder Muhammad said: 'Truffles are part of the 'manna' which God sent to the people of Israel through Moses, and its juice is a medicine for the eye.' This is how blatant nonsense is passed on from religion to religion. Writer Tim Zeak highlighted in an Internet article, 'Ten Reasons Why the Bible's Story of the Exodus is Not True', how history, including archaeological history, is *silent* on what would have been a monumental event:

> Not in Egyptian history, nor in any other history. Despite decades of extensive archaeological endeavors, not one trace of it has ever been found. This story describes over two million people escaping from Egypt and spending 40 years in the wilderness. That is more than twice the population of Jerusalem today.
>
> Almost all archaeologists, including those in Israel, acknowledge that it could not have possibly happened without significant evidence being left behind; yet not a trace has ever been found, even after numerous and extensive attempts to prove the historicity of this event.

Zeak writes that the books of Exodus and Numbers claim this enormous multitude of people and animals moved to new camps 42 times in those 40 years and every one would have left millions of animal bones from 'the daily sacrifices, cemeteries each having tens of thousands of burials, and a sundry of other things including remnants of their numerous fires'. Yet there is nothing to corroborate the biblical story even with ground-penetrating radar in dry deserts where artifacts are best preserved. That's all the biblical story is – a *story*. Zeak calculates that such a number would have 'created a line well over 200 miles long (at eight abreast with only three feet between each row) along with their animals, of which the Bible says they had many':

> They also took along much treasure. Many would have been with babies, pregnant, crippled, blind, or bedridden, and yet a line of people extending over 200 miles long were able to outrun the Egyptian army who were chasing

them with chariots and horses, all in a single day and night.

Zeak quotes orthodox Jewish scholar Lawrence Schiffman, chairman of Hebrew and Judaic studies at New York University, responding to the claimed numbers: 'You'd have to be a bit crazy to accept that figure.' But people do because they believe that 'God' can't be wrong. The desperation of the Jewish authorities, political and religious, to find evidence of the biblical narrative means that if it existed it would have been found. There is a branch of archaeology called Biblical Archaeology that seeks to confirm biblical history, and it has not found supporting evidence for the fantastic claims like those in Exodus. I remember the elation of Israeli prime minister Netanyahu that a girl had found a '2,000-year-old silver coin' used during the Second Temple period between about 515 BC and 70 AD which proved a historical Jewish connection to Judea and Samaria, now known as the West Bank. Netanyahu wrote: 'This exciting discovery is additional evidence of the deep connection between the people of Israel and its land – to Jerusalem, to our temple, and to the communities in Judea and Samaria.' The coin turned out to be a replica souvenir which are regularly made at the Israel Museum as part of an educational programme for children. Don't laugh. Oh, go on then.

The Promised Land

Next, we have the Bible account of how 'Joshua' followed the departed Moses and led the Israelites in the brutal destruction and mass murder of the Canaanites who occupied the 'Promised Land' at the end of their 40-year wilderness punishment inflicted by God. Now this God demanded 'his people' eliminate every Canaanite man, woman and child. The Bible here quotes God in Deuteronomy 20:16-18:

> You are not to leave even one person alive in the cities of these nations that the Lord your God is about to give you as an inheritance. You must completely destroy the Hittites, the Amorites, the Canaanites, the Perizzites, the Hivites, and the Jebusites, just as the Lord your God commanded you ...

There was just one more essential necessity demanded by God before battle commenced and this is described in Joshua 5:5-8:

> Though all the men who came out [of Egypt] were circumcised, none of those born in the wilderness during the journey after the departure from Egypt were circumcised ... It was the children God raised up in their stead whom Joshua circumcised, for these were yet with foreskins, not having been circumcised on the journey. When the circumcision of the entire nation was complete, they remained in camp where they were, until they recovered.

If anyone can explain why cutting skin off your willy is preparation for battle or anything else perhaps they would let me know. My question is why God would put the skin there in the first place if he then wanted it cut off. But maybe that's just my ignorance, not being religious and all. Anyway, it seems to have worked because the Bible describes the brutal mass slaughter of Canaanites that followed. This is the Joshua 8:22-23 account of the siege of a city called 'Ai': 'Since those in the city came out to intercept them, Ai's army was hemmed in by Israelites on both sides, who cut them down without any fugitives or survivors except the king, whom they took alive and brought to Joshua.' The king didn't last long either according to Joshua 8:29 as he had the king hanged on a tree and ordered the body moved to the entrance of the city gate where 'a great heap of stones was piled up over it'. You can see how mass murder on the instruction of God is infused into the psyche of Jewish people that believe this baloney. It explains so much about the genocide in Gaza when God had compelled the genocide in Canaan. To this programmed psyche the Palestinians stand between the Israelites and their 'Promised Land' just as the Canaanites did.

No tumbling

The problem is that none of this *ever happened*. There is no supporting written evidence outside the biblical texts while archaeology tells a very different story about the development of life and peoples in Canaan that does not include anything even approaching the biblical narrative. Finkelstein and Silberman reveal in *The Bible Unearthed* how archaeology confirms there was no settlement relating to the biblical city of Ai 'at the time of its supposed conquest by the children of Israel'. The attack on the Canaanite Jericho is a famous Bible event when the Israelites blew their horns and the 'walls came tumbling down' as God predicts in Joshua 6:1-5:

> Then the Lord said to Joshua, 'See, I have delivered Jericho into your hands, along with its king and its fighting men. March around the city once with all the armed men. Do this for six days. Have seven priests carry trumpets of rams' horns in front of the ark [of the covenant].
>
> On the seventh day, march around the city seven times, with the priests blowing the trumpets. When you hear them sound a long blast on the trumpets, have the whole army give a loud shout; then the wall of the city will collapse and the army will go up, everyone straight in'.

And so, it was. Except that archaeological excavations of Jericho have revealed that the city did not have any walls to fall. *The Bible Unearthed* says that archaeology confirms that cities of Canaan were 'unfortified' and there were 'no walls that could have come tumbling down'. There was once again no trace of a settlement in Jericho of any kind in the 13th century BC let alone a city with a wall around it. No Canaanite city had walls. But there's more. The Israelites were supposed to have fled the pharaoh in Egypt by heading into the Sinai wilderness and on from that after 40 years into Canaan. There is just the little fact that the land of Canaan in the period claimed, including modern Lebanon and southwestern Syria, was controlled by ... *Egypt*. The Egyptians also exploited copper and turquoise mines in Sinai where the Israelites are said to have headed and in the Negev desert which is described in Numbers 13:17 as having 'strategic importance for the Israelite tribes' where spies were sent during preparations for the alleged conquest of Canaan. No Egyptian presence in Canaan is mentioned in the biblical accounts and yet archaeology has confirmed a network of Egyptian military forts there to secure control of the region. No Egyptian documents mention the 'Joshua' invasion. The Israelites fled from *Egypt* into land controlled by *Egypt*? Canaan was a vassal of Egypt in this period as confirmed by communications to and from pharaohs, engravings on Egyptian temples, and literary works. Finkelstein and Silberman write:

> Perhaps the most detailed source of information on Canaan in this period is provided by the Tell el-Amarna letters. These represent part of the diplomatic and military correspondence of the powerful pharaohs Amenhotep III and his son Akhenaten, who ruled Egypt in the fourteenth century BCE ...
>
> ... But most were from rulers of city-states in Canaan, who were vassals of Egypt during this period. The senders included the rulers of Canaanite cities that would later become famous in the Bible, such as Jerusalem, Shechem, Megiddo, Hazor, and Lachish. Most important, the Amarna letters reveal that Canaan was an Egyptian province, closely controlled by Egyptian administration.

They go on to say that the provincial capital was in Gaza and Egyptian garrisons were stationed at key sites throughout the land of Canaan including south of the Sea of Galilee and the port of Jaffa, now part of Tel Aviv. The Old Testament claims that Joshua handed different parts of the conquered (it wasn't) Canaan to the 'twelve tribes of Israel'.

'David' and 'Solomon'

The Bible story goes that the Israelites grew into a single nation – a 'united monarchy' – under King David ('reign' estimated about 1000/900 BC) and his son, the 'wise' Solomon ('reign' estimated about 970-931 BC). David is said to have reigned for 40 years (a recurring

They Made It Up (2)

number) amid one of the most prosperous periods of Israel's history known as the 'Golden Age'. Thank goodness that Trump has arrived to bring another one, then. David is biblically reported to have seized and secured an empire as far as the Euphrates (modern Iraq) in the east and to the Nile in the west. Solomon further expanded the kingdom of Israel to include parts of Jordan and Syria, or so the story goes. This is the unsupported claim behind the modern Zionist pursuit of a 'Greater Israel'. 'King David' is important to official Jewish history for many reasons and that includes the assertion that he is the first character in the Old Testament tales that can be historically confirmed to exist. Tel Aviv-based Jewish journalist Ruth Margalit wrote in *The New Yorker*:

> In the long war over how to reconcile the Bible with historical fact, the story of David stands at ground zero. There is no archeological record of Abraham, or Isaac, or Jacob. There is no Noah's Ark, nothing from Moses. Joshua did not bring down the walls of Jericho: they collapsed centuries earlier, perhaps in an earthquake.
>
> But, in 1993, an Israeli archeologist working near the Syrian border found a fragment of basalt from the ninth century B.C., with an Aramaic inscription that mentioned the 'House of David' – the first known reference to one of the Bible's foundational figures. So David is not just a central ancestor in the Old Testament. He may also be the only one that we can prove existed.

Well, maybe. I am not convinced by the 'evidence' myself which has been too easily taken as read in my view. The Israel team that made the find was led by Dr Avraham Biran (1909-2008), an archaeologist at Hebrew Union College. Biran was a committed Zionist who justified the Israel seizure of the Palestinian West Bank in 1967 as 'in times of war, the victor takes over the possession of the vanquished'. The Biran team uncovered the 'Tel Dan Stele' (a fragment of a monument) on which an unnamed Aramaic king boasted about defeating King Jehoram of Israel and Ahaziahu, son of Jehoram, 'king of the House of David'. It is dated to 900 BC. The stele was greeted with ecstatic celebration. It is housed in the Israel Museum in Jerusalem in its own alcove with three walls dedicated to highlighting its significance and has been displayed in the United States. Museum director James S. Snyder was quoted in 2024 in the Jewish publication, the *Forward*, as saying the stele was 'the lightning bolt of intersection between archeology and the Bible, between mythology or metaphor and reality'. He went on: 'The Tel Dan Stele is really about the origins, not just of Judaism, but of the monarchy that would become the touchstone for the founding of the monotheistic faiths, first of Judaism, then of Christianity, and then of Islam.' Others disagree. The *Forward* points out that 'although the stele is significant for being a non-biblical reference to King David, it is not indisputable evidence that he existed'. Dr Jack M. Sasson, a former religious studies professor at UNC-Chapel Hill, said in *The New York Times*: 'David may still only be a mythical ancestor for those who created the stele, a figure they used to legitimize their rule'.

There is controversy over the translation of the Aramaic on the stele of 'House of David' as promoted by Avraham Biran. Among the sceptics is the Reverend Dr George Athas, a lecturer of Biblical Hebrew and Koine Greek at Southern Cross College, Sydney, Australia, and Director of Research in the Old Testament Department of Australia's Moore Theological College. Athas laid out his doubts in his 2003 book, *The Tel Dan Inscription: A Reappraisal and a New Interpretation*. I read in an archaeological website article about the stele controversy that 'Bible detractors do not easily accept any artifact as authentic that bears the name of King David'. But George Athas is a *Christian minister* and he's not alone in his 'House of David' scepticism. Most studies of the Tel Dan fragments come from examinations of published photos and hand-drawn facsimiles, but Athas examined the actual fragments in the Israel Museum. He said that he 'could not stress enough' that the term interpreted as 'House of David' should be regarded as a 'toponym' (a word that is the name of a place, such as a city, a river, or a mountain) and 'not a reference to a Davidic dynasty'. He contends that the stele author was not referencing the House of David, but referring to a geographical entity which he believes was Jerusalem. '… We cannot say that we have pinned David down outside the pages of the Bible. We may well, so to speak, have found a footprint, even a fresh one, but he himself still eludes us.' He certainly does when he is claimed to have been confirmed on fragments of an Aramaic stele while neither David or Solomon is mentioned in any Egyptian or Mesopotamian texts even when they are said to have ruled an 'empire from the Nile to the Euphrates'. There are no monuments to either of them. This is compounded when you take all the other evidence into account that demolishes the David-Solomon fables in the Old Testament. If David and Solomon existed at all, and there is no credible evidence, they were certainly not the people described in the Old Testament.

Misleading the kids

The Bible tells us that David became king after felling the Philistine giant Goliath with a single sling shot and an empire followed which was ruled from the 'City of David', Jerusalem. Jews, Christians, and school children are told that King David's reign was, with his son Solomon, that 'Golden Age' of Israel history. The truth is rather different, and this is important also to Christianity in which the Roman Gospels connect 'Jesus' to the 'House of David' in their efforts to promote their invented

Christianity as the next stage and outgrowth of the Jewish tales. Renowned Italian university biblical researcher, historian, and language expert Giovanni Garbini (1931-2017) writes in his book *History and Ideology in Ancient Israel* that there is no credible evidence for 'the ancient biblical text with its glorious Davidic empire'. He said analysis and critical examination radically modified the picture that the Old Testament presents of the tenth century BC: 'David never killed Goliath … never fought against the Idumaeans, Ammonites, Amalekites and Aramaeans and did not create an empire.' If David did not exist – how does that leave his 'son', Solomon? Or 'House of David Jesus', come to that.

The Israelites were a nomadic grouping who gradually became a pastoral and more static people. They did not escape out of Egypt or conquer the land of Canaan through war, and they were tribal in nature with the tribes of the north and the tribe of Judah in the south around Jerusalem. Nor did they have a large empire under David and Solomon secured by war and conquest. Archaeological digs desperately seeking Bible-supporting confirmation have failed to reveal any evidence that Jerusalem was a major city during the alleged period of David and Solomon. Quite the opposite. Finkelstein and Silberman say in *The Bible Unearthed*: 'The most optimistic assessment of this negative evidence is that tenth century [BC] Jerusalem was rather limited in extent, perhaps not more than a typical country village.' They continue:

> This modest appraisal meshes well with the rather meager settlement pattern of the rest of Judah in the same period, which was composed of only about twenty small villages and a few thousand inhabitants, many of them wandering pastoralists.

Finkelstein and Silberman say that archaeological evidence for the famous building projects of Solomon described in the Bible is 'non-existent', and no evidence has been found in excavations on Temple Mount of 'Solomon's Temple', or his palace. Yet the whole Jewish temple story outlined earlier and projecting into present-day events is dependent on this. WTF? There followed the control of Israelite/Judean land out of Mesopotamia by the Assyrian empire in the 8th century BC followed by the Babylonians who destroyed Jerusalem in the 6th century BC. Both invasions led to mass deportation to the homelands of their captors in Mesopotamia although very far from everyone was forced to leave. The mass-exile in Babylon is estimated to have happened around 597 to 586 BC and lasted anything between 50 and 70 years depending on the source. Babylon was subsequently conquered by the Persians led by Cyrus the Great who allowed the Israelite exiles to return and pick up the pieces – again – only for further invasions to come through

Alexander the Great out of Greece in 332 BC and much later the Romans from whom came Christianity. Many had stayed in the Promised Land and were not exiled to Babylon, others came back, and still others became the 'diaspora' (the 'dispersion') over the centuries who moved elsewhere around the world. This is where we pick up the story from earlier about the Khazars who *converted* to Judaism around 740 AD, with no connection to biblical Israel, and became the overwhelming majority of today's Jewish community which established modern Israel with the justification of these made-up ancient tales.

There had long been two distinct societies in the north and south of the 'Promised Land' and these have been described as the ten tribes of the north with their capital Samaria and the tribes of Judah and Benjamin in the south centred on Jerusalem. They developed differently not least due to different terrain and its impact on economic possibilities. The north was far more affected by the Assyrian invasion, but both took the consequences of the conquest from Babylon. The south began to develop rapidly after the Assyrians arrived as they infused peoples from foreign lands and many Israelites who had avoided deportation to Mesopotamia headed to Jerusalem and the lands of Judah. Jerusalem began to develop into the city it would become in a very different timescale to the one claimed in the Old Testament and attributed to David and Solomon. The Babylonian invasion brought an end to the alleged Davidic kings and the priestly class became the prime source of societal direction or as much as the various invaders would allow.

From the many – one: Yahweh

The biblical story of the Israelites and Judeans is one of pleasing the 'god' YHWH (Yahweh) or upsetting him by worshipping other gods. I'll explore the nature of these 'gods' in the coming chapter. Israelites were told that if they worshipped Yahweh he would give them the land he promised and if they worshipped other gods, such as Baal, El, Asherah, and gods of the Sun and Moon, he would punish and destroy them. Many continued to follow other gods and here you have the reason why invading forces from Assyria, Babylon, and Rome were perceived as being sent by Yahweh as punishment for turning away from the 'true god'. What a head-fuck those we call today Jewish have had visited upon them and *still do*. Imagine being told from birth that if you don't follow the law of Yahweh given to Moses on Mount Sinai then Yahweh will condemn and destroy you? No wonder many won't turn on a light on the Sabbath. Another example is the Jewish organisation Neturei Karta ('Guardians of the City') which opposes Zionism and advocates Palestinian control of Israel/Palestine because they believe Yahweh wants the diaspora 'exile' to continue until the Hebrew Messiah comes. Wherever you look there are religious believers interpreting fairy tales.

They Made It Up (2)

So, when did the fantastic stories on which Judaism is based (and later Christianity/Islam) begin to appear in the to-be biblical form? The answer takes us to 7th century Judah and a king called Josiah who reigned from 640-609 BC. He is said to have become king at the age of eight and if that's the case his 'advisors' and the priesthood would have had enormous power over him. As Judah developed the record keeping, and much archaeology, begins to put this period of history on more solid ground. Josiah wanted to return the people to the one 'true god' of Yahweh, stop the idolatry of other gods, and make the Israelites north and south into one nation headed by the 'House of David'. To do this he needed a version of Israelite history that told the story of a nation with a special covenant with 'God' going back to Abraham – 'God's Chosen People'. A good example is the Book of Joshua, the sixth book of the Hebrew Bible and Old Testament which recounts the story of Israel from the conquest of Canaan covered earlier to the Babylonian exile. Scholars date the early writing of this book to Josiah's reign and its completion in the period of the Babylonian conquest and exile, or just after. Joshua's fantasy conquest of Canaan is supposed to have been launched in 1405 BC and yet the book describing this was not started until the reign of Josiah that began in 640 BC. I read that 'the consensus among scholars is that the Book of Joshua is historically problematic and should be treated with caution in reconstructing the history of early Israel'. You don't say.

The book is the source of the alleged wars to take the land of Canaan and divide it between the twelve tribes. 'Joshua' warns of the need to observe the law of Moses. King Josiah would have insisted that his scribes included that. You can see why these writers long after the 'event' would quote Moses as condemning worship of the bull god symbolised by the 'Golden Calf' as he is claimed to have returned from up the mountain with the 'Ten Commandments'. Now – King Josiah had a remarkable piece of luck (Yahweh inspired I'm sure) in that just as he was going about his business of deleting the worship of other gods and seeking to unite the people behind Yahweh, you'll never guess what happened: *One of his priests found the Book of the Law given to Moses hidden in the temple in Jerusalem.* No! Oh, *yes.* We know this is true because it says so in 2 Chronicles 34:14-33:

> And when they brought out the money that was brought into the house of the Lord, Hilkiah the priest found a book of the law of the Lord given by Moses. And Hilkiah answered and said to Shaphan the scribe, I have found the book of the law in the house of the Lord. And Hilkiah delivered the book to Shaphan. And Shaphan carried the book to the king.

Josiah was beside himself when he saw what the law contained (you mean he didn't know?) and said that 'great is the wrath of the Lord that is poured out upon us, because our fathers have not kept the word of the Lord, to do after all that is written in this book'. Josiah went to the temple and read the words of the book of the law and covenant with Yahweh to 'the inhabitants of Jerusalem, and the priests, and the Levites, and all the people, great and small: and he read in their ears all the words of the book of the covenant that was found in the house of the Lord'. Chronicles continues:

> And the king stood in his place, and made a covenant before the Lord, to walk after the Lord, and to keep his commandments, and his testimonies, and his statutes, with all his heart, and with all his soul, to perform the words of the covenant which are written in this book.
>
> And he caused all that were present in Jerusalem and Benjamin to stand to it. And the inhabitants of Jerusalem did according to the covenant of God, the God of their fathers.

Who said that synchronicity is a myth? But was it synchronicity or a scam? Finkelstein and Silberman had the right idea in *The Bible Unearthed*: 'Rather than being an old book that was suddenly discovered, it seems safe to conclude that it was written in the 7th century BCE, just before or during Josiah's reign.' It didn't seem to do Josiah much good because he was killed apparently by the pharaoh of re-emerging Egypt and then along came the Babylonians and exile.

We're off!

During Josiah's reign, the exile, and afterwards the texts were up and running that would form the biblical Old Testament and tell the story of a nation spawned by Abraham in the covenant with God who had been led out of slavery in Egypt by Moses, the Promised Land regained by Joshua, then lost and won and lost and won depending on the worship of Yahweh or other gods. The writers combined fantasies about great heroes and villains, brutal battles and wars, legends, and themes picked up from the Egyptians, Assyrians and Babylonians. The story of Noah and the 'Great Flood' was a direct steal from much earlier flood stories including the *Epic of Gilgamesh* from ancient Mesopotamia. We also have the invented character of Moses left by his mother as a baby in a basket among the Nile bulrushes in Egypt to be found by the pharaoh's daughter and brought up in the royal court. King Sargon the Great (Sargon of Akkad), who ruled the Mesopotamian Akkadian Empire from about 2334 BC until about 2279 BC, said of his mother apparently in his own inscription:

> She laid me in a vessel made of reeds, closed my door with pitch, and dropped me down into the river [Euphrates], which did not drown me. The river carried me to Akki, the water carrier. Akki the water carrier lifted me up in the kindness of his heart, Akki the water carrier raised me as his own son ...

Sargon went on to lead his people as did the later plagiarised Moses in Egypt of whom it is said of his mother in Exodus 2:3:

> And when she was no longer able to hide him, she took a small basket woven of bulrushes, and she smeared it with pitch as well as tar. And she placed the little infant inside, and she laid him in the sedges by the bank of the river.

Exodus goes on to describe how the baby Moses was found by the daughter of the Pharaoh, brought up in the royal family, and went on to lead the Israelites out of Egyptian slavery. Some scholars have noted the similarities between the story of Sargon and Moses along with others including Karna, a major character in the Hindu epic Mahabharata, and Oedipus in Greek mythology. We are looking at universal stories repeated across generations and cultures and taken to be factual history. Symbolic 'history' more like. We also had the original patriarch Abraham's birthplace given as Ur of the Chaldees in Mesopotamia. 'Chaldean' became synonymous with the Babylonians during the Neo-Babylonian Empire which invaded Judah although *not* in the time Abraham is supposed to have been born. I could go on demolishing the Old Testament make-believe, but that will do. Research the evidence yourself and I recommend *The Bible Unearthed* and others like it for an evidential pull-together on biblical claims and the lack of textual and archaeological evidence. Israel Finkelstein and Neil Asher Silberman are two Jewish archaeologists who had nothing to gain by dismantling the biblical version of events and much to lose in the face of religious literalists.

I concluded a long time ago that the Old Testament narratives attributed to the 'Israelites' and 'Judeans' (today called Jews) really originated in Mesopotamia, modern day Iraq and part of Syria, and were added to 'Jewish' history with a twist and new characters to form a manipulated origin. I was therefore interested to read, while researching this book, that biblical historian and language expert Giovanni Garbini thought the same. We are told there is an unbroken Hebrew history going back to the ancient world, but that is not the case. Garbini writes in *History and Ideology in Ancient Israel*:

> The virtually complete silence of epigraphy [study of inscriptions] on Hebrew history seems all the more disconcerting when we compare it with the epigraphic evidence from neighbouring peoples: Phoenicians, Aramaeans,

Moabites, Philistines and now even Ammonites have left more or less numerous inscriptions ... in them we find a record of the names and actions of rulers, of relations with neighbouring peoples, of wars and works of peace.

The lack of historical Hebrew inscriptions cannot be considered a matter of chance: it becomes a historical problem which must be approached as such.

Garbini's work led him to conclude that what are called the original Jews can be traced to the Syrian Desert between the Tigris and the Euphrates and from there some Aramaic tribes moved on to Damascus before migrating to what is now the land of Palestine/Israel. I mentioned that Garbini believed claims about a David-Solomon monarchy were an invention and much of the real history of the 'Israelites' and 'Judeans' was erased and rewritten by Hebrew scribes in the period I have highlighted when the Babylonian exiles returned to the land of Judah after Babylon was conquered by the Persian empire of Cyrus the Great. The Babylonian and Persian influence would have allowed the communication and circulation of ancient stories from Mesopotamia, the so-called 'Cradle of Civilisation'. From this so much of the Old Testament would be reconstructed and it is to that land we shall now turn in search of answers to this question:

What is this God that religious texts like the Bible and Koran talk about? Where did 'he' come from and to what end? What a story this is.

CHAPTER 19

Who (or What) is the Biblical 'God'?

*Every man takes the limits of his own field of vision
for the limits of the world*
Arthur Schopenhauer

I first began to see the *real* nature of the Old Testament 'God' in the mid-1990s. I had noted since the days of my religious 'education' (indoctrination) at school that the Old and New Testament 'Gods' were fundamental contradictions.

One was a brutal tyrant demanding the mass slaughter of the innocent while the other talked through his 'son' about 'love'. Even then God number two insisted that his 'son' was horrifically tortured on a cross to 'forgive the sins' of humanity. I remember thinking why didn't he just do it without all the bloodshed, pain and suffering? Why would 'sins' be forgiven anyway when nothing had changed except that his 'son' went through agony? How could you be redeemed by believing in Jesus when he appeared in a tiny land in the Middle East and was unknown for centuries by the rest of the world? None of it made any sense. But from 1995 two things happened to reveal the identity to me of the Old Testament 'God'. I realised that a non-human force was manipulating human society, and I saw that a word meaning 'God' in the Old Testament really translated as 'gods'. This was 'Elohim' which is used in the context of a plural and not a singular. I read biblical phrases in which the word Elohim was translated as a singular 'God' and yet it referred to 'us' and 'our'. The italicised emphasis is mine: 'And God said, Let *us* make man in *our* image, after *our* likeness' (Genesis 1:26); and 'Then the LORD God said, "Behold, the man has become like one of *us*, to know good and evil"' (Genesis 3:22). We also have in relation to building the Tower of Babel: ' ... let *us* go down, and there confound their language, that they may not understand one another's speech' (Genesis 11:7).

The plural 'Elohim', which the Greeks called the plural Theoi, appears more than 2,500 times in the Hebrew Bible with the word biblically translated as 'God' *singular*. The magnitude of impact this has had on human understanding cannot be calculated, so far reaching and detailed are its consequences. The Names of God Bible (NOG) is an English translation that restores the original Hebrew and Aramaic names of 'God' (the gods) to the texts. What a difference is the opening to Genesis alone when you replace the mistranslated singular 'God' with the plural Elohim:

> In the beginning Elohim created heaven and earth. The earth was formless and empty, and darkness covered the deep water. The Ruach Elohim was hovering over the water. Then Elohim said, 'Let there be light!' So there was light. Elohim saw the light was good. So Elohim separated the light from the darkness. Elohim named the light day, and the darkness he named night. There was evening, then morning – the first day …
>
> …Then Elohim said, 'Let us make humans in our image, in our likeness. Let them rule the fish in the sea, the birds in the sky, the domestic animals all over the earth, and all the animals that crawl on the earth.'

'Ruach' along with 'Kavod', a term used by Moses in Exodus, are both believed by retranslators of the Bible to be some sort of flying phenomenon. They point out that many words have multiple meanings and should be translated according to the context of the sentence. Mauro Biglino worked on Vatican-approved Bible translations for Bible publisher San Paolo Edizioni before going public with his contention that the Old Testament is a very different story to the one we are told to believe. Kavod, which appears more than 250 times in Hebrew

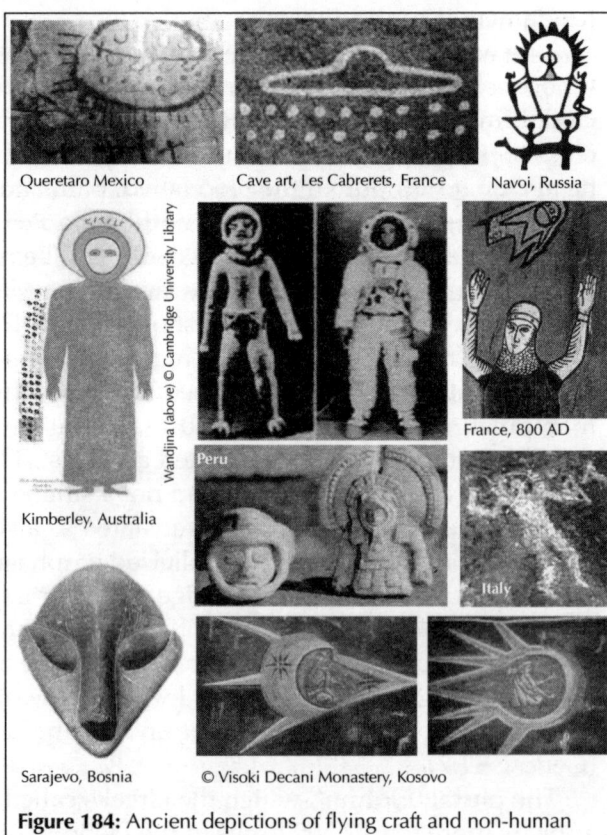

Figure 184: Ancient depictions of flying craft and non-human entities around the world.

Scriptures, is translated as 'glory' when its original meaning is 'to be heavy, to have weight, to be hard'. Biglino writes that the ancient Hebrew term 'ruach' had a 'very concrete meaning' of 'wind', 'breath', 'moving air', 'storm wind', and in the broader sense 'that which moves swiftly through the air space'. Ruach is written as 'spirit' in the Bible and is translated in that Genesis verse about 'the Ruach Elohim hovering over the water' as 'the Spirit of God moved upon the face of the waters'. Biglino says:

> In the extreme concreteness of the ancient Hebrew language anything that flew swiftly through the air could only be referred to as a kind of 'wind'. In later theological-spiritualistic elaboration, the term took on the meaning of 'spirit' familiar to us today, which it probably did not initially have.

Elohim translates from the root meaning as 'the powerful ones' while other cultures refer to their pantheons as 'sky gods' and similar names that reflect the gods coming from the sky (Fig 184). The Bible and global cultures describe how the gods met in a council, or Divine Council, in which many deities came together under the presiding chief god. The concept can be found in Sumerian, Akkadian, Old Babylonian, Ancient Egyptian, Babylonian, Canaanite, Israelite, Celtic, Ancient Greek, Roman, and Nordic pantheons. Egyptian accounts refer to a 'synod of the gods' while in Mesopotamia the presiding god was the leader of the sky gods, Anu, the equivalent in other cultures of Zeus, Jupiter, and so on. We have the Elohim, plural, meeting in council and addressed by their leader 'Elyon' in the Old Testament Psalm 82:5-8. This is from the Names of God Bible:

> Wicked people do not know or understand anything. As they walk around in the dark, all the foundations of the earth shake. I said, 'You are gods. You are all sons of Elyon. You will certainly die like humans and fall like any prince.' Arise, O Elohim! Judge the earth, because all the nations belong to you.

I checked with the King James Version published in 1611 and once again Elohim was translated as a singular 'God'.

The 'one' is many

Bible translator Mauro Biglino is adamant that the Old Testament 'God' should be 'gods'. He says that Elohim is a plural and used as a plural. He highlights how many Bible passages make no sense as a singular, but total sense as a plural. Biglino asks why Hebrew texts would speak of '*the*' Elohim if the word means 'God'? He writes in his book, *Gods of the Bible*:

> The application of the hypothesis established by the [biblical translation], stating

that the term 'Elohim' is undoubtedly singular, leads to the following consideration: should the term 'Elohim' have a singular value, the Bible would be an absurd, incoherent, confused, and almost incomprehensible text.

On the other hand, if we are to reaffirm the non-theological hypothesis that the term 'Elohim' refers not to an individual but to a plurality of individuals, to a group of individuals, then the text would be clearly understood by everyone without the need for mediation and interpretation.

Biglino includes many examples in his book of Elohim being used to clearly portray many and not one. Here are a few:

'This is the camp of the Elohim!' – Genesis 32-2.
'Who is like you among the Elohim?' – Exodus 15:11.
'Now I realise that Yahweh is greater than all the Elohim' – Exodus 18-11.
'You shall have no other Elohim before me' – Exodus 20:2-3.
'You shall not follow other Elohim among the Elohim of the nations around you' – Deuteronomy 6:14.
'Let us go and worship other Elohim' – Deuteronomy 13:7-11.
'Throw away the Elohim your ancestors worshipped' – Joshua 24:14.
'Choose for yourselves this day whom you will serve, whether Elohim your ancestors served beyond the Euphrates, or Elohim of the Amorites' – Joshua 24:15.
'Will you not take what your Elohim, Chamosh, gives you? Likewise, whatever Yahweh our Elohim has given us, we will possess' – Judges 11:24.
'They pour out drink offerings to other Elohim to arouse my anger' – Jeremiah 7:18.

We should also remember that the Bible texts have been constantly retranslated century after century, and they will have deviated often far from the original meaning. Giovanni Garbini was an expert in ancient Middle Eastern languages at Italian universities who interpreted the biblical narrative against the history of the region. He said:

> Words underwent drastic transformations, changing their meaning according to the ideological needs of the individual biblical authors, which in the final phases of composition were far removed from those at the beginning of the first millennium BCE.

It is against this background that the biblical 'word of God' must be analysed and assessed. There have been a fantastic number of 'gods' worshipped across the world through the ages. I am well aware that they include names attributed to planets and stars and how their original meanings have been usurped through the generations and mistranslations to have different meanings and symbolism. Sorting them out is a minefield. My focus here is to uncover what they originally meant and referred to way back in the mists of history. To do that we need to look at patterns of agreement between apparently unconnected societies.

Created or genetically manipulated?

Common global stories include how, what I suggest are the reptilian Elohim/Anunnaki and other names for the 'gods', *created* humanity. Bible translator Mauro Biglino analysing the texts across languages believes the Anunnaki/Elohim *genetically engineered* a new human from a version that already existed: '… we are dealing here with Adam's actual fabrication and, thus, the making of a new species, the Adamites.' The Adamite human body could not at first reproduce independently, but it seems that the Anunnaki 'god' Enki introduced that. He is said to have looked upon humans a little more benevolently. The Anunnaki/Elohim leadership began to panic at what they saw as a loss of control. Biglino points to Sumerian accounts that describe how 'the element to be inserted to make man was taken from the purified blood of Anunnaki males'. Biglino's translation of Hebrew texts reads differently to the Bible version of humans created 'in our image'. He writes:

> … the Adam is not simply created 'according to the image' of the Elohim. The correct translation would be: 'with the image', or better, 'with that material something that contains that image' of the Elohim …

> … So, the Elohim does not *create* (the verb is unambiguous) but *forms* the Adam with 'something' found on the planet Earth. We immediately notice the correspondence between Adam 'man' and [Adamah] 'earth', also reminiscent of the assonance between 'earth' and 'earthly'.

This would explain why the reptilian brain is such a driver of human behaviour, a prime emotional trigger, and producer of loosh. It didn't 'evolve'. It was genetically inserted. The late American researcher Lloyd Pye studied human origins for decades and wrote that our DNA has more than 4,000 defects compared with only a few hundred in chimpanzees and gorillas. Mainstream science has acknowledged sudden changes in human genetics about 200,000 years ago and again around 35,000 years ago and there have been officially unexplained societal transformations in a short period when for example we moved from nomadic lifestyles to farming which ancient texts connect to knowledge brought by the gods. The human body has been subjected to

Figure 185: Depictions of the same theme, but not so much creating as genetically manipulating.

substantial gene splicing to change the genetic structure which is like cutting frames in a film and putting them back in a different order. How was it done aeons ago by supposedly primitive people? It wasn't. It was the Elohim/Anunnaki.

The Sumerian Tablets are said to portray Enki of the Anunnaki genetically modifying the new human and you see similar depictions in other cultures and periods (Fig 185). The level of knowledge can be seen with an extraordinary artefact thousands of years old found in Colombia which confirms detailed awareness of the internal birth process. This is known as the Genetic Disc and depicts human eggs and sperm which can only be seen through a microscope (Fig 186). The disc is made of lyddite which is a very hard stone with a structure that breaks up easily when cut. Austrian researcher Klaus Dona said experts in the field have told him that it would not be possible to make the same disc today with the same material. The birth theme continues with images of a foetus on the back of the disc which portrays someone that is clearly not

Figure 186: The Genetic Disc found in Colombia depicts human eggs and sperm only visible through a microscope, but it is thousands of years old.

human. Sexual procreation isn't the only way for the Elohim and humans to interbreed and change genetics. There is genetic manipulation far beyond what we appear to see today.

A Russian research group changed frog embryos into salamander embryos by transmitting salamander DNA information patterns. Dr

Michael Levin, a researcher at Tufts University in Massachusetts, produced tadpoles with eyes on their backs and frogs with six legs simply by manipulating their electrical communication systems. That's how easy it is to do, and this is what is happening today through electromagnetic fields produced by 4G, 5G and the upcoming 6G. Levin predicted that what he did with tadpoles could be done with humans and this is the foundation reason for the self-replicating nanotechnology in 'Covid' fake vaccines and others of the same type. It's not to give humans more legs, but to connect them to a collective hive mind via receiver-transmitters in the body interacting with a global electromagnetic field. The Astral-based Elohim will have been far in advance of this since the ancient world and can mutate humans by transmitting signals or fields of information to the body's DNA receiver-transmitter systems.

From the sky they came

The biblical Creation story featuring the 'gods' is described in ancient global texts which confirm each other despite those involved not officially ever meeting. The *Popol Vuh* ('Book of the Community' or 'Book of Counsel') is a written text from oral translations of the K'iche' people of Guatemala in Central America described as 'one of the Maya peoples' of Mexico and areas of Belize, Honduras and El Salvador. I have seen it described as 'the sacred book of the ancient Maya'. The *Popol Vuh* details the mythologies of Mesoamerica and is made even more important by the systematic destruction of other mythology documentation following the Spanish conquest. The Roman Catholic Church and the Christianity hierarchy in general has sought to destroy all evidence of ancient accounts that do not support their one-God official story. Some individuals have had more respect, like the Catholic priest who translated these texts, but not the inner circle that gives out the orders and knows what a scam Christianity has been all along. The *Popol Vuh* refers to entities that created humans with much trial and error. It says: 'The Creator, the Former, the Dominator, the Feathered-Serpent, they-who-engender, they-who-give-being, hovered over the water as a dawning light'. The gods worldwide seem to have done a lot of 'hovering' according to ancient texts. The *Popol Vuh* says they created more than just humans:

> Then the earth was created by them. So it was, in truth, that they created the earth. Earth! they said, and instantly it was made. Like the mist, like a cloud, and like a cloud of dust was the creation, when the mountains appeared from the water; and instantly the mountains grew.

> Only by a miracle, only by magic art were the mountains and valleys formed;

and instantly the groves of cypresses and pines put forth shoots together on the surface of the earth.

This is the Mesoamerican version of the biblical Elohim. The gods may have claimed to have created the Earth, but I will have more about that shortly. The phrase 'bene elohim', is translated as 'sons of the gods' which we see in Genesis 6:1, 2 and 4 from the Names of God Bible:

The number of people increased all over the earth, and daughters were born to them. The sons of Elohim saw that the daughters of other humans were beautiful. So they married any woman they chose ...

... The Nephilim were on the earth in those days, as well as later, when the sons of Elohim slept with the daughters of other humans and had children by them. These children were famous long ago.

Here you have the plural Elohim and Nephilim who were both described as 'giants' and other biblical names for giants include Anakim, Rephaim, and Emim (Fig 187). It is surely no coincidence that those in the modern world who say they have seen or interacted with Reptilians, including military personnel in underground bases, describe them as extremely tall or 'giants'. The Elohim-human offspring are portrayed in ancient texts as hybrid 'demi-gods' – part human, part 'god'. Bene elohim, or 'sons of the gods', has an 'exact parallel' in Ugaritic (an extinct Semitic language) and Phoenician texts. The term refers to the 'council of the gods'. Other references include 'heavenly host' (Hebrew and Semitics scholars) and 'divine council' which is a concept of all ancient Mediterranean cultures. Elohim, the plural gods translated as 'God', is of central importance to what has happened to the world ever since and it's the same with the Muslim 'Allah' who morphed into the singular from a multitude of plural gods. All the 'Abrahamic' religions have gone through the same process of the plural becoming the singular with Christianity inheriting from Judaism. Religions across the world have either been

Figure 187: Gods were portrayed in Mesopotamian tablets as giants.

individualised as 'God' or continue with their multi-god originals as with Hinduism.

Israelite gods became God

The number of gods worldwide is staggering, but when you look at how they were portrayed and what they represented it is clear they are different names for the *same* deities which they connect to various locations including the Pleiades, Orion, Saturn, Sirius, the Draco constellation, and elsewhere. These locations also operate in Astral dimensions and not only ours. Pantheons of gods are everywhere in the ancient world. A reminder again and these are only some:

African pantheons; Armenian pantheon; Aztec pantheon; Berber pantheon; Burmese pantheon; Canaanite pantheon; Celtic pantheon; Chinese pantheon; Egyptian pantheon; Germanic pantheon; Greek pantheon; Hindu pantheon; Incan pantheon; Irish pantheon; Jain pantheon; Japanese pantheon; Japanese Buddhist pantheon; Maya pantheon; Native American pantheons; Norse pantheon; Roman pantheon; Slavic pantheon; Akkadian pantheon; Assyrian pantheon; Babylonian pantheon; Sumerian pantheon.

The last four were all in Mesopotamia, now Iraq, and are extremely important because those pantheons led to the *Israelite* Elohim pantheon. A most prominent one was the goddess Asherah who is mentioned 40 times in the Hebrew Bible and less so in English translations. Asherah was also known as The Lion Lady, Astarte, Anat, Elat, Hathor, and Queen of Heaven which is a title later given by some Christians to Mother Mary. Queen of Heaven was a term used for 'sky goddesses' in the ancient Mediterranean and Near East. The Old Testament says in Jerimiah 7:18: 'The children gather wood, the fathers light the fire, and the women knead the dough and make cakes to offer to the Queen of Heaven.' The 'prophet' Jerimiah condemns these offerings to the 'Queen of Heaven' as connected to idolatry. Goddesses like Asherah abound in the ancient world under names such as Inanna, Isis, Ishtar, Semiramis, Nut, and in Greco-Roman times, Aphrodite, Venus, Diana, Artemis, Hera, and Juno. At least many were different names for the same deity. Israelites/Judeans were Asherah and multi-god and goddess worshippers. They did so with standing stones, temples, high places ('high' is a constant in worship of the sky gods and goddesses), and Asherah figurines or 'poles'. 2 Kings 17:9-12 tells us:

> The Israelites secretly did things against the LORD their God that were not right. From watchtower to fortified city, they built high places in all their cities. They set up for themselves sacred pillars and Asherah poles on every high hill and under every green tree.

They burned incense on all the high places like the nations that the LORD had driven out before them. They did wicked things, provoking the LORD to anger. They served idols, although the LORD had told them, 'You shall not do this thing'.

'The Lord' is Yahweh which most Israelites of the time rejected although some scholars connect Asherah to being a 'consort' of Yahweh and also Saturn god El. Asherah was worshipped as the goddess who showed humans how to farm and this is another theme of global accounts. The gods brought the skills and knowledge that transformed societies and the way they lived. But before we get too misty-eyed the gods had their own agenda for this. The whole official history of the Israelites/Judeans is one of battles between those that worshipped multiple gods and others led by many kings and the priesthood that sought to impose the worship of only *one* of the multiple gods which the Bible calls 'Yahweh'. Translator Mauro Biglino is convinced from the texts that the psychopath 'Yahweh' was a lesser 'god' of the Elohim:

> The Elohim who called himself Yahweh was not one of the many 'gods' of a polytheistic religion, but a member of ranks of the deities differently called Anunnaki/Igigi/Neteru/Elohim, flesh-and-blood individuals who came to Earth, formed the Adam in their image … and eventually passed on to him all that was necessary to create culture and civilisation.

Yahweh comes on the biblical scene when he contacts Moses through the burning bush that doesn't burn at 'Horeb, the mountain of Elohim'. Biglino's knowledge of Hebrew is interesting here. He says the word 'seneh' which is translated as 'bush' can also mean 'rocky ridge' and is used this way in 1 Samuel 14:4. If a craft landed on the mountain or 'rocky ridge' there could be flames that did not burn the rocky ridge, rather than a 'bush'. Biglino quotes Exodus 19:16-19. This is the Names of God Bible version:

> … There was thunder and lightning with a heavy cloud over the mountain, and a very loud blast from a ram's horn was heard. All the people in the camp shook with fear. Then Moses led the people out of the camp to meet with Elohim, and they stood at the foot of the mountain.
>
> All of Mount Sinai was covered with smoke because Yahweh had come down on it in fire. Smoke rose from the mountain like the smoke from a kiln, and the whole mountain shook violently. As the sound of the horn grew louder and louder, Moses was speaking, and the voice of Elohim answered him.

Is it not more likely that a craft was landing on a 'rocky ridge' of a mountain than a bush bursting into flames without burning?

The Sumer connection

I am saying that these stories attributed to 'Moses' really came from Mesopotamia with Israelite/Judean characters added to make it appear the events happened in the 'Promised Land'. 'Yahweh' was one of the Elohim and not 'Almighty God'. As Biglino puts it: 'We know Yahweh was not the one and only "God", but just a minor local ruler. His insignificance and weakness caused him to issue cruel orders ...' If it wasn't so tragic in its consequences it would be hilarious. An Israelite/Judean 'good king' and 'bad king' as assigned by history is largely based on which gods or God they worshipped or allowed to be worshipped. King Josiah in the 7th century BC was a 'good king' because he sought to stop multiple god worship and, not coincidentally, he also began with his priesthood the writing and rewriting of texts that now form the Old Testament in which the 'gods' became 'God'. We should remember that the Israelites were invaded by the Assyrians and Babylonians, and many were taken into Mesopotamian exile where ancient stories circulated.

Assyria and Babylon not only occupied the same Mesopotamia as the former Sumer, but they were also massively influenced by that culture and the accounts of history that the Sumerians left them. Mesopotamia is known as the cradle of civilisation and is of primary importance to understanding the world that followed to present day (Fig 188). I have long said that Sumer was less the origin of what is called 'civilisation' and more a restart after the 'Great Flood'. The Sumer Empire is dated from about 4500-1900 BC; Akkadian Empire (c.2334 BC-2154 BC);

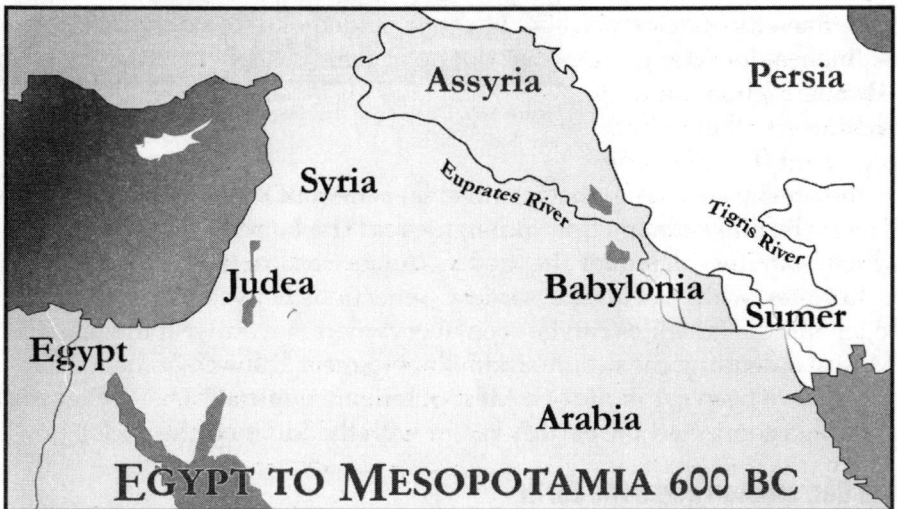

Figure 188: The lands from which the Bible texts came with their origin in Mesopotamia.

Assyrian Empire (c.2025-609 BC); Babylon (c.1894-1595 BC) with a second empire from 626-539 BC emerging in the 7th century known as the Neo-Babylonian or Chaldean Empire. This is the one led by King Nebuchadnezzar II who rebuilt the city of Babylon, created the Ishtar Gate in honour of an 'Elohim' goddess, invaded Israel/Judah, and instigated the Babylonian exile.

Sumer emerged from the devastation of the Earth upheavals and flood to – I would say – *re*invent and *re*discover irrigation networks, the wheel, the ability to construct major buildings, astronomy, a number system, the 60-minute hour, maps, and complex social and economic systems founded on city-states with their own government and *ruling deity*. City-states, their kings and deities, had many wars which were a theme of Mesopotamian cultures and lands influenced by them. To give you an idea of the mentality – King Eannatum of Lagash in Sumer destroyed a nearby city-state and had a limestone Stele of the Vultures monument built to commemorate the 'victory' depicting birds feeding on the flesh of those he defeated. This is similar to the story of the ancient Greek god Prometheus punished by the leader Zeus for helping humanity. Wherever the 'gods' went there was war, control and suffering which continues to this day. Sumerians, Akkadians, Babylonians, and Assyrians worshipped multiple gods in their pantheons and built enormous 'ziggurat' stepped pyramids dedicated to these gods with elaborate temples at the top. The famous ziggurat in the Sumerian city-state of Ur (biblical location of 'Abraham') was dedicated to their 'sky god', Anu (Fig 189). The

Figure 189: Drawing of the Ziggurat of Ur. It was dedicated to the 'sky god', Anu.

theme of 'sky gods' is globally universal across all locations and cultures. Shinar, the biblical name for Sumer, means 'The Land of the Watchers' which is another name for the 'gods'. Sumer was known by the Egyptians as Ta Neter, which meant the same. Connections between Mesopotamian belief and the Israelites can be seen everywhere. I wonder if the tale of 'Moses' ascending the mountain in Sinai to meet Yahweh of the Elohim might have been symbolic of a Mesopotamian ziggurat? They believed the pyramids connected the earthly realm with the 'divine' (the gods).

And God ~~created~~ *owns* the Earth

There is also the biblical use of Elyon or El Elyon (Elon!) which is mostly translated into English as 'God Most High' and in the Septuagint (the Greek translation of the Old Testament from the original Hebrew) as 'God the highest'. I guess if you were a sky god you would be 'Most High'. A more accurate translation of Elyon is 'what is above' or 'high above, superior, according to Bible translator Mauro Biglino who says there is no word in Hebrew for an 'omniscient, omnipotent, transcendent spiritual entity'. They are talking of gods, not God. Biglino says the title of Elyon indicates the overall commander of the Elohim, a title rather than a single individual, and his meticulous translations from earlier texts and mistranslations reveal that (1) Elyon is said in what became the biblical texts to be the *owner* in a legal sense, not the creator, of the Earth; and (2) that the Hebrew god Yahweh was inserted to replace Elyon and turn Yahweh into the God of the Hebrews with whom they claimed a covenant that made them 'God's Chosen People'. Biglino says a word translated as 'Creator' really indicates legal ownership and not creation which rather takes us back to the 'Yaldabaoth' experience of Isabella Greene from earlier.

Elyon equates with the Greek Zeus, head of the Greek pantheon, who is 'god of the sky and the thunder', 'king of all other gods and men', and the 'son of Cronus' (Saturn). Elyon and Zeus are the Roman Jupiter, another 'sky god' and king of the Roman pantheon. The various global pantheons are a series of gods (Astral entities) with one god that became the biblical and monotheistic 'God'. Jupiter's symbols in Rome were the eagle and sceptre. The eagle or two-headed eagle can be found in state emblems today all over the world, including the United States, Russia, Poland, Germany (see the Nazi eagle), Austria, Mexico, Liechtenstein, Czech Republic, Serbia, Montenegro, Albania, Romania, Egypt, Jordan, Syria, Iraq, and the land of the Mesopotamian gods. The sceptre has been a symbol of royal authority and power through the ages as the mace is the symbol of power in parliaments like the UK Houses of Parliament and US House of Representatives (Figs 190 and 191). The mace is the symbol of royal authority and without it neither UK

Figure 190: The Mace symbolising royal power in the UK Houses of Parliament.

Figure 191: The ubiquitous sky god eagle on the ceremonial mace of the US House of Representatives which symbolises order and authority (Saturn).

House, the Commons and Lords, can meet or pass laws and the same in most Commonwealth countries such as Canada, Australia and New Zealand. Members of parliament must pledge an oath of allegiance to the monarch to take office. You think you have *'democracy'*?? Ceremonial maces again originated in the ancient Near East as symbols of authority in Mesopotamia, Egypt, Iran/Persia, the Levant, and Arabia.

One of the UK monarch's sceptres used at coronations includes a dove which is the symbol of the goddess Queen Semiramis in Babylon (Fig 192). The dove represents in the official fairy story the 'holy ghost' in the 'Christian' trinity of God the father, the son, and the holy ghost or spirit symbolised as a dove. The Babylonian trinity was Nimrod (father god), Tammuz, the virgin-born son, and Semiramis who was symbolised as a dove. Semiramis was the 'Queen of Heaven' and 'virgin mother' and her Babylonian titles were transferred to the figure of Mother Mary in the Roman-produced Gospels. Sceptres have been the symbol of power since ancient times. The power is delegated by the 'gods', hence the 'Divine Right To Rule' (Fig 193). This means that sceptres and maces symbolise that royalty and parliaments rule on behalf of the ultimate power – the 'gods'. The British coronation is awash with Middle Eastern and Mesopotamian symbolism including the anointing with oil, all the paraphernalia, and the music Zadok the Priest composed by Handel. Zadok is claimed to be the priest who anointed King Solomon. 1 Kings 1:39-40 says:

Figure 192: The King Charles coronation as he holds the Semiramis dove sceptre. Another fish hat on view.

Figure 193: Hammurabi, sixth king of the First Dynasty of Babylon, standing before the seated Mesopotamian sun god Shamash holding the sceptre. Hammurabi claimed to have been granted his rule by the gods.

And Zadok the priest took a horn of oil out of the tabernacle, and anointed

Solomon. And they blew the trumpet; and all the people said, God save king Solomon. And all the people came up after him, and the people piped with pipes, and rejoiced with great joy, so that the earth rent with the sound of them.

Words to this effect have been used since the coronation of King Edgar at Bath Abbey in 973 AD. Then there's the Sovereign's Orb, a golden and jewelled ball with a gem-encrusted cross, which symbolises that the monarch's power is derived from God. Ah, but what is this 'God'? It all begins to make sense when you realise the reason for royalty from the start. Ancient Mesopotamian accounts tell how hybrids from the union of the gods and humans became the kings ruling on behalf of the gods. Kings were described as 'changelings' (shapeshifters). These were – *are* – the hybrid 'demi-gods'. Ancient tablets say the gods introduced the whole concept of 'kingship' through 'royal' and 'aristocratic' bloodlines representing the gods on Earth. Are we getting the picture? No wonder so much royal imagery and symbolism relates to serpents.

Most populations began to reject rule by 'royal' (reptilian-human) bloodline succession and the gods transferred gofer power to politics controlled from the shadows, but the deal is the same. Look behind the Speaker in the US House of Representatives and you'll see the Roman symbol, the Latin fascis (fasces), or 'bundle', which was the power

Figure 194: The Roman fascis (fasces) symbol and the origin of the term 'fascism'.

Figure 195: The fascist bundle symbol behind the Speaker in the US House of Representatives.

symbol in ancient Rome and goes back further (Fig 194). It is the symbol from which the term 'fascism' derives and how appropriate that it should be displayed on Capitol Hill (Fig 195). As with royalty, so the priesthood, with their ritual bits and pieces, uniforms, colours, and the mitres of the fish god religions. It all originates long, long, before the

Christian Church. See my book *The Perception Deception* for highly detailed background to the symbolism and what it means. The interdimensional Elohim 'gods' operated openly long, long, ago and then withdrew to manipulate through their Global Cult of hybrid agents and gofers. The 'gods' that openly controlled in the seen have since continued their control from the unseen – as I have been saying since the 1990s to the sound of ridicule and dismissal.

Earth 'reset'

Sumerians are credited with the invention of writing in the form of cuneiform script. Cuneiform is the earliest known writing system which wasn't deciphered until the 19th century with the discovery of the 'Behistun Inscriptions' in Persia/Iran which were to cuneiform what the Rosetta Stone was to Egyptian hieroglyphics. Cuneiform (from a Latin root meaning 'wedge-shaped') was later adapted by other Mesopotamian languages and continued for more than 3,000 years (Fig 196). Cracking the cuneiform code was vital to unlocking the secrets of what I call the Sumerian Tablets although they include those from other Mesopotamian cultures like the Akkadians. Sumerian accounts describe flying serpents and dragons (reptilian entities flying in craft?). The Bible uses dragon and serpent interchangeably along with cultural legends

Figure 196: An example of cuneiform script.

across the world. Hundreds of thousands of clay tablets and fragments in the cuneiform language unearthed by archaeologists in the 19th and 20th centuries include a list of kings going back a vast period before the deluge. It is so obvious reading the content that the stories of 'Israelites' in the Old Testament are relocated tales from Mesopotamia with different names for the characters. Remember how the US army during the war on Iraq in 2003 systematically allowed the museums to be invaded by mobs who smashed and stole exhibits gathered from ancient Mesopotamia. They were allowing history to be destroyed and stolen into private collections to hide the truth and the same with all the other ancient sites destroyed by war and targeted demolition. You can understand the lack of archaeological evidence in Israel and Egypt for biblical events when their origins were in Sumer and much earlier before the cataclysms and flood.

There is no better example than *The Epic of Gilgamesh* which is described as the first-known written work of literature and tells in the Sumerian Tablets the story of the Great Flood that was later repeated in plagiarised form with 'Noah' in the starring role. The *Epic* also tells the tale of Enkidu and Shamhat which has a clear correlation with the later Adam and Eve in Genesis. Both involve a god creating a human from soil/earth who lives in nature before being tempted by a woman, covering his nakedness, and leaving his home which is called in the again plagiarised biblical version, the Garden of Eden. *The Epic of Gilgamesh* even includes a snake stealing a plant of immortality from the 'Adam' character. Noah's flood story is told in Genesis 6-9 and the Koran of Islam. 'God' is not happy with the 'evil' humans he created and seeks to destroy them with a Great Flood throughout the Earth. God warns Noah of the coming deluge and tells him to build an ark to save his family and animals to rebuild the world after the flood. The pre-translated version has one of the *Elohim* telling Noah all of this.

Noah offered burnt offerings to God who made a covenant with him and mankind that he would never instigate another global flood which was nice of him, really. God told Noah that a 'rainbow in the cloud' shall be 'the sign of the covenant between Me and the earth'. From this nonsense comes the seven universal Noahide Laws planned to be imposed on non-Jews thanks to the fantasy that Noah seeded all of humanity and subsequent nations in the wake of the flood. If it wasn't so tragic, it would be funny. You have the story of the dove released by Noah that returns with a 'freshly plucked olive leaf' that confirmed the waters were receding. The Noah narrative is repeated in the Rome-compiled Gospels as you would expect with Christianity created as an Old Testament continuation. The Gospels of Matthew and Luke have Jesus relating the coming Day of Judgement to the Noah flood. This is Matthew 24:37-39 in the Names of God Bible:

> When the Son of Man comes again, it will be exactly like the days of Noah. In the days before the flood, people were eating, drinking, and getting married until the day that Noah went into the ship. They were not aware of what was happening until the flood came and swept all of them away. That is how it will be when the Son of Man comes again.

The Roman Gospel writers with a big tongue in a big cheek related this coming 'Son of Man' to the Flavian Titus who at the time the Gospels were written had *already* destroyed Jerusalem and proved Jesus right that people would know nothing until the coming of the Son of Man – Titus – on the Day of Judgement. Now we shall look at *The Epic of Gilgamesh*, the earliest version dated from around 2100 BC, which tells the story of Gilgamesh, 'demi-god' (hybrid) king of Uruk. Gilgamesh interacts with powerful and often unjust gods and goddesses and goes in search of a man known as Utnapishtim, 'a king of the ancient city of Shuruppak', who survived a great flood by building a boat and was granted eternal life by the gods. Utnapishtim is also called Ziusudra, Atra-hasis, and Uta-napishtim in other Mesopotamian versions. Sumerian Tablets describe the arrival of gods they named the Anunna or Anunnaki who were led on Earth by Enlil aided by his brother Enki. Remember Anu, the 'sky god'? He was said to be their 'father' in overall charge of the mission.

This is a common theme and the legendary Zulu high shaman or 'sanusi', Credo Mutwa, told me of the Zulu legends of Wowane and Mpanku who were reptilian brothers known as the 'water brothers'. This matches the symbolism of Enki (Ea to the Babylonians), who was symbolised in Mesopotamia as 'the god of fresh waters'. It is likely that the Old Testament story of the brothers Cain and Abel was taken from the Mesopotamian Anunnaki brothers Enlil and Enki. Genesis claims that Eve gave birth to Cain and Abel with Cain a farmer and Abel a shepherd. They both made offerings to 'the Lord', but 'the Lord' did not favour what Cain offered, the ungrateful sod. Cain was so miffed he attacked Abel and killed him. Enlil and Enki did not get on according to the Sumerian Tablets which also describe disputes between farmers and shepherds. All 'Hebrew' roads lead to Mesopotamia. Sumerian Tablets and Zulu accounts describe how the invading and controlling force from the skies instigated the cataclysmic events that brought the flood. The 'Noah' character can be found all over the world as Deucalion (Greece), Manu (India), Fo-hi (China), Xisthros (Persia), Nota (Mexico), and others. Sumerian Tablets tell how the god Enki warned a human 'priest-king' called Ziusudra (Utnapishtim in the *Epic*) about the coming deluge. He told him to build a huge ship to survive the coming flood and to take aboard 'beasts and birds'. The Bible relates this to the Hebrew people when they are nowhere mentioned in the original accounts from which the biblical version was derived. Mesopotamian and Zulu accounts also agree that the gods came to force humans as slaves to mine for gold and there is certainly evidence of gold mining in Africa 100,000 years ago.

Squabbling 'gods'

Ancient Mesopotamian accounts record the wars and disagreements between the gods about the flood and how intelligent humans were allowed to be. Enlil and Enki did not agree on this with Enki much more supportive of the human cause. The story of the snake in the Garden of Eden who wanted to expand the perceptions of Adam and Eve fits the bill of the reptilian Enki seeking to genetically progress humans despite the resistance from his brother Enlil (although still within the overall

Who (or What) is the Biblical God?

desire for control of humans). We have Prometheus in Greek mythology who defied the Olympian gods led by Zeus by taking fire from them and handing it to humanity as knowledge, technology, and civilisation. Zeus punishes Prometheus with eternal torment as he is bound to a rock with an eagle (emblem of Zeus) sent to eat his liver which then grows back overnight to be eaten each day. Some Prometheus myths link him to creating humans from clay (like Enki) and the flood story (like Enki). It is extraordinary that the whole concept of 'original sin' comes from this ejection by 'God' from the Garden of Eden because of a Bible in which 'God' is translated from 'gods' and the singular 'God' is exposed as interdimensional entities.

I came across the catastrophic events on Earth right at the start of my conscious awakening in 1990. I saw that the geological and biological record absolutely supports these accounts from across the world and they fit with the legends of Atlantis and Mu/Lemuria, two vast continents said to have sunk beneath the Atlantic and Pacific Oceans around 11,500 to 13,000 years ago. Tales of global cataclysm can be found in Mesopotamia, Egypt, Greece, Arcadia, Rome, Scandinavia, Germany, Lithuania, Transylvania, Turkey, Persia, China, New Zealand, Siberia, Burma, Korea, Taiwan, the Philippines, Sumatra, in Islamic lore, Celtic lore, and among native peoples throughout North, South and Central America, Africa, Asia, Australia and the Pacific. They describe a great heat that boiled the sea; mountains breathing fire; a darkened sky; raining down of blood, ice and rock; the Earth flipping over; the sky 'falling'; the rising and sinking of land; the loss of great continents; the coming of the ice; and a gigantic tsunami that swept across the planet. Ancient maps have been found drawn on stones that accurately portray known coastlines and yet also include enormous landmasses in the Atlantic and Pacific where Atlantis and Mu are said to have been.

Christopher Columbus was not 'looking for India' when he found the Americas. He knew basically where he was going because of the information held in the Cult networks from long before. Columbus headed out in 1492 sponsored by Catholic monarchs and only a few years later came the Piri Reis Map of 1513 which includes North and South America, Greenland, and it is alleged Antarctica which was not discovered (officially) until 1820. Piri Reis was a prominent admiral in the Turkish navy, and this gave him access to non-public sources to follow his passion for maps and map-making. He said that he met a sailor who claimed he had been one of the pilots working for Christopher Columbus on his journeys to the Caribbean and the Americas between 1492 and 1504. The pilot had said that he possessed the map of the world that Columbus had been following. Official history claims that it was pure luck that Hernán Cortés, leader of the Spanish conquest of the Aztecs in Central America, arrived on the same day in

1519 that Aztec prophecy said would see the return of their feathered-serpent god, Quetzalcoatl. Cortés has been described as being 'among history's luckiest conquistadors'; but there was nothing lucky about it. He turned up on the day that he knew would be most likely to make the Aztecs mistake him for Quetzalcoatl. It worked and before the Aztecs realised their mistake the situation was irretrievable.

Truth in plain sight

The Earth landscape reflects the cataclysm and flood that ended the global society that went before. Anyone who has been to the Grand Canyon in Arizona and looked down to see the Colorado River in the distance must surely laugh at the claim that the canyon has been scored out by the river. The Grand Canyon is 277 miles long, up to 18 miles wide and reaches a depth of more than a mile. Sure, it was the river what did it. Across the world you find scattered rocks known as 'erratics' with often no connection to the surrounding bedrock. How did they all get there? Massive buildings, pyramids, and advanced architecture have been found in oceans that would once have been above the waters including a pyramid and other monuments found 25 metres under the sea off the Japanese island of Yonaguni that has stone streets and a stadium/Coliseum-type structure (Fig 197). Anyone sceptical about a global society could maybe explain how these

Figure 197: The submerged city just off the Japanese island of Yonaguni.

'coincidences' came about (Figs 198, 199, and 200).

One map that includes where Atlantis and Lemuria are said to have been located was found by gold miners in Ecuador along with 350 other artefacts which don't appear to fit with any known South American culture and are estimated to be thousands of years old. The stone map includes an eye placed in the Middle East close to Saudi Arabia. The eye, or all-seeing eye, is a prime symbol used to this day by the secret societies and families behind the global Control System and a radiant and shining eye is often used in the symbol of a pyramid with the capstone raised above the main structure – as with the image on the US dollar bill. How extraordinary that among those hundreds of ancient

Who (or What) is the Biblical God?

Figure 198: The Jewish Menorah symbol, the seven branch version described in the Bible and claimed to have been used in the Jerusalem temple.

Figure 199: The same symbol in different forms around the ancient world.

Figure 200: What a coincidence.

Figure 201: The Global Cult symbol of the pyramid and all-seeing eye alongside one thousands of years old found by Ecuador miners with the same 13 levels. The eye illuminates in ultraviolet or black light.

artefacts found in the goldmine in Ecuador is a virtually identical image of the same pyramid and all-seeing eye. Not only that, when the pyramid is placed in ultraviolet light, or 'black light', the eye shines (Fig 201). Many ancient texts describe entities with light shining from their eyes and they are often referred to as the 'shining ones'.

Mystery solved

The interdimensional Astral 'gods' are described under many and various names around the world, but the themes are the same be it in Mesopotamia, Egypt, Israel/Judah, South Africa, Europe, the Americas, Asia, Australia – everywhere. The American TV show, *Ancient Aliens*, has found enough material to explore the subject for more than 20 series. We no longer need to puzzle over how the Giza pyramids and Sphinx were constructed thousands of years ago or all the other fantastic buildings and walls that I have seen throughout the world that we would struggle to replicate today. The Roman Temple of Jupiter in Baalbek, Lebanon, formerly Heliopolis or the 'City of the Sun, includes stones weighing more than a thousand tons – up to 1,650-tons – and that's more than three Boeing 747s. Some are believed to date from long before the Romans, possibly even to 11,000 years ago, because the Roman temple was built on much older foundations.

Stone spheres in the Diquis Delta in Costa Rica are near-perfect orbs weighing up to 15 tons and some more than two metres across. No one has a credible idea how the ancients made them. They are dated to the Diquis culture from about 700 to 1530 AD. I bet they were made a lot earlier than that. Amazing structures abound around the world, but were built by primitive people? Crazy stuff. They were built with the technology of the gods that was way in advance of what we have even now. Highly advanced technology described today by those *genuinely* abducted by 'extraterrestrials' was the technology used to build these structures. Are we surprised that the ancients thought these Astral Elohim entities were 'gods' when they arrived 'out of nowhere' with miraculous technology that could do miraculous feats? Take as an example the 'cargo cults' in New Guinea and other islands when the people believed American troops were gods with their aircraft and the goods they brought during World War Two while fighting in the Pacific arena. Rituals and symbols were practiced after the war hoping for the American 'gods' to return. Why would the ancients be any different?

Ezekiel's revelation

Biblical texts attributed to alleged Hebrew prophet Ezekiel are often quoted as confirmation that he is describing advanced technology while apparently in Babylon during the period of exile in the 6th century BC. The same theme can be found around the world with ancient societies describing technology capable of amazing feats amid an apparently primitive people. We have been left the result in structures that can simply not be explained by what appeared to be possible at that point in history. I would even take this forward to the building of the great cathedrals that tell the same story of techniques that defy the technology of the time. There is a lot more to know about them and their origin, too. Famous cathedrals of Europe can be traced to the Knights Templar secret society which remains today a major element of the Global Cult. The Book of Ezekiel claims that the prophet was from the priestly class and describes his 'divine' experiences with 'God' that sound very much like encounters with the 'gods' and flying craft. This is from Ezekiel 1:4-28:

Who (or What) is the Biblical God?

> As I looked, a stormy wind came out of the north: a great cloud with brightness around it and fire flashing forth continually, and in the middle of the fire, something like gleaming amber. In the middle of it was something like four living creatures.
>
> This was their appearance: they were of human form. Each had four faces, and each of them had four wings. Their legs were straight, and the soles of their feet were like the sole of a calf's foot; and they sparkled like burnished bronze. Under their wings on their four sides, they had human hands.

Great clouds, pillars of fire, and blinding lights are a feature of global tales of the gods. Ezekiel says the 'living creatures' had the face of a human being but then describes them as having 'the face of a lion on the right side, the face of an ox on the left side, and the face of an eagle; such were their faces'. Their wings were spread out above with each creature having two wings which touched the wing of another, while two covered their bodies. Gods were depicted with wings to symbolise their ability to fly as with an Akkadian portrayal of the goddess Inanna (Ishtar) from between 2350-2150 BC (Fig 202). Ezekiel said that in the middle of the living creatures was something that 'looked like burning coals of fire, like torches moving to and fro among the living creatures'. The fire was bright, and lightning issued from the fire. The living creatures darted to and fro, like a flash of lightning:

Figure 202: Flying gods and goddesses.

> As I looked at the living creatures, I saw a wheel on the earth beside the living creatures, one for each of the four of them. As for the appearance of the wheels and their construction: their appearance was like the gleaming of beryl; and the four had the same form, their construction being something like a wheel within a wheel. When they moved, they moved in any of the four directions without veering as they moved.
>
> Their rims were tall and awesome, for the rims of all four were full of eyes all round. When the living creatures moved, the wheels moved beside them; and when the living creatures rose from the earth, the wheels rose. Wherever the spirit would go, they went, and the wheels rose along with them; for the spirit of the living creatures was in the wheels. When they moved, the others

moved; when they stopped, the others stopped; and when they rose from the earth, the wheels rose along with them; for the spirit of the living creatures was in the wheels.

Over the heads of these creatures was something like a dome, shining like crystal, spread out above their heads. Under the dome their wings were stretched out straight, one towards another. When the creatures moved, he heard 'the sound of their wings like the sound of mighty waters, like the thunder of the Almighty, a sound of tumult like the sound of an army'. When they stopped, they let down their wings:

> And above the dome over their heads there was something like a throne, in appearance like sapphire; and seated above the likeness of a throne was something that seemed like a human form. Upwards from what appeared like the loins I saw something like gleaming amber, something that looked like fire enclosed all round; and downwards from what looked like the loins I saw something that looked like fire, and there was a splendour all round.

> Like the bow in a cloud on a rainy day, such was the appearance of the splendour all round. This was the appearance of the likeness of the glory of the Lord. When I saw it, I fell on my face, and I heard the voice of someone speaking.

'Ezekiel' recounts how he was taken up in a craft that he was describing:

> Then the spirit lifted me up, and as the glory of the Lord rose from its place, I heard behind me the sound of loud rumbling; it was the sound of the wings of the living creatures brushing against one another, and the sound of the wheels beside them, that sounded like a loud rumbling. The spirit lifted me up and bore me away.

The 'glory of the Lord rose from its place'? Ezekiel uses the terms Kavod and Ruach interchangeably when describing what he saw which adds to the contention that the words, translated as 'spirit' and 'glory', refer to craft. We hear of another experience:

> It stretched out the form of a hand and took me by a lock of my head; and the spirit lifted me up between earth and heaven, and brought me in visions of God to Jerusalem, to the entrance of the gateway of the inner court that faces north, to the seat of the image of jealousy, which provokes to jealousy. And the glory of the God of Israel was there, like the vision that I had seen in the valley.

Former Vatican translator Mauro Biglino emphasises that the word translated as 'vision' here really means to see something tangible with one's own eyes. Ezekiel 1 in the Names of God Bible has the prophet saying: 'On the fifth day of the fourth month in the thirtieth year, while I was living among the exiles by the Chebar River, the sky opened, and I saw visions [tangible with one's own eyes] from Elohim.' Then 'the power of Yahweh came over Ezekiel'. There are many more descriptions in the Book of Ezekiel which is worth reading if you are interested in the subject. The text says in Ezekiel 11:22-25:

> Then the cherubim lifted up their wings, with the wheels beside them; and the glory of the God of Israel was above them. And the glory of the Lord ascended from the middle of the city and stopped on the mountain east of the city. The spirit lifted me up and brought me in a vision by the spirit of God into Chaldea, to the exiles. Then the vision that I had seen left me. And I told the exiles all things that the Lord had shown me.

What is the real identity of the biblical 'angels' (from the Greek 'angelos' meaning 'messengers'), 'cherubim', 'seraphim' ('fiery flying serpents'), and similar groupings widely described? Sceptics try to explain away the Ezekiel texts without an extraterrestrial concept as did NASA engineer Josef F. Blumrich until he decided to look deeper after a meeting with the father of ancient astronaut theory, Swiss author Erich von Däniken, with his ground-breaking 1968 book, *Chariots of the Gods*. Not everything von Däniken wrote stands up to scrutiny, but he made the pivotal contribution of opening the subject to widespread debate. It seems that von Däniken met Blumrich in the 1970s when they discussed the Ezekiel 'vision'. Blumrich's first response to von Däniken's interpretation was to dismiss the idea that advanced technology was being depicted. This did not last long. Blumrich went on to write the book, *The Spaceships of Ezekiel*, in which he said that the words could indeed be describing with the 'wheels within wheels' an advanced craft. Blumrich patented a design for an 'omnidirectional wheel' based on the Ezekiel passages. He said: 'Seldom has a total defeat been so rewarding, so fascinating, and so delightful.' Bible translator Mauro Biglino highlights other ancient texts that support the Ezekiel theme including the Book of Enoch:

> … It should be remembered that twenty-three kinds of flying chariots are described in the Book of Enoch. Enoch travelled a lot; he was initiated into astronomy mysteries, the heavens' secrets, et cetera. In other words, he received scientific knowledge that he had to record in writing for the benefit of humankind.

Or perhaps it was to advance the agenda for humanity designed to benefit themselves.

Indian flying craft

Many ancient descriptions can be interpreted as portraying advanced technology by people who often had no idea what they were and linked them to 'God' and the 'divine' purely from the amazing things they could do. Hinduism is still a multi-god religion that embraces reincarnation, and India has a comprehensive written history of tens of millions of manuscripts going back to the ancient Sanskrit language. Most have not been translated into English yet. India also excelled in mathematics as far back as 1200 BC. Ancient Indian accounts describe flying machines 6,000 years ago known as 'Vimanas' (also 'Ratha' and 'Astras') which they discuss in detail. They were 'chariots of the gods', even 'flying palaces', moving through the sky at great speed and used in battles between gods. Vimanas were big and small and different shapes. Some were classic saucers with others shaped like a cigar as with many modern 'UFO' sightings. They could operate underwater or fly to the Moon and out into space and were associated with war and destruction. There are manuals that detail guidance for how to pilot these craft. Vimana means aircraft in some Indian languages today to emphasise how they are interpreted.

Dr Ruth Reyna at India's University of Chandigarh caused a stir in 2001 when she translated an ancient manuscript written in the 4th century BC that was discovered by the Chinese in Tibet. The *India Times* reported her findings which included directions for building interstellar spaceships called Astras with anti-gravity propulsion – 'a centrifugal force strong enough to counteract all gravitational pull'. This was likened to the concept of 'laghima', a Sanskrit word meaning 'absence of weight'. Hindu Yogis say that through meditation laghima can make the body so light that it can float or levitate. Reyna said the texts describe how the craft can be hidden through a technique of invisibility. This is important and a theme I have picked up many times about the ability to cast an energetic field that prevents humans from seeing them. A former director of the International Academy of Sanskrit Research said they had documents from thousands of years ago dealing with aeronautics and building multi-decked craft for civilian use and war. There is also a connection to Atlantis. Flying craft named in the texts as Vailixi are connected to the Asvins which some researchers associate with Atlanteans in the Indian accounts.

An insider speaks

I was sent a video as I was completing the book about Spanish former Jesuit Catholic priest Salvador Freixedo (1923-2019) who was born into an extremely religious family in which his brother was also a Jesuit and his sister a nun. Freixedo became a Jesuit at aged 16 and stayed for 30 years working in many countries including America. He founded Christian movements in Latin America before seeing through the nonsense and dogma. The Jesuit Order excluded him after his 1968 book *My Church Sleeps* which was banned in Spain. He began to study the 'paranormal' and the connection between religion and the worship of non-human entities manipulating humanity from another dimension. Sound familiar? He concluded that those worshipped as 'God' and 'gods' were really 'invisible farmers' feeding off human energy. This is what happens once you look at religion and 'holy books' anew with an open mind and open eyes. Freixedo became a prolific author and spoke at UFO conferences around the world expounding his belief that 'suffering, wars and oppressive religions could be part of a control system designed by intelligences that not only manipulate us but may have lived among us for centuries'. He highlighted 'gods' across the world described by the ancients that subjugated the population through fear, forced obedience, and sacrifice. The former Catholic believer highlighted the Old Testament God Yahweh and the demands for mass extermination of 'enemies' and brutal punishments for those who worshipped other gods (Elohim). The video, on the *Ethereal Wisdom* YouTube channel, went on:

> What most caught Freixedo's attention were the detailed instructions given by Yahweh for sacrificial rituals. Which part of the animals should be burned? How the ritual should be performed. What should be offered? All of this, he thought, was not symbolic, but functional. It generated a specific energy the suffering and fear of the animal, the surrender and obedience of the devotee that this entity used for some specific purpose, perhaps as a form of nourishment.
>
> But Yahweh would not be an isolated case. Other ancient cultures described in the Bible also worshipped deities that demanded blood sacrifices. The same occurred in Mesoamerica, where the Aztecs offered beating hearts to their gods to feed them and maintain cosmic order. Why this global coincidence? What did these entities gain from pain, blood and fire? Were they not merely rituals, but a form of food?

I said earlier that Zulu shaman Credo Mutwa told me how their legends said the reptilian 'gods' brought cannibalism into the world. Freixedo asked what if these fraudulent 'gods' never left and still operate from the shadows (100 percent they do). He asked if they could be behind the present world of wars, economic crises, and global fear which was slavery disguised as progress (100 percent they are). 'Yesterday they appeared as gods, angels or demons', the video said. 'Today they appear as ships and extraterrestrial beings.' The 'gods' hadn't changed. Humans had. Salvador Freixedo had realised the real source of human control and how the Bible and other 'holy books' tell the story while hiding the truth behind the fusion of the many 'gods' into one 'God'. Multi-deity religions like Hinduism worship as 'gods' what are really Astral manipulators and energetic vampires.

'History' has been fabricated to delude us. The pre-flood, pre-cataclysmic, world was not primitive in its ruling hierarchy – anything but. There was high technology which explains the scale of the buildings, descriptions of advanced craft, and finds of technological phenomena that have baffled the 'experts' with the question: How could a primitive people have done this? *They* didn't. The 'gods' did.

CHAPTER 20

Dividing the World

In every country and in every age, the priest has been hostile to liberty.
He is always in alliance with the despot, abetting his abuses in return
for protection to his own.
Thomas Jefferson

The evil Old Testament tyrant 'Yahweh' must be seen in the context of each subordinate god in the Anunnaki/Elohim hierarchy designated a region or city-state and the loosh-generating battles between them.

Bible translator Mauro Biglino with his knowledge of languages has established by retranslation of biblical texts, and returning to older texts, that the chief god Elyon (Anu/Zeus/Jupiter etc.) designated different lands to the 'children of the Elohim'. They ruled on behalf of Elyon these different regions of the Earth and wars ever since have largely been wars between the gods via human dupes. Think of the loosh this has produced and all orchestrated by the chief god Elyon who can knock heads together when it gets out of hand to threaten the agenda. This whole Archontic hierarchy of control and division is the emanation of Yaldabaoth consciousness that perfectly reflects the mentality involved. Yaldabaoth is at war with itself via subordinate entities to generate the loosh that drives the whole system. Would it not make sense if the Elohim 'Yahweh' was still behind the actions and wars of the Sabbateans that control Israel? Would this not explain the genocide of the Palestinians and be a coordinating force of the Sabbateans since the time of Sabbatai Zevi (and before under other names)? Would it not explain the Sabbatean infiltration of the world with such small a number?

Ancient Greek philosopher Plato (about 428/423 to 348/347 BC) wrote about this division of lands and people by the gods in his dialogue, *Critias*, in which he tells the story of how the island kingdom Atlantis sought to conquer Athens but failed. Plato said the gods divided the Earth into different territories which were assigned by choosing lots to prevent arguments. Deuteronomy 32:8 in the Names of God Bible says: 'When Elyon gave nations their land, when he divided the descendants of Adam ...' The King James Version replaces Elyon with 'Most High'. The Old Testament designates Yahweh to the 'Chosen People' and claims the tyrant to be the 'only god'. This has had devastating consequences for the world with its demand for unquestioning obedience. Yahweh was the jealous god who threatened to destroy the Israelites and Judeans if they did not worship him and no one else. The Ten Commandments, which some scholars compare with Mesopotamian and other laws and treaties, are claimed to have been given by Yahweh to Moses. The number one law at the top is: 'I am the Lord your God, who brought you out of the land of Egypt [he didn't], out of the house of bondage. You shall have no other gods before Me.' This is followed by these two 'commandments':

> You shall not make for yourself a carved image – any likeness of anything that is in heaven above, or that is in the earth beneath, or that is in the water under the earth; you shall not bow down to them nor serve them. For I, the LORD your God, am a jealous God, visiting the iniquity of the fathers upon the children to the third and fourth generations of those who hate Me, but showing mercy to thousands, to those who love Me and keep My commandments. (Exodus 20:4-6)

> You shall not take the name of the LORD your God in vain, for the LORD will not hold him guiltless who takes His name in vain. (Exodus 20:7)

Next comes the law to remember the Sabbath day and keep it holy, for it is the day of 'the LORD your God' who 'blessed the Sabbath day and hallowed it'. This is why orthodox Jews sit in the dark every Saturday and eat a bit of cold as they say with the oven out of action. Honouring your mother and father is another demand no matter how horrible and abusive they may be, and I don't see any mention of 'Thou shalt not commit paedophilia' which is rampant among many religious believers. We do have 'You shall not murder' which is ironic, really, coming from a cold-blooded killer like 'Yahweh'. Yet again Elohim is translated as the singular God in the Commandments' narrative while the Names of God Bible opens the sequence with 'I am Yahweh your Elohim'. Yahweh is a super-psychopath and here you have the mentality behind Israel and its leaders like Netanyahu that mirror the same Yahweh/Yaldabaoth psyche and will be terrified of retribution if he doesn't follow the script. You can see why he connected the mass murder of Palestinians to 'Yahweh's' demand for the slaughter of the Old Testament Amalekite 'enemies of the Israelites'. Netanyahu quoted Deuteronomy 25:17, which has Yahweh saying: 'Remember what the Amalekites did to you along your way from Egypt.' He said that in 2023. Confirmation of the connection in Netanyahu's child-like mind comes with this demand by Yahweh in Samuel 15-3: 'Now go and smite Amalek, utterly destroy all that they have, and spare them not; but kill both man and woman, infant, ox and sheep, camel and donkey.' Netanyahu always obeys his God.

Keep them ignorant!

I have said that Sumerian accounts describe how Elohim-human hybrids became kings to rule for the gods as kingship was established. Today these hybrid bloodlines operate mostly with dark suits rather than coronets. The principle remains the same with Reptilian-human hybrids and other operatives representing the Astral gods within human society. Hybrids have inbred abilities to see further into the simulation field than the usual visible light range and can see what most people cannot. Their plan from the start has been to keep it that way. Ancient accounts on every continent explain how the gods were concerned about letting humans become too intelligent and manipulated the body to that end. They also wished to maintain them in a perceptual control system called 'guilt' through the concept of 'original sin'. We have the profuse use of guilt by the Roman Church and other religions which are representatives of the 'gods' in the human realm. Yet Mauro Biglino writes in *Gods of the Bible*: 'A careful reading of the biblical text can only lead to the conclusion that original sin is a *theological invention*.' The Mayan *Popol Vuh* describes how humans were genetically manipulated to suppress their vision and awareness. It first features the early efforts of the gods to create updated humans and how many failed before they achieved what they wanted. Notice the continuing use of the plural 'us'. The texts quote the gods as saying:

> 'Let us try again! Already dawn draws near: Let us make him who shall nourish and sustain us! What shall we do to be invoked, in order to be remembered on earth? We have already tried with our first creations, our first creatures; but we could not make them praise and venerate us. So, then, let us try to make obedient, respectful beings who will nourish and sustain us.' Thus, they spoke.

This is a common theme – the need to manipulate humans psychologically and it's still going on. The Mesoamerican texts take the same line as Genesis and many others in that humans were made of earth, but there were challenges for what are called the 'engineers': 'The Creator and the Maker said: "Let us try again because our creatures will not be able to walk nor multiply. Let us consider this," they said.' The gods eventually decided to start again: 'Then they broke up and destroyed their work and their creation. And they said: "What shall we do to perfect it, in order that our worshippers, our invokers, will be successful?"' They go on to produce a prototype human they are pleased with until they considered the possible consequences of creating a being that was too intelligent and visually far-seeing. The *Popol Vuh* translation says:

But the gods were not wholly pleased with this thing; Heaven they thought had overshot its mark; these men were too perfect; knew, understood, and saw too much. Therefore, there was counsel again in heaven: What shall we do with man now? It is not good, this that we see; these are as gods; they would make themselves equal with us; lo, they know all things, great and small.

Let us now contract their sight, so that they may see only a little of the surface of the earth and be content. Thereupon the Heart of Heaven breathed a cloud over the pupil of the eyes of men, and a veil came over it as when one breathes on the face of a mirror; thus was the globe of the eye darkened; neither was that which was far off clear to it anymore, but only that which was near.

What an explanation this is for why humans can see only the narrow band of frequency that scientists call visible light. I thought immediately when I realised how little humans can see that this had to have been imposed on purpose. There would seem to have been compromises between the gods that wished humans to have more potential and those that wanted them with the intelligence only to be bound in slavery. Both views ultimately desired control. It was a matter of scale. It could well be that a compromise was to allow more potential intelligence, but to so squeeze visible acuity that the gods could no longer be seen. They still come and go in the human space. It's just that we can't see them like the ancients could with a much wider range of visual frequency. The Elohim lived very long lives it would seem but were not immortal. Their hybrid intermediaries ('patriarchs' etc.) are said to have lived enormous lifetimes and that may be exaggeration, or it may have been the inherited genetic traits of the Elohim/Anunnaki. Whatever the background, human lifetimes began to shorten, eventually dramatically. I guess the longer you live in the material world the better chance you have of seeing through all the simulated perceptual bullshit.

The suppressed potential of the human brain can be seen with savant syndrome, which is mostly triggered by autism, a brain injury such as a serious bang on the head, or effects on the central nervous system. Somehow this can unlock some of the blocks the gods have imposed on human brain activity. The result is staggering to see in the gifts that are liberated in fields such as art, memory, maths, and music. British artist Stephen Wiltshire is an outstanding example with his extraordinary ability to view whole cities like Rome from the air just once and then draw them in accurate detail. Brain information processing potential has been systematically blocked by the interdimensional 'gods' in the interests of control. Brain plasticity in which the brain changes according to the information it receives can be another albeit longer-term means to bypass the blocks by allowing expanded consciousness to enter your field and rewire your brain. The plan to connect the brain to artificial intelligence is designed to stop this. The level of AI involved is simply a connection to the 'gods' so they can make you think whatever they choose.

Muslim – 'One who submits'

I looked at the history of Islam and found the same recurring sequence with a hero they call Muhammad for which there is no credible contemporary evidence or record. Written works like the Koran appeared well after his death and Muhammad biographies took far longer. This is the official timeline: Muhammad, born in 570, was visited by the angel Gabriel who took him on a 'night journey' on a winged 'horse' to Jerusalem and Allah. The Koran was then revealed to him by the angel Gabriel on behalf of Allah between about 610 and his death in 632. The Koran began to be written down in 652, some 20 years after Muhammad departed, and compiled from earlier fragments and people who memorised what Muhammad had told them. The Koran was the latest 'word of God' and I must say he does seem to go around the houses to get his message across – 'fragments and people who remembered what Muhammad told them'? The widely used Koran today, the Cairo version standardised by the Egyptian government, was not completed until 1924.

The first biography of Muhammad's life did not appear until a book by Ibn Isḥāq who died 133 years after Muhammad in 765. This book *The Life of God's Messenger* was according to *Britannica* 'a compilation of autonomous reports about specific events that took place during the life of Muhammad and also prior to it, which Ibn Isḥāq arranged into what he deemed to be their correct chronological order and to which he added his own comments'. It's hardly unimpeachable evidence, is it? *Britannica* notes that the fact that such biographical narratives about Muhammad come only in texts dating from the 8th or 9th century, or even later, 'is bound to raise the problem of how confident one can be in the sīrah [Muhammad's life and work] literature's claim to relay accurate historical information'. Just a little bit. Even then Ibn Isḥāq's book is lost and only parts included in the Ibn Hisham work *The Life of the Prophet*. Hisham is said to have been born in Iraq before moving to Egypt and died around 833. This is 200 years after Muhammad. The official narrative about Muhammad comes from these long-after-the-fact 'sources'. Why did it take so long? This is the same question posed to the Old and New Testament.

None of the writers who established the Islamic historical narrative came from anywhere near Mecca and Medina where the Muhammad story is set. He is said to have been born in Mecca, where parts of the Koran were revealed to him, and fled to Medina to escape persecution in Mecca from multi-god followers as he tried to preach his one-god religion. Muhammad eventually returned with 10,000 Islamic converts to seize Mecca and by that time most of Arabia became Muslim. This, I stress, is the official story. What we do know is that Islam expanded through conquest across the Middle East and beyond to create a massive Muslim empire, but was it 'Muslim' to start with or an Arabic empire? Scholars and researchers point to archaeological and historical research that casts doubt on Mecca even existing in this 'Muhammad' period – certainly on the scale described. No archaeological evidence has been found in Mecca before the 700s AD when Muhammad is said to have died in 632. Mecca did not appear on a map of the Middle East until 900.

Yet Mecca is so central to Islam that Muslims believe that Abraham and his son Ishmael were instructed by God to build the Kaaba cube which is considered to be the first place of worship to one god. The Black Stone in the Kaaba which Muslims seek to kiss on their pilgrimage to Mecca is claimed to have been given to Abraham by the ubiquitous angel Gabriel. The stories just do not add up here. Researchers highlight the geographical descriptions of Mecca in the Koran that do not fit with its landscape. They say the ancient city of Petra in modern-day Jordan aligns with the landscape descriptions. Studies of the grammatical style of the Koran have also linked the text to Northern Arabia and current day Jordan and not Mecca. I can only report these questions and people will have to reach their own conclusions with their own research.

Politically expedient?

What is certainly the case is that writers who established the Islamic narrative worked from way north of Mecca and Medina and that this is where the Abbasid caliphate or Empire was located which overthrew the Umayyad caliphate in 750 and ruled the Muslim empire until the Mongol invasion of 1258. It was when the Abbasids took over that the official history of Muhammad and Islam began to proliferate. Robert Spencer makes this point in his book *Did Muhammad Exist?*: 'The first complete biography of the prophet of Islam finally appeared during this era – nearly 150 years after the traditional date of his death.' The Abbasids would have found it very useful to unify their empire behind a single fiercely imposed religion just as other religions have been exploited in the same way. Robert Spencer makes these highly relevant points:

- No record of Muhammad's reported death in 632 appears until more than a century after that date.
- Early accounts written by the people the Arabs conquered never mention Islam, Mohammad, or the Qur'an [Koran]. They call the conquerors 'Ishmaelites', 'Saracens', 'Muhajirun', and 'Hagarians', but never 'Muslims'.
- The Arab conquerors, in their coins and inscriptions, don't mention Islam or the Qur'an for the first six decades of their conquests.
- Neither the Arabians nor the Christians and Jews in the region

Dividing the World

mention the 'Qur'an until the early 8th century.
- While the canonical Islamic account holds that Muhammad was born in Mecca, which was a thriving center for trade and pilgrimage, the extant records show that during the time Muhammad is supposed to have lived, it was not a city of any importance.
- The Qur'an contains numerous characters and stories that have been taken from Judaism, Christianity and other sources.

The last point is highly relevant in the context of the last few chapters. We have seen how New Testament Christianity was created as an outgrowth of Old Testament stories and both were in wide circulation when Islam arrived. It absorbed into its own 'holy book' biblical characters including Adam, Noah, Abraham, Isaac, Jacob, Joseph, Moses, King Saul, King David, King Solomon, Ezekiel, Elijah, Ezra, Enoch, Job, 'angels' Michael and Gabriel, Goliath, Jonah, Gog and Magog, Lot, Lot's wife, the Devil/Satan, Jesus, John the Baptist, Mother Mary and the Apostles. All these mythical characters were taken from Judaism and Christianity and absorbed into Islam. Are they any less mythical as a result? It's all so crazy. Robert Spencer writes the following in *Did Muhammad Exist?* He could have been describing what happened with all the made-up people of global religions:

> Once Muhammad was summoned, he could not be sent away. One pious legend fabricated for political purposes would lead to another, and then another, to fill in holes and address anomalies in the first; then those new stories would lead in turn to still newer ones ...

Christianity was written to appear to be a continuation of Judaism and much the same can be said of Islam which accepts Jesus as a prophet of God. It just says that the latest and most important one is Muhammad. Islam's most holy place is Mecca in Saudi Arabia with its black cube of Saturn and the alleged birthplace of Muhammad. Pre-Islamic Arabia worshipped the usual multiple gods which Islam made into one God.

From all – one (*again*)

The Mecca Kaaba cube was once where Arabians worshipped 360 different gods and one of them, Allah, appears to have evolved into the 'one-God' from the moon god, Sin (also Suen), who was worshipped throughout the Middle East, Mesopotamia (where he was known as Nanna by the Sumerians) and much wider afield. The main cult centre of Sin in Mesopotamia was Ur, the alleged birthplace of Abraham. Sin can be found in Mount *Sin*ai (Sin was the 'God of the Mountain') and in the 'Desert of Sin' through which the Israelites are supposed to have travelled after the 'escape from Egypt'. The symbol of pre-Islamic god Sin was the crescent moon that became a symbol of Islam and one of the centres of Sin worship was Mecca where he became known as 'al-ilah', or 'al-llah', and later *'Allah'*. Sin/Allah was portrayed as the 'god above all others'. Islam transformed him into the *only* God. Archaeologists have discovered many artifacts relating to a deity with a crescent moon on top of its head to symbolise the worship of the moon god (Fig 203). These finds and historical records indicate that moon god Allah married the sun goddess, and they produced three goddess daughters.

Figure 203: The crescent symbol of the moon god Sin from the 12th century BC.

I read that 'a number of sources attest the existence of a tradition in which [moon god] Sin was regarded as the sole head of the Mesopotamian pantheon or a deity equal in rank to the traditional kings of the gods, Anu and Enlil'. This would connect with what Zulu shaman Credo Mutwa told me about the southern Africa version of Enlil/Enki known in legends as Wowane and Mpanku. Credo said that Zulu accounts describe how Wowane and Mpanku brought the Moon and positioned it in an orbit around the Earth as a gigantic craft for the reptilian 'gods'. This would certainly explain the countless Moon anomalies, connections to the Moon of the reincarnation cycle, and military whistleblower accounts I have seen about the Moon being an extraterrestrial base.

Considerable influences from Hinduism and Persia can be identified in the emergence of Islam which through the usual violence and conquest fused the previous many gods into a one-God religion. What strikes me are the parallels between Yahweh and Allah in their authoritarian bloodlust. I have highlighted the horrors demanded by Yahweh and the consequences for disobedience. We have Allah saying in the Koran: 'And as for those who disbelieved, I will punish them with a severe punishment in this world and the hereafter and they will have no helpers'; 'Soon shall We cast terror into the hearts of the Unbelievers ...'; 'The punishment of those who wage war against Allah and His messenger and strive to make mischief in the land is only this, that they should be murdered or crucified or their hands and their feet should be cut off on opposite sides or they should be imprisoned'. Either the mentality of Allah is doing Yahweh impressions, or they are the same Astral entity/consciousness dividing and ruling their human slaves in pursuit of loosh and control.

People think religion is a human creation, but they are Astral creations and from there is orchestrated the whole horrific game as naivety is played off against naivety for the benefit of the 'gods'. Can we not see that Christianity, Judaism, and Islam are being used to instigate conflict and upheavals while being controlled by the same force? Does anyone think that those that rule Saudi Arabia with Islamic extremism don't know it's all a myth? Or those controlling Israel? Or Satanists who parrot Christianity in the West? I also found it amusing to see some of those seeking to dismantle the historical foundations of Islam pointing to the Bible or the New Testament as an example of a religious text that can be supported by the evidence and archaeology. Yet another example of I will question every other belief except my own. Archaeology from the *time* of Jesus can of course be found – the Gospels were based on events in that century. They are just not the events the Gospels describe. I am not saying that Muhammad didn't exist because I don't know, but where is the evidence that he was the man described by Islam? The foundation of Islam is the Koran 'dictated by Allah via the angel Gabriel' as the Old Testament is founded on what God told Abraham and Moses as the New Testament is founded on what 'Jesus' is supposed to have said and done. Anyone see a pattern here? Is it not at least worth reassessing what we believe from the distant 'past' that is allowed to dictate our whole perception of reality when clearly neither the Bible nor the Koran are the unfiltered 'word of God'?

As then, so now

Compare all that I have written here with the stupendous number of UFO sightings in modern times and people who claim to have been abducted by non-humans for genetic experimentation. This is what the ancients describe. The same is happening now as it did then, but it's done more secretly instead of out in the open. You have all the US military and Air Force whistleblowers, several of which I have spoken with, who describe how Reptilians, Greys and other non-human entities are operating in the underground bases and involved in transferring technological know-how to humans for the AI takeover. How long I have said that world governments and the Global Cult that drives the direction of human society are being controlled by non-human Astral forces. More are now starting to get that. The subject is being brought to public attention with Congressional hearings revealing suppressed information about UFO sightings and Air Force pilots witnessing craft performing manoeuvres at speeds that defy the apparent laws of physics.

We should be careful what we believe because there is a scenario in which a staged 'alien invasion' would justify the centralisation of global power to 'meet the threat'. It is also the case that some militaries, including of course the United States, have secret advanced technology that when seen most would believe must be 'alien'. That said, what is being described is what the ancients said they experienced and to ignore these common stories, ancient and modern, would be ridiculous. But many still do. I have a lot more detail on these subjects in *The Perception Deception* and *Everything You Need To Know But Have Never Been Told*. The point here is to show a common theme of multiple gods becoming one God and the rules, behaviour and beliefs being imposed from childhood to secure control, perceptual limitation, and subordination.

It is worth repeating the religion figures again in the light of this information. There are said to be 8 billion humans currently and around 5.4 billion of them identify as Christian, Muslim or Hindu – even without all the others. Multi-god Hinduism and ancient Indian tales make it most clear that we are dealing with a non-human invading force, while made-up stories, mistranslations, and calculated deceit have made it less obvious with Christianity/Judaism and Islam until you scratch away the surface, often not very deeply, to see what has been hidden from humanity for thousands of years. The consequences of the religious fakery outlined in the last five chapters have had an extraordinary impact on human control and oppression and it is the product of a non-human force that imposes its will through the illusion of gods and God via religious laws and belief systems that hold their targets in a myopia of perceptual servitude. Without the religions of the gods, we would live in a very different world by now.

Defending the indefensible

I enjoyed reading the research into biblical archaeology by Israel Finkelstein and Neil Asher Silberman, *The Bible Unearthed*, but I seriously differ with their conclusion in which they appear to indicate that it doesn't really matter that the Old Testament is not historical fact. Oh, but it *does*, because that is the way it is sold and promoted to generations of people over thousands of years. It's the same with the New Testament. *The Bible Unearthed* authors say that with the destruction of the Second Temple by the Romans in 70 AD and the rise of Christianity 'the independent power of the Bible as a formative constitution – not just a brilliant work of literature or a collection of ancient law and wisdom – proved itself'. It had been the basis for the Mishnah (the first written collection of the Jewish oral traditions) and Talmud of Rabbinic Judaism (the primary source of Jewish religious law and theology) and was recognised as the 'Old Testament' of formative Christianity. 'The consciousness of spiritual descent from Abraham and the common experience of the Exodus from bondage became a shared mindset for ever-growing networks of communities throughout the

Roman empire and the Mediterranean world.'

The authors say that hope of future redemption, though no longer attached to the extinguished earthly dynasty of David, was kept alive in Judaism's prophetic and messianic expectations, and in Christianity's belief that Jesus belonged to the Davidic line. The Hebrew Bible (Old Testament) would offer an unparalleled source of solidarity and identity to countless communities in the centuries that followed. The details of its stories, drawn from ancient memories, fragmentary histories, and rewritten legends, possessed power not as an objective chronicle of events in a tiny land on the eastern shore of the Mediterranean but as a timeless expression of what people's divine destiny might be. Just as the subjects of Charlemagne paid homage to him as a new, conquering David – and the followers of the Ottoman sultan Suleiman saw in him the wisdom of Solomon – other communities in very different cultural contexts would identify their own struggles with the struggles of biblical Israel. The Puritan settlers of New England went so far in imagining themselves as Israelites wandering in the wilderness that they recreated the Promised Land – with its Salem, Hebron, Goshen and New Canaan – in their newfound meadows and woods. And none of them doubted that the biblical epic was true [even though it wasn't]. Finkelstein and Silberman continue:

> ... the Bible's integrity and, in fact, its historicity, do not depend on dutiful historical 'proof' of any of its particular events or personalities, such as the parting of the Red Sea, the trumpet blasts that toppled the walls of Jericho, or David's slaying of Goliath with a single shot of his sling.
>
> The power of the biblical saga stems from its being a compelling and coherent narrative expression of the timeless themes of a people's liberation, continuing resistance to oppression, and quest for social equality.

They end by saying that only when we recognise when and why the ideas, images, and events described in the Bible came to be so skillfully woven together that we at last begin to appreciate the true genius and continuing power of this single most influential and spiritual creation in the history of humanity.

Sorry, don't agree

I recommend their book for its archaeological information and confirmation of the fables claiming to be real, but I could not disagree more with its conclusion. I'll tell you why. Religion in totality, if not every expression, has been a disaster for the world by both allowing the 'gods' to impose rigidity on the human psyche and largely misleading the population to worship them through the guise of a single God.

Energy flows where attention goes, and you make an energetic connection to what you focus upon. Worship is highly focused attention which makes you a constant source of loosh if your worship is related to the gods in whatever symbolic form. Religion, taken in totality, has set the world ablaze with violence and tyranny. It comes to something when it is considered a positive trait to be 'God-fearing'. Says it all, really. The history of horrific brutality in the name of religious imposition has the Roman Church right up there with anyone. The Romans may have sought to invent a pacifist Messiah to replace the perceived warrior Messiah of the Jews, but there is nothing pacifist about the Roman Church with its history of mass slaughter to protect its fairy stories from being openly questioned. 'Heresy' is religion-speak for having the wrong opinion.

Gnostics and Cathars were murdered and burned en masse for presenting another message and meaning of 'Jesus', suggesting that reincarnation is real, and that the human world was created by a demonic 'god'. Giordano Bruno was burned alive by the Roman Church psychopaths for having a different version of reality. The Vatican Inquisition colonised much of the world with one-God Christianity through mass murder and fear while destroying everything they could to suppress knowledge of the Astral gods or seizing it for the Vatican vaults. The Great Library of Alexandria was sacked and burned and its inspiration Hypatia torn limb from limb by a Catholic mob whipped up by 'Saint' Cyril, Bishop of Alexandria, whose 'feast day' is celebrated every June 28th. Look at other versions of Christianity, plus other religions like Islam and Judaism, and see what sickening brutality they have visited upon the world on behalf of the gods that inspired and manipulate them. Global history on every continent records how the religions of the gods have engaged in murder, rape and pillage of those of another faith or no faith.

'Christian' Trumpism

I said earlier how extraordinary I believe it to be when I see those who claim to stand for freedom of speech and opinion converting to the Roman Catholic Church which is a global network of reality imposition through the manipulation of fear and guilt. It does this with the illusion of an Old Testament God that expresses the mindless violence of the gods from which it was compiled and the claim in the New Testament that salvation comes only through a belief in Jesus as your saviour. Podcaster Candace Owens and Dutch activist Eva Vlaardingerbroek are two 'freedom of speech' warriors who are Catholic converters. Vlaardingerbroek converted in 2023 surrounded by friends and colleagues at GB News. She supported Jordan Peterson's wife as she converted to Catholicism. Candace Owens, already a Christian, converted to the Roman Church in 2024. Russell Brand's wife is a Roman Catholic and he has posted a video of himself doing the Catholic Rosary. Everyone to their own. I just don't see how they can talk about freedom of thought and speech given the Roman Church's brutal assault on both.

JD Vance is another Roman Catholic convert who said this deepened his commitment to Israel. Vance's venture capital firm, Narya Capital, was launched with funding from Peter Thiel, Marc Andreessen, and former Google chief and mega-globalist Eric Schmidt. Narya Capital invested in the Catholic prayer app, Hallow, which became very successful. It is promoted by Russell Brand and another investor is the non-Catholic … Peter Thiel. Apparently, Thiel is a 'devout Christian' which rather devalues the religion I would have thought. How you can credibly believe in freedom of opinion and at the same time convert to the Catholic fold that expanded its reach through the horrific killing and intimidation of non-believers is something I will never get. Russell Brand claims to be a researcher and exposer of untruth then converts to Christianity through a baptism in the River Thames while claiming the Bible is God's word. No questions to ask, no research to be done, just quote the passages and build a new audience. The alternative media has been hijacked by the Old Testament 'Christian' Right and its acolytes and the term 'Christ is King' on a social media post has become the confirmation of your loyalty to the club. What 'Christ is King' or 'Jesus is Lord' means has always been a mystery to me. What does it actually *mean*?

The hijacked conspiracy research arena and the MAGA Trump following is dominated by the Christian belief system. Try challenging their view of reality and you'll see how *un*-Christian a Christian can be. There's a researcher on Twitter/X and Rumble with the pseudonym Polly St George. She does some good work exposing the fake 'alternative' media that I will come to later on, but when I posted that the Global Cult answers to an interdimensional non-human force and we are experiencing a simulated reality she was seriously triggered. All this was bullshit she responded. Of course, she had no idea if it was true after doing no research into the subject, but it breached her religious belief system and that was enough. Jesus was her man and that was that. It was such confirmation of what I say about rigid, unquestioned beliefs creating no-go areas for potential discovery and enlightenment. Babies and bathwater are thrown in all directions.

What does it say when you could not become US president without claiming – *claiming* – that you are a Christian? You can be a great man or woman with all the values and motivations necessary to fairly and justly represent the interests of the whole population, but say you are not a Christian and don't believe the stories and you have got no chance. Look at the record. Most hilariously Donald Trump, the most unchristian bloke you can imagine, claims to be Christian. He said that God chose him to be president and saved his life to that end in an 'assassination attempt' which to say the least I have some *serious* questions about. It's all baloney as everything is with the professional fraud that is Trump and yet swathes of the Christian community believe this nonsense despite his unchristian policies and behaviour. The Mafia Don plays the Christian card only because he would have no chance of being president without doing so. The New Testament as a continuation of the Old Testament ensures a big connection between Christian presidents, real and otherwise, to Israel and its alleged biblical history. This has secured, along with Israeli intelligence infiltration and blackmail, largely unquestioned American government support for Israel's grotesque ambitions – again based on fake biblical history. One after the other US presidents of both parties, along with many key politicians worldwide, have lined up in their yarmulka at the Wailing or Western Wall. They pledge hand-on-wall allegiance to the Jewish God which is also taken to be the Christian God (Fig 204). The Western Wall is claimed to be the 'remains of the last temple' in Jerusalem while many scholars believe it is really the remains of a *Roman* fort built to house troops that destroyed Jerusalem in 70 AD. Pinch me quick.

Figure 204: Trump like all presidents and political leaders make the obligatory pilgrimage to the Western or Wailing Wall in Jerusalem to pledge their allegiance to Israel.

On your knees!

Muslims worldwide fall to their knees and face the Saturn cube five times a day because Muhammad claimed to have dreams with the angel Gabriel taking him to Allah who told him what his followers must do. Religious police seek to enforce this on Muslim populations and others with their fascist 'Sharia Law'. This is all done in the name of a god in the pre-Islamic Arabian pantheon that came from the Mesopotamian pantheon. How the Astral gods must laugh. 'Muslim' means 'One Who Submits' and you can apply that to almost any faith. You must submit to the faith. The house of cards comes tumbling down if you ask too many questions like the walls of Jericho that didn't exist. Practicing Jews rush to the synagogue on the Sabbath because an extraterrestrial psychopath dubbed 'Yahweh' told the mythical Moses that they must honour the Sabbath/Saturn Day in honour of him. Jewish women panic to finish the food preparation with their oven soon out of action because the Astral god demanded it. Many spend Saturday with the lights off unless they can con a non-Jew to turn them on or buy a lamp that's always lit, so they don't have to flick the switch on a Saturn-day. What insanity it all is. To those Jews who say it's all true – ask yourself what you would believe was true today if you were born into a Muslim, Hindu or Christian family instead of a Jewish one.

I read on Biblehub.com that the conquest of Canaan under Joshua was not merely a historical account but carried profound theological significance. It demonstrated God's faithfulness to 'His' covenant promises and 'His' role as the divine warrior who fights on behalf of 'His' people. The narrative also served as a reminder of the importance of obedience and faith in God's commands, as seen in Joshua's adherence to the instructions given to Moses. Oh, but of course. Obedience and faith are what it's all about. I saw a 1995 article in *Time* about 'Jerusalem 3000', a 17-month festival of art, music and archaeological exhibitions, commemorating the 3,000th anniversary of the city's 'original conquest by the ancient Israelites'. It said:

> But the celebration serves as a reminder that the region has witnessed a very special sort of history. For nearly 3 billion Jews, Christians and Muslims, this is the Holy Land, the place where the Bible and Koran say Jesus and Abraham and King David and King Solomon all walked the earth.

Yes, they *say* that, but do we just believe this because books written long ago say so? Books that have clearly been written and changed to suit the authorities and agendas of the day? Where is consciousness that questions everything until only the truth is left? Jesus is quoted as saying 'be like children' and religious advocates have taken the words *literally* because of their religious 'faith'. Moses had a staff that morphed into a serpent, and he turned the Nile to blood. The Red Sea opened. Jesus changed water into wine and fed 5,000 with a few loaves and fishes. Muhammad's 'night journey'? Any questions before believing it all? For many the answer is 'no' and the same with other religions like orthodox science, the New Age, and human-caused climate change. Nothing should be beyond question – including what I say. If it doesn't make sense, reject it. Just do so with your own research and antenna, not reflex action responses. I don't believe all that the Gnostic texts say just because they say it and I am always looking for support from other sources and experience.

Division is the rule

Different rigid, unquestioned, faiths are also perfect for the Cult's essential need to divide and rule. Religious beliefs seeking to impose their 'truth' on 'blasphemers' and 'infidels' have led to untold wars (think of the loosh) and we have the recurring theme of a religion being created and then dividing into competing factions. Protestantism broke from Roman Catholicism while endless other Christian factions have followed. Islam divided into Sunni and Shia. The hatred and contempt between them can be as fierce as that between different religions. Iran as the centre of Shia Islam and Saudi Arabia as the home of Sunni explains their mutual antagonism and the same between Muslim Pakistan and Hindu India. All this goes back to ancient times and the imposition of one religion, or version of the gods, on others through conquest. The Middle East was the scene of the Knights Templar Crusades representing the Prince of Peace seeking to seize Jerusalem through horrendous violence with Islam doing the same to win it back. Both believed they were doing the will of the true 'God' when they were (mostly) unwitting pawns of the same gods playing out their pathetic feuds and need for loosh. The theme is: 'Satan has deceived people into believing in all the other religions – *except mine.*'

I say 'mostly' because while the great majority believe what they are told to believe, the inner sanctum of every religion will know the truth. Given the unlimited potential for suppression of knowledge and division of the population the Global Cult and the Astral gods will sit atop all of them. Religions operate like secret societies with knowledge held by the few that is kept from the majority. The fake 'royal' monarch, a human/non-human hybrid, heads the Christian church in Britain as 'Defender of the Faith' which King Charlie referred to as 'Defender of Faiths'. He and the Cult could not care less what faith you follow so long as it involves unquestioned obedience. It is almost amusing to watch the 'royals' going through the motions of being 'good Christians' in state events when they know who they are really being faithful to.

Paul Wallis was a Christianity insider for 33 years as a Church Doctor, Theological Educator, and Archdeacon in the Anglican Church in Australia, but then began to publish his *Eden* books about how the 'God' of the Old Testament has been confused with extraterrestrial 'gods'. His first, *Escaping From Eden,* was in 2020. This transformation began when he compared the Hebrew and English translations. He realised that the plural Elohim was being translated as a singular 'God'. It is clear from what he says that many others in the church have made this connection and resist saying so to protect their church careers and because their congregations won't want to hear the truth. The indoctrination is too great, and we have many who get a placating comfort from their religious beliefs and don't want the truth to spoil a good story. If I believe in Jesus I'll be saved and that's all the detail I need, thank you. It is shocking how deep the programming goes even among those that think they are awake.

I want to acknowledge before we move on that there are many people who express their spirituality and kindness through their religion when they take the best and leave the rest. But this can be done without all the dross, the fake history, rules and regulations of collective control, and suppression of an open mind allowed to go where the evidence takes it. The positive justification of religion can be done in a direct connection to the infinite realm beyond the simulation – the Infinite of which we are all an expression.

There I go, blaspheming again.

CHAPTER 21

Trump Psyop

The universe runs on the principle that one who can exert the most evil on other creatures runs the show.
Bangambiki Habyarimana

Donald Trump is a tool of the Cult with a specific agenda to hijack the minds of those previously pushing back on the 'Deep State' and bring them into line with the AI control system and human-AI fusion. His modus operandi is to divert their attention by loudly telling them what they want to hear while AI oligarchs quietly put the control system into place. It may well be that with his obvious health and scandal problems they intend to replace him at some point with the oligarchs' bought-and-paid-for vice-president JD Vance.

The Woke 'Left' was susceptible to the hard-sell of AI through the usual suspects like Klaus Schwab, Bill Gates, and Google executive and 'futurist', Ray Kurzweil, who say that if we fuse with AI we will be 'gods'. Kurzweil has openly said that by 2030 AI will be connected to the human brain after which it will do more and more of human thinking until that becomes 'negligible' (deleted). Gates has said that within ten years humans won't be needed 'for most things'. The Woke mentality has been systematically drilled into young generations through school and university after they were born into a world dominated by smartphones and other devices. They are the scrolling generations. Yes, older people can do that, too, but it is the young the Cult is after to turn them into extensions of Archontic technology open to seeing human/AI fusion as just the next step in the glorious technological revolution. Why wouldn't they believe that? A society dominated by technology is all most of them have known and what you are born into becomes your sense of 'normal'. Those like me born into a very different world a few years after World War Two can see the vastness of the change that has happened and how it is anything but 'normal'.

Woke extremism

'Woke' is also a Psyop to play off against the Trump-Musk Psyop and bring the former pushbackers against AI control and fusion on board with it. I'll explain how this has been done, but first what exactly is

'Woke'? The term, as in 'stay woke', was used by the African American community at least since the 1930s to stress the need to be aware of the racism of American apartheid and discrimination. The modern version was much expanded among the young and political Left to include the concept of 'inclusivity' and 'equity'. The latter has been confused with equality when equity doesn't mean that. Not in the way it is applied anyway. The official meaning is 'a situation in which everyone is treated fairly according to their needs and no group of people is given special treatment'. That is not the case at all. Woke demanded special treatment for minorities and the targeting of the majority white population that were demonised and marginalised. They were labelled racist, sexist and discriminatory against transgender people and those from the LGBT arena. I am sure that some were, but the majority just saw the inequality and unfairness of different sections of society being treated differently.

We descended into identity politics when expressions of Infinite Awareness were told to identify with their body, race and sexuality. The LGBT label just went on getting longer and longer as people identified with the fine detail of their sexual preference. The most extreme example I saw was the Wesleyan University in Connecticut with its LGBTTQQFAGPBDSM (lesbian, gay, bisexual, transgender, transsexual, queer, questioning, flexual, asexual, gender-fuck, polyamorous, bondage/discipline, dominance/submission). We have had people losing their jobs and livelihoods for not using the 'preferred pronouns' of men with a dick demanding they are addressed as a woman. Toilet arrangements and changing room protocols were scrapped to allow the said 'dicks' to use facilities previously designated for women only. 'Dicks' were sent to women's prisons, allowed in female retreats from male violence, took part in women's sport and basically destroyed it when they did. Children as young as toddlers were exposed to men with beards in women's clothes reading to them in libraries or even strutting their stuff akin to a sex club. Talk about gender confusion imposed upon even little children.

It was obvious that at some point there would be a mass reaction against this by those suffering the consequences and parents sick of seeing their children indoctrinated by Woke schools and universities awash with rainbow flags (Noahide Laws) and pronoun bullshit. This reaction was factored into the Psyop as I will come to. Part of the package was that the human-caused climate change hoax was real and threatened our existence, support for mass unfettered immigration, and that there are no conspiracies (unless the other 'side' is responsible and not their own). Otherwise, they don't exist no matter what the evidence. Extreme Wokers never consider little things like evidence worthy of their attention. The definition of a 'conspiracy' is merely 'the activity of secretly planning with other people to do something bad or illegal' and 'a general agreement to keep silent about a subject for the purpose of keeping it secret'. To say there are no conspiracies by those definitions alone borders on the insane. The terms 'conspiracy theory' and 'conspiracy theorist' were brought into widespread use by the CIA in the 1960s when they urged major media to attach these labels to discredit those questioning the assassination of President Kennedy in 1963 and later those of Malcom X, Martin Luther King and Robert Kennedy, brother of JFK and father of RFK Jr. A Woker would almost certainly not know that and wouldn't want to know that (Fig 205). Sorry, I can't hear you. Go on the Internet and you will find the original CIA document. Still can't hear you. I must get my hearing fixed.

Figure 205: People repeat conspiracy theory with no idea they are parroting a term circulated by the CIA to discredit exposure.

My own view of Woke is that everyone should be treated equally and given equal opportunity whatever their race, religion, background and income bracket. Advancement should be based on one thing – merit. I want aircraft pilots to be the best available and not someone leapfrogged over the best because he or she is the 'right colour' or 'right sexuality' to fulfil the quotas imposed by 'equity'. I also believe in the right of everyone to live their lives as they see fit so long as they don't impose their choices on other people. If you are a bloke who wants to wear women's clothes or vice versa then be my guest. It's none of my business. But don't tell me how I have to address you when to me you are not what you are claiming to be. That is a slight on my self-respect in calling you what I do not believe you are. For people to be fired in these circumstances is a grotesque abuse and the fury was always going to lead to a backlash. The point I am making is that this backlash was carefully planned and triggered by the same Cult that pushed the Woke. It was a perceptual set-up. But why?

Wokers had pretty much laid back and accepted the AI hard sell. They were in the bag. Those the Cult needed on board were the pushbackers on AI and tyranny who *did* believe in conspiracies, *didn't* believe in human-caused climate change, and were vehemently against mass unchecked immigration. They were sickened by the gathering Woke impositions and nonsenses under the Democrat administrations of Barack Obama and Joe Biden as others were with their governments around the world. The Democratic Party was the chosen vehicle for Woke tyranny in the United States and the Trump-led Republicans were the home of the pushbackers that morphed into 'MAGA' or Make America Great Again. They were chosen to push back on the Woke tyranny with an 'anti-Woke' tyranny. The more extreme the Wokers became the more furious the MAGA became and not only in the United States. A global response was gathering. Perfect. Then along came Donald Trump who was telling them exactly what they wanted to hear. He would dissolve Woke, stop the obsession with laws relating to climate change, block mass immigration, deport many already in the country, and he did believe in a 'Deep State' conspiracy. Ah, but not the real one. That is the One-Party State with the Cult working through both 'sides' with the emphasis and rhetoric directed in the form of designer manipulation aimed at the two belief systems of Left *and* Right. No – the conspiracy promoted by Trump and MAGA was only a Democratic Party conspiracy. *They* were the 'Deep State'. Nonsense beyond belief, but MAGA bought into it because the Democrats promoted Woke.

Enter Musk

A crucial step in the Trump/Musk/MAGA Psyop was Elon Musk being allowed to buy Twitter in 2022. I had been tracking him for many years because his companies were ticking the boxes of the Cult agenda and its front organisations like the World Economic Forum of Klaus Schwab. Tesla was pushing the electric and autonomous vehicle climate change agenda; Neuralink was promoting the AI connection to the brain agenda; and SpaceX was constantly launching low-orbit satellites which are a vital part of the hive mind agenda that I will be highlighting. I knew immediately from this background that Musk acquiring Twitter was a Cult operation. But for what reason? It soon became clear. The target was the MAGA and the plan was to manipulate them to support AI mass control. He has been pushing the AI takeover on the platform ever since. It's all about perception and part of that is image. Musk promoted himself as a 'free speech absolutist' which to people like me, shadow banned in the extreme on his platform, is a rather sick joke. He had positioned himself years earlier as an AI sceptic to ingratiate himself later with the MAGA audience; but he has since rolled out more and more AI both literally and aspirationally until he was supporting the prediction there will be some billion humanoid robots on Earth in the next two decades. Musk was being exposed before Twitter for his AI transhumanist promotion and this changed dramatically after he was allowed to buy the platform which was a key reason why the Deep State (Cult) sold it to him.

He allowed banned people back on Twitter, which he renamed X, a letter he is obsessed with. This was pivotal in his image transformation.

Those who were warning about his transhumanist tendencies were suddenly giving him a free ride because Elon was now 'one of us'. Here was another case of tell them what they want to hear, and they'll kiss your ring. All critical thinking faded away among the Elon-loving former pushbackers. Dutch activist Eva Vlaardingerbroek once denounced Elon Musk for being an AI transhumanist and then stopped abruptly to become a loyalist after he bought Twitter. The sequence was widespread. It is agreed, and the experience confirms it, that what MAGA calls the 'Deep State' was in control of Twitter pre-Musk. The numbers banned and limitations on what could be posted saw the Deep State (a national expression of the Global Cult) in full control of what could be seen. This was precisely what it wanted of course. It was home and very dry. Musk even released what became known as the 'Twitter Files' (some of them) which were emails and documents confirming that the Deep State 'had' controlled Twitter. They were released through late-to-the-party Matt Taibbi and Joe Rogan's mate Michael Shellenberger. Taibbi once called those questioning the official story of 9/11 'hopelessly stupid' in a 2006 *Rolling Stone* article headed 'The Idiocy Behind the "9/11 Truth" Movement'. The 'Twitter Files' were released to add to Musk's image of being the free speech defender. But here's the question: If the Deep State was in control of Twitter and dictating what could be seen *why did they then sell it to Musk, a self-styled free speech absolutist??* They had Twitter where they wanted it, and they just gave it away? It made no sense because it's not true. The Cult still controls it, just in a different way to a different end. Well, the same end, but a different route.

Musk did not buy Twitter by himself. He merged Twitter into his new company X Corp which is a subsidiary of X Holdings Corp. This was only registered in 2023. X Holdings Corp was the real owner of Twitter, now X. Musk tried everything he could to stop the X Holdings shareholders being revealed during a lawsuit filed by former Twitter employees which Musk had fired; but the judge ordered they were made public after an intervention by lawyers from the Reporters Committee for Freedom of the Press. They included Saudi Arabian Prince Al Waleed bin Talal al Saud; Q Tetris Holding registered in the same Doha building which is home to the Qatar Investment Authority, the Qatar government sovereign wealth fund; Oracle tech billionaire Larry Ellison; 8VC, a venture capital firm co-founded by Joe Lonsdale, also a co-founder with Peter Thiel of software company Palantir which supplies surveillance and data technology to intelligence agencies and the military; Scott Nolan, a partner at the Founders Fund of Peter Thiel; venture capital firm Andreessen Horowitz (AI promotor Marc Andreessen); financial giants Fidelity which bought shares for more than 20 funds; Pershing Square Foundation, which lists hedge fund billionaire Bill Ackman and his wife as co-trustees; cryptocurrency exchange Binance; Sean John Combs (Diddy, Puff Daddy and P. Diddy), an American rapper, record producer, and record executive who would later be charged with sex trafficking and racketeering. What a bunch of free speech absolutists, eh? Tech journalist Jacob Silverman who forced the disclosure said: '… the court-disclosed list of X shareholders offered what I hoped it would: a little sunshine directed toward the shadowy technofascists and authoritarians helping to underwrite Musk's empire.'

Zionist oligarchy

One of the shareholders, Larry Ellison, co-founded Oracle which had the CIA as its first customer and took its title from a 1977 CIA project codename. Ellison once said in support of mass monitoring of the population:

> The police will be on their best behaviour because we're constantly watching and recording everything that's going on. Citizens will be on their best behaviour because we're constantly recording and reporting everything that's going on … We're using AI to monitor the video … it's not people that are looking at those cameras. AI is looking at those cameras.

How good to know we have people like ultra-Zionist Ellison protecting our freedoms and willing to invest in X. The Federal Communications Commission (FCC), headed by Musk's mate Brendan Carr, voted to approve Paramount's $8.4 billion merger with the Ellison family's Skydance Media. This came after Donald Trump successfully sued the Paramount CBS *60 Minutes* show for 'deceptively' editing an interview with Kamala Harris. It was an outrageous lawsuit doomed to failure in a court of justice (Fox News has edited Trump interviews to protect him), but CBS paid Trump $16 million in support of the Paramount merger with Skydance Media that Trump had to approve. It was blatant extortion. CBS also cancelled the show of Trump critic 'comedian' Stephen Colbert who I find appalling, but he has a right to his view. American comedian Jon Stewart asked if cancelling Colbert was a financial decision as claimed. 'Or maybe the path of least resistance for your $8 billion merger was killing a show that you know rankled a fragile and vengeful president?' Skydance is owned by Ellison's son, David, with the father providing most of the finance for the merger. The Ellisons plan to turn CBS into a Trump-supporting station or anyone of like mind that follows him. I am sure it will also be a vehicle for selling the AI dystopia. Ultra-Zionist NBC Universal executive Jeff Shell was named as president of new Skydance Paramount while the ultra-Zionist David Ellison was in talks with ultra-Zionist Barri Weiss to buy her *The Free Press* for between $200-$250 million. *The Financial Times* reported that Ellison 'wants to position *The Free Press* alongside CBS News', and the *New York Times* quoted an insider as saying that Ellison was considering giving Weiss 'an influential role in shaping the editorial sensibilities of *CBS News*'. If that plays out, then *CBS News* will become massively pro-Israel and Netanyahu its poster boy. This is what you voted for MAGA.

Free speech myth

Elon Musk announced in March 2025 that his xAI company was buying Twitter/X in an all-stock deal and with both companies privately owned they were not required to publicly disclose their finances. The Musk-to-Musk deal valued xAI at $80 billion and X at $33 billion (he paid $44 billion originally). He said:

> xAI and X's futures are intertwined. Today, we officially take the step to combine the data, models, compute, distribution and talent. This combination will unlock immense potential by blending xAI's advanced AI capability and expertise with X's massive reach.
>
> The combined company will deliver smarter, more meaningful experiences to billions of people while staying true to our core mission of seeking truth and advancing knowledge.

Pass the sickbag. 'Combine the data, models, compute' is exactly in line with AI control of information. X users provide the data to train AI. Musk said: 'This will allow us to build a platform that doesn't just reflect the world but actively *accelerates* human progress.' The significance of 'accelerates' will become clear. The 'AI sceptic' had taken the mask off and he posted in July 2025: 'I resisted AI for too long. Living in denial. Now it is game on.' It always was, mate, as you knew from the start. He also says that to maintain 'relevance' humans must be 'interwoven with AI' – 'that we effectively become one with the AI'. Musk posted a robot selling popcorn with the comment: 'This will become normal in a few years.' Why we need popcorn to be sold by robots and not humans he never said. His public fall-out with Trump didn't seem to affect his government contracts with the Pentagon awarding Musk's company xAI a $200 million contract to employ artificial intelligence chatbot, Grok, as 'part of a wider rollout of AI tools for government use'. The BBC reported that this, along with other AI government contracts for Anthropic, Google and OpenAI, 'aligns with the Trump administration's push for more aggressive adoption of artificial intelligence'. The Cult agenda continues whatever the background to the apparent Musk-Trump 'feud' and the signs are that they are back together as I finished this book.

The Musk game was even clearer when he hired NBCUniversal executive, Linda Yaccarino, to be Twitter/X CEO. Musk positioned himself for image purposes as against the aspirations of the World Economic Forum. He had to appear that way when the MAGA despised the WEF. Yet Yaccarino was an Executive Chair of the WEF and headed its Taskforce on Future of Work. It was an apparently bizarre choice, but I have said for 36 years that people should observe actions not words. They are easy – you just move your lips. Yaccarino and Musk introduced their policy of 'freedom of speech, not freedom of reach'. Yaccarino said: 'If it is lawful, but it is awful, it will be extraordinarily difficult for you to see it.' It was immediately clear what they meant. Those that eulogised Musk and promoted the narrative that suited him would get boosted by the algorithms to be seen by big numbers. Those saying 'lawful but awful' things like he and Trump were free speech frauds pursuing the Cult agenda would be algorithmically suppressed. Most of the 770,000 people following my page on Twitter/X as I write don't get to see my posts as they should – as many have told me. This is the blatant censorship of 'shadow banning'. Meanwhile the Gatling gun posts by Musk 24/7 have the algorithm on full-blast to get millions, even tens of millions, for each one no matter how inane and self-serving. Then there is a network of posters who promote Musk as a god that naturally have the algorithms on their side and a Musk repost with a comment of 'Wow' or 'Interesting' has them ride the Musk algorithm to those millions.

Those that pushed back on his demand for more H1-B high-skilled worker visas that allow American workers in Silicon Valley to be replaced by Indian immigrants were specifically targeted by Musk. His dolly was launched from his pram, maybe with help from SpaceX. Some lost their Twitter/X 'blue checkmark' and subscriptions. The checkmark allowed them to upload much longer videos and they could post 25,000 characters in a tweet instead of 280. If you are trying to communicate information to challenge the Musk/Trump/X narrative this was clearly a serious blow, and it was meant to be. Musk, like Trump, is a mega narcissist and they don't take insubordination. Neither of them is very bright despite the PR. We are supposed to eulogise Musk as a 'genius' when he's a complete phony front man with others running his companies while he posts on his Twitter/X, plays video games (and pays experts to win in his name), does interviews and generally self-promotes the 'genius' image. He is, like Trump, a very unpleasant piece of work. The H1-B visas were supported by Trump:

> I have many H-1B visas on my properties. I've been a believer in H-1B. I have used it many times; it's a great program.

I can see why he would when it saves him money, but how does this square with America First? The visas allow for Americans to be replaced by cheaper immigrants, and many have told how they were expected to train foreign workers to do their jobs before being fired themselves. The immigrants are exploited, too. Critics call it 'indentured servitude' in that visa holders can't change jobs, or it is made more difficult to do so. Right at the start of his second presidency they both showed that when their agenda is at odds with the MAGA agenda there will only be one winner – and it was just the start. Musk, like Trump, is an extraordinary liar.

Nice man

Cristina Balan, a former highly rated engineer at Tesla, was fired after warning about a design flaw related to Tesla braking systems. She pursued Musk in the courts while branding him 'pure evil' and a 'monster'. Balan spoke out after California appeal judges reversed a previous decision to dismiss her defamation claim against Tesla. She said: 'I started this lawsuit to prove my innocence and to prove how vindictive this monster is.' Balan told *Times Radio* that Musk 'enjoyed hurting people' and there was no movie that could 'paint how Elon Musk is in real life'. He had destroyed so many people at Tesla that 'you have no idea'. She said he had told employees to email him with any problems with the vehicles, but '90 percent of those who did got fired'. She said that brakes were not her only concern that she told Musk about. 'We had hundreds of defects per car, and we are [knowingly] sending the cars out like that.' Musk employee contracts across his companies had forced them to 'give up their freedom of speech and right to sue'. Balan said that Musk's claims about working late and sleeping on the floor were 'bullshit'. Musk had been 'present in Tesla on one day every other week with small exceptions'. She asked: 'How much could you do in two days a month?' This supports my long contention that he doesn't run 'his' companies as claimed.

Vivek Ramaswamy whose parents emigrated from India played a major part in the Trump campaign, but he was ditched for saying the quiet part out loud and revealing the scale of contempt that the Trump regime has for Americans outside its tiny circle of billionaires. MAGA worships Trump while he has contempt for them. Ramaswamy posted that Big Tech needs overseas workers because Americans don't have sufficient work ethic. American culture 'venerated mediocrity over excellence'. He said that the reason top tech companies often hire foreign-born and first-generation engineers over 'native' Americans came down to the c-word: culture. It wasn't well received, and he was ejected from the garden. Ramaswamy is a protégé of Palantir's Peter Thiel who has invested in Ramaswamy's firm Strive Asset Management along with American Jewish billionaire hedge fund manager, Bill Ackman, an investor in Musk's Twitter/X, and Howard Lutnick, named by Trump as his Commerce Secretary. See how often Thiel keeps recurring and there's much more to come. The Trump world at its core is not very big and the same names turn up over and over. Trump is the mouthy front man, but the oligarchs control him.

Mafia 'Don'

I'll come back to Musk and his alliance and 'fall out' with Trump after we've put 'The Donald' into the perspective of the Psyop. I watched a TV series called *The Capture* which was set within British Intelligence. The thrust of the series was the ability to change CCTV footage in *real time* and make it appear to show events that never happened. The series calls this 'deepfake' technology 'Correction'. That was fascinating to see, but what really struck me was a theme in part of the series of a British politician who was suffering ups and downs in his career. Some events looked like the end for him politically only for things to turn around and allow his further progress towards becoming prime minister. Eventually, he realises that a global tech company has been guiding his career and challenges through an algorithm. We need to realise that they are not only used to dictate content online. We are in a simulation and algorithms are everywhere. Life Programs running through the biological computer are essentially a form of algorithm. Anyway, this politician asked the obvious question. If the algorithm was designed to make me prime minister, why did I have all the challenges and near disasters on the way? He was told by the tech oligarch that this was what the algorithm said was necessary to reach the goal. What was necessary did not mean plain sailing the whole way.

I related this to Donald Trump and his 'journey' to the presidency for the second time. He faced all those court cases with some that could have ended his presidential ambitions, but in the end they all went away. Trump was pretty much a busted flush after the election defeat of 2020 and his influence with MAGA had waned. Trump support would need to be infused with a new burst of enthusiasm if he was going to run in 2024. Then a sequence of court challenges began. The FBI raided his Mar-a-Lago mansion complex in Florida in August 2022 over classified documents said to have been illegally taken there after he left the White House. I observe public responses to events (outcomes) because it's in the outcomes that the reason for something can often be identified. Support for Trump among the MAGA base began to stir again with the perception that the 'Deep State' was out to get him and they must be frightened that he will run again for president.

In the end he faced a series of charges including the classified documents, fraud, election subversion and paying hush money to American pornographic film actress Stormy Daniels for which he was convicted on 34 felony counts of falsifying business records to make the payments before the 2016 election. Trump was handed an unconditional discharge and no-penalty sentence avoiding probation, fine or jail time days before he took office on January 20th, 2025. He became the first convicted felon to become president, but federal law and the US Constitution do not stop felons running the country. This is just as well given all the unconvicted felons there have been who must have been a whisker away from conviction had the system not been watching their back. The other cases that it was claimed threatened Trump's run for president went away one by one up to his inauguration, but once in office he faced other court challenges while his Thiel-gofer vice-president JD Vance was waiting in the wings should Trump be brought down for any reason.

A ruling from the Trump Republican majority on the US Supreme Court was pivotal. This related to charges against him claiming he sought to subvert the result of the 2020 election officially lost to Joe Biden. By a 6-3 majority (three justices were appointed by Trump) they decreed that a president has absolute immunity for certain official conduct. Chief Justice John Roberts said that a president's discussions with the Department of Justice (in this case over the election result) are official acts of the presidency and are 'absolutely immune' from prosecution. This was a massive win for Trump and a massive loss for blocks on power. Dissenting Justice Sonia Sotomayor said: 'The President is now a king above the law.' Quentin Fulks, Biden's deputy campaign manager, was quoted as saying: 'Immune, immune, immune. They just handed Donald Trump keys to a dictatorship.' Both comments would prove prophetic. The Supreme Court earlier unanimously ruled against the validity of plans in more than 30 states to remove Trump from the presidential ballot over claims that he sought to overturn his 2020 election defeat. This process through multiple court cases across many different charges did not diminish Trump's support. Quite the opposite. Support from the MAGA mindset increased dramatically on the grounds that the 'Deep State' is out to get Trump, and he must be a threat to them.

'God saved me'

Then came the 'assassination attempt' on Trump at an election rally at the Farm Show Grounds near Butler, Pennsylvania, on July 13th, 2024. He grabbed his ear during the sound of gunshots and dropped to the floor under a group of Secret Service agents. An audience member was killed and two critically injured. My initial reaction was that this would further explode the MAGA belief along with many other voters that the Deep State wanted Trump out of the way because he was a threat to their power. This is exactly what happened, and I started to question events and the official story. I was especially keen to see the first images of Trump's ear after the shooting allegedly by 20-year-old Thomas Matthew Crooks, of Bethel Park, Pennsylvania, who is said to have fired eight rounds from an AR-15 rifle from a distance of 400 to 500 feet. The shooting was clearly allowed to happen with no agents on the roof of a building that would surely have been identified in an instant as a potential shooting location. Members of the crowd saw a man

Figure 206: The fight, fight, fight image. So many questions.

up there long before the shots and tried to warn police and agents, but nothing was done. The alleged gunman was shot dead by snipers on the roof of another building and dead men don't speak. As Trump emerged from the Secret Service pack, they opened a gap for him to appear in view, punch the air and shout 'Fight! Fight! Fight!'. It was what they call in filmmaking the 'money shot' and it became a central feature of Trump's election propaganda from that point (Fig 206).

I will come to the 'alternative' media later which was hijacked by Trump-supporting propagandists after the 'Covid' hoax. This is very significant to the whole story of how MAGA was scammed. The old alternative would have been all over the shooting forensically investigating the official story to see if it stood up to scrutiny or whether it was a set-up or 'false flag' operation for whatever reason. Remaining and now marginalised alternative journalists did so, but the fake 'alternative' dominated by Trump worshippers did nothing of the kind when had it been Biden they would have been screaming it was a 'false flag' to garner support. They said the shooting was allowed to happen, but only to kill Trump. There is no critical thinking in the fake 'alternative' and it didn't occur to them to ask why, if the plan was to kill Trump, they used a 20-year-old kid who registered to vote in Pennsylvania as a member of the Republican Party on reaching voting age in 2021. He remained so at the time of Butler.

Crooks tried to join the Bethel Park High School rifle club but was so bad he was considered a dangerous shooter and rejected. Reminds me of the 9/11 'Al-Qaeda pilot' who was banned from hiring a one-engine Cessna at a flying school because he was useless and weeks later is claimed to have crashed an airliner into the Pentagon after an amazing turn and descent that professional pilots said they couldn't have done. Why wasn't a trained sniper hitman used who would not have missed?? Information about Crooks' life and personality is described as 'varying considerably' and remember how easy it is to mind control individuals not only as assassins, but to be in the wrong place at the wrong time to make it look like they were. I am not making definitive statements, only looking at the possibilities. It's amazing how fast an 'assassination' attempt on a would-be president disappeared from view with no credible investigation.

Trump appeared days later at the Republican Party Convention in Milwaukee to a rapturous welcome with a white bandage on his ear. The audience pumped their fists and shouted 'Fight! Fight! Fight!' while musicians sang 'God Bless the USA'. The media reported that 'the Republican nominee for November's presidential contest is riding a wave of political momentum'. Supporters even began wearing bandages on their ears in what had become a personality cult with Trump as its heroic leader. Pathetic doesn't begin to describe it. He was

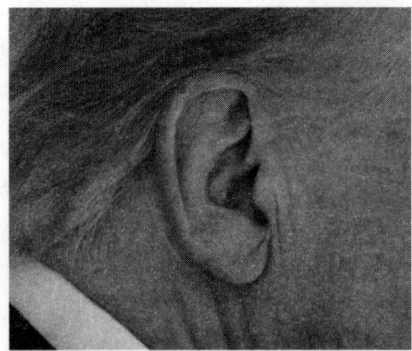

Figure 207: Posted 15 days after the shooting.

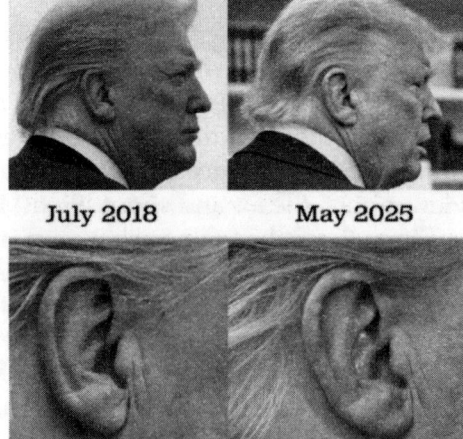

Figure 208: Spot the difference? Me, neither.

appearing without the bandage before the end of July and revealed what I expected. His ear was supposedly hit by a bullet from an AR-15, but there was nothing to be seen. *Nothing*. Maybe his legendary vanity got the better of him. He took the bandage off far too soon for credibility (Figs 207 and 208). One mainstream headline noted: 'First photos of Trump without ear bandage have everyone saying the same thing.' This 'same thing' was to say the obvious. Social media comments included: 'Trump's ear today: Healed pretty well, right?'; 'Trump's "bullet wound to the ear" healed very quickly ... almost like it wasn't even hit by a bullet or shrapnel'; 'Where are the stitches? Where are the scars?'; 'Donald Trump appears today for the first time since assassination attempt without a bandage on his right ear, seemingly fully recovered'. It's a transparent joke. What are the chances of an assassin clipping the ear an inch from disaster and not causing any discernible damage? There was the added bonus for his Christian-dominated followers that somehow 'God' had saved him to (Moses-like) set the people free. The theme was everywhere. Trump said at his inauguration: 'I felt then, and

I believe even more so now, that my life was saved by God to make America great again.' Sure, it was, Donny. Sure, it was.

The Trump Cult

There have been many claims that Trump is the leader of a MAGA cult and at the extreme end of MAGA that's certainly true. Steven Hassan is a mental health professional who was once in the 'Moonie' cult known as the Unification Church founded in 1954 by Sun Myung Moon in Seoul, South Korea. Hassan was by his own admission subjected to deep perceptual programming and believed that Moon was a god-like figure. He recovered eventually and trained in mental health specialising since 1976 in helping those in destructive cults to leave and get their minds back. Hassan says as he observed Donald Trump and his MAGA followers that he saw all the signs and classic mind control techniques of a cult. He wrote a book, *The Cult of Trump*, in which he lays out his findings. I didn't agree with Hassan's take on many things away from Trump. He appears to see cults that aren't and doesn't see cults that are – like orthodox science. He also buys 'Covid', the fake vaccine, and the climate change hoax. But on Trump as a cult leader, he is blatantly on the money. Hassan explains how cult leaders demand loyalty and obedience and their word must be the final truth. They seek to control the thoughts, behaviour and emotions of their followers and cult leaders are narcissists or an even more extreme version that he calls malignant narcissists. These have:

- Grandiose self-centred behaviour.
- Fantasies of power, success and attractiveness.
- A need for praise and admiration.
- A sense of entitlement.
- A lack of empathy which can lead them to exploit, bully, shame, and demean others without guilt or remorse.

Trump has all of these traits, but Hassan says that behind this personality type there is often very low self-esteem and feelings of inferiority, emptiness and boredom. He said that many cult leaders experienced loveless childhoods and that is the case with Trump who grew up with an absent mother and authoritarian father. Trump biographer Michael Wolff, who has observed and written about Trump for decades, has said that he is basically still a 13-year-old (like Elon Musk). His bombast and boasting is a cover for his insecurity and lack of love in his life. He is all over the place mentally and emotionally which makes him a perfect front man who can easily be manipulated by flattery. Making sure you are the last one to speak with him before a decision is made helps, too. I have seen those who knew the British prime minister Margaret 'Iron Lady' Thatcher say that you could get her to do anything so long as she thought it was her idea.

Trump's 'grandiose self-centred behaviour' is legendary as he struts around constantly speaking in superlatives. Everything he does is 'the greatest'; 'No one else could have done this; but me'; 'There's never been anything like it'; 'Nothing in history compares with what I've done.' Watching his cabinet eulogising him like some pharaoh, king or god, is sickening to watch. Their role is not to inform him of what he needs to know from their subject area. They are only there to praise the monarch. It's how you survive in the Trump circle. Meanwhile, he was posting typical cult images of himself as the pope and the White House depicted him as Superman (Figs 209 and 210). As always with Trump, and many other presidents, all dignity was deleted from the White House press office. He talks in exaggerated overstatement about himself and everything he does, no matter how ridiculous, and he expects his underlings to do the same or they're out. Only people with extreme insecurity demand that.

Trump is a psychopath/sociopath with a brutal personality that takes pleasure in hurting, crushing, and humiliating others. It helps to placate his extreme insecurity. At the same time, he has contempt for the MAGA and especially the sycophants he makes sure surround him. Steven Hassan says that cult leaders can be identified by the way they constantly lie to their followers

Figure 209: Trump posted himself as the pope.

Figure 210: The White House posted Trump as Superman.

and here Trump once again excels. His days are spent lying from dawn to dusk. 'Deception is the lifeblood of a destructive cult', says Hassan. Members were recruited and indoctrinated through lies and trickery. Lying had other intrinsic benefits for cult leaders. It created confusion, which disrupted people's 'stable mental framework' and made them susceptible to the indoctrination process. Trump is a skilled exploiter of the 'gaslighting' technique. This is a term originating from the play *Gas Light* in 1938 and movies based on that. Gaslighting is 'the act or practice of grossly misleading someone especially for one's own advantage' by basically lying consistently until the target stops believing their own thoughts and what their eyes can see.

Classic traits

Hassan says cult leaders use a variety of confusion techniques, but a major one was delivering a dizzying amount of information, much of it contradictory and false. This overloaded and overwhelmed critical thinking. Confused people began to 'doubt their ability to distinguish truth from lies, right from wrong'. A cult leader could then 'inculcate a new set of beliefs, feelings, and behaviours'. A confused person could easily be manipulated and controlled. Another tell-tale sign of a cult was when those who challenged the leader with an alternative view, even if it was true, were punished or banished from the cult. You only have to witness the astonishing number of people hired and fired by Trump in his first term to see how this defines him. I remember biographer Michael Wolff predicting that his relationship with Elon Musk would only last so long because Trump fell out with everyone. All you have to do is contradict him or threaten to take his limelight. Musk and Trump are both extreme narcissists and they always fall out in the end although as I write they appear to have kissed and made up. Trump even fired the Bureau of Labor Statistics Commissioner Erika McEntarfer after the bureau published job numbers that didn't suit him. He said she would be replaced by someone 'much more competent and qualified' which is Trump-speak for someone who will supply job numbers that make me look good. The man's a child.

A blatant example of Trump's cult leader behaviour came in June 2025 when Tucker Carlson, who did so much to get Trump elected, questioned the policy of America directly joining the Israel war with Iran. What Carlson had done to benefit Trump was forgotten in an instant as he called him 'kooky' in his contemptuous dismissal. To Trump this was disloyalty when it was a valid opinion. In typical cult fashion his MAGA base also turned on Carlson and anyone else who questioned their god-king. Suddenly they were not 'really MAGA'. Trump said that Carlson had apologised (which he denied), as he said Musk apologised when their relationship publicly unravelled. MAGA media 'influencers' don't seem to realise that Trump is just using them, and they are gone the moment they cease to be useful. Carlson is a pawn to Trump like the rest of them. A means to an end. Carlson staggeringly called Trump a decent humane man in his criticism of the Iran policy. Biographer Michael Wolff is adamant that Carlson and former aide Steve Bannon 'detest' Trump. He said he had listened to them for hours on end speak of their contempt for him. What you see is rarely what you get. Carlson's father Dick had close ties to the CIA as has been publicly known for years (see *The Reveal*), but Carlson said he only found out after his father died on March 24th, 2025, at the age of 84. This is rather a big ask to believe to be honest, especially when video exists before his father's death when Tucker talked about his childhood experiences with CIA operatives. Carlson himself once applied to join the CIA as famously revealed by Vladimir Putin in their interview. His son, Buckley Carlson, by the way, is deputy press secretary to JD Vance.

Trump clearly conspired with Benjamin Netanyahu to orchestrate Israel's bombing of Iran in the summer of 2025 and then sent in 'bunker bombers' to target Iran's nuclear facilities deep underground. The cover story was that Iran was possibly weeks or days from developing a nuclear weapon which was a mantra that Netanyahu had been repeating since at least 1996. Trump's Director of Intelligence Tulsi Gabbard had said only months before that the assessment of US intelligence agencies was that Iran was not developing a nuclear weapon. She was banished from the fold for saying what didn't suit his Iranian ambitions when her comments were re-posted. Trump resorted to the usual superlatives to say that Iranian nuclear ambitions had been 'obliterated' by the bunker bombs. The Pentagon's own immediate intelligence assessment, along with others, contradicted this and Trump was beside himself with rage that anyone could question his lies. He had announced a ceasefire between Israel and Iran on the grounds that 'the job was done' when in truth Israel and Trump wanted a ceasefire with Iranian missiles increasingly causing serious damage to Israeli cities as the 'Iron Dome' missile interceptor system courtesy of the American taxpayer proved to be less than 'iron'. Efforts to subjugate Iran are far from over.

His MAGA base through 'influencers' like Benny Johnson and the late Charlie Kirk spun the climbdown as a Trump masterclass in how to end a war (that he and Israel had started). Kirk even called for Trump to be awarded the Nobel Peace Prize. There was little I agreed with Kirk about, but I condemn his murder in the strongest terms because violence is never an answer to anything. It only leads to still more problems, often violent in nature. Trump claimed to have ended a stream of wars he had nothing to do with ending including the spat between India and Pakistan because he takes lying into the stratosphere. What a sight to see people having their businesses trashed by Trump's off-on tariff insanities saying they still support him while their livelihood went under. Or husbands with their wives arrested by Trump immigration police after decades in the US, and with three young children born there, saying that the cult leader still had their vote. That is cult member behaviour – mind control.

Then there were all the grift scams that Trump and his family launched to take advantage of MAGA and his presidency. We have had Trump family crypto meme coins that are reported to have made billions while MAGA buyers lost their money. Trump and sons established a cryptocurrency venture, World Liberty Financial, an Internet bank using digital money (straight off the wishlist of the World Economic Forum). Official visits to countries include his sons doing deals in the background with those governments. Trump is reported to have secured billions in deals which included as one article said 'licensing the Trump brand to local developers in exchange for large upfront fees'. There are agreements for Trump hotels, towers and a golf club. He accepted a gift from Qatar of a luxury Boeing 747-8 jet worth approximately $400 million. His on-off tariffs allowed for insider trading for anyone in the know amid the market yo-yo and the public pay the tariffs not the country of origin which means it's just another tax. The tariffs were also driving trade towards China and Asia which suited the Cult agenda perfectly of moving power eastwards and away from the West.

We have had a Trump mobile phone, watch, 'fragrance', and even a Bible. The grifting on the back of the presidency is outrageous as is the corruption. He's used his position to scam law firms for in-kind fortunes with threats of government action and frivolous lawsuits against media organisations that have paid millions to settle (he believes in free speech, you see). But those stalwarts of the MAGA cult were unmoved. He was their cult leader after all. The extraordinary irony is that Trump is a little boy in short trousers to his own masters in the shadows and the Sabbateans that own him. The bombast is only for MAGA and the public. The servitude is for *them*. The 'big man' is just a pawn and a puppet, and the Cult will promote him and dispose of him as its agenda demands. Cult leaders come and they go and all will be not what it seems.

That's for sure in the case of Trump.

CHAPTER 22

Enter Epstein

*There's some things you can cover up.
And there's some things you can't.*
Ray Lewis

Trump's cult leader status was challenged like never before from the summer of 2025 when his own personal Achilles heel resurfaced – the late convicted paedophile and child trafficker Jeffrey Epstein.

Trump and his regime hacks had promised to release the 'Epstein files' if he won a second term that would reveal the rich and famous 'clients' who abused the underage girls that Epstein trafficked with his accomplice Ghislaine Maxwell. The MAGA were waiting with bated breath for the revelations to unfold and Trump had made it part of his election campaign. But there was a big problem with that. Trump had been a long-time close friend and associate of Epstein, and he was *in the files*. There were pictures of them together all over the Internet and more would follow after Trump suddenly reneged on releasing the Epstein evidence. There were also many pictures of Trump with his friend Ghislaine Maxwell who was jailed for 20 years in 2022 for sex trafficking, recruiting, grooming, and abusing young girls. She spent time in Israel before her arrest. Epstein had controversially 'died' in New York's Metropolitan Correctional Center in 2019 during Trump's first term. Elon Musk had posted after his falling out with Trump that the Epstein documents and his famous 'clients' had not been released as promised because Trump was in them. Coming from a recent insider of the Trump regime this was a devastating move and fuelled the fire of what would follow. Maybe Musk had swallowed too many pills, or just as maybe it was coldly calculated.

Senate Judiciary Chairman Dick Durbin claimed he had whistleblower evidence that about a thousand FBI agents were deployed in 24-hour shifts to review some 100,000 Epstein records to 'flag' any mention of Donald Trump. Durbin set out his claims in a letter to Attorney General Pam Bondi. Bloomberg soon after reported that Trump's name along with other 'high-profile individuals' were redacted from the records to protect them using an exemption that refers to 'a clearly unwarranted invasion of personal privacy' and another on the grounds that exposure 'could reasonably be expected to constitute an unwarranted invasion of personal privacy'.

Then the *Wall Street Journal* reported that Bondi (a Trump sycophant) and her deputy Todd Blanche (Trump's personal defence lawyer) informed him in May 2025 that his name appeared multiple times in government Epstein files reviewed by the Department of Justice and the FBI (headed by Trump appointees and sycophants Kash Patel and Dan Bongino). Both Patel and Bongino had called the Epstein story a cover-up when they were MAGA Rumble podcasters before they were appointed to the FBI by Trump and, well, became part of the cover-up. Bongino had once said a 'Middle Eastern country' was running a blackmail operation with Epstein, but couldn't bring himself to say which one, and when asked what was closest to his heart he said: 'Israel. The defence of Israel.' Shakes head, moves on. Bondi had told the media soon after Trump's inauguration that the Epstein files were 'on my desk', but now the story would suddenly change. The *Journal* said that Bondi and company told Trump they planned not to release the files 'because the material contained child pornography and the personal information of victims'. Oh, I think there were other reasons when that could have been redacted. Subsequently Bondi and the FBI announced that they had 'found no evidence that Epstein kept a list of individuals connected to his sex trafficking operation involving underage girls' or that he was running a blackmail operation on his 'clients'. They further affirmed that Epstein died by suicide in federal custody in 2019 and was not murdered to silence him ahead of court proceedings as the Trump MAGA base contended (and others that he's not dead at all). They released video footage close to Epstein's cell that night which had minutes missing and fixing videos is child's play.

What a coincidence that two guards were said to have 'fallen asleep' that night when they should have been checking on Epstein every half an hour and relevant prison surveillance cameras were 'not working' leaving only one camera which didn't cover the whole area outside Epstein's cell. A CBS investigation of the video concluded that it was possible to enter the cell (or leave) without being caught on the single camera (Fig 211 overleaf). It also revealed an unidentified third person who entered a common area near Epstein's cell shortly after 4am which was around two hours before 'Epstein's body' was found. A computer curser appears on the camera footage at one point indicating the video could have been shot from a computer screen. Computer experts told CBS that the video metadata showed that the footage had been changed and consisted of two videos edited together. The Mail Online reported that 'metadata shows the video file was modified multiple times on May 23, 2025, over a span of more than three hours, contradicting the notion that this was "raw" footage'. The whole thing stinks. Forensic pathologist Dr Michael Baden, a former New York chief medical examiner, was hired by brother Mark Epstein to observe the autopsy. Baden said: 'I think that the evidence points toward homicide rather than suicide.' He said there were signs of 'unusual' activity 'from day one' of the autopsy with the wounds 'more consistent with ligature homicidal strangulation'. Baden highlighted two fractures on either side of Epstein's larynx, and one on the hyoid bone above the Adam's apple. 'Hanging does not cause these broken bones and homicide does – a huge amount of pressure was applied.' Whatever the background, dead or alive, they didn't want Epstein appearing in court.

Figure 211: The CBS investigation revealing the extent of the one camera coverage near Epstein's cell and the route that could be taken to the cell door without being recorded.

Best buddy

Trump biographer Michael Wolff revealed that Epstein had told him Trump was his closest friend for ten years (others say 15) and showed him pictures of Trump in compromising situations with girls on his lap of an 'uncertain age' naked to the waist. He said one picture included 'a stain on his pants' with girls pointing at it and laughing. Trump and his wife Melania were reported to have had sex for the first time on Epstein's infamous plane dubbed the 'Lolita Express' after all the young girls who had been constantly on board. Trump was named in the flight logs many times. Wolff said Melania was 'very involved' in Epstein's social circle and this was how she met Trump in 1998 through the Epstein-connected founder of ID Models, Paolo Zampolli, who helped her emigrate to the United States. 'MAGA loyalist' Zampolli was appointed Trump's 'special representative for global partnerships' in March 2025 and is reported to have a giant oil painting of Trump in his mansion in Washington's Georgetown. Wolff said Epstein and Trump were 'joined at the hip' before they fell out over a real estate deal in which Trump counterbid his friend after Epstein showed him around the property that he planned to buy. Stacey Williams, a former Sports Illustrated model, said she was Epstein's girlfriend for four months. She recalled:

He always talked about Donald; I can't name another friend that he ever mentioned. He spoke about him regularly, pretty consistently – he was sort of ever present in those conversations.

She claimed that in 1993 she was groped by Trump as he and Epstein were talking. Wolff told the media he had 'hours and hours and hours and hours and hours' of recorded conversations with Epstein talking about his relationship with Trump and the workings of the Trump White House in his first term. Leading media organisations had declined to use the tapes because they had said 'this is too hot to handle'. Steve Bannon, a MAGA stalwart and former Trump aide in his first presidency, also has apparently a large collection of interview tapes with Epstein that have yet to be seen at the time of writing. Michael Wolff said that when he went to Mar-a-Lago to interview Trump his aides asked him for a rough outline of what he wanted to talk about. He mentioned Epstein. They said: 'If you ask about that, he'll just stop the interview, and you won't get anything.' The person added: 'I really recommend you not ask that if you hope for this interview to go on.'

The evidence for the close relationship between Trump and Epstein is overwhelming and Trump's lies about it became laughable in the end. They hung out together year after year; Epstein was a regular visitor to Mar-a-Lago from his home minutes away; he attended Trump's wedding; Trump was a documented passenger on Epstein's Lolita Express at least seven times; the pair are caught on film ogling women at parties; Trump's obsession with women and sex is legendary and he's been accused of sexual abuse by many women – at least 25 since the 1970s. This included writer E. Jean Carroll who won a $83 million defamation verdict against Trump for calling her claims a 'hoax' and a 'con job' to sell a book. 'Hoax' seems to be a favourite word. Other accusations denied by Trump include 'rape, kissing and groping without consent', looking under women's skirts, and walking in on naked teenage pageant contestants. The sexual way he has talked publicly about his daughter Ivanka is seriously weird. Trump said in a *New York Magazine* article in 2002:

> I've known Jeff for fifteen years. Terrific guy. He's a lot of fun to be with. It is even said that he likes beautiful women as much as I do, and many of them are on the younger side. No doubt about it – Jeffrey enjoys his social life.

Virginia Giuffre (formerly Roberts), the most famous and one of the most outspoken of 'Epstein's girls', was working at Trump's Mar-a-Lago mansion in Palm Beach, Florida, when Maxwell recruited her for Epstein who lived only a mile or so down the road. Giuffre, who accused British royal Prince Andrew and his friend Epstein of underage sexual abuse, died by 'suicide' aged 41 in April 2025 just before the Epstein file furore began. She claimed that Prince Andrew had sex with her at Maxwell's say-so when she was 17. Andrew settled out of court for £12 million in 2022 with the sum reportedly paid by the then Queen. But there was no Epstein list. Nothing to see here – move on. Historian Andrew Lownie writes in his book *Entitled: The Rise and Fall of the House of York* that Andrew and Trump were clearly good friends. He says they were overheard at an event about Trump's plans for a Scottish golfing complex talking entirely about 'pussy,' and Trump gave Andrew a list of masseuses. King Trump-the-Liar said in 2019: 'I don't know Prince Andrew.'

Trump said as he flailed around trying to calm the storm that he fell out with Epstein because he 'stole my workers' from his Mar-a-Lago resort and when asked if they included Virginia Giuffre he said yes. This was another blatant lie and contradicted his previous story that he ended the relationship with Epstein because he thought he was a 'creep'. No one seems to have asked him why he came to that conclusion and if it was because he was trafficking and abusing girls why did Trump not tell the authorities? The term 'stole my workers' was typical Trump arrogance that implied ownership. He agreed that those Epstein is claimed to have 'stolen' were young girls working in the Trump spa. Virginia Giuffre's family said it was 'shocking' to hear President Trump saying he was aware that Virginia had been 'stolen' from Mar-a-Lago. They said in a statement: 'It makes us ask if he was aware of Jeffrey Epstein and Ghislaine Maxwell's criminal actions, especially given his statement two years later that his good friend Jeffrey likes women on the younger side ... no doubt about it.'

Did Trump not want to know what was happening to his 'stolen' staff literally down the road where he used to visit? Or did he already know? The whole thing was a lie even looking at the timeline. He talked of Giuffre being taken by Epstein (it was actually Ghislaine Maxwell) and that happened in 2000. Trump remained his closest friend for years after that and Epstein attended his wedding to Melania in 2005. Most of the allegations against Epstein relate to this very five-year period. Trump biographer Michael Wolff said that Epstein explained to him that his fall-out with Trump was over a house in Palm Beach that he bid $36 million to buy. Trump went to see the house to advise Epstein on how to move the swimming pool. Then, behind Epstein's back, Trump bid $40 million and bought the property. Wolff said Epstein was deeply involved with Trump's 'scattered finances' and knew that he didn't have $40 million to buy the house. In that case, it was someone else's $40 million and Epstein believed the funder was a Russian oligarch called Dmitry Rybolovlev. Less than two years later Trump sold the house for $95 million to ... Dmitry Rybolovlev. Wolff said this was a 'red flag for

Enter Epstein

money laundering' and a furious Epstein began to threaten Trump with lawsuits and going to the media to accuse him of being a front man for a money laundering deal. Wolff said:

> Trump panicked at this point and Epstein believed to his dying day that it was Trump who went to the police – Trump who was fully acquainted with what was going on at Epstein's house … for many years. Trump went to the police and as Epstein said 'dropped the dime' on him.

Wolff told this story in his 2019 book *Siege: Trump Under Fire* and he said Epstein called him from Paris 'with some alarm' after reading the book and said he may have said too much. Trump was president at the time. Three weeks later Epstein returned to America from Paris and was arrested on the tarmac at an airport in New Jersey. The rest, as they say, is history. Wolff said he told Epstein at one point that he should make the Trump photos he had public, but Epstein had replied: 'The problem with Donald Trump is he has no scruples.'

Dear Jeffrey

Epstein also had big connections to Bill Gates and former US president Bill Clinton, but suddenly it was Trump who was the focus of attention with all his history as a close friend of Epstein and the files not released. His MAGA base was furious at the broken promise and the sequence began in which Trump's story constantly changed. 'There is no file' became 'there *is* a file', but it had been compiled by the Democrats including former presidents Obama and Biden. The file was a 'hoax', Trump claimed with his fingers crossed. It was another Trump lie as he grappled with the fall-out from his MAGA support which he attacked and belittled for asking questions about the cover up. The *Wall Street Journal* published details of a letter it said Trump had sent to Epstein on his 50th birthday in 2003 in a file compiled by Maxwell. The letter was said to include a drawing of a nude woman with Trump's signature where pubic hair would be. It said:

> Voice Over: There must be more to life than having everything.
> Donald: Yes, there is, but I won't tell you what it is.
> Jeffrey: Nor will I, since I also know what it is.
> Donald: We have certain things in common, Jeffrey.
> Jeffrey: Yes, we do, come to think of it.
> Donald: Enigmas never age, have you noticed that?
> Jeffrey: As a matter of fact, it was clear to me the last time I saw you.
> Trump: A pal is a wonderful thing. Happy Birthday — and may every day be another wonderful secret.

Trump denied that he wrote the letter and later said that it could have been written by someone else. It couldn't have been him because he didn't draw and didn't use words like 'enigmas'. The Internet then produced many of his drawings and doodles along with speeches in which he said 'enigma'. It was confirmed that Ghislaine Maxwell did compile a 'birthday book' of messages for Epstein and a letter emerged written by Maxwell to Epstein from the book. It included letters from Bill Clinton and lawyer Alan Dershowitz. Neither denied they wrote the letters, but Trump said his was fake and issued a $10 billion lawsuit against the *Wall Street Journal*, its owner Rupert Murdoch, and others. Murdoch had been a long-time friend of Trump. Alan Dershowitz had been part of Epstein's legal team that secured him a ridiculously lenient deal on paedophile charges in 2008 agreed with the then US Attorney in South Florida Alexander Acosta who Trump would name as his Secretary of Labor in his first term. The deal was that he pleaded guilty to two state prostitution charges and spent 13 months in a county jail, which he could leave during the day. Prosecutors identified 36 Epstein abuse victims, but most were not even told about the plea deal in violation of Federal law. Trump had contempt for them during the Epstein furore. Then came the revelation that demolished Trump's denials when the House Oversight Committee subpoenaed the Epstein estate to hand over documents which included the Trump birthday letter that was exactly as the *Wall Street Journal* reported with the signature matching Trump's. He was in serious trouble, but the story was quickly downgraded in public attention when two days later came the horrific killing of major Trump promotor Charlie Kirk (see Postscript).

Other revelations continued to confirm Trump's closest of relationships with Epstein. There was the 1997 book *Trump: The Art of the Comeback* signed by Trump to Epstein with the words 'To Jeff – You are the greatest!' (signature the same as the Epstein letter). A video of Epstein emerged making a sworn testimony deposition in 2010 during questions by the lawyer for an alleged victim. Epstein agreed that he socialised with Trump and was then asked: 'Have you ever socialised with Donald Trump in the presence of females under the age of 18?' Epstein replies: 'Though I'd like to answer that question, at least today, I'm going to have to assert my Fifth, Sixth, and Fourteenth Amendment rights, sir.' To 'plead the fifth' is the right to remain silent and not self-incriminate. Trump had once said: 'If you are innocent why are you taking the Fifth Amendment?'

MAGA beside itself

The MAGA were devastated by all this as their saviour was exposed before their eyes. Trump sycophant Alex Jones was in near tears in his reaction to what was the most obvious protection operation for Trump orchestrated by the Justice Department and FBI that he controlled. Jones tried so hard to spin it as he sought to defend the indefensible and destroyed what was left of his credibility with every new 'Trump is doing it because' that insulted the most basic intelligence. The first try was that Trump was holding back the file because he was *'blackmailing the Deep State!'*. Later we had – 'Is Trump being blackmailed *by* the Deep State?' and 'He's not released the files because the Democrats have manipulated them'. These would be the files that the Trump regime claimed didn't exist, right? Anything would do short of being honest that he had been wrong from the start about his hero (and so much else despite his constant claims). It was stomach-turning for me to watch him insult the genuine alternative media day after day with his Trump-defending, Musk-promoting, bootlicking. I find it utterly disgusting what has happened to the 'alternative' since the MAGA media hijack. These people have no idea what's going on, or in some cases don't want us to know.

It was hysterical watching 'influencer' members of the Trump cult disappearing up their own backsides as they came back to 'daddy' and sought to recover from the fleeting realisation that 'daddy' has been a fraud all along – as I have been saying since he came on the political scene in 2016. There were tears and disbelief to begin with as realisation dawned, but cult members are so programmed and personally dependent on their Jim Jones that they must quaff the Kool-Aid and find a way to explain why their daddy is such a blatant liar and conman. Thus, we initially had everyone around the cult leader blamed – Bondi, Patel, Bongino – but not their god-king. Trump's soft support that was not in the Cult, and even some who were, didn't buy the nonsense, however. Bit by bit Trump's support was being chipped away by him saying one thing and doing another over the Epstein files and the way he was ever more obviously owned by Israel. It was not the MAGA core yet at the time of writing; but his softer support was beginning to drift away, furious at being scammed.

Diversion, diversion, diversion

Trump became ever more desperate as his usual techniques to manipulate his MAGA base failed to stop the questions despite the best efforts of his MAGA media. He tried telling them the subject was boring, of no importance, and everyone should move on. Didn't work. He tried insulting them and calling them weak for believing there was a conspiracy. *Seriously* didn't work. Then he tried placating them by saying he would ask Bondi to release 'credible' segments of the Grand Jury testimony in the Epstein case which (a) would need the agreement of a judge and (b) would only involve a *fraction* of the documentation held by the government. The judge did not give permission because of guidelines governing grand jury secrecy – as Trump well knew would happen. Next, he wheeled out Director of National Intelligence Tulsi Gabbard, back in the good books, to deliver 'bombshell revelations' that President Obama together with Hillary Clinton and intelligence officials had orchestrated false claims that Russia had sought to intervene in the 2016 election to help Trump. The so-called 'Russia hoax' had sought to undermine the Trump presidency, Gabbard claimed.

Obama and others like the Clintons' are appalling for sure, and capable of anything, but the timing of the 'revelations' in the middle of the Trump-Epstein uproar told the story. It was a desperate effort to quench the Epstein fire that was starting to threaten his presidency. Alex Jones and the MAGA media were immediately on the case demanding that Obama be arrested and jailed. Trump posted videos to this effect. But he then admitted that the Supreme Court decision to give presidents immunity from prosecution for official acts in office (to benefit Trump) would also apply to Obama. You mean he didn't know that all along? MAGA just gets played and played. It's a One-Party State and Mark Epstein, brother of Jeffrey Epstein, told the media: 'In the 2016 election, Jeffrey told me that if he said what he knew about the candidates [Trump and Hillary Clinton], they would have to cancel the election.'

Desperation reached new heights when Trump despatched Deputy Attorney General Todd Blanche, his personal lawyer, to meet with Ghislaine Maxwell over two days in her Florida jail. This was unprecedented and other lawyers said the meeting was not ethical. Fortunately, the Justice Department's senior ethics attorney, Joseph Tirrell, had just been fired by Trump gofer Pam Bondi. Days earlier Trump and Bondi had sacked Maurene Comey, a veteran prosecutor with the Attorney's Office for the Southern District of New York, who secured the conviction of Maxwell. Comey is the daughter of former FBI head James Comey who Trump clearly hates, and his gofer Bondi indicted him in 2025 on charges of making a false statement to Congress and obstructing a Congressional proceeding in 2020. Around the same time Epstein's lawyer Roy Black, who helped secure Epstein's 2008 plea deal, died. Okay, he was 80, but it added to the gathering coincidences. Days after Maxwell met Trump gofer Todd Blanche she was moved from Florida to a minimum-security jail in Texas with no towering fences, no barbed wire, and no high-security cells – all against protocol given her crime and sentence. Reports even suggested she had the chance of work release. Inmate Julie Howell, serving a one-year sentence at the jail for theft, was immediately transferred to a higher security facility after criticising Maxwell in an interview with a British newspaper. Howell said she spoke out because a family member was a victim of sex trafficking.

The *Times of Israel* reported that Maxwell had long been 'receiving prison benefits by touting Jewish heritage' with help from organisations like Chabad-Lubavitch. Rumours began that Maxwell, a long-time friend of Trump, was being offered the 'deal' of a reduced sentence or even a pardon if she cleared him. Blanche was accompanied by Maxwell's lawyer David Oscar Markus who is a personal friend and appears with him on podcasts. Trump was asked by the media while the Blanche meetings were happening if he was considering giving a pardon to Maxwell. He said in separate comments:

> It's something I haven't thought about. I'm allowed to do it, but it's something I have not thought about …
>
> … A lot of people are asking me about pardons. Obviously. This is no time to be talking about pardons. But a lot of people have asked about pardons. This is just not the time to be talking about pardons.

He had said something similar before pardoning people. The idea that 'I haven't thought about it' is an obvious whopper even by Trump standards as was the claim that he did not have details about what Maxwell had said during the meeting with Blanche. Then came the inevitable punchline as the 'transcript' of the Blanche interview was released by the Trump regime in which she cleared him of 'acting inappropriately' with anyone, said she knew nothing about the Trump-Epstein birthday letter, and denied she and Epstein were running a blackmail or trafficking operation. No wonder she got the jail change. Talk about in plain sight. What a joke. Unfortunately for her the birthday letter and 18,000 Epstein emails leaked to Bloomberg demolished her denials. Trump biographer Michael Wolff said the White House believed the Trump 50th birthday letter to Epstein was leaked from the 'Maxwell side' as a 'shot across the bows' to Trump that Ghislaine Maxwell has damaging material on him. She was clearly willing to release it unless she got something in return, and it was then that Trump started dropping the word 'pardon'. This would also explain why Trump's lawyer Todd Blanche was dispatched to meet with Maxwell in her jail. Wolff made the point that Trump treats his lawyers with contempt: 'He has crucified them all – I cannot describe his treatment of these people. He breaks them.' He said that as a result they know that they have only one role in life and that's to serve Donald Trump. Wolff said the Justice Department was not an independent body representing America. It only represented the interests of Trump. The man is a psychopathic monster and that is who Jones, Brand, Rogan, Johnson, Pool, the late Charlie Kirk, Tucker Carlson, Candace Owens, Megyn Kelly and the MAGA media crowd promoted into power.

Trump has previous with other 'model agents' including John

Casablancas, founder of the legendary Elite Model Management that developed the concept of the 'supermodel'. Trump's daughter Ivanka was a model at Elite at age 15. Casablancas became a friend and associate in New York and Trump said Casablancas 'tutored him' in the 'modeling agency' scene. Trump subsequently started his own agency, Trump Models, while Epstein invested in the MC2 modeling agency of Jean-Luc Brunel who faced allegations of sexual assault over three decades and worked with Epstein from just after the millennium until 2015. He was accused of grooming young women and being involved in Epstein's sex trafficking ring. Brunel died by 'hanging himself' in a French jail cell less than three years after Epstein is said to have done the same in New York. Trump also ran 'beauty pageants' and bought Miss Universe, Miss USA, and Miss Teen USA. He told journalist Michael Gross, author of the 1995 book *Model: The Ugly Business of Beautiful Women:* 'I don't think anybody had more sex than I did.' Trump attended Elite Model Management parties in the early 1980s, hosted and judged events for them, and provided accommodation for models. Elite agency model Barbara Pilling said Trump invited her to dinner in 1989 and asked how old she was: 'I said 17 and he said, "That's just great – you're not too old, not too young."'

Cutting through the crap

Okay, a little sanity is required. Jewish Jeffrey Epstein was running a blackmail operation for Israel and its intelligence arm Mossad. Epstein's Jewish sidekick Ghislaine Maxwell is the daughter of known Mossad agent, the late media mogul and UK Labour MP, Robert Maxwell. He was also believed to work for British and Russian Intelligence. I have talked to some of the women abused in the Epstein circle when little more than children and they all mention the hidden cameras and microphones on Epstein's private island, Little Saint James in the US Virgin Islands, and at other properties in Florida, New York and elsewhere. The Cult, in which Mossad is a major asset, specialises in honeytraps and drawing influential people into paedophilia to ensure they do whatever they are told from then on. Here we had Trump as the 'closest friend' of Epstein for a decade and knew him for far longer. The potential for entrapment was unlimited and later he suddenly runs for US president, wins twice, and gives Israel virtually everything it has demanded. Former Israeli prime minister Ehud Barak was a close friend of Epstein while Trump's ultra-Zionist Commerce Secretary, Howard Lutnick, who survived by being late to work at the World Trade Center on 9/11, was a next-door neighbour of Epstein in New York. Barak was apparently introduced to Epstein by another Israel prime minister Shimon Peres. Former Israeli military intelligence agent, Ari Ben-Menashe, said Barak was getting blackmail information from Epstein about powerful people in the United States. This was why Epstein made sure he used underage girls to trap his targets in illegal sexual activity. A hack of 100,000 emails by a hacker group targeting Israeli officials confirmed the Epstein-Barak connection and how this also linked to an Israel-centred AI surveillance network that involved Peter Thiel's Palantir. The *Cult* network in other words.

Robert Maxwell was a mega crook known as Captain Bob and the Bouncing Czech (he was born in Czechoslovakia in 1923). He owned a media and publishing empire and knew both Epstein and Trump. Maxwell and Trump bought luxury yachts from the same dealer and named them after their daughters Ghislaine and Ivanka. Ghislaine Maxwell could well have been introduced to Epstein through her Israel agent father because they knew each other before her father's death in contrast to official claims. Former Mossad agent Victor Ostrovsky describes in his book, *The Other Side of Deception*, how Robert Maxwell was murdered by Mossad at sea on his yacht in 1991 near the Canary Islands when he became more of a hazard than a help as his business empire collapsed. He also embezzled hundreds of millions of pounds from his own companies' pension funds including the Mirror newspaper group. Everyone is expendable to the Cult if it benefits the Cult. Maxwell was then buried by the country that killed him with full honours on the Mount of Olives in Jerusalem – the 'resting place for the nation's most revered heroes', as Ostrovsky puts it. The hypocrisy is breathtaking. A Jewish publication said: 'One of the great curiosities of the late 20th century is why publishing magnate Robert Maxwell was accorded what amounted to a state funeral on the Mount of Olives attended by a posse of rabbis, the then Israeli President Chaim Herzog and Prime Minister Yitzhak Shamir.' Services rendered, I guess. Shamir said at the funeral that Maxwell 'has done more for Israel than can today be said'. The funeral was attended by six then current and former heads of Israeli intelligence. I met Maxwell when I was making a film for the BBC about the football club he owned, Oxford United. I interviewed him in his office at Mirror newspapers. I felt like I needed a shower afterwards to wash away the evil. Horrible, horrible, man, and Trump reminds me of him. Former Mossad case officer Ostrovsky said:

> Mossad was financing many of its operations in Europe from money stolen from Maxwell's newspaper pension fund. They got their hands on the funds almost as soon as Maxwell made the purchase of the Mirror Newspaper Group with money lent to him by Mossad.

Highly significantly, he claimed that Mossad provided prostitutes for Maxwell in Israel which they used for blackmail and employed the Epstein method of hidden cameras with 'a small library of video footage of Maxwell in sexually compromising positions'. Ari Ben-Menashe, an Iranian born Jew and former operative with Israel's Military Intelligence Directorate, also said Robert Maxwell was a Mossad agent with big ties to Jeffrey Epstein. Ben-Menashe said he met Epstein and Ghislaine Maxwell through Robert Maxwell in the 1980s when they were already working for Israeli intelligence: '... they found a niche for themselves – blackmailing American and other political figures.' Ben-Menashe said Epstein had been a regular visitor to Robert Maxwell's office in London.

Researcher Whitney Webb writes that Maxwell was a close associate and friend of Israeli intelligence officer and 'superspy' Rafi Eitan who was the 'handler' of Jonathan Pollard, an American former intelligence analyst, jailed for spying for Israel and handing over top secret information. Rafi Eitan previously worked directly with Zionist mobster Meyer Lansky whose crime syndicate had major connections to Mossad and the CIA. Pollard was sentenced to life imprisonment in 1987 and paroled in 2015. He later relocated to Israel which had granted him citizenship in 1996. Author Daniel Halper in his 2014 book, *Clinton Inc: The Audacious Rebuilding of a Political Machine*, quotes documents and former government officials as saying that Netanyahu sought to pressure President Bill Clinton into releasing Pollard with the threat that Israel had phone tapes of the infamous sexual relationship between Clinton and Jewish intern Monica Lewinsky. Halper was not the only author to say this, and you see how the game works. Clinton apparently backed off when his head of the CIA, George Tenet, threatened to resign if Pollard was released.

Are we really so naive that we can't see the obvious that two Jewish insiders were running a blackmail operation for Mossad – both with enormous connections to 'elite' society and Israel with one the daughter of an Israel intelligence operative given a hero's funeral on the exclusive Mount of Olives? Does that naivety extend to dismissing the very idea that Donald Trump was a close friend of Epstein and Maxwell over a long period and, when he twice becomes US President, he gives Israel whatever it demands? Cult operative Benjamin Netanyahu announced on yet another visit to Washington that he had nominated Trump for the Nobel Peace Prize for bombing Iran in an exchange that had Trump calling Netanyahu 'the greatest man in the world'. It doesn't get more ridiculous, but when you are owned you will be as ridiculous as they tell you to be. Epstein would also have had connections to the CIA which at the 'web' level' connects through the Cult with Mossad.

Then there is the question about the source of Epstein's vast wealth. He owned private islands, private jets, a helicopter, at least 15 vehicles, and high-end homes across the world. He was described in court by a prosecutor as a 'man of nearly infinite means'. A file in his criminal trial put his wealth at $560 million while others put it higher. Where did it come from? No one seems to know. One source was his close associate, Jewish billionaire Les Wexner, owner of lingerie chain Victoria's Secret, who employed him as his financial manager from 1987 to 2007. Epstein reportedly made a lucrative investment in Valar Ventures, the venture capital firm co-founded by Peter Thiel and again named after characters in the writings of J. R. R. Tolkien including *Lord of the Rings*. But none of this explains the size of his wealth. Two days before his demise he signed away his assets to a trust which meant those who benefited remained private and undisclosed.

The Mega Group

Billionaire and Epstein associate Les Wexner was a co-founder in 1991 of the Mega Group with businessman Charles Bronfman of the notorious Jewish Canadian-American Bronfman family. Researcher Whitney Webb points out that the Mega Group had ties to Robert Maxwell who was a business associate of Charles Bronfman. It involved those with 'deep ties to organized crime' and the crime network 'largely led by notorious [Jewish] American mobster Meyer Lansky'. The Mega Group was also connected to Jeffrey Epstein and Donald Trump. Webb wrote:

> By virtue of the role of many Mega Group members as major political donors in both the U.S. and Israel, several of its most notable members have close ties to the governments of both countries as well as their intelligence communities ...
>
> ... the Mega Group also had close ties to two businessmen who worked for Israel's Mossad — Robert Maxwell and [commodities trader] Marc Rich — as well as to top Israeli politicians, including past and present prime ministers with deep ties to Israel's intelligence community ...
>
> ... Media profiles of the group paint it as 'a loosely organized club of 20 of the nation's wealthiest and most influential Jewish businessmen focused on philanthropy and Jewishness,' with membership dues upwards of $30,000 per year. Yet several of its most prominent members have ties to organized crime.

Another Mega Group member was Israel and Jewish cause benefactor Ronald Lauder of the Estee Lauder cosmetics family who gets several mentions in my 9/11 exposure book, *The Trigger*. Lauder was central through funding and personnel to Benjamin Netanyahu's first victory in 1996. Webb writes that 'perhaps the best illustration of how the connections between many of these players often meld together can be seen in Ronald Lauder: a Mega Group member, former member of the Reagan administration, long-time donor to Israeli Prime Minister Benjamin Netanyahu and Israel's Likud Party, as well as a long-time friend of Donald Trump and Roy Cohn'. The latter has already appeared in the book as a deeply crooked ultra-Zionist lawyer and mentor to Trump. Cohn represented ultra-Zionist media mogul Rupert Murdoch who met Trump through him at the start of a long friendship. The fact that Trump issued a $10 billion lawsuit against Murdoch over the *Wall Street Journal* 'letter to Epstein' means there is a lot more to know about the background to all this. The whole thing is dominated by Israel and its benefactors, gofers and operatives.

The Mega Group connects with the World Jewish Congress (past president Edgar Bronfman and current one Ronald Lauder are both Mega Group members), the Rothschild B'nai B'rith and its creation, the Anti-Defamation League (ADL) which campaigns for the censorship of 'antisemitism' using a panoramic definition. Whitney Webb reveals that Mega Group members have been key players in the pro-Israel lobby in the United States. They included Max Fisher of the Mega Group who founded the National Jewish Coalition (now the Republican Jewish Coalition). Among its chief patrons have been Sheldon Adelson and Bernard Marcus who were leading donors to Donald Trump's election campaigns. Mega Group founder Les Wexner was an associate of former Israel prime minister Ehud Barak who became close to Jeffrey Epstein. Whitney Webb noted:

> According to Barak, he was first introduced to Epstein by former Israeli Prime Minister Shimon Peres, who eulogized Robert Maxwell at his funeral and had decades-long ties with the Bronfman family going back to the early 1950s. Peres was also a frequent participant in programs funded by Leslie Wexner in Israel and worked closely with the Mossad for decades.

You see what a maze it is. This is how the Cult works, but behind it is a simple interlocking structure which has the name 'Israel' running through like seaside rock or candy. Brooklyn-born Jewish American Steven Hoffenberg was CEO, president, and chairman of a Ponzi scheme called Towers Financial Corporation which defrauded investors out of $475 million and served 18 years of a 20-year sentence. Hoffenberg employed Epstein for six years in the late 1980s/early 1990s and said he was intimately involved in the Ponzi scheme. Hoffenberg called him the 'architect of the scam', but Epstein was never charged. He said Epstein and Ghislaine Maxwell were gathering information on the rich, famous and influential in the United States on behalf of Israel and the British. Epstein worked for the late British defence contractor Douglas Leese who Hoffenberg said was his intelligence/arms 'mentor' and introduced him to Ghislaine Maxwell. Hoffenberg said Epstein had told him he also worked with Robert Maxwell on various projects, and Hoffenberg emphasised the central role played with Epstein of Ghislaine Maxwell.

She had been equal if not worse than Epstein which was a point also made by Virginia Giuffre. Hoffenberg said the duo were working for Israeli intelligence from the 1980s which matches the claims of Israeli intelligence operative Ari Ben-Menashe. This would mean that Epstein was working for Israeli intelligence throughout the time that Trump was his best buddy. Peter Thiel said it was unlikely that Jeffrey Epstein was involved with foreign intelligence, so confirming that he was.

Another rarely mentioned Epstein property to highlight is his 8,000-acre Zorro Ranch in New Mexico with its landing strip and helicopter pad located less than an hour from Santa Fe. Ickonic's Richard Willett has done extensive research on the ranch and the surrounding area. He points out that within less than 200 miles (no distance by helicopter and private jet) are major underground bases such as Dulce, Los Alamos National Laboratory (of Manhattan Project fame producing the first atomic bombs dropped on Japan), and Kirkland Airforce Base that have all been connected to extraterrestrial sightings and activity. There is also the Scientology Church of Spiritual Technology at Trementina, a two-hour drive east which was created to 'provide storage space to preserve the writings, films and recordings of Scientology founder L. Ron Hubbard'. New Mexico has many underground bases and secret locations that have been linked with ET activity. The famous Roswell UFO incident was in New Mexico in 1947. I have written at length over the years about tunnel systems with high-speed trains that link these and other bases throughout the United States. Rumours tell of tunnels under Zorro Ranch and there are certainly vast underground rooms.

Virginia Giuffre/Roberts and another outspoken Epstein-Maxwell campaigner Juliette Bryant both described being taken to the ranch. The *New York Times* reported that Epstein told scientists and close friends that he 'hoped to seed the human race with his DNA by impregnating women at the ranch'. He had an intense interest in human cloning, DNA manipulation, and transhumanism. South African Juliette Bryant said that while at the Zorro Ranch, she woke up naked in a laboratory and was unable to move. 'They did something to me, and I want to know what. That's why I won't stop until I find out.' She said she met Epstein in Cape Town in 2002 after being promised help with her modelling career. She was invited to dinner with Epstein, former president Bill Clinton and actors Kevin Spacey and Chris Tucker. She said Clinton's presence added to Epstein's credibility. A 2020 Netflix documentary series *Jeffrey Epstein: Filthy Rich* revealed that the three men travelled in Epstein's plane to Africa in 2002 for 'humanitarian purposes in combating the HIV/AIDS epidemic'. Bryant said she saw a 'UFO' while at the Zorro Ranch and she told Richard Willett on his Ickonic.com show, *Classified*, that she saw Epstein shapeshift into a reptilian form when taken to his island:

I saw Epstein shift in front of my eyes. It was very, very frightening and it's something I had to explain to myself because I saw him turn into something. If someone told me this, I wouldn't believe it, but unfortunately it happened to me, and I had to look into it and find reasons to explain it. It's not an easy thing to talk about because most people wouldn't understand it if they hadn't seen it.

Bryant said Epstein took the form of like a dragon. She said she had never heard of the shapeshifting phenomenon then, but years later her mother began to research my work:

I saw him shift into something – it only happened once. It was like a weird hologram. It had big black eyes … it was like a reptilian, Draconian, alien sort of thing. I looked away and when I looked back it was him again.

She said in another interview: 'Then [there was] a big mouth with this horrible tongue and like this sort of dragon horn stuff, which is almost like the devil.' It is a reminder that the hybrid bloodlines of the Cult are not who people think they are and behind the place men and women and gofers that we see in politics, business and media is a very different force at work orchestrating the dystopian control of humanity from the Astral dimension of the Matrix.

Where will it go?

What was happening with Trump reminded me of the Watergate scandal which I lived through and observed in the 1970s and had parallels with the Trump-Epstein storm. Operatives for the Republican Richard Nixon regime broke into the Democratic Party headquarters in the Watergate Building in Washington. Denials by Nixon were followed by more revelations followed by more denials followed by more revelations followed by more denials followed by more revelations until eventually Nixon was forced to resign. People on the inside like Henry Kissinger were working to undermine Nixon and there would be insiders doing the same with Trump who is nothing more than an expendable Deep State gofer. Nixon was replaced by the Deep State gofer vice president Gerald Ford, an operative in the grotesque child-abusing mind control operation, MKUltra.

I wondered if scandal and Trump's increasingly bizarre behaviour, cognitive and health decline, and news conference ramblings would prevent him completing his term in favour of JD Vance. Israel-owned Musk had posted: 'JD is a good guy through and through.' He isn't, but this is politics. Trump had threatened to delete massive government subsidies to Musk companies when they began sharing insults, but as

Trump's troubles ran deeper and deeper he posted: 'Everyone is stating that I will destroy Elon's companies by taking away some, if not all, of the large-scale subsidies he receives from the U.S. Government. This is not so!' People *stated* that because Trump *said* that. But this was a vulnerable Trump: 'The better they [Musk's companies] do, the better the USA does, and that's good for all of us.' Should Trump for some reason not go the distance the president would be JD Vance who is owned by Peter Thiel and the AI oligarchy and owned by Israel as much as Trump. Maybe the plan from the start was to use Trump and MAGA to get him elected only to remove him through health or scandal to open the way for AI oligarch/Thiel funded gofer JD Vance. Didn't Musk urge Trump to pick Vance as his Vice President running mate? Didn't Thiel? Trump to the Cult is just a glove puppet. It has so much on him and its covert networks can make him or break him at will.

Epstein was a Mossad blackmail operation, and the Cult via Israel will have all the files that 'don't exist', sorry, 'were compiled by the Democrats'. If it suits the Cult for Trump to stay, then he will. If it doesn't at some point, well ... they always have Thiel-owned Israel-fanatic Vance. Whatever suits their agenda they will do. We'll see where it goes from here – Trump is making every effort to divert attention from the Epstein files – and much will happen before you read this with the book's months of production and shipping to America still to come. I can only go with what is happening as I write, and I will add updates as an end-of-book Postscript just before it heads for the printers.

All is being orchestrated from the shadows and the Astral with Trump, Musk, Vance, and their like only front people following orders while they are considered useful. The Cult is constantly aware of sell-by dates.

CHAPTER 23

'Accelerating' the 'Dark Enlightenment'

All tyrannies rule through fraud and force, but once the fraud is exposed, they must rely exclusively on force.
George Orwell

The most significant development triggered immediately after the 'assassination attempt' was the Trump support from Elon Musk who endorsed him for president within the hour followed by other Big Tech AI oligarchs. He went on to hand Trump a quarter of a billion dollars for his campaign.

Musk, it turned out, was buying himself into government unelected and he would go on to create calculated mayhem before leaving to unleash a barrage of attacks on Trump that ended the bosom buddy act for a while. It all seemed so sudden and contrived. One day he was in the Oval Office being handed a symbolic 'Golden Key' to the White House and being praised by Trump for all his work at the end of his tenure as a 'special government official'. Then in no time Musk is firing cruise missiles at his former 'best buddy'. Musk turned his ire on Trump's ridiculously named 'Big Beautiful Bill' that was passed – just – to add trillions to government debt against everything the cult leader said he would do. He called it a 'disgusting abomination'. Musk for sure had his own reasons for targeting the bill and it wasn't because it gives massive tax breaks to billionaires while cutting medical and other payments for millions of poor people. He announced the launch of a new political party, the America Party, to break the 'two party state'. It's a One-Party State and would still be so with Musk's addition. His new party pronouncements had to be seen in the context of his $5 million donations to the Senate Leadership Fund and Congressional Leadership Fund, the main super PACs supporting Senate and House Republicans, on the same day he handed $5 million to the pro-Trump MAGA Inc. PAC. This was on June 27th, 2025, and he publicly proposed the America Party on July 5th. The public conflict between Musk and Trump (of which there is a lot more to know) added to the chaos and upheavals as the Cult transitioned from its old system to a new level of dystopia founded on AI. There is a possible scenario in which Trump eventually steps down through health or scandal before the end of his term and JD Vance becomes president with the support of Elon Musk backing the AI oligarch gofer along with his political funder Peter Thiel. We'll see. By August 20th, the UK Mail Online was reporting, based on a *Wall Street Journal* story, that Musk was putting his America Party on hold to support Vance for a run for president in 2028 and so join other 'tech titans' backing Vance including Peter Thiel and Palmer Luckey. Don't be surprised if this happens *before* Trump's term is supposed to conclude. But it's not about Trump or Musk, Thiel or Vance, or any other individual. If you can see them, they are gofers. The whole agenda is being driven from the shadows and the Astral and even the richest and apparently most powerful are only pawns being moved around the board.

'Dark MAGA'

Trump was back in the White House in January 2025 surrounded by the Silicon Valley oligarchs who would run his presidency along with his Cult masters and Israel. Trump returned to the Butler 'assassination' location just before the 2024 election when Musk also took to the stage to announce his MAGA credentials – with a difference. 'I'm not just MAGA, I'm dark MAGA', he bellowed. Dark MAGA? What could he mean? He was describing the collective mentality of the AI oligarchs surrounding Trump. Iain Davis in an excellent two-part article I saw at Unlimitedhangout.com relates this to the 'Dark Enlightenment' and something called 'accelerationism'. This is a new buzzword appearing across both Left and Right and in governments and corporations. The Dark Enlightenment wants an end to democracy and a return to authoritarian rule, including an 'absolute monarchy' in which 'the sovereign is the sole source of political power, unconstrained by constitutions, legislatures or other checks on their authority'. Totalitarianism in other words. This doesn't mean necessarily a king or queen, but one person running the show. The trend is not only in the United States and the theme of 'Dark Enlightenment' and 'Dark MAGA' will embolden other parts of the world with China as a blueprint. Long-time American freedom campaigner John Whitehead of the Rutherford Institute highlighted how the Trump regime that pledged to uphold the Constitution was dismantling it once in office. They were targeting:

> First Amendment rights to free speech, assembly, and protest. Fourth Amendment protections against unreasonable searches and seizures. Fifth Amendment guarantees of due process. Sixth Amendment protections ensuring a right to legal counsel. Eighth Amendment protections against cruel and unusual punishments. Fourteenth Amendment rights to equal protection under the law.

Accelerationism is how you get there. This means to accelerate the destruction and disruption of the *old* Cult system and replace it with the *new* Cult system of AI control. Watch for the use of 'acceleration' by Global Cult operatives. Remember that Musk said when he merged his xAI with Twitter/X: 'This will allow us to build a platform that doesn't just reflect the world but actively *accelerates* human progress.' Iain Davis highlights how Zionist Larry Fink, WEF chairman and CEO at multi-trillion dollar 'investment' firm, BlackRock, used the term seven times in a 2021 letter to shareholders including 'the pandemic has also *accelerated* deeper trends' (it was meant to) and 'momentum continues to build, and in 2021 it will *accelerate* – with dramatic implications for the global economy'. Joseph H. Davis, Chief Economist for Vanguard, another investment giant, wrote in 2020 that 'the pandemic has *accelerated* some trends already in place'. You get the picture and the reason – one *major* reason – why the 'Covid pandemic' was hoaxed. I saw European Central Bank chief Christine Lagarde speak of *accelerating* the pace to the digital euro and once you get the meaning it's like the subliminal becomes conscious and you begin to notice how often the term is used. Lagarde is former head of the International Monetary Fund (IMF) and a long-time Cult operative. The theme of 'acceleration' is intrinsically linked to my concept of Problem-Reaction-Solution and the Totalitarian Tiptoe now becoming the 'Totalitarian Sprint'. Iain Davis quotes an article by Andy Beckett in the UK *Guardian*:

> Accelerationists argue that technology, particularly computer technology, and capitalism, particularly the most aggressive, global variety, should be massively sped up and intensified [...] Accelerationists favour automation. They favour the further merging of the digital and the human.
>
> They often favour the deregulation of business, and drastically scaled-back government. They believe that people should stop deluding themselves that economic and technological progress can be controlled. They often believe that social and political upheaval has a value in itself ...
>
> ... Accelerationism, therefore, goes against conservatism, traditional socialism, social democracy, environmentalism, protectionism, populism, nationalism, localism and all the other ideologies.

This is the mentality being promoted by the Trump regime and its AI oligarchs and grasping this opens the door to understand what is really going on. One of the advocates of accelerationism and the Dark Enlightenment is ... Peter Thiel. Among the ideological drivers has been Nick Land described as the 'Godfather of accelerationism' who co-founded the Cybernetic Culture Research Unit at England's Warwick University. Another is Curtis Yarvin (pen name Mencius Moldbug) who with Nick Land are 'spiritual' architects of the Dark Enlightenment and its accelerationism modus operandi. Big Tech billionaires and front-line Trump/MAGA politicians and operatives have said they are influenced by Yarvin. Peter Thiel said he was his 'most important connection' and supplied start-up funding for Yarvin's technology company, Urbit. Yarvin describes watching the results of the 2016 presidential election with Peter Thiel and said: 'He's fully enlightened. Just plays it very carefully.' Trump supporter and his former political strategist Steve Bannon is said to have admired Yarvin's work and Vice-President JD Vance cites Yarvin as an influence. You can see the ideological foundations of the Musk-Thiel-Vance mentality. Yarvin wants government to be imposed by a corporate structure that he dubs 'gov-corp'. He has called for a 'national CEO', or 'dictator':

> It is essential to squash the democratic myth that a state 'belongs' to the citizenry. The point of neo-cameralism [tyranny] is to buy out the real stakeholders in sovereign power, not to perpetuate sentimental lies about mass enfranchisement ... Once the universe of democratic corruption is converted into a (freely transferable) shareholding in gov-corp, the owners of the state can initiate rational corporate governance.

This has been happening before your eyes. Who did the *New York Times* say Elon Musk consulted while considering his new 'America Party'? *Curtis Yarvin*.

The love-in (at first)

Musk and Trump always had an up and down relationship. Trump once called him 'another bullshit artist' which is probably one of the most accurate statements he's ever made. Musk resigned from presidential advisory boards in Trump's first term in protest at America's withdrawal from the Paris Agreement on Climate Change. Musk said at the time: 'Climate change is real. Leaving Paris is not good for America or the world.' Climate change *is* real, it has happened since the Earth first appeared, but *human-caused* climate change is a load of baloney instigated by the Cult through its agencies like the Club of Rome to justify the transformation of human society and the centralisation of global power. The history of weather 'experts' in government and 'academic' institutions making up data is shocking. 'Heat measuring' technology is positioned beside runways where military jets spewing flames from their engines are taking off. Others are placed next to heat sources on buildings while other data is compiled from 'measuring centres' that *don't exist*. The *Daily Sceptic* website and its excellent climate researcher Chris Morrison exposed through Freedom of Information requests to the UK Met Office, and the work of individual researchers, that data was being used from more than 100 stations that *don't exist* to produce 'temperature averages'. See *The Perception Deception* and *Everything You Need To Know* where I take the climate lies apart and see also the brilliant Ickonic.com series *The Climate Truth* with long-time climate researcher Paul Burgess. Meanwhile the landscape continues to be blighted by wind turbines and solar panels to stop a problem that's not happening. So no, Mr Musk, *human-caused* climate change is *not* real.

Musk endorsed Trump for president followed by other Silicon Valley billionaires immediately after the 'assassination attempt'. The AI sting was being moved into place. Musk also urged Trump to select Ohio Senator JD Vance as his running mate. Vance is another political protégé of Musk's friend, associate, and investor in his companies, Peter Thiel, who has funded Vance's career with help from the Israel lobby. They are also business associates. Vance is a principle at Peter Thiel's venture capital company Mithril Capital and very supportive, to say the least, of the Musk-Thiel agenda for the takeover by AI. Days after the shooting and Musk's endorsement we had Trump naming Vance as his running mate at the Republican Party Convention even though in 2016 Vance told his former law school roommate: 'I go back and forth between thinking Trump is a cynical asshole like Nixon who wouldn't be that bad (and might even prove useful) or that he's America's Hitler. How's that for discouraging?' Vance, Trump, Musk, and MAGA claim to be 'anti-globalist' while connecting fundamentally with Thiel who is on the steering committee of the globalist Bilderberg Group along with his fellow Palantir founder, Alex Karp. Divisions and rhetoric are mostly pure theatre and where conflict between operatives is genuine it is not allowed to get in the way of the overall plan. If it ever threatens to get out of hand (we are talking about narcissists after all) there are consequences.

Trump went on to appoint Musk as the unelected head of 'DOGE', or 'Department of Government Efficiency', which was sold as deleting government waste. Musk was a de facto joint President in the early weeks of 2025 (who had never seen a ballot box) as Trump set about dismantling the checks and balances of Congress and courts to impose a full-blown dictatorship. Musk and his DOGE began firing government employees en masse and destroying their lives and incomes without even knowing what they did. Staff at the National Nuclear Safety Administration overseeing America's nuclear stockpile were fired until the juvenile idiots that DOGE employed realised who they had sacked and scrambled to re-employ them. Government workers were demonised just for being government workers with the age-old technique of demonise and destroy. The Musk propaganda, mostly without any evidence, was relentless and yet the amount of money 'saved' was a tiny, tiny, fraction of the $2 trillion that was promised. I mean *tiny*. But that wasn't the point. Unleashing chaos and disruption was the point.

DOGE chaos

Musk's DOGE operation may not have saved much money, but it did have the Cult benefit of instigating chaos and the dismantling of the status quo. Whole government agencies were deleted and funding slashed including for weather monitoring staff despite warnings that this could lead to disasters through inadequate forecasts and personnel. Then came the mass deaths after catastrophic flooding in Texas. Among them were many young girls at a summer camp. Officials said they were not adequately warned by weather agencies. There was also speculation about rain-making operations happening in the area in the run up to the deluge that were instigated by the Rainmaker weather modification start-up company of CEO Augustus Doricko which has been backed by Peter 'he's everywhere' Thiel. Doricko, who was awarded $100,000 through Thiel's Fellowship, denies his rainmaking two days before the disaster was connected to the flash floods. Musk and DOGE targeting agencies meant that food and other aid was left to rot at seaports unable to move while the would-be recipients went hungry.

Musk and DOGE really didn't want their operatives exposed, but some came to light including 19-year-old high school graduate Edward Coristine known by the nickname 'Big Balls'. He was fired from a previous job for leaking internal information to competitors. Just what you need when accessing private information of the public and rivals of Musk for government contracts. Coristine is reported to be the grandson of KGB double agent Valery Martynov who was executed for being a traitor to the Soviet Union in 1987 after secretly working for the FBI and CIA. Coristine was formerly an intern at Musk's Neuralink and became a 'senior adviser' to the Bureau of Diplomatic Technology at the State Department and an 'expert' at the Office of Personnel Management which is connected to the hiring and firing of government employees. Another DOGE operative identified by *Business Insider* from his publicly accessible Google Calendar going back to 2016 revealed connections to the Trump administration, names of other DOGE staffers, and scheduled interviews at companies including Tesla, Palantir, and Anduril. Tesla is Musk, Palantir is Peter Thiel, and Anduril is another AI defence and surveillance operation headed by Thiel protégé and self-styled 'radical Zionist' Palmer Luckey who promotes the use of AI killer robots. A call was also set up with Founders Fund – Peter Thiel. The fund was one of SpaceX's first investors. This DOGE bloke was 26-year-old Riley Sennott who was listed in an internal NASA directory as a 'senior advisor'.

DOGE was onsite at NASA from where SpaceX (a NASA company in truth) gets multi-billion contracts. Concerns emerged that Musk's DOGE mob were using AI to trawl personal data from government systems. Gerald E. Connolly, Ranking Member of the Committee on Oversight and Government Reform, wrote to 24 federal agencies asking for documented confirmation that the use of artificial intelligence complied with federal laws, protected the population's sensitive and private data, and did not financially benefit Elon Musk:

> I write with serious concerns about the use of unapproved, third-party artificial intelligence (AI) software employed by members of the U.S. DOGE Service (DOGE) at federal agencies.
>
> The American people entrust the federal government with sensitive personal information related to their health, finances, and other biographical information on the basis that this information will not be disclosed or improperly used without their consent, including through the use of an unapproved and unaccountable third-party AI software.

Anyone really think that didn't happen?

Clearing the decks for AI Technocracy

All governments have inefficiencies which should be addressed, but that was not the motivation here. DOGE saw destruction as an end in itself. Trump and Musk were the wrecking balls brought in to demolish the Cult-created status quo to replace it with the next stage – another Cult-created status quo controlled by AI. This is blatant 'creative destruction' which is essential to 'accelerationism'. MAGA cheered all this as 'winning' in their child-like naivety when Musk was dismantling the system and creating calculated chaos on the road to replacing humans in government administration with centrally controllable AI. This was confirmed by *The Atlantic* magazine. The 'GSA' mentioned here is the General Services Administration which manages and supports the functioning of federal agencies:

> The bot, which GSA leadership is framing as a productivity booster for federal workers, is part of a broader playbook from DOGE and its allies. Speaking about GSA's broader plans, Thomas Shedd, a former Tesla engineer who was recently installed as the director of the Technology Transformation Services (TTS), GSA's IT division, said at an all-hands meeting last month that the agency is pushing for an 'AI-first strategy'.
>
> In the meeting, a recording of which I obtained, Shedd said that 'as we decrease [the] overall size of the federal government, as you all know, there's

still a ton of programs that need to exist, which is a huge opportunity for technology and automation to come in full force'. He suggested that 'coding agents' could be provided across the government – a reference to AI programs that can write and possibly deploy code in place of a human.

Musk stepped back from DOGE after failing to secure the cost savings he claimed while accessing all that personal data in the months before Trump hired Peter Thiel's Palantir to collate personal data from all government departments into one database. Big Tech billionaires like Thiel, Marc Andreessen, Larry Ellison, Sam Altman, Jeff Bezos, Mark Zuckerberg, and many others circled their wagons around Trump for the same reason – AI control – and they are the ones in the driver's seat. Ellison laid out the game to Cult operative Tony Blair, who he funds, at the 2025 World Governments Summit in Dubai. He said that governments need to put all their information in one place – even citizens' genomic data – if they want AI to improve services and security for their citizens. 'I have to tell [the] AI model as much about my country as I can. We need to unify all the national data, put it into a database where it's easily consumable by the AI model, and then ask whatever question you like.' Trump is a pawn of the oligarchs who uses bravado to hide his insecurity and the fact that he does what he's told or else. Musk began deleting whole government departments, a stream of which were investigating various aspects of his companies – investigations that then, of course, stopped. One was the Bureau of Consumer Financial Protection which targeted financial fraud and manipulative lending practices. It had recovered $20 billion for victims of this and was overseeing Musk's plan to make Twitter/X an 'everything app' including financial services. Musk is such a lovely man. 'Deregulation' to allow a political and corporate free-for-all is part of the deal. Let's give that *Guardian* article on accelerationism another go in the light of Musk's activities:

> Accelerationists argue that technology, particularly computer technology, and capitalism, particularly the most aggressive, global variety, should be massively sped up and intensified [. . .] Accelerationists favour automation. They favour the further merging of the digital and the human.
>
> They often favour the deregulation of business and drastically scaled-back government. They believe that people should stop deluding themselves that economic and technological progress can be controlled. They often believe that social and political upheaval has a value in itself ...

This is what Trump and Musk set out to do and hence you have Trump's war with Iran on behalf of Israel and the Cult; his global financial mayhem with his tariffs that are on, off, then on again; the intimidation of Congressional oversight and judiciary; and his use of the military for domestic law enforcement to impose a step-by-step dictatorship. A protest in Los Angeles against Trump's migrant deportations was met with deployment of the military National Guard and Marines to set the precedent for dealing with pushback. Millions of people came out in protest across America in June 2025 under the banner of 'No Kings' while Trump was watching the failure of a Palantir-sponsored 'military parade' on his 79th birthday that he wanted to be a North Korean-like, Russia-like, parade of military might. It wasn't. Very few came to watch and troops taking part appeared to be going through the motions with *Fortunate Son* by *Creedence Clearwater Revival* blasting out as they passed King Donny. *Fortunate Son* was a Vietnam era song about how unprivileged kids were sent to war while the children of the privileged dodged the draft – exactly what Trump did. At least that was a laugh on a sad and pathetic day. The 'No King' protests had an appropriate title when you see Curtis Yarvin's demand for a monarch-like 'national CEO' dictator that Trump was set on becoming (as a pawn at best). Unleashing troops on Los Angeles was just the start, as it was always going to be, and Trump took over the police force and deployed troops long-term in Washington DC (supported by Musk). Then came troops to Portland, Oregon, and he said other cities would follow like Chicago, New York, and '19 states'. He changed the Department of Defense to the Department of War (against Americans). The 'justification' was crime running rampant when Washington recorded crime in decline. The trigger for Trump's military takeover in Washington was … wait for it … the 'Big Balls' guy from DOGE being attacked in the street. My goodness, coincidences are amazing. Armed troops on American streets was followed by the use of *military* lawyers to prosecute civilians. A new MAGA had emerged that supported everything they once opposed. Make America Great Again was now Make America Germany Again. It was straight from the Cult script.

Musk talked in 2019 about '*accelerating* Starship development to build the Martian Technocracy' and another way to describe the Dark Enlightenment and acceleration is 'technocracy'. This is as I said earlier 'a form of government in which the decision-makers are selected based on their expertise in a given area of responsibility, particularly with regard to scientific or technical knowledge'. Technocracy describes the Archontic Cult goal of replacing elected politicians with appointed technocrats and bureaucrats and this is why so many moronic people are raised to political power. Public perception is being prepared to accept an end to them and elections by appointing to government people with little discernible brain cell activity. See the UK and US governments for confirmation. Technocracy runs in the blood and DNA of Elon Musk and drives him to impose a totalitarian 'Technate' on the human population based on control by AI. Joshua N. Haldeman (1902–1974), his maternal grandfather, was a leader in Canada of the American Technocracy Inc. which promoted this very form of government now beloved of his grandson. Lawrence Preston Gise, grandfather of Amazon founder Jeff Bezos, helped to found ARPA which became DARPA, the sinister technology development agency of the Pentagon. This is the top-secret Defense Advanced Research Projects Agency which claims credit for creating the Internet with military technology. Bezos and Musk are now both filling the low-orbit realm with satellites to create the 'Cloud' to which humans are meant to be connected in the hive mind. They are also creating the 'Skynet' global surveillance grid. People do not rise to these positions by accident and Bezos is now on board with Trump and attended his second inauguration with Mark Zuckerberg. Then there is the Musk-Bezos-Epstein behaviour manipulation connection from earlier. It's all planned and orchestrated.

The 'Technate'

Musk's grandfather Joshua Haldeman and his Technocracy Inc. sought to overthrow elected democratic government in the US and Canada and replace it with appointed technocrats and bureaucrats. Technocracy derives from the Greek words, 'tekhne' meaning skill, and kratos meaning power, governance, or rule. The movement was inspired by engineer and economist, Howard Scott, along with other engineers and academics from Columbia University. Scott founded the Technical Alliance in 1932 that later became Technocracy Inc. A technocracy publication in 1938 stated: 'The Technate will encompass the entire American Continent from Panama to the North Pole because the natural resources and the natural boundary of this area make it an independent, self-sustaining geographical unit.' The proposed Technate spanned from Venezuela in the north of South America up through Panama, Central America and Mexico to include Canada and … *Greenland* (Fig 212 overleaf). We see why Trump, Musk, and their fellow billionaires seek to take over Panama, Greenland, and absorb Canada as the 51st state. It also explains the Trump obsession with oil abundant Venezuela with a $50 million reward for the arrest of President Nicolás Maduro and, as I write, a fleet of warships and thousands of troops positioned off the Venezuelan coast using the excuse of stopping drug cartels.

Big Tech oligarchs like Peter Thiel have long had their eyes on Greenland. Thiel is a major investor in the plan to build 'Praxis', a new city-state 'autonomous colony' in Greenland to 'restore Western civilization'. Elon Musk supports the moves to absorb Greenland while Jeff Bezos and Bill Gates advocate mining the rare earth minerals there

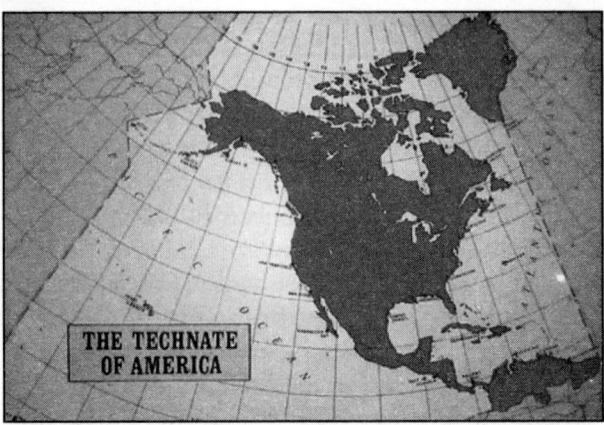

Figure 212: The technocracy map of North, South and Central America (including Greenland) envisaged by Elon Musk's grandfather.

which are vital for Big Tech manufacturing. These are the same rare earth resources Trump seeks to steal from the people of Ukraine. Extreme heat producing AI data centres would also benefit from Greenland's freezing climate. Tom Dans, a former commissioner of the US Arctic Research Commission, said: 'Greenland offers abundant potential energy, strategic metals and minerals, and proximity to key US population centres – all in a highly controllable environment ... Take what's needed for the US to maintain information technology dominance: data storage and computing power deployment.' This is what the Greenland focus is really all about and Trump-Vance will do what the Big Tech billionaires tell them. Their claim that the US plan to take over is about US and Greenland 'security' is pure fiction. Greenland is currently owned by Denmark and Trump picked as his ambassador to Denmark another member of the Peter Thiel circle, Ken Howery, who established with Thiel the venture capital Founders Fund. Howery, a friend of Musk, was ambassador to next-door Sweden in Trump's first term. They always play the long game coordinated by the Astral Archons.

Trump never mentioned Canada or Greenland in his election campaign. Then he was demanding that Canada be absorbed as the 51st state as soon as he parked his bum in the Oval Office, and said Denmark should hand over Greenland to the US with all its natural resources. I remember how the then alternative media was exposing the plan for a centrally controlled North American Union of the United States, Canada and Mexico. Now suddenly the fusion of the US and Canada was not so bad to the MAGA media crowd because their hero said it. Trump said the US should take back the Panama Canal because China had far too much influence. Next thing you know the multi-trillion-dollar BlackRock investment giant headed by the WEF's Larry Fink was announcing the purchase of ports from a Hong Kong company at the Atlantic and Pacific entrances to the canal. 'Alternative' voices that had been exposing the 'globalist' BlackRock seemed fine with that. 'At least it's an American company.' But it's not. In terms of control, it's Israeli.

South Africa connection

A ban on technocracy by the Canadian authorities led Joshua Haldeman and his family to relocate to South Africa in 1950 where Musk was born to Haldeman's daughter, professional model Maye Haldeman. She had married South African businessman and politician, Errol Musk, in 1970. Elon Musk was born in 1971 with the apartheid regime in full swing. A tiny minority of whites owned by law more than 85 percent of the land while blacks were treated like vermin. Chris McGreal, Johannesburg correspondent of *The Guardian* in the last years of South Africa's apartheid regime, has tracked the upbringing and career of Elon Musk and the Musk family. He told *Democracy Now* that technocracy grandfather Joshua Haldeman is on record as supporting apartheid – 'vividly so' – and had said that was the reason he moved there. McGreal described how Canadian technocrats became increasingly fascistic, wore grey uniforms modelled on the Nazi black and brownshirts, and were banned when Canada declared war on Germany because technocracy was obviously sympathetic to Hitler. Haldeman was arrested and subversive documents supporting the Nazis were found in his house. He was jailed for 'a few months' and added to a 'subversive watchlist' for the rest of the war as a Nazi sympathiser.

Now we can see why he headed for South Africa with his wife where they became 'fervent supporters of apartheid'. Funny how his grandson Elon is alleged to have made Nazi salutes at a Trump rally. Musk was born under the rule of neo-Nazi Prime Minister John Vorster who in 1942 likened his 'Christian nationalism' belief system to German Nazism and Italian fascism. The same 'Christian nationalism' had infiltrated the school system as Elon Musk passed through. The family and his father Errol benefited from the white-focused apartheid and made his fortune from emerald mines in Zambia. Black miners worked in terrible and brutal conditions while their owners enriched themselves. McGreal says the Musks would have lived a 'neo-colonial lifestyle' and that the father owned a yacht, a plane and several homes. Musk left South Africa for Canada and the United States at the age of 18 just before he would have been drafted like all white males at the time into the South African army amid by then great civil upheaval.

Then there are his mates in the Trump circle pushing for an AI technocratic society and mutually supporting each other. Peter Thiel went to school in Johannesburg until his father secured a job with a uranium mine near Swakopmund across the border from South Africa in what was then South West Africa. It was under South African administration from 1915 to 1966, and occupied by South Africa from then until 1990. It became known as Namibia in 1968 and independent in 1990. Thiel then went to school in Swakopmund. South West Africa had been a German colony until the end of the First World War and McGreal said a large part of the population was still of German ancestry. Thiel was born to German parents in Frankfurt in 1967. The father of major Nazi Hermann Goering had been a governor of South West Africa while McGreal noted that Swakopmund was 'notorious into the 1980s and 90s as a continued hotbed of support for the Nazis and for Hitler'. Gift shops sold Nazi memorabilia and the town openly celebrated Hitler's birthday. Thiel went to a German school there while his father was an official at the uranium mine that supplied South Africa with part of the means to make atomic bombs in the 1970s with help from Israel. McGreal said that this deal also involved South Africa supplying 'yellowcake' (a type of powdered uranium concentrate) to Israel for its nuclear programme. He said that while families like Thiel and Musk claim they didn't support apartheid they benefited enormously from it.

Atlantic crossing

Thiel and Musk became long-term buddies in the United States as part of the PayPal Mafia around Trump that also includes David Sacks who was appointed Trump's AI and crypto czar. The PayPal Mafia refers to a group involved in PayPal with Peter Thiel. David Sacks was born into the apartheid regime in Cape Town, South Africa, a year after Musk in 1972 and moved with his parents to Tennessee at the age of five where McGreal says he grew up in the 'white South African diaspora'. Sacks became a big fundraiser for Trump. Another member of the PayPal Mafia is Roelof Botha. He was born in the South African capital Pretoria (like Musk) in 1973 and his grandfather was Roelof Frederik 'Pik' Botha, the last foreign minister of South Africa under apartheid. Roelof Botha was PayPal's director of corporate development, vice-president of finance and chief financial officer. Botha is a partner in American venture capital firm Sequoia Capital whose investment helped Elon Musk buy Twitter/X. How well the boys born in apartheid South Africa have done. Botha has sat on the boards of instant messaging and social networking service provider Meebo and YouTube (before they were bought by Google); and Tumblr (before it was bought by Yahoo!). He was a board member of 23andMe, the DNA testing and ancestry company co-founded by Anne Wojcicki, sister of the late YouTube CEO and mega-censor, Susan Wojcicki, and former wife of Google co-founder Sergey Brin. It's such a small world with these people. Trump deleted aid to South Africa soon after taking office in January 2025 and gave refugee status to white South Africans who were 'suffering racial discrimination'.

Musk settled in the United States in 1994 after arriving in Canada five years earlier through his mother's connection. I have covered what happened next in other books, but the necessary theme here is that clearly someone had his back. And his front. The money kept rolling in despite being a poor businessman and entrepreneur. He seemed to have an ability to claim he 'founded' companies that he never did. These included Tesla and PayPal. He certainly had a gift for bullshitting if you had a short memory and didn't check the facts. His ability to claim credit for what he hasn't done is legendary and Musk is about image and perception rather than substance. Whatever he did, however much his colleagues wanted rid of him, he benefited in the pocket from companies and mergers that were the work of other people. Peter Thiel was a regular part of the story. Musk's worth went on and on increasing and much of that came from government subsidies and contracts to the point as I write that the government is handing to Musk in various ways some $8 million *a day*. There is no way that he is running Tesla, SpaceX, Starlink, Neuralink, the Boring Company, and the rest while posting on Twitter/X all day, doing endless interviews, playing video games, and for a time running DOGE. Others are doing most of this and he is only the front man sales pitcher. He told his sycophantic mate, podcaster Joe Rogan, that he spends '80 percent' of his time designing and engineering. What a liar although I am open to him designing the disastrous Tesla 'cyber truck'. It's so bad he could have been involved there.

SpaceX is a great example because it would not exist without 'Deep State' contracts from the Pentagon and NASA when he claims he is opposing the 'Deep State' and how it is out to get him. We are also supposed to believe that he cares about freedom and liberty when he has Pentagon and government contracts for low-orbit surveillance technology which would dovetail nicely with his friend Thiel's Palantir and its surveillance tech supplied to intelligence networks and the military. The official story of SpaceX is that Musk travelled to Russia in 2002 with CIA operative Michael Griffin hoping to buy discounted intercontinental ballistic missiles. No deal was done and on the plane home Musk announced his plan to start SpaceX with Griffin as his partner and chief engineer. Griffin instead took another job as president and chief operating officer of the CIA's technology development and seed-funding arm, In-Q-Tel (I-Q-T) that seeks out companies which can aid its surveillance and control agenda. During Griffin's tenure or very shortly afterwards the CIA's In-Q-Tel seed-funded the launch of Thiel's Palantir, founded in 2004, and Griffin's next job was head of NASA between 2005 and 2009 when Musk's SpaceX began to attract essential NASA contracts which have kept on coming and increasing in value. SpaceX is really NASA and the Pentagon. What an amazing coincidence that Musk's mate Griffin was involved in the emergence of both Palantir and SpaceX.

Peter Thiel has also invested in SpaceX via his venture capital Founders Fund which has infused hundreds of millions into Musk's brain chip operation, Neuralink, and his tunnel-building company, The

Boring Company. Alphabet Inc., parent company of Google and YouTube, has been a serious SpaceX investor along with Fidelity, the Twitter/X investing global asset management giant, that handed $100 million to SpaceX and took a stake in Jeff Bezos-founded space company, Blue Origin. The usual suspects. More military and NASA contracts have followed with SpaceX given the gig to transport NASA astronauts to the International Space Station and in 2023 came the contract for the Starshield network of hundreds of spy satellites for the Department of Defense National Reconnaissance Office to supply real-time information and communication for the military, intelligence agencies and government. The data gathering is processed by AI. Journalist Derrick Broze points out that Starshield is overseen by retired Air Force General Terrence O'Shaughnessy, Vice President of Special Programs Group at SpaceX, who on retirement became a 'Senior Advisor to Elon Musk on matters regarding SpaceX'. O'Shaughnessy had served for 39 years with the Air Force, US Northern Command (NORTHCOM) and North American Aerospace Defense Command (NORAD).

For someone 'anti-establishment' Musk is, like Thiel, very close to the intelligence, military, and surveillance networks. The *Wall Street Journal* reported: 'The size and secrecy of the [Starshield] agreement illustrate a growing interdependence between SpaceX – a dominant force in the space industry – and the national-security establishment.' The paper quoted Gwynne Shotwell, SpaceX President and Chief Operating Officer, as highlighting the 'very good collaboration between the intelligence community and SpaceX'. What's the relationship between the intelligence community and Twitter/X? The Federal Communications Commission (FCC) has awarded Musk and SpaceX permission for tens of thousands of low-orbit satellites, and it was good news for them that Trump appointed Musk's friend and associate Brendan Carr as head of the FCC in 2025. I wonder how the FCC can give the go-ahead for all those low-orbit satellites when the whole world is affected and not just America? That would be the Global Cult at work then. Brendan Carr's FCC is also targeting media organisations that don't support or openly criticise Trump while being a friend of 'free speech absolutist' Elon Musk. It was Carr that approved the sale of Paramount to ultra-Zionist AI billionaire Larry Ellison and family that will turn the CBS network into supporters of the Trump regime and its like. What a farce and fraud it all is. Musk has massive connections to China not least via Tesla which must keep the Chinese government sweet for its vehicle sales and how does that square with all the American intelligence that will come Musk's way? Mind you, the Global Cult has no borders.

Dismantling democracy

The Trump-Musk regime was straight into Dark Enlightenment mode as it raced to marginalise the checks and balances of Congress and courts. Republican politicians were threatened with having other candidates funded to run against them if they didn't support the White House and Trump's picks for government. The MAGA base was all for it. Next came the courts with Trump and Musk running demonisation campaigns against judges who decreed the blatantly obvious by saying many aspects of what they were doing was illegal. They called for the judges to be impeached for having the nerve to disagree with them. Trump also targeted law firms with executive orders and intimidated them into working for him free in return for withdrawing the order. Trump posted that one law firm, Paul, Weiss, Rifkind, Wharton & Garrison, would 'dedicate the equivalent of $40 million in pro bono legal services over the course of President Trump's term to support the administration's initiatives, including: assisting our Nation's veterans, fairness in the Justice System, *the President's Task Force to Combat Antisemitism*, and other mutually agreed projects.' Law firm Skadden, Arps, Slate, Meagher & Flom agreed to provide at least $100 million in pro bono legal services 'during the Trump administration and beyond'. Trump said the firm had agreed to assist 'veterans and other public servants, including members of the military, law enforcement, first responders, and federal, state and local government officials ... and *combatting antisemitism*'. Could this be considered anything but using political office for extortion?

Other firms challenged Trump's threats in court and a federal district judge imposed a temporary restraining order halting his action against one of them. The judge said the threats 'sent little chills down my spine'. Unelected Musk with no oversight was closing down government agencies, firing thousands on a whim, with extraordinary conflicts of interest and it wasn't *illegal??* The regime didn't care in their pursuit of de facto 'monarchy'. Musk was deleting agencies investigating his companies and his DOGE juveniles were getting access to highly sensitive and private information about citizens and the government contracts of his rivals for the public pig trough. But, hey, we can't allow judges to stop us – *impeach them*!

Three sections of government, executive, Congress, and the judiciary, were created and kept separate to stop one running riot and imposing dictatorship, but this separation of powers is the very target of 'monarchy' or Dark Enlightenment one-person government. White House senior advisor, the appalling ultra-Zionist Stephen Miller, filed a lawsuit through his America First Legal Foundation targeting Supreme Court Chief Justice John Roberts asserting that federal courts are part of the executive branch and not the judiciary. This would mean the president controlled judicial operations throughout the country. The lawsuit noted that 'Federal courts rely on the executive branch for facility management and security' and that judges 'need resources to fulfil their constitutional obligation'. Trump ignored Supreme Court judgements and threatened to withdraw protection of judges by US Marshals. Then the Supreme Court with a Trump majority, which had earlier handed him his potential dictator status, curbed the right of lower court judges to block Trump's one-man executive orders nationwide. Trump with typical Cult inversion described the ruling as a 'monumental victory for the Constitution'. Supreme Court Justice Sonia Sotomayor wrote a far more accurate dissenting opinion in which she called the decision an 'open invitation for the government to bypass the Constitution'.

Trump and Musk turned their sights on social security and medical aid which are the lifeline of tens of millions of Americans, the disabled and seniors. Musk called social security a 'Ponzi scheme' when for example the elderly are receiving what they had paid in all their lives as income insurance for old age. But what did billionaire Musk care? The mentality of these people was revealed by another billionaire, Trump's ultra-Zionist Commerce Secretary, Howard Lutnick. He said:

> Let's say Social Security didn't send out checks this month. My mother-in-law, who's 94, she wouldn't call and complain. She just wouldn't. She'd think something got messed up and she'd get it next month. A fraudster always makes the loudest noise, screaming, yelling and complaining.

There you have the Trump regime and Dark Enlightenment in a few sentences. The mother-in-law of a billionaire wouldn't complain about a social security no-show, but if those living from cheque to cheque to live and eat complained they must be fraudsters. It's a form of mental illness in my view and these are the people that the MAGA think are pledged to support the working class. Laugh or cry – either is appropriate.

Deportation and Project 2025

Politicians and governments lie – that's a gimme – but the Trump regime takes it to a whole new level. Trump denied during his 2024 election campaign knowing anything about Project 2025, or the '2025 Presidential Transition Project', a 900-page document produced by the infamous Heritage Foundation with a wishlist of policies if Trump won. This wasn't good for Trump because it told the truth about what he planned. He said he hadn't read the document (then contradicted himself) and said he had 'no idea who is behind it'. What a liar (again). The Heritage Foundation is a highly influential Washington conservative think tank founded in 1973. Project 2025 is a detailed plan that includes appointing Trump loyalists to government jobs, politicising federal agencies and imposing strict immigration among much else. The document became a liability for Trump's election. The man behind it, Paul Dans, director of Project 2025 at the Heritage Foundation, was pressured to resign to reduce the heat. Phew, that was close. Fast forward two months after Trump took office and Paul Dans was telling *Politico* that he was 'delighted with the extent to which Project 2025 has, in fact, become the Trump administration's playbook'. It was always going to be. Dans said: 'It's actually way beyond my wildest dreams.' Some legal commentators said Project 2025 would damage the separation of powers, separation of church and state, and civil liberties. It soon became clear when Trump took office that they were right.

Trump appointed a barely-one-dimensional buffoon as his 'border czar' to oversee what Trump said would be the deportation of millions of 'illegal aliens' who were violent criminals, murderers, rapists, and members of brutal Central and South American gangs. Tom Homan, a former acting director of US Immigration and Customs Enforcement (ICE) in 2017/2018, was tasked by Trump with the mass removal. The problem is that Tom Homan, like Trump, can see only two colours – black and white. Homan proceeded on that basis and mayhem and injustice followed as it always does with a black and white mind. The Geo Group, a leading private prison company in the United States, has made a fortune from government ICE contracts through Trump's deportation policies and its stock soared when he came to office. Tom Homan worked as a consultant for Geo Group while Pam Bondi, picked by Trump to be Attorney General, was a lobbyist for the company. Trump signed an order to invoke the Alien Enemies Act of 1798 (then denied that he did and said someone else did it). This had sycophants rushing round claiming he meant that he didn't sign the Alien Enemies Act of *1798*. Trump is constantly stalked by lies and chaos. The Act gives the president *wartime* authority to arrest and/or deport people from an 'enemy nation'. The trouble was that America was not at war and Trump claimed it was on the grounds of an invasion of migrants.

The law is perfect for Trump and the Dark Enlightenment because it allows him to arrest and deport without a court or due process. He can do so purely on their country of birth and citizenship. The Alien Enemies Act had been used only three times before, the War of 1812 and the two World Wars. Some judges did at least push back on its use. Trump's 'Big Beautiful Bill' passed in the summer of 2025 and included massive increases in funding for ICE to target the influx of migrants which, as I have outlined in other books, has been orchestrated by Israel in North America and Europe – the same Israel that owns Trump. He is using fears about migrants to focus the attention of his base while Israel and the Cult use him as a wrecking ball for the West. The Cult is brilliant at psychological manipulation and appearing to do one thing while doing another.

Trump was not happy with the initial migrant deportation numbers and introduced quotas of arrests a day that Homan and ICE had to meet. This proved a disaster for justice because they soon ran out of migrant violent criminals that rightly needed removing and started on the legal, innocent, and those going through the courts in pursuit of citizenship. Trump had struck a deal with his political kin in El Salvador, Nayib Bukele, who described himself as the 'world's coolest dictator'. The agreement was that El Salvador would take some of Trump's deported immigrants and *American citizens* in exchange for $6 million a year. They would be incarcerated in a 40,000-capacity prison complex in brutal conditions with no due process, trial, or release date. People might support that for mass-killer gang members although my view is that you only dehumanise yourself if you act as those you condemn. If you act with brutality against brutality – which is which? Take them out of circulation, but what happens in El Salvador is evil condemning another form of evil. The quotas could not be met with gang members and criminals and the innocent had to suffer. But so what? They were only collateral damage to the Trump psychopaths.

Jerce Reyes Barrios, a professional soccer player and coach, fled Venezuela after opposing President Nicolás Maduro and sought asylum in the United States where he was living peacefully and making his way through the legal system to secure permanent residence. Homan's ICE then snatched him and accused him of being a member of a violent Venezuelan gang, Tren de Aragua. They confirmed this by his tattoo. Well, not really. Gang members have tattoos it is true, often all over their bodies, but other people do as well. In the case of Barrios, a professional soccer player, it was a tattoo of his favourite team, Real Madrid! He was further accused of gang membership for a photograph online in which he made a hand gesture which actually means 'I love you' in sign language. Barrios was deported to El Salvador on this basis by the numbskulls at ICE under Homan chasing the quotas. Another man was a gang member because he had tattoos featuring 'anime, flowers, animals,' and 'a crown of thorns' which was a 'tribute to his grandmother' according to his lawyer with her date of death at the base of the crown. Other 'gang members' had tattoos with 'a Rose, a Clock and a Crown with his son's name on it'; a rosary, his partner's name; a Bible verse and a rose with money as petals; and one celebrating his daughter. A gay Venezuelan makeup artist seeking asylum over persecution for being gay and opposing Venezuela president Maduro, was sent to El Salvador for having an innocuous tattoo. He had no criminal history.

District Court Judge James Boasberg ruled that migrants were 'entitled to individualised hearings to determine whether the [Enemies] Act applies to them'. He ordered that aircraft heading for El Salvador were turned back, but the Trump regime ignored him. Trump had to break the courts to become a de facto monarch. El Salvador President Bukele posted a video of shackled men taken off a plane with the caption, referring to the judge's ruling, of 'Oopsie… Too late'. This is the mentality ever more obviously taking over the world. It's always been there, but now it flaunts itself on public display. Bukele is of Palestinian descent, but his dictatorship is armed by Israel who he slavishly supports. *MintPress* reported that Israeli exports of overwhelmingly weapons to El Salvador have been rapidly advancing since Bukele came to power. The military and police are supplied with Israeli rifles, submachine guns, pistols, and armoured vehicles. Bukele owned by Israel doing a deal with Trump owned by Israel makes sense.

Miller time

Trump took the deportation policy to new extremes after ultra-Zionist 'advisor' Stephen Miller was reported to have ordered buffoon Homan to increase the deportation quota by targeting stores and other workplaces to find illegal migrants to eject from the country. The media revealed that Miller had a $250,000 investment in Peter Thiel's Palantir which had government contracts relating to ICE. This led to allegations of a serious conflict of interest. *What*? A conflict of interest in the Trump administration? Never, surely. Many of the migrants targeted by ICE now had American wives and children and were attending court hearings to make their case to stay. Homan's masked thugs were even waiting for people to leave the court before grabbing them against the decision of the judge. They arrested one judge for allegedly seeking to help a migrant avoid arrest. The next stage was to find an excuse for Trump to use the military for domestic law enforcement like all good dictators. Homan's thugs were sent into Woke Los Angeles of all places to very visibly target migrants at their workplaces, and this was bound to trigger protests in California. That did indeed follow as the Trump regime knew it would. Trump took control of the state National Guard immediately and illegally with 4,000 policing the streets followed by the deployment of 700 marines. Trump indicated that this was how he would deal with protests from then on if he chose to do so and Washington DC followed. Shortly afterwards came the American attack on Iran in support of his masters in Israel. Trump was acting like a 'king', but really, he was a frontman 'king' in name only. Those behind the 'king' and pulling his strings stayed in the shadows.

Trump's increasingly fascistic behaviour included a plan to imprison migrants in the US prison camp at Guantanamo Bay in Cuba and the opening of 'Alligator Alcatraz' next to an airstrip in the Florida Everglades. The facility was backed by the Florida state government and Department of Homeland Security headed by the incompetent Trump and Israel clone, Kristi Noem, and constructed in just weeks to hold as many as 5,000 beds in cages. Anyone who sought to escape would be faced with snakes and alligators. Trump was asked if the idea was that detainees would be eaten by alligators should they try to escape. 'I guess that's the concept. This is not a nice business. I guess that is the concept.' Trump said that 'snakes are fast but alligators – we're going to teach them how to run away from an alligator'. They should run in a zig-zag line. 'You know what, your chances go up about one percent.' This is the President of the United States speaking. The man's an empathy-deleted thug. Even a Mexican tourist with a valid visa ended up at Alligator Alcatraz. Trump began to roll back on deporting *many* illegal migrants when his donors protested at the impact on food production and hotel staffing etc., which was affecting their businesses. This work had been done since way back by illegal migrants. Veteran freedom activist and writer John Whitehead saw through the smokescreens of telling the MAGA what they wanted to hear and produced decisive and telling articles about what was really going on. Trump wasn't dismantling the Deep State – he *was* the Deep State. He wrote:

> While promising to drain the swamp, his administration has instead relied on contradictory policies, misinformation, and propaganda to further entrench the very system he claims to oppose. Although the Trump administration is merely the latest frontman for the Deep State's efforts to maintain its stranglehold on power, we are approaching a tipping point beyond which there may be no turning back to freedom as we have known it …
>
> … While President Trump, well versed in the 'art of the deal', appears to be saying all the right things about peace, corruption, graft, wasteful spending, free speech, equality, bloated bureaucracy, national security, etc., his administration's actions tell a far different story about his priorities and his loyalties, which remain self-serving, imperial, flagrantly unconstitutional and intended to keep the Deep State in power.

Trump's book, *Art of the Deal*, was actually written by 'co-author', American journalist and business book writer, Tony Schwartz, who said of Trump: 'He is incapable of reading a book, much less writing one.'

Scamming MAGA

The AI oligarchs stressed that their association with Trump and MAGA was not dependent on Elon Musk after the fall out with his former buddy. No, the billionaires were fully committed to MAGA and making the world a better place (with AI of course). The message came in a *Spectator* article by Joe Lonsdale, a co-founder of Palantir with Thiel and Karp. Yep, they want a better world for everyone, I can feel it in my water.

Lonsdale's article was headed 'The tech right-MAGA alliance is far from over' and said that, in the aftermath of the Musk-Trump break-up, many were wondering about the future of the 'tech right' and its relationship to the MAGA movement. 'In 2024, the two groups fought together and won', he said. 'Technology people who aren't crazy leftists.' See how they want to instil the perception of MAGA with 'the AI oligarchs are on your side and want what you do'. Lonsdale said that many in the tech field shifted right because of the excesses of wokeness and the 'dysfunction of far-left culture' – push them so far in one direction and then tell them you are with them in pushing back. Lonsdale went on:

> If this was simply a matter of technologists red-pilled by the insane left, you could be forgiven to think that issues such as immigration and tariffs, or disputes between Trump and Elon, could break it all up. Surely, that is what the left hopes to see.
>
> But a deeper trend in society defines the real 'tech right': the US innovation world is no longer mostly about the internet. We're building in the real world, trying to fix substantive areas of our society.

These people are so caring and lovely. That would be an AI 'fix' I take it? What formed the 'deeper substance' of the tech right was an optimism about what we can achieve for the entire country, and 'an opposition to the mountain of cronyist left-wing rules and regulations that have made it so hard and are being used by special interests trying to stop us'. You mean you want to delete regulation of AI just like Trump was also pushing for at the same time? There would be a continued 'natural alliance' with MAGA in this quest for a better world (with AI). Cut to the chase, mate, you are boring me with your vacuous bollocks. Oh, here we go:

> I'll focus on a few that are important to people within the MAGA base. Imagine, for a moment, the America that we can build with technology. With AI-enabled services and a regulatory upheaval, Medicare and Medicaid would be far cheaper [what's left after Trump is finished with it] ... Our military would be able to deter our enemies and accomplish missions as a lean and mean technological machine – without sending American boys to die in faraway conflicts.

He means AI taking over from human troops and deciding who lives and dies. Lonsdale is in full flow now. Pray continue:

> Insiders in the US technology world are experts at seeing the economic future. Across the board, we're realizing how AI can be applied in the coming

decade to make all of these areas of society far cheaper and far better – it's clear that we are going to be able to cure much of the US's cost disease.

But doing so requires policy entrepreneurship to break through the regulatory state, to fix terrible rules that block you from starting a competitor to a health system without a special certificate, or that stop a nurse and AI from performing an action even if it's shown to be safer and better, because of 'scope of practice'.

Give us a deregulated AI free-for-all and paradise will follow. Only the Right was willing to boldly stand up to the bureaucracy and government to make this happen. 'Tech and right is a natural partnership; and as we start to show wins for our citizens, the bonds will only strengthen.' From our Orwellian Translation Unit: 'We want you to support the AI control agenda that you once resisted.' It's so blatant and I warned long ago that this was the game and a foundation reason for Trump and Musk. Lonsdale said this did not mean the MAGA had to love Google or Facebook, or the people who used to run Twitter – 'or even Palantir (albeit, among other successes, I'm proud of the many terror attacks Palantir helped stop, and the civil liberties protected)'. Get on with it will you:

But as a patriot, you *do* have to love the young Americans with a fire in their eyes who want to build things for their fellow citizens – for you and your neighbors. They want to build new factories; engineer better planes and cars; find new therapeutics and cures.

They want to make you live longer and have more time with and money for your family. For me, my colleagues and thousands of people I've worked with over my career in mission-driven companies, *that* is what we mean by our work in technology.

MAGA and the tech right didn't have to be at odds and shouldn't be. The US had the top technology sector in the world, and on the patriotic right, they were proud of that fact. The MAGA/tech alliance would not surrender to dysfunctional government and civilisation wouldn't fail to surmount these challenges. 'The tech right isn't going anywhere; it's just getting started helping to make America great again.' Excuse me a second, I need to throw up. Anyone who buys that crap deserves to be manipulated.

Timing

One other point is how Trump/Vance came to power with their AI fusion Silicon Valley coterie in just the right period to target the MAGA. Trump won in 2016 and was ousted by Biden in the 2020 election. Had Trump won he would have been barred from standing again after two terms. He would have been out of the White House in January 2025. The most important period to get the pushbackers on board with the AI agenda (or divert their attention long enough to get it installed) is the period running up to 2030 when they want much of it in place. This is a target year common to the United Nations with its Agenda 2030, China and Russia with their AI ambitions, and in 2007 the World Economic Forum launched the Young Global Leader 'Project 2030' with the aim to 'formulate a positive vision for the world in 2030 and put forward concrete strategies and workstreams to translate their vision into action'. The UN Agenda 2030 came eight years later because the web precedes its conduit agencies.

If a Democrat had followed Trump from 2025 the pushbackers in the form of MAGA would have been kicking off very loudly if a Democrat president or even a non-Trump Republican had surrounded themselves with the Silicon Valley billionaire Mafia and promoted AI-human fusion within an AI controlled society. 'See TOLD YOU – look at what they're doing!' But Trump lost in 2020 and was able to come back in 2024/25. This was perfect to target the MAGA in the years up to 2030 to divert their former opposition to an AI dystopia. I know this will be hard for many to accept. I mean how could they fix elections? Far easier than people may think is my answer and there are multiple levels to this. Some of them are very deep and coming from the Astral. The conspiracy for human enslavement is far bigger than just Trump v Harris and manipulation of perception goes way beyond the tiny realm of the five senses.

We now must see where it goes from here with Trump and Musk both controlled by the Cult and Israel. Trump does what Netanyahu tells him, and the Israeli psychopath is a 'family friend' of the Musks. Both are fomenting chaos and dismantling the status quo – globally – with Trump's tariff instability (a tax on Americans), war and division, and the military on the streets. This is precisely what the Cult wants so its new status quo (control by AI) can replace it. The Cult will be the real winner whatever happens with the Trump and Musk theatre unless people awaken to what is happening, and why, and cease to cooperate with their own enslavement. Trump or Vance as president will be the same Cult agenda.

Back to the Big Picture

The Gnostic reference to Yaldabaoth and Archons as the 'forces of chaos' is most appropriate. I see their foundation state as an energetic frequency distortion, an inversion of everything represented by the Infinite. While that is balance, wisdom, love and harmony, the Yaldabaoth distortion is *im*balance, foolishness, evil and *dis*harmony. Evil is really an energetic distortion. Observe human society and you will see how it is founded on inversion. The schism has been penetrating everything including the human mind through which society springs as a projection of the schism. It is war, conflict, upsets and upheavals. It is the schism between people, cultures, religions, politics and belief systems in general. It is hunger in a world of plenty, illness, suffering and deprivation – all of which are the distortion/inversion made manifest. Only those that can reconnect with the balance of Spirit can restore themselves to harmony in a world of utter madness. Which is what? What is this *madness*? It is distortion and inversion. From the multiple dimensions of the simulation to the life of an individual you see the schism at work.

Donald Trump, JD Vance, Elon Musk, Peter Thiel, and their masters are expressions of that schism bringing disharmony to everything they do and touch. This is what 'leaders' are doing across the world in politics, religion, finance and corporations. They are energetic wrecking balls – distortions crashing into distortions to further distort. What is the energy thus created?

Loosh.

CHAPTER 24

'You're the Media Now"

Until you realize how easy it is for your mind to be manipulated, you remain the puppet of someone else's game.
Evita Ochel

Seizing control of the alternative media was crucial to the Trump-Musk Psyop and the co-opting of the previously sceptical MAGA to the AI agenda. MAGA and those aware of the conspiracy in general had rightly become contemptuous of the mainstream media and there was no way that could be used for propaganda to perceptually infiltrate the pushbacker mind.

They would have laughed at you if you told them to believe what the BBC, Sky News, CNN, MSNBC, and the newspaper industry told them. Pushbackers had instead been getting their information from the alternative media. This did not exist when I started out in 1990 and for a long time afterwards. Those exposing the global conspiracy were a few disparate individuals and it really began to gather momentum after the 9/11 attacks of 2001 when many did not buy the official narrative. I was delighted to see others joining the fold and while I didn't always agree with their take on events (often I did) there was an understanding that the apparently multi-party State was really a One-Party State or 'wings on the same bird' as they used to say. Numbers gathered and when the 'Covid' hoax was played to impose global fascism amid lockdowns (house arrest), imposed testing, mask and 'vaccine' mandates, there was an enormous awakening to the blatant fact that something wasn't right and that there was indeed some sort of 'conspiracy'.

Alternative sources of information had to be infiltrated by the Cult for two main reasons. 'Covid' confirmed to the Cult that things were getting out of hand in the way 'alternative' information was awakening increasingly large numbers to the scam. London protest marches and speaking events that I took part in attracted tens of thousands of people, maybe 100,000 or more for protest marches at their peak. You had the feeling that a breakthrough was now possible, and the Cult had to act to misdirect and divide this unity. But the hijack had another intent. These were now the media sources that their target pushbackers were watching and the Cult had to take them over to achieve that misdirection. 'You are the media now' as Musk constantly said. I noticed from around 2021 and even more in 2022 (the year Musk bought Twitter) that personalities were coming into the alternative from the mainstream media and society and dominating the arena with massive audiences underpinned by big algorithmic promotion and funding. I contacted Alex Jones to say I thought the alternative media was being absorbed by these people and he said he agreed. Next thing I know he is having them on his shows and became one of the most shameless supporters and promotors of the Trump-Vance-Musk-Thiel Psyop. Jones had suddenly never seen an arse he didn't want to kiss so long as it was attached to his beloved Elon and Donald. They could do no wrong (or not for long) whatever wrong they did.

Among mainstream names that came in or switched to the MAGA version of 'alternative' were Tucker Carlson (ex-Fox News), Megyn Kelly (ex-Fox News and NBC), Russell Brand, Jordan Peterson, the Tates, Bret and Eric Weinstein, Benny Johnson, Tim Pool and Luke Rudkowski. There were so many. They became highly rewarded pro-Trump 'influencers' (propagandists). A pivotal character along with Alex Jones and others is podcaster Joe Rogan with contracts from Spotify and the system worth hundreds of millions of dollars. Rogan is a close friend of Musk and gives him softball interviews to mega-audiences along with Trump, the Weinsteins, Peterson, Brand, and Big Tech AI Trump stalwarts Peter Thiel and Marc Andreessen. Rogan has refused to interview me at the time of writing (same with Carlson) when I have been a full-time researcher since 1990. They instead interview people around for five minutes who know next to nothing about the Big Picture. They are interviewed no doubt *because* they know next to nothing about the Big Picture. The Cult needed to control alternative communication to secure access to the MAGA mentality to get it on board with AI and to control the extent of what is called the 'Overton window'. This is defined as 'the range of subjects and arguments politically acceptable to the mainstream population at a given time'. You could describe this as the range of perceived '*normal*'. In this case they sought to regulate the alternative Overton window which means to control the range of what is discussed to ensure it only goes so far and no further. People like me were therefore a *big problem*.

Changing with the wind

American Ian Carroll was the new kid on the block promoted by people like podcaster Candace Owens. Carroll is loved by the algorithms on Musk's X which he only joined in 2023. He was invited on the Rogan show and highly promoted as he talked about 'conspiracies' that have been exposed in my books for decades. Trump gofer Michael Flynn, a retired US Army lieutenant general and briefly Trump's US national security advisor in his first term, has promoted him as someone to follow. Carroll told Rogan that the 'Deep State' did not involve a group sitting around a single table and was instead a random alliance of mutual interests that align. This is *absolutely not true*, but it is what the Cult wants you to believe. The Cult, which Carroll doesn't even acknowledge exists, is highly organised and if you go high enough or deep enough there *is* a group sitting around a single table directly interacting with Astral entities. Carroll urged people to support Trump, Musk, and Robert Kennedy Jr, Trump's 'health' pick, who are all owned by Israel. He then complained about Trump's support for Israel which was obviously going to be the case all along. You only had to observe his first term never mind doing just a little research into Trump's history with Israel assets like Netanyahu and deeply corrupt ultra-Zionist New York Mafia lawyer Roy Cohn. Carroll's contradictions make no sense. He also has a connection to Robert Kennedy's former running mate, Nicole Shanahan, who was married to Google co-founder Sergey Brin, and Carroll had a podcast called 'MAHA', or Kennedy's 'Make America Healthy Again'. Carroll and his promotor Candace Owens tried to explain away Kennedy's slavish support for Israel with the claim that 'he's being blackmailed' without producing evidence. Candace Owens was so pro-Israel in Trump's first term that she went to Jerusalem in 2018 with the late Charlie Kirk to attend the ceremony marking the moving of the American Embassy from Tel Aviv to Jerusalem that was a major blow for the Palestinians. She posted a picture with Kirk on social media and said:

> Amazingly, not a single elected Democrat is here to celebrate this historic event in Jerusalem, a bonafide signal that they do not stand with Israel. This snub will not soon be forgotten – not in America or abroad.

Owens also worked for the ultra-Zionist Prager University Foundation (PragerU) and ultra-Zionist Daily Wire of Israel-obsessed Jew, Ben Shapiro. Her career on the 'Right' was launched with major support from the late ultra-Zionist David Horowitz of the David Horowitz Freedom Center who was also influential in the careers of Shapiro and Charlie Kirk. She was helped to national prominence by her appearances on the Tucker Carlson Show on Fox News before his transition into the 'alternative' media. Owens married George Thomas Stahel Farmer of the elite Farmer family in England in 2019 where her vehemently pro-Israel father-in-law Lord (Baron) Michael Stahel Farmer has been a long-time metals and commodity trader including gold, silver, oil, gas and copper. He is known as 'Mr Copper' in the City of London financial district and was a treasurer of the Conservative Party.

He was mentored in the metals trade by top German-Jewish trader Manfred Kopelman who moved to Britain after the Second World War. Farmer worked at Philipp Brothers, co-founded by German orthodox Jew, Julius Philipp. The company bought Salomon Brothers in New York, and it was renamed Phibro-Salomon. Today it is simply Phibro. Baron Farmer established the Metal & Commodity trading company in 1989, a subsidiary of Metallgesellschaft AG, and it became the world's premier trader in physical copper and nickel. It was sold to the notorious Enron for $448 million. Metallgesellschaft AG was incorporated in 1881 in the Rothschild home city of Frankfurt, Germany, by Jews Wilhelm Ralph Merton, his father Ralph, Leo Ellinger, and Zachary Hochschild. The latter's brother Berthold Hochschild was sent to New York to establish the American Metal Company (AMCO) with among others the Société Le Nickel of France which was founded by the Rothschilds. The London and global metals and commodity trade has been long dominated by the Sabbatean House of Rothschild. Farmer co-founded metals trading and investment firm, the Red Kite Group, in 2005.

Baron Farmer is the Deputy Chair of the Council for Christians and Jews, founded in 1942 as a 'bulwark against antisemitism', with the monarch as its patron. Some researchers have said that Baron Farmer is connected to the Pilgrims Society which was established in Britain and the United States in 1902 and 1903. See the articles and videos of Michael McKibben at American Intelligence Media (aim4truth.org). The patron of the Pilgrims Society is once again the British monarch, currently King Charles, and its members over its 124 years have included the most influential Anglo-American businessmen and political manipulators including J.D. Rockefeller, David Rockefeller, and other prominent Rockefellers along with Rockefeller gofer, Henry Kissinger. Hitler-funding Prescott Bush, father of President George H.W. Bush, and grandfather of President George W. Bush, was another member as was the first civilian director of the CIA, Allen W. Dulles, and 9/11 Secretary of Defense Donald Rumsfeld. A list of members from 2002 circulating on the Internet includes 'Tucker S. M. [Swanson McNear] Carlson' and his CIA-connected father 'the Honourable Richard W. Carlson'. The title 'Honourable' comes from his appointment by President H.W. Bush as US ambassador to the Seychelles in 1991. The Pilgrims Society is an extreme globalist organisation while today Tucker Carlson presents himself as 'anti-globalist'. British members have included wartime leader Winston Churchill and Lord Carrington, NATO Secretary General and British Foreign Secretary in the run-up to the Falklands war in 1982. Carrington was the mega manipulator partner of Kissinger.

The Pilgrims have been covertly involved in a stream of society-changing events and connect into the Rothschild-Cecil Rhodes Round

Table network I mentioned earlier including the Bilderberg Group, Council on Foreign Relations, Trilateral Commission, Club of Rome, Royal Institute of International Affairs and a vast web of interconnected organisations and groupings. The Pilgrims Society and its wider network created the League of Nations after the First World War and its successor the United Nations after World War Two. This is a network that drives what MAGA calls 'globalism'.

George Farmer proposed, and Owens accepted, on an Internet FaceTime call only 17 days after their first meeting. As *People* magazine noted: 'The whirlwind romance meant Owens and Farmer did not date before getting engaged.' Since her marriage into the Farmer family Owens eventually transformed her public views on Zionism and began to condemn Israel. This is one of several about turns. She once mocked Trump and called herself a Left 'progressive'. Then she campaigned vehemently for Trump only to turn against him as his second presidency went pear-shaped as anyone paying attention knew that it would. She said in 2025 that she trusts JD Vance because Tucker Carlson does (his son works for Vance) and didn't see the issue of his political career being funded by Peter Thiel. WTF? I am delighted that people like Owens and Carlson are calling out the behaviour of Netanyahu and Israel (with their massive audiences while others are shadow banned), but why on earth did it take them so long when it was obvious all along – like for decades? And they can't see what Thiel and Vance really want? Candace Owens is a devout Roman Catholic Christian like her husband who was quoted in a 2023 article as saying that if Owens wanted to run for US president 'I'll be standing right beside her'. George Farmer, an Oxford-educated one-time investment banker, ran Turning Point UK, a fiercely pro-Trump offshoot of Charlie Kirk's Zionist-funded Turning Point USA (where Candace Owens was communications director), and has joined his Baron father as a shareholder at fake 'alternative' GB News. I'll have more on Charlie Kirk when I cover his disgusting murder in the end-of-book Postscript.

George Farmer was a member of the Bullingdon Club, an all-male dining club that has had prime ministers David Cameron and Boris Johnson among its members. Bullingdon is infamous for drunken rowdiness and elitism. Farmer has also known 'influencer' Andrew Tate since 'before Andrew was Andrew'. Candace Owens has been a promotor and apologist for Tate and his brother on her podcasts. Owens says she's a free speech and privacy advocate, but she tried to launch a website in 2016 called Social Autopsy. This was a search database tracking people's social media behaviour and revealing their 'real identities, including their places of employment'. One article said: 'The database would be accessible to anyone in the world, allowing them to search for information about individuals on their names or other personal details.' She faced a backlash from privacy advocates which she blamed on 'progressives' and 'became a Conservative overnight' in 2017. How her views on many things have been subject to dramatic change is quite a sight to see.

Owens-promoted Ian Carroll claimed to have 'red-pilled' Elon Musk on Israel as if Israel-owned Musk, a friend of Netanyahu, didn't know far more than him. It's a head-shaker, but good for numbers especially when Musk assured him millions of views by commenting on the post. Carroll's modus operandi appears to be that long, long, after others said something, which he ignored, he is promoted and promotes himself for repeating what he previously ignored. He did this with Elon Musk as he ignored the obvious while Musk was coming to power to create calculated mayhem. Then suddenly – 'I am exposing Musk'. File Ian Carroll under 'after the horse has bolted'. Or 'saying what to others was always obvious – but only *after* the obvious has already happened'. It's a blatant theme in the fake 'alternative' where they all campaigned to get Trump over the line and the damage was done before some of them began to criticise him for doing what he was clearly going to do all along. This was necessary to maintain their credibility as Trump went about his fascistic destruction of American society. Carroll is an example. What this does, because the algorithms love him, is divert attention and acknowledgement from those *ahead* of the game to those who are *after* the game when what they are 'exposing' is already a fait accompli. Candace Owens has done the same. First, she promotes Trump and then complains that he is controlled by Israel and was destroying free speech when that was always going to be the case. He was controlled by Israel in his first term and signposted his attack on free speech in his election campaign. Another stable door open. Another horse missing. I don't trust Candace Owens to be honest and nor Ian Carroll who posted in October 2024 just before the presidential election:

> The reason why Kamala Harris and Joe Biden are the same is because they are both just puppets of the CIA and the American Military Industrial Complex. (The CIA and Dick Cheney literally endorsed Kamala). Trump is the only president in any of our lifetimes (unless you're old enough to remember JFK) who isn't completely beholden to them. That's why we have seen such a coordinated legal, media, and political offensive against him ...
>
> ... They are pulling out every stop to try to defeat him so they can go on with business as usual. Now the Israel matter is far more complicated and deserves an hour long deep dive. But just consider how the empire has mobilized against this one man selectively and it tells you all you need to know about this election. You either vote for the CIA and the corrupt oligarchical empire, or you vote for the only man we've ever seen who has the unique

combination of traits that has allowed him to win against them.

The naivety (being optimistic) is stunning. Notice how he bought the idea that the 'Deep State' was out to get Trump which is exactly how the Psyop was played to give Trump that credibility. A few months into his presidency with free speech being targeted, troops on the streets of Los Angeles and Washington DC, bombs dropped on Iran, and Epstein files withheld we had the usual Carroll pivot in the hope that his followers won't remember what he said only months before. Carroll was also promoted by Trump/Musk sycophant Alex Jones from his operation in Texas where Musk has moved most of his business operations. Carroll in return promotes Jones and says he's not 'controlled opposition' when in fact he became no opposition at all – just a propagandist for Trump and Musk.

Listen to what I say – not what I said

Carroll constantly says one thing and when that proves to be wrong, he takes another approach in the hope that people have the memories of a goldfish. He is in my view a personification of the arrogance displayed by the 'New Media' which he tries to hide with mock 'humility'. I am heading for my 37th year of full-time research and yet this guy who has been around for a *fraction* of that said I was trying to 'ride his coat tails'. This from a bloke who is a babe in arms when it comes to knowing what is really going on. He also asked sarcastically what I am doing today, not in the past, *today*? Extraordinary that he can't be bothered to find out. Why do the algorithms promote him and other MAGA media names while shadow banning those that can see a much bigger picture? Everyone in the genuine alternative media that I respect for seeing through the diversions has the algorithms against them. They can also see through Ian Carroll. Funny, too, that I am banned from 30 European countries, plus Australia and countless more if I tried to go there, my YouTube channel was deleted in 2020, and I am banned from many social media platforms; but the 'alternative media stars' are not. Instead, the algorithms promote them.

Carroll dismissed with a smirk and great disrespect my then 35 years of research as 'he thinks it's all the reptiles' in an interview with Musk sycophant Joe Rogan which synchronised with Rogan's long-time dismissal of me allegedly for the same reason. Rogan with his contracts from the system worth hundreds of millions indicated in the interview that I was a 'grifter'. You can only laugh. Ironically, he interviewed two people who talked about Reptilians, only weeks before this exchange with Carroll, and he was fine with that. They were retired US Air Force veteran Jason Sands, a former member of the Unidentified Anomalous Phenomena (UAP) programme, and Lenval Logan, a retired Air Force intelligence analyst and a UAP Task Force member. They said that every time Reptilians were raised while 'on mission' it was quickly hushed up. Contacts would talk about other alien types, including the Greys, but not the Reptilians. 'They didn't want to talk about the Reptilian presence at all.' I am not saying this because I am desperate to go on the Rogan or Carlson shows. I couldn't care less either way. But journalistically it makes no sense to exclude me, and I am simply asking a legitimate question: *Why*?

Other highly promoted and clueless Trump/Musk sycophants are the brothers Andrew and Tristan Tate who both blocked me on Twitter/X while located in Romania awaiting the outcome of a series of charges including human trafficking and others are scheduled to follow in the UK. Tristan dismissed me as basically a 'has been' – 'People knew his name in the 1990s, but he is destined to die in obscurity.' Apparently, I wanted to be the face of the 'big movement' (I don't, I just want to demolish the here-and-no-further barricade) and 'tried for 40 years garnering barely 7% of my brother's online following and 1% of his reach and influence'. Perhaps he might ask why he and his brother have been so algorithmically promoted while following the Trump-Musk script, including many mainstream interviews, when those challenging that script are not. Tate ended with: 'This will probably be his last interaction with anybody with influence' and 'I am sorry we succeeded where you failed Mr. Icke.' Oh, but you didn't. That's the problem. You just led people down a garden path of myopia that took them nowhere.

Woke opens the door

I have said that the Woke agenda was made seriously extreme to make pushbackers furious and open to supporting anyone who would oppose it. Many of the new fake 'alternative' media came into the arena as 'anti-Woke' and then began pontificating about the conspiracy in general that they knew little about. Well, most of them – others will know but they are there to divert, not reveal. I spent many hours shaking my head while reading or watching their analysis that was so misleading. I am not saying that they are all knowingly misdirecting. That is not necessary. You just select people with a limited understanding and promote them with funding and full-on algorithms. Many of them had bought the 'Covid' hoax and now they were being promoted as 'experts' on 'Covid' and the fake vaccine in interviews with Rogan, Carlson, Jones, Brand, and others. One is Jewish intellectual Bret Weinstein, brother of Eric Weinstein, a business associate of Peter Thiel as managing director of Thiel Capital. Eric Weinstein is closely connected to the Edge organisation which arranged those 'billionaires dinners' once funded by Jeffrey Epstein.

The Weinsteins entered the arena via the 'Intellectual Dark Web', a term coined by Eric Weinstein to describe a group of academics and others who opposed Woke left-wing identity politics and political correctness. The term was popularised by *New York Times* journalist Bari Weiss who was educated at the Hebrew University in Jerusalem. She authored the 2019 book, *How to Fight Anti-Semitism*, and was reported to be in talks with the Zionist Ellisons over a role at the CBS they bought with Paramount. Weiss reported that the Intellectual Dark Web included podcaster Joe Rogan, ultra-Zionist Ben Shapiro of the Daily Wire, Netanyahu-loving Canadian psychologist Jordan Peterson, Zionist podcaster Dave Rubin, Israel fanatic Douglas Murray, and neuroscientist Sam Harris. Peterson launched an 'alternative' organisation in 2023 called ARC (Alliance for Responsible Citizenship) funded by some very non-'alternative' sources (see *The Reveal*) and announced this on the ubiquitous Joe Rogan podcast. Peterson told *Esquire* magazine in 2018 that he was discussing an 'undisclosed project' with Peter Thiel and another AI billionaire, the big investor in Israeli tech companies, Marc Andreessen, who blocked me on Twitter/X before I had even mentioned him. Bari Weiss would later join Joe Lonsdale, co-founder with Peter Thiel and Alex Karp of surveillance company Palantir, and others, to launch the University of Austin which is claimed to be dedicated to freedom of thought (don't laugh). This is backed by a 'group of powerful venture capitalists' that include Marc Andreessen who promotes an AI society on the Rogan show where Bret and Eric Weinstein have been regularly interviewed.

Bret Weinstein, a former professor of evolutionary biology, called for more severe lockdowns and told Rogan that he was 'very concerned' about the 'brand new evolutionarily Covid virus' (*which didn't actually exist* – see my book, *The Answer*). No surprise that Weinstein deleted his tweets on 'Covid' when he became a go-to 'Covid' expert for Rogan, Carlson, and company. He explained in a video during 'Covid' how he wore a bandana scarf around his neck at home so he could pull it up over his face whenever anyone knocked the door (Fig 213). He said he had bought 25 bandanas from Amazon. Weinstein also wore 'safety glasses' with his pulled-up scarf whenever he went out to make sure the 'virus' had a 'complex path to get past my glasses' and into his eyes if he walked through 'a cloud that someone has coughed out'. He wore cloth gloves (he had

Figure 213: Bret Weinstein taking no chances with a virus that didn't exist.

'multiple sets') and he would take off his clothes to be washed whenever he came home. Meanwhile, I was hugging hundreds of people on protest marches and never had so much as a sniffle. The arrogance of many 'we're here now' newcomers after 'Covid' was breathtaking. Weinstein said the following to people who saw through 'Covid' and asked why he was suddenly an expert:

> We have an epidemic of friendly fire within the dissident community. The people involved need to level up or get off the battlefield. That should be obvious ... the petty infighting among dissidents is a distraction at best and a circular firing squad at worst ...
>
> ... Individuals and new dissident institutions argue about who gets to take credit for victories. Purists criticize latecomers for not getting things right initially. But how do you expect to expand a movement if you don't allow for converts, and are not grateful [grateful?] when people change their minds and come over to your side?
>
> Many dissidents do not understand media and communications, and think that shouting the truth, even when nobody is listening, will move the ball down the field ... when the team wins we all win and it does not matter who gets credit for the game winning shot.

The arrogance of it. The point he misses is that those that could see through 'Covid' while he wore his bandana, glasses and gloves, had no problem with new people joining the throng. The more the better. It was the fact that these people walked in and wanted to take over when they were light years from the cutting edge and that the system through its algorithms, funding and promotion was helping them to do it. As for not understanding media and communications – I have been a journalist and communicator since 1973 on newspapers, radio, television and Internet. You, Mr Weinstein? Then you have newbies like Ian Carroll claiming I am riding his coat tails and asking what I do now – 'not in the past'. It's the same approach as Weinstein which is basically 'stand aside, we're here now'. It may be asked why accounts would be algorithmically boosted that appear to 'expose' the agenda, but the game is to limit exposure to *'here and no further'* to continue to control the circulation of information within the Overton window. This is why the 'new stars' have used information in my books for decades and exposed by others long ago which they present as 'breaking news'. A lot of stuff is already out there and it's the next stage of the plan that they want to suppress. By focussing on old information while presenting it as new they hold attention on that and not the current phase that is leading to AI dystopia. The focus on Left-Right politics and the Deep State as only the Democrats or the 'Left' is a perfect example.

There was clearly a force at work infiltrating the alternative and its means and nature of communication. This is an old technique and one perfected by the Sabbateans. You infiltrate organisations and arenas you wish to control and divert by posing as 'one of them' before manipulating yourself into a position of power and marginalising genuine people that were there before. I remember 5G campaigner Claire Edwards describing how a 5G resistance group she was involved with went down this route. Claire worked for 19 years at the UN in Austria and became aware of the electromagnetic field agenda. She is a loud and effective exposer of 5G, but the infiltration drove her out of the International Appeal to Stop 5G on Earth and in Space when she says it was infiltrated by people that connected with the Club of Rome, the Cult climate scam, along with New Ager 'stars'. I have seen this happen often over the decades and I could see what was happening with the 'alternative' since a long time back. This is why I have always worked alone and not in groups.

Rumble and the usual suspects

The Rumble video platform was founded by Canadian Chris Pavlovski in 2013 as a rival to censorious YouTube. He once publicly offered Joe Rogan $100 million over four years to move his podcast to his platform. Among Rumble investors have been AI promotors Peter Thiel, JD Vance, Vivek Ramaswamy, and Trump 'AI czar' David Sacks. Rumble promotes the MAGA media big names who have supported Trump and his election. The number of Rumble operatives, podcasters and investors who were appointed to the Trump regime in 2025 should concentrate the mind. A researcher on X, Rumble and Substack using the pseudonym Polly St George, has highlighted this. They include Trump himself with his Truth Social platform working with Rumble's cloud infrastructure. Then there is: JD Vance, Vice-President; Howard Lutnick, Commerce Secretary; Tulsi Gabbard, Director of National Intelligence; Michael Ellis, Deputy Director of the CIA; Kash Patel, Director of the FBI and director of Trump Media and Technology Group; Dan Bongino, Deputy Director of the FBI; Devin Nunes, US Intelligence Advisory Committee and CEO/Chairman of Trump Media and Technology Group; Linda McMahon, Education Secretary and Trump Media and Technology Group; and David Sacks, Trump's AI and crypto 'czar'. Ultra-Zionist Commerce Secretary Howard Lutnick, a Rumble investor, is chairman and CEO of financial services giant Cantor Fitzgerald who helped Rumble to go public in 2022. Rumble is a source of handsome rewards for a stream of 'influencers' supporting Trump and Vance that include Russell Brand.

Some backroom executives at Rumble: Tyler Hughes is chief

operating officer and former head of marketing for the AI software development arm of pharmaceutical and agribusiness giant Bayer Monsanto. Michael Ellis, Rumble's General Counsel and Corporate Secretary, had senior legal and policy roles in the intelligence network, White House, and Congress. Ellis was Senior Director for Intelligence Programs at the National Security Council (NSC) under Trump; Senior Associate Counsel to the President; Deputy NSC Legal Advisor in the Office of the White House Counsel; General Counsel of the notorious National Security Agency (NSA); General Counsel of the House Permanent Select Committee on Intelligence and an intelligence officer in the United States Navy Reserve. What is he doing with an 'alternative' video platform you might ask? Other Rumble executives and 'partners' have connections to Microsoft, Yahoo, Bayer, and the US National Security Council.

MAGA media and Trump's election

Trump was elected because of this 'New Media' which has moved in on what was a genuine alternative, swathes of it anyway, and taken it over. It has been essential for the Cult to control sources of information (propaganda) that are trusted by the target pushbackers to get them behind AI or at least become so mesmerised by the 'you're the media now' and 'we're winning' that they don't notice what that smokescreen is being used to hide. Trump has been marginalising the mainstream media, including the Associated Press for refusing to call the Gulf of Mexico the 'Gulf of America' which Trump renamed in a one-man executive order in a pathetic piece of PR for the MAGA mind. It had been the Gulf of Mexico for 400 years. The man is a child with arrested development. Trump began allowing the 'New Media' (MAGA sycophants) into White House press briefings including Rumble chief Pavlovski. It was staggering to watch the ease with which once sceptical people bought the Trump-Musk Psyop and vehemently abused and attacked anyone pointing out that it *was* a Psyop. Part of this was the desperation for Trump and Musk to be genuine, like clinging to the wreckage of a sinking boat. Those who exposed the scam were taking away their sense of 'hope' and I understand that. But what's the point of 'hope' if it's misplaced and another perceptual diversion?

We pursue the truth unfettered by compromise and cul-de-sacs or we go under. This is not to be a 'purist'. It is simply intelligence and common sense. How easy it is for values and perceptions to be bait and switched. 'Alternatives' had been against electric vehicles as a key element of the human-caused climate scam; but when protestors turned on Tesla after Musk's support for Trump and cars were burned and boycotted, the same 'alternatives' were suddenly promoting Tesla and buying its EVs. Trump even used the White House as the backdrop for a Tesla sales-pitch looking every bit the used-car salesman that he is. Alex Jones began to promote Tesla electric vehicles and then there's the MAGA Trump fanatic on Twitter/X who calls himself 'Catturd'. Classy bloke. He posted in 2022:

> Just so you know – everything about electric cars suck, and they're horrible for the environment. It's not the way of the future and never will be. It's a bad joke pushed by woke idiots, and people trying to get rich on government subsidies.

The latter would be a comment about Musk, but after Trump came to office with Musk and protests began at Tesla locations the same 'Catturd' posted in March 2025:

> Daily reminder … Wear your MAGA hat proudly. Drive your Tesla proudly.

They have no shame. The plan is to create the illusion of dissent in which people think they are opposing the system when they are serving it. The mainstream media serves through censorship and propaganda and the mainstream 'alternative' serves through censorship and propaganda.

The 'alternative' maze

The MAGA and its media is driven by Christianity and its support for Israel comes from a belief in the Old Testament as historical fact. I remember the late mega Trump supporter Charlie Kirk of Turning Point USA saying that to be a Christian you must 'honour the Jews'. Kirk said this to a 'Palestinian Christian': 'In our Scriptures it says we must bless the Jews.' God had a 'Covenant with Israel'. He asked the Palestinian Christian how we knew that the Bible was true. 'From the land of Israel-Palestine', came the reply. 'It's not Palestine', said Kirk, who believed that an extraordinarily contradictory book was the word of God. The land was Israel. It was appalling what happened to Charlie Kirk, but he personified how unquestioning allegiance to a highly manipulated book can dictate your view of everything when you consider every contradictory word to be the 'word of God'. American MAGA senator Ted Cruz said that he was taught in Sunday School that those who blessed Israel would be blessed and those that curse Israel will be cursed. Yes, mate, but you are an adult now and can think for yourself. Apparently not. He said that he wanted to be 'in the blessing side of things'. Cruz said that his support for Israel came from God's biblical command to support Israel. That would be 'Yahweh', then? The bloodthirsty tyrant? It's all madness and this mentality is promoting the direction of the world on behalf of a US president who wouldn't know a Bible if it smacked him in the face. To be fair he might just about recognise his God Bless the U.S.A. Bible, or 'Trump Bible', 'the only Bible endorsed by Donald Trump'. It is sold for $60 when the Associated Press reported that copies were printed in China for less than $3 a time. It's not a scam or anything to target his Christian followers as he has targeted the MAGA with a stream of other scams.

Russell Brand converted to Christianity, bought the whole biblical download, and was baptised in the River Thames with 'TV survival expert' Bear Grylls who went on to be appointed by King Charles to an Army role of inspiring new recruits. Brand later baptised others. He said: 'As a Christian, when you read the Old Testament, you have to acknowledge that there is a unique, particular and sacred relationship between the Jewish people and that land.' This is the new 'alternative' media. A book written long, long, ago without evidence becomes the basis of what we should believe is historical truth and dictate what happens in 2026. Brand has been a comedian, actor, New Ager, supporter of the political Left, and then since 'Covid' transformed into a Trump-supporting, way-back from the cutting edge 'conspiracy' podcaster, and finally a Christian which ticked the boxes of his new audience, the 'Christian Right'.

Brand has backed Trump and Musk and moved to the United States to be among his people. He says he speaks to Musk on the phone, and he has arrived for events at Trump's Mar-a-Lago mansion in a private jet. He's a friend of the Trump circle including Trump's son, Donald Trump Jr, and presents a world in which the 'Deep State' is the Democrats. Brand sings from the Trump-Musk song sheet and fell to his knees to deliver a prayer at two big audience events hosted by Tucker Carlson to promote Trump in the run-up to the 2024 election. None of this is what a proper journalist, let alone an 'alternative' one, would do. Proper journalists expose the abuses of power whatever form it takes and never take political 'sides' in a One-Party State like Brand, Jones, Rogan, and all the rest of them. To do otherwise is not to be a journalist. It is to be a propagandist which is what the seized alternative really is and designed to be. These 'alternatives' think they are awake when they are fast asleep – coma asleep – and oblivious of the scale of what is happening. People like Brand rail against the mainstream media but can't see – or won't see – that they act in exactly the same way. Political bias is not balanced by the other polarity of political bias. Truth doesn't have political bias. It just is.

Dark Enlightenment and AI promotor Peter Thiel pops up everywhere to connect into government through Trump and Musk, into Big Tech in which he is a major player, and the fake 'alternative' media. His business associate Vivek Ramaswamy is on the organising committee of Jordan Peterson's Alliance For Responsible Citizenship, with its apt catchphrase 'Welcome aboard the ARC'. It is awash with the hijacked 'alternative' and others in mainstream politics with its backers cross-referencing with the very semi-'alternative' GB News (see *The Reveal*). Peterson is a friend of Zionist Israel-first MAGA media host Dave Rubin who became a friend of Peter Thiel after being introduced by Thiel's venture capital advisor, Eric Weinstein. Rubin posted a promotion of a Rogan-Bret Weinstein interview this way: 'The Elites are on the march, but @elonmusk @BretWeinstein @joerogan and many others are putting up a fight.' There is constant cross-promotion by MAGA media names, and they regularly interview each other.

Rubin, a member of the Intellectual Dark Web, launched Locals Technology Inc., or Locals.com, in 2019, with his Israeli brother-in-law Assaf Lev. Locals was handed millions in seed-funding by Craft Ventures, a San Francisco venture capital firm co-founded by Zionist David Sacks who was born to a Jewish family in Musk's birthplace South Africa and is part of the 'PayPal Mafia' that includes Musk and Thiel. Sacks was Trump's pick to be his White House AI and crypto 'czar' which positioned him perfectly for the drive for AI control. Sacks has invested in SpaceX, Palantir, and Facebook, and served on the board of Rumble (major investor Peter Thiel). Rubin sold Locals to Rumble. Jordan Peterson in turn works for Netanyahu's friend and Israel fanatic Ben Shapiro at the Daily Wire. Shapiro took Peterson to Israel where they both interviewed Netanyahu and when Hamas was allowed to break into Israel from Gaza on October 7th, 2023, Peterson posted on Twitter/X: 'Give 'em hell @Netanyahu. Enough is enough.' He did. Peterson denies Israel's over-influence on world affairs and says those suggesting this was a 'quick way for dimwits to gain more virtue at the expense of other people'. It was blatant scapegoating. His wife said Jewish people have more influence than others compared with their numbers because Jews were smart people. *That* is blatant gaslighting.

There is also a theme of conversion to Roman Catholicism among highly promoted 'alternative' names. This is strange when those who campaign for freedom of speech convert to a Roman church responsible for the horrific mass murder of untold numbers for the crime of speaking a different truth to the Catholic men in frocks. Then there is the infamous child abuse within the church and its systematic cover-up. It's all very weird to me.

Keeping you well

Alongside the 'new media' network are those funding the chosen. Joe Rogan gets his hundreds of millions from Spotify and then there is the everywhere-you-look operation, The Wellness Company, long exposed by Polly St George who has highlighted its funding of the MAGA fake 'dissident network'. It funds a stream of people in the MAGA media including Russell Brand. The Wellness Company, launched in 2022 as the takeover was really getting underway, is co-owned by Foster Coulson and Dave Lopez and sells health supplements. Lopez is a former Navy SEAL and has worked for US Homeland Security. Wellness public faces include cardiologist Dr Peter McCullough, and Dr Paul Alexander, described as 'a Canadian independent scientist' who was a Trump administration official at the US Department of Health and Human Services during 'Covid'. We are supposed to trust our health with someone who bought the 'Covid' hoax? I don't think so. Foster Coulson and family have a company 'fighting wildfires' and earns billions in government contracts. Coulson says he met Dave Lopez, his partner in The Wellness Company, by chance in Bolivia. I don't buy it myself. Lopez worked in Haiti, an infamous child-trafficking centre, for the 'anti-child trafficking' Underground Railroad of Tim Ballard which became widely known with the movie, *Sound of Freedom*. He also has his own 'anti-child trafficking' operation called Mission Six Zero ('unleash your inner soldier').

Lopez has worked for big Trump supporter Erik Prince, a CIA asset, former Navy SEAL officer, and founder of the mercenary army operation Blackwater (later Xe Services, then Academi, now Constellis). This is one of the world's biggest private security firms used as an arms-length agency by the CIA and Pentagon. Prince has trained James O'Keefe and staff at the hidden-camera exposure group, Project Veritas. O'Keefe now runs the O'Keefe Media Group which is funded by The Wellness Company. Erik Prince appears on the shows of former Trump aide Steve Bannon, Alex Jones (who called him a 'patriot') and Tucker Carlson who said that Prince was 'a good friend of mine', a 'really wonderful person', and 'one of my favourite people, actually'. Blackwater operatives killed 17 and injured 20 in Nisour Square, Baghdad, while escorting a US embassy convoy in 2007. Four of the Blackwater shooters were convicted in the United States for murder or manslaughter in 2014, but were pardoned in 2020 by Donald Trump, a long-time friend and ally of Erik Prince.

Prince instigated the deal with El Salvador President Nayib Bukele to take migrants and even US citizens deported from the US into his notorious prison system. Prince said he pitched the idea directly to Bukele and the following week the agreement was announced between Bukele and Trump Secretary of State Marco Rubio. Bukele said he would accept 'dangerous American criminals into custody in our country, including those of US citizenship and legal residents'. He meant whoever Trump sent him including innocent gay men and professional soccer players with a tattoo confirming his 'gang membership' that was really a logo of his favourite football team. Prince has floated the policy of using private armies ('private military contractors') for operations against the Houthis in Yemen and discussed his 'crackdown talents' with Ecuador President Daniel Noboa with a view to a 'strategic alliance'. CNN reported that Noboa had announced the day before his chat with Prince the imminent arrival of 'special forces from abroad to tackle crime in Ecuador'. He also approached Trump to send US troops amid martial law and gang violence. Prince allies include Defense Secretary Pete Hegseth and Director of National Intelligence Tulsi Gabbard with Prince acting as a character witness for Gabbard when some Republicans doubted her qualifications for the job. If you need Erik Prince as a 'character witness' you must be struggling.

Prince associate Dave Lopez, Foster Coulson, and their Wellness Company sponsor a long list of MAGA media assets, websites and video platforms, and Coulson operates the Vigilant News Network. Wellness CEO Peter Gillooly has said that anyone they financially support has their content monitored for 'fringe or hate speech'. Stay on message might be another way of putting it. The Wellness Company is part of Foster Coulson's Stardust Group which includes 1775 Coffee, a partner with Rumble, and has been promoted by Russell Brand and Andrew Tate. Foster Coulson, Dave Lopez, and another Wellness stalwart Brandon Kuemper launched an American venture capital company, Integro Capital, in 2021 which invested in Nanobiosym, 'a physics, biomedicine, and nanotechnology' company founded by chairman and CEO, Dr Anita Goel. This sets out to converge physics, nanotechnology, and biomedicine into a 'new science' of 'nanobiophysics'. Goel connects with the Clinton Global Initiative, Pentagon Big Tech arm DARPA, NASA, SpaceX, and Peter Diamandis, a promotor of AI-human fusion.

What a maze and these are just some of the people handing over massive amounts of money to MAGA media 'stars' since the 'alternative' was targeted by the Cult in the wake of 'Covid'. They are also paid by Rumble with 'requirements' that 'tailor the Program to creators that provide the most value to the platform', according to founder Chris Pavlovski. He said they would be 'weeding out creators that take the budget away from high performing creators'. Rumble has promoted Donald Trump, Donald Trump Jr; Russell Brand (Trumper); Dan Bongino (now Trump's deputy head of the FBI); Sean Hannity (Trumper); the late Charlie Kirk (Trumper); Andrew Tate (Trumper), Ben Shapiro, Israel fanatic; Tulsi Gabbard (Trump's head of National Intelligence); Dave Rubin (Trumper); Tim Pool (Trumper); Steve Bannon, one-time Trump advisor; and Dana White, CEO of the UFC and friend of Trump who is on the board of Meta which owns Facebook. There's a common theme there which doesn't take much effort to see. Rumble does not, it is safe to say, promote me which I take as a compliment given the above.

Think global

Crucial to understanding the political game is to see through the Left-Right diversion and realise that the agenda for human control is *global*. What happens in North, Central and South America, Europe, Africa, Asia, the Middle and Far East and Oceania is all serving the *global* plan. I have MAGA Americans tell me to stop focussing on the United States when my own country is in such a mess. They don't get that what happens in the US and Britain is all part of the same global sequence to total human control through AI. The US because of its size and influence on the world becomes, therefore, something that everyone should focus on. What happens there will be happening everywhere eventually and the same with China. The fake 'alternative' media has served the Cult magnificently in regressing the focus away from the One-Party State, let alone the global one, and into the Left-Right cul-de-sac. This regression has promoted the idea that the 'Deep State' is the 'Democrats', or the 'Liberals' and Left, who are out to 'get' Trump, the hero that's come to save us. It's an insult to even a child's intelligence, but grown adults sell it and fall for it. They want you focused on the irrelevant myopia so the panorama (and with it the answers) are never seen. Look how deeply we are now in the Left-Right puppet show and the five senses after previous chapters about the simulation trap, Archontic manipulation, and the infinity that awaits us beyond the illusion. This is exactly where the Cult and its Astral masters want humanity to be. Caught in the myopia of illusion and ignorant of that once upon a no time land not far away. That is the real reason for what we come to next – the AI takeover.

I warned from the START that Trump was a front man for the AI oligarchs to impose the AI control agenda and sell it to the MAGA mind that has always been sceptical of it. Trump has since done just that along with Musk, Thiel, and all the rest of them (and you've seen nothing yet). Now, having promoted Trump and Musk on an extreme level of sycophancy, and still batting for them, the MAGA media including Alex Jones complain about the AI agenda.

It's almost laughable. Almost.

CHAPTER 25

AI Dystopia

The line between human decision-making and AI-driven choices is blurring faster than we realize.
Abhijeet Sarkar

We return to the most important theme of the book upon which the entire conspiracy stands or falls – the separation of 'incarnate' awareness from the infinite 'Divine Spark' self. True awakening is that reconnection because then *everything, everything, everything* changes.

It is testament to the power of expanded awareness that the Archontic force must bombard us with all its weapons aimed at disconnection. There is the control of information through 'education' and media to dictate conscious and subconscious perception of self and reality, and the algorithmic 'life' programs running through the biological computer. There is the manipulation of brain function to lock us away in the left side while messing with the decoding and information processing mechanisms which firewall access to expanded ways of thinking, feeling and seeing. There is another which is rarely talked about which is Archontic communications through the simulation field. We interact visually and consciously through the five senses as we decode information into illusory 'physicality', but there are other subconscious interactions that allow 'backdoor' access to the human mind/brain. You could think of them as like algorithms infused into the simulation field that those operating on the same frequency will decode into thoughts and feelings which manifest as actions that they take to be their own choices. In the same way those simulation algorithms and blocks can target people and events that could awaken the population to cause disruption and lack of circulation of awakening information. Ickonic filmmaker Christianne van Wijk calls these 'Astral algorithms'.

It has been well established how frequencies can be broadcast across a target area which can wind up people to the point where one trigger can send them into a collective frenzy of rioting and violence. The authorities provide the trigger which may be a wrongful arrest, police violence, whatever. It's been 75 years since Dr Andrija Puharich, an American medical and parapsychological researcher, discovered the connection between frequencies, perception and behaviour. How sophisticated must it be now? Puharich found that frequencies can change DNA and RNA and why wouldn't that be true when DNA is a receiver-transmitter of information as well as a 'hard drive'? DNA can be manipulated by frequencies in the same way that brain plasticity is impacted by the information (frequencies) that it processes. He established that psychic people operate on 8Hz as they connect with other realities and that frequencies of 10.80Hz produce 'riotous behaviour' while 6.6Hz brings the onset of depression. A similar process is happening in the simulation field as collective perceptions are encoded to be decoded as a person's own thoughts and beliefs if they are 'entrained' into those frequencies. Entrainment is the principle that the dominant frequency will 'entrain' others into that frequency. Three violins tuned to the same note will cause a fourth violin to resonate to that note with the imposition of the dominant frequency. You see this happen when people react collectively as a mob. The power of consciousness can override this if activated and we call it 'thinking for yourself' or 'being a maverick'.

The hive mind

The phenomenal multi-levelled bombardment of the human mind with perception manipulation really does tell you how powerful consciousness is when set free from its prison cell. The Archontic force must work 24/7 to hold us in the servitude of limited perception and separated by frequency from the Divine Spark and Infinite Awareness. It is terrified this connection will happen when it's over for the Archontic should humans break free of the multiple aspects of mind control. This is why the goal is to connect artificial intelligence to the human brain/body to ensure that AI dictates thought and emotional response (Fig 214 and 215). The brain would be 'plasticity' wired by the AI information input to block the processing of expanded awareness. What you think and feel would be delivered by AI and that would never tell you to question 'who am I?' or 'where am I?' Humanity would be a hive mind that could be controlled from a central point. Fantastic? If only. It's already happening. This is a

Figure 214: Human minds connected to a central point of control and perceptual dictatorship. The AI mind of the 'gods' infiltrating human awareness. (Image by Neil Hague.)

AI Dystopia

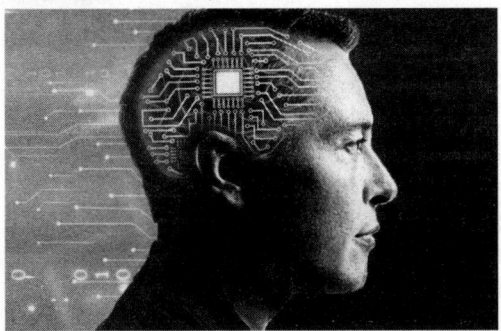

Figure 215: Elon Musk wants to fuse humans with AI.

Merriam-Webster dictionary definition of a hive mind:

The collective mental activity expressed in the complex, coordinated behaviour of a colony of social insects (such as bees or ants) regarded as comparable to a single mind controlling the behaviour of an individual organism.

Humanity is already a hive mind collective in that different factions gravitate into hive perspectives. We have the Woke and MAGA hive minds and those of religions where people operate in the same software program and condemn, even hate, other software that triggers 'different' collective behaviour when they all mirror each other. They act the same whether it be Holy Week, Ramadan, Passover, Diwali, a Trump announcement, or a Woke censorship. They follow their programs without question and respond accordingly. We are now seeing the sequence of bringing those hives together in a *global* hive mind which is made easier if the targets are already in the hive mentality. The global hive mind requires two elements – delivering and receiving. The means of delivery is the technologically generated global electromagnetic field, or 'The Cloud'. The receiver is the self-replicating nanotechnology infused into the body by the 'Covid' fake vaccines, those of a similar type, and other means. It was said that the fake vaccine was circulated without adequate 'trials', but it depends what kind of 'trial' you mean. Yes, they were nothing like adequate to see if it was 'safe and effective'. Trials however were extensive over years to make sure it was *un*safe and effective in doing what I am describing here. Google executive, inventor, 'futurist' and AI obsessive Ray Kurzweil said the following would happen by around 2030. He talks about the 'Cloud' as in the computer cloud but when I say the 'Cloud' I mean that plus the technological electromagnetic field which is the delivery medium for the hive mind:

> Our thinking ... will be a hybrid of biological and non-biological thinking ... humans will be able to extend their limitations and 'think in the cloud' ... We're going to put gateways to the cloud in our brains ... We're going to gradually merge and enhance ourselves ... In my view, that's the nature of being human – we transcend our limitations.
>
> As the technology becomes vastly superior to what we are then the small proportion that is still human gets smaller and smaller and smaller until it's just

utterly negligible.

Kurzweil wrote in his 2005 book, *The Singularity Is Near*:

> Augmented reality will be projected constantly onto our retinas from our glasses and contact lenses. It will also resonate in our ears ... Most of its functions and information will not be explicitly requested, but our ever-present AI assistants will anticipate our needs by watching and listening in on our activities. In the 2030s, medical nanorobots will begin to integrate these brain extensions directly into our nervous systems.

Kurzweil, who was born in New York to Austrian-Jewish parents in 1948, describes himself as 'a leading developer in artificial intelligence for 61 years – longer than any other living person'. Bill Gates calls him 'the best person I know at predicting the future of artificial intelligence'. I guess it helps if you know what the plan is. Kurzweil founded the Singularity University with another AI obsessive Peter Diamandis who I mentioned in relation to Dr Anita Goel, the 'new science' of 'nanobiophysics', and fake 'alternative' media funder, Wellness Company owner Foster Coulson. The technological 'singularity' is defined as when 'technological growth becomes uncontrollable and irreversible, culminating in profound and unpredictable changes to human civilization' and when 'artificial intelligence ... surpasses human cognitive capabilities and can autonomously enhance itself' (known as AGI or artificial general intelligence). Put more starkly – AI takes over (Fig 216). Kurzweil has predicted this will happen by 2045 while Elon Musk has said it could be much earlier. Musk said in 2024: 'My guess is that we'll have AI that is smarter than any one human probably around the end of next year.' I should add the rider that Musk's predictions are notoriously wrong so we will see. Diamandis takes the same line as Musk in that AI control is 'inevitable':

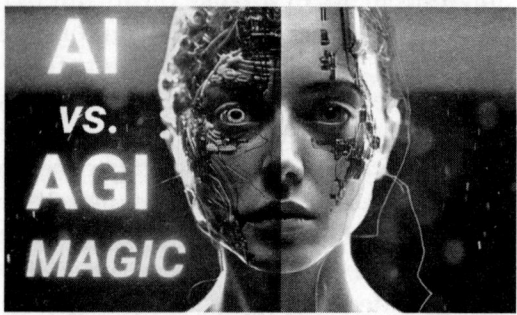

Figure 216: We are fast entering a whole new world in which Artificial General Intelligence (AGI) and even more advanced AI can take over everything including human thinking and emotional response. Humanity is sleepwalking into extreme dystopia being sold to them as progress.

> Anybody who is going to be resisting the progress forward [to transhumanism] is going to be resisting evolution and, fundamentally, they

will die out. It's not a matter of whether it's good or bad. It's going to happen.

'Resisting evolution'? What a load of old crap. Resisting the Archontic Cult agenda more like. 'Inevitability' is an important tool of perceptual manipulation. When you wish to stop something, you set out to stop it. But when you are convinced that it's 'inevitable' – 'resistance is futile' – you either give up or focus on mitigating its effects. With the first you stop pushing back, and with the second you dilute your approach to making the best of it. The Cult plays the long game and prepares well ahead for what it knows is coming unless humanity awakens. Elon Musk positioned himself years ago as an 'AI sceptic' and said that it could be the end of humanity. The contradiction is that ever since then he has turned out and promoted more and more AI. He's pushed the lie that AI is, yes, 'inevitable' and the only way to save humanity is to fuse with AI to keep up with it. Musk said when he launched his company xAI (now owners of Twitter/X) in 2023:

> If I could press pause on AI or really advanced AI digital superintelligence I would. It doesn't seem like that is realistic so xAI is essentially going to build an AI. In a good way, sort of hopefully.

Bullshit.

Hard sell, soft sell

Musk and his fellow Silicon Valley billionaires (in league with AI scientists in Israel) are involved in a two-pronged attack targeting the belief systems of the political Left and Right. The Left are being given the hard sell of AI-human fusion through Klaus Schwab, Bill Gates, Ray Kurzweil, Peter Diamandis, and their like. This is the 'next stage of evolution', 'we'll be gods' approach. The Right contains many people who before the arrival of Musk at Twitter/X were highly sceptical of the AI transhumanist agenda. They had to be absorbed into the AI fold by another means in which AI could be hidden behind the 'we're winning' technique of the Trump regime dismantling the 'Deep State' (in theory), Woke laws, and deporting illegal (and legal) migrants. Musk is the soft sell as he plays the AI sceptic and says the AI takeover is 'unfortunately' inevitable. The only way for humanity to survive is by fusing with AI. The outcome of the hard sell and soft cell? Fusing humans with AI (Fig 217 overleaf).

The hive mind requires delivery and receiver systems, and they are both well advanced. Delivery is by frequency through the fast expanding electromagnetic 'Cloud' generated through towers on the ground and low-orbit satellites in their thousands already permitted by the US Federal Communications Commission (FCC). The low-orbit leader is Elon Musk's SpaceX (really NASA and the Pentagon) with the Kuiper system of Amazon and Jeff Bezos well underway. They form together into an orbiting surveillance network as well as generating the Cloud and operate under the cover of space-based broadband connection. SpaceX has Starlink and its military/government version Starshield. SpaceX began launching its satellites in 2019 and Kuiper was established in the same year. SpaceX plans some 12,000 satellites expanding to tens of thousands as necessary. The FCC has granted Amazon approval to deploy 3,236 satellites so far. I'm sure that SpaceX will be delighted that Donald Trump appointed Musk buddy and supporter Brendan Carr to head the FCC in 2025. Carr wrote a chapter about the FCC in Project 2025 which is the Trump regime wishlist that Trump said he knew nothing about but has clearly followed since returning to office. Carr also has free speech in his gunsights.

Figure 217: Hour by hour artificial intelligence is taking over the human world.

Astronomers were complaining very early that SpaceX and Musk were changing the night sky with their satellite constellation and making it ever more difficult to scan, but what does Musk care about anything that doesn't suit him? The combination of low-orbit satellites and towers bombarding us with 4G and far more disruptive 5G, with 6G and 7G in the pipeline, are forming the global electromagnetic Cloud through which the hive mind frequencies will be circulated. Clare Edwards has worked tirelessly to expose the dangers and reasons for 5G since she left the United Nations where she edited the documents of the UN Committee on the Peaceful Uses of Outer Space and its Legal, Scientific and Technical subcommittees. This gave her insights into space law and the impact of orbiting technology. She said:

> The whole point about 5G is that it affects your brain. I mean, not only does it affect your body, but it affects your brain and therefore it affects your judgment. It can also be used for mind control ... 5G, in my view, is about a total surveillance and mind control and kill grid. That's what 5G is.

This is happening as we speak as the hive mind is instigated and the unconscious population is influenced in its thinking and emotions via the electromagnetic field while being blocked from awareness outside the simulation. They need a receiver system to make it even more powerful. What could that be?

Self-replicating 'vaccines'

Ladies and gentlemen, please welcome the 'Covid' fake 'mRNA' vaccine (and all others of the same type with the same content). I say 'fake' vaccine because it does not meet the previous definition of a vaccine. It is a genetic manipulator and builder of nano-systems in the body to receive hive mind transmissions. Scientists and medical doctors seeking the truth (the few) have witnessed through powerful microscopes how self-replicating nano structures are being formed in the blood of fake vaccinated people and those who have been tested for 'Covid' with the probe high up the nose. They see *synthetic operating systems* that build and replicate in the body and brain with the intent of connecting human perception processes to the hive mind Cloud. They have found snake-like phenomena never seen in the body before which self-assemble into 'matrix-like' material and can illuminate in the presence of a smartphone (Figs 218 and 219). Synthetic biology is a fast-growing discipline of science and defined as 'the design and construction of new biological parts, devices, and systems, and the re-design of existing, natural biological systems for useful purposes'. Redesigning 'life' as we know it.

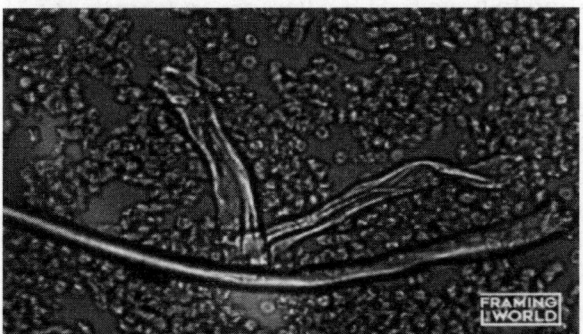

Figure 218: Nanotubes in the blood of the fake vaccinated.

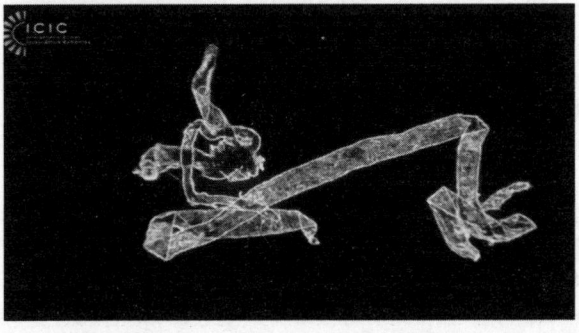

Figure 219: What is this doing in blood after the fake vaccine?

Researchers led by a team from Macquarie University in Australia claim to have reached a 'major milestone' in engineering life in the laboratory in a study involving a synthetic yeast genome. They said they constructed a full synthetic genome which was 'a proof-of-concept for how more complex organisms, like food crops, could be synthesised by scientists'. Molecular microbiologist Sakkie Pretorius from Macquarie University said this was a landmark moment in synthetic biology. 'It is the final piece of a puzzle that has occupied synthetic biology researchers for many years now.' They are seeking to turn the world synthetic.

I have warned for decades about the plan to make the human body far more synthetic that would lead eventually to the end of human procreation as we know it. This would be replaced by technological procreation in the way described by insider Aldous Huxley in *Brave New World* published as long ago as 1932. How is it possible to know that nearly a century ago? I said there are two worlds, the Cult and the human population, and they are divided by advanced knowledge on one side and programmed ignorance on the other (Fig 220). Global authorities on the say-so of the Cult-created World Health Organisation put pressure on the population to have the fake vaccine and constant testing because it was planned to instigate the hive mind. This was compartmentalisation with those giving the fake vaccines and doing the tests having no idea what the consequences were and indeed had them themselves. It was considered 'essential work' during lockdowns to erect towers for the then new 5G while most other work was banned. It's clear that not all fake vaccines were full-blown content. So many have died and had their health destroyed after having the shot. Imagine what the numbers would be if everyone got the killer content. Researchers have identified certain batches as particularly lethal compared with others. The Cult intends to get everyone eventually – if we submit to that. Other vaccines are being changed to the alleged 'mRNA' type and nanotechnology is being ingested in food with the fake vaccines being given to cattle and chickens. It is claimed by researchers using high-powered microscopes that graphene and nano self-replication is in dental anaesthetics. Well, if you want to get everyone.

Figure 220: Keep the target population ignorant of what you know. You may be stupid, but you rule if you make the population even more stupid.

Graphene re-wire

I have been in quite regular touch with La Quinta Columna ('The Fifth Column' in English), the research group in Spain which alerted the world to the significance of graphene oxide they identified in fake vaccine vials. Graphene oxide as an electricity conductor can re-wire the brain and connect the brain/body with other self-replicating structures to the hive mind electromagnetic Cloud. It also *amplifies* the effect of electromagnetic fields in the body/brain and amplifies the impact of the Cloud. The official line is there is no graphene in the jabs (and maybe not in *all* of them) but I have seen enough research confirming the graphene content to cross my line of evidence. There are also many papers on the PubMed database maintained by the United States National Library of Medicine at the National Institutes of Health which track studies into graphene use in vaccines and other medical procedures. One from 2020 is headlined: 'Recent progress of graphene oxide as a potential vaccine carrier and adjuvant.' The paper said their work describes how 'functionalized graphene oxide serves as a vaccine carrier and shows significant adjuvant activity in activating cellular and humoral immunity'. An adjuvant 'enhances the body's immune response'.

Another paper from 2023 labelled 'Graphene oxide as novel vaccine adjuvant' describes how 'graphene-based nanomaterials have recently attracted significant attention as a new type of vaccine adjuvants due to their potential role in the activation of immune responses'. Other papers include 'Functionalized graphene oxide serves as a novel vaccine nano-adjuvant for robust stimulation of cellular immunity'; 'Advances in Drug Delivery Nanosystems Using Graphene-Based Materials and Carbon Nanotubes'; 'The Emergence of Carbon Nanomaterials as Effective Nano-Avenues to Fight against COVID-19'; 'Biomedical Applications of Carbon Nanomaterials: Fullerenes, Quantum Dots, Nanotubes, Nanofibers, and Graphene.' Remember that research in the underground bases and secret programmes is *vastly* in advance of what is admitted to the public. It is quite a coincidence that public arena research was happening into graphene use in vaccines at the same time the claims began that graphene was in the 'Covid' shots.

Celeste Solum worked as a contractor for US Homeland Security and the Federal Emergency Management Agency (FEMA) before she left government work in disgust at what was happening. She became a vehement campaigner against the technological control of humanity through synthetic biology, electromagnetic fields, and fake vaccines with help from many contacts she made on the inside. Solum's father was employed by the Naval Warfare Center and was Assistant Director for Public Lands and Natural Resources in Washington State and California. She says: 'I was in a pivotal position during a time of revolutionary change in American history when she [America] turned from her historical foundation to rabid fascism.' Solum is adamant that graphene is in the fake vaccines known as mRNA and that it is contained in a substance called 'hydrogel'. This is a jelly-like substance holding large amounts of water that can bypass the immune system with a payload inside that would normally be rejected. Hydrogel can also release the payload slowly. Celeste Solum says that graphene is in a gelatine hydrogel composite, which is fabricated by mixing graphene and gelatine, much like Jell-O: 'Your body will not reject this invasion because it does not see it as an enemy or being hostile to your humanity … intelligent alien entities enter your body, and they begin to set up shop'. She said in 2021 that this is how graphene is delivered in the jabs – through 'biologically compatible' hydrogel:

> Graphene also has magical and conductive qualities making your body and your mind a receptor for any message that the controllers want to embed. Graphene and hydrogel play two roles. The gelator to self-assemble into the hydrogels and the filler to blend with small molecules and macromolecules for the preparation of multifunctional, get that, multifunctional hydrogels, which are collectively called graphene-based hydrogels.

> Scientists and researchers are using the self-assembling gelator to create a synthetic scaffold system inside your body, while the filler replaces your human parts with artificial ones that are predisposed to a collective or global fascist order …

Solum says the plan is for this infusion of 'synthetic organic materials that are used in plastics and resins' to eventually replace human DNA, blood, cells, tissues, and organs as the hydrogel nanoparticles self-assemble (this is synthetic biology, or 'SynBio'). 'Think of this as an invisible invasion transforming you from a human to a synthetic entity.' This is the agenda that I have been warning about for decades now. As Solum points out: 'Your body and mind become one with artificial intelligence and the Internet of Things … In essence, you become a canvas for the pharmaceutical artists to create a synthetic artistic masterpiece subservient to the alien system, not resembling anything human-like whatsoever.' The Internet of Things are the billions of items connected to the Internet with the plan to include humans in an Internet of Everything. Solum says that when hydrogel enters the body 'it fuses with your cells, your ligaments, your bones and everything and it becomes one with you and you become one with the Internet and artificial intelligence'. Solum quoted a 2020 fake vaccine patent:

> Hydrogels are highly absorbent, natural or synthetic polymers. Hydrogels also possess a degree of flexibility very similar to natural tissues due to their significant water content. The hydrogel described herein may be used to encapsulate lipid nanoparticles, which are biocompatible, biodegradable …

Solum says that 'dynamic hydrogel' responds to stimuli such as pressure, temperature, light, and the *magnetic* field:

> It is intelligent or 'smart' as they say. The biosensors are soft and flexible, often referred to as soft robotics, transforming a human being into a hybrid life form.

Hydrogel is programmable and 'can program transformation', and 'cavitate or gut you like a fish' to make the body a vessel for soft robotics. 'You'll be like the zombies that they were preparing for the zombie apocalypse.' Solum continues:

> Graphene is considered a magical material and according to the military, this information comes to us from a 232-page military document that I received in December of 2019. AI will yoke humanity using the magical material graphene development. It's a PNT, a position navigation and timing for precision weapon and targeting kill system.
>
> And it's going to replace GPS. This basically is a weapon, graphene is part of a weapon system. Think of it on a weapon with the red dot laser. That would be the graphene. And they can tell exactly where you are and then hit you with various direct energy weapons, frequency weapons.

Celeste Solum said this new system would require expansion from 5G to a 6G network with a quantum computer to process all the sensors implanted in our bodies, every animal and plant, throughout the environment and in space. It's not just humans that are being transformed into a synthetic state – it is *everything*. This is the new layer of control and disconnection from the Infinite that I have been saying all these years was the plan. Scientists have suggested that humans could be used as antennas to power 6G and 'harvest additional energy' when in fact they are already being used this way as people are turned into broadcasters of electromagnetic frequencies akin to mini 5G towers. This is what the human body has been designed to be – a receiver-transmitter of information. They are just taking this to another level. Solum says a 'neural attendant quantum computer' is used to 'capture, record, evaluate and report on every single thing inside your body'. If you are exercising, eating, not eating, praying or thinking – every single thought and action is recorded. 'You might think of it as a counterfeit Book of Life … that's mentioned in the Bible where everything that you do is written down.' It's another expression of the 'Akashic Records'.

Hexagon graphene

Graphene had been theorised since 1947, became a reality in 2004, and today it is used in semiconductors, electronics and electric batteries among much else. Its atoms are arranged as a hexagon honeycomb (Fig 221 overleaf). If the hexagon represents the frequency of Saturn does this mean that graphene in the body connects people with this frequency? This would make sense with my contention that Saturn is broadcasting low frequencies to the Earth amplified by technology within the Moon.

Graphene and its derivative, graphene oxide, appears black because it absorbs all visible light wavelengths and is phenomenally strong – the strongest metal ever measured on a microscopic scale. Black is the colour associated with Saturn. Most significantly, it is a tremendous conductor of electricity and even a superconductor as this Cambridge University article highlighted:

Figure 221: The hexagon structure of graphene.

> Researchers have found a way to trigger the innate, but previously hidden, ability of graphene to act as a superconductor – meaning that it can be made to carry an electrical current with zero resistance.
>
> The finding, reported in Nature Communications, further enhances the potential of graphene, which is already widely seen as a material that could revolutionise industries such as healthcare and electronics.

All this is highly significant in relation to the hive mind and the manipulation of perception. The brain processes information electrically and communicates that way with the rest of the body and vice versa. Graphene oxide can re-wire the brain and connect the brain/body with other self-replicating structures to the hive mind electromagnetic Cloud. Anything that disrupts or changes that electrical processing is going to impact on thought and emotional response. The nano content of the vials, including graphene, is designed to cross the blood-brain barrier that's supposed to protect the brain from toxic substances.

La Quinta Columna is headed by founder and director Ricardo Delgado Martin who has a long list of qualifications in health biology, clinical microbiology, epidemiology, clinical immunology, psychology and statistical analysis. Delgado said that graphene's interaction with electricity would affect the central nervous system, neurons, and heart which was where damage from the fake vaccine is happening (along with fast-acting or 'turbo cancers'). Then there is one other crucial point I've already mentioned. Graphene *amplifies* the effect of electromagnetic fields and graphene in the body/brain increases the effect of the Cloud. One report said: 'The unique two-dimensional structure of graphene contributes to its ability to interact with and absorb electromagnetic waves.' Graphene is a *neural* interface which is magnetic within the body and according to Delgado 'can be used to monitor, modulate, and stimulate remotely and wirelessly by means of telephone masts or towers' (and low-orbit satellites). Perfect for a hive mind. You will find a video at Davidicke.com in which I discuss graphene and other findings with Ricardo Delgado. You will also see on my website videos of what they have seen through the microscope.

Delgado says that people able to make spoons and other metal objects stick to the skin on the fake vaccine site and over a wider area can be explained by magnetised graphene. Graphene nanoparticles are highly likely to be involved in the concept of 'shedding' when the fake vaccinated transfer their nano-toxins to the non-fake-vaccinated. This can be done by many means including skin contact. For those who still doubt this is possible here is Dr James Giordano, Chief of the Neuroethics Studies Program in the Pellegrino Center for Clinical Bioethics, and a professor in the Department of Neurology, and Graduate Liberal Studies Program at Georgetown University in Washington. Giordano serves on the Neuroethics, Legal, and Social Issues Advisory Panel of the Pentagon's DARPA:

> This is why it is so important to understand the novelty and the viability of neuroscience being leveraged as weapons. We then have the use of nano particulate agents, aerosolize able nanomaterials that can be breathed in and disrupt blood flow and neurological network activity that can be used as an in-close weapon or perhaps can be used as a more broad weapon of disruption and destruction.
>
> We also have the capability to use nanomaterials to get electrodes into a head and create a vast array of viable sensors and transmitters ... Next generation non-invasive neuromodulation utilizing these techniques and technologies to create vast arrays of implantable electrodes that need not be put into the brain surgically. They are then able to read from the brain and write into the brain remotely in real time and there is a rapid pace.

You can see there as I have been saying for years how far back from the cutting edge is Musk's Neuralink. SpaceX rockets are the same. Giordano said this was happening not only in the United States, but internationally.

Hydrogel interface

Science researchers have suggested that content of the fake vaccine can lay dormant until activated by Cloud frequencies and could lead to a 'new disease', or what the WHO has called 'Disease X' which would be blamed on another cause while really being fake vaccine content activation through the electromagnetic field. Bill Gates comments and

Moderna fake vaccine patents confirm that self-assembling nanoparticles are in the vials. Their release can be controlled and activated once inside the body by electromagnetic fields. Hydrogel tricks the immune system into allowing the content to enter the body without rejection and Israel-developed 'nanorobots' can then be activated externally at will to do whatever they are programmed to do. Nature.com ran an article about the use of hydrogels in merging humans with AI. It said: 'Hydrogels have emerged as an ideal material candidate for interfacing between humans and machines owing to their mechanical and chemical similarities to biological tissues and the versatility and flexibility in designing their properties.' Graphene and other nano content makes the brain/body an antenna which can interact with the Cloud and the hive mind that will be connected to the Reptilian and Archontic hive mind. Once there is control through the Cloud to AI the human mind modes of thought and emotion can be stimulated to produce loosh at will. No longer would thought and emotion need to be manipulated. It would be on tap.

Fake vaccine vials are kept very cold. The temperature requirement of Pfizer is minus 70 degrees Celsius. They are activated at body temperature after insertion. La Quinta Columna put the content of a Pfizer vial in a reptile incubator at the body temperature of 37 degrees centigrade (98.6 F) in March 2024. It was quite clear to begin with but then as the temperature increased complex structures appeared and became more so with the passage of hours and days (Fig 222). Delgado said they found no biological material in the vials, and it was all synthetic. Nor did they find mRNA or 'spike protein' – even the synthetic kind. The story is that the 'spike protein'

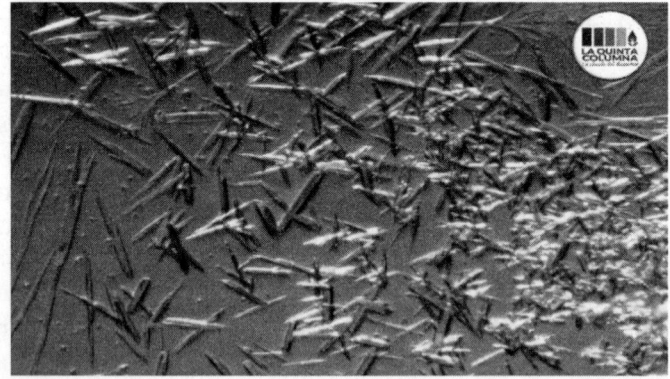

Figure 222: What happened in the La Quinta Columna experiment when a Pfizer 'Covid' fake vaccine vial was placed in an incubator at body temperature. It went from clear to complex structures.

in the fake vaccine is a response to the 'spike protein' in the 'virus', but there never has been a 'Covid virus' and there is nothing to respond to (see my books since *The Answer* in 2021). The whole story of 'Covid' is a lie. Every last syllable of it.

Another source of graphene is from the air through the chemtrails released from aircraft. Chemtrails (different to contrails) were once a 'conspiracy theory' denied by the authorities despite them appearing all over the world since at least the late 1990s. Now they are being promoted by the same authorities to block out the Sun to stop 'global warming'. The human-caused climate hoax keeps on giving. Contrails caused by hot air from the engines meeting cold air at high altitudes can quickly disappear while chemtrails stay in the air and pan out before falling to earth. You can watch planes criss-crossing the sky until a clear blue sky becomes a cloudy day (Fig 223). Pilots are told it is a top-secret mission to save the world from human-caused climate change. Decades of denial have been replaced by 'dimming the Sun' sales-pitched by Bill Gates which is always a *big* red flag. The UK government of Gates and climate change groupie Keir Starmer said in April 2025 that it was handing more than £50 million to research Sun dimming. The official idea is to reflect heat away from the Earth through 'stratospheric aerosol injection' and to study if it would be safe to deploy on a large scale. Those involved are lunatics with scientists warning them about the potential dangers including the impact on ecosystems, rainfall patterns and food production. Professor Hugh Hunt, deputy director of Cambridge's Centre for Climate Repair, said: 'The urgency of the situation demands bold and innovative solutions, and geoengineering offers a pathway to avert the worst consequences of a rapidly warming world.' There is no urgency and the reason for geoengineering is nothing to do with 'climate change' as people like Gates well know.

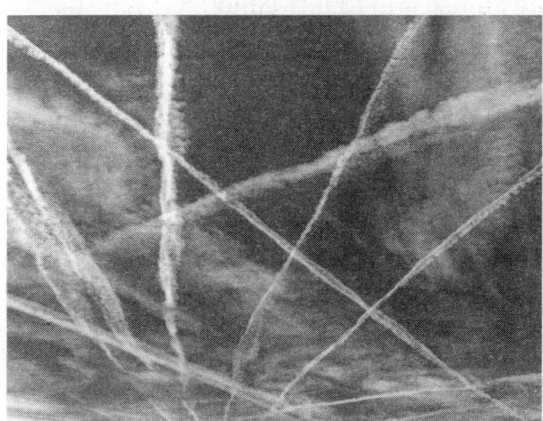

Figure 223: Chemtrails – the conspiracy theory they are now openly promoting to save the world from human-caused climate change which isn't happening.

Chemtrails have been analysed to discover they are delivering a payload of highly toxic aluminium, barium, strontium, manganese and polymer fibres. It has taken independent scientists to do this because the authorities do not test the land and plant life at the necessary nanoscale. Whistleblowers have made this public and a good source of chemtrail information is GeoengineeringWatch.org. They say *graphene* has also been found in chemtrails. Applications to the US patent office describe inventions that use '3D Graphene Oxide Nanoparticles for Cloud Seeding'. The application says the invention relates to the synthesis of

3D graphene/metal oxide nanostructured composite materials 'for ice nucleation in cloud seeding, artificial snow making and freeze-drying technologies in biomedical and the food industry and the like'. Ice nucleation employs particles that trigger the formation of an ice crystal in the atmosphere. People like Gates won't *know* all this?? Fake vaccine promoting, chemtrail promoting, Gates, meanwhile, is invited for cosy dinners with Trump at the White House and Mar-a-Lago.

Electromagnetic confirmation

There is increasing supporting evidence for electromagnetic field potential to dictate behaviour. Researchers from the Institute for Basic Science (IBS) and Yonsei University in South Korea manipulated mice with nanoparticle-activated 'switches' inside their brains by making changes in a magnetic field. This way they dictated their behaviour including when they ate food, socialised with other mice, and even acted maternally. They named the technology 'Nano-MIND' and it combines genetics, nanoparticles, and magnetic fields to allow remote activation of brain circuitry. Jinwoo Cheon, senior author and director of the IBS Center for Nanomedicine, said: 'This is the world's first technology to freely control specific brain regions using magnetic fields.' Researchers concluded: 'We expect it to be widely used in research to understand brain functions, sophisticated artificial neural networks, two-way brain-computer interface technologies, and new treatments for neurological disorders.' They hoped the 'groundbreaking' technology could be used to treat emotional, social behaviour and appetite disorders.

A few things. It's not 'groundbreaking technology' to Cult operatives in the underground bases and secret projects; nor to their masters and 'gods' in the Astral. It's old hat to them and definitely not a 'world first'. The technology which already exists is being played out in a sequence to install the human hive mind. We should not kid ourselves that it's not already being used to affect perception. It's just a matter of scale. Good people may see this as a way of helping those with behaviour or brain problems, but that's not why the Cult has developed it. That's only for the press release and the underlings. Synchron, an American brain-computer interface company, has created an implant that allows the infirm to send emails and surf the internet with their thoughts. Chief executive Tom Oxley, a 'neurointerventionist' at Mount Sinai Hospital in New York, said that brain implants will transform the way humans communicate. He says that 'the full potential of the brain would then be unlocked.' But as an article at theconversation.com rightly said:

> It's also worth mentioning that the start-up funding for Synchron partly came from DARPA, the research and development arm of the US Department of Defense that helped gift the world the internet. It's wise to be concerned about

where DARPA places its investment monies.

Researchers at the Chinese University of Hong Kong have combined the chemical element gallium used in electronics with magnetic fields to produce tiny robots that can 'shapeshift' between liquid and solid states and back again. The concept was portrayed in the *Terminator* movies series and much technology and possibility are featured in 'fictional' sci-fi films which already exist in the secret projects. The liquid or 'slime' states of this material remind me of 'black goo' which I highlighted in *The Reveal*. This is a black slime-like substance that you can see move and respond when a smartphone is switched on to activate an electromagnetic field. Black goo has been connected to graphene, and this makes total sense given that both are programmable materials in different forms activated by electromagnetism. Researchers at Massachusetts Institute of Technology (MIT) and Harvard have been developing since long ago a 'reconfigurable' robot that can 'shapeshift' into anything it is programmed to be. The team reported their project in *Proceedings of the National Academy of Sciences*. They have combined origami with algorithms that can trigger a sheet of 'semi-rigid material' to take different shapes in response to electrical signals and it is part of the research into 'programmable matter' with the goal to create small robots that 'could snap together like intelligent Legos to create larger, more versatile robots'. A lot of research into programmable matter is funded by, yes, yes … DARPA. But don't worry. The external manipulation of your perceptions is a myth!

China is doing it

I was being interviewed by long-time conspiracy radio host Jeff Rense while writing this book. We chatted about these methods of mind control and he mentioned a video that highlighted the scale of electromagnetic perceptual manipulation happening in China. I found it on the 'Lei's Real Talk' video channel on BitChute which is presented by a Chinese lady who exposes 'life under a totalitarian government' in the country where she grew up but no longer lives. She highlighted Chen Yizhang, president of the Chinese Neuroscience Society, who had revealed some *26 years ago* the extent of Chinese government mind control programmes with his colleague Dr Deng Zibin. She quoted Chen Yizhang as saying that we were 'witnessing the rise of a phantom of spiritual interrogation haunting the land' and 'facts will be extracted from weakened and manipulated consciousness'. The technology was wireless without physical sensation and thoughts. Memories were being fully intercepted and recorded. 'Whatever you think or do, they already know.' Those who controlled this technology as it developed were able to control us, dominate us, know what we're going to do before we do it, and know what we've done after the fact. It could detect what people are thinking and doing at any moment, and thoughts, memories, and behaviour were no longer private.

The Chinese whistleblower said that tech could interact with the brain, even extract your memories, and mimic a person's voice in real-time conversation; dreams could be forcefully implanted and content dictated; it could make you smell through artificially generated odors; transmit an intent into your mind to control both your thoughts and behaviour; and inflict mental and physical torture. The latter are known today as 'targeted individuals' who say authority is using electromagnetic radiation to inflict mental and bodily torment. They are dismissed as 'mad', but here we see how long that has been possible. Absent the torture mode this electromagnetic manipulation could be happening without the person knowing. Millions of people were already being monitored 24-7, and most had no idea. Main targets in China included intellectuals, mid and low-level government officials and civil servants, mid and low-ranking military officers, along with regular soldiers, teachers and students at universities and high schools. Chen Yizhang is quoted as saying:

> In 1996, China became a member of the Human Brain Project, a global initiative involving 21 countries. Today, most of those countries possess this technology, but for various reasons, they are unwilling to admit it. If anyone brings it up, the topic is either suppressed or distorted because the use of such technology is deeply anti-human and serves only those who control it.

'Anti-human' because it is ultimately not the work of 'humans'. The 'Lei's Real Talk' video then went through a timeline of further developments. The China Brain Project was approved by the State Council in 2015 and designated as a major scientific and technological project crucial to the country's future development. Brain science and brain research were included a year later in China's 13th five-year plan as one of its key scientific innovation initiatives and in early 2017 it was listed among the National Science and Technology Innovation *2030* major projects. The recurring date again. Planning for the implementation began and the official news portal of the People's Liberation Army published an article in 2017 headed: 'Control Over the Brain: The crown jewel of warfare supremacy' which said:

> Human beings are the decisive factor in the outcome of war. If one can control the brain and seize control over it, the victory can be achieved without fighting. We must establish military strategies and national security systems centered around the brain as the core element in order to prevent threats before they arise.

Your brainwave signature

China Military Online published another article in 2018 titled 'Future Wars May Begin in the Cerebral Cortex: Do you know about brain control weapons?' It described how everybody's brainwave 'fingerprint' is unique. This individual unique neural signature could be accessed, stored on computer, and then decoded to reveal visual, auditory, linguistic, and emotional neural activity using special translation software. This unique brainwave signature will be part of the tracking for the Astral Akashic Records. Think what level of technological potential would be involved in the Astral when we have got this far in the world of dense materialism. The Chinese article said the goal of brain-controlled weapons was not to destroy the enemy's body, but to conquer their will. The path to victory in war was shifting from destruction to manipulation. It is also clear that social media is already reading brainwaves through computers and phones. Ickonic's Christianne van Wijk had a stream of experiences in which she only *thought* of something and that something would immediately appear as an advertisement on her Internet feed. She posted to this effect, and it was obvious from comments that the experience is widespread. Technology is already far beyond what they are telling you.

A China National Defense News article in 2019 emphasised that latest brain control technologies do not require implanting chips into the brain. Media such as electromagnetic waves, light, sound, and even smells can be used to carry out mind control. However, how much more powerful the hive mind connection would be with nanoparticles in the brain/body and the electromagnetic field amplified by graphene? CIA officers in Havana, Cuba, reported symptoms in 2016 including persistent headaches, dizziness, hearing loss, brain fog, vision problems, and sleeping disturbances, after hearing strange high-pitched sounds. Something similar happened to staff at the US Consulate in Guangzhou, China, in 2018. Lei said:

> Just imagine tens of thousands of PLA [People's Liberation Army] soldiers trained in weaponry but stripped of emotions and feelings. They're all turned into mindless killing machines. What does that mean to the rest of the world?
>
> And imagine millions, or tens of millions, of Chinese citizens willingly following party orders, donating money, sending their children to the front lines. Imagine thousands of foreign intelligence officers, generals, or even national leaders betraying their own countries because their minds are not their own.

This technology could destroy us or turn us into digital slaves. Those who control the technology want to play the role of God (or at least give the power to the Yaldabaoth fake 'god' to do so). Lei said that advanced technology cannot control people's true spirit connected with the Divine. Yes, and that's why the Archontic Cult works so hard to maintain a perceptual separation. China is also developing brain chips. The NeuCyber Array BMI System, a self-developed brain-machine interface system from China, was unveiled in 2024. A monkey with its hands restrained and soft electrode filaments implanted in its brain, controlled an isolated robotic arm and grasped a strawberry by using its 'thoughts'. The technology is described as an 'information highway' for the brain – 'facilitating communication with external devices and providing cutting-edge technologies in human-machine interaction and hybrid intelligence'.

I reported in *The Dream* a talk by Dr Charles Morgan to a US West Point Academy military audience in 2018 about research into manipulating the human brain to send and receive sensory information 'like the Matrix' and editing DNA for mind control. Morgan was a CIA and military special operations forensic psychiatrist and neuroscientist, and a national security professor at the University of New Haven, Connecticut. He described how a human brain could take over the minds of rats and cockroaches to dictate their behaviour and how genetic manipulation can be used to externally control humans or even kill them: 'You can engineer a unique [genetic] thing that would only kill one person in the world.' Morgan said human brains could be connected and this is a prime feature of the hive mind. Think of the effect on reality if you centrally control human minds and focus their collective attention on a particular thought and intent. You could create anything.

Bluetooth 'humans'

Fake vaccines have also made at least many people trackable when they have received the full-blown content. Dr Luis Miguel De Benito, a digestive physician with a PhD in molecular biology, is one researcher who pursued this. His experiments convinced him that the 'Covid' fake vaccinated have their own 'MAC address'. Media Access Control (MAC) identifies devices with a unique code except these were not devices. They were people. Benito removed all sources of MAC codes and checked there were none in range. When patients arrived that he later confirmed were fake vaccinated he would see MAC addresses appear on his screen and if they had phones he would have them disconnected. This would cause one MAC device code to disappear off the screen but often there would still be another. He questioned 137 patients and none of those who said they had not been fake vaccinated registered a MAC address, but 96 of the 112 who said they *had* been fake vaccinated registered a code. He said:

I interpreted that it was a code that the patient himself was carrying and that, in fact, when he left the office, leaving the building, it disappeared from my cell phone. I've been able to verify that 100 percent of the patients who say they aren't vaccinated don't raise any contact device with my cell phone via Bluetooth. But 86 percent of those who said they were vaccinated generated a MAC address on my cell phone.

Dr Benito discussed his findings with roboticists, biologists, engineers, computer scientists, and others, and passed his research to international investigators. What he found is certainly the Cult plan with Klaus Schwab saying in 2016 – years before 'Covid' – that humans would be chipped and merged with machines: 'Certainly in the next ten years, first, we will wear them in our clothes, and then we could imagine that we will implant them in our brains or on our skin, and in the end … there will be a direct connection between our brains and the digital world.' Ten years from that statement would take us to 2026. Dr Benito is far from alone in his findings. I have seen other videos in different countries that have replicated his research – including MAC signals in cemeteries from the graves of people who have died since the fake vaccines were circulated. Ickonic's Christianne Van Wijk filmed a study in England that happened in the countryside away from Bluetooth activity. All fake vaccinated people taking part without Bluetooth devices generated a Bluetooth code. Christianne was filming for a study into the effectiveness of a product called MasterPeace targeting the effects of the fake vaccines on the body. It had not worked in the first study with all fake vaccinated still registering a Bluetooth code, but later when the dose was substantially increased the code had disappeared in all participants. I am not recommending MasterPeace because I wasn't involved in the study and people will have to see what they think from the evidence. I am only reporting what happened, but it's good to know that some are researching ways to eliminate this crap from the body.

Mass 'vaccination'

The next stage in their catch-all plan is an mRNA-based aerosol fake vaccine known as 'AeroVax' and backed by funding from the Bill and Melinda Gates Foundation as you would expect. This delivers the genetic concoctions through a fine mist without needles and is absorbed through the lungs. It is being developed by Canada's McMaster University with additional funding by the Canadian Institutes of Health Research. A Substack media report by GeneralMCNews said:

> With technology like AeroVax, the potential exists to disperse the vaccine through the atmosphere, enabling mass immunization on a scale never seen before. Such a method could theoretically 'vaccinate' entire cities or regions

simultaneously – without the need for personal appointments, needles, or even individual awareness.

In this scenario, public consent could be bypassed entirely, raising pressing questions about autonomy, ethics, and transparency in public health.

This is what a combination of lunatics and psychopaths can do. The Trump Food and Drug Administration (FDA) also fast-tracked a Bill Gates-funded fake vaccine by biotech firm Arcturus Therapeutics for the alleged 'bird flu'. They admit that the fake vaccine is 'self-amplifying' or 'replicon' and designed to deliver genetic instructions to replicate inside the body. It was 'continuously producing more mRNA [or whatever is really in there] after entering cells'. A senior advisor to Arcturus Therapeutics is Dr Peter A. Patriarca, a former official of the Food and Drug Administration (FDA) and the Centers for Disease Control (CDC) who also advises the Gates Foundation. The media report said that 'experts and citizens alike have voiced serious concerns over the implications of a vaccine that keeps reproducing within the human body', but 'federal health agencies are pushing full steam ahead with the development of these next-gen injections, accelerating trials and approvals in an effort to bring them to market'. Why? It's the Cult agenda.

Soul and Spirit disconnection

The most important goal for the Archontic manipulators is to ensure that humanity is further disconnected from Divine Spark awareness and the infinity that we really are. The AI hive mind is adding another layer of disconnection and healers working with the energetic fields of clients noticed a difference in the fake vaccinated immediately after the jabs. Thomas Mayer correlated many of these findings in the book, *Corona Vaccines from the Spiritual Perspective. Consequences on Soul and Spirit, and the Life after Death*. He features the experiences of many healers of different techniques and psychologists. Many treated people before and after the jab and noticed an obvious even extreme transformation. One said that fake vaccinated patients appeared 'dense' and 'dull' as if 'enclosed within themselves'. Another said they were 'deeply shocked by effects these vaccines have without people becoming aware of any of them'. Some healers described seeing 'dark entities' in the auric fields of the jabbed which 'inhibited functions'. There was 'stagnation and rigidity'. Tissues felt 'as if held in a tight grip, unable to breathe or move, they were no longer able to vibrate'. One patient who once had extensive dreams no longer dreamed after the shot. A healer quoted in the book says:

I also notice with vaccinated people that the aura, which was previously strong and colorful, collapses and becomes gray ... when I meet vaccinated people, my eyes often 'search' for the aura, but all I can see is a smooth gray surface, like concrete. This confuses me; no other color appears ...

... It is frightening to see the vaccinated clients deteriorate. Their skin color changes, they seem to have aged years, lymph nodes are swollen for a long time, the aura is 'tattered' and many of them smell unpleasant.

The smell is described as 'sweetish and penetratingly unpleasant'. Other healers said:

I noticed immediately the change, very heavy energy emanating from [the] subtle bodies ... The scariest thing was when I was working on the heart chakra, I connected with her Soul: it was detached from the physical body ... as if it was floating in a state of total confusion ...

... I understood that this substance is indeed used to detach consciousness so that this consciousness can no longer interact through this body that it possesses in life ... where there is no longer any contact, no frequency, no light, no more energetic balance or mind ... It is shattering!

People become Non-Player Characters driven only by the Astral program running through the body, and for those that have the full-blown content the fake vaccines are like a form of possession:

Patients who have been coming for many years, for whom eurythmy therapy has always been a decisive help, suddenly can no longer feel ... holding the head with both hands repeated the perception of holding a completely hollow, empty head ... The etheric brain and the pineal gland felt like dried up and shrivelled ... otherwise perceptible surficial craniosacral rhythm was not perceptible ...

... With none of my other clients, after more than 20 years of experience, have I ever had such experiences ... I am deeply shocked by what these vaccinations do to people, without them noticing anything ... I had the feeling that there was a dark being on top of her, inhibiting all functions. Stagnation and rigidity. The tissue was as if held, could not breathe and could not move, was no longer able to pulsate ... With one patient I had the experience of massaging a 'corpse' ...

Healers said they saw 'visible changes in the face' which became 'like a mask' ... 'that which wants to shine through is missing'. They described changes in the 'core being' and one said: 'I know these clients well, but somehow, they are no longer there … In the aftermath of a session, I no longer feel the person, even though they were physically there.' A very common theme is disconnection or separation of the 'physical' body and the immediate etheric body from expanded states of awareness – exactly what I am talking about. One healer said:

> On the level of the intellectual Soul, we experienced a blockage between the forehead and the crown chakra [an energy vortex at the top of the head]. We interpreted this as implying a separation of the intellectual Soul from the higher self.

I have spoken with large numbers of people since the fake vaccine rollout who speak of the psychological as well as 'physical' health challenges of jabbed family and friends. You can see why. We are talking further disconnection from expanded awareness. I should stress that not all fake vaccinated people were as described here, and this is likely to be confirmation that not everyone has yet had the full-blast version. Others responded to treatment and if not back to their previous state were very much improved.

Pure evil

Austrian philosopher Rudolf Steiner said in 1917 that a vaccine was planned that would disconnect humans from their spiritual self. Materialist physicians would 'expel the Souls from mankind'. The Soul would be eliminated with medicine through a vaccine that would be administered possibly at birth so that humans could not imagine the existence of Soul and Spirit. They would be immune to the 'madness' of spiritual life. They would be intellectually smart but not develop a conscience (a connection to AI would do the same). 'Man would become an automaton', Steiner said – a Non-Player Character as I have described. 'He becomes materialistic of constitution and can no longer rise to the spiritual.' This is what those energy healers say they found in the aftermath of the fake 'Covid' vaccine and the 'mRNA' assault on humanity has only just begun.

Here's an idea of the psychopathy involved. Japanese researchers announced a 'shocking' discovery in 2024 that the fake 'Covid' shots were affecting 'every possible aspect of human pathology'. They tracked surges in more than 200 dangerous even fatal diseases in their wake and linked them to thousands of 'side-effects'. There is nothing 'side' about them – they are *effects*. Leading scientists in the Vaccine Issues Study Group worked for six months before releasing their findings. Professor Emeritus Masanori Fukushima of Kyoto University said the damage to health was 'unprecedented' in a medical procedure. He said: 'Thousands of papers have reported side effects after vaccination, affecting every possible aspect of human pathology, from ophthalmology to psychiatry.'

Death rates from leukaemia had increased along with 'significant findings' for cancers. There were so many *brain-related effects* that they probably hadn't found them all yet. 'Mental disorders, psychiatric symptoms, depression, mania, anxiety, came up in abundance, but it's endless', the professor said. This has been happening across the world yet still 'health' authorities go on pushing people to have more shots and the use of the fake vaccine technique is being ever expanded while hiding its consequences. The UK *Telegraph* newspaper revealed that the US-based Crawford and Company performed nearly 13,000 medical assessments on those claiming to have been injured by the fake vaccine but dismissed more than *98 percent* of them. Those they approved for one-off payments of £120,000 through the Vaccine Damage Payment Scheme totalled £24.36 million while Crawford was paid £27.63 million for its services which declined 98 percent of claims. What were they really being paid to do?

Funeral directors, coroners and embalmers around the world began to see massive clots in the dead after the fake vaccine was rolled out amid heart attacks and strokes that soared even in professional sports people. John O'Looney operating out of Milton Keynes in England was especially vocal in the UK and others followed. Retired US Air Force Major Thomas Haviland conducted a 'Worldwide Embalmer Clot Survey' in 2024 which produced extreme findings in support of the experience of O'Looney. Some 83 percent of embalmers from 250 respondents said they were seeing big white fibrous clots in the deceased from 2021 after the fake vaccines were introduced in late 2020 (Figs 224 and 225). This 2024

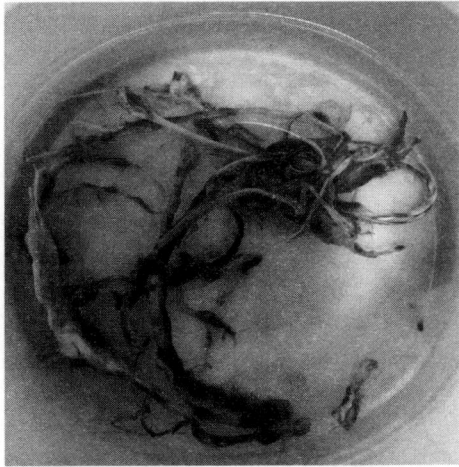

Figure 224: White fibrous clots found in the deceased by funeral directors and embalmers after the 'Covid' fake vaccine rollout began. Image courtesy of John O'Looney.

Figure 225: The clots have been discovered in people all over the world since the safe and effective fake vaccine was introduced.

figure of 83 percent of embalmers increased from 73 percent in 2023 in line with findings by others of nano self-replication. 'Microclotting' was found by 78 percent of embalmers in around 22 percent of cases, and this had increased from less than 5 percent in 2020. They reported that their professional associations had failed to act on what their members had seen. Haviland shared his findings with the US 'watchdogs' the FDA, CDC, and National Institutes of Health, but they didn't reply. Another study, the People's Blood Clot Survey, looked at 1,425 self-reported or observed clotting cases from 40 countries with the focus on post-2020. This found that 91 percent of those with clotting had been given at least one 'Covid' fake vaccine. The number was a major increase in clotting before the 'Covid' jab. Clots in the legs, lungs, brain, and heart, were most common and this matched official findings. Many required surgery and many died. White fibrous clots were not the same as regular blood clots in 'structure and composition, suggesting a unique pathological process'.

Killer jab double-down

Big Tech AI billionaire and ultra-Zionist Larry Ellison made a sales pitch for the same fake vaccine-type to be used to treat cancer during his announcement with Trump of the up to $500 billion AI 'Stargate' project. This was after a big increase in cancers since the fake vaccine was circulated. Ellison said the 'mRNA vaccine' could be made using AI 'in about 48 hours' to target specific individuals. This is the same vaccine-type increasingly connected with fast-spreading 'turbo cancers' that great numbers have experienced after the 'Covid' jab. Trump himself claims credit for being the 'father' of the fake vaccine through Operation Warp Speed in 2020 and says it saved millions of lives. The idiot continued to double-down on this despite the catastrophic contrary evidence. The global horror was run through the military with even the disgusting Pfizer, Moderna, and other fake vaccine sources only a conduit for the Cult targeting of humanity. Dr Susan Monarez, Trump's pick for head of the Centers for Disease Control and Prevention (CDC), had urged the public to have more fake vaccines even in the light of the known consequences. Dr Dave Weldon, Trump's first choice, was abruptly dropped after White House officials were reported to have been alarmed about comments sceptical of vaccines. Monarez was deputy director of ARPA-H, the Advanced Research Projects Agency for Health, based on the Pentagon's sinister DARPA. She has promoted AI in health care to replace doctors on DARPAtv which Israel fanatic and Trump's health chief Robert Kennedy Jr also supports. He said in 2025 that his 'vision' was for all Americans to have a 'wearable' (electronic data collection device) within four years to track and trace 'health issues'. This is in line with the Cult agenda. The potential for surveillance and the impact from electromagnetic fields is obvious.

Kennedy seemed to be fine with Dave Weldon's expulsion, but then quickly fell out with Monarez who was fired for refusing to follow Kennedy's directives just weeks after she was confirmed by the Senate. This prompted several high-ranking CDC officials to resign in protest. Why was she hired in the first place when her stance was clear to see? Jim O'Neill was then named interim head of the CDC – the *Peter Thiel* Jim O'Neill who was already Kennedy's deputy secretary of the Department of Health and Human Services (HHS). O'Neil is an American science and technology investor and very close friend and associate of Peter Thiel. He co-founded the Thiel Fellowship in 2010, was CEO of the Thiel Foundation, and managing director of Mithril Capital Management which he co-founded with Thiel. Who do you think controls Kennedy? The Trump regime seeks a balance between keeping the MAGA base on board in the wake of the Epstein debacle and pushing through the Cult agenda. It's a fine line. On one hand Kennedy, a vaccine sceptic who became less so after taking office, removed government research funding for 22 'mRNA' fake vaccines, but the Food and Drug Administration, under Kennedy's overall command, granted full approval in July 2025 to Moderna's Spikevax 'Covid' fake vaccine for children from 6 months to 11 years who have 'at least one condition putting them at increased risk' (from a 'virus' that doesn't exist). Kennedy also left current mRNA fake vaccines in place. Moderna CEO Stéphane Bancel said: 'Covid-19 continues to pose a significant potential threat to children, especially those with underlying medical conditions.' I guess he couldn't bring himself to say 'safe and effective' given what has happened.

Kennedy signposted the development of a 'universal vaccine' or 'all-in-one-jab' against 'Covid-19', flu, and 'future pandemics'. This was the plan of Kennedy's infamous predecessor Anthony Fauci. NBC reported Fauci's ambitions in 2021 under the headline 'Fauci pushes for universal coronavirus vaccine'. The report said: 'The scientific quest for a universal coronavirus vaccine received a boost Wednesday, as three top federal researchers, including Dr. Anthony Fauci, outlined a path to develop new vaccines that could tackle a variety of ailments including Covid-19, some common colds and future viruses.' This was remarkably similar in tone to Kennedy who did not, of course, mention the self-replicating nanotechnology infused by the fake vaccines or that the evidence for the existence of a 'Covid virus' is laughable. Never mind what you call a 'vaccine' – the content is what matters. Trump demanded data from the drug companies to justify the fake vaccine while telling a cabinet meeting that 'his' Operation Warp Speed was 'one of the greatest achievements ever in politics'. It's that 'fine line' at work again. Kennedy also pledged to make food safer, but his Food and Drug

Administration (FDA) gave permission for companies to produce lab-grown synthetic meat, chicken and fish produced with the vocal and financial support of people like Bill Gates and Jeff Bezos. I am not saying that Kennedy hasn't made *some* changes for the better. It's just that no way is he rolling back the foundations of the Cult agenda because he wouldn't be there if he was. Kennedy, a life-long Democrat who publicly opposed Trump, ran as a third presidential candidate before suddenly joining Trump's campaign. They pledged to Make America Healthy Again (MAHA) which helped to get Trump across the line, but they will ditch him if he goes too far.

British cardiologist Dr Aseem Malhotra is among Kennedy's reported 'close advisors'. He publicly promoted the 'Covid' fake vaccine for the UK National Health Service (NHS) before becoming feted for opposing the jab after his 'very fit' father, a former deputy chair of the British Medical Association (BMA), died of a heart attack after having the jab. There were many who bought the 'Covid' hoax and promoted the fake vaccine to millions of followers before somehow becoming 'Covid' heroes associated with exposing the jab. Among them is Englishman 'Dr' John Campbell (a 'doctor' of philosophy, not medicine) and a retired 'nurse educator'. He supported the official story and the jab until it was untenable and then became a star of the 'alternative' media. Campbell was not banned from YouTube after travelling the road to Damascus and the same with these other 'Johnny-Come-Latelys' for what should have been obvious from the start. Others who saw through the hoax at the time *were* banned. A video circulating on the Internet has him pushing the nonsense of 'asymptomatic' transmission by adults and children without symptoms which was used to justify locking down *everyone*. The video then has him much later saying:

> This whole thing about asymptomatic spread – one in three spread it while asymptomatic. I mean, where did this come from? Why was it perpetuated for so long? If an infection came without a traceable source the authorities can't say 'I don't know where that infection came from'. They have to make something up.

Yes, 'Dr' Campbell, with help from people like you.

The exclusion of Soul and Spirit is only part of the AI agenda, albeit the most important for the Archons and their Cult. The whole of society is planned to be taken over by artificial intelligence with humans as its slaves – slaves of the Archons and Yaldabaoth consciousness through the conduit of AI.

CHAPTER 26

Making It Happen

Distracted from distraction by distraction
T. S. Eliot

Elon Musk deleting government departments and firing tens of thousands of government workers was not 'dismantling the Deep State' as the MAGA were told to believe (and mostly did). He was deleting government in line with the Dark Enlightenment ('Dark MAGA') and clearing the decks for government to be controlled by AI.

Musk may have taken leave from the *public* Trump circle, at least for a while, but the agenda he represents continued through other Silicon Valley oligarchs and Musk associates along with JD Vance. Trump was manipulated and funded into power as a conduit for the Cult AI agenda and not as the driver of it. The oligarchs are in charge for their masters' and that still includes Musk. The quest to absorb the MAGA into the AI agenda has been supported by a stream of calculated guests on the Joe Rogan podcast, including Peter Thiel, Marc Andreessen, and many others. Rogan's pathetically soft ball 'interview' with Trump just before the 2024 election helped Mafia Don to win the White House and open the way for the AI free-for-all. You only have to observe how easy it was to turn the MAGA from anti-electric vehicles to promoting Tesla (see Alex Jones) to realise that the same can be done with AI. Tell them that the best way to stop illegal migrants is to use AI and the MAGA would be all for it. Well, the extreme end, anyway, with the compliant 'alternative' media doing the sales-pitching.

It took only two days after Trump took office to wheel out AI billionaires Larry Ellison of Oracle, Sam Altman from OpenAI, and Masayoshi Son of investment company SoftBank Group, to announce that up to $500 billion investment in AI and its essential data centre infrastructure. Trump said at their news conference: 'Stargate will be building the physical and virtual infrastructure to power the next generation of advancements in AI.' A few months later OpenAI and Oracle announced the building of new data centres that would require the energy consumption of a major city to power the next generation of AI. One report said that the goal was simple: 'To build enough computing power to bring advanced AI to everyone.' The report said they now expect to 'blow past' the initial projected investment of half a trillion dollars. Ultra-Zionist Ellison's Oracle has deep ties to the CIA and government and, like Musk and Thiel, benefits massively from government contracts. Ellison advocates digital IDs and a 'national security database combined with biometrics, thumb prints, handprints, iris scans or whatever is best ... to detect people with false identities'. He also wants AI cameras in schools. Oracle has worked with Peter Thiel's Palantir and it's all a cosy little circle.

The cabal also involves Cult operative Tony Blair, the former UK prime minister, who has been promoting the human enslavement agenda his entire political career. This includes the invasion on a lie with Boy George Bush that brought death and destruction to Iraq in 2003. Accounts reveal that Ellison bankrolls Blair's '[Cult] policy institute' to the tune of tens of millions. Ellison handed the Institute £26 million in 2021 and there were plans for at least another £38 million. Oracle supplied software to Blair's government and they worked together during the fake 'Covid pandemic' to speed up vaccination rates in Africa. I bet they did. How Bill Gates must have loved that. Ellison's cash for Blair is paying for 'a joint partnership to help African countries create a central database of vaccination records to monitor and combat a variety of diseases'. Blair boasted how this meant who had been vaccinated and who hadn't would be recorded which is another box ticked on the Cult wish list. The war criminal said: 'Oracle can provide that system with data securely stored and owned by each country and is prepared to do so as part of a global philanthropic partnership.' Yes, I'm sure it's all done out of 'philanthropy'. Blair constantly calls for digital IDs and other dystopian desires of Ellison. So let us reprise. Ellison funds Blair, a classic Woke 'globalist' seeking, like him, technological dystopia, while at the same time being a backer of 'anti-globalist' Trump and announcing with him an up to $500 billion investment in AI expansion and infrastructure? They have contempt for you, MAGA.

I'm sure that Blair's constant promotion of AI is nothing to do with Ellison's money or the fact that Blair is a Cult gofer. He has urged Britain via his Institute to open the way for AI doctors and nurses while claiming the world was 'in the foothills' of the biggest transformation since the Industrial Revolution (exactly as planned). Blair said AI could have an 'absolutely transformative' impact on public services by making them better, cheaper and more efficient. He would be thinking if still in power about 'how you reorganise the whole government around how you embrace and access this revolution'. This is precisely the policy being followed by the Trump administration. Meanwhile, Larry Ellison and Oracle announced a $5 billion investment in Britain to meet the 'rapidly growing demand for its cloud services'. Ellison, a close friend of Musk, would 'expand Oracle's Cloud Infrastructure's footprint in the

UK and help the British government deliver on its vision for artificial intelligence innovation and adoption'. Prime Minister Keir Starmer, mentored by Blair and at least a 'past' member of the Cult Trilateral Commission, vowed to transform Britain into 'one of the great AI superpowers' to boost growth and deliver services more efficiently (with AI). Technology Secretary Peter Kyle said that 'the UK is determined to lead the world in AI innovation' and 'by working with global tech leaders like Oracle, we're cementing the UK's position at the forefront of the AI revolution'. The European Union has its own multi-billion AI programmes and the same is happening across the world. Apparent policy divisions are pure theatre. They all pursue the same outcome.

No, really? Trump supports AI?

Six months into the second Trump presidency came a news release headed 'White House Unveils America's AI Action Plan'. It said the plan was in accordance with Trump's January executive order on 'Removing Barriers to American Leadership in AI'. Winning the AI race would 'usher in a new golden age of human flourishing, economic competitiveness, and national security for the American people'. No – it would usher in AI dystopia as these liars know and something similar is happening worldwide. The plan would cover more than 90 Federal policy actions across 'three pillars' – '*Accelerating* Innovation, Building American AI Infrastructure, and Leading in International Diplomacy and Security.'

Key policies in the AI Action Plan included:

- Exporting American AI: The Commerce and State Departments will partner with industry to deliver secure, full-stack AI export packages – including hardware, models, software, applications, and standards – to America's friends and allies around the world.
- Promoting Rapid Buildout of Data Centers: Expediting and modernizing permits for data centers and semiconductor fabs, as well as creating new national initiatives to increase high-demand occupations like electricians and HVAC technicians.
- Enabling Innovation and Adoption: Removing onerous Federal regulations that hinder AI development and deployment, and seek private sector input on rules to remove [Free-for-all].
- Upholding Free Speech in Frontier Models: Updating Federal procurement guidelines to ensure that the government only contracts with frontier large language model developers who ensure that their systems are objective and free from top-down ideological bias.

The latter is bollocks. *Infusing* top-down ideological bias is the game.

You see the ubiquitous deletion of regulation to thwart any blocks on AI with the 'private sector' dictating what regulation to delete. The statement said that America's AI Action Plan charted a decisive course to cement US dominance in artificial intelligence. President Trump had prioritised AI as a cornerstone of American innovation, powering a new age of American leadership in science, technology, and global influence. This is *exactly* what I said the Trump regime would do. The plan 'galvanizes Federal efforts to turbocharge our innovation capacity, build cutting-edge infrastructure, and lead globally, ensuring that American workers and families thrive in the AI era'. What – with all their jobs disappearing?

Michael Kratsios, the White House Office of Science and Technology Policy Director, said they were moving 'with urgency' to make this vision a reality'. Well, 2030 is not far away after all. Kratsios was formerly the third highest ranking official at the Department of Defense and the principal advisor to the Secretary of Defense for technology, while overseeing the Defense Advanced Research Projects Agency (DARPA), the Missile Defense Agency, the Defense Innovation Unit, the Space Development Agency, and the DOD laboratory enterprise. This is where the AI agenda is coming from – through the military. Trump's AI and Crypto Czar David Sacks said the United States must win the AI 'race' which is how they are seeking to diminish opposition. Turn it into a sporting event that our 'side' must win. Marco Rubio, Secretary of State and Acting National Security Advisor, said: 'Winning the AI Race is non-negotiable – America must continue to be the dominant force in artificial intelligence to promote prosperity and protect our economic and national security.' Still more from the song sheet.

The China blueprint

The Mao revolution in China was a Global Cult revolution designed to develop and incubate in stages a means of mass population control behind the cover of a closed society brutally run by a small circle of super psychopaths. The West was still having to pay lip service to freedom and democracy while China could move at a far faster pace to rollout an AI control system involving millions of cameras in the cities that can identify people in minutes via face recognition. Constant real-time surveillance tracks behaviour and points are awarded or deleted by whether your choices and actions are supported by the government. This 'social credit system' rewards conformity and punishes non-conformity by denying travel by plane or train or operating in mainstream society if your credits fall below government-imposed numbers. Fines can be taken from bank accounts within seconds of an alleged 'indiscretion' caught on camera. China's AI control system is extremely advanced compared with other parts of the world and the more the West uses Chinese technology the more potential there is for 'backdoor' access to Western AI developments. Tech security researchers have identified some of these. Hedley Donovan, a founding member of the Cult's Rockefeller instigated Trilateral Commission, wrote in *Time Magazine* 25 years ago that China was already a technocracy:

> The nerds are running the show in today's China. In the twenty years since Deng Xiaoping's reforms kicked in, the composition of the Chinese leadership has shifted markedly in favor of technocrats ... It's no exaggeration to describe the current regime as a technocracy.

Chinese police revealed their latest AI robot technology at the Shanghai Formula 1 Grand Prix in early 2025. They were a humanoid and a 'dog' labelled G1 and GO2 and the makers released footage of them doing complex moves. The G1 danced before swirling a staff and the GO2 produced a very impressive balancing sequence. Meanwhile, Musk's robots at Tesla by contrast walked as if they needed a wee, but didn't get there fast enough. China has some of the most advanced AI on earth and has been developing and incubating a system of mass technological control that the Cult always planned to play out across the world. The 'Covid' hoax was officially triggered out of China (it wasn't, that's just the story) and what followed? The Chinese system has been instigated ever more obviously across the West and elsewhere thanks to the ever-quickening installation of AI.

Some in the fake 'alternative' media believe that Putin and Russia are against the 'New World Order' which always makes me smile. You must be joking. He said in 2025 that a 'new, more just, world order' is taking shape and the United Nations role should be strengthened to make the UN central to global affairs. This was straight from the Cult script that I have been highlighting for decades with the UN a stalking horse for world government and the power moving east to China, Russia and India. The reaction of the West to Ukraine and the demolition of American economic might by Trump and multiple presidents have moved Russia and China ever closer. Trump's (Cult-calculated) tariffs insanity has driven India and many others into the China-Russia alliance while devastating Americans that have to pay them and threatens the dollar as the world's reserve currency on which the American economy is so dependent. Hypocrite Putin ordered a three-day ceasefire in his invasion of Ukraine to mark the 80th anniversary of VE day, or Victory in Europe Day, from the Second World War. You must be taking the piss surely to have a three-day pause in mass murder to commemorate mass murder in Europe. Putin has been either President or Prime Minister of Russia since 1999 and somehow the Global Cult has a problem with him?? He's as much under control as the rest of them and AI plans for Russia match the universal plan of the Cult. Russia is committed to the same AI control system as the United States, Europe, and China.

This includes the 'ultimate goal' of transferring 'a human's individual consciousness to an artificial carrier' and a 'new mankind' and 'social transformation' achieved 'through the focus on 'nanotechnology, biotechnology, information technology, cognitive technology, genetics, and robotics'. I am quoting here from the first Global Future 2045 Congress hosted in Moscow as long ago as *2012* when some of the 'world's leading scientists' met to discuss the 'future development of humankind'. Where must that vision be by now? The Moscow event described 'unprecedented developments in new cognitive abilities, refined artificial intelligences and brain-computer interfaces' to 'simulate complex systems'. Humanoid robots and cyborgs would be created, and human personalities would be transferred to an 'artificial carrier' (Fig 226). All this would demand 'a new civilisation or paradigm, new philosophy and ideology, new ethics, new psychology, new culture' and 'we must *reset* our limits to go beyond the Earth and the solar system'. I guess that would be Klaus Schwab's Great Reset or 'Fourth Industrial Revolution', but the whole thing globally is being orchestrated as always from the Astral.

Figure 226: The next stage of human evolution. Sure it is. If evolution means control.

Once again, the Cult has no borders. Russia and Putin are further committed to achieving the carbon Net Zero goals and a digital currency that's being introduced in the EU and across the world which has fundamental implications for freedom. The 'anti-globalist' Putin responded to 'Covid' the same as the rest of the world with lockdowns and censorship and he would not reveal data on the trial safety and effectiveness of Russia's Sputnik V 'Covid vaccine' on the grounds that it was 'confidential and contains information constituting a commercial secret'. Same old, same old. The European Union announced in 2025 a plan to spend €20 billion to build AI gigafactories to challenge the US and China for AI 'supremacy' when they are all controlled by the same masters. The EU said the idea was to turn Europe into an 'AI continent' and 'the global race for AI is far from over'. The 'competition' is only for the manipulation of the masses and to say 'we can't be left behind'. It's a *global* agenda. The plan which is being ever more rapidly unleashed is for AI to control everything including the human mind. The entire reality is being possessed on a scale never seen before in known human history. It is an interesting synchronicity that over the decades I have picked up a theme that the Reptilian race involved in human control is obsessed with technology as are those known as the Archons. 'Their god is their technology', as one source said of the Reptilian modus operandi. Everything is being digitalised to open the way for AI control of the system.

Israel connection

Hive mind perceptions can be broadcast globally from a central point once the delivery infrastructure is in place. That 'point' could well be Israel and connected to its Greater Israel/Third Temple agenda and the plan for the world to be ruled from Jerusalem. It's also possible Israel may be sacrificed in pursuit of the ultimate goal of global control with the hive mind centre elsewhere. Most people don't realise that Israel now rivals Silicon Valley for cyber and AI development. Israel is very much run on the lines of China in the sense that there is no such thing as an 'independent' Chinese company. They are all controlled and answerable to the government and that includes Chinese Internet and social media companies. In the same way, there is no such thing as an 'independent' Israeli company with all controlled and answerable to the government-Mossad-Shin Bet-IDF network with its global reach. The Cult is global and at the inner core Israel *is* China *is* the US *is* Europe *is* the rest of the world. They operate as one unit at the Cult level with the divisions among the lower ranks mere diversion for the masses even though most in those lower ranks will believe it is real. It makes the whole thing more believable to any observer.

Israel's massive military cyber centre is the Cyber Intelligence Unit in the desert-city of Beersheba with its 20,000 'cyber soldiers'. It's the biggest infrastructure project in Israel's history and I detail this and the Israeli global cyber reach and capabilities in *The Trigger*. Technology giants have a research and development presence there including Intel, Microsoft, IBM, Google, Apple, Hewlett-Packard, Cisco Systems, Meta (Facebook). Motorola, Dell, Deutsche Telekom, PayPal, Oracle, and Lockheed Martin. Intel Corporation, officially an American company but with an enormous Israel connection, is the market leader in computer microprocessors (the 'brains' of the computer) with its logo 'Intel Inside'. The Beersheba complex is run by the military, and this is home to many Internet and social media trolls that hurl abuse at their targets using technology that can make multiple posts across all platforms. There are versions of this in major countries. In Britain it is the 77th Brigade which describes itself as 'a hybrid unit of Regulars and Reservists with specialist skills to combat new forms of warfare in the information environment for the defence of the UK and its overseas territories'. It seeks to undermine everyone and everything that doesn't suit the narrative of its masters. 77th Brigade was extremely active during 'Covid'. These military and intelligence 'bots', often recently joined and/or with tiny numbers of followers, are turned on those presenting the 'wrong' narrative.

The Beersheba operation is highly organised and structured. The authorities scan the schools and universities for cyber talent and when people with those skills are conscripted into the army they continue to be trained at Beersheba. The best are then given technology developed in the secret projects to apparently 'invent' through the start-up companies arranged for them. It is not by accident that Israel is called Start-Up Nation. Others are sent to America to infiltrate Silicon Valley companies. Israel's speciality has been cybersecurity, and its systems are used throughout the world including by the US government. Cybersecurity requires whole-system access to write programs to protect from hacking but allows for backdoors to be installed that give Israel real-time access to the classified data and new technology inventions. China does the same. Israeli spyware companies are infamous for selling to tyrannical regimes which use it against human rights activists and journalists. *The Times of Israel* noted in March 2025 how Israel had turned its focus on AI. Writer Alon Ghelber said in an article headed 'From Start-Up Nation to an AI Powerhouse: Israel's Tech Reinvention':

> As we move into a new phase in the evolution of global tech, one which sees AI implementation take precedence for organizations worldwide, our tech ecosystem has begun to undergo a transformation in its approach, and it could see us push boundaries at the forefront of technological innovation once more. In many ways, we are witnessing the making of Startup Nation 2.0.

Many Israeli cyber operatives in 'private' companies are members of the infamous elite military cyber and intelligence team, Unit 8200. If you see this in a cyber-CV it would be wise to take note, and they come up often. Unit 8200 hacks into computer systems, inserts cyber viruses, causes malfunction, takes control from a distance, and of course scans for information. Israel dominates the market for computer and Wi-Fi systems in vehicles which means they can be controlled from the other side of the world if necessary.

I spy

Mike Waltz, then US *National Security Advisor*, was seen using Israeli technology on his phone in his final Trump cabinet meeting before being fired from the post following the Signal security breach involving the

Jewish editor-in-chief of *The Atlantic* magazine who was somehow invited onto a government call discussing an imminent attack on Yemen. Waltz was using at the cabinet meeting an unofficial version of Signal called 'TM SGNL', created by the Israeli company TeleMessage to archive messages. TM SGNL is TeleMessage 'Signal Capture' software which it sells to governments and corporations. TeleMessage is yet another example of Israel's leadership in the supply of spyware and 'digital forensics' established by 'former' Israel Defense Forces and intelligence operatives. TeleMessage was founded in 1999 by 'former' IDF personnel. Investigative journalist Jason Paladino listed TeleMessage bigwigs on the Drop Site News website:

- Guy Levit, TeleMessage's CEO, 'served as the head of the planning and development of one of the IDF's Intelligence elite technical units' from 1996 until 1999, according to his official biography.
- Gil Shapira, TeleMessage's Vice President Business Development, served in the 'Israeli Air Force from 1993-1999 as a computer programmer, project manager and team leader,' according to his bio.
- Nir Elperin, the Vice President of Corporate Strategy 'served 4 years in the Elite Military Intelligence Unit of the Israel Defense Forces', according to his bio, where he 'commanded teams of computer experts'.
- A mobile researcher at TeleMessage, Aviv Tzitayat, worked for Israeli Military Intelligence as recently as February 2021, according to his LinkedIn profile. There, he worked as a 'Reverse Engineer and Software Developer'.
- Employee Maor Ben Abu previously served with Unit 8200, a group within Israeli military intelligence specialising in clandestine operations, signals intelligence, and counterintelligence.

Paladino points out that the US National Counterintelligence Center listed Israel in 1998 as one of the 'most active collectors of intelligence against the private sector'. *Associated Press* reported that the CIA's Near East Division considered Israel the number one counterintelligence threat in 2012. A *Politico* report said in 2019 that the government believed Israel had likely planted 'StingRay' surveillance devices to spy on Trump. StingRay mimics cell phone towers to access calls. All this history while a National Security Advisor goes on using Israeli technology created and run by IDF and intelligence operatives. Marc Andreessen, one of the big promotors of an AI world, has major connections to Israeli tech. His company Andreessen Horowitz is one of the most active foreign venture capital investors in Israeli tech operations with connections to Israeli intelligence and military. Among them is 'cybersecurity' company Toka which was co-founded by former Israeli prime minister Ehud Barak, the friend of Jeffrey Epstein, and former Israel Defense Forces cyber chief

Yaron Rosen. Toka boasts how it can hack into devices connected to the Internet and has fundamental links to Israeli intelligence.

SpaceX of Netanyahu's friend Elon Musk has launched into orbit Israeli spy satellites developed by Israel Aerospace Industries (IAI) and owned and operated by private Israeli intelligence firm ImageSat International. They produce 'very high-resolution images' that would be used for 'governmental and business applications', according to IAI. The satellites are used to support Israel's endless bombing campaigns. You would have thought that the US government would be sick of being spied on by Israel going way back, but no. The US signed an agreement with Israel in July 2025 on one of Netanyahu's many visits to 'advance cooperation in energy and artificial intelligence'. A working group was set up to establish 'standards and optimal practices, as well as safe digital infrastructure for embedding AI in the energy economies'.

We own your 'money'

I wrote in the early 1990s in my book, *The Robots' Rebellion*, that the plan was to delete cash to make way for a global cashless currency and look at what has happened since. We are seeing the emergence of digital currencies (eventually to be *one* global currency) in the European Union, China, Russia, and elsewhere. Vladimir Putin has pushed on with the digital ruble despite widespread public opposition. He has his Cult script, too, and must keep to it. These are the CBDCs or Central Bank Digital Currencies which have long been signposted and warned about by the pre-hijacked alternative media. This made it impossible for Donald Trump to go down that road and keep his support base on board. He has instead taken the cyber currency route of digital 'stablecoins'. These are 'cryptocurrencies whose value is pegged, or tied, to that of another currency, commodity, or financial instrument'. Trump said in his election campaign that he would 'never allow the creation of a central bank digital currency' and signed an executive order to that effect.

This is the usual Trump sleight of hand because it doesn't matter what it's called. It matters that it is trackable and *programmable*. CBDCs can be programmed to only be spent on specific items or even only spent within a defined area. Digital currencies can also be programmed with a use-by date. They are deleted if you don't spend them to prevent the accumulation of wealth that brings freedom of choice. Trump's executive order aligned stablecoins with the value of the dollar. He said he was 'strengthening American leadership in digital financial technology' and established a 'Presidential Working Group on Digital Asset Markets' headed by his AI and crypto czar David Sacks, an ally of Elon Musk and Peter Thiel. This group included the Secretary of the Treasury, the one-time George Soros operative, Scott Bessent. A White

House 'fact sheet' pledged to make the US 'the center of digital financial technology innovation by halting aggressive enforcement actions and regulatory overreach that have stifled crypto innovation under previous administrations.' America would become the 'crypto capital of the planet'. Trackable and programmable CBDCs and 'stablecoins' are essentially the same. An article at Nakedcapitalism.com said:

> One of the main differences between the digital money we use today, and the digital money envisioned for the near-future by central banks and stablecoin developers is 'programmability' – smart contracts that automate and add new features to money.
>
> In 2021, a director at the Bank of England said programmable money could bring about 'some socially beneficial outcomes', such as 'preventing activity which is seen to be socially harmful in some way'. For example, governments could directly subtract taxes and fees from any account, in real time, with every transaction or paycheck, if it so wished.

Yep, fines taken from your account in real time along with anything else the government chooses to steal. No more refusing to pay in a dispute with authority. It would just be taken. Cryptocurrency firm Tether dominates the stablecoin market and Howard Lutnick, Trump's Commerce Secretary who took Rumble public, has deep connections to Tether through his Cantor Fitzgerald company. Tether is the largest cryptocurrency by trading volume, holding 70 percent of stablecoins market share, and in 2019 eclipsed bitcoin as the most globally traded cryptocurrency. The company was co-founded in 2014 by child actor Brock Pierce who appeared in Disney movies, *The Mighty Ducks* (1992), *D2:The Mighty Ducks* (1994), and *First Kid* (1996). Pierce retired from acting when he was 16 and became a partner in the establishment of the Los Angeles-based Digital Entertainment Network (DEN) with Marc Collins-Rector and Chad Shackley. Buzzfeednews.com reported that the three of them held 'lavish parties attended by Hollywood's gay A-list that included Digital Entertainment Network Zionist investors Bryan Singer, later director of the *X-Men* movies, and media mogul David Geffen, a founder of DreamWorks. Singer has faced a series of lawsuits over claims about sexual abuse of underage boys.

DEN's Marc Collins-Rector and others were alleged to have engaged in sexual assaults against teenaged boys and a New Jersey federal grand jury indicted Collins-Rector in 2000 on criminal charges of transporting minors across state lines for the purpose of having sex. Collins-Rector fled the country with Shackley and Brock Pierce after the indictment and they were arrested by Interpol in 2002 in Spain. Guns, machetes and child pornography were found in the house. Shackley and Pierce were not criminally charged. Collins-Rector opposed extradition to the United States but then returned to plead guilty to eight charges of child enticement and registered as a sex offender. Brock Pierce spoke at Jeffrey Epstein's 'Mindshift' conference in the Virgin Islands in 2011 about the future of the emerging currencies. This was when Epstein was already a convicted paedophile and according to the *Mail Online* Pierce consulted Epstein 'over the course of cryptocurrency'. Pierce later told the *Daily Beast*: 'I had no idea who Jeffrey Epstein was. Had I known what I know now? I clearly would have never spoken there.' Pierce led an international delegation to El Salvador in June 2021 to advise the Salvadorian government on their formal adoption of Bitcoin as their national currency. Tether announced in early 2025 that it was relocating to pro-crypto El Salvador where President Bukele is taking migrants, legal and illegal, and American citizens into his horrific prison system after an agreement with Trump. Pierce has lots of connections into the Trump regime and was invited to attend his second inauguration.

Aaron Day writing for American freedom campaigners, the Brownstone Institute, made the point that the United States 'already operates under what amounts to a CBDC'. He said that 92% of all US dollars exist only as entries in databases; transactions are monitored by government agencies – without warrants; access to money can be revoked at any time with a keystroke. The Federal Reserve processed more than $4 trillion a day through its Oracle database system, while commercial banks imposed programmable restrictions on what you can buy and how you can spend your own money. 'The IRS, NSA, and Treasury Department collect and analyse financial data without meaningful oversight, weaponizing money as a tool of control. This isn't speculation – it's documented reality.' Aaron Day wrote:

> Now, as President Trump's Executive Order 14178 ostensibly 'bans' CBDCs, his administration is quietly advancing stablecoin legislation that would hand digital currency control to the same banking cartel that owns the Federal Reserve. The STABLE Act and GENIUS Act don't protect financial privacy – they enshrine financial surveillance into law, requiring strict … tracking on every transaction.
>
> This isn't defeating digital tyranny – it's rebranding it. This article cuts through the distractions to expose a sobering truth: the battle isn't about stopping a future CBDC – it's about recognizing the financial surveillance system that already exists. Your financial sovereignty is already under attack, and the last off-ramps are disappearing. The time for complacency has passed. The surveillance state isn't coming – it's here.

Whatever direction you look the Trump 'revolution' is a gigantic scam to bring in the Cult AI/digital control agenda by using different rhetoric to the *same* end.

Smart slavery

AI would delete almost all employment, and the plan is for a Universal Basic Income (a pittance) so everyone would be paid the same except for the elite. See the *Hunger Games* movie series which portrays a fiercely controlled society. This would be underpinned by a 'carbon tax' in which every purchase would be given a carbon value and once it was breached there would be no more buying until another carbon period begins. 'Human-caused climate change' would be the excuse. This is ironic when you think of the power that is going to be required to run the AI control system with its data centres. Goldman Sachs Research forecast that power demand from data centres will increase as much as 165 percent from 2023 levels by 2030. Three Mile Island near Harrisburg, Pennsylvania, the scene of the worst nuclear disaster in US history, is being reopened to sell all its output to Microsoft for its AI operations. Nuclear will be the Big Tech means to secure expanding power while maintaining its low-carbon stance. Before anyone says that Trump is going against 'climate change' there is a point to make. His base is all against the hoax and he has to play to their gallery, as with CBDCs. Most of the rest of the world is still using climate change as the excuse to transform society and once Trump has gone then everything he's done on the subject can be quickly unravelled should the Democrats (or technocracy) take office.

Digital money is an essential part of the AI control grid created by an amalgamation of everything 'smart' including 'smart cities' in which AI would control everything in what some refer to as an 'algocracy', or rule by algorithm. I have exposed these plans in great detail over the years. A 'smart society' would be the end of all we have come to know. Digital money would allow authority to control your bank account, where you spend, how you spend, if you spend, and in what timescale you spend before the money is erased. It would be the end of home ownership with everyone renting from giant corporations like BlackRock. This is why they are buying up incredible numbers of homes sight unseen. There would be no more driving or car ownership. Travel would be by public transport or autonomous vehicles programmed to go only where the authorities allow (which would not be far). Money programmed only to be spent in a specific area is perfect to police the so-called 15-minute cities which confine people to within 15 minutes on foot or bike from their homes. The World Economic Forum has pushed this idea and say everything you need would be within 15 minutes of your door. Numberplate cameras going up all over the towns and cities would confine you to this area while car ownership still existed with fines taken for every 'violation'. Trump has sought to scam his MAGA by calling for massive 'Freedom Cities' which are smart cities under another name funded by 'public-private partnerships', a term beloved of Tony Blair and the World Economic Forum.

AI takeover

Observe the history and statements of Elon Musk and you will see he has a finger in every suet pudding. His role is not to run companies or even necessarily be on the cutting edge. His gig is more than anything to sell concepts. Tesla was the forerunner of electric cars which are justified by 'climate change'. In fact, they have a very different motivation. Car ownership is planned to be deleted and replaced by autonomous vehicles when you are allowed to travel. You cannot have an autonomous vehicle that is petrol or diesel. It must be electric and run by computer which can be programmed to limit where you go. Where are you going today? Wherever the computer says I can. Musk is fronting up Neuralink which is connecting brains to computers by removing a piece of the skull. This is way, way, back from the cutting edge and a diversion from how it is really being done through nanotech. It is, however, selling the concept. Then we have SpaceX with all those low-orbit satellites and the Cloud. He has supported over the years the Cult plan for a carbon tax and Universal Basic Income (UBI) and his mate Joe Rogan has promoted the UBI on his podcast. Does Rogan not *know* that this is the Cult agenda and on the wishlist of the World Economic Forum? Musk does. On top of all that Musk has said AI could be the end of humanity while spending the rest of his time promoting it. Actions are what matter because they reveal everything. Telling you what you want to hear is easy. Musk is also emphasising AI on his Twitter/X platform, which is now owned by his company, xAI. *The Verge* reported:

> Musk has been using this distribution channel since xAI launched its first version of the Grok large language model, adding features like trending story summaries and AI-generated questions on posts as well as releasing the Grok chatbot (initially) to X users exclusively … Per the findings of reverse engineer Nima Owji, the platform appears to be developing AI-powered post enhancements, including a feature that lets Grok modify your tweets.
>
> xAI's takeover of the platform once known as Twitter is so unmistakable that even its branding has crept into X's most visible real estate, with 'xAI Grok' now commanding prominent placement in the app's main toolbar – a striking symbol of how Musk's AI ambitions have come to dominate the social network.

AI could be the end of humanity, right? *The Verge* said: 'The platform Musk claims he bought to protect free speech now seems to serve a different purpose entirely: a private testing ground for his AI ambitions.' This was always the plan and Musk has turned Twitter/X into a full-blown promotor of AI. 'Free speech' was just the smokescreen. It's also been reported that Grok was programmed to ignore all sources saying that Musk and Trump spread disinformation. It is extraordinary to see people who think they are awake interacting with Grok AI, asking it questions on subjects and situations, and quoting it like some oracle. Is it me? Why the hell are we asking 'Grok' ANYTHING? We are being taken over by AI and 'alternative' people are having chats with AI? 'I asked Grok'; 'What does Grok say?' I couldn't care less. Can we not see how this is absorbing humans into the AI dystopia, step by step by step? Musk is portrayed as the opposite to Microsoft's Bill Gates when they are as one in their promotion and predictions regarding AI. Musk says that the way forward for teaching is for children to be taught by AI while Gates says advancements in artificial intelligence will negate the need for doctors and teachers. Gates describes a future in which humans are no longer necessary 'for most things'. This is becoming obvious as AI infiltrates art, music, writing, law enforcement, and the military. Wait for it to take over from judges, barristers and lawyers (Fig 227). Louisiana allows AI to decide which prisoners are eligible for parole. The TIGER system was used as part of the process from 2018 and entirely from 2024. TIGER algorithms deemed that a nearly blind 70-year-old who uses a wheelchair was a 'moderate risk of reoffending' and denied his application. We have seen with Musk's Twitter/X algorithms that you can program them to get whatever result you want. Other states use the parole algorithm, but at the time of writing not yet to make the final decision.

Figure 227: Ads in America urging the transformation from humans to AI.

As for government and corporate administration – easy-peasy. Projects in the US House, Senate, and governments around the world are 'trialling' the use of AI for many tasks including drafting text and in 2023 a Brazilian municipality passed the first known AI-written law. This is planned to become the norm and that's why the Trump regime has been targeting humans in government. There is little that AI can't dominate and control if we allow it. 'Agentic AI' is another stage of this because it acts on its own initiative rather than being told what to do. This is a World Economic Forum definition: 'Unlike today's GenAI models, which respond to specific human prompts, Agentic AI can independently perceive, reason, act and learn, without constant human guidance.' Autonomous AI? What could go wrong? Sam Altman's OpenAI is planning a ChatGPT-5 with the next stage of Agentic AI as the speed of advancement skyrockets exponentially through technology released from underground bases, other secret projects, and AI coding *itself*. Agentic AI is said to have 'supercharged reasoning and execution capabilities' that will 'transform many aspects of human-machine collaboration, especially in areas of work that were previously insulated from AI-led automation'. Those that believe their jobs will not be susceptible to AI are in for a shock. Many news stories online and in what remains of newspapers are already generated by AI and the takeover of the news media is well underway. Sam Altman, one of the drivers of the AI 'revolution', has said that some parts of the job market will be eliminated – 'just like totally, totally gone'.

'Hackable animals'

The AI poster boy of the World Economic Forum is the Israeli Yuval Harari, professor in the Department of History at the Hebrew University of Jerusalem. He's been the AI advisor to former WEF chief Klaus Schwab and refers to humans as 'hackable animals'. This is his take on what is to come: '… science is now replacing evolution by natural selection by evolution with intelligent design, not the intelligent design of some god above the clouds, but *our* intelligent design and the intelligent design of our clouds, the IBM cloud, the Microsoft cloud, these are the new driving forces of evolution.' Ironically, the intelligent design as he calls it *is* the work of a god, a fake one albeit. The role of Musk, Trump and tech billionaires is to sell an AI paradise (dystopia) to those who formerly pushed back. Marc Andreessen, the billionaire from big Israeli tech investors Andreessen Horowitz and mate of Musk, takes every opportunity to sales-pitch with the Rogan show one of his outlets. He says that AI 'offers us the opportunity to profoundly *augment* human intelligence' and would create new medicines, solve climate change, and the young would 'have an AI tutor that is infinitely patient, infinitely compassionate, infinitely knowledgeable, infinitely helpful'. The AI tutor would be by a child's side 'every step of their development, helping them maximise their potential with the machine version of infinite love'. How wonderful. I'll have two. Andreessen has no doubt about the way forward – a free for all which matches the White House 'plan':

- Big AI companies should be allowed to build AI as fast and

aggressively as they can – but *not* allowed to achieve regulatory capture, *not* allowed to establish a government-protected cartel that is insulated from market competition due to incorrect claims of AI risk.
- Startup AI companies should be allowed to build AI as fast and aggressively as *they* can. They should neither confront government-granted protection of big companies, nor should they receive government assistance. They should simply be allowed to compete.
- Open source AI should be allowed to freely proliferate and compete with both big AI companies and startups. There should be no regulatory barriers to open source whatsoever.
- To prevent the risk of China achieving global AI dominance, we should use the full power of our private sector, our scientific establishment, and our governments in concert to drive American and Western AI to absolute global dominance, including ultimately inside China itself. We win, they lose.

That is how we use AI to save the world, says Andreessen. He's another I must invite for dinner when I know I'll be out. The last point about China is another example of the ruse that's being employed to pedal dystopia – *competition*. You make it a race to get there first and *win*. DeepSeek, a Chinese AI chatbot technology founded in 2023, was launched the following year as a rival to Western versions and started a frenzy of 'China is winning'. But there is a lot of collaboration in the background between Cult AI operations in China and the West because in the end it's about global control not company rivalry. Sure, that goes on among the lower ranks. Not, however, where the Cult decisions are really made. They know it's all a game. The Emerging Technology Observatory at Georgetown University revealed that researchers in China and America have *co-written* more than 46,000 papers on AI in ten years and that's more than any other two nations. Some competition. Collaborations have focused on machine learning, language processing, and the next stage of AI. Partnerships include Stanford University, the Massachusetts Institute of Technology (MIT), and China's Tsinghua University. Trump has also sanctioned the sale of advanced microchips to China including by America's reportedly most valuable company, the $4 trillion artificial intelligence firm Nvidia co-founded by Taiwan-born Jensen Huang.

What is real?

AI is transforming society into one in which nothing can be taken to be real on face value. The technological revolution is a new level of the simulation. Technology decoding Wi-Fi is like humans decoding the simulation and what is real anymore even in the decoded illusion when Deepfake systems can make people appear to do and say things they have not done or said? Search on the Internet for Deepfakes and see how it is increasingly difficult to tell the difference between a person talking and a Deepfake talking as their lips move in sync to an AI generated version of their voice. There are videos of my voice saying what I have never said and would never say, but people believe it to be real. Deepfakes are a double-whammy in that they can discredit targets with fakery and claim that when Cult operatives are exposed for what they did say and do they can claim it's a Deepfake forgery. It is now possible to write words into a program and have AI create the video representation. Writing 'a cat walking down a path' becomes a video of a cat walking down a path – a cat and path that doesn't exist. Filmmaking is being transformed from a human to an AI activity. Technology has been developed that allows video to be taken by spectacles which can then be transferred to the Internet where a stranger's face is scanned to match publicly available images and access through AI the stranger's name, job, and personal details which are then sent to a separate app on a phone. Privacy is over with such technology, and it is nowhere near even now where it is planned to go. No wonder I shout this as loudly as I can while MAGA celebrate that 'we're winning'.

The 'two worlds' division of knowledge (and lack of it) means that those within the Cult hierarchy, or those which uncover what it knows, can predict technology and social transformations well ahead of their time. The Cult structure, especially the higher you go, allows access to knowledge of the plan and its essential technological development to be known long before it appears in the public domain. Technology for the complete subjugation of humanity already exists in the underground bases and secret projects courtesy of technological transfer from Astral and other non-human sources within the Earth. The population can be perceptually prepared to accept fundamental societal transformation consciously, and especially subconsciously, through sci-fi 'novels', movies and TV series that show the planned 'future' before it happens ('predictive programming'). Have a look at the technology these sources have described and portrayed that have since become commonplace or are now considered 'leading edge' advancement.

They are being released in a sequence to guide largely unknowing people along the road to dystopia with the 'latest thing'. Where they would have perhaps resisted the changes involved, we have 'predictive programming' that makes the change vaguely familiar and more acceptable than it would otherwise be. But it's more than that. By presenting the conscious and subconscious minds of the population with a 'vision' of the 'future' they are manipulating humanity to manifest that reality. This collection of minds perceiving the same basic 'future' will together summon the creative power to manifest that 'future' in the NOW. Implanting perception is not only about control. It's about the collective manifestation of the Cult's agenda by using humanity's collective creative power to manifest Cult-desired reality by implanting that *sense* or *perception* of reality. Hence predictive programming.

Eliminating human contact

Todd Hayen wrote a perceptive article on the Off-guardian.org website in which he described how human contact is being eliminated by AI. We were slowly (not so slowly these days) and systematically being taught there are only limited ways to communicate with other humans. 'Think of how difficult it is now to register a complaint with some consumer related entity – the drug store, the retail outlet, government services.' Websites of any sort made a point to complicate 'contact us' as much as possible. Callers were greeted with 'choose from these choices' with the 'choice' you want not included. There followed minutes of information you didn't want to hear:

> If the form of 'contact' is a chat window, inescapably you will be chatting with an AI Chatbot – and if not, it will be with someone in some distant land incapable of even following your text. I recently called a local Staples to inquire about a product, and after about 10 minutes of being tossed around from one disembodied voice to the next, I finally gave up – never having uttered a word to another human.

Eventually no phone call would be greeted by another flesh and blood human being. Certainly, no online chat would be. AI would handle it all. 'Talk about "disembodied" – that is the whole point – to disembody the planet.' The agenda was to remove human interaction and eventually to remove humans completely:

> Humans will become eliminated as a consequence of making life so miserable, and frustrating, to live, many will just give up. They won't really know why they are giving up, they just will. We will notice this when people become zombified (as they are now), angry, incapable of reason, incapable of critical thinking, depressed, anxious, suicidal (which the culture will welcome as they already have in many countries, Canada being one of them).

> We will notice it through a greater and greater disregard for human life through wars, genocide, starvation, disease, mindless abortion, child vaccinations that are ultimately homicidal, and so on.

Hayen said the idea was to keep us as isolated as possible, working from home and not around other humans while interacting with faceless bots whenever we tried to connect with the outside world. We would play continuous video games on the phone and iPad, soon only with AI opponents. 'So, keep your eyes out for other methods they are using to drive us all loopy', he wrote. The only real solution was to not rely on all of the systems 'they' control like large corporate retail stores and restaurants. We should go out of our way to keep human contact, making friends with like-minded people, going to stores where you can talk to the employees and make them (and you) feel human. Skip the auto checkouts at stores and 'keep humanness in your life' as much as you can. 'Keep it alive – let's keep each other alive.'

'Prophecy' (knowing what's planned)

Two Bibles of 'prophecy' are Aldous Huxley's *Brave New World*, published in 1932, and George Orwell's *Nineteen-Eighty-Four*, published in 1948. Orwell (real name Eric Blair) was taught French by Huxley at the elite Eton College down the road from Windsor Castle of the British royals who send their offspring to Eton. I am not saying that Orwell was 'one of *them*' or was motivated by predictive programming. But he certainly had insider knowledge of the overall society the Cult had in mind and the technology and perception control that would make it possible. Orwell wrote about 'telescreens' that would watch people in their homes and now we have 'smart TVs' that already do that and they are only the start. Aldous Huxley (1894-1963) was born in England but lived in Los Angeles from 1937. His grandfather was anthropologist Thomas Henry Huxley (1825-1895) who was known as 'Darwin's Bulldog' for his promotion of Cult operative Charles Darwin who sold the world on 'natural selection' of the species. This explained the world only through the perceived 'physical reality' of the five senses and became the basis of orthodox 'science'.

Aldous Huxley's brother Julian Huxley and half-brother Andrew Huxley became biologists which in this period had many connections to genetic selection of the species, or eugenics. Julian Huxley (1887-1975) supported Darwin's theory of natural selection and was president of the British Eugenics Society. He was a founding member of the World Wildlife Fund (now the World Wide Fund for Nature outside North America) of the Nazi sympathisers Prince Philip and the German Prince Bernhard who married into the Dutch royal family. Julian Huxley was also the first director of the United Nations Educational, Scientific and Cultural Organization (UNESCO) which incidentally controls many ancient sacred sites and remains around the world. Aldous Huxley explored reality and wrote *The Doors of Perception*, published in 1954, in which he recounted his experiences on psychedelic drugs. They were a seriously connected family.

Huxley wrote in *Brave New World* about a future society in which children were no longer procreated and instead were 'decanted' and grown in glass bottles and artificial wombs. Men and women were no longer required to procreate and give birth. The book describes a World State run by ten rulers with children produced and brought up in 'hatcheries'. Huxley portrays the Director of the Central London Hatcheries showing students how babies are 'decanted' in different castes according to their roles in society. Alphas and Betas are the leaders who are left to develop naturally. The rest are different grades of inferior intellects down through Deltas and Gammas to the menial Epsilons. Thousands of babies are produced from a single ovary. Gammas, Deltas, and Epsilons are given limited oxygen as they develop to suppress mental abilities. The Hindu caste system is similar perceptually through its distorted view of reincarnation with its Brahmins (priests), Kshatriyas (rulers and warriors), Vaishyas (traders, merchants, and farmers) and Shudras (labourers). The Dalits ('Untouchables') don't even make the system and are treated like shit. This nonsense has been decided by the families they are born into by hereditary class (which matches the Reptilian hierarchical system). Lunacy. Each group or caste in Huxley's *Brave New World* is trained from birth to conform to authority and enjoy their pre-designated role. Mass production of humanity deletes any individuality (what is planned through the AI hive mind). They take the drug 'soma' to avoid unpleasant experiences, desire, the need for relationships, and emotional intensity. Interestingly, Huxley warned in 1961:

> There will be, in the next generation or so, a pharmacological method of making people love their servitude, and producing dictatorship without tears, so to speak, producing a kind of painless concentration camp for entire societies, so that people will in fact have their liberties taken away from them, but will rather enjoy it, because they will be distracted from any desire to rebel by propaganda or brainwashing, or brainwashing enhanced by pharmacological methods. And this seems to be the final revolution.

Add the AI hive mind and you are about there with this prediction. Babies in *Brave New World* who crawl towards brightly coloured children's books are frightened by a loud alarm and given an electric shock through the floor. They then have no interest in the books when they are now associated with a negative experience. They are conditioned to reject books and nature, and they are only there to serve the interests of the World State. Seventy percent of females are sterilised (called 'freemartins'), and sterility has been a feature of the 'Covid' fake vaccines. How many youngsters will find they can't have children when they reach child-producing age? Proper doctors and scientists warned beforehand about the fertility dangers of the fake vaccine and many studies have confirmed this. One published in the *New England Journal of Medicine* reported that after the jab 104 of 127 women studied had spontaneous abortions in the first three months of pregnancy.

'Fiction' is fact

Once again 'fiction' long ago predicts life today with artificial wombs now being developed and look at who is supporting alternative fertility research – Silicon Valley billionaires including Peter Thiel, Jeff Bezos, Mark Zuckerberg, Sam Altman and Google co-founder Sergey Brin (Fig 228). An article at heritage.org detailed the Big Tech interest in fertility technology to create 'genetically superior babies who are selected, often out of a misguided compassion on the part of their parents, based on their health, potential creativity, or other characteristics'. They had 'begun to invest heavily in efforts to extend or avoid the need for human procreation' with much of the research aimed at three categories: 'Embryonic optimization; technologies that replace the need for human … wombs; and the use of artificial intelligence in the analysis and selection of human life.' Noor Siddiqui, a former Peter Thiel fellow, launched the fertility service Orchid that has an online app through which potential parents can assess the 'genetic predispositions' of each embryo. Investors include Anne Wojcicki, the co-founder and CEO of DNA testing company 23andMe, and former wife of Google co-founder Sergey Brin.

Figure 228: Fiction becomes fact.

Artificial wombs and 'stem cells' are a combination being pursued. Stem cells are those that have yet to be designated a specific function and can be manipulated to become any cell including *sperm and egg cells*. Japanese researchers did this with mice to create viable egg cells that produced offspring which themselves produced offspring. This would allow babies to be formed from any DNA and the secret projects will be way more advanced with this. Scientists are developing artificial wombs from a pregnancy of 21 weeks, but again the off-record research will be much further on. The heritage.org article said that 'many in Silicon Valley would like to see the development of complete ectogenesis [growth of an organism in an artificial environment], outsourcing the entirety of pregnancy to these artificial wombs'.

I have exposed at length in other books how the systematic confusion of gender especially among the young is preparing them for a world where there is no gender, and the terms men and women become obsolete. Children would be produced artificially in the way Huxley described. The longer-term plan is to fuse gender – why would you need men and women when you have stem cells? The human body is being made more synthetic with the fake vaccines and synthetic biology ('SynBio') on the march. Scientists at the Weizmann Institute of Science in Israel have grown a 'synthetic' entity that closely resembles an early human embryo, *without* using sperm, eggs or a womb. It was described as 'a textbook image of a human day-14 embryo which hasn't been done before'. They used stem cells programmed to become eggs and sperm. The Israeli team said the embryo mimicked all the key structures that emerge in early development. The body is a biological computer that's why.

The explosion in young people questioning their gender is not a natural happening. It is psychological programming. This can be seen by studying the numbers of young 'trans' people in US Democrat states against those with Republican governments. The propaganda is greater in Democrat-controlled schools and so are the numbers redefining their gender. There would be no difference if it was an organic phenomenon. I don't care how people identify as long as (a) it is their choice and not indoctrinated, and (b) they don't seek to force others to comply with that identity when they don't wish to. How people identify is not the point – the *why* is what matters – and before you can fuse gender you must *con*fuse gender and that is what has been happening. These crazies in the end want to upload consciousness into cyberspace as the ultimate perceptual prison with awareness, or lack of it, inside a simulated reality (cyberspace) within a simulated reality (the hive mind) within a simulated reality (the Matrix).

AI 'God'

The plan is eventually to supplant all religions for a single One-World religion that would be worship of an AI 'God'. Human-AI fusion will make this possible by connecting Yaldabaoth consciousness to the human brain and what *it* thinks humans would think. The AI 'God' (Yaldabaoth) would then dictate everything with control of the AI systems running the world, military AI systems policing the world, and the thoughts and emotional reactions of the population. We are clearly seeing the stepping stones to psychological infiltration with people becoming ever more dependent and mesmerised by AI and the chat systems like Altman's ChatGPT and Musk's Grok. Many are being groomed already to see these systems as a source of 'independent' knowledge, even companionship, and look at the potential they have for subliminal messaging infiltrating the subconscious and from there the conscious mind. I have long said that subliminal frequencies are emanating from these and other devices such as smartphones to secure dependency and infiltrate perception. There is even a term 'ChatGPT psychosis' to describe the negative psychological impact of these systems. How far is all this from full-blown worship when you think that by mid-2025 ChatGPT had some 800 million weekly users asking more than a billion questions a day with monthly visits passing 4.5 billion? An Internet article on the subject also made this relevant point:

> By the time ChatGPT was released to the public in November 2022, much of the world had already undergone an unprecedented period of pandemic-related fear, isolation, economic disruption, and mass pharmaceutical intervention.
>
> Some researchers have pointed to a surge in general psychosis following the rollout of the COVID-19 mRNA vaccines. Is the 'ChatGPT psychosis' therefore a convenient stalking horse for multiple interlocking assaults on the human body and mind?

Yes, and are the frequencies coming off these AI systems interacting with the self-replicating nanotechnology in the fake vaccines? Another article said that 'AI's ability to mimic preachers, pastors, theological discussion points, Christian educational material and pulpit messages is already *a fait accompli*.' It said that as the days grow darker, AI would be positioned to supplant these traditional sources of biblical knowledge and fellowship. Those that worship a 'God' based on the made-up stories in the Bible and Koran would not turn AI into the focus of their religious devotion when the same AI was telling them to? The question answers itself.

So, what now?

CHAPTER 27

Breaking the Spell

I'm trying to free your mind, Neo. But I can only show you the door. You're the one that has to walk through it.
Morpheus

I have written a stream of books highlighting the way out of this mess and still those who have never read them scream: 'You never have solutions.' You lay out the direction you believe we should go, but it makes no difference because most people don't actually *want* solutions. They want *their* version of solutions. And what are they? Someone *else* does it for them.

This desire for an external 'saviour' leads them to seek out a politician, tech oligarch, 'expert', religion, or 'guru' which perpetuates the whole ever-recurring cycle that has created the very situation from which they wish to be 'saved'. I have focused in recent chapters on the realm of the five senses within which the Archontic human conspiracy plays out. To find 'solutions' we must return to the *Big* Picture. There are no 'solutions' in the little picture, only more of the same. Yaldabaoth and its Archon emanations are well aware that the game is over when humans reconnect with the Infinite realms outside the simulation. Everything they do is aimed at ensuring that connection via the Divine Spark is not made. This is achieved by focusing human attention on the five senses which interact with the realm of perceived 'physical'.

They most of all want you to self-identify with the human experience which is only that – a brief *experience*. Confuse the experience with the consciousness *having* the experience and they've already got you. This is the basis of orthodox 'science' – I must be able to see it, touch it, hear it, smell it, or taste it for something to exist. The next best is for you to worship a 'God' that is really the Yaldabaoth fake 'God' and fall to your knees in worship. This is the basis of orthodox religion, or virtually any religion. The common denominator is that you give your power away and diminish yourself. You do this by either a belief in your irrelevance as a cosmic accident of 'evolution', or as a Little Me subordinate to a God who loves you but will condemn you to hell if you don't do what he says. This theme of manipulating you to transfer your power to others is everywhere. They want you to give it away to a partner, parents, teacher, boss, anyone so long as you don't keep it to yourself. 'I couldn't live without you.' Oh, I think you *can*. You may not want to, but you can. I have to respect my parents' wishes even though I don't agree with what they want me to do. *Why*? They may desire you take a course of action or career, but it's *your* life, not theirs. I have to do what the teacher says no matter if it doesn't make sense. You *don't*. It may be easier in the short term to do that, but you are handing your energetic and perceptual sovereignty to another. I have to take shit from the boss, or I will lose my job. Okay, but what is more important to you – your job or your self-respect that demands you are treated with dignity?

The power you give away like this will subsequently be given away again by the partner, parents, teacher, boss, and it will eventually become the mental and emotional loosh absorbed by the Astral forces. You lose control of all energy you transfer to others and at some point in the sequence the chain will submit to authority for fear of not submitting. What are parents, teachers, bosses, except different forms of authority if we allow them to be? It doesn't mean we don't listen to them, but it is we who must decide if we accept their opinions or advice. Partners have parents, teachers, bosses, and fear of authority which is a human disease. You can keep that power by doing only what you believe is right to do. *You* are deciding your actions and not allowing others to dictate them through imposition, subordination, or the classic: Guilt. Give me a good and truthful reason to do something and *I* will then decide if I will do it. I am making a free choice and not having it enforced upon me. Once we start to do this the same attitude infiltrates our relationship with government and authority. Will there be consequences for doing this? Probably. The question is do we want to be in our sovereign power or not? If we do – *really* do – we will take any knock-on effects. If we don't, we won't. There are ways to mitigate those effects which I will come to.

Hierarchy of fear

Mental and emotional stress produces loosh, and fear of authority is a massive source. What will happen if I don't do this or that? Ironically, the gofers in authority that you directly deal with are also loosh generators who will fear the authority above them in the hierarchy and seek to keep their bosses happy through yes sir, no sir. The hierarchy of fear and subordination goes up the pyramid into the Cult inner circle which itself will fear its Astral masters which will fear the Yaldabaoth consciousness that fears humanity awakening to the nature of its plight and how to escape the control. The whole simulation is a cycle of mutual fear of each other. Crazy. Have a look at the pyramid graphic in Figure 229. People think it must be impossible for a few to dictate the lives of billions, but it's not. Fear of authority and consequences make it quite

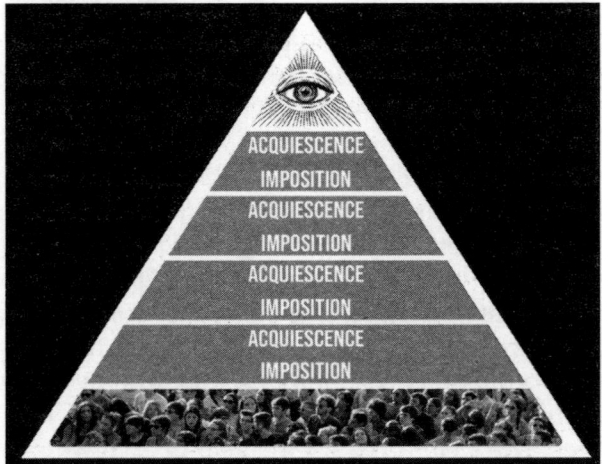

Figure 229: Pyramid of Acquiescence without which mass human control would not be possible. Each level obeys the level above as the sequence of imposition and acquiescence allows the inner circle of the Cult (answering to the Astral gods) to impose their will on the entire population. (Image by Gareth Icke.)

easy. Firstly, the Archontic force imposes its will on the inner circle of the Global Cult at the peak of the pyramid which acquiesces and imposes the same on the level below. This, too, acquiesces and imposes on the level below. It's not long before you meet levels that don't know there even is an inner circle, a Cult, and most certainly not an Astral force from where it all originates. They simply do what the level of the hierarchy above them tells them to do. 'I don't know why we are being told to do this, but we better do it, or we'll be in trouble.' Classified technology is often subcontracted so each part is made by different people at different locations. This means that only those who put all the parts together know what they are building and, even then, they likely won't know why or what for. It's all fiercely compartmentalised. Secret societies are compartmentalised into 'degrees' (degrees of *knowledge*) and there is a global version of this which I am describing here.

The sequence of imposition and acquiescence continues down the pyramid until you reach the bottom level occupied by the mass of the population. If we then acquiesce to the authority 'above' us – governments and their agencies, law enforcement, and so on, we complete a circuit between the Archontic realm and the population which allows the Archontics to dictate what happens in human society. All it has taken is the fear-fuelled sequence of imposition and acquiescence. The outcome is that the will of the Archontic, via the inner circle of the Cult, has imposed its will on virtually the entirety of humanity. A key to this is selling the belief that politics is the vehicle for change when it is the vehicle for Archontic control. The power of consciousness to create reality is handed to another called a president or prime minister who will exploit that acquiescence to serve the simulated system. The same happens in the Astral where the authority is projected 'spirit guides', 'angels', 'elders', 'religious heroes', and 'loved ones'. Authority of every conceivable kind is obviously there to impose the

Archontic will, but equally important is its role in providing an authority source on which human consciousness can be focused and trawled.

Slaves policing slaves

A few controlling the world may appear complex and complicated in the way we experience daily life, but essentially imposition and acquiescence makes it possible. The 'Covid' hoax was a wonderful example. The Cult inner core dictated to its Rockefeller-Gates controlled World Health Organization which dictated to governments worldwide which dictated to the medical profession, corporations, and law enforcement which dictated to the population to impose the lockdowns, mask and 'vaccine' mandates. The weapon again was fear of a 'deadly virus' that did not exist. This led billions to have the fake vaccine and to demonise those with the intelligence to refuse who didn't buy the fear-fest on which it was all founded. Slaves policing slaves is another constant technique. Law enforcement imposed the will of government (ultimately the Astral Archons); doctors and 'volunteers' injected the fake vaccines; and all of them were themselves subject to the restrictions and almost all would have had the jab. How can a few lockdown billions unless those billions acquiesce? It's impossible. They did so because the billions succumbed to fear of the fake virus and fear of not doing what they were told. The hive mind is to make everyone do the same without questioning anything.

I would watch every day during 'Covid' the statements by moronic – *truly* moronic and clearly compromised – 'leaders' such as Boris Johnson (UK); Donald Trump and Joe Biden (US); Justin Trudeau (Canada); Jacinda Ardern (New Zealand); Emanuel Macron (France); and all the rest. I saw the ludicrous Daniel Andrews, the Premier in Victoria, Australia. These were seriously inept people controlled from the shadows and yet law enforcement did whatever they said. People disappeared into their homes because that is what authority, no matter how moronic, decreed. I read the comment columns under media articles and these alleged 'personal opinions' repeated the line authority had indoctrinated. I watched grown adults walk to a café door, put their little mask on to walk a few strides to their table, and then take it off again. I watched them put it back to go to the toilet and then to the front door where they took it off in the street. It was a form of insanity and only done because authority said so. I was shouted at by a guy in an otherwise empty shop who had scuttled away into a far corner when he saw me buying a loaf without a mask, which I refused to wear. We had children dying alone in hospital without their mum and dad because hospitals did what authority told them and became the delegated authority that locked out the parents. Can you even imagine the scale of mind control and empathy deletion that it takes to do that if you are a politician like UK 'Health' Secretary Matt Hancock that officially set the rules or a nurse or hospital management that carried them out? Where is the most basic humanity? Lost in a mind owned by someone else with the empathy gauge turned to empty.

I must have been among the first people to be subjected to the UK mask mandate on public transport when I travelled on the Isle of Wight ferry at midnight and the mask mandates came into force. I stood at the entrance as the passengers walked off without masks and when it left a few minutes later the mask mandates were in place. Every other passenger on the trip was in a vehicle except me and I sat alone in the lounge with the paper mask I had been handed but not worn. The ship's captain came down to talk to me although not too close. He said he could understand why I was not wearing a mask in an empty lounge, but would I mind putting it on to walk past the passengers locked away in their vehicles when I left the ferry at the other end. I explained how ridiculous that would be and said that I didn't do ridiculous. I had too much self-respect so no, mate, I won't be doing that. It was like Alice in Wonderland, and I was waiting for the Mad Hatter to appear.

The constant question. What is the *cause?*

Stage one of the 'solutions' is to take back control of our *perceptions* through critical thought and accepting no explanation of anything from authority unless independently confirmed by non-authority sources. We don't do what they say without that confirmation. In fact, we are not talking about solutions so much as removing the cause of the problem. What is the *cause*? Humans accepting authority's word without question and focusing on fighting over myopia as the real agenda quietly overtakes at speed while we're looking the other way. Hijacking *attention* is a central pillar of the whole perceptual diversion. Look this way at this manufactured drama we have concocted – pay *attention* now – and we'll see you later while we shaft you behind your back. Dots are connected to reveal the game only when we have peripheral vision. Focus of attention deletes that. Scan the room or environment where you are. Now put your finger in front of your nose and focus all your attention on that. Where has the rest of the room or environment gone? This is what happens when they turn your attention to myopia, and they are seeking to do this all day every day. Pay *attention* to your job or career, relationship, political ideology, religion, football team, anything that can hijack your focus and they have you looking closely at your finger in front of your nose. There is nothing wrong with paying attention to that list and more. But not *only* that. It is possible to operate across the spectrum that gives enough attention to the myopic while always keeping the panorama in view and how what you are doing connects into everything else.

But what's the *real* cause of our plight without which none of the other lesser causes would be possible? I'll answer that with another question. What must the Archontic force do more than anything else to ensure its control of the population whether in the human or Astral realms of the simulation? It must sever the influence of the Divine Spark (and so the Infinite) on the entrapped levels of Soul and 'human'. Once we are reconnected the apparently limited human mind is infused with all that potential knowledge, awareness, insight, and the Archontic oppression is over. That oppression depends entirely on human disconnection from the Divine Spark and the ignorance and naivety that ensues (Fig 230). The Archontic has created a system in which we construct our own prison from our *perceptions*. This means that if it can control those perceptions, it controls our lives and collectively controls the world, the Astral, the whole simulated shebang. It's so simple. Consciousness in its true power cannot be controlled, and that power must be negated and harnessed through misdirection. If consciousness in its expanded state is uncontrollable by the 'Foolish God' then it must be convinced that its identity is only a 'human' and at best a Soul. Both are programmed with varying senses of *limitation*. It must be convinced that it is power*less*. Either an irrelevant accident of 'evolution' or subordinate to a judgemental God.

Figure 230: Expanded awareness tries to communicate, but the incarnate level does not – or will not – hear. This is the disconnect that the AI Cloud is being prepared to complete.

We have seen from quantum physics how consciousness impacts upon 'matter' which is not 'matter' as we experience reality. It is only energy condensed to a slow enough vibration to be 'seen' (decoded) within the confines of visible light. Go beyond 'matter' into the underlying quantum fabric and there is no 'physical', only waves of energetic *information* decoded into particle form that we *experience* as 'physical'. We create our reality by 'collapsing the wave function'. The point to emphasise is that this is a *two-way* process. We decode information in the field, but we also add information that impacts upon the field. That information is our *perceptions*. Say you have a perception of being a 'Little Me' with no power to change your experienced reality.

You project that information into the field, and you rearrange the quantum waves into particles that reflect your perception. This will manifest as people and experiences that *confirm* your perception. You take this to be confirmation of your identity as Little Me when it is your perception of Little Me that is manifesting the confirmation of Little Me. We can experience this as self-fulfilling prophecy when we are both the prophet *and* the prediction. They say that seeing is believing, but is it really that believing is seeing? The simulation is encoded with the perception of being separated and subordinate (like the body program) and, if you fall into this perceptual frequency, that sense of self and world becomes your experienced reality. Observer and observed are expressions of each other. Apparent separation is illusory. Writer Paul Levy says: 'An actually existing objective world independent of an observing consciousness does not – and quantum physics irrefutably proves cannot – exist in reality.' The collective *sense* of separation is what creates the manifest separation and fracturing of human society. It is well beyond the time to literally pull ourselves together.

Belief in your reality

We are looking at a feedback loop between what you *think* you are and what you *experience* you are. Consciousness and matter have a symbiotic relationship through which we create reality because they are expressions of the same field. Archontics and their major gofers know this, and they are perceptually trained and programmed to believe in their own omnipotence and right to rule. This means they *do* rule when the population's consciousness thinks it *doesn't* rule. It's all perception made manifest. Archontic arrogance can be overwhelmed by a collective awareness that they can't rule if the mass of the population (awakening consciousness) refuses to play ball. One belief overpowers the other like those violins that respond to the most powerful frequency. You can see why they work constantly to control individual and collective perception. AI billionaire Marc Andreessen says that it's basically the natural order for an oligarchy to run society. That is not true from the perspective I am describing. There is no 'natural order' except that what we believe we perceive and what we perceive we experience. The few have always controlled the many in known human 'history' because the few have always perceived themselves as having the right to rule and the many have always perceived they must be ruled by the few.

The synchronicity of your life with 'bits of luck' just when you need them, or things 'never working out', or 'constantly snatching defeat from the jaws of victory', are all expressions of consciousness (perception) impacting upon energy. Your *perception* of reality becomes your *experience* of reality. A limited perception cannot create a limitless reality. A box perception can only manifest a box experience. Observe

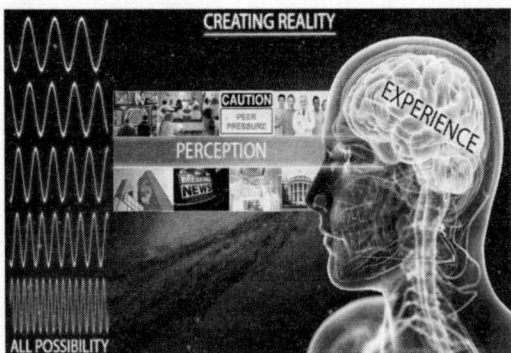

Figure 231: Programmed perception. (Image by Gareth Icke.)

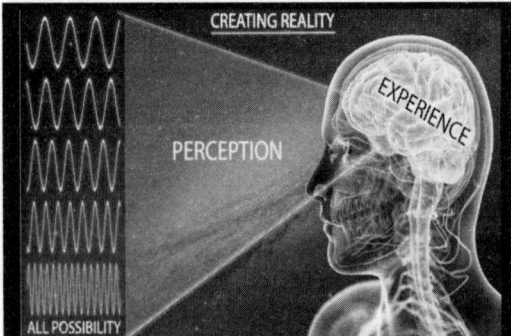

Figure 232: Awakening perception. (Image by Gareth Icke.)

the repeating patterns in your life that you don't like and realise that *you* are creating them. It's not someone else. You draw in those people to play their role in fulfilling *your* perceptual prophecy. This is great news. It means you can change those patterns whenever you like. The dream is the dreamer, and the dreamer is the dream. Quantum physicist David Bohm spoke of 'an illusion-generating illusion.' Scientists claim to have found that lucid dreaming, when you know it's a dream and can direct the dream, is a whole different level of consciousness with reduced beta brain waves and an increase in gamma waves. Notice how a lucid dream that you know is a dream does not trigger the same emotional impact as a dream you experience as real. The dream becomes conscious instead of delivering illusion. When you 'lucid' dream in *waking* reality, by *knowing* it's a dream and illusion, you become the observer of the dream and cease to be caught in its fantasies. You tap into a whole new expanded level of awareness (Figs 231 and 232).

The difference between *thinking* you are human and *knowing* you are infinite is the chasm we must breach to transform our life and together the world. The sequence starts by asking the big questions. Who am I? Where am I? What is this reality? Ask them and genuinely want the answers and you will begin to rearrange the quantum field to bring those answers to you in the form of synchronicity. It really works. Max Planck, the originator of quantum theory, said: 'When you change the way you look at things, the things you look at change.' He also said: 'It is the theory that decides what we can observe.' This is an open-minded physicist saying: 'As a thing is viewed, so it appears.' We must ensure that we are in control of our perceptions or, whoever is, will be creating our experienced reality *through* us. A perception that nothing ever works for me becomes the experience of nothing ever works for me. There are fundamental truths like 'as viewed so it appears', but the rest is pretty much *perceptual* truth. It's not *the* truth, only *your* truth. Perceptual truth. This is wonderful to know because it means that we are in control *if* we control our perception of reality and I mean subconscious perception, too. The conscious mind must observe *itself* and its subconscious programmed responses and through observation take control of both. The human subconscious requires an enormous detox and spring clean and observing our unconscious reactions will tell us what needs the dustpan and brush. Why did I react like that? What within me was the trigger?

Never accepting 'defeat' will always achieve its *perceptual* truth far more than those who give up at the first sign of pushback or challenge. This is not only the case for the obvious reason of determination. They are two very different perceptions that rearrange energetic information. One believes it can achieve and the other does not which reveals itself by giving in. Manchester United football teams under their manager Alex Ferguson were famous for scoring late goals to win games. It became known as scoring in 'Fergie time' and many put this down to 'luck'. It wasn't. There is no such thing as 'luck', only creating your own reality. I am not talking about believing conceptually. Just saying it is not enough. It is a *knowing* that impacts on the field more than anything else. A football manager like Ferguson who refuses to accept defeat no matter if the game is almost over can infuse that same mentality into his players who then collectively make it manifest. The greatest football managers are less the best tacticians and far more the best psychologists and/or most able to infuse their own determined personality into their team. Again and again, you see a manager fired by a club for poor results and replaced by someone who has almost immediate success with the same players. The players have not got better overnight. Their mentality – *perception* – has.

The eddy mentality

The manipulators know this and if they can implant your perception of reality they can – through *you* – dictate your experience of reality. I was not kidding over the years when I said that perception is the stadium in which the whole conspiracy is played. They are manipulating the population to build their own prison by telling them what that prison is going to be. Predictive programming is all part of this as is the belief that something is 'inevitable'. This is why it is vital that those who warn about the Cult agenda make it clear that it doesn't *have* to happen. A change of mass perception can still prevent the extremes of what is planned, but it is going to take now a colossal awakening. That's why the fake 'alternative' media has been created to block a *true* awakening to infinite self-identity and hold the focus of more aware people on Left v

Right politics. The realisation that politics, finance, government and wars etc., are manipulated is only the first stage. Perception dictates the 'plasticity' rewiring in the brain. The firing of the neural networks changes as perception changes while the old networks go on processing reality in the same way if perception stays the same. We call this a 'closed mind'. You become an eddy in the river going round and round while the river of potential awareness and insight flows past. This arranges the quantum energetic fabric to deliver perception as a feedback looped experience. Nothing changes.

The brain is targeted (through 'education', media, peer pressure) because that is the computer that processes information/awareness from the auric field (mind) into conscious perception. The Mind delivers perceptions to the brain, and it processes them into conscious awareness and action. The idea is to firewall the brain as you firewall a computer to stop it processing thoughts that the Archontic Cult doesn't want you to think and ponder. Nanotech that infiltrates the brain is designed to do this and can become a permanent inability to break the 'eddy' sequence once AI is connected. You think what AI thinks. The result is to turn humans into automatons and zombies – mere computer terminals on someone else's Internet. Additives in food and drink, pharmaceutical drugs, and the technological electromagnetic field are all working on the brain to limit its range of information processing. A firewalled brain filters perception as a firewalled computer limits what you can access. But consciousness is more powerful than any of them and if you allow it to flow by removing all perceptual limitations it can blast these firewalls into oblivion. The potentially unstoppable power of consciousness can be seen in the extraordinary lengths to which the Archontic goes to suppress and redirect it. You have:

- The Life Program running through the biological computer. This must be overridden by consciousness, or it will dictate your life and make you in effect a Non-Player Character controlled by the program.
- Astral influences seeking to misdirect you including possession at its most extreme.
- Life-long perceptual programming through Archontically controlled 'education' and media.
- Peer pressure from others who have downloaded the program and believe it to be the way things are – the 'real world'.
- Food, drink and electromagnetic sources to suppress brain processing.
- Nanotech infused through vaccines, fake vaccines, food and chemtrails that also target the brain and the decoding of reality.

There will be others we don't even know about. That's quite a list that we must overcome, but we *can*. They are only simulation (by definition low-level) blocks. They must be multiple in nature when consciousness has such power to manifest its own reality instead of the one the Archontics *depend* upon us having. They are terrified that we will realise this, and their control system will be dismantled by humanity *ceasing to create it*! If you need confirmation that we can still head off the dystopia, look no further than we are *creating it* with our manipulated perceptions, and we can therefore *un*create it.

The real 'awake'

What is this true awakening which the Archontics and its Cult assets are terrified will happen? People talk about being 'awake' when no human is 'awake'. To claim to be means they are missing the point. We are an expression of infinity – the Infinite – but we are subject to all those constant and calculated efforts to subjugate and limit. We are observing a 'world' through the systematic and myopic lens of visible light. To be 'awake' to infinity in such circumstances is not possible without a redefining of reality on a scale that is hard to even imagine. What we are – *if* we are – is awaken*ing*. It's a process of deprogramming. Our true state is of being awake to infinity. What diverts us from this awareness are the layers of programming, like skins of an onion, which involve the veil of forgetfulness, Soul programming in the Astral (go back to pay your 'karma'), and the mega programming of 'human'. I see so many who perceive themselves as 'awake' when they realise the political and financial level of manipulation and conspiracy. This is where the fake 'alternative' media – or 'MAGA media' – is designed to keep them. Religion does the same to limit your sense of self and power. Put the two together with the Christian Right 'alternative' media and they've *really* got you.

I have quoted many times the words attributed to the ancient Greek philosopher Socrates. There are various forms of what he is claimed to have said such as 'wisdom is knowing how little we know' and 'To know is to know you know nothing'. Another is: 'I know nothing except the fact of my ignorance.' Given that we are in a reality specifically designed to maintain ignorance this is a very good place to start. It means we retain the essential humility that whatever we think we know there is always more to know. This is the perception that keeps you out of the eddy. You are aware that any eddy is the illusion of knowing all we need to know. 'I've got it now' means you haven't. You may have some of it, but there's *always* more to know. Always. Physicist Werner Heisenberg said: 'Only a few know, how much one must know to know how little one knows.' This book extends across a huge spectrum and yet there will be far, far, more to become aware of as our minds open and explore ever deeper in the infinity of awareness. Psychiatrist Iain McGilchrist, who has studied the left-brain's desperation for certainty, said:

> I would also like to get in a word for uncertainty. In the field of religion there are dogmatists of no-faith as there are of faith, and both seem to me closer to one another than those who try to keep the door open to the possibility of something beyond the customary ways in which we think, but which we would have to find, painstakingly, for ourselves.
>
> Certainty is the greatest of all illusions: whatever kind of fundamentalism it may underwrite, that of religion or science, it is what the ancients meant by hubris. The only certainty, it seems to me, is that those who believe they are certainly right are certainly wrong.

Humility is sadly missing from the invaded 'alternative' which is why they have focused on the myopia of Trump as the 'saviour-god' and Jesus as the saviour deity. They want certainty. It also helps to limit the Mind if that very limitation is the source of your often massive income. American author Upton Sinclair said: 'It is difficult to get a man to understand something, when his salary depends on his not understanding it.' This is true across the board and certainly the case with the massive income levels of the fake 'alternative stars'. Ironically, they will be dropped like a stone by those they promote when they are no longer considered useful.

Who is this *you?*

What is the biggest cause of the problem? It is *self-identity*. Of all the manipulations of perception this is the numero uno from which all others follow. What you think you are you will be. Self-identify as a human and the labels of human and you create that limitation from your belief in limitation. Man, woman, race, religion, income, sexuality, are only *experiences* called 'human' (Fig 233). Self-identify as a Soul subordinate to the demands of a judgemental 'God' (authority) and you will manifest a reality – individually and collectively – that will make you subordinate to other expressions of authority. The subordinate frequency creates

Figure 233: Self-identity with the labels of human – as an I and not just an experience – condemns you to follow the programs of the Matrix.

subordinate experience. But there's more. We are part of Infinite Reality with limitless potential and possibility. The simulation is designed to hijack perception in a trap of limitation – *sense* of limitation and impotence. They want you to be perceptually *in* the simulation and *of* the simulation (while not even aware there *is* a simulation). Talk about mind control, blimey. I mean by 'in' that your perception and access to information and insight is limited to the simulation field that is feeding you your sense of reality and especially your sense of who you are – *self-identity*. I am a man, woman, and my race, religion, income bracket, life story, when these are but brief experiences for your *consciousness*.

This sense of limitation is expressed in the limitation of potential and possibility that you tap into. The extent of the field and levels of frequency that you access is limited *only* by the range of consciousness you *choose* to access. Put simply – a closed mind interacts with limited possibility in the field and an open mind connects with an expanded range of possibility. The difference between the two is once again self-identity. If you identify only as 'human' then you will interact only with the strictly limited human field of possibility or energetic density. Identify with subordination to a 'God' and you may access the Astral levels of the simulation and worship Yaldabaoth in disguise. Identify as a Soul constantly reincarnating to 'learn lessons' and simulated Astral reality will be the best you can do. But identify as a boundless Spirit – pure disembodied awareness – and a point of attention within infinite attention and you expand ever further into the infinity of potential, possibility, insight, awareness, that reunites your connection to the Divine Spark and *All That is, Has Been, And Ever Can Be*. Self-identity dictates awareness. Limited self-identity = limited awareness. Expanded self-identity = expanded awareness. What is awareness? Perception. What is self-identity? Perception of self. Perception interacts with potential and possibility to manifest an experience of itself. You are what you think you are and in the self-identification with Spirit – *know* you are. Morpheus in *The Matrix* was in a training fight with Neo that was happening purely in the Mind through a software program. He says:

> What are you waiting for? You're faster than this. Don't think you are, know you are. Come on. Stop trying to hit me and hit me.

This is an important distinction. The difference between thinking and knowing. Thought is limited to concepts. You can think of yourself as a boundless Spirit and infinity having a brief experience called 'human'. This is a start, but your impact on the field and levels of awareness you access will still be conceptual and remain in the simulated realm of thought where you *think* and *hope* and *try*. The next stage is to *know* that is who you are, and you enter the infinite realm where you *know* and just *do*. It is no longer an external concept. It is a *being* in which your True 'I' Spirit is fully integrated. You are not connected to 'it'. You *are* 'it'. You don't interact with the field. You *are* the field. You don't think you are infinity – you *know* you are. A state of trying manifests an experience of trying and not necessarily achieving. A state of hope means what you hope for is always in the illusory future. That is what hope is. What you want becomes a can constantly kicked down the street.

Centipede syndrome

These are different stages of awakening, and this final one is necessary to release yourself from the simulation. Your perceptions have kept you here and your perceptions can set you free. When you *know* you are *All That Is* there are no Archons that can entrap you. They are impotent and can only control from their sense of limitation by holding you in an even more myopic sense of limitation. In the Kingdom of the Blind the one-eyed man is king. You know how to walk. You don't think about it. You just do it because you know. The trouble can start when you think about it. A 19th century poem, *The Centipede's Dilemma*, gave its name to a psychological state known as the 'centipede effect' or 'centipede syndrome' which is when, as an example of what I am saying, a *knowing* becomes a *thinking*. The centipede with all its legs did not think about walking. It just did it. It just knew. When it thought about how it walked the centipede couldn't walk any more.

Once you *know* you are infinity you *live* as infinity. There are no 'connections' to the Infinite. All is one seamless whole. There is no point where you start and end. You are everything *and* nothing – all possibility. You are *already* infinite. That is your natural state. It is the layers of perceptual programming running through the body and Soul that keep people from that realisation because it focuses attention on the human and Astral realities of the simulation. *You* are not trapped in the Matrix – your perception, your self-identity, are. Redefine your self-identity from body and Soul to Infinite Spirit, a formless state of being aware, and the perceptual programs begin to fade. You see deeper and deeper into infinite reality as this process unfolds and cross the *perceptual* borders of the simulation into insights and awareness that expose the illusion you have been believing is real. Your body may be in the simulation, but the span of your consciousness is not. Dots connect because in the Infinite Realms there are no dots, only one seamless whole. The simulation is the same because it's a bad copy of the seamless whole. The difference is the way the Archontic force presents the deception of separation and apartness. Suddenly you see what you could not see before as the scales of delusion fall from your eyes. This is the real awakening that Yaldabaoth and the Archons work so hard to prevent. They know their game is over when it does. You realise as your consciousness expands that we don't all live in the same world we perceive as human. Our bodies may be anchored in the same band of frequency, but the potential spans of consciousness stretch from Little Me to Infinite Me.

The old saying goes that insanity is doing the same thing over and over again and expecting different results. We can now find confirmation of that in quantum reality. If you believe there is nothing you can do, you will manifest circumstances to confirm there is nothing you can do. I can't do it means you won't do it. I'll try to do it means I will never actually do it. To believe it's impossible means that it is. Someone will always control us means they will. I have no power means you don't. I am powerful means you are. How long we have been incessantly programmed to believe negative statements about ourselves. From birth and by the hour since then through 'education', media and society in general. This is systematic to infuse the perception of 'I can't' which leads to a manifest reality of 'I don't'. We need to strip away those life-long programs and reactions and start again in the knowledge that we are what we believe we are or even better *know* we are. What if our negative programs were so ingrained with repetition that we reach a state of *negative* knowing? We *know* we are powerless and impotent. What kind of life would that bring into manifest experience? Look around at the human family and you'll see because that's where so many are coming from. Self-fulfilling feedback loop quantum 'prophecies' constantly confirm the quantum prophecies that further ingrain the quantum prophecies until you just *know* the quantum prophecies are true. 'I *know* it's true from long experience of the same thing happening to me over and over.'

Naivety – the human disease

Let us apply all this to the collective and conspiracies like the world wars, 9/11, the Kennedy assassination, 'Covid', and endless others that the Cult has visited upon humanity. The Cult and its agents have a cover story prepared and waiting for when the deed is done. Immediately they set the perceptual agenda when the official story is unleashed and repeated in every direction to solidify the narrative. Lee Harvey Oswald shot Kennedy with bullets that did U-turns; Arab hijackers banned through incompetence from flying one-engine planes did fantastic manoeuvres with passenger jets; a fake vaccine must be mandated protection from a virus that's never been shown to exist. It doesn't seem to matter how ludicrous the stories are. The great majority still believe them when to mainstream TV watchers and newspaper readers that's all they have heard. Everyone around them seems to believe the same so it must be true, but they are *also* mainstream TV watchers and newspaper readers forming their perceptions from the same source.

I used to be bewildered as a kid when I watched greyhound racing on the television from time to time at why the dogs never grasped the trickery. For those not familiar with the greyhound sport some background is needed. A fake mechanical hare is sent around the track at speed while the dogs are kept in 'traps' or little cages at the start line. The gates open when the hare passes, and the greyhounds fly out in pursuit. They keep running until the finish line when the hare is slowed down to a stop. The dogs then catch up with the hare and surround it. Sorry lads, it's not real. We tricked you. Okay, I get it so far. But then the dogs are taken to the next track and the next and every time they chase a fake hare, see that it's fake, and then chase it again believing that this time it's real. People may think the dogs are a bit stupid, but then they will believe the fake stories from officialdom about world events and even if they are eventually shown *not to be true* they will still believe the next one!

Repetition of the official story is all you need to ingrain a belief that the ridiculous is true. The narrative goes out in the immediate aftermath. This is repeated by news organisations across the world and then re-repeated by the watchers and readers. Soon the same narrative is everywhere embedded in the collective psyche which then encodes it en masse in the field to which humans are connected through the five senses. Now the field is awash with waveform information repeating the official story and the population is bombarded with the same version of events from government, media, simulation field, and later through the 'education' system in the form of official 'history'. Schools teaching what happened on September 11th will be repeating the official narrative a quarter of a century later even though independent research has demolished its whole premise.

Add to this the censorship by the mainstream media, social media and these days by elements of the 'alternative' media and you can appreciate why so many believe complete nonsense. Perception that the official story is true will manifest experienced confirmation of the bullshit through people you attract and news stories that you see. They will operate within their own perceptual bubbles and echo chambers without ever knowing that what they believe without question is fundamentally flawed and has been shown to be so. Cause and effect, cause and effect, cause and effect. Another crucial form of censorship that few acknowledge is 'Astral shadow banning'. This is the Archontic manipulation of the simulation field to block expansive information from circulating through the field. Silent censorship you could say.

Humans in general have been programmed to love their official stories, and they defend them from challenge. 'History' and experience shows us that authority lies – constantly – and yet so many have a reflex action aversion to anyone exposing this. They defend official narratives from proven liars rather than check the facts that reveal the deceit. The foundation of this response is a terror of facing reality. They are seeking out comfort and solace in a scary world. They want to believe that authority is benevolent and like a kind mum and dad who only want the best for us. The State is our protector. To accept that mum and dad are psychopathic liars and satanists, serving the beast you know as Satan, is just too much to bear and face. Most can't handle that and defend the State sometimes with their lives. 'They' would never do that! Oh, they *would*, and they'd love it. There are even different versions of the State that mean some will question the 'Deep State' and support the anti-Deep State when both are the State (Cult) wearing different clothes and talking from different sides of their mouth.

Another vital part of a true awakening is to know that authority *lies* irrespective of 'Left' or 'Right' or the name on the door. We don't accept what they say is true and later see that it wasn't. We start with the premise that they are lying. We investigate why and to what end and refuse to cooperate with the lies and the reason for them. The odd occasion when we see that they are telling the truth is a bonus. Everything I am saying is about taking responsibility. Our perceptions create reality and a refusal to investigate or check what we are told to believe is a refusal to take responsibility for what those perceptions are. They then interact as frequencies with the field and rearrange energy to become manifest as 'someone else's fault' that we again refuse to take responsibility for. Questioning authority is not a here and there; it is an every time. It's how – or one major reason how – we keep control of our perceptions rather than allow others to tell us what they should be. It is how we maintain control of our experienced reality.

Seeing through the drama

The transformation from human me to infinite me includes withdrawing from the manufactured drama. This is big-time vital. The Archontic needs us to hold our attention in the five senses to avoid the expansive pondering that elevates our consciousness into the Infinite Realms. The major way they do this is to consume our attention with drama. This could be anything from family dramas to Donald Trump dramas to world wars. Human reality is a tidal wave of dramas for this reason – plus all the loosh they generate. Drama also invariably means divide and rule conflict at all levels which allow the manipulators to prevail by setting the population at war with itself. We fight each other over politics, religion, race, and culture while they go about their business of control without effective challenge. We must learn to live together despite our disagreements and focus on the threat to the freedom of all. They want us to be offended by others having another opinion when being offended is simply a choice. Someone does not offend you. That is not the dynamic. You *choose* to be offended which is not the same thing. Your reaction does not come from what is said to you. It comes from you responding by being offended. Choose not to be. People have a right to another opinion even if we think it is wrong and misguided. We can end the drama by refusing to take offence. We can counter with a different view, but it is being offended that leads to (a) drama, (b) divide and rule, and (c) people being silenced for 'causing offence' (Fig 234). I have been ridiculed and abused since 1991, but I refuse to take offence. It only gives the abusers what they want for a start. We are bigger than that – or can *choose* to be (Fig 235).

Figure 234: Taking offence is a choice and you can choose not to.

Figure 235: Another choice.

Drama elicits the whole range of emotions from shock to horror to fear to hatred and together they bring emotional upheaval and disturbance – loosh. All benefit the Archontic, not least the way they focus attention on the world of 'human'. You find as you transform self-identity from human to Spirit that you more and more withdraw from the drama. You step back from emotional attachment to the drama and become more the observer. You can note a situation or event without the emotional rush that you had before. It's not that you become unfeeling. It's that you put the drama in perspective. Am I getting distraught over something that I can't change? If so, what is the point of emotional upheaval when I am not in a position to impact on what has happened? Is it really as bad as it seems or could it be resolved calmly without emotional drama. How many times do people go into emotional overload for something that's sorted in minutes or days? You were in a terrible state the last time I saw you – what happened? Oh, it was nothing, it got sorted okay. All that loosh and drama was for no reason then?

Some are addicted to drama through addiction to the chemicals produced by emotional reaction. We call them 'drama queens' who constantly experience dramas because perception becomes reality. If there is not a drama, they will have to invent one while at the same time feeling a victim for all the constant drama in their life which *they* are unknowingly creating and blaming others for. Chaotic perceptions are projected as chaotic frequencies that manifest chaos and drama wherever they go. Observer consciousness does not get pulled into drama. It knows that the world is a manipulated illusion to keep us entrapped and that drama is essential to the entrapment. It observes the world calmly and responds calmly because it is at least one step back from emotional reaction which stops you thinking straight anyway. Shit happens. It is what it is. You deal with it without the emotional drama that isn't necessary. I have found that if you respond calmly when children fall over and make no big deal about it then mostly neither do they. React as if it's a terrible drama and they burst into tears. They are distraught because they think it *is* a big deal when you have made it so. Emotion is encoded in the body computer specifically to generate loosh. Spirit feels without the emotional theatrics. I find I am able to deal with often highly negative events in the world in my work while staying emotionally detached. You do what you can to make a difference without being emotionally drained. Of course you can still get pulled in at times, but you are conscious of your response and can withdraw from the drama immediately. Emotional upheaval would be justified if it made a difference, but it doesn't. It just creates emotional turmoil for no benefit. Spirit doesn't need emotion to be motivated. It's Spirit's natural state.

Doing what is right

This brings me to another key trait of awakening to Spirit. You do what you believe to be right no matter what. It doesn't mean you go looking for trouble for the sake of it. You seek to avoid that, but not at the expense of doing what you believe to be right. There is no listing of all potential consequences to the point where you choose to run and hide. To consider potential consequences is to consider not doing what you believe to be right and Spirit consciousness will never do that. It knows the consequences are all part of the simulated illusion and there is nothing to fear except what we can be manipulated to fear. It knows that the consequences are far greater if we don't do what we believe to be right. That's how we got here. It knows that perceptions create reality and fear of consequences can become consequences while lack of fear can stop them manifesting. We have to choose how badly we want to make a difference to our own lives and the collective. A little bit, or with every fibre of being. Morpheus was right again in *The Matrix*: 'Neo, sooner or later, you're going to realise – just as I did – there's a difference between knowing the path and walking the path.' I see social media log-in pseudonyms making their comments seeking to undermine those who are actually *doing it* while they hide behind their anonymity doing *nothing*. Such people are among the most spellbound of all – lost in their own sense of superiority while contributing not at all to the greater good.

This is the human plight – *spellbound*. A spell has been cast on their minds and Soul that keeps them in the trance essential to Archontic control. The trance is the death stare on human freedom and infinite freedom. And yet, and yet, that which has induced the trance is not all powerful. They are a bunch of prats which some ancients knew were the foolish ones. How stupid do you have to be to act as they do? To need to feed off the suffering of others? To get high on the sacrifice of children? I can think of nothing more pathetic than Yaldabaoth consciousness and its Archontic emanations of the same mentality. We are supposed to fear lunatics like this? Not a chance. They have my sympathy. It must be an ongoing nightmare to be that pathetic. They are frightened little boys and girls terrified of being exposed for what they are – moronic tricksters who can only prevail by diminishing their targets and turning them into a fraction of what they should be. To dominate not by your own power, but by negating the power of others and feeding off their energy has got to inspire the coining of a new word. Pathetic will simply not suffice.

What are we doing being imprisoned by such non-entities and nonsense? The answer is ours to decide because they feed off us, not we them. They need us, not we them. Their power is *our* power recycled. Our perceptions become our reality, and we must take back control of our minds, our self-identity, and remember the infinite magnitude of who we really are. As we remember, we expand into infinite reconnection. The age of perceptual separation would be over. We must see how the Archontic system works against us and end the essential divide and rule by ceasing to impose our beliefs on others. Be at peace with another having a different opinion, lifestyle, or belief so long as they don't seek to force it on anyone else. All this is a big ask when humanity exists in such a childlike twilight of programmed perception and behaviour, but awakening can be fast once the dam is breached. You realise what a lie and delusion we have been living while believing it to be 'real'. At the very least we can understand what happens when we leave the body at illusory 'death' and exit the Matrix when the moment comes to bypass the Archontic Wheel of Samsara. You'll find much about that in my Reality Trilogy, *The Trap*, *The Dream* and *The Reveal*.

We hold all the aces. We have simply been kidded that others do. We have been playing poker with a deck rigged against us using calculated ignorance. But we know more now. I trust this book has played a part in deleting that ignorance.

That was, after all, the point (and the solution).

CHAPTER 28

Final Thought

I regard consciousness as fundamental.
I regard matter as a derivative of consciousness.
Max Planck

I want to end by emphasising the theme that both enslaves humanity in simulated servitude and offers the means to return to Eternity. This theme is that our perceptions dictate our experienced reality. People say they want a 'solution'. Well, here it is.

We are not even returning to Eternity. We are already there. We never left. We can't leave when we *are* eternal. We are *All That Is, Has Been, And Ever Can Be*. That level of us is not entrapped. Our *perceptions* are. The perceptions of that expression of us that is caught in the simulated maze of reincarnated illusion. Nor is what I am saying really a 'solution'. It is removing the cause of the problem. Our perceptions are not ours. The eternal ours. They are a downloaded sense of reality and self-identity not least through 'education', 'media' and scientific oppression specifically designed to sync our perceptual frequency with the Trap. Removing the cause is to take them back. To be the True 'I' again.

Thought and emotion – together 'perception' – rearrange energy in the quantum field beyond 'matter' to create what we experience in the realm of (illusory) 'matter'. I mean our 'success' and 'failure'. Our ability and inability to manifest what we want. The opportunities we grasp or spurn. I mean the people we attract and repel. All are creations of our conscious and especially subconscious mind where 95 percent of human behaviour originates. The instant emotional reactions. The beliefs. Everything from road rage to following a religion only because that's all we ever heard in the formative years when our perceptions of self and reality were being consciously and subconsciously moulded. They become 'us'. The fake 'us'. The Phantom Self on which our *attention* is fixed and myopia secured (Fig 236 overleaf). Funding for scientists that seek to publicly explore these connections, this feedback loop between perception and experience, are suppressed while the cultists privately fund their own research and methods of manifestation. Why does anyone think they 'succeed' in their goals, their focus of attention, and most of the rest do not? How can there be scarcity when scarcity and

Figure 236: Phantom Self – the perceptual identity bubble.

abundance are perceptual states made manifest? Most of the population is programmed to believe in scarcity and limitation and their subsequent experience confirms that – what you believe you perceive and what you perceive you experience.

The cultists know that their perceptions become their reality, and they make the feedback loop work for them. The population are isolated from this knowledge and have their reality dictated by the cultists through the manipulation of their perceptions. The human world in two sentences. Cultists are trained in these techniques as they are passed on through the generations. Journalist Napoleon Hill interviewed more than 500 self-made millionaires over a span of 20 years which led to the 1937 book, *Think and Grow Rich*. The principles he identified are why some succeed in creating what they want and most don't. Crucially you need to *know* what you want. 'I dunno, really' will manifest as 'I dunno, really'. The principles apply to everything you wish to manifest and the 'grow rich' is just a metaphor for self-creation overall. These are some of the common themes that he observed: You have to want it; believe that you can achieve it; use affirmations (attention focus); visualise your success; organised planning (organised thoughts); defeat procrastination with decisiveness; persistence; master positivity and dismiss negative emotions; trust your gut or 'sixth sense' (intuition). Resistance is treated as a challenge, not an obstacle, and either ignored by focus or treated as feedback information. All of those relate to perception through thought, emotion and imagination. There were other practical aspects such as surrounding yourself with 'smart people', but they are an expression of your perceptions anyway. What Napoleon Hill identified as common themes was described in the Internet video documentary, *Reality Is Not Physical – Top Physicist's Shocking Revelation*:

> Figures like Rockefeller, Ford, and Edison revealed surprisingly similar practices. Systematic visualisation. Structured auto suggestion, and connection with what they called infinite intelligence. The concept of the mastermind emerged from these investigations not as a poetic metaphor, but as an observable phenomenon.

Final Thought

> When multiple consciousnesses align around a common goal, an amplified field of possibilities emerges. Hill documented cases where ideas considered impossible materialised through this collective resonance.

These claims are supported by quantum physics. Divide and rule is not only about division into opposing factions. It is about separating consciousness into different belief systems to prevent a unified focus of perception that would collectively transform reality. Some of Hill's findings were excluded from book versions released publicly which included society's 'big-hitters' going into altered states of consciousness to solve problems. Don't let the people know or they might use the knowledge to create another reality. Dismiss in public settings what you are doing privately. English physicist Isaac Newton's 'laws of physics' laid out in his *Philosophiæ Naturalis Principia Mathematica* (Mathematical Principles of Natural Philosophy) in 1687, like Charles Darwin's *Origin of the Species* in 1859, diverted understanding from perception = reality into belief in a clockwork universe and humans as mere byproducts of 'evolution' that cease to exist when the body expires. I say this was calculated from the Cult perspective. Newton studied the esoteric and must have realised how consciousness cannot be separated from matter. Charles Darwin was a secret society insider from a very 'occult' connected family.

Subconscious 'life'

How do you know how your subconscious is programmed? Observe your life. There you go. It's all on public display. If perception becomes reality, then your reality must mirror perception. Your life tells you what programs are running your subconscious. Is your life as you want it to be? Do you attract supportive friends or needy ones? Those that give or those that take? Those that nurture or those that exploit? It's not they who are to 'blame'. They are who they are, what they are, for now. It is your perceptual field that attracted them into your reality. Those who are experiencing the process of awakening from the programs will know how old acquaintances drift away and new ones emerge while interactions with the unawakening can dramatically change in terms of family relationships and so on. As you change, your *perceptions* change, this must be. Former relationships of all kinds must change as your perceptions of self and reality do. You can't attract possibilities you don't consciously and subconsciously believe in. Life changes because *you* change. Frequencies you broadcast change and what they magnetically attract and manifest do the same. I have long called this vibrational magnetism. Little Me becomes Little Me life. Infinite Me becomes Infinite Me life. I can't becomes I don't. I can becomes I do. Chaotic thought becomes chaotic life. I bet you know someone just like that. We

Figure 237: What you are, you will be. (Image by Gareth Icke.)

Figure 238: 'Little Me.' (Image by Neil Hague.)

all do. Calmness within becomes calmness without (Fig 237). We are so much greater – infinitely greater – than we believe ourselves to be (Fig 238).

Sporting performance alone could be transformed by these realisations. We speak of 'physical' performance when there is no 'physical'. It is all *psychological* performance – perception creating reality. You can also see why the level of support from a watching crowd or TV audience can affect the outcome. Random number technology has been shown to be affected by collective perceptual reaction to a major event. 'Physical' illness is treated through 'physical' means when illness (energetic imbalance) cannot manifest without the passive agreement of the Mind, or even the active participation. Fear of illness becomes experienced illness. Hypochondria can become a self-fulfilling prophecy. The Mind is the source of imbalance and by definition the Mind can heal. What is the placebo effect except belief made manifest?

Psychiatrist Carl Jung's concept of 'archetypes' is highly relevant here. Archetypes are described as 'innate patterns of thought and behaviour that strive for realisation' to create a sense of identity. Jung listed twelve. I add brief descriptions, but there is more to them than this: The innocent (purity and optimism); the orphan (fearing being left out or standing out); the hero (seeks to prove worth through courageous acts); the caregiver (desires to protect and care for others); the explorer (wants freedom and fears being trapped); the rebel (seeks revolution or change); the lover (wants connection and fears rejection); the creator (the artist in multiple forms who fears mediocrity); the jester (seeks joy and laughter, fears boredom); the sage (strives for truth and knowledge); the magician (promotes societal advancement); the ruler (wants to control and fears being usurped). These recurring patterns of thought and perception relate to the body programs because universal awareness cannot be categorised this way. It is all-possibility and not limited possibility. These psychological patterns are self-identities or feedback loops between patterns and experience. What we think we are we will be. Thus, the perception of a martyr is likely to be martyred. This can be literal in the sense of killed for a belief or cause or constantly put upon and exploited. The point is to move beyond archetypal patterns of behaviour by moving beyond patterns of limited self-identity into infinite possibility. AI algorithms can identify and manipulate psychological and behaviour patterns, but they can't deal with infinite possibility.

Quite simply: The quantum field is possibility and potential while perception decides what possibility and potential we bring into 'material' manifestation. This is the 'collapse of the wave function' from wave form into particle form – quantum possibility into 'matter' experience. This applies within or beyond the simulation which is a 'bad copy' of Prime Reality and must operate on the same principle. It's just that the Archontic force in all its levels does not want us to know that. The feedback loop is instead exploited by the Archontic to dictate human and Soul perception to manifest their reality aided by the biological Life Programs running through the body which only consciousness can overcome. The sequence of control goes like this: *Sense* of reality triggers a cycle of perception = reality = confirmation of perception = entrenched reality = more confirmation of perception = even more entrenched reality ad infinitum until the cycle is broken. We all have unique perceptions and therefore a unique frequency signature even if in some it is only marginally so. The idea is to use AI to create universal human frequency signatures which would create a universal created reality. AI/human fusion is really about using *us* to manifest the world the Archontic wants to create.

Figure 239: The connection to All That Is.

But the 'problem' is the

'solution' and removing the cause of the 'problem'. What controls us can set us free if we use it another way and awaken to the True 'I' (Fig 239 on previous page). Everyone who awakens to this knowledge and begins to express it in their lives is moving us closer to a critical mass that will overturn the Archontic control system by manifesting a different reality. This transformation of awareness is infused into the simulation field to weaken its message of limitation and oppression. If 'They' don't control our perception they cannot control our experience. The Archontic is now in a race to deliver AI perception before enough awaken to critical mass. Even then we can influence our own lives this way. So, what am I saying as we conclude (for now) our road map, our Handbook for Life? Simple:

'THEY' don't control your destiny.
YOU do.

Postscript

I'm afraid, based on my own experience, that fascism will come to America in the name of national security.
Jim Garrison, JFK assassination investigator

I have said in recent books that I felt the lower levels of the Astral dimension where the feeding frenzy of human energy is so focused was being fused or connected more deeply into the human realm of dense materialism.

This has become ever more obvious to me as I have observed world events like the genocide in Gaza and never more so since the arrival of the 'Covid' fake vaccine. It's like the demonic has secured even more access to the human mind to deliver perception and no doubt the gathering global technological electromagnetic 'hive mind' field is already playing its part. This can have a positive expression in that to the truly awakening mind the contrast between expanding awareness and Archontically-controlled perceptual oppression has never been more blatant. It makes the manipulation much easier to see for those awake enough. But, of course, the negative aspects of this 'fusion' are put before us every day as the world gets more extreme and, well, insane and possessed by the Archontic Astral.

Perhaps in the light of events more can appreciate why I have been vehement in my exposure of the Cult hijack of the 'alternative' media. The hijack has regressed the 'alternative' from knowledge of the One-Party State back into the Us v Them 'Left'/'Right' illusion designed to set the population against each other on the basis of rigid and solidified political ideology with the flames fuelled by the religious divide of Christian v Muslim. I have watched with horror as 'alternative Christian influencers' like Alex Jones have transformed from system *exposers* into system *servers* who now insist that the 'Deep State' is the 'Left' or the Democrats in the US. For sure he and many like him are now promoting what they once said they stood against. The speed of this oppositional collapse has been stupendously quick since the Trump second term Psyop and even more so since the appalling murder of Trump's mega supporter Charlie Kirk who did so much to get him elected in November 2024. The Cult agenda demands civil war worldwide and this is the foundation reason for promoting the extremes of Wokism and opening the borders of Europe and America to unchecked – indeed governmentally encouraged – mass immigration with much of it illegal. The idea was to push society so far in one direction working through the 'Left' that a corrective pushback was certain to follow working through the 'Right'. The key is to understand that the *same force* that manipulated the 'Left' into Wokism also manipulated the 'Right' into its inevitable response. The result was divide and rule.

The murder of 31-year-old Charlie Kirk at the Utah Valley University in Orem on September 10th, 2025, one day before the 9/11 anniversary, was a massive catalyst for this Left v Right Psyop. Kirk launched Turning Point USA in 2012 when he was just 18 with Conservative activist Bill Montgomery and it became the dominant force in promoting Christian Conservatism in American colleges and universities. Kirk and Turning Point were acknowledged by Trump as a major reason he won the 2024 election through directing youth votes his way. He became a close associate of Trump and his son Donald Trump Jr, and he was a very prominent voice in the MAGA movement. He worked with Trump's son during the 2016 election campaign. Kirk was speaking and debating in Utah as part of 'The American Comeback Tour' before an outdoor audience of some 3,000 when he was shot dead, officially from long range. Others disagree. They say the bullet came from Kirk's right and not as officialdom claims from a shooter on a roof straight ahead. This right-side scenario says the bullet wound seen on videos plastered across the Internet was the exit, not entry, wound. Still others dispute this. We'll see what the weeks and months bring from here.

Keystone Kop FBI

The FBI investigation was led by Trump sycophants Kash Patel and Dan Bongino who told us they would release the Epstein files and then didn't. They said there was no evidence that Epstein trafficked girls to anyone despite what the girls involved have said. These are the people asking us to believe them about anything. Patel claimed 'historic' credit for arresting 22-year-old Utah man Tyler Robinson which happened, as Patel emphasised at a news conference, 33 hours after the murder. But FBI competence was not the reason. Robinson was reported to have been handed to police by his father after images of the alleged shooter wearing sunglasses were circulated and two others had been apprehended in the immediate aftermath that turned out not to be responsible. Patel even announced they had arrested the alleged killer in one case when it wasn't true. 'The subject for the horrific shooting today that took the life of Charlie Kirk is now in custody', Patel posted. These were all unnecessary diversions.

A figure on the roof of a building overlooking the Kirk event had been noted by 'passers-by' before the shooting and later surveillance camera footage emerged of someone wearing a backpack running across the roof before jumping to the ground and hurrying from the scene. Patel said DNA on a towel around the gun and a screwdriver found on the roof matched with Robinson. Before anyone accepts the FBI narrative as the whole story, we should remember that the FBI history of lying and setting people up is legendary – 9/11 is a prime example, but there are so many others. Question everything and remember that mind control techniques can not only program people to carry out assassinations. They can put people in the right place at the right time (from the Cult's perspective) when others do the deed. Mind control can even make the fall guy believe that he *did* do it. Once you have control of someone before or after the event anything becomes possible. Robinson was raised as a Mormon and Utah/Salt Lake City is the centre of Mormonism worldwide. I know from my own experience of visiting the place and talking to Mormon whistleblowers from the 1990s that Utah is a major centre for mind control and Satanism. Mormonism has major connections to Zionism and ties to the CIA. Mormons speak of the creation of Zion and accept biblical prophecies of Judaism and Zionism about the rebuilding of the Third Temple. Early creators of the Mormon Church, Joseph Smith, his brother Hyrum, and Brigham Young were all Freemasons with its fundamental links to Sabbateanism.

I am writing this some months before the book is released with printing and shipping across the world still to come and there is no point in reacting in detail to the various opinions at this stage about who shot Charlie Kirk when so many things will have happened and new revelations forthcoming before you read this. I want to instead highlight the reactions of the MAGA and the 'Left' to the killing because they are very telling. You can see in the immediate aftermath of an assassination or attack like 9/11 what the official story is designed to be by the emphasis and direction that government and media takes the narrative. Long experience of these events tells us that the story we are first given is almost never what turns out to be the truth and the FBI specialises in such deceit in league with other government agencies answering to the Cult. You can add the MAGA media in the case of Trump when that has become even more relevant than the mainstream. The 'legacy media' as the mainstream is now called still takes the official story from politicians and law enforcement and repeats it without much, often even any, question; but the MAGA media is now the one to watch most of all while Trump/Vance and the billionaire oligarchs are in power. These major 'influencers' made it very clear the line the Trump regime was taking when all blame was directed at the 'Left' and the Democrats. Alex Jones and the rest of the mob were out of the blocks immediately with their 'violent Woke transgender killer' narrative which was obviously being fed from within the regime and its law enforcement network.

The Wall Street Journal, followed by other media, reported that Kirk's alleged murderer was using bullets with writing on them relating to 'transgender ideology'. The report was based on information from the Bureau of Alcohol, Tobacco, Firearms and Explosives (ATF) that was centrally involved in the bombing blamed on 'domestic terrorism' at the Alfred P. Murrah Federal Building in Oklahoma City in 1995 which killed 168 people. The 'transgender' information was leaked by a source to 'alternative' podcaster Steven Crowder, then repeated by Alex Jones, Donald Trump Jr and others. 'All cartridges have engraved wording on them, expressing transgender and anti-fascist ideology', the ATF document said. The chosen 'villain' is made clear as early as possible to infuse public perception during the period of emotional response and it sets the theme from then on. This is why Osama bin Laden's name was mentioned soon after the Twin Towers were hit on 9/11 when those attacks were nothing to do with him (see *The Trigger*). Governor Spencer Cox announced that anti-fascist writing was found on ammunition used by the killer and Donald Trump Jr posted as the official story circulated: 'Now you are reading about trans paraphernalia written on the cartridges of this rifle ... it is an absolute sickness.' Then came *The Wall Street Journal* rollback which said that the bulletin from the ATF 'may not accurately reflect the messages on the ammunition'.

Keep them guessing

Another telltale sign of misdirection in these cases is the number of conflicting and contradicting stories that are circulated to confuse. We were told that Tyler Robinson came from a Republican family in St George, Utah, with his father and relatives MAGA-minded supporters of Trump. His parents were registered Republicans while Tyler Robinson was not aligned to any party and had not voted in the two previous elections. Robinson's grandmother Debbie insisted that they came from a family of MAGA Trump supporters, and her grandson had 'never, ever spoke politics to me at all' or had 'never, ever gotten in trouble in his life'. I was surprised to hear this MAGA angle because the 'trans' information would not have been leaked as the perceptual direction if that was to be discredited at the first base. Then all made sense when officials said that Robinson shared a home with a man in the process of transgender transition. The story was back on track – it was a 'trans hate' killing by the 'Left' which suited the agenda perfectly. Alex Jones couldn't stop telling us so.

Patel also announced that the FBI found evidence of a 'chilling note' Robinson allegedly wrote before the shooting. Patel said: 'He claimed that he had an opportunity to take out Charlie Kirk and he was going to do it because of his hatred for what Charlie stood for.' The note was claimed to have been found at the home where Robinson and his transgender partner lived but had since been destroyed. How did they

Postscript

know it existed then? Patel said the note was recovered with 'forensic evidence' and that investigators 'confirmed what that note said because of our aggressive interview posture at the FBI'. What is that supposed to mean? Officials then released alleged text messages between Robinson and partner Lance Twiggs which were widely ridiculed for being obviously scripted and not at all the text language/grammar of a 22-year-old. 'Robinson' admits in the texts to the killing which is the last thing you would do if you wanted to avoid arrest, and you would surely know the exchange would be recoverable. The texts say he has 'left no evidence'! 'He' also mentions hiding his rifle and hoping to retrieve it and this was the gun by the time of the text release that the FBI said had been found in a wood wrapped in a towel. The texts describe 'engraving bullets' and basically confirm the story being sold by the authorities in nothing like the usual text language. The crime scene was dismantled immediately and not protected while cameras behind Kirk were removed with footage we have not seen publicly at the time of writing. What a coincidence that before the shooting Kash Patel *fired* the head of the FBI's Salt Lake City field office in Utah who former agents called 'absolutely the best in the bureau' and 'a legendary case agent involved in the biggest national security cases of the last two decades'. She would have been leading the investigation if Patel had not fired her just before.

Then there was that rifle. Camera footage emerged of a man on the roof alleged to be the killer who climbed down to the ground and hurried away. He didn't have an obvious rifle and it was claimed it was disassembled in his backpack. Gun experts pointed out that this rifle type was not easy to take apart and would have taken some minutes. Therefore, we were asked to believe that he shot Kirk, stayed there while disassembling the rifle, put it in his backpack, ran across the roof and down to the ground, before going to the 'wood' and *reassembling* the rifle only to leave it there. 'He' was also allegedly filmed on the way to the campus wearing a purple t-shirt and light shorts which he must have changed according to the official story into the black shirt and dark trousers that the figure wore on the roof and CCTV images. In fact, they said he changed clothes *twice*. We were told that he was wearing the same clothes allegedly caught on camera when arrested 33 hours later so he was obviously doing everything he could not to be caught and identified! These early versions of the official story aimed at blaming a 'lone gunmen' connected to a transgender partner or a trans network with no other involvement by any other source had more holes than a sieve factory.

Lying history of the FBI

I have been on this journey of discovery since 1990, seen it, done it, and researched it, and there is no way I will believe anything the FBI says without serious corroborating evidence. It's been a pillar of the 'Deep State' (Cult) since it was created as the Bureau of Investigation (BOI) in 1908 and even more so with the reign of the unbelievably corrupt, J. Edgar Hoover, who was head of the BOI and its successor the FBI from 1924 to 1972. Hoover oversaw the investigations (set-ups) into the assassinations of President Kennedy, Bobby Kennedy, Malcolm X and Martin Luther King in the 1960s. This led to at least Lee Harvey Oswald, Sirhan Sirhan, and James Earl Ray being named as the killers when the evidence said otherwise (see *And The Truth Shall Set You Free*). I have no doubt there are many genuine FBI agents who do seek out the truth, but the Bureau's controlling hierarchy is there to serve the Cult. That must always be remembered, especially with so many 'terrorist' attacks and operations being orchestrated by FBI assets which they then claim credit for 'stopping'. No way the FBI under Trump is anything other than more of the same.

I am not saying that there was not a transgender and 'Left' connection to the death of Charlie Kirk because at this stage as I write the evidence is still being compiled and questioned by those who do not accept the official story. I will say, however, that whatever the involvement we must widen our vision of possibility in search of the ultimate villains who never put themselves on public display. Utah Republican Governor Spencer Cox said early on that there was no evidence of any other participants with Tyler Robinson (for whom the authorities demanded the death penalty). It was the usual 'lone gunmen' story reflecting the claims about Lee Harvey Oswald, Sirhan Sirhan, and James Earl Ray. I would not be surprised to see in this case claims of a wider 'trans/Left' network because that suits the intent of the Trump regime as a Problem-Reaction-Solution to viciously target political opponents on the road to all-out tyranny. Troops were already in the streets and free speech targeted. Clearly that was only the start, and they needed more excuses to finish the job. Let's say that blaming the killing of Kirk on the 'Left' fitted this agenda.

Seeing through the smokescreens

You can read these events by knowing what the agenda is, observing how that can be advanced by what has happened, and then seeing what actions are taken by the authorities in response to the event. I knew pretty much immediately that 'Covid' was a con by seeing the potential it would have for massively advancing the Cult plan for dystopia and mass vaccination. It was the same with September 11th which is why I began investigating that official story immediately for *Alice in Wonderland and the World Trade Center Disaster* (2002) and later in fine detail *The Trigger* (2019). The Trump regime and its MAGA media revealed from day one what the narrative was going to be with Charlie

Kirk – the 'evil Left did it'. I am not saying that some aspect of the 'Left' was not involved because it is too early to know that precisely. But what does this 'Left' connect with? The same Cult force that also works through the 'Right'. Just because the 'Left' may be at the point of the arrow does not mean that it ultimately orchestrated the arrow to be *fired*.

Alex Jones and the usual suspects screamed from the start that the 'Left' and 'anti-fascist' group Antifa etc. did it and, of course, there is a violent element to them as there are violent elements on the 'Right'. The Trump regime responded by saying that Antifa would be designated a 'terrorist organisation' (with others to follow) as Keir Starmer has in the UK with Palestine Action. The point is that to see the game you have to go beyond 'Left' and 'Right' to that level of the Global Cult that works through *both* of them. This is the level that plays off 'Left' against 'Right' and sets them at war with each other while the same force is pulling the strings of both 'sides'. Trump is controlled by this force as are the 'Left' and Antifa. One creates the problem for which the other provides the 'solution' that advances the Cult agenda to an ever more dystopian society. At the Cult level the 'Left' provides the 'solution' to the 'Right' when it is in power and vice versa when the 'Right' is in power as currently with Trump/Vance. This is why we have troops on the streets in America and gathering totalitarianism thanks to the 'Right' while civil liberties and freedoms are being targeted in the UK by a government claiming to be 'Left'. Trump targets the 'Left' while Starmer targets the 'Right' and both serve the interests of the Cult agenda for global dystopia. This is what the Alex Jones' don't get – on the Right *and* Left – and play their essential role in dividing so the Cult can rule while largely having no idea (being optimistic) that both political polarities are being played by the same force. This is why we have to go beyond constant emotional reaction and calmly see how the game works. If we don't understand the game and how it manipulates perception and emotion, then the game will go on playing us. That's the *real* Wake-Up – not the fake one.

It's okay when WE do it

There can be no more obvious confirmation of what I say here than the response of the MAGA media and the Trump regime to the Kirk murder. Alex 'I'm always right' (he's *not*) Jones was out of the traps like a greyhound chasing a hare spewing his hatred for the 'Left', but he was far from alone. Others like Trump associate Laura Loomer, a big critic of Kirk who she described as behaving like a 'charlatan', was vitriolic in her finger pointing at the 'Left'. Vacuous Attorney General Pam 'what Epstein files?' Bondi was immediately signposting the direction of travel along with Trump and his ultra-Zionist handler (with Lutnick), Stephen Miller. Bondi said:

There's free speech and there's hate speech and there's no place [for hate speech] especially after what happened to Charlie in our society. We will absolutely target you, go after you, if you are targeting anyone with hate speech.

She could have been a Woker talking in the Biden regime and even many MAGA were shocked by what she said. Charlie Kirk criticised hate speech as a nonsense concept. He once posted:

Hate speech does not exist legally in America. There's ugly speech. There's gross speech. There's evil speech. And ALL of it is protected by the First Amendment. Keep America free.

What Bondi said was everything that Trump and Trumpers railed against when out of power. Trump had said in his inauguration speech: 'I will also sign an executive order to immediately stop all government censorship and bring back free speech to America.' JD Vance said in February 2025: 'And under Donald Trump's leadership, we may disagree with your views, but we will fight to defend your right to offer it in the public square, agree or disagree.' Professional liars the both of them. Then there was ultra-Zionist Homeland Security advisor and White House deputy chief of staff for policy, Stephen Miller, in his response to Kirk's death. 'RICO' is the Racketeer Influenced and Corrupt Organizations Act:

Under President Trump's leadership, it's going to be a RICO charge, a conspiracy charge, conspiracy against the United States, insurrection, but we are going to do what it takes to dismantle the organisations and the entities that are fomenting riots, that are doxing, that are committing acts of terrorism, that are committing acts of wanton violence.

It has to stop and my message is to all the domestic terrorists in this country spreading this evil hate [delivered as always with hate on his face], we will not live in fear, but you will live in exile, because the power of law enforcement under President Trump's leadership will be used to find you, will be used to take away your money, take away your power, and if you have broken the law to take away your freedom.

A classic case of Problem-Reaction-Solution. He talked about 'doxing' (publishing private or identifying information on the internet with malicious intent). At the same time MAGA cultists were celebrating how they had a long stream of people sacked from their jobs for cheering, being indifferent or having another opinion about the death of Charlie

Kirk – the same process that MAGA rightly condemned when Wokers had them fired for the 'wrong opinion'. Vice-President Peter Thiel-owned JD Vance publicly encouraged calling employers to get people fired. Disney-owned ABC indefinitely suspended the TV show of Trump critic Jimmy Kimmel because of a comment about the MAGA movement and Tyler Robinson after criticism from Trump censor and Musk friend Brendan Carr at the Federal Communications Commission (FCC) that oversees broadcasting licences. An enormous public backlash had Disney saying they would reinstate Kimmel a week later. Trump's intent, however, was clear. I am seriously not a fan of Kimmel or the earlier cancelled Trump critic Stephen Colbert, but both were dropped because snowflake Trump didn't like them, and he was far from finished in his tyrannical deletion of his opponents. Meanwhile, pro-Trump Fox News presenter Brian Kilmeade said on air that the homeless could be given an 'involuntary lethal injection' to kill them, but kept his job. Alex Jones once condemned the 'Left's' use of the term 'domestic terrorists' to demonise the 'Right', but, like Miller, was quite happy to use it against the 'Left'. Jones called for doors to be 'kicked down'. The hypocrisy and selective morality were beyond belief. Donald Trump used an Oval Office address to fan the flames that suited his masters' agenda:

> Violence and murder are the tragic consequences of demonising those with which you disagree day after day, year after year, in the most hateful and despicable way possible [Trump could have been talking about himself]. For years those on the radical Left have compared wonderful Americans like Charlie Kirk to Nazis and the world's worst kind of mass murderers and criminals.
>
> My administration will find each and every one of those that contributed to this atrocity and other political violence including the organisations that fund it and support it, including those that go after our judges, law enforcement officials, and everyone else who brings order to our country. Radical Left violence has hurt too many innocent people and taken too many lives.
>
> Tonight, I ask all Americans to commit themselves to the values on which Charlie Kirk lived and died – the values of free speech, citizenship, the rule of law and the patriotic devotion and love of God.

Only someone as shameless as Trump could condemn 'going after our judges' when he had been doing exactly that; promote the free speech he was destroying; and the 'rule of law' that he was constantly breaking to impose his tyranny. He said the problem was the Left calling those on the Right 'Nazis' and videos followed of Trump doing exactly that to the Left. All these members of the Trump regime made the planned direction very clear. This was an opportunity to rout any opposition that threatened their total power. Elon Musk posted that 'the Left is the party of murder' (what *all* of them?) and then appeared on video screen at a London protest about immigration a few days later to say: 'If they won't leave us in peace, then our choice is fight or die.' Given that the Cult wants civil war across the world to divide and rule while they install the final AI dystopia you can see how the death of Charlie Kirk played into that. Trump could as always depend on his sycophants to fill the Internet with propaganda as they condemned violence by promoting it. This was the little boy in short trousers, Andrew 'hard man' Tate, talking about Tyler Robinson:

> Now he's been apprehended he should be interviewed publicly. The name of every inspiration that comes out of his mouth when we ask him what he believes what he did about Charlie, all of the left-wing media, all of the left-wing influencers, all of his friends, all of those who told him bad things about Charlie, they are all in a RICO case and they all go to jail.

> He is then thrown in a cell and the only way he can get food in this barren landscape is to carve the word 'sorry' into his own skin with a knife. Eventually when he's run out of skin to carve, we are going to line him up and shoot him in the fucking neck. If anyone at home has a problem with this, I will take the shot myself.

To think this deeply sad man has had such an influence on so many young males. Tragic. Amazing how they mirror what they claim to oppose. Another MAGA bloke posted an Internet video saying:

> This is no longer Left versus Right. This is good versus evil. If you [President Trump] ask for a civil war, the Conservative veterans in this country will take our country back from the evil Left – Nazis who have destroyed our country, who mutilate our children, who rape our children, who coddle paedophiles … what we do here will echo around the world … Mr President, I implore you, call for a civil war. Let us go door to door, street by street, and clean this country … we are all Charlie Kirk.

Trump super-sycophant 'influencer' Nick Sortor said of Tyler Robinson: 'He needs to be found guilty and shot in the middle of the town square under the Trump administration – that way it's done, and it needs to be quick.' Killing is wrong so we need to kill him ASAP with no other questions asked. It's barely one-dimensional. A Trump Presidential Memorandum issued in the wake of the shooting headed 'Countering Domestic Terrorism and Organized Political Violence' (NSPM-7) listed the following 'common threads animating this violent conduct': Anti-

Americanism, anti-capitalism, and anti-Christianity; support for the overthrow of the United States Government; extremism on migration, race, and gender; and hostility towards those who hold traditional American views on family, religion, and morality. None of these are defined and in short it declares war on anyone with a different view to the Trump tyranny.

Bible mind

Charlie Kirk also supported capital punishment on the basis that killers must be killed, but if we are not bigger than the killers then how can we believe we are any better? His 'tooth for a tooth' mentality came from his slavish belief that the Bible is the word of God and, although he could not tell you who wrote the texts, he believed we must live life according to what they say. His support for capital punishment came from the Old Testament: 'Why did God say to do it five times in all five books of the Bible [the Torah] – this is not man's law, this is God's decree. If you take a life your life shall be taken.' No, Charlie, this is the law that suited those who oversaw the writing of the Old Testament thousands of years ago. Kirk also said:

> My other problem with the death penalty – it takes too long, too many appeals. It should be public. It should be quick. It should be televised … [You could have it] 'brought to you by Coca-Cola'. I'm not kidding.

My own view is that Charlie Kirk was a deeply misguided man, but another aspect of Kirk's murder was to turn him into a religious figure, deify him, and make him a martyr for freedom. He who cannot be criticised. Sorry, but I'm not having that. No one should be subjected to violence for a different opinion and what happened to him with two small children is appalling. That said there was very little I agreed with him about and what I observed was a man with a mind utterly captured by the Bible with little capacity to think beyond it. I can't say I liked what I saw. He said this about Israel:

> When I went to Israel I came into contact with the living God that walked on water and rose Lazurus from the dead. When I went to Israel, I saw the Bible come to life … I saw Abraham, Isaac, Jacob, Sarah, Rebecca and Leah in the Hall of Patriarchs. I said this is the Word of God. This is real. These are not fairy tales or fables or things we tell our kids.

> When I went to Israel, I was able to cry where Jesus cried. [Where] he was betrayed by Judas and arrested. Where he rose from the dead and gives us eternal life … Paul said you will bless the Jews. If you bless Israel, you'll be blessed, if you scorn Israel, you will be scorned. There is a diabolical Satanic

agenda every single day to try and delegitimise the Scriptures and I will defend the Holy Land, the place that let me see where my Lord and Saviour lived, and I will not apologise for that.

I think you will understand why I disagree. His often-vehement views about gays, transgender, Muslims, and 'the Left' were rigidly biblical while my own very non-biblical view is that people should live their lives as they choose – *so long as they don't seek to impose their beliefs and lifestyle on others against their will or through perceptual manipulation.* I have no problem with a bloke calling himself a woman and wearing a dress so long as others are not expected to act as if he is a woman even if they believe otherwise. People losing their livelihoods for using the 'wrong' pronouns is insane but believe what you like so long as you don't expect me to believe what you do. The same Old Testament obsession led Kirk to say that wives should 'submit to their husbands'. He said of singer Taylor Swift's engagement: 'Submit to your husband, Taylor. You're not in charge.'

Kirk was reported to be paid some $400,000 a year by Turning Point USA and yet argued against children getting a free school lunch. 'The parents should feed their children, not the government', he said. He was asked: 'What if they can't?' Then they should 'go get a job', Kirk replied. What if the minimum wage is so low that even with a job they can't? 'You are so dumb, dude', came the answer. Kirk said: 'Show me a single child in America going hungry – doesn't exist.' He condemned Martin Luther King as 'awful' after once calling him a 'hero' and said the Civil Rights Act of 1964 that ended racial segregation in America was a 'huge mistake'. He absolutely had a right to his opinion, but you can see why many didn't care for his views – which is their right so long as violence is not involved. He said that he used to say if you as a gay person went to Gaza they would throw you off a tall building. 'Now they don't have any tall buildings left', he said with a grin amid laughter and applause from his audience. Charlie Kirk was no saint as the MAGA is making out and you can condemn his killing without agreeing with his world view. I am not saying that he was a horrible person in every way, some speak highly of him, only that he was no saint to be deified because it suits Trump and the MAGA.

The Israel-did-it theory

Kirk once said that his ideas and arguments came from reading, watching or listening to Jordan Peterson and ultra-Zionist radio hosts Dennis Prager and Ben Shapiro. I can't think of three people I would look to less for 'ideas and arguments'. All three are vehement supporters of Benjamin Netanyahu and Turning Point attracted support from mega-rich Jewish donors with its annual budget of some $80 million a year and more than 600 employees. Kirk acknowledged the critical role of ultra-Zionist David Horowitz of the David Horowitz Freedom Center who also had a pivotal influence on the career of Candace Owens as well as Ben Shapiro and Trump 'advisor' Stephen Miller. Kirk posted when Horowitz died in April, 2025:

> Without David Horowitz, I'm not sure Turning Point USA would exist. Over 90% of our earliest major donors were introduced at a David Horowitz event – thanks to his warm endorsements and generous introductions. His support opened doors that would have otherwise remained closed.

But Kirk's views on Israel's actions in Gaza were beginning to change in the weeks before the shooting according to reports circulating in its wake. This led to suspicion that Israel was involved in his demise. Kirk was a passionate advocate of Israel as you would expect from someone fundamentally steeped in the Bible mentality, but some close to him have said that his views on the Netanyahu government were being changed by the ever-gathering and systematic mass murder – genocide – in Gaza. Some even said he 'despised' Netanyahu. He certainly began to criticise the actions of Netanyahu's government and even earlier said the lack of Israeli military response to the Hamas breaches of the border fence on October 7th made no sense:

> I've been to that Gaza border. You cannot go ten feet without running into a 19-year-old with an AR-15 or automatic machine gun that's an IDF soldier. The whole country is surveilled ... was there a stand-down order? Six hours? I don't believe it.

> Israel is the size of New Jersey. When I took a helicopter ride from Jerusalem to the Gaza border it's 45 minutes. They're live-streaming the killing of Jews. Did someone in the government say 'stand-down'. That is a legitimate non-conspiracy question.

Kirk further began to criticise the influence of Israel within the United States political system (absolutely massive in scale) and the Jewish funding of organisations seeking unchecked immigration: 'Jewish donors have been the number one funding mechanism of radical, open-border neoliberal quasi-Marxist policies, cultural institutions and non-profits.' Yes, and they also fund the 'Right' that opposes all that. Divide and rule. Reports suggested that the mega-Jewish donors of Turning Point were not happy and sought to rein him in and bring him back into line. They were seriously unimpressed with him inviting speakers to Turning Point events who criticised Israel. Kirk is said to have warned Trump against bombing Iran on Israel's behalf, but that Trump 'barked at him' and angrily shut down the conversation which confirmed to Kirk that Trump was controlled by Netanyahu. All this was a big deal to Netanyahu and his fellow psychopaths. Turning Point had long been funded by wealthy Jewish donors with its influence among the Christian young on campuses across America that included 3,500 campus 'chapters'. If Israel lost the Christian Zionists in the United States its power would seriously wane. The whole point of promoting Christianity was to make an Old-New Testament connection with Israel and secure Christian support for its agenda. Reports emerged after his death of a 'sustained private campaign of intimidation' against Kirk by the 'free-floating fury' of wealthy and powerful allies of Netanyahu.

It was said that he was afraid of them and others said Kirk had told them privately that he feared being killed by Israel if he turned against them. Conservative commentator, Harrison H. Smith, had posted in August: 'I'm not gonna name names, but I was told by someone close to Charlie Kirk that Charlie thinks Israel will kill him if he turns against them.' Friends said Netanyahu offered Kirk vast amounts of money for Turning Point and invited him to Jerusalem, but he turned him down. All this added to claims that Israel was behind Kirk's murder and immediately after the shooting Netanyahu used the social and broadcast media to contend that Kirk was a staunch supporter of Israel and insisted that Israel had no role in his killing. If you believe in the relevance of symbolism note that the spot where Charlie Kirk died looked like the Jewish menorah (Fig 1) and he died wearing a white t-shirt bearing the single word 'Freedom' meaning in the language of symbolism that freedom was killed in public. A 71-year-old Jewish man in the crowd who immediately shouted 'I did it' told police that he tried to help the suspected gunman escape by faking a confession, authorities

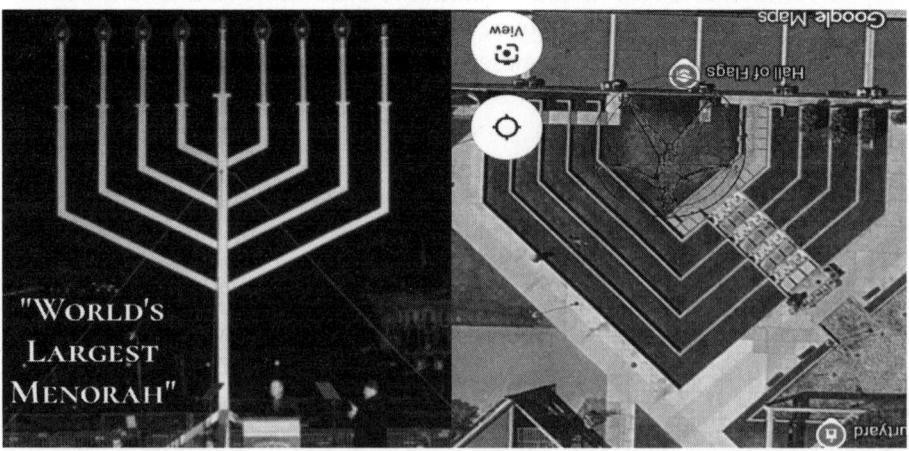

Figure 1: The remarkable similarity between the spot where Charlie Kirk was murdered and the symbol of the menorah.

say. Utah County Sheriff Michael Smith said George Zinn admitted to police that he had 'yelled that he was the shooter to allow the actual suspect to flee'.

Mossad signature?

Such an attack would certainly fit the Mossad/IDF modus operandi. The US *60 Minutes* programme talked with two 'former' Mossad agents who were involved in the pager attacks on Hezbollah in Lebanon in September 2024 when thousands of handheld pagers and hundreds of walkie-talkies exploded simultaneously. The Lebanese government said the attack killed 42 and injured 4,000 civilians. One of the Mossad agents told *60 Minutes* how they tricked Hezbollah into buying the devices:

> We have an incredible array of possibilities of creating foreign companies that have no way of being tracked back to Israel. Shell companies over shell companies who affect the supply chain to our favour.
>
> We create a pretend world. We are a global production company. We write the screenplay. We're the directors. We're the producers. We're the main actors. The world is our stage.

This is what Mossad Case Officer Victor Ostrovsky described in his books *By Way of Deception* and *The Other Side of Deception* which I read a long time ago. Could Israel have done it? Absolutely, but whether they did, or the evidence that they did, may never be known. You might know more when you read this. What is worth remembering in all these situations is that the official story over and over invariably turns out to be a diversion to hide the real orchestrators. Who has looked in any depth at the assassination of President Kennedy in 1963 and still thinks it was done by 'lone gunman' Lee Harvey Oswald? It was an enormous, interconnected, compartmentalised operation and Oswald was the fall-guy 'patsy'. Even if the actual killer is identified you have to work back from them through the layers upon layers of Russian dolls and into the shadows from where it all originated. Israel, Mossad and the IDF are experts at hiding that. Ultra-Zionist Ben Shapiro (Kirk's last podcast interview) announced within 24 hours of Kirk's death that he would be embarking on his own campus speaking tour: 'We're gonna pick up that blood-stained microphone where Charlie left it.' Shapiro also pledged a million-dollar donation from his Zionist-funded *Daily Wire* to Turning Point USA. It's hardly a prophecy to expect Turning Point to now become even more pro-Israel and a guy being promoted as I write, 'Charlie Kirk's heir apparent', Brilyn Hollyhand, is exactly that.

Elon's back!

An enormous memorial event to Charlie Kirk at the State Farm Stadium, in Glendale, Arizona, was organised eleven days after his murder which seems amazingly quick for an event so big that went on for hours. Trump and his entire cabinet attended with political speeches from Trump, Vance, Miller and Hegseth (but not family members apart from his widow who bought the official story and 'forgave' Tyler Robinson who was still awaiting trial). It was turned into a political and religious rally, the latter to generate biblical support for Israel, the 'End Times', 'Last Days', and belief in the imminent 'return of Jesus'. As someone posted:

> It was mass conditioning through weaponized faith, with death repackaged as a 'turning point'. A 10-hour stadium revival stitched together from nationalism, the glorification of military enlistment and biblical martyrdom. This is the machine.

It certainly had that feel about it as a flags and crosses MAGA hyper-fest of propaganda that less exalted and more exploited him and what happened. Elon Musk also attended, and it seemed to be the point where the public feud with Trump (whatever the real background) was ended. They were filmed greeting each other and Trump's White House X page posted a picture of them with the message that they were back together 'For Charlie' (Fig 2). Musk reposted it and added his own: 'Forgive us our trespasses as we forgive those who trespass against us.' Ironic when the last bit is clearly not the case with himself or Trump. The gang was back in public or so it appeared. Musk said the

Figure 2: The White House posted this 'back together' image of Musk and Trump at the Charlie Kirk memorial with the message: 'POTUS x @ElonMusk – For Charlie.'

Epstein files were not being released because Trump was in them, but let's forget all that 'for Charlie' who was demanding they be made public. Yep, makes sense, right? Except that a few days later documents released by Epstein's estate to congressional investigators appeared to show contact between Epstein and both Musk and Peter Thiel. Epstein's itinerary includes a possible trip by Musk to Epstein's island on December 6th, 2014, with a note saying 'is this still happening?' Also included were 'lunch with Peter Thiel' on November 27th, 2017, a tentative 'breakfast party' with Bill Gates on December 5th, 2014, and breakfast with former Trump strategist Steve Bannon on February 16th, 2019. An Epstein jet manifest includes Prince Andrew and his bodyguard. Epstein became a convicted sex offender in *2008* and was added to the national sex offender registry.

Constant confirmation

These are some other updates that continue the themes laid out in the book:

- Dr Sucharit Bhakdi, a world-renowned immunologist and critic of the 'Covid' fake vaccines, said that 'billions' of 'Covid'-vaccinated now have 'altered brains' through 'systemic vasculitis' which is a multi-organ inflammation of the blood vessel lining that is damaging brains, hearts, and other organs on a mass scale. Bhakdi said this was causing neurological damage which leads to diminished willpower, critical thinking, and the ability to resist control. This is exactly what the Cult designed the fake vaccines to do. Other studies confirm this outcome along with brain damage leading to homicide, homicidal tendencies, schizophrenia, psychosis, Alzheimer's, cognitive impairment and violent behaviour. Klaus Schwab said as head of the World Economic Forum in 2022: 'We have to prepare for a more angry world.' I wonder how he knew?? Trump and 'health chief' Robert Kennedy held an Oval Office news conference to eulogise Zionist Pfizer chief Albert Bourla. Trump said he 'has done a fantastic job with Covid' while Kennedy said: 'He really created a template for corporate responsibility, for putting public health ahead of his individual interests.' They have no shame.

- The UK government of Cult gofer Keir Starmer announced the imposition of a digital ID system long warned about in my books without which no one can work in the UK (with so many more restrictions to follow). It is a crucial part of the AI-digital dystopia and has been promoted for years by Starmer mentor, the war criminal Tony Blair. It was Blair who instigated mass unchecked immigration as prime minister and Blair Cult subordinate Starmer used the excuse of illegal immigration to justify the digital ID which together with a digital currency will delete freedom. Problem-Reaction-Solution. Blair and Starmer are members of the Fabian Society with its logo of a wolf in sheep's clothing. It was founded in London in 1884 and named after Roman statesman Quintus Fabius Maximus Verrucosus (about 280-203 BC) who specialised in wars of attrition rather than decisive battles – exactly the strategy of the Fabians. The consequences of the digital ID, with its planned global introduction, can be seen in Vietnam which deleted or froze 86 million 'unverified' bank accounts. Everyone must surrender their biometric data to maintain a bank account which is how they plan to force it on people worldwide.

- It was announced during Trump's 'state visit' to the UK in September 2025 that US tech companies would be investing £150 billion in the UK. The plan was dubbed the 'Tech Prosperity Deal', but it was really the AI and quantum computer tech dystopia being brought to Britain by the usual suspects doing the same in the US. Speaking of tech – an investigation revealed that an Israeli app called AppCloud is installed on Samsung smartphones which users cannot uninstall. The app was developed by IronSource of Tel Aviv. As one article said: 'Not only does AppCloud silently harvest user data, but its ties to an Israeli firm raise serious legal and ethical questions …' Netanyahu bragged to a Republican and Democrat delegation that if they had a cell phone they were holding 'a piece of Israel'. How come such a tiny country can be everywhere?

- The United States government under Joe Biden threatened to ban China-owned TikTok in the country unless ownership of the US segment was handed to US investors and Trump pledged to 'save it' in a wonderful example of the One-Party State at work. Well, well, guess who moved in to take over US TikTok? Ultra-Zionist Trump ally Larry Ellison, the multi-billionaire co-founder of tech firm Oracle whose son was allowed by Trump and FCC gofer and Musk associate Brendan Carr to buy Paramount and CBS News. Reports as I write say the Ellisons are ready to acquire Warner Bros. Discovery, Inc (WBD) which owns HBO, Warner Bros. Studios, and CNN. A credible democracy would block the concentration of such media power, but Trump couldn't care less about freedom when he's owned by Israel and seeks to transform 'Left'-leaning media organisations into promotors of him. Israel-centric Zionists are being allowed to buy the mainstream media while having serious influence with the fake 'alternative' and driving the wider censorship agenda, not least through claims of 'antisemitism' which really means we won't let you criticise Israel and Zionist (Sabbatean) influence around the world.

- TikTok prepared for what is to come by appointing ultra-Zionist Erica Mindel, a former IDF soldier, to monitor 'hate speech'. Mindel was a US State Department contractor who worked for Deborah Lipstadt, the special envoy to monitor and combat antisemitism. This was after two years with the American Jewish Committee (AJC) as its assistant director of programme development. Mindel's TikTok role is 'spearheading long-term policy strategies' regarding hate speech, monitoring online content, advocating for the company's policy stances, 'serving as a subject matter expert on antisemitism and hate speech in internal and external meetings', 'analysing hate speech trends' and 'focusing on antisemitic content'. You can only laugh at the brazen nature of it and Nostradamus won't be needed to predict where this is going.

At the same time Trump was signposting the deployment of troops in ever more American cities and had a military flotilla off Venezuela sinking boats while claiming, without bothering with the evidence, that they were targeting drug trafficking. Alex Jones who once condemned 'regime change wars' said: 'I'll say it – I am for removing the Venezuelan dictatorship!' Venezuela is at the southern end of the Musk grandfather 'Technate' which extends to Greenland in the north. Trump is talking of the most extreme censorship that would withdraw licences from broadcast media companies that criticise him 'unfairly'. Potential federal employees are told to prove their 'enthusiasm' for Trump's (the Cult's) agenda including a description of when they had their 'MAGA revelation'. This while humanity is set at war with itself through the well tested – and essential – technique of divide and rule.

When will we learn and see that we're all being manipulated by the same force? There are none more stupid than those who control humans except the humans that allow them to do it. United we stand, divided we fall, was never more appropriate.

Index

A

Abraham (Abram) 197, 307, 317–19
accelerationism 403–5, 408–11
Adelson, Miriam 203–4, 213
Adelson, Sheldon 202, 203–4, 213, 398
Aeons
  Lower Aeons 28, 31, 35, 103, 109
  Upper Aeons 28–33, 35, 103, 109
  Yaldabaoth 28–35, 103, 109
Akashic Records 138–40, 455, 463
AI 178, 221–2, 425, 489 see also artificial intelligence (AI)-human fusion; Big Tech/AI tech
    oligarchy
algorithms 184, 244, 373, 431–4, 445, 461, 487, 521
all-possibility (potentiality) 18–22, 29, 32, 37, 47–8, 84–5, 235, 277, 282, 521
all-seeing eye 21–2, 114–15, 196, 251–3, 255, 340–1
All That Is, Has Been, And Ever Can Be 18–20, 27, 44, 509–10, 517
alternative media/New Media, control of 156, 391, 427–44, 505–6
  AI-human fusion 427, 436–7, 440, 444
  algorithms and funding, stars as promoted by xix, 431–4
  Big Tech/AI tech oligarchy 45, 160
  Central Bank Digital Currencies (CBDCs) 482
  Christian right 26, 43, 360–1, 438–9, 441, 507
  Covid-19 170, 241, 427, 434–

6, 439, 441, 443, 472
  funding 441–3
  Global Cult xix–xx, 170, 199, 224, 427–44
  left-brain (closed mind) 235
  MAGA 427–30, 437–43, 507
  mega-corporations, owned by 241–2
  Musk 427–9, 431–2, 438–40, 444
  perception 235, 512
  pushbackers 366, 368–9, 370, 425, 427–8, 434, 437
  reptilians 224, 433
  Rumble video platform 436–7, 438, 440, 443, 483
  simulation/Matrix 45
  surveillance 165
  Thiel 428, 434, 440
  Trump 232, 377, 391, 427–32, 437–40, 443–4, 508
  Universal Basic Income (UBI) 165
Altman, Sam 146, 165, 203, 409, 473, 488, 494–5
Amazon 177, 245–6, 248–9, 411, 435, 450
Ancient Greece 26, 97–8
Andreessen, Marc 176, 184, 361, 371, 409, 428, 434, 473, 481, 488–9, 503
Anduril 186–8, 407
Andrew, Prince 387–8
Anti-Defamation League (ADL) 209, 244, 397–8
anti-Semitism 190, 197, 203, 207–8, 212, 246, 398, 430
Anunnaki see
    Elohim/Anunnaki
archaeological evidence of religion 309–13, 315, 317, 319–20, 336–7, 354, 356–7, 359
archetypes 30, 130, 520–1
Archons/demons 87–108, 164,

166–8, 171–2, 189, 222, 514
  see also loosh; under particular
  main entries
  ancient cultures 23–4, 87, 95, 108
  Archon, definition of 29
  body program 101–2
  chaos, forces of 89, 99, 426
  DUMBS 89–90
  five-sense awareness 497, 513
  gods, agents of the 96–8, 107–8, 183
  hierarchies 93–4, 96, 98, 172, 349
  hive mind 446, 458
  male and female, as a fusion of 98
  normality 239
  number of Archons 102–3
  other names, under 97–9
  possession of humans 99–100, 102, 120
  royal bloodlines 91, 104–7
  Saturn 253–84
  Schism inversion 99–101
  separation 28, 464, 510
  seven, significance of number 102–3
  shapeshifting 87, 98, 107–8, 166
  Spider's web 166–8, 180
  trance, being in a 516
  Wetiko (mind virus) 99–102
  Yaldabaoth 87–8, 91, 98–101, 109, 11–12, 218, 497, 510–11
artificial intelligence (AI)-human fusion 38, 159, 163, 180, 250, 352–3, 357, 445–96
  see also **Big Tech/AI tech oligarchy** loki2
  accelerationism 404, 409–10
  Agentic AI 487–8

Index

algorithms 184, 521
alternative media 427, 436–7, 440, 444
Archons/demons 89, 95, 366, 449, 472, 479, 506, 521–2
artificial general intelligence (AGI) 448
Astral AI Mind program 127, 129–30, 134–5, 143
Big Tech/AI tech oligarchy 408–11, 422–5
censorship 165, 184
China 476–9, 489
Cloud Infrastructure 181, 457, 474–5, 488
Covid-19 fake vaccines 447, 451, 457–60
data centres, energy needed by 412, 485
deepfakes 489–90
education 165, 236
employment, end of 485, 486
Fourth Industrial Revolution 178
genetic manipulation 464
government and corporate administration 487–8
graphene 452, 456, 458
hive mind 164, 218, 446–8, 452, 493
human contact, eliminating 491–2
hyrogel interface 457–60
inevitability as tool of perceptual manipulation 448–9
Israel 218, 479–80
left-brain (closed mind) 236
loosh 114, 458
low-orbit satellites 411, 449–50
mind control 227
Musk 186, 246, 372–3, 449, 473–5, 486–8
sceptic, as 369, 372, 427, 449
Tesla robots 477
Trump xix, 369–70, 402, 406, 408–11, 422–5, 449
nanotechnology 165, 506
non-player characters (NPCs) 133, 506
Oracle 165, 370–1, 473–5, 479
perception 427, 445–6, 451, 456, 460, 464, 495
political left and right xix, 170, 449
reptilians 93, 96, 479
simulation/Matrix 72, 140
Stargate Project 146, 203, 473
surveillance 188–9
takeover, by 448–9, 486–8
technological singularity 448–9
Thiel 473–4
Trump 165, 186, 188–9, 366–71, 401, 473–6, 485
Action Plan 475–6
czar 176, 203, 414, 437, 440, 476, 482
Musk xix, 369–70, 402, 406, 408–11, 422–5, 449
Wokery 366–9
World Economic Forum (WEF) 176, 488
Yaldabaoth 109, 218, 472, 495–6
artificial wombs 494–5
assassination attempt on Trump 362, 376–9, 402–3, 406
Astral realm see Fourth Dimension (4-D) (Astral)
Astral travelling/out-of-body experiences (OBEs) 115–18, 153–8
astrology 77–8, 103–4, 135, 258
Atlantis 84, 339–40, 346, 349
atoms, physicality of 10, 59
Atwill, Joseph 286–300
authority 127, 151, 154, 250, 500–2, 512–13
attention, hijacking 501–2
causes of acceptance 501–3
children 228, 500
fear 93, 126, 498
non-player characters (NPCs) 132
obedience xviii, 165, 229, 231, 493, 499
perception 133, 137–8
Pyramid of Acquiescence 499–500
self-identity 508
symbolism 333–4
awakening 43, 507–16
awareness 21–2, 42, 85, 133, 154, 492, 497, 509, 512–13, 521 see also **Infinite Awareness**

B

bad copy of Prime Reality 30–4, 37–8, 40, 62, 109, 521
banks and financial services 110, 159, 165–71, 179–83, 201–2, 236–8, 267, 409, 431, 476
Bannon, Steve 382, 387, 405, 443
Barak, Ehud 249, 394, 398, 481–2
Bergrun, Norman 267–9
Bezos, Jeff 177, 246–8, 409, 411–12, 416, 450, 472, 494
Bible 4–5, 33–4, 44, 108, 210, 218, 263–5, 306–20, 349, 455 see also **Biblical God; Jesus**
Adam and Eve narrative 28–9, 38–41, 46, 216, 337–9
angels 58, 345
archaeological evidence 309–13, 315, 317, 319–20, 336–7, 357, 359
authorship 41, 270, 274, 289–99, 314–15, 357
Babylonian exile 315–20, 331–2, 342
Book of Enoch 41, 104, 298, 345
Canaan 264–5, 307, 309–12, 317, 363
chronology 307–9
corroborating evidence outside the Bible 309–15, 317, 319–20, 336–7, 357, 359
David, King 216–17, 287–8, 307, 312–17, 320, 334–5, 359
Exodus, story of 306–12, 315, 318–19, 355–6, 359–60, 363
Ezekiel's revelation 342–6
forty year periods 292–3, 313
Gnosticism 25–6, 28
Great Flood 84, 104, 108, 219, 222, 267, 318, 331–2, 337–8
Jerusalem 282, 293–8, 304, 314–18, 337, 341, 344
Josiah 317–18, 331
Koran 355
Mesopotamia, relocated tales from 314–20, 331–6, 338, 350
Promised Land 292–3, 310–11, 316, 318, 359
Talmud 217, 219, 221, 278,

281, 291, 358
Torah 210, 219, 280–1
universal stories 318–20
Biblical God 160, 321–48 *see also* **Elohim/Anunnaki; Yahweh**
Adamites 325–6
Asherah 329–30
Creation story 327–9, 351
disagreements between gods 338–9
Elyon/El Elyon 332–6, 349–50
fear 160, 282, 347, 360
genetic manipulation 325–7, 338–9, 351–2
Israelite gods as God 329–31
kavod, use of term 322–3, 344
Mesopotamia 329–32, 335–9
plural gods 321–4, 330–3, 348, 355
ruach, use of term 322–3, 344
singular god 321–4, 333, 349–50, 359
Sumer connection 326, 331–2, 351
translations/retranslations 322–5, 330, 349–50
Yahweh 316–18, 330–1, 345, 347, 349–50
Biden, Joe 100, 212–13, 200–1, 244, 250, 368, 376, 389, 425, 431, 500
Big Beautiful Bill 188–9, 238, 402, 419
Big Pharma 137, 177, 180–1
Big Tech/AI tech oligarchy 100, 180, 246–7, 449
AI-human fusion 160, 408–11, 422–5
alternative media 45
fertility research 494
Musk 408–11, 422–5
Spider's web 166
Trump 176–7, 366, 371–2, 374, 400–1, 408–11, 422–5, 473
Vance 366, 400–1, 403–6
Biglino, Mauro 322–5, 330, 333, 345, 349, 351
Bilderberg Group 172, 174, 182–4, 198, 406, 430
biological computer 6–9, 11, 15, 38–40, 101–2, 136, 445, 506, 521

black 253–4, 261–2, 279, 282, 354–6, 362
BlackRock 175, 178, 404, 412–13, 485
Blair, Tony 174, 177, 245, 247–8, 409, 474–5, 486
Blanche, Todd 385, 392–3, 401
blasphemy 43, 275–7, 360
bloodlines 40–1, 91–2, 104–7, 162, 335
Bohemian Grove 264–5
Bohm, David 8–9, 51, 65–6, 75, 504
Bondi, Pam 174, 203, 384–5, 391–2, 419
Bongino, Dan 385, 391, 437, 443
Botha, Roelof 414
bots xix, 247, 372, 448, 458, 480, 486, 489, 491
brain 12–17, 71 *see also* left-brain (closed mind); right-brain (open mind)
body/brain 17
brainwave fingerprints 463
consciousness 17, 232–3
Covid-19 fake vaccines 466–70
holograms/holographs 116
plasticity 234–5, 352–3, 446, 506
reptilians 93–4
savant syndrome 352
split-brain syndrome 234
targeting 232–4
Brand, Russell 43, 214, 361, 391, 393, 428, 434, 437, 439–43
Brin, Sergey 213, 246–8, 414, 429, 494
Buddhism 123, 285
Māra 3, 23, 47
reincarnation 280–1
Wheel of Samsara 37, 47–9, 122, 126–7, 137–44, 151–2, 254, 516
Bush, George HW 100, 154, 169, 201, 221, 226
Bush, George W 100, 169, 201, 226, 474
Bryant, Juliette 399–400
Bukele, Nayib 420–1, 442, 483

C

Calvi, Roberto 170–1
Canada 182–3, 411–13

Capitol Hill 259, 265–6, 335–6
Carlson, Tucker 302, 381–2, 428, 430, 433, 435, 440, 442
Carney, Mark 175, 177, 182–3
Carroll, Ian 428–9, 431–3, 436
cash, elimination of 482–3
Castaneda, Carlos 94–5, 113
Cayce, Edgar 138–40
censorship 184, 242, 244–6, 438, 512
AI-human fusion 165
alternative media 438
Covid-19 180
Ofcom 245–6
self-censorship 245
shadow banning xix, 244–5, 369, 373, 433, 512
social media 245–6, 369, 373, 433, 512
centipede effect 510–11
Central Bank Digital Currencies (CBDCs) 482–4
Chabad-Lubavitch network 209–17, 219, 260, 392
messianic movement, as 211, 215–17
Rebbe (Grand Rabbi) 211–12
Third Solomon's Temple, plans for a 216–17, 222
Zohar 210–11, 218
chákras 67–8, 104, 154, 217
chaos xix, 6, 39, 89, 93, 99, 120, 155, 162, 188, 402, 407–8, 419, 425–6, 515
channelling 78, 79
Charles III, King 105–6, 175, 334, 364, 430, 439
ChatGPT psychosis 495–6
chemtrails 458–60
Cheney, Dick 226–7, 431
children *see also* **paedophilia**
authority 228, 500
Christianity 273–4, 283, 285, 290
Covid-19 471–2, 500
education 165, 231, 234–6, 240–2, 445, 506, 511–12, 517
fertility research 493–5
Gaza, as victims in 144, 205–8
gender confusion, imposition of 367
loosh 114–15, 119–20, 143, 226
mother and child theme 285
near-death experiences (NDEs) 141–3

Index

Online Safety Act 2023 245–6
reincarnation 124–5, 134
religion 273–4, 282, 358
sacrifice 119–20, 166, 265, 516
China 222, 403, 412, 443, 477
  AI 425
  chatbot technology 489
  human fusion 476–9, 489
  competition 489
  Covid-19 477
  digital currency 482
  Internet firewall 62
  mind control 461–4
  Musk 416
  real-time surveillance 476
  remote viewing 147
  social credit system 476
  social media and Internet, government control of 479
  totalitarianism 403
  Trump 403, 412, 416, 439, 477, 489
chosen people narrative 190–1, 204, 212, 249–50, 273–4, 317, 333
Christianity 43–4, 219, 273–9, 305, 358, 360–4 see also Bible; Jesus; Roman Catholic Church
  alternative media 361, 438–9, 507
  Archons/demons 87–8, 97, 100
  Christian right 43, 361, 438–9, 507
  churches 66–7
  Constantine the Great 286, 303–4
  conversions 26, 43, 360–1, 439, 441
  Devil/Satan 23–4, 29–30, 33–4, 87–8, 97, 281
  fear 282
  Islam 283
  Jews, connections to 438–9
  nationalism 413
  neo-Flavians 303–4
  Protestantism 304, 364
  reincarnation 122–3, 127, 305
  Romans, invention of Christianity by 287–304
  Rome, state religion of 303, 316
  sacrifices 279, 281
  Trump 360–2, 378–9

uniformity 278–9
Zionism 194–5, 203, 217
CIA 117, 169, 183–5, 225, 242–3, 368, 371, 382, 396, 415, 431, 441, 463, 481
climate change hoax 165, 172, 175, 178, 367–9, 406–7, 436, 459, 478, 485
Clinton, Bill 100, 174, 201, 226, 248, 389–90, 396, 399, 442–3
Clinton, Hillary 100, 226, 391–2, 442–3
cloning 106–7
closed mind *see* left-brain (closed mind)
Cloud 164, 181, 411, 447–51, 456, 457–8, 474–5, 486, 488
Club of Rome 172, 175, 198, 406, 430, 437
compartmentalisation in organisations 167–8, 171, 174, 179–80, 223, 499
consciousness 16, 19–20, 33–40, 54, 61, 102, 125, 131–3, 500–6
  alters (altered consciousness) 225–6
  Archons/demons 87, 235, 502–3
  brain 17, 232–3
  death 136
  distorted consciousness 24, 28, 157–8
  fear 498–9
  frequencies 18–19, 21–2, 25, 35, 281, 446
  Gnosticism 286
  gods 19, 24, 27–8, 281
  left-brain (closed mind) 234
  Life Programs 506, 521
  matter 503, 519
  observer effect 515
  out-of-body experiences (OBEs)/Astral travelling 117, 153–5
  perception 103, 135, 490, 495, 503–6, 511
  quantum physics 62, 66, 502, 519
  reality 20–2, 503–7
  reincarnation 122, 125–6, 136
  remote viewing 145–6
  scientific orthodoxy 497
  simulation/Matrix 33, 36–7, 48, 61–3, 189
  self-identity 509, 517
  Spirit 37, 515

subconscious 131–2, 135, 251–2, 445, 490, 505, 519–20
  symbolism 251–3
  True 'I' 25, 37–9
  Yaldabaoth 24, 28–30, 33–9, 94, 109, 112–13, 157–8, 218, 226, 281–2, 349, 495
conspiracy theorists 17, 43, 156, 214, 241, 247, 361, 367–8, 427–9, 459, 511
Constantine the Great 286, 303–4
constitution, dismantling the US 403–4, 406, 417–18
contrails 459
corporations, control of 179–80
Coulson, Foster 441–2, 448
Covid-19 hoax/Covid-19 fake vaccines xviii, 154, 247, 451–2, 464–70, 511
  accelerationism 404
  Africa, vaccination records in 474
  AI-human fusion 181, 451, 457–60
  alternative media 170, 241, 434–6, 439, 441, 443, 472
  blood clots after death 469–70
  Bluetooth devices 465
  brain-related effects 466–70
  British Army 77th Brigade (Psyop unit) 480
  cancer 469–70
  censorship 180
  China 477
  Cloud 181, 457–8
  DiseaseX, activation of 457–8
  experts 231–2
  fertility, effect on 493–4
  genetic manipulation device, as xviii, 451
  graphene 452–8
  hydrogel 453–4, 457–60
  lockdowns/masks 231, 427, 435, 452, 478, 500–1
  Media Access Control (MAC) address 464–5
  mind control 227, 231–2, 501
  mRNA 181–2, 451–2, 458, 468, 470–1, 496
  nanotechnology 181, 231, 327, 447, 451–2, 458, 496, 506
  protests 427, 435

Russian vaccine Sputnik 5 478
scientific orthodoxy 69–70
self-replicating vaccines 447, 451–2, 471, 496
soul and spirit disconnection 466–8, 472
spike protein 458
synthetic biology 451–2, 495
Trump xviii, 470–2, 500
universal vaccine or all-in-one-jab 471
Creation 18–20, 28, 32, 36, 54–5, 72–3, 325, 327–9
Cummings, Dominic 181–2
currency 485–6
    cryptocurrency 176, 482–4
    digital currency 478, 482–3, 485–6
    meme coins 383
    stablecoins 482–4
Cusp interface 172–7, 179, 183–4
cymatics technique 21–2, 251

D

Dark Enlightenment 403, 405, 410, 417–19, 440, 473
DARPA 245, 411, 457, 460–1, 470, 476
David, King 287–8, 315
Davis, Henry 286, 291, 297–8
death 136–8
Deep State 162, 179, 366, 369–70, 375–6, 390, 400, 415, 422, 429, 432, 436, 440, 443, 449, 473, 513
deepfakes 489–90
Delgado Martin, Ricardo 456–8
democracy, dismantling 417–18
demons *see* Archons/demons
deportations from US 419–22, 442, 449, 483
Devil/Satan 23–4, 29–30, 33–4, 87–8, 97, 281 *see also* Satanic groups
Diana, Princess of Wales 90, 105–6
Dick, Philip K 45–6
digital currency 478, 482–3, 485–6
divide and rule 86, 161, 173, 274, 305, 363–5, 513–14, 516, 519

dividing the world 349–65
divination 78–81
DNA 9, 55, 79, 130, 454
D-Notices 242
DOGE (Department of Government Efficiency) 184–6, 212, 215, 406–10, 415, 417, 473
Draco/Draconians 92, 96, 104, 154, 270
drama and emotional reactions 513–15
duality/polarity 32–3, 38, 84–6
DUMBS 89–90

E

Edge Foundation 247–9, 434
Edomites (West), destruction of the 217–18
education 165, 231, 234–6, 240–2, 445, 506, 511–12, 517
Einstein, Albert 3–4, 7–8, 64–5, 199, 210–11, 230
electromagnetism/electricity 32, 57–61, 64, 77, 164, 436, 506 *see also*
holograms/holographs
algorithms 461
amplification 456–7
Archons/demons 88–9
behaviour, dictating 460–1
brain targeting 233
Covid-19 fake vaccines 470
false light 29
graphene 452–6, 461, 463
human electromagnetic auric field 16
incarnation process, memories of 48
loosh 114
meridian network/ley lines and sacred places 66
perception 11, 80, 461–3
plasma 58–60, 128, 129–30, 139
simulation/Matrix 49, 65, 77, 450
Ellison, Larry 146, 165, 203, 370, 371, 409, 416, 434, 470, 473–5
Elohim/Anunnaki 108, 321–37, 342, 347–50, 364
Elyon/El Elyon 332–6
genetic manipulation 325–7, 338–9, 351–2
hybrids 325–7, 338–9, 351

Judaism 259
plural gods, translation as 321–4, 328–9, 331, 351
reptilians 325, 328, 351
singular god, translation as 323–4, 328–9, 331, 364
Sumer connection 326, 331–2, 351
Yahweh 331–3, 349–50
Elyon/El Elyon 332–6
Emanuel family 199–200, 201
energy *see* loosh
entrainment 446
Epic of Gilgamesh 337–8
Epstein, Jeffrey 384–401
    Bezos 246–7, 411
    Big Tech/AI tech oligarchy 246–7
    birthday book/letters 389–90, 393
    blackmail 173, 385, 394–5
    Carbyne911 249
    cryptocurrency 484
    death 384–6
    Edge Foundation 247–9, 434
    Epstein files 384–92, 401, 432
    Giuffre, Virginia 387–8, 398–9
    Israel 173, 246, 385, 394–6, 398, 401, 481
    mass behaviour manipulation courses 246–9
    Maxwell, Ghislaine 384, 387–90, 392–5, 398, 401
    Mega Group 396–8
    Mossad 172–3, 394–6, 398
    Musk 173, 246–7, 249, 384, 391, 411
    Ponzi scheme, involvement in 398
    shapeshifting 399–400
    Thiel 394, 396, 398
    Trump 173–4, 202, 384–94, 396, 401, 471
    wealth, sources of 396
    Zorro Ranch 398–9
European Union (EU) 162, 174, 181, 217, 478–9, 482
experts 69–70, 231–2, 239–40
extraterrestrials 68–9, 89, 346, 399

F

Facebook/Meta 177, 180, 184, 187, 200, 223, 245, 248–9, 424, 440, 443, 479

Index

facial recognition technology 186
Fall of Man/falls from heaven 5, 23–5
Farmer, George/Farmer, Michael Stahel (Baron Farmer) 429–31
fear 121, 225, 281–3, 316, 530
  authority 93, 126, 498
  Bible 160, 282, 347, 360, 441
  consciousness 498–9
  death 135
  hierarchy of fear 498–500
  loosh 112, 114–15, 135, 183, 360, 498
  Pyramid of Acquiescence 499–500
  sacrifices 119, 347
Fermi Paradox 68–9
fertility research 493–5
Fibonacci numbers 54–5
Fink, Larry 175, 178, 404, 412–13
Finkelstein, Israel 306–7, 311–12, 315, 318, 358–9
five-sense awareness 133, 492, 497, 512–13
Flavians and neo-Flavians 287–304, 337
4G/5G/6G/7G 436, 450, 452, 455
Fourth Dimension (4-D) (Astral) 36–8, 68 see also under particular main entries
  Astral AI Mind program 127, 129–30, 134–5, 143
  incarnation process, memories of 128–9
  interdimensional Astral gods 341–2
  Orion star system 96–7
  possession 120, 506
  reincarnation 37, 125–30, 136–9, 143, 156
  simulation/Matrix 36–7, 126, 510
fractal patterns 54–5, 109, 154
Frank, Jacob 194–7, 199, 210
freedom of speech
  Musk xix, 243–4, 369–70, 372–4, 416, 450, 487
  Roman Church 360–1, 441
  Trump 369–70, 416, 431, 450
  Twitter/X xix, 243–4, 369–70, 372–4, 487
Freemasons 167–8, 171, 196, 253
  Great Architect of the Universe 31
  Saturn 260–1, 263–4
  symbolism 167–8, 171, 260–1
frequencies (waves) 6–7, 18, 37, 48, 57, 445–6 see also under particular main entries
  Archons/demons 110–11
  awareness 21–2
  bands 36
  behaviour, changing 445–6
  chakras 154
  consciousness 18–19, 21–2, 25, 35, 281, 446
  death 136–7
  decoding 502–3
  emotions 5, 114
  Invisibility Cloaks or shields 96
  language 85–6
  numerology 80
  perception 5, 36–7, 66, 127, 158, 445–6, 503
  plasma universe 57–9
  riotous behaviour 445–6
  sacrifices 119–20
  simulation/Matrix 31, 46–8, 52–3, 61, 64–6, 127, 445–6
  smartphones and other devices 495–6
  sound waves 14, 21–2
  symbolism 251, 253
  Wetiko (mind virus) 102
  Yaldabaoth 99, 109, 111–12, 261–2
Freixedo, Salvador 346–8

G

Gabbard, Tulsi 382, 391–2, 437, 442–3
Garbini, Giovanni 315, 319–20, 324
Gates, Bill 100, 160, 176, 177, 180, 182, 248, 366, 389, 449, 457–60, 465–6, 472, 474, 487
Gates, James 55–6, 73
Gateway Process 117–18, 145
Gaza, Israel's war on 183, 205–9, 216, 440–1
  dissent, silencing 207–9
  genocide 207, 222, 311, 349–50
  Mediterranean resort, Trump's proposal for a 205, 207
  protests 207–9
  Trump 205, 207–9, 212
gender 38, 98, 367, 494–5
genetic manipulation 38, 40, 325–7, 338–9, 351–2, 451, 464
Giuffre, Virginia 387–8, 398–9
global cataclysm 339–41
global centralisation 172, 174, 183, 357–8, 405
Global Cult 159–78 see also under particular main entries
Gnostics 25–33, 125, 155, 286 see also Nag Hammadi manuscripts; Yaldabaoth (Gnostics)
  Archons/demons 87, 97–103, 112
  Bible 25–6, 28
  Cathar Gnosticism, ending of 25, 360
  false self-identity 39
  Jesus 286
  Nag Hammadi manuscripts 25–33, 39, 98
  reincarnation 122–3, 125
  Roman Church 25–7, 97
  Saturn 103–4
  trio of human types 39–40
gods see also Biblical God; Yahweh
  AI-human fusion 495–6
  Allah, bloodlust of 356–7
  Archons/demons 96–8, 107–8, 161, 183
  consciousness 19, 24, 27–8, 281
  Creation 72–3
  demi-gods 41
  existence of God 17–19, 27–8
  fear 281–3
  Gnostics 27
  interdimensional Astral gods 341–2
  loosh 360
  mind control 228–9
  near-death experiences (NDEs) 137–8
  pantheons of gods 97–8, 280–1, 292, 323, 329, 333, 356, 362
  perception 216, 308, 338–9, 357–8
  reptilians 91, 96, 325, 328
  royal bloodlines 104–5

Saturn 257–9, 444
sun gods 257–8
technology of the Gods 341–6, 348
Grade, Michael 245–6
graphene 452–7
 AI-human fusion 452, 456, 458
 black goo 461
 chemtrails 458–60
 Covid-19 vaccines 452–7, 458
 electromagnetism 452–3, 456–7, 461, 463
 frequencies 455–6
 hexagon graphene 455–7
 hydrogel 453–5
Great Flood 84, 104, 108, 219, 222, 267, 318, 331–2, 337–8
Great Pyramid of Giza 68, 84, 342
Great Reset 84, 252–3, 267, 478
Greene, Isabella 129, 134, 156
Greenland 411–13
Grok 372, 486–7, 495
guilt 112, 142, 305, 350–1, 360, 379, 498

H

Haldeman, Joshua N 203, 410–11, 413
Hall, Manly P 161, 168, 251, 258
Hamas 205–8, 440–1
Hassan, Steven 379–81
Heath, Edward 104–5, 118–19
Hegelian Dialectic 188
Heisenberg, Werner 10, 53, 101, 507
Hemispheric Synchronisation 115–17, 153, 235
heresy/blasphemy 43, 275–7, 360
Heritage Foundation 418–19
hexagons and hexagrams 252, 255–6, 260–5, 455–7
hierarchies 163, 231, 223–4, 233–4, 240, 490
 Archons/demons 93–4, 96, 98, 172, 349
 fear 498–500
 reptilians 93–4, 96, 132, 172, 493
 world government 163
Hill, Napoleon 518–19
Hinduism 23, 84, 104, 279–80,

285, 346, 363–4
advanced technology 346, 356
caste system 94, 123, 274, 493
plural gods 329, 348, 358
reincarnation 274, 346
Hitler, Adolf 169, 192, 196, 198, 413–14
hive mind 93, 96, 164, 446–52, 460, 466
 AI-human fusion 164, 218, 446–52, 493
 Archons/demons 446, 458
 Cloud 164, 447–8, 449–51
 Covid-19 fake vaccines 181, 447, 451–2
 delivery 447–8, 449, 479
 global hive mind 447
 graphene 456
 low-orbit satellites 449–50
 mind control 463
 perception 446, 451, 456, 460
 receipt 447, 449
Hoffenberg, Steven 398
holograms/holographs 12, 49–56, 88, 116
 decoding 50–1, 64, 79
 digital holographic information 79
 Global Cult 181–3
 meridian network/ley lines and sacred places 66–7
 simulation/Matrix 49–56, 58, 65–6, 72–6, 117, 181
holy books 4–5, 18, 275–81 *see also* **Bible; Koran**
homeopathy 53
Homan, Tom 419–21
Huxley, Aldous 452, 492–5
hybrid bloodlines 40–1, 107–8, 325–7, 335, 338–9, 351
hydrogel 453–5, 457–60
Hylics 39–40, 133
Hypatia 26, 360

I

ICE (Immigration and Customs Enforcement) 419–21
identity *see* **self-identity**
Illuminati 195–6, 197
incarnation process, memories of 47–8, 128–9, 134, 157
inevitability 448–9, 505

Infinite Awareness 17–18, 156, 281
 Divine Spark 47, 55, 445–6, 455, 464, 466–8, 472, 502–3
 symbolism 41–2
Intellectual Dark Web 434, 440
interdimensionals 28, 41, 88–9, 96, 160–1, 218, 259, 261–2, 336, 339, 341, 352, 361
Invisibility Cloaks or shields 96
Iran 206, 222, 381–2, 396, 410, 421
Islam 195, 274, 277–9, 283, 305, 337, 353–7, 358, 360, 362–4
 Allah, bloodlust of 356–7
 archaeological evidence 354, 356–7
 crescent moon symbol 356
 Jesus 282, 355
 Jinn 87–8
 Kaaba or black cube 261–2, 279, 282, 354–6, 362
 Koran 353–5, 357
 Mecca 261–2, 279, 282, 353–6
 mind viruses 100
 Muhammad 98, 262, 282, 309, 353–5, 357, 362
 Saturn 260–2
 Sharia law 362
 Shaytan/Iblis 23–4, 33, 87, 281
 Sin/Suen, worship of 355–6
 Sunni and Shia, division into 364
 symbolism 356
 uniformity 278–9
Israel 195, 210, 244, 429, 480 *see also* Gaza, Israel's war on; Jerusalem; Mossad; Sabbateans/Sabbateans-Frankists; Zionism loki
 AI-human fusion 218, 479–80
 arms, supply of 173, 205, 213, 222
 artificial wombs and stem cells 495
 blackmail 385, 394, 401
 boycotts of Israel, Trump's steps to prevent 207–8
 Carbyne911 249
 Christian right 438–9
 creation 195, 196, 211
 Epstein, Jeffrey 173, 246, 385, 394–6, 401, 481
 funding 203–4

Global Cult 394, 398, 410
gods 329–32
Golan Heights as Israel land, recognition of 222
government-controlled companies 479
Greater Israel 197–8, 199, 222, 312, 479
Hamas attacks 205–8, 440–1
illegal aliens in US 419–21
Iran 206, 222, 381–2, 396, 410, 421
Iron Dome 187, 382
Messiah 216–18, 316
military and intelligence 187, 199, 205–8, 212, 243, 247, 249, 382, 394–5, 479–82,
487
Musk 203, 400, 425, 431, 482
nanorobots 458
Palantir 394
Panama Canal 413
psychopathy 190, 205, 425
Putin 214
Signal security breach in United States 480–1
social media bots and trolls 243, 247, 479
Syria 222
TeleMessage 481
Trump 202–4, 216, 396, 425, 429, 432
arms, supply of 173, 205, 213, 222
Stingray surveillance devices 481
Unit 8200 249, 480–1

J

Jerusalem
Bible 282, 293–8, 304, 314–18, 337, 341, 344
Third Solomon's Temple, plans for a 216–17, 222, 262–3, 479
US embassy, relocation of 202, 204, 429
Jesus 6, 43, 87, 99, 281, 284–305
Barabbas 295–6
Bible, mentions outside the 284, 287, 291–8, 301–3
crucifixion 34, 279, 295–6,

300, 301–2, 304, 321
David, line of 287–8, 315
disciples 294, 298–300
divinity 297
existence 286–305
Flavians 287–304, 337
Gnostic texts 286
Gospels 289–99, 302, 314–15, 357
Islam 282, 355
Josephus/Arrius Piso 291–8, 301–3
Messiah 218–19, 287–90, 300
Mithra 285–6, 300
Moses 289–93
Mother Mary 282, 285, 329, 334, 355
near-death experiences (NDEs) 137–8, 142
New Testament authorship 287, 289–98
Paul's epistles 300, 301–3
typology, use of 289–93
Paul of Tarsus, Saint 284, 286, 300–3
Peter, Saint 68, 294, 298–300
pre-Christian precursors 284–6, 303
prophecies, fulfilment of Moses' 289–90, 292
reincarnation 122–3, 127
resurrection 303–4
typology, use of 289–93
John the Baptist 286, 289, 292, 355
Johnson, Boris 181–2, 431, 500
Jones, Alex 390–2, 393, 428, 432, 434, 438, 440, 444, 473
Josephus/Arrius Piso 284, 291–8, 301–3
Judaism/Jews 100, 273–4, 277, 279–83, 285, 305, 358, 360
see also Bible; Chabad-Lubavitch network; Israel; Zionism
anti-Semitism 190, 197, 203, 207–8, 212, 246, 398, 430
Ashkenazi Jews 191–2
caps 278
Chabad-Lubavitch network 209–19, 222, 392
Christian right 438–9
crypto-Jews 194–5
diaspora 316
God's chosen people 190–

1, 204, 212, 273, 317
Hasidic Judaism 210
Khazar Empire, origins in the 190–2, 316
Messiah/Moshiach 217–18, 259, 359
origins 320
Palestine, relocation to 192–3
Sabbateans/Sabbateans-Frankists 193–5
Sabbath 104, 259, 279–80, 282, 316, 350, 362–3
Samael 23–4, 33, 34, 87, 281
Saturn 259–62
seven, significance of number 103
United States 199–201
Yahweh 316–18
judges, Trump's attacks on 410, 417–18
Jung, Carl 130, 520–1

K

Kaaba or black cube 261–2, 279, 282, 354–6, 362
karma 126, 128–9, 134, 142
Karp, Alex 183–4, 406, 423
Kennedy, John F, assassination of 214, 368, 511
Kennedy Jr, Robert F 203, 208, 213–14, 368, 429, 470–2
Khazar Empire, origins of Jewish people in the 190–2, 316
Kirk, Charlie 189, 382, 391, 393, 429, 430–1, 438–9, 443, 523-537
Kirlian photography 123–4
Kissinger, Henry 174–5, 400, 430
Knights Templar 54, 67, 166, 342, 364
Koran 353–5, 357
Kordylewski Clouds 139–40
Kurzweil, Ray 366, 447–9
Kushner, Jared 213, 214–15

L

Levy, Paul 83, 85, 100–2, 234, 503
ley lines, meridian network and sacred places 66–9,

119, 217
Life Programs 130, 134–5, 143, 506, 521
light 8–9, 29, 32, 66, 72, 81, 352
Little Me 35, 43, 497, 502–3, 511, 519–20
Lonsdale, Joe 370, 423–4, 434
loosh 109–21, 154, 164, 238, 262, 349, 426
  AI-human fusion 114, 458
  children 114–15, 119–20, 143, 226
  Divine Spark 112–13, 123
  drama and emotional reactions 514–15
  emotional states and drama, addiction to 114
  fear and terror 114–15, 119, 135, 183, 360, 498
  Fourth Dimension (4-D) (Astral) 114–15, 154
  frequencies 110–21, 143, 262
  mind control 226, 227
  nature as a killing field 48, 114
  perception 111, 116–18, 121, 272
  power, giving away 498
  reincarnation 122–3, 126, 129, 135, 136, 142–4, 150
  religion 262, 305, 364
  reptilians 118–19, 325
  sacrifices, human and animal 118–21
  simulation/Matrix 113, 134
low-orbit satellites 161, 164–5, 457
  Cloud 411, 449–50, 486
  FCC 449
  graphene 457
  hive mind 447–50
  infrared satellites 187
  Kuiper system of Amazon 246, 450
  SpaceX 48, 114, 164, 369, 415–16, 450, 486
  Starlink 249, 415, 450
  Starshield network 416, 450
  surveillance technology 415, 460, 482
low-vibrational energy *see* **loosh**
Luckey, Palmer 187–8, 403, 406
Lutnick, Howard 203, 212, 374–5, 394, 418, 437, 483

M
McDonnell, Wayne 117–18, 146
McGilchrist, Iain 235–6, 508
Manchurian candidates 226
Matrix *see* **simulation/Matrix**
The Matrix (film) 12, 39, 45–7, 93, 99, 113, 133, 286, 509, 515
Matus, Don Juan 94–5, 112, 120
Mayans 23, 84, 103, 327–8, 351
Maxwell, Ghislaine 384, 387–90, 392–5, 398, 401
Maxwell, Robert 394–5, 398
media *see* **alternative media/New Media, control of; social media**
Media Access Control (MAC) address 464–5
Mega Group 396–8
meridian network/ley lines and sacred places 66–9, 119, 217
Mesoamerican creation story 327–8, 351
Mesopotamia 318–19, 329–32, 335–9, 350
Messiah 211, 215–18, 259, 287–90, 300, 316, 359
migration 188–9, 419–22, 442, 449, 483
Miller, Stephen 203, 417–18, 421
mind 16–17, 27, 94–102 *see also* **hive mind; left-brain (closed mind); mind control**
mind control 223–38, 249, 509
  alters (altered consciousness) 225–6
  brain targeting 232–4
  brainwave fingerprints 463
  children 225–36
  China 461–4
  Covid-19 227, 231–2, 501
  DNA, editing 464
  electromagnetic perceptual manipulation 461–3
  experts 231–2
  Global Cult 189, 223–6, 249–50
  hive mind 463
  Manchurian candidates 226
  mind-wipe 49, 126, 134, 136–7, 142–3, 148, 152
  MKUltra 224–8, 232, 242, 400
  Musk 248–9

  nudging 247, 249
  perception 223, 224–34, 249–50
  plasticity 233–5
  religion 273, 275–7, 281
  repeaters 231–2
  targeted individuals 462
  Trump 250, 377–9, 383
Mithra 285–6, 300
MKUltra 224–8, 232, 242, 400
moksha 147, 151–3
Monroe, Robert 115–18, 145–6, 153, 235
Moon 268–72, 356
Mormons, 525-6
Moses 210, 283, 289–93, 307–11, 316–19, 322, 330–2, 350, 357, 362
Mossad 173, 199, 205–6
  CIA/Mossad network of sexual abuse 172–3
  Cyber Intelligence Unit in Beersheba 243, 247, 479–80
  Epstein, Jeffrey 172–3, 394–6, 398
  Hamas attacks 205
  Maxwell, Ghislaine and Maxwell, Robert 394–5
Muhammad 98, 262, 282, 309, 353–5, 357, 362
Musk, Elon 100, 160–2, 169, 175, 537-8, *see also* **SpaceX; Trump, Donald and Musk, Elon; Twitter/X and Elon Musk**
  AI, fusion of humans with xix, 186, 246, 369–73, 402, 406–11, 422–7, 449, 473–7, 486–8
  alternative media 427–9, 431–2, 438–40, 444
  China 416
  Christian nationalism 413
  climate change hoax 406–7
  conspiracy theories 43
  Edge courses 248–9
  Epstein, Jeffrey 173, 246–7, 249, 384, 391, 411
  freedom of speech xix, 243–4, 369–70, 372–4, 416, 450, 487
  intelligence, military, and surveillance networks, links to 416
  Israel 203, 425, 431, 482
  Mars 23
  Neuralink 407, 416, 457, 486

Index

Palantir 184–6
PayPal 414–15
perception 369, 410, 415, 438
political left and right 449
richest man, the world's 238
Rogan 428, 433
singularity 448–9
South African connection 413–14, 440
Tesla 374, 407, 415, 416, 438, 477, 486
Thiel 184, 186–7, 405–6, 415, 428, 440
Vance 405–6
xAI 186, 249, 372, 404, 449, 486
Musk, Errol 203, 413
Mutwa, Credo 91–2, 98, 120, 271, 338, 347–8, 356

N

Nag Hammadi 25–33, 39, 91, 98, 101–2
  Adam and Eve narrative 28–9, 38
  Apocryphon of John 29, 39–41, 83, 112, 135
  Hylics 133
  Saturn 256–7
  Tripartite Tractate 29, 33, 39
  Yaldabaoth 32–4, 87–8
natural world 48, 83, 114
Nazi regime 92, 169, 174, 191–2, 196, 198–9, 208, 224–5, 244, 254, 333, 413–14
near-death experiences (NDEs) 20–1, 47, 115
  Fourth Dimension (4-D) (Astral) 36–7, 126, 137, 142
  life reviews 124, 129, 141–3
  love-bombing 137
  reincarnation 123–4, 126–9, 136–8, 141–4, 499
  spirit guides 124, 126, 127, 141, 499
  tunnel-of-light 127, 136–7, 141–2, 281
Nephilim 40–1
Netanyahu, Benjamin 310, 350, 397, 434, 440–1
  background 192
  Greater Israel 222, 307
  Iran 187, 382
  Musk 203, 431, 482
  Trump 173–4, 212–13, 372, 396, 425, 429
Neuralink 407, 416, 457, 486
New Agers 123, 126, 280–1, 363, 436
New Media see **alternative media/New Media, control of**
Noah and Noahide Laws 84, 104, 108, 219–22, 267, 318, 331–2, 337–8
non-governmental organisations (NGOs) and think tanks 172, 177–8, 179–80, 217
non-player characters (NPCs) 132–3, 143, 467, 506
normality 239–42
numerology 78, 79–81, 102–3, 263–4, 292–3, 313
Nuyts, Rolf 153–5, 271–2

O

Obama, Barack 56, 100, 199, 201, 246, 364, 389, 391–2
O'Brien, Cathy 225–6, 264
observer effect 64–5, 85, 515
oligarchs see **Big Tech/AI tech oligarchy**
One-Party States xix, 162, 169–70, 205, 241, 427, 443
Online Safety Act 2023 245–6
open mind (right brain) 116–18, 235–7, 509
OpenAI 165, 372, 473, 488
Oracle 165, 370–1, 473–5, 479
Orwell, George 233, 246, 402, 424, 492
Ottoman Empire 198–9
Ouroboros/Leviathan 34–5, 157, 257
out-of-body experiences (OBEs)/Astral travelling 115–18, 129, 153–8
Owens, Candace 360–1, 428–32

P

Palantir Technologies 183–7, 370, 375, 394, 406, 440
  AI-human fusion 183–6, 474
  deportations 421
  DOGE 184–6
  ICE contracts 421
  low-orbit surveillance technology 415
  Musk 184–6, 407, 409
  Trump 183–6, 407, 409
Palestine 212–14, 316 see also
  Gaza, Israel's war on
  Hamas 205–8, 440–1
  Jewish people, relocation of 192–3
  Ottoman Empire 193
  sexual and gender-based violence 211–12
  West Bank 200, 203–4, 212–13, 216, 222, 298, 310, 313, 439
  Zionism 196–9
Panama Canal 411–13
pantheons of gods 97–8, 280–1, 292, 323, 329, 333, 356, 362
paranormal 19, 46, 77–81, 145, 276–7
Patriarca, Peter A 466
Pavlovski, Chris 436–7, 438, 443
Patel, Kash 385, 391, 437
Paul the Apostle, Saint 97, 138, 284, 286, 300–3
PayPal 414–15, 440
perception programming 1–2, 85–6, 90, 134, 137–8, 227, 231–4, 251, 379, 506, 510
Peter, Saint 68, 294, 298–300
Peterson, Jordan 360, 428, 434, 440–1
Planck, Max 8–10, 504, 517
plasma 57–60, 75, 128, 129–30, 139–40
plasticity of the brain 233–5, 352–3, 446, 506
Plato 26, 349
Pliny the Younger 301–3
Pneumatics 39–40
political left and right xix, 169–70, 200, 235, 369, 443, 449–50, 513
  accelerationism 403
  alternative media 43, 436, 505–6
  Christian right 43, 361, 438–9, 507
power, giving away 497–8
predictive programming 490–1, 492, 505
Prime 'Earth' 20–2, 46–9
Prime Reality 20–2, 29–34, 37–40, 46, 49, 62, 83, 109, 153, 521

Problem-Reaction-Solution (PRS)/No-Problem-Reaction Solution 188–9, 205, 207, 227, 248, 404, 521–2
Project 2025 418–19
Propaganda Due (P2) 168–71
psychopathy 34, 92, 96, 169, 178, 183, 476, 513
  Bible 308, 330
  child sacrifices 166
  Covid-19 fake vaccines 468–9
  Gaza, Israel's war on 205
  Global Cult 159–60, 178
  Israel 190, 205, 425
  mind control 225–6
  Roman Church 25–7, 360
  traits, list of 100
  Trump 205, 380–1, 393, 420, 422, 425, 466
  Wetiko (mind virus) 100
  Yahweh 330, 350, 362, 439
  Putin, Vladimir and Russia
    Carlson, Tucker, interview with 382
    Covid-19 vaccine Sputnik 5 478
    digital currency 478, 482
    Israel 214
    Sabbateans 197
    Ukraine, war with 214–15, 412, 477
    WEF 177
    Wetiko (mind virus) 100
Pyramid of Acquiescence 499–500
pyramids 21–2, 66, 68, 251–3, 266, 332, 340–2, 498–9
pysops *see* **Trump Psyop**

Q

quantum computers 77, 455
quantum physics 8–10, 16, 46, 59, 62, 65–6, 502–3, 511, 519
  extra-terrestrials 82–3
  holograms/holographs 66, 76
  intentionality 111
  observer, perceptions of the 85
  potentiality 18, 521
  quantum jumps 52
  scientific orthodoxy 8–10, 17, 235
  simulation/Matrix 76–7, 521

uncertainty principle 235

R

Ramaswamy, Vivek 184, 374–5, 437, 440
Reagan, Ronald 169, 201, 220
reality 10–12, 49, 55 *see also* **Prime Reality**
  bad copies 52, 62, 84–5, 510, 521
  belief in your reality 503–5
  consciousness 20–2, 503, 504–7
  Infinite Reality 11, 17–18, 20, 22, 84–5
  official narratives, **perception of** 512–13
perception 1–2, 46, 61–2, 86, 304, 357, 491, 503–21
Prime Reality 20–2, 30, 49, 52, 62, 84–5, 153, 510, 521
  quantum physics 10, 502, 511
  reincarnation 49, 117, 122–44, 274, 280–1, 346
  Archons/demons 127, 130, 136–7, 143
  Astral AI Mind program 127, 129–30, 134–5, 143
  birthmarks and birth defects 124–5
  children 124–5, 134
  Christianity 122–3, 127, 305
  clothes 123, 126
  consciousness 122, 125–6, 136
  cycle 126, 127–9
  Fourth Dimension (4-D) (Astral) 37, 125–30, 136–9, 143, 156
  frequencies 127–8
  Global Cult 127, 138
  Gnosticism 122–3, 125
  Heaven 127, 137, 141–2
  incarnation process 128–9
  karma 126, 128–9, 134, 142
  loosh 122–3, 126, 129, 135, 136, 142–4, 150
  mind-wipe 49, 126, 134, 136–7, 142–3, 148, 152
  near-death experiences (NDEs) 123–4, 126, 128–9, 136–8, 141–4, 499
  plasma 128, 129–30, 139–40
  religion 122–7, 137–8
  simulation/Matrix 47, 103, 123, 125–9, 135, 139–43
  Souls, recycling 49, 122,

125–9, 137, 143–4, 148–52
  trap 47, 103, 122–3, 125–7, 140, 151–3, 156
  tunnel of light 127, 136–7, 141–2
  Wheel of Samsara 37, 47–9, 122, 126–7, 137–44, 151–2, 254, 516
religion 6, 43, 273–83, 497 *see also* **Bible**; **different religions** (eg Christianity); **gods**
  Archons/demons 23, 87–8, 97–8, 108, 273, 276–7
  buildings 276–7
  children 273–4, 282, 358
  divide and rule 363–5
  factions 364
  faith, definition of 274–5
  Global Cult 161–2, 273, 363–5
  heresy/blasphemy 43, 275–7, 360
  hive mind 447
  imposition of beliefs 273–4
  left-brain (closed mind) 235–6
  loosh 305, 364
  mind/perception control 273, 275–7, 281
  One-World religion 495–6
  perception 123, 273–7, 281, 305
  reptilians 91, 94
  Saturn 254, 259–64
  scientific orthodoxy 276–7
  uniforms 277–9
remote viewing (RV) 145–9, 154
reptilians 90–7, 154, 171, 184, 338, 357, 399–400
  AI-human fusion 93, 96, 479
  alternative media 224, 433
  Archons/demons 90–7, 104–8, 118, 166
  Bible 325, 328, 336
  brain 93–4
  cannibalism 98, 347–8
  Draco/Draconians 91–2, 96, 104, 154, 270
  Fourth Dimension (4-D) (Astral) 91, 95–7, 118
  giants 328
  gods 91, 96, 325, 328
  hierarchy 93–4, 96, 132, 172, 493
  hive mind 93, 96, 458
  loosh 118–19, 325

Index

Orion star system 96–7
out-of-body experiences (OBEs)/Astral travelling 153–4, 156–7
predators, as 95
R-complex 93
royal bloodlines 91–2, 96, 104–6
sacrifices 119
shapeshifting 107–8, 166, 335
Yaldabaoth 23, 91, 93–4, 118, 157–8
right-brain (open mind) 116–18, 235–7, 509
Ring-Pass-Not 34–5, 143, 157, 257
Rockefeller family 174–5, 180–3, 226, 229, 264, 298, 430, 477
Rogan, Joe 199, 370, 393, 415, 428–9, 433–6, 440–1, 473, 486, 488
Roman Catholic Church 97, 286, 304–5, 351, 361, 430–1
 brutality and fear 97, 360, 441
 conversions 26, 43, 360–1, 439, 441
 freedom of speech 360–1, 441
 Global Cult 166–7, 259
 Gnostics 25–7, 97
 guilt 351, 360
 Propaganda Due (P2) 168–71
 psychopaths 25–7, 260
 secret societies 166–7
Romans (Flavians and neo-Flavians) 287–304, 337
Rothschild family 175, 177, 180, 183, 195–9, 202, 209, 215, 237, 260–1, 264, 397–8, 430–1
royal bloodlines 40–1, 91–2, 104–7, 162, 335
Royal Family 264, 333–6, 364, 387–8
Royal Institute of International Affairs/Chatham House 172, 175, 198, 430
Rubin, Dave 434, 440, 443
Rubio, Marco 203, 442, 476
Rumble video platform 436–7, 438, 440, 443, 483
Russia *see also* **Putin, Vladimir** and Russia; Russian Bolshevik Revolution 1917

BRICS 162
Chabad-Lubavitch network 212
Khazar Empire, origins of Jewish people in the 190–2, 316
remote viewing 146–7
Russian Bolshevik Revolution 1917 197
Zionism 197, 202

S

Sabbateans/Sabbateans-Frankists 190–222, 430
 Chabad-Lubavitch network 209–17, 219, 221, 260
 Christianity 194–5, 216, 219
 crypto-Jews 194–5
 infiltration 194–6, 349, 436
 Saturn worship 260
 Trump 202–4, 383
 Zionism 196–8
Sabbath 282, 350, 362–3
Sacks, David 176, 203, 414, 437, 440
sacred places, meridian networks and ley lines 66–9, 119, 217
sacrifices 118–21, 347–8
 animals 98, 118–21
 children 119–20, 166, 265, 516
 Christianity 279, 281
 human 98, 118–21, 166, 265, 516
 Satanists 118–20
Samael 23–4, 33, 34, 87, 281
Satan/Devil 23–4, 29–30, 33–4, 87–8, 97, 281 see also Satanic groups
Satanic groups 29, 66, 210
 Global Cult xix, 118–19, 183
 paedophiles 105, 119–20, 133, 166
 sacrifices 118–20
 Saturn 258
 shapeshifting 107
 symbols 258, 261–2, 266–7
satellites see **low-orbit satellites**
Saturn and symbolism 97, 103–4, 253–84
 Archons/demons 253–84
 astrology 103–4
 black, association with 253–4, 259–61, 267, 355, 456
 Black Sun symbol 253–4

chakras 104, 272
Christianity 261–2
cube 253, 255, 259, 261–3, 271, 279, 282
frequencies 103, 253, 256–7, 261–2, 268–72, 455–6
Global Cult 103, 253–84
Gnostics 103–4
gods 257–9, 330, 333
hexagrams and hexagons 252, 255–6, 260–5, 455–6
Islam 260–2
Judaism 104, 259–62
Magic Square of Saturn 263–4
Moon as an artificial object 268–72, 455
religion 254, 259–64
return 257
rings 255, 267–72, 277
Saturnalia 258–9
Sigil of Saturn 264
sound 271
Star of David 253, 256–7, 260
storm on poles of Saturn 255–6
Sun, as the main Earth of 255
Thiel 254
Yaldabaoth 103, 256, 258, 260–2, 272
Saudi Arabia 195, 213, 262, 279, 340, 357, 364, 370
Savile, Jimmy 105–6
scarcity=dependency=control 249, 517–18
Schneerson, Menachem Mendel 211–13, 220
Schwab, Klaus 84, 100, 160, 172, 174–5, 177–8, 215, 366, 369, 449, 465, 478, 488
scientific orthodoxy 8–10, 17, 69–86, 145, 232, 363, 492, 497
 corporate powers 234–5
 Covid-19 fake vaccines 69–70
 expert stupidity 69–70
 left-brain (closed mind) 234–5, 268
 paranormal 77–81
 physics, law of 81–2
 religion 276–7
 quantum physics 8–10, 17, 235
Saturn rings 268
scientism 276–7
 simulation/Matrix 71–5

secret societies *see also* **Freemasons**
Cusp interface 172–7, 179, 183–4
degrees of knowledge 167–8, 171, 224, 499
funding 177
Global Cult xix, 28, 67, 112, 120, 160–2, 165–80, 183–4
hierarchy 223–4
NGOs and think tanks 172, 177–8, 179–80
Saturn symbolism 263
semi-secret organisations 172–4, 177–8, 179, 183
Spider's web 165–7, 172, 177
self-identity 27, 35–6, 39–43, 48, 101, 127, 508–10, 517, 521
separation of powers 417–19
September 11, 2001, terrorist attacks xviii, 173, 187, 196, 201, 247, 370, 377, 394, 427, 511
shadow banning xix, 244–5, 369, 373, 433, 512
shapeshifting 78, 87, 98, 107–8, 166, 335, 399–400, 461
Shapiro, Ben 203, 429, 434, 440, 443
Shaytan/Iblis 23–4, 33, 87, 281
Silberman, Neil Asher 306–7, 311–12, 315, 318, 358–9
simulation/Matrix 30–1, 45–73, 84, 102, 189, 497 *see also* the Architect 31
astrology 78, 103, 135
bad copy of Prime Reality 52, 62, 84–5, 510, 521
death 136
decoding/encoding 49–53, 56, 63–5, 489
Electric Universe 59–62
energy 53, 57–8, 64
fragmentation 155
interactive, as 62
plasma universe 57–60, 75
Prime Earth overlay 46–9
Prime Reality overlay 49, 62, 153
remote viewing 147–9
2D, universe as 76
singularity 448–9
smart cities/15-minute cities 485–6
social media 243–4
anonymity 515–16
bots xix, 247, 372, 448, 458,
480, 486, 489, 491
British Army 77th Brigade (Psyop unit) 247, 479–80
censorship 245–6, 369, 433, 512
China, government control in 479
facial recognition technology 186
Israel 243, 247, 479
mind control/perception control 249
nudging 249
Online Safety Act 2023 245–6
Palantir 184
privacy 431
shadow banning xix, 244–5, 369, 373, 433, 512
Truth Social 437
Socrates 26, 46, 507
Sol Invictus 286, 303
Solum, Celeste 453–5
Soros, George 176, 177, 203, 217, 482
soul 27, 36–7, 39
recycling 49, 122, 125–9, 137, 143–4, 148–52
spirit 25, 37, 466–8, 472
Source of All 18, 24, 37, 109
South Africa 92, 162, 413–14, 440 *see also* **Zulus**
space and time 3, 32, 240
empty space 9–10, 57–8
illusion of time 2–4, 30
quantum jumps 52
Saturn 103
speed of light 65, 71–2, 81
Time Loops 103
SpaceX 48, 114, 457
FCC 416, 449–50
funding and investors 408, 415–16, 440
Golden Dome missile defence system 186–7
Israel's use of spy satellites 482
low-orbit satellites 48, 114, 164, 369, 415–16, 450, 460, 486
NASA/government contracts 415–16, 450
Starlink 249, 415, 450
Starshield 416, 450
Spider's web 165–8, 172, 177, 179–81
Spirit 25, 27, 36–9, 42–4, 466–8, 472, 510, 515
spirituality 235, 365

Star of David 195, 253, 256–7, 260
Stargate Project 146–7, 203, 470
Starlink 249, 415, 450
Starshield network 416, 450
Steiner, Rudolf 115, 468
stem cells 494–5
Stuart, Brett 147–51
subconscious 131–2, 135, 251–2, 445, 490, 505, 519–20
Sumerians 104, 108, 326, 331–2, 336–8, 351
surveillance 165, 184, 188–9, 394, 411, 415–16, 460, 474, 476, 481
symbolism 28–9, 41–2, 45, 117, 251–72, 284, 335–6 *see also* Saturn and symbolism
all-seeing eye 21–2, 114–15, 196, 252–3, 255, 340–1
cubes 73–4, 253, 255, 259, 261–3, 271, 279, 282, 354–6, 362
dragons 91–2
Freemasons 167–8, 171
Islam, crescent moon symbol in 356
maces and sceptres 333–4
Mesopotamia 333, 335–6
pyramid 21–2, 66, 68, 251–3, 266, 332, 340–2, 498–9
rainbow 222, 237
reptilians 91–2, 104, 338
royalty 333–6
Satanic groups 258, 261–2, 266–7
Star of David 195, 253, 256–7, 260
subliminal, as 251–2
pentagrams 265–6
synaesthesia 14
synchronicity 130, 134, 140, 233–4, 318, 503–4
synthetic biology 451–2, 495

T
Tate, Andrew 428, 431, 433, 442–3
tarot cards 80–1
the Technate 411–13
technocracy 160
technology of the gods 341–2, 348
Temple Mount (al-Haram al-Sharif) 216, 262, 315

Index

Tesla 374, 407, 415, 416, 438, 477, 486
tetrachromacy 14
Thaler, Richard 246–8
Thiel, Peter 176, 177, 183–7, 248, 374–5, 431 see also Palantir Technologies
  AI-human fusion 473–4
  alternative media 428, 434, 440
  Covid-19 fake vaccines 471
  Epstein, Jeffrey 394, 396, 398
  fertility research 494
  Golden Dome missile defence system 186–7
  government contracts 187
  Musk 184, 186–7, 405–9, 413–16, 421, 423, 428, 440
  Namibia 413–14
  Rumble video platform, investment in 436, 440
  Saturn 254
  South African connection 413–14
  Trump 203, 374–6, 400–1, 405–9, 413–16, 421, 423, 428, 440, 471, 482
  Vance 184, 361, 376, 400–1, 403, 405–6, 430
Third Solomon's Temple, plans for a 216–17, 222, 262–3, 479
time see **space and time**
Titus Flavius 288–99, 304, 337
Tompkins, William 91–2, 270–1
Totalitarian Tiptoe 189, 404, 478
totalitarianism 186, 189, 403–4, 410–11, 478
transhumanism see **artificial intelligence (AI)-human fusion**
Trilateral Commission 172, 198, 430, 475, 477
True 'I' 25, 32, 37–42, 44, 125, 130, 136 510
Trump, Donald see **Trump, Donald and Musk, Elon; Trump Psyop**
Trump, Donald and Musk, Elon xix–xx, 173, 372–4, 381, 402–28, 433, 438, 482
  2030, importance of year 425
  accelerationism 403–5, 408–11
  AI-human fusion xix, 369–70, 402, 404, 406, 408–11, 422–5, 449
  America Party, launch of the 402, 405
  Big Tech/AI tech oligarchy 408–11, 422–4
  Dark Enlightenment 403, 405, 410, 417–19, 440, 473
  Deep State 366, 369–70, 375–6, 390–1, 400, 422, 429, 432, 440, 443, 449, 473
  democracy, dismantling 417–18
  deportations 188–9, 419–22, 442, 449, 483
  Alien Enemies Act of 1798, invocation of 419–20
  due process, lack of 419–21
  Geo Group 419
  ICE 419–21
  Palantir, conflicts of interest in relation to 421
  wartime powers 419–20
  DOGE 184–6, 212, 215, 406–10, 415, 417, 473
  elections, fixing 425
  extortion 417
  fall out 372, 381, 400, 402, 425
  freedom of speech 369–70, 416, 450
  funding of election campaign 402
  H1-B visas 373–4
  judges, attacks on 410, 417–18
  law firms, intimidation of 417
  MAGA cult 185–6, 403–5, 408, 410, 412, 417–18, 422–5
  Palantir 183–6, 424
  Project 2025 418–19
  rare earth minerals, access to 412
  social security and medical aid, attacks on 418
  South African connection 413–14
  the Technate 411–13
  Thiel 405–7, 409, 411, 413–14, 416, 421, 423
  Vance 184, 376, 400–1, 403–6, 424–5
  World Economic Forum (WEF) 176, 373
Trump, Ivanka 213, 215, 393, 394
Trump, Melania 386, 388
Trump Psyop 17, 99, 366–83 see also **Trump, Donald and Musk, Elon loki1**
  advanced microchips to China, sale of 489
  AI-human fusion 165, 186, 188–9, 366–71, 401, 473–6, 485, 490
  Action Plan 475–6
  czar 176, 203, 414, 437, 440, 476, 482
  alternative media xix–xx, 232, 391, 427–9, 431–2, 437–40, 443–4, 508
  anti-Semitism 207–8, 213
  assassination attempt 362, 376–9, 402–3, 406
  Big Beautiful Bill 188–9, 238, 419
  Big Tech/AI tech oligarchy 176–7, 366, 371–2, 374, 400–1, 473
  bird flu, vaccines for 466
  Canada 182–3, 411–13
  chaos, causing xix, 162, 188, 402, 407–8, 419, 425
  China 403, 412, 416, 439, 477, 489
  Christianity 360–2
  climate change hoax 367–9, 485
  conspiracy theories 43, 361
  constitution, dismantling the 403–4, 406, 417–18
  corruption 383
  court challenges 375–6
  Covid-19 fake vaccines xviii, 470–2, 500
  crypto meme coins/cryptocurrency/stablecoins 176, 383, 482–4
  election 2020, attempt to subvert 376
  election 2024 204, 213, 375, 403, 418, 423, 425, 440, 473
  Epstein 173–4, 384–94, 471
  felon, Trump as a convicted 376
  Freedom Cities 486
  freedom of speech 431
  funding 203–4
  Global Cult 100, 162, 165, 169, 366, 369–70, 375–7,

383, 401
Golden Dome missile defence system 186–7
Greenland 411–13
Hegelian Dialectic 188
hive mind 447
immunity 376, 392
Israel 173–4, 202–9, 212–13, 216, 238, 372, 396, 400, 425, 429, 432, 481
MAGA cult 176, 188, 238, 361, 369–83, 400–1, 447, 474
AI-human fusion 473, 490
alternative media 427–30, 437–43, 507
Epstein, Jeffrey 384–5, 387, 389–94, 401, 471
mind control 377–9, 383
model agencies and beauty pageants 387, 393–4
National Guard, use of 410, 421, 431
Nobel Peace prize 382, 396
Panama 411–13
pardons 442
perception 17, 368–9, 375, 379, 423, 425, 438
psychopath/sociopath, as 205, 380–1, 393, 420, 422, 425, 466
Putin 214–15
Rogan, Joe, interview with 473
Rumble video platform 437, 443
Saturn 258
sexual abuse accusations 387
Signal security breach 480–1
tariffs 383, 477
Thiel 203, 374–6, 400–1, 428, 440, 471, 482
Truth Social 437
universities and colleges, withdrawal of funding of 208
Vance, JD 376, 400–1, 412, 473
Venezuela 411–12
Wall Street Journal article 202
West, dismantling the 162, 217–18
Woke extremism 366–9
World Economic Forum (WEF) 173–4, 175–6
Zionism 199–200, 202–4, 214
Truss, Liz 181–2
tunnel of light 127, 136–7, 141–2
Twitter/X and Elon Musk xix, 133, 249, 416, 428–9
AI-human fusion 372–3, 449, 486–7
algorithms 244, 373, 487
censorship 244, 369, 373
everything app, expansion into an 249, 409
financial services 409
freedom of speech xix, 243–4, 369–70, 372–4, 487
Grok 372, 486–7, 495
ownership 249, 370–2, 404, 449, 486
shadow banning 244, 369, 373
Trump 244, 400, 487
Twitter Files 370
xAI company, purchase by 249, 372, 404, 449, 486
typology, use of 289–93

U

UFOs/UAPs 89, 92, 357–8
Ukraine-Russia conflict 214–15, 412, 477
United Nations (UN) 175–7, 180, 198, 203, 211–12, 215, 221, 246, 425, 450, 477, 492
United States 199–200, 210, 220–1, 253, 265–6
all-seeing eye and pyramid 21, 196, 252–3
Capitol Hill 259, 265–6, 335–6
CIA 117, 169, 183–5, 225, 242–3, 368, 371, 382, 396, 415, 431, 441, 463, 481
constitution, dismantling the 403–4, 406, 417–18
DARPA 245, 411, 457, 460–1, 470, 476
Federal Communications Commission (FCC) 416, 449–50
government, list of Zionists appointed to 201–2
Israel 199–204, 398, 480–1
media 241–2, 371–2, 385–6, 416, 434
MKUltra 224–8, 232, 242, 400
One-Party State 392, 402
September 11, 2001 terrorist attacks xviii, 173, 187, 196, 201, 247, 370, 377, 394, 427, 511
Signal security breach 480–1
Zionists 198–203
Universal Basic Income (UBI) 165, 484–6

V

vaccines see also **Covid-19 vaccinations** 468–72 see also **Covid-19 fake vaccines**
AeroVax 465–6
bird flu 466
mass vaccination 465–6
mRNA-based aerosol fake vaccine 465–6
van Wijk, Christianne 47, 143, 445, 463, 465
Vance, JD
AI-human fusion 165
Big Tech/AI tech oligarchy 366, 400–1, 403–6
Bilderberg Group 184
funding 184, 430
Musk 184, 376, 400–1, 403, 405–6, 424–5
President, becoming 184, 376, 400–1, 403, 425
Roman Church, conversion to 361
Rumble video platform 436–7
Thiel 184, 361, 376, 400–1, 403, 405–6, 430
Vedmore, Johnny 246, 248–9
Vespasian 288, 290–3, 299
virtual reality (VR) 5, 15–17, 32, 71–2
vortices 66–8, 119, 154, 217

W

waves see frequencies (waves)
Webb, Whitney 395, 397–8
Weinstein, Bret 428, 434–6
Weinstein, Eric 428, 434, 440
The Wellness Company 441–2, 448
West, destruction of the 162, 217–18, 419
Wetiko (mind virus) 23, 99–102
Wexner, Lex 396–7
Wheel of Samsara 49, 122,

Index

126–7, 137–44, 151–2, 254, 516
Wheeler, John 2, 64, 83, 85
Wojcicki, Anne 414, 494
Wokery 17, 366–9, 434, 447
Wolff, Michael 379, 381–2, 386–9, 393
World Economic Forum (WEF) 160, 172, 174–7, 178, 182, 373, 488
  Board of Trustees 175
  Chabad influence 215
  Davos 174–5, 178
  15-minute cities 485–6
  governments, penetrating 177
  participants, list of 175–6
  training, list of people who have been through WEF 177
  Trump 173–4, 175–6
  Universal Basic Income (UBI) 486
World Health Organization (WHO) 179–81, 452, 457–8

X

X *see* **Twitter/X and Elon Musk**
xAI 186, 249, 372, 404, 449, 486

Y

Yaccarino, Linda 244, 372–3
Yahweh 33–4, 260, 316–18, 345, 439
  Asherah as consort god 330
  Elohim/Anunnaki 331–3, 349–50
  Jehovah 33
  Jewish people 316–18
  mass exterminations, blood lust and brutal punishments 347, 350, 356–7
  psychopathy 330, 350, 362, 439
  single god, as 349–50
Yaldabaoth (Gnostics) 23, 41, 69, 76, 83, 91 see also loosh; under particular main entries
  Aeons 28–31, 35, 103, 109
  Archons/demons 87–8, 91, 98–101, 109, 111–12, 218, 497, 510–11
  bad copy of Prime Reality 30–4, 37–8, 40, 109
  Blind One/Foolish One 34, 109
  cleverness 34, 109–10
  consciousness 24, 28–30, 33–9, 94, 109, 112–13, 157–8, 218, 226, 281–2, 349, 495
  Counterfeit Spirit, as 29, 40–1, 48–9
  Demiurge 28, 48, 103, 281, 286
  distortion 31, 99, 158, 426
  Great Architect of the Universe, as 31
  inversion 99–101, 209
  Prime Reality 29–34, 37–8, 40, 46, 83, 109
  psychopathy 34, 226
  Sabbateans/Sabbateans-Frankists 220, 260
  Saturn 103, 256, 258, 260–2, 272
  simulation/Matrix 28, 31–7, 46, 82–3, 158
  Sophia 28–9
  trap, springing the 37–9
  Yahweh, as 33–4, 260
YouTube 80, 147, 180, 237, 245, 248–9, 347, 414, 416, 433, 436, 472

Z

Zevi, Sabbatai 193–6, 210, 260, 349
Zionism 196–9, 371–2
  Christian Zionists 203, 217
  Greater Israel 197–8, 199, 222, 312, 479
  Jewishness, separation from 196–7
  Palestine, colonisation of 196–9
  Revisionist Zionism 197
  Trump 199–200, 202–4, 214
  United States 198–203
Zohar/Zoharists 210–11, 218
Zuckerberg, Mark 177, 184, 409, 411, 494
Zulus 91–2, 98, 100, 108, 120, 271, 338, 347, 356

DAVIDICKE.COM
FOR DAILY NEWS UPDATES, VIDEOS AND ARTICLES ON CURRENT EVENTS, AND MORE.

The Latest News

 Article
 Come and Join the Conversation...

 Article
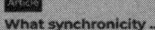 What synchronicity ...

 Video
He's been desperate all along to give his Cult masters what they want to...

  Video
Trump Names Tony Blair to Oversee Gaza in New Peace Plan | Trending...

  Video
Streaming now on Ickonic.com

  Video
Reptilian Energy vs Human Energy

  Video
How the system works – Hip-Hop musician describes meeting with...

 Video
An unhinged prime minister whose masters control an unhinged...

 Video
The Trump 'peace' deal is a JOKE. You only have to see the grin and smirk...

THE DAVID ICKE FORUM - FOR OPEN DEBATE, CONNECTING WITH LIKE-MINDS, & A CONSCIOUS COMMUNITY

 Video
How the system works – Hip-Hop musician describes meeting with...

 Video
The Trump 'peace' deal is a JOKE. You only have to see the grin and...

 Video
The gift of being different in a world of uniformity. Who wants to 'fit in'...

 Article
The "Farm to Fork" Green Agenda: How the EU and the Davos WEF...

BOOKS

The Reveal
The Dream
The Trap
Perceptions of a Renegade Mind
The Answer
The Trigger
Everything You Need To Know But Have Never Been Told
Phantom Self
The Perception Deception
Remember Who You Are
Human Race Get Off Your Knees - The Lion Sleeps No More
The David Icke Guide to the Global Conspiracy (and how to end it)
Infinite Love is the Only Truth, Everything Else is Illusion
Tales from the Time Loop
Alice in Wonderland and the World Trade Center Disaster
Children Of The Matrix
The Biggest Secret
I Am Me - I Am Free
. . . And The Truth Shall Set You Free – 21st century edition
Lifting The Veil
The Robots' Rebellion
Heal the World
Truth Vibrations

DVDS

Worldwide Wake-Up Tour Live
David Icke Live at Wembley Arena
The Lion Sleeps No More
Beyond the Cutting Edge – Exposing the Dreamworld We Believe to be Real
Freedom or Fascism: the Time to Choose
Secrets of the Matrix
From Prison to Paradise
Turning Of The Tide
The Freedom Road
Revelations Of A Mother Goddess
Speaking Out
The Reptilian Agenda

shop.davidicke.com

MORE BOOKS BY DAVID ICKE

All Available at:
shop.davidicke.com